Collins
GEM
Dictionary

Bahasa Malaysia · English
English · Bahasa Malaysia

Revised Edition

Haji Abdul Rahman bin Yusop

HarperCollins*Publishers*

first published in this edition 1975

© William Collins Sons & Co. Ltd. 1964, 1975

Latest reprint 1994

ISBN 0 00 458655 7

General Editor
W. T. McLeod

Printed in Great Britain by
HarperCollins Manufacturing, Glasgow

CONTENTS

FOREWORD TO THE REVISED EDITION

Thanks to Almighty God for the opportunity to revise the Dictionary with the new revised spelling system. In this edition new terminology has been included and some archaic words omitted. It is hoped that the rules of the new spelling system which have been included would be useful to readers.

Haji Abdul Rahman bin Yusop

PENDAHULUAN CETAK YANG DIBAHARUI

Syukur ke hadrat Allah kerana taufik dan hidayah-nya beroleh peluang menyambungkan tenaga menyemak akan kamus ini dengan menggunakan sistem ejaan baharu. Dalam kerja itu telah diambil kesempatan bagi menambah perkataan-perkataan yang baharu tercipta dan meninggalkan mana-mana perkataan yang sudah jarang digunakan. Dalam edisi yang baharu ini telah dimuatkan peraturan sistem ejaan yang baharu moga-moga menjadi faedah kepada pengguna Kamus ini.

Haji Abdul Rahman bin Yusop

FROM THE FOREWORD TO THE FIRST EDITION

Many uses will be found for this dictionary but I hope that it will be of special use to pupils in Malayan schools. In the English to Malay section many words are included that ordinarily would not be given in a dictionary of this nature. For example, the

English names of many flowers, birds, animals, fabrics, etc are explained as 'a kind of . . .' (sejenis . . .). These renderings are not translations, but may be of value when the words are met in English books. Similarly, many of the more complex terms have been given renderings that are more in the nature of explanations than translations.

While this dictionary is an entirely new work and takes full account of the many changes which have affected both languages in recent years, I am very conscious of the debt I owe to editors of earlier works.

PENDAHULUAN

Diharapkan kamus ini akan berfaédah kepada umumnya lebih-lebih lagi kepada murid-murid sekolah. Dalam bahagian daripada bahasa Inggeris kepada bahasa Melayu telah dimasukkan banyak perkataan-perkataan yang jarang didapati di dalam kamus yang setara dengan kamus ini. Untuk menyenangkan nama-nama bunga, burung, binatang, kain dll. diterangkan dengan cara menyebut 'sejenis . . .'. Ini nyatalah bukan terjemahan, tetapi haruslah mendatangkan faédah apakala berjumpa perkataan-perkataan itu di dalam buku-buku Inggeris. Bagitu juga perkataan-perkataan lain yang rumit diberi ertinya yang lebih berupa keterangan daripada terjemahan.

Walaupun kamus ini adalah semata-mata lunas baharu dan mengandungi ciptaan baharu tetapi saya terhutang budi juga kepada tenaga penyusun yang lebih dahulu.

PRELIMINARY NOTES

Malay is written in two scripts, namely (*a*) in the Jawi script and (*b*) in the Rumi or Romanized script.

THE NEW SPELLING SYSTEM FOR BAHASA MALAYSIA

A new spelling system which has been reformed in Malaysia is as follows:—

1. The Alphabet

The letters used in the romanized alphabet of Bahasa Malaysia are as follows:

a	A	j	J	s	S
b	B	k	K	t	T
c	C	l	L	u	U
d	D	m	M	v	V
e	E	n	N	w	W
f	F	o	O	x	X
g	G	p	P	y	Y
h	H	q	Q	z	Z
i	I	r	R		

(Note: **q** and **x** will only be used to spell certain foreign words which are not changed to the Malay phonemic system. The pronunciation of the alphabet will remain as usual).

2. The Vowel System

There are six vowel phonemes (or distinctive sounds) in Bahasa Malaysia and the vowel letters used to represent these phonemes are as follows:—

a   i   u   e   o

(Note: Letter e symbolizes 2 phonemes, that is, the e pepet which is pronounced as [ə] as in 'err' and the e taling which is pronounced as [E] as in 'day').

2.1 The Use of Vowels in Final Close Syllables

i. Vowels ı and u are used in final close syllables if the preceding syllables consist of vowels **a, i, u, e**. Examples:

Penultimate position	Final syllable	
a	i	kasih, balik, habis
a	u	basuh, bakul, catur
i	i	bılik, piring, fikir
i	u	riuh, pikul, tidur
e pepet	i	lebih, petik, sepit
e pepet	u	ketuk, betul, telur
u	i	putih, cungkil, tulis
u	u	tubuh, pucuk, pukul

ii. Vowels o or é (taling) are used in final close syllables if the preceding syllables consist of vowel o or é (taling). Examples:

Penultimate position	Final syllable	
o	o	gopoh, pokok, borong
o	é (taling)	boléh, kolék, bogél
e	o	témpoh, bélok, sérong
é taling	é	léceh, gélék, géntél

vii

iii. Exceptions shall be made in spelling foreign words or terms recently introduced into Bahasa Malaysia. These are limited to vowels o and e in final syllables. The purpose is to retain the visual shape of the foreign words or terms. Examples:

(a) atom (atom) *not* atum
rektor (rector) *not* rekter
sistem (system) *not* sistim

(b) The spelling of monosyllabic words does not change when prefixes are added to the words. Examples are:—
stor (store) *when prefixed becomes* menyetor (*not* 'menyetur')
brék (brake) *when prefixed becomes* membrék (*not* 'membrik')

iv. The vowels in final syllables do not influence the type of vowels in the preceding syllables. Example:
déwan (hall) *not* diwan
orang *not* urang

v. The form ye is substituted by vowel i in such words as the following:
ayér *becomes* air
cayér *becomes* cair

vi. In writing disyllabic words or words with two syllables which are separated by vowels, the method of spelling shall follow Rule one (i) above. Example:
kuéh (cake) *becomes* kuih

3. Consonants

Twenty-four (24) consonant phonemes are in current usage in Bahasa Malaysia and these are symbolized by 24 consonant letters as follows:—

letters examples

p	pandai	sampai	siap
b	batu	lambat	sebab
t	tanah	kertas	sukat
d	dekat	kedai	tekad
k	kerat	tangkap	tumbuk
g	gemuk	bagus	beg
c	cakap	lucut (*not*: chakap, luchut)	
j	jalan	panjat	kolej
s	surat	masam	keras
h	habis	tahan	kasih
m	makan	lama	dalam
n	nakal	senang	telan
ny	nyamuk	senyap	
gh	ghaib	maghrib	mubaligh
z	zaman	izin	Mahfuz
ng	nganga	mangkuk	menang
l	lama	bulu	gatal
r	rambut	barang	tukar
f	fikir	sifat	motif
v	volta	universiti	
sy	syarat	masyhur (*not*: sharat, mashhur)	
kh	khabar	akhlak	tarikh
w	wayang	sawah	
y	yatim	bahaya	

3.1 Changes in Consonant Letters

Changes in consonant letters are as follows:—

Examples

ch *becomes* **c**	chachat *becomes* cacat
sh *becomes* **sy**	sharat *becomes* syarat
dh *becomes* **d**	dharab *becomes* darab
dz *becomes* **z**	dzalim *becomes* zalim
th *becomes* **s**	Ithnin *becomes* Isnin

(ε) when it is at the beginning of the syllable, the symbol is abolished 'alam *becomes* alam

ta'at *becomes* taat

when it is at the end of the syllable, the symbol is replaced by k ra'yat *becomes* rakyat

tama' *becomes* tamak

(' = hamzah) when it is at the beginning of the syllable, the symbol is abolished masa'alah *becomes* masa-alah

when it is at the end of the syllable, the symbol is replaced by k ra'yat *becomes* rakyat

3.2 Letter V

Letter v is used to spell foreign words borrowed in Malaysia. Examples are as follows:—

v in initial position such as variasi
v in medial position such as universiti

ve in final position of foreign words, is replaced by f in the new spelling. Examples are as follows:—
positive [positiv] *becomes* positif
active [æktiv] *becomes* aktif

4. Diphthong

There are 3 diphthongs in Bahasa Malaysia. These are au, ai, oi and their method of spelling does not change. Examples are:—

au—pulau, pukau, pisau
ai—pakai, gulai
oi—amboi

5. Prefixes Di- and Sa-

The new system is as follows:—

i. **di-** as prefix is joined to the word that follows; the hyphen symbol (-) is abolished. Examples are as follows:—

New method	Old method
dimakan	di-makan
dijalankan	di-jalankan

ii. **sa-** as prefix is changed to se, and is joined to the word that follows; the hyphen symbol is also abolished. Examples are as follows:—

New method	Old method
seorang	sa-orang
sebatang	sa-batang

6. Prepositions di-, ka-, kapada

The new rules are as follows:—
i. **di-** as preposition is written as a separate word

from the word that follows; the hyphen symbol is abolished. Examples are as follows:—

New method	Old method
di rumah	di-rumah
di atas	di-atas

ii. **ka-** as preposition is changed to **ke** and is written separately from the word that follows. Examples are as follows:—

New method	Old method
ke rumah	ka-rumah
ke atas	ka-atas

iii. **kapada** is changed to **kepada**

7. Particles -lah, -kah, -tah and pun

The new rules are as follows:—

i. Particles **-lah**, **-kah**, and **-tah** are written without the traditional hyphen symbol. They are joined to the preceding words. Examples are as follows:—

New method	Old method
ialah; iakah	ia-lah; ia-kah
adalah	ada-lah
adakah	ada-kah
apatah	apa-tah

ii. **Pun** is joined to the word that follows except when **pun** means 'also', 'too' or 'even', in which case it is written separately from the word that follows. Examples are as follows:—

Examples of **pun** which is written without the hyphen:

(a) adapun cerita ini asalnya dari 'Hikayat Melayu'.

(b) sungguhpun orang itu miskin, sifatnya pe-murah.

(c) sekalipun dia orang miskin, hatinya baik.

(d) bagaimanapun, biarpun, meskipun, walaupun dan lain-lain.

Examples of **pun** meaning also, too or even

(a) dia pun hendak ikut saya ke kedai. (He too wants to follow me to the shop.)

(b) Jepun pun kalah dalam pertandingan bolase-pak Piala Merdeka. (Even Japan was defeated in the Merdeka Cup football match.)

(c) Cik Pun (nama orang) pun turut serta dalam pertandingan itu. (Even Cik Pun (name of a person) *or* Cik Pun too took part in the competition.)

(d) sudah pun dia membuat kerja itu. (He has finished the job after all.)

(e) meja ini baik, tetapi meja itu pun baik juga. (This table is good, but that table is also good.)

(f) tahu pun awak membuat kerja ini! (You know how to do the work after all!)

8. The forms kau, ku, mu, nya

The short forms kau, ku and mu are written together with the base words—either in initial position or in final position. Examples are as follows:—

kauambil	rumahkau
kuambil	rumahku
rumahmu	

The form nya which is a particle as well as a pronoun is joined to the base word. Examples are:—

rumahnya	rupanya
sesungguhnya	agaknya

9. Compound Words

The rules regarding the spelling or writing of compound words are as follows:—

i. When two or more words are placed between two affixes, the words are combined. Examples are:—

pemberitahuan *not* pemberi-tahuan *or* pemberi tahuan.

persuratkhabaran *not* persurat-khabaran *or* persurat khabaran.

ketidakadilan *not* ketidak-adilan *or* ketidak adilan.

ketidaksempurnaan *not* ketidak-sempurnaan *or* ketidak sempurnaan.

mengalihbahasakan *not* mengalih-bahasakan *or* mengalih bahasakan.

ii. All words which take foreign affixes must be written together with the affixes. Examples are as follows:—

Initial Affixes

(Prefixes)	Examples
maha	mahasiswa
tata	tatabahasa
dwi	dwibahasa
eka	ekabahasa
pra	prasejarah
pro	prodemokrasi
anti	antikomunis
panca	pancaindera

Final Affixes

(Suffixes)	Examples
wan	bangsawan
man	seniman
wati	seniwati (actress)

iii. Two or more words which have hitherto been
      written as one word shall continue to be written
      in the traditional manner. Examples are:—
jawatankuasa *not* jawatan kuasa *or* jawatan-kuasa
setiausaha *not* setia usaha *or* setia-usaha

10. Reduplications

Reduplicated words are written in their complete
forms by using the hyphen (-). The traditional use
of the numeral 2 is abolished. The methods of spelling
such words are as follows:—

i. The hyphen is inserted between the reduplicated
    form such as:—
tiap-tiap *not* tiap2
kanak-kanak *not* kanak2

ii. In the case of partial reduplication, the hyphen
     is inserted between the base word and the part
     or form that is reduplicated.
berjalan-jalan *not* berjalan2 *or* ber-jalan2
buah-buahan *not* buah2an.

iii. Words which are reduplicated by a process of
      phonemic change are written as follows:—
gunung-ganang
bukit-bukau

GRAMMATICAL NOTES

The Malay Adjective

There is no *article* such as 'a' or 'the' in Malay. To indicate a definite object the demonstrative adjectives 'ini' (this, these) and 'itu' (that, those) are used and should follow the word they qualify, eg The house = rumah itu; this book = buku ini.

The *attributive adjective* follows the noun, eg rumah besar = a large house.

There is no verb 'to be' in Malay. Rumah besar is also translated 'the house is large'. It is only intonation that will say whether the adjective is used attributively or predicatively.

The Malay Noun

The Malay noun is either singular or plural according to context:

    Saya naik kapalterbang (I fly in an aeroplane).

    Saya makan kacang (I eat pea-nuts).

When it is necessary to indicate plural, this is done in the following ways:

(a) By numerals, eg Saya ada lima ékor ayam (I have five hens).

(b) By words like banyak (many) and sedikit (a few), eg Di padang itu banyak lembu (There are many oxen in the field). Sedikit sahaja orang datang (Only a few came).

(c) Reduplication, eg Ramai murid-murid belajar di sekolah itu (There are pupils attending the school).

The Malay Verb

There is no change in the form of the Malay verb to indicate person or number:

xvi

Saya minum air (I drink water).
Abdul minum air (Abdul drinks water).
Budak minum air (The children drink water).

There is no change in the Malay verb to indicate tense:

Saya makan (I eat *or* am eating; I ate *or* was eating; I shall eat).

There is a system of affixation in Malay which is employed to give various meanings to the verbs. The affixations are di; me; ber; per; ter; kan; i; lah; kah; nya.

Di- is used to turn the verb into a passive.

Daging dimakan anjing (The meat is eaten by the dog).

Note: Another function of this prefix is prepositional.

Saya tinggal di Kuala Lumpur (I live in Kuala Lumpur).

Prefixes

The prefixes me, mem, men, meng, meny are used:

(a) To express continuance of action.
Emak menganyam tikar (Mother is weaving a mat).

(b) To express purpose.
Dia datang membawa khabar (He comes with news).

(c) To make a verbal noun.
Suka melihat-lihat (Like seeing).

(d) To put emphasis on the doer.
Dialah yang membuatnya (It was he who did it).

(e) To make the finite verb of a statement.
Orang itu pun membuat kerjanya dengan cepat
(He did his task speedily).

me *before* **l, m, n, ng, ny, r**
  lawan becomes melawan (fight)
  makan becomes memakan (eat)
  nanti becomes menanti (wait)
  ngantuk becomes mengantuk (sleepy)
  nyanyi becomes menyanyi (sing)
  raba becomes meraba (grope)

mem *before* **b, (p)**
  buat becomes membuat (to do)
  pasang becomes memasang (to fix) (Note the p is
  dropped).

men *before* **d, (t), ca, j**
  dapat becomes mendapat (to obtain)
  tanya becomes menanya (to ask) (Note the t is
  dropped).
  cari becomes mencari (to search)
  jaga becomes menjaga (to guard)

meng *before vowels and* **g, h, (k)**
  atur becomes mengatur (arrange)
  ela becomes mengela (to drag)
  embik becomes mengembik (bleat)
  ikut becomes mengikut (follow)
  usik becomes mengusik (to disturb)
  garu becomes menggaru (to scratch)
  harung becomes mengharung (to wade)
  karang becomes mengarang (to compose) (Note
  the k is dropped).

xviii

meny *before* **(s)**

> sapu becomes **menyapu** (to sweep) (Note **s** is replaced by **ny**).

The prefix **ber**. This prefix involves no change in the initial letter of a word. It indicates:

(a) The reflexive (to do something for oneself) eg **berjalan** (to walk).

(b) Reciprocal action (involving oneself with another) eg **bertengkar** (altercation with another).

(c) Possession, eg **berbaju** (to have a coat).

(d) Repetition, eg **berpuluh-puluh** (in tens).

(e) Continuity of action, eg **bermesyuarat** (to discuss).

The prefix **per** denotes the doing of an action, eg **perbuat** (to do); **perdalam** (to deepen).

The prefix **ter** denotes completion, intentional as well as accidental, ability and the superlative:

(a) Completion, eg **tertutup** (closed).

(b) Accidental completion, eg **tertiarap** (accidentally falling).

(c) Ability, usually negative, eg **tiada terkira** (beyond enumeration).

(d) Superlative, eg **terkaya** (richest).

Suffixes

The suffix **kan** is derived from the word **akan**, meaning for, towards, to. Its uses are:

(a) Forming causative verbs, eg **mencantikkan** (to beautify).

(b) Forming transitive verbs, eg **membawakan** (to take along).

The suffix **i** differs from the suffix **kan** as illustrated by the following examples:
  menaiki besikal (riding a bicycle).
  menaikkan besikal (raising, lifting a bicycle).

The Possessive Pronoun

nya

The possessive pronoun **nya** is derived from **dia**, his, her, etc and this is inseparable from, and follows, the word it qualifies, eg
  Emaknya minum (His mother drinks).

lah

The particle **lah** is used as a means of emphasizing a word, eg
  Dialah yang jahat (It is he who is naughty).

kah

This particle is attached to interrogative words, eg
  Mahukah dia pergi? (Will he go?)

NUMERALS

Numeral Coefficients

The following are the numeral coefficients commonly used:
  orang, eg **Dua orang Melayu** (Two Malays).
  ekor, eg **Tiga ekor kambing** (Three goats).
  buah, eg **Empat buah rumah** (Four houses).
  biji, eg **Enam biji telur** (Six eggs).
  batang, eg **Tujuh batang rokok** (Seven cigarettes).
  helai, eg **Lapan helai kertas** (Eight sheets of paper).
  keping, eg **Sembilan keping papan** (Nine pieces of plank).

Cardinal Numbers

1 satu		19 sembilan belas	
2 dua		20 dua puluh	
3 tiga		21 dua puluh satu	
4 empat		same order is followed	
5 lima		up to	
6 enam		99 sembulan puluh	
7 tujuh		sembilan	
8 delapan		100 seratus	
9 sembilan		101 seratus satu	
10 sepuluh		1000 seribu	
11 sebelas		10,000 sepuluh ribu	
12 dua belas		100,000 seratus ribu	
and so on up to		1 million satu juta	

Ordinals

first	pertama
second	kedua
third	ketiga
fourth	keempat
fifth etc	kelima dll

YEAR OF THE HIJRAH

(The year of the Hijrah began in 622 A.D.)

Muharam	30 days
Safar	29 days
Rabiulawal	30 days
Rabiulakhir	29 days
Jamadilawal	30 days
Jamadilakhir	29 days

Rejab	30 days
Syaaban	29 days
Ramadan	30 days
Syawal	29 days
Zulkaidah	30 days
Zulhijah	30 days

Measures and Weights

Gelen = gallon (4.5 ltr) (of petrol etc)
Gantang = gallon *or* bushel
Cupak = quart (approx 1 ltr) (holding about 2 lb of rice)
Kati = catty (approx 600 gr)
Pikul = picul (approx 60 kilograms)

Time

Jam hour, clock.
Pukul to strike; o'clock.
Pukul berapa? What's the time?
Pukul dua two o'clock.
Lima minit five minutes.
Suku jam quarter of an hour.
Setengah jam half an hour.
Tiga suku jam three-quarters of an hour.
Satu jam setengah one hour and a half.
Pukul dua pagi two o'clock in the morning.
Pukul dua belas tengah hari twelve noon.
Pukul empat petang four p.m.
Pukul tujuh malam seven p.m.
Pukul sembilan setengah malam nine-thirty p.m.

The Malay States

States	Capital
Johor	Johor Baharu
Kedah	Alor Star
Kelantan	Kota Bharu
Melaka	Melaka
Negeri Sembilan	Seremban
Pahang	Kuantan
Pulau Pinang	Georgetown
Perak	Ipoh
Perlis	Kangar
Selangor	Syah Alam
Terengganu	Kuala Terengganu
Wilayah Persekutuan	Kuala Lumpur

Abbreviations used in this book

abbr	abbreviation
anat	anatomy
approx	approximately
Ar	Arabic
astr	astronomy
cf	compare
col	colloquial
comp	comparative
eccl	ecclesiastical
eg	for example
esp	especially
etc	et cetera
excl	exclamation, interjection
fig	figuratively
geog	geography
gr	gram
HM	His (Her) Majesty

ie	that is
k.l.	about, approximately
lb	pound
lit	literal
liter	literature
ltr	litre
m	metre
med	medicine
mil	military
Mr	Mister
mus	music
naut	nautical, naval
old	old-fashioned
o.s.	oneself
oz	ounce
pej	pejorative
pol	politics
pp	past participle
print	printing, typography
pt	past tense
rail	railways
rel	religion
sch	school
sl	slang
s.o.	someone, somebody
sth	something
sup	superlative
tech	technical
theat	theatre
US	American usage
zool	zoology

BAHASA MALAYSIA-ENGLISH

DICTIONARY

A

abad era; century; eternity; endless future: berabad-abad for centuries.

abah I direction; mengabah to direct one's course to.

abah II father.

abah III abah-abah, harness.

abai, mengabaikan to have a low opinion of; to neglect; terabai neglected.

abaimana anus.

abang eider brother, male cousin or friend older than o.s.

abar, mengabar to brake, slow up speed or progress; slack, flapping.

abau large swamp tortoise.

abdas ritual ablution before prayer.

abdi slave; mengabdikan diri to make o.s. the humble servant; Abdullah 'Servant of God'.

abiad(z) white.

abid I everlasting, eternal.

abid II pious, godly.

abjad alphabet.

ablor crystal.

abnus ebony.

absen absent.

absterak abstract.

abu ashes, cinder, dust, fine powder; menang jadi arang, kalah jadi abu win you become charcoal, lose you become ashes; mengabui mata to throw dust in the eye,

cheat; proper name **Abu Bakar.**

abuan share, portion.

abuh I bustling.

abuh II swollen.

abuk dust; **bunga** pollen; abuk kayu sawdust.

abur, mengabur to squander, lavish; hambur, tabur to spring, scatter.

acah, mengacah to tease, make feints at an opponent.

acak quickly, hurriedly.

acan, mengacan to mimic; decoy roused by tapping.

acang - acang trusty messenger.

acap I, acap kali often.

acap II submerged; buried to the top.

acar pickles; sink, rubbish hole.

acara traditional conduct, established usage; agenda, programme of a function.

acaram betrothal ring.

acau, mengacau to have a nightmare, rave; *also* racau, cacau.

Aceh Acheen a district in North Sumatra.

aci done, ready; tak aci it's off; elder sister; aci-aci lever by which the boom of a Malay boat is turned to fold up sail.

acu, mengacu to threaten with a weapon; attempt; test; try; acuan matrix, mould, pattern.

aouh heed, care.

acum, mengacum to provoke, libel; acuman incitement.

1

acung, mengacung to kick (sepak).

ada to be, be present, exist; possess; **ada orang** there are people present; **mengadakan** to create; **keadaan** position, state; **berada** to be somewhere; be rich; **adalah** word introducing a narrative; **adapun** concerning.

adab manners, courtesy; **kurang adab** unmannerly; **beradab** courteous, cultured.

adai-badai dish cover.

adalat justice.

Adam proper name; **bani Adam** humanity, mankind.

Adan Eden, Aden.

adang, mengadang to intercept, obstruct; barring a passage; **mengadang musuh** to keep the foe at a distance; **adang-adang = kadang-kadang** at times, sometimes.

adap = hadap.

adas, **adas manis** aniseed, fennel.

adat custom; customary law; customary behaviour; **adat istiadat** ceremonial customs; **pada adatnya** customarily; **adat Temenggung** patrilineal custom; **adat Perpatih** matrilineal custom; **beradat** customary, traditional.

adawat enmity, hatred.

adegan scene.

adem cold, tasteless.

adi excellent; noble; eminent; especially in titles; **Askar Melayu' Diraja** Royal Malay Regiment; some titles, **adipati**, **adiraja**.

adib polite, courteous.

adik younger brother or sister; cousin or friend younger than o.s.; **adik-beradik** brothers and sisters; **adik kakak** both younger and older; **adik ipar** husband or wife of younger sister or brother

adika = andeka respectful you; **seri adika** having authority, noble.

adil just, fair, impartial; **keadilan** justice; **mengadilkan** to decide a case fairly; **pengadil** magistrate; **Pengadil Keamanan** Justice of the Peace.

adinda court and literary form of **adik**.

ading younger brother or sister (in Malay-Javanese literature); variant of **adik**.

adipati ancient exalted title used in Java.

adiraja very royal; royal by descent; also **diraja**.

adiratna jewel.

adiwarna glowing with colour, resplendent.

administrasi administration.

administrator administrator.

adu, mengadu to pit match in a contest; lodge a complaint; **aduan** plaintiff; yang kena adu defendant; **pengaduan** plaint; **peraduan** contest; **beradu** to sleep (of royalty); **peraduan** royal bed; bedroom.

aduh exclamation of pain or wonder; **mengaduh** to utter such a cry.

aduhai alack, alas.

aduk, mengaduk to knead, mix; **campur aduk** mixture; miscellaneous.

adun, mengadun to knead; **adunan** dough; **adunkan pengantin** to deck out a bridegroom.

adzab sorrow, pain; troubles; torture; **mengazabkan** to cause trouble.

afal conduct, behaviour.

afiat healthy; **sihat wal afiat** in good health; **afiatkan** to restore to health.

Aflatun Plato.

aflun opium.

afrit evil; giant; spirit.

afsun sorcery.

afuah spiritual power.

afzal, terafzal eminent.

agah, mengagah to make a baby crow; **beragah-agah** to keep crowing (of baby); **beragah-agahan** facing each other gesticulating before a fight.

agahari = ugahari.

agak, mengagak to guess; **agaknya** approximately; **agak-agak** fairly; **agak kecil** pretty small; **tidak teragak** unthinkable.

agal leathery turtle.

agam manly, big, stout, tall.

agama, igama, ugama religion; **agama Islam** Islamic religion.

agan, peragam intentional; **mati beragam** dead from no visible cause.

agar I in order that, so that.

agar II, agar-agar edible seaweed; jelly.

agas sandfly; **tali agas** bedcord for a woman in labour to raise herself.

agih, mengagihkan to divide; to distribute the share to be allotted to anyone.

agresi aggression.

agresif aggressive.

aguk breast ornament worn by children and at wedding by women.

agul, mengagulkan to boast.

agun, mengagunkan to give security.

agung large, main, important; **menteri agung** cabinet minister; **mesyuarat agung** general meeting; **Duli Yang Maha Mulia Seri Paduka Baginda Yang Di Pertuan Agung** His Majesty the King.

agus fair, handsome.

agut-agut crow-pheasant.

ah ah!, oh! (exclamation of pain or annoyance).

Ahad, Ar one, first; **hari Ahad** Sunday; **malam Ahad** Saturday night; **ahli-al-Ahad** people of the covenant.

ahkam laws; **Majmu-alahkam** digest of laws.

ahlan welcome!

ahli member; expert; **ahli al-kitab** persons who have a sacred book; **ahli mesyuarat** members of council; **ahli sukan** athlete; expert in; **ahli al-nujum** astrologer.

ahmak stupid, dense; miser.

ahmar red.

ahwal things, events; **segala hal ahwal** all the facts.

aib shame, disgrace; **memberi aib** to put to shame.

aidin iodine.

aidoform iodoform.

ain eye; spring of water; **nur al ain** light of the eye; **ain-ul-banat** kind of fabric.

air water, liquid, juice, sap; **air bah** floodwater; **air batu** ice; **air keras** spirit; **air madu** honey; **air mata** tears; **air muka** expression of face; **air surut** the falling tide; **air pasang** the rising tide; **air terjun** waterfall; **buang air besar** to defecate; **buang air kecil** to urinate; **tanah air** fatherland.

airloji, (h)arloji clock.

aiwan hall of audience.

aiyar swindler, cheat.

ajaib wonderful, strange; **ajaib khanah** museum.

ajak, mengajak to invite, urge, persuade to action.

ajal destiny allotted span of life; **sudah sampai ajainya** he has died.

Ajam Persia.

ajar, mengajar to teach, instruct; warn, advise; **mengajarkan** to teach (a subject); **belajar** to learn; **pelajaran** learning, education; **pelajar**

student; **terpelajar** educated; **kurang ajar** ill-bred; **ajaran** doctrine.

ajenda agenda.

ajeng gracious; title of princesses in Java.

aji, mengaji to study religious works, recite the Koran; **pengajian** study.

ajnas miscellanies, sorts; **tuhfatul-ajnas** gift of various articles.

aju, mengajukan to offer, bring forward a proposal.

ajuk to ridicule by mimicry; **mengajuk** to mimic.

ajun farthest from the mark, last in competition; **mengajun** to plan to do, propose, put forward.

ajung assistant.

akad contract; **akad nikah** marriage contract.

akaid dogma.

akal intelligence, tact, understanding, mind; **berakal** intelligent; resourceful; **akalkan** to deceive, get the better of.

akan to, with reference to; *word indicating future tense*; **tunjuk akan dia** show him; **akan hal itu** as for that matter; **dia akan belayar** he will sail; **kedai itu akan dijual** that shop is to be sold; **seakan-akan** just like, resembling; **akan tetapi** but.

akar root, fibre; climbing or creeping plant; **tiada rotan, akar pun berguna** if you cannot get a rattan any fibre will be useful (half a loaf is better than no bread); **berakar** having roots; **harimau akar** leopard cat.

akas I lively, nimble, deft.

akas II returned, reverted, on the contrary.

akat to settle, conclude, put through; **akat nikah** marriage contract; *also* **akad**.

akbar most great, almighty; **Allahu akbar** God is almighty; **tahun haji akbar** Great Pilgrimage year; a year in which the first day of the Haj ceremony falls on a Friday.

akhbar news, newspaper.

akhir end; last; **akhirnya** finally; **akhir zaman** the end of time.

akhirat the life to come, the next world; **dunia akhirat** this world and the next.

akhwan, ikhwan brothers.

aki grandfather, grand-uncle (addressed to any old and respected man); *see* **kakek**.

akibat consequence, result.

akidah belief, faith.

akik agate, cornelian, coral.

akikah ritual head-shaving of an infant a few days after birth.

akil intelligent, clever; **akil baligh** adult.

akmal perfect (*of* God).

akrab near, close, intimate; *see* **ikrab**.

aksa distant; **masjid al-aksa** the farthest mosque.

aksara letter, alphabetical symbol.

aktip active.

aktiviti activity.

aku I, me, myself; **akan daku** to me; **aku semua** we; **aku sekalian, mengaku** to admit; accept; confess; **pengakuan** admission; confession.

akus elephant goad.

al the; **al-kesah** the story is; **al-marhum** the deceased.

ala on, upon; according to; **ala kadarnya** to the extent of his ability.

alabangka crowbar.

alaf one thousand.

alah to be worsted, lose; **mengalahkan** to defeat; **dialahkan** defeated; **alahan** old riverbed.

alaihi upon him, to him.

alaikum upon you, to you.

alak to urge on, encourage; see **galak**.

alam I world, universe; **ilmu alam** geography; **syah alam di rimba** king of the forest world.

alam II to know; **wa Allahu alam** and God knows; **alami** to experience; **pengalaman** experience.

alamat sign, signal; address; **alamat surat** address on envelope; **beralamat** addressed; **mengalamatkan** to address.

alan advertisement; **mengalankan** to advertise.

alan-alan jester, clown in the makyong play.

alang crossbar; to thwart; **alangan** obstacle, river bar; **mengalangi** to thwart; slight in importance, of little account; **alang-alangan** half-hearted.

alap sedate, slow, quiet.

alar born slave.

alas foundation, basis, framework, stand; **alas baju** coat lining; **alas kaki** footstool; **alas rumah** foundations of a house; **alasan** pretext, excuse.

alat equipment, instruments; **alat kerajaan** regalia; **alatan perang**, **alat senjata** military equipment; **alat tulis** stationery; **mengalatkan**, **mengalati** to equip.

alau-alau hornbill.

album album.

Alcoran Koran; see **Al Kuran**.

alf(u) thousand; **Alfa lailah wa lailat** The 1001 Nights.

algibra, **aljibra** algebra.

algojo executioner.

alhamdu lillah praise be to God.

ali, **ali-ali** sling, catapult; **anak ali**, **batu ali** the stone thrown.

Alias Elias.

alif first letter of the Arabic alphabet.

alih, **mengalih** to move, shift; **alih kata** change of topic; **alih sila** to move one's seat; **beralih** to shift; **alih haluan** to alter her course; **alih-alih** then it happened that.

alik, **olak-alik**, **ulang-alik** backwards and forwards.

alilintar thunderbolt.

alim learned, religious; **orang alim** learned, pious.

alin, **mengalin** to massage with dough, flour or eggs to dispel illness.

aling, **ulang-aling** motion to and fro, backwards and forwards; **mengaling** screen from light.

alir I, **mengalir** to flow (of blood, water etc); **aliran** current of water, air; trend of opinion.

alir II a bait for crocodiles.

alis eyebrow.

alit, **mengalit** to make a fine mark; touch up with kohl.

alkali alkali; alkaline.

alkimbri inmost heart.

alkah embryo; inmost heart.

alkari sealing wax.

alkemis alchemist.

alkonya surname.

alku procurer, pimp.

Al Kuran Koran.

Allah God; **Allah Taala Goa** Most High; **la ilaha illa Allah** there is No God but God; **Allahumma** Oh God.

almanak almanac.

almari wardrobe, cupboard.

almas diamond.

alon-alon slowly; quietly.

alongan tank, pond.

alot tough, hard to break or tear.

alpa careless, negligent; forgetful; **mengalpakan** to forget, neglect.

alperes ensign; deputy district officer.

alti smart, clever.

alu pestle, pounder; **mengalu-ngalukan** to greet ceremoniously.

alum, mengalum to wither, waste away (*of persons*).

aluminium aluminium.

alun long rolling waves; **beralun** billowy; **alun-alun** esplanade in front of a Javanese palace.

alur fairway of a river, channel; trench round flower bed; groove in pattern; **alur gajah** elephant's trail; **beralur** grooved; **alur kunci** keyway.

alwah aloe extract.

am general, universal; **amnya** generally.

ama atom; insect, plant parasite.

amah Chinese nurse *or* maid; Tamil mother.

amal works; **beramal** performing good works; **meng-amalkan** to do, practise, execute; **amalan** good works.

aman peaceful, safe; **kurang aman** unsettled; **mengaman-kan** to pacify; **pengaman** pacifier; **keamanan** peace, security.

amanah charge, trust; mandate; **menaruh amanah** to leave a charge; **pecah amanah** breach of trust.

emang I tungsten and other impurities in tin ore.

amang II, mengamang to threaten, menace by gesture.

amar command, injunction; **amaran** warning, caution.

amat very; **teramat** surpassingly; **mengamati, meng-amat-amati** to look very closely at; **amatan** percept.

amatur amateur.

ambai purse net fixed in estuary.

ambak, tambak to bank up.

ambal mat, prayer rug;

ambalan group; **berambal-ambalan** to move in procession.

ambang lintel of a door; doorstep; **mengambang** to hover in the air as moon or sun above the horizon.

ambar amber, ambergris; **tawar ambar** insipid.

ambau bamboo float fixed to the side of the boat.

ambek=ambil.

amben couch.

amber girdle.

amberok to fall, collapse.

ambil, mengambil to fetch, take away; bring; **ambil tuladan** to take as example; **ambil berat** to take seriously; **ambil dihati** to take to heart; **tanah ambil** earth carrying tin ore; **ambil alih** to take over.

ambin I, mengambin carrying in a sarung slung over a shoulder.

ambin II sleeping platform.

ambing udder.

amblas to be submerged in water.

amblop envelope.

amboi hullo, oh (*exclamation of astonishment*).

Ambon Amboyna.

ambring vague, vanishing.

ambu mahout's 'rise' to an elephant.

ambul, mengambul to rebound (*as a ball*); froth up.

ambung back-basket of bark or rattan; **mengambung** to surge up (*of waves*); bounce; **terambung-ambung** bobbing up and down of a ship.

ambus, mengambus to run away.

Amdan Hamadan.

amil I recipient or collector of religious titles.

amil II, amil lamil mollusc.

amin amen, be it so; **meng-aminkan** to say amen; agree to.

amir emir, commander; **ami-**

rul-bahar admiral; **amir al mukminin** commander of the Faithful.

amit, pengamitan bride-groom's gift to his parents-in-law on leaving their house.

emma, baku after that, and then (*in letters*).

ammi illiterate; = **buta huruf**.

amonia ammonia.

ampai loose and swaying; **ampaian kain** clothes line; **ampai-ampai j** llyfish; **meng-ampaikan kain** to hang clothes on a line; **terampai** hung to air.

ampang easy, light = **gampang**; *also* **empang** = dam.

ampean secondary wife.

ampek gasping for breath.

ampel bamboo.

ampit, anak ampit fighting fish.

ampo edible earth; = **nampal**.

ampu, mengampu to hold up, support; **pengampu** support.

ampuan, tengku ampuan ruler's principal wife.

ampuh submerged in water.

ampuk a bird.

ampul, mengampul to swell out, be blown out.

ampun pardon, forgiveness; **minta ampun** to ask forgiveness; **ampun kurnia** royal grace and bounty.

ampung floating, bobbing about in water, drifting; *see* **apung, lampung.**

amput to copulate; *also* **hamput.**

amra hog plum.

amril emery.

amris gullet, windpipe; **urat amris** muscles and blood vessels.

amsal example.

amtenar civil official.

amuk, mengamuk to go mad, attack fiercely in battle, run amuck.

amung only sole.

ana i, me.

anai-anai white ants, termites.

anak child, offspring, young of an animal, fish *or* plant; **anak angkat** adopted child; **anak bini** wife and child; **anak tiri** step-child; **anak laki-laki** son; **anak perempuan** daughter; **anak Melayu** a Malay; **anak negeri** native; **anak kunci** key; **anak mata** pupil of the eye; **anak panah** arrow; **beranak** to bear a child; **memperanakkan** to bear, give birth to.

anakanda court and literary form of **anak.**

analisa analyse.

analoji analogy.

anam, enam six.

ananda son; *variant of* **anak-anda.**

anasir element, agent.

anatomi anatomy.

anbar ambergris; = **ambar.**

anbiak prophets; *pl of* **nabi.**

anca handicap, disadvantage.

ancai crumbling, fragile; **meng-ancaikan** to crush to bits; = **cuai** careless.

ancak offerings of food placed in basket for evil spirit; **buang ancak** to make such offerings.

ancam, mengancam to threaten; **terancam** threatened.

ancang, mengancang-ancang to prepare to jump, dive.

ancu large raft; cross beams under flooring.

ancuk, berancuk to pair, copulate.

ancung glazed earthen pot.

anda I musk gland in a civet; **anda kasturi** name of Malay sweetmeat.

anda II you, your; **rumah anda** your house.

andai I, andainya supposing for example.

andai II, handai friends.

andak, pandak short; meng-andakkan layar reef of sail; diandak reefed; andak fourth child.

andaka wild bull.

andal, unduk-andal in swift succession.

Andalas, Pulau Andalas Sumatra.

andam dressing of the hair above the forehead; the fringe of a bride.

andang rough palm-frond torch.

andapita cake.

andar, mati andar to perish for nothing.

anderak pit dug to catch elephants.

anderiguru Bugis captain.

andika you, sir, your honour; sanctity of pre-Muslim rulers; title of chief; also adika.

andil share.

anding grey mullet = belanak.

Andoman Hanoman; also Doman.

anduh to support by means of a sling; anduhan sling for injured arm; tali anduh lashings of a gun carriage.

anduk towel.

andun, mengandun perang to go to war.

andung a plant, dracaena.

andur buffalo sleigh.

aneh strange, odd; wonderful.

aneka kinds, species; serba aneka of various kinds, of all sorts.

anfas valuable.

ang you.

angah, terangan panting.

angan-angan thoughts, ideas, ideals; angan-angan sahaja imaginary; berangan-angan day-dreaming.

angga tine (of deer).

anggabaya, ratu anggabaya title.

anggai-anggai sign, signal = isyarat.

anggal lightly laden; not fully occupied; menganggalkan to lighten.

anggap I consider, view as: anggapan view, opinion.

anggap II, menganggap invite to drink, dance; berang-gap-anggapan inviting to one another in turn.

anggar, menganggar to calculate, reckon; anggaran estimates, budget.

anggara wild (of beast); also angkara.

anggau, anggau-anggau white egret = bangau to clutch at.

anggerik orchid.

anggerka, baju anggerka long buttoned undercoat.

anggit, menganggit to fasten with rattan; rotan penganggit atap.

angglap to steal.

anggota limbs; members of any body; anggota tentera soldiers.

angguk, mengangguk to nod in assent; mengangguk-ang-gukkan kepala to keep nodding the head.

anggul, mengangul to pitch teranggul-anggul pitching.

anggun elegant in dress.

anggung, mengangggung to lift, raise (head).

anggur vine; wine; buah anggur grapes; menganggur to transplant; penganggur one without work.

angguri, kain anggur cloth used for a pilgrim's jubah (gown).

anghun red tobacco.

angin wind, breeze, current of air; angin darat land breeze; angin puting belrung whirlwind; angin sakal contrary wind; angin timba ruang wind abeam; **negeri di atas angin** land above the trade wind belt; **cakap angin** to talk hot air; **kepala angin** flighty; **makan angin** to go for an airing, enjoy o.s.; **menganginkan** to air; **tempat peranginan** balcony; place to take the air.

angka cypher; digit; figure; **angka dua** the figure two; reduplication mark; **perangkaan** statistics; **angka kandungan** multiple.

angkak, angkak-angkak joke.

angkap flue for smoke.

angkar sacred; haunted (of place).

angkara violence, brutality; breach of court etiquette.

angkasa the region of the air, heavens; **unggas angkasa** bird of the air; **angkasa lepas** outer space; **angkasawan** astronaut.

angkat, mengangkat to raise, lift; **anak angkat** adopted child; **angkat sembah** to raise hand in homage; **angkat-angkat** gait, bearing.

angkatan armed force; **angkatan laut** navy; **angkatan raja diraja** royal hearse; **berangkat** to travel, set out (of princes); **mengangkat-angkat** to flatter.

angkatap constant.

angkin woman's belt of cloth.

angkit, mengangkit to lift a light object.

angklung bamboo musical instrument.

angkong game with three cards.

angku form of address to maternal uncle.

angkuh proud, haughty.

angkuk figurehead of native boat.

angkup forceps, tweezers; pincer-like; **mengangkup** to hold in forceps; **terangkup-**

angkup opening and shutting.

angkus elephant goad.

angkut, mengangkut to lift; **mengangkut nanah** to come to a head (of boils); **pengangkut** carriage; **pengangkutan** to transport.

anglo brazier.

anglung pavilion, summer house.

angsa goose.

angsama pimp, procuress.

angsana yellow-flowered roadside tree.

angseg, mengangseg to intrude.

angsoka name of a tree.

angsur, ansur, berangsur-ansur by instalments; gradually; **bayar berangsur** to pay by instalments; **bertolak-ansur** to compromise.

angut recurring (of fever); **mengagut** to doze.

anhu upon him.

ani part of a loom; **mengani** to arrange the pattern on a weaver's loom.

aniaya injustice, tyranny; **menganiaya** to oppress; **teraniaya** oppressed.

aning-aning, naning large wasp.

anis aniseed.

anja ship's halyard; = **tali anja**; **teranja-anja** spoilt (of child).

anjak, menganjak to move slightly; **beranjak** shifted.

anjal, menganjal to rebound, spring back.

anjang, Anjang name of a fourth child in a family.

anjar anchor.

Anjiman, kapal Anjiman East Indiaman (ship).

anjing dog; **menganjing** to treat like a dog; **anjing air** otter; **anjing hutan** wild dog; **anak anjing** puppy; **saudara anjing** half-brother by same mother of different father.

anjir fig (*the fruit*).

anju to aim at, try to jump.

anjung projecting front room over a porch.

anjur, menganjur to project (*as a headland*); **menganjurkan** to bring forward; urge, propose; **penganjur** propagandist, promoter, leader (*esp pol*).

anona custard apple; = **nona**.

ansar helpers of the Prophet Muhammad when he left Mecca.

ansur = angsur.

anta existence, nature; **anta-beranta empyrean; negeri anta-beranta Utopia; Anta boga** a great serpent.

antah rice grains left unhusked among the husked after pounding; **antah-antah** descendants of the fifth, sixth and seventh generation; **antah-berantah** fairy.

antak to stamp on.

antan pestle; **antan patah, lesung hilang** pestle broken and mortar lost (misfortune after misfortune).

antap heavy for its size.

antara between; **antara ini dengan itu** between this and that; **antara ada dengan tiada** hardly; **tiada berapa lama antaranya** after a short interval; **perantaraan** medium.

antar-antar, **antar-antar senapang** ramrod; **antar-antar gobek** pestle of areca nut pounder.

antari, baju antari inner vest under pilgrim's gown.

antelas, kain antelas satin.

anteng quiet, not crying (*of infants*).

antero the whole; **antero dunia** all over the world.

anti– anti-; **anti kerajaan** anti-government.

antih, mengantih to spin; *also* **kantih.**

antik antique.

antil, untal-antil swaying; loosely.

anting pendant and swaying; **batu anting** pendulum of clock; **anting-anting** ear pendant; **burung anting-anting** large racquet-tailed drongo.

antuk, berantuk to collide; knocking against; **terantuk** in collision; **mengantuk** feeling sleepy; **sudah terantuk baharu tengadah** to look up after collision (to shut the stable door after the horse has bolted).

antul, mengantul to bounce, rebound (*of balls*).

antun, berantun to be particular about one's dress.

antung-antung hanging holder (*for creese*).

antup sting of an insect.

anu, si anu so and so; **di kampung anu** at such and such a place.

anugerah bounty of God, gift from prince, favour, endowment; **menganugerahi** to bestow gift on; **menganugerahkan** to give to a person.

anum young.

anut, menganut to follow religion; **penganut** follower.

anyal resentful.

anyam, menganyam to plait; **anyam tikar** to make a mat; **anyam sasak** to make wickerwork for walls and fences; **anyaman** plaiting, matmaking.

anyang spiced uncooked fish *or* meat.

anyar new.

anyih unseemly.

anyik, onyak-anyik loose, shaking (*as loose tooth*).

anyir = hanyir.

apa what; **apa dia?** what is it?; **siapa dia?** who is he?; **apa lagi?** what else?; **apa fasal?,**

apa sebab? for what reason?; **tidak apa, tidak mengapa** never mind, no matter; **apabila** when; **apa pun jadi** any one will do; **berapa** how many, how much?; **berapa harganya** how much is the price of it?; **beberapa** some, several; **seberapa** as many as; *see* awat.

apak, hapak frowsy, sweaty (*of persons*).

apal, mengapal to learn by heart.

apam cakes of steamed rice flour.

apar-apar jellyfish.

apas smart appearance.

api fire, light; **api neraka** hellfire; **batu api** flint; **bunga api fireworks**, spark; **bara api** embers; **kayu api** firewood; **keretapi** train; **mengapi** to make trouble; **periuk api** bomb, mine; **semut api** stinging ant; **berapi** flaming.

apik smart, neat; **cakap upak-apik** inconsistent; name given to Chinese hawking food in village.

apilan gun shield.

apit, mengapit to press between two surfaces; **apitan** printing press; **pengapit** best man at a wedding; **pengapit bicara** assessor at a trial; **apit-apit** pincer trap.

apiun raw opium.

apran apron.

April April.

apung flotsam; **laksana apung di tengah laut** like driftwood on the waves; **apungan** buoy, float; **terapung-apung** to drift about.

ara generic name for Ficus species; **utang kayu ara** fig-tree debt, never likely to be repaid; **menanti ara tak bergetah** waiting for the sap of ara tree which has none (till doomsday).

Arab Arabian; **tanah Arab** Arabia; **orang Arab** the Arabs.

arah direction, course; **arah ke laut** towards the sea; **mengarah** to direct one's course; **tidak tentu arah** in confusion; **pengarah** director of a company.

arai, arai-jemarai hanging loosely.

arak I, arrack rice spirit, alcohol.

arak II, berarak to walk in procession; **perarakan** procession.

arakian furthermore, again.

aral obstacle, accident; **aral melintang** accident intervened.

aram I, mengaram to bear a grudge; **araman** grudge.

aram II scaffolding, temporary structure.

aram III, aram-temaram clouded over (*of moon*).

arang charcoal; **arang batu** coal; **kayu arang** ebony; **sapu arang di muka** to cause shame, disgrace.

aras rising to a level with; **mengaras** to rise to; **air mengaras lutut** water rose to one's knee.

arau, mengarau to stir liquid.

arba, hari arba, (Rabu) fourth day, Wednesday.

arbab viol.

arca image.

arek young girl.

aren sugar palm.

arghawani ruby red.

argus guinea pig.

ari, kulit ari epidermis, outer skin; **ari-ari** the pubes.

aria to lower away boats.

arif learned; wise; **arifin** the wise.

arih, mengarih to put out hand.

arik to pull (*var*).

aring I stinking, foul (*of urine*).

aring II fretwork in a kris blade under the guard.

ariningsun younger sister; darling (in *literature*).

arip sleepy.

aris boltrope; noble, prince.

Aristatalis Aristotle.

aristokerat aristocrat.

arit sickle; **mengarit** to cut grass; tap a palm.

arkan articles of Islamic faith.

arloji, harloji clock.

armada fleet of warships.

arnab rabbit.

arpus resin for rubbing strings of instruments.

aruah = **arwah**.

aruan, ikan aruan edible freshwater fish.

aru–aru, hantu aru-aru malicious forest spirit.

aruda rue (*plant*).

aruh, pengaruh influence, authority; **berpengaruh** influential; **terpengaruh** influenced; **mempengaruhi** to influence.

aruk, mengaruk to create disturbance, wreak havoc.

arun, mengarun to mix, stir.

arung, mengarung to wade, ford, traverse; **mengarung darah** to wade through blood; **arungan** sea.

arus = **harus**.

arwah souls of the dead; baca arwah, arwahkan to hold prayers for the dead; kenduri arwah feast for all souls; hilang arwah, terbang arwah to lose consciousness, faint.

arzi the earth.

asa hope; putus asa disappointed; asa-asaan in suspense.

asabat nerve(s); sakit asabat nerve disease.

asad lion.

asah, mengasah to grind, whet, file down; batu asah whetstone; **asahkan** to whet, grind down.

asahan Persian earthenware.

asai weevil; rotten (*of wood*); **mengasai** to moulder, be worm-eaten, decay, rot.

asak, mengasak to cram, stuff, crush; berasak-asak crushed.

asal I source; **asalnya** origin of it; originally; asal kata root word; asal-usul origins, antecedents.

asal II so long as, provided that; asal ada as long as there is one.

asam acid, sour, acid fruits; asam jawa tamarind; asam dengan garam like acid and salt (good mixers); perak asam bad-coloured silver alloy; asam-asaman sour fruits; pengasam keris to clean kris with acid.

asap smoke, steam, fog, fumes; **mengasapi** to fumigate; perasapan censer; berasap smoky, misty, steaming; bintang berasap comet.

asar I afternoon, hour of afternoon; sembahyang asar afternoon prayer.

asar II usages set up by the Prophet's companions.

asas foundation; pada asasnya basically; berasas founded on; **menasaskan** to found; pengasas founder; asasi basic.

asfal low (*of person*).

asfar cream-coloured.

ashab disciples, companions.

asi treacherous, rebellious; **mengasi** to care, heed.

asid acid.

asimilasi assimilation.

asin salty, briny; **mengasinkan** to soak in salt; asin-asin vegetable treated with salt.

asing part, separate; bangsa asing foreign race; **mengasingkan** to separate, segregate; perasingan segregation.

askar troops.

asli original; well-born.

asmak names.

asmara passion, love.

asmaradanta white (of teeth).

asnad credentials, authorities for a statement.

aso, mengaso to rest (from work).

asrafin seraphim.

asrama hostel; dormitory.

assalamu alaikum peace be with you.

asta eight.

astaga, astagfirullah God forgive me!

astagina manual training.

astaka, balai astaka open canopied dais for royal ceremonies.

astakona octagon; **nasi berastakona** rice dished up in octagonal form at a wedding; **bintang astakona** many pointed stars.

astana palace; seat.

asu, gigi asu canine teeth.

asuh, mengasuh to nurse infants; **pengasuh** a nurse; **asuhan** nursing, upbringing.

asuk male dancer at a rong-geng.

asung, mengasung to incite; **asungan** incitement.

asut, mengasut to agitate; incite, egg on; **pengasut** instigator; **asutan** incitement.

aswad black; **hajar al-aswad** the Black stone at Mecca.

asyik enamoured, infatuated; busy; **asyik dengan maksyuk** loved and beloved.

asyhadu I testify; **asyhadu Allah ilaha ilalah** I affirm there is no God but Allah.

asyura 10th Muharram in honour of Hassan and Hussein descendants of Prophet Muhammad.

atak, mengatak to arrange, order.

atal = hartal.

atap roofing (esp of thatch); **atap genting** tiles.

atar, minyak atar perfume.

atas top, upper part; **di atas** above.

atau, atawa or, either.

atek to practise; cultivate.

atendam auxiliary.

ati–ati to beware.

atlas, antelas satin; map, atlas.

atma = utama.

atom atom.

atung, teratung-atung to be calmed; drifting (of steamers broken down).

atur, mengatur to arrange; **beratur** in order; **peraturan** arrangement; **aturan** rule.

aub to kick the bucket (die); **telangkup aub** to upset (of boat).

aulia saints, holy men.

aum, mengaum growling (of a tiger).

aur bamboo; **mengaur-aurkan** to scatter, throw about.

aurat sexual organs; parts of the body that should be covered.

auta lying, boasting; bluff.

autonomi, otonomi autonomy.

auzu billahi I take refuge with God!

Awa, Ava Burma.

awa, pinang awa areca nut with the end cut off.

awah payment half in cash and half on credit.

awai to wave the hand.

awak body, person; you, I; **awak perahu** crew of a ship; **perawakan** posture.

awal beginning; early; **awal tahun** beginning of the year; **awal amat** too early; **awalan** grammatical prefix.

awam general, common; **orang awam** civilian.

awan cloud; **mengawan** to

ascend to the clouds; **berawan** in the clouds.

awang young fellow; **perawangan** class of royal pages.

awang-awangan space between earth and sky.

awas keen-sighted, careful; **mengawas** to supervise; **pengawas** comptroller, supervisor; **pengawasan** to control; oversight.

awat, apa buat? why?; ridge between furrows.

awet lasting.

awewe woman, wife.

awi bamboo.

ayah father; **ayah bonda** parents; Indian nurse.

ayahanda father (*in courtly language*); = ayah.

ayak, mengayak to sift; **ayakan** sieve.

ayam hen, cock, fowl; **ayam betina** hen; **ayam denak, ayam hutan** jungle fowl; **ayam jantan** cock; **ayam-ayam** watercock.

ayan iron.

ayanul-sabita the essences of things, fixed prototypes.

ayap to eat; **ayapan** victuals.

ayat verse, sentence, phrase.

ayu beautiful; elder sister.

Ayub Job.

ayuh to come along.

ayuhai ho!, alas!

ayuk to copulate.

ayum to abet; **ayuman** collusion.

ayun, berayun, mengayun to rock, sway; **ayunan** hammock, cradle; **matahari ayun-temayun** afternoon.

ayut, mengayut to copulate.

azab sorrow, pain, trouble, torture; *also* adzab.

azal beginning of time, endless past.

azam I intention; purpose.

azam II great, exalted.

azan muezzin's call to prayer.

azim sublime.

azimat talisman, amulet.

aziz dear, darling.

azmat awe-inspiring.

azza glorious; **azza wa-jalla** may he be honoured and glorified.

B

ba second letter of the alphabet.

bab chapter, main division of a book.

baba Chinese born in Malaya.

babad episode; scene in play; round in boxing; chronicle, history.

babak act; episode in tale; scene in play.

babal young jackfruit.

babang gaping wide, agape.

babar, membabarkan to spread (*sail*); unfold (*plan*); **terbabar** stretched out.

babas, terbabas driven past one's goal; driven out of its course.

babi pig; **membabi buta** be reckless; **babi hutan** wild pig; **gila babi, pitam babi, sawan babi** epilepsy; **bintang babi** evening star.

babil, berbabil to dispute, wrangle; quarrelsome; **perbabilan** wrangle.

babit, membabitkan to implicate another; **terbabit** involved.

babon hen.

babor broad (*of blades*).

babtis to baptize.

babu Javanese female domestic.

babuk dense, dull, stupid.

baca, membaca to read, recite; **bacaan** reading; **pembaca** reader (*person*).

bacak wet, slushy.

bacang horse mango.

bacar voluble, eccentric; abusive.

bacin stinking (*as fish-paste*).

bacuk joint of bamboo used as a receptacle for water.

bacul timid; spiritless; ayam bacul cock which will not fight.

bad wind; bala bad=di atas angin.

bada Malay cake of fried banana; bada-bada willy-nilly; tidak terbada-bada unbearable.

badai sudden gale, hurricane; membadai to rage (*of gale*).

badak rhinoceros; tapir; badak raya, badak sumbu large one-horned rhino; badak tampung, badak tenuk, badak murai tapir.

badan body; organization; sihat badan healthy; badan perahu hull of ship.

badang round tray for winnowing.

badar full moon; name of plain near Mecca; edible sea and freshwater fish.

badi evil influence haunting a place, animate thing or corpse; *also* bahadi.

batik small straight dagger.

Badui Bedouin; pagan hill-folk in Bantam, Java.

baduk clumsy; bulky; shapeless (*of person*).

badut clown, buffoon; membadut to clown.

bafta woven fabric.

bagai sort, kind; berbagai-bagai various types; dan sebagainya and so forth; bagaimana how.

bagak brave, bold.

bagal too big; clumsy.

bagan open platform for drying fish; quay; fishing village.

bagas continuous gale, strong wind, blast.

bagat pockmarks; ikan bagat a fish.

baghal a mule.

bagi to give; for; as for; rumah bagi orang house for people; bagi perkara itu as for that matter.

bagih seance without music.

baginda king, prince, ruler; Seri Paduka Baginda Yang Di-Pertuan Agung His Majesty the King.

bagini=bagai ini in this way; so.

bagitu=bagai itu in that way; thus.

bagoh, ikan bagoh a fish.

bagong big; clumsy (*of people, boats*).

bagor coarse weaving (*of palm fibre*).

baguk overgrown; clumsy; ikan baguk marine catfish.

bagur overgrown (*of the young*); clumsy.

bagus fine, handsome.

bah inundation; air bah flood water; musim bah the wet season.

bahadi=badi.

bahaduri knightly, gallant.

bahagi, membahagi to share, deal out; bahagian division, share, part.

bahagia happiness; happy; berbahagia fortunate.

bahak, terbahak guffawing.

bahala=bala disaster.

baham, membaham to eat without masticating.

bahan to beat, thrash; kena bahan to get beaten; raw material; bahan cerita material for a story.

bahana noise confused murmur of many sounds; echo.

bahang glow of fire; glowing hot.

bahar sea, large expanse of water.

bahara a weight = 3 pikul.

bahari beautiful, splendid; the old days; old customs.

baharu, baru new, recently, only then; **baharu tadi** a moment ago; **dia minta baharu saya beri** not till he asked did I give it; **membaharui** to renovate, renew.

bahas = bahath discussion; debating; **perbahasan** discussion; consideration.

bahasa language; **bahasa kebangsaan** national language; **bahasa daerah** dialect; **bahasa pasar** bazaar language; **bahasa dalam** court language; **bahasa kacukan** mixed language; **simpulan bahasa** idiom; **juru bahasa** interpreter; **berbahasa** polite, cultured.

bahawa the story is, the facts are; **bahawa sesungguhnya** truly, verily.

bahaya danger; **merbahaya, berbahaya** dangerous; **membahayakan** to endanger.

bahkan certainly; moreover.

bahri marine, of the sea.

bahtera vessel, ark.

bahu shoulder.

bahwa = bahawa.

bai form of address to Bengalis, Punjabis and Pathans; baby.

baid distant (*of kin*); **karib dan baid** close and distant relatives.

baiduri opal; generic name for a number of precious stones such as opal, cat's eyes *etc.*

baik good, useful; well, recovered from illness; **orang baik** honest person; **jaga baik-baik** to take good care; **sebaik-baiknya** the best; **membaiki** to mend things; **memperbaiki** to repair.

bainat bayonet.

bairup beacon, buoy.

baisikal bicycle.

bait abode; house; **bait ullah** the temple at Mecca; **bait ulmal** state treasury.

baja I manure; **membaja** to manure.

baja II steel; **besi baja** steel; **berbaja** of steel.

bajak plough; **mata bajak** ploughshare; **membajak** to plough a second time.

bajan(a) basin.

bajang evil spirit, familiar spirit; spirit malignant to pregnant women and infants.

Bajau, Orang Bajau coastal tribe in Borneo.

bajau to strike; **berbajau, dibajaukan** was hit; **fabulous bowl of gold awaiting a digger.**

baji wedge; **membaji** to insert a wedge.

bajik, kebajikan philanthropy; virtue; welfare; **kebajikan umum** public welfare.

bajing squirrel; **bajingan** pilferer.

baju coat, upper garment; **baju dalam** singlet; **baju panas** overcoat.

bajul crocodile; thief, pilferer.

bak = ba' like, resembling; Chinese ink.

baka I heredity, inherited character; stock.

baka II eternal, everlasting; **dari negeri yang fana ke negeri yang baka** to die.

bakai, mandi bakai to wash in fresh water after bathing in the sea.

bakal prospective; future; **bakal raja** prospective ruler; **bakal isteri** future wife.

bakap, ikan bakap dark murrel.

bakar, membakar to set fire to; **terbakar** alight; burnt; **dibakar** burnt intentionally.

bakat traces; inherited characteristic talent; **awan bakat hujan** clouds portending rain; **berbakat** having marks, traces; talented.

bakau mangrove trees; **hutan**

bakau mangrove swamp; **ular kapak bakau** species of viper.

bakda after; **bakda-hu** afterwards.

bakdul halter for horses.

bakhia sewing with long stitches.

bakhil miserly, mean.

bakhtiar fortunate.

baki balance, left over, surplus, residue.

bakiak clogs.

bakik a pepper.

bakir sour (*of milk*).

baksi, layar baksi mizzen sail.

baksut buckshot.

bakti meritorious service; **berbuat bakti** to show devotion; **berbakti** to serve; **kebaktian** devotion.

baku genuine; acknowledged; **harga baku** standard price.

bakuk stupid; inattentive; dense; **ikan bakuk** herring.

bakul basket hamper.

bakung large white lilylike flower.

bakup swollen (*of face*) by inflammation.

bala affliction; **bala bencana** disaster and trouble; **tolak bala** rite to avert calamity.

balad country; ballad.

balah, berbalah disputing, quarrelling; **perbalahan** argument.

balai hall; **balai penghadapan, balai besar** audience hall; **balairong, seri balai dais** in audience hall; headman's court; **balai polis** police station; **balai angkat-angkat** royal bandstand; **balai gambang** houseboat; **balai-balai** topsyturvy.

balak large piece of timber.

balam banded ground dove; dim; **berbalam, membalam** to loom vaguely.

balan internal ailment.

balang bottle with a long narrow neck; **hembalang** to hurl.

balap blind.

balar albino whiteness; pinkness; **kerbau balar** pink buffalo; **cakar-balar** scratched all over.

balas, membalas to send back; return; **balasan** requital; revenge; **balas surat** to reply to a letter.

balau, pokok balau large tree.

baldi bucket.

balet ballet.

balgham mucus, phlegm.

Bali Bali; **limau bali** pomelo, shaddock.

baligh adult; **akil baligh** years of discretion; puberty.

balik to go back; behind; the reverse; **di balik** behind; **balik ke pekan** to return to town; **terbalik** inverted; **sebaliknya** on the contrary; **berbalik** to return; **membalikkan** to turn upside down.

baling, membaling throw at; **berbaling** rotate; **baling-baling** wind-vane.

Balkis, Puteri Balkis Queen of Sheba.

balon balloon.

balsam balsam.

balu widow, widower; immune from a disease.

baluarti stone rampart.

baluh wooden frame of a drum.

balui quits at games; stagnant (*of tidal water*).

baluk a small boat; **berbaluk** to argue, dispute.

balun, membalun to thrash with cane or bamboo; **membalun** to roll up, coil up; **naga balun** coiling dragon.

balung cock's comb; **balung kulit** to loose bark; **buang balung** to circumcise a girl.

balur dried skin.

balut, membalut to wrap up.

bam crosspiece; bar of cart.

bambang, terbambang spread wide; bambangan kuala where the estuary widens out.

bambangan, ikan bambang- an sea perch.

bambu bamboo = buluh.

bambun Malayan mongoose.

bami dish of vermicelli with prawns and cress; also mami.

bamper bumper.

banang, duku banang a popular fruit.

banar, sinar-banar radiant; radiating (of rays of the sun).

banat, membanat to thrash; ainul-banat a precious cloth; hutan banat wild forest.

bancah perplexed.

bancang to hold up, stop.

banci roll, census, enumera- tion.

bancuh to mix, knead.

bancut projecting; terbancut mata with eye thrust out intently.

bandan, ikan bandan a fish; main bandan child's dance.

bandang, ikan bandang sal- mon herring.

bandar seaport, town; syah bandar port officer; Majlis Bandaran Town Council.

bandarsah, also **madara-sah** small Muslim chapel.

bandea salver.

bandel to be obstinate, be stubborn.

bandela bale, pack.

banderek drink made from ginger.

bandering sling for stones.

banding comparison; tiada tolok banding incomparable.

bandot he-goat.

bandu friend, companion.

bandul pendulum of a clock; membandul to swing like a pendulum.

bandung joined as a pair; rumah sebandung semi- detached house.

bandut, membandut to put a band round (cracked porcelain, fragile gun barrel).

bang I muezzin's call to prayer.

bang II = abang brother.

bangai, terbangai abandoned dish left uncovered.

bangar putrid; ingar-bangar great uproar.

bangat quick; bangat-bangat very quickly.

bangau egret; Chinese pond heron.

bangbang crimson, red.

bangbun = bambun.

bangga proud; conceit; mem- banggakan to be proud of.

banggelo bungalow.

banggi perverse, disloyal; zaman banggi ini this de- generate age.

banggul, bunggul low hill.

bangir pointed, sharp.

bangka stiff, hard; tua bangka old and stiff.

Bangkahulu Bencoolen, old port in Sumatra.

bangkai carcass of animal.

bangkang wide apart; tanduk bangkang horns which are wide apart; contradictories; membangkang to oppose; bangkangan objection, protest.

bangkar snag in river; skin and bone; stiff, hard.

bangkas speckled yellow and red (of fowl).

bangkerap bankrupt.

bangking large round urn- shaped lacquered box for clothes.

bangkir, bongka-bangkir turning topsy-turvy.

bangkit to rise up; bangkit berdiri to rise; membangkitkan to raise; kuih bangkit pastry.

bangku bench, stool.

bangkung, parang bang-kung heavy chopper; pokok bangkung wild cempedak tree.

bangkut stunted in growth, stumpy.

bangor mischievous; brutal.

bangsa race; good birth, good stock; kind, sort; bangsa China the Chinese; sebangsa of the same race, stock or kind; kebangsaan national.

bangsai rotten (of timber exposed to weather).

bangsal shed, booth; cooly lines.

bangsang, membangsang to excite, anger.

bangsat destitute; orang bangsat vagrant.

bangsawan of good family; Malay opera.

bangsi bamboo flute; berbangsi to play the flute.

bangta, anak bangta child born to a ruler after his accession.

bangun to get up, rise; jatuh bangun falling and rising; bangunan building; structure; membangunkan to rouse.

bangus pig's snout.

bani children; bani Adam human kind.

baning tortoise.

banir buttresslike projection at the base of the trunk of some trees.

banjar rows; range; berbanjar in rows; banjaran gunung mountain range.

Banji glazed earthenware lattice work.

Banjir flood; flooded; membanjir to come in a flood; membanjiri inundated.

bank bank (for money).

bantah quarrelling, altercation; berbantah to quarrel; berbantahan wrangling, arguing; bantahan opposition; perbantahan dispute.

bantai, membantai to slaughter; belabour; bantai lari to run; pembantai butcher.

bantal pillow, cushion; bantal panjang bolster; berbantalkan lengan to sleep on one's arm.

bantang, bunting-bantang big-bellied, advanced of pregnancy.

bantar, membantar to resist; avert disease; terbantar averted.

bantat doughy (of badly baked bread).

banteng the wild Gaur=seladang.

banter quick, fast, high (of price).

banteras, membanteras to fight against.

banting; membanting to thresh, beat; banting kepala to bother one's head; banting tulang to work hard.

bantu, membantu to help; wang bantuan financial help.

bantun, membantun to uproot; terbantun uprooted.

bantut frustration; rendering abortive; bantutkan nipping in the bud.

banyak much, many; quantity; banyak orang number of persons; sebanyak as many as; kebanyakan most; majority.

banyau foul.

banyul farcical; membanyul to play the clown.

bap sound of a flop.

bapa father; emak bapa, ibu bapa parents.

bapet worthless.

baptis to baptize.

bara embers; bara api live coals; jijak bara to walk delicately; sara-bara topsyturvy.

barah abscess; tumour, cancer.

baral, terbarai loosened.

barak barracks; patah barak broken in (of elephant); reformed (of persons).

baran low swampy undergrowth; **babi baran** wild pig infesting such undergrowth; **panas baran** peculiar habit (*of person*).

barang commodity; thing; luggage; one's belongings; anything; any; **barang apa** whatever; **barang bila** whenever; **barang siapa** whoever; se-**barang** whatever; **barang** belian chattel.

baras leprosy.

barat west; **barat-daya** southwest; **barat-laut** north-west; **bintang barat** evening star.

barau, **burung barau-barau** yellow-crowned bulbul; **ikan barau-barau** carp.

barbur plunging in waters; **orang barbur** plunger.

bareng together, along with; **berbarengan** in company.

bari God the creator; **bari-bari** fruit flies; moveable for unloading a Malay boat.

barid messenger.

barik mottled, veined; water-marked.

baring, **berbaring** to lie down, be reclining; **membaringkan** to lay down.

baris row, line; **berbaris** in rows; to drill; **barisan** lines.

barkas launch.

barnis varnish.

barometer barometer.

barongan mask of lion with a body manipulated by an actor concealed in it.

baru I = baharu.

baru II fibrous shrubs.

baru pimp, pander.

baruh lowland near river or sea; **di baruh bukit** below the hill.

barung, **barung-barung** booth, stall.

Barus, **kapur Barus** camphor; Sumatran port.

barusan just now, newly.

barut long bandage; **bodice**

worn by children; **membarut** to swathe.

barzakh, **alam barzakh** Hades.

basa-basi etiquette, manners.

basah wet, moist; **basah kuyup** wet through; **kain basahan** clothes used for bathing in; **basahkan** to wet.

basal dropsy; wet; beri-beri.

basau hard (*of boiled potato, yam etc*).

basi I musty, stale, mouldy.

basi II something extra; discount; interest; **mengambil basi** harus to make allowance for the current when crossing a stream.

basikal bicycle.

Basir all-seeing God.

basit all-embracing.

basmi, **membasmi** to destroy, obliterate.

basuh, **membasuh** to clean with water, wash; **air basuh tangan** water for washing the hands.

basung corklike root; friable wood; dry rot; **kayu basung** touchwood; **bual basung** empty talk; **membasung** to kick a ball high.

basut, **membasut** fountain, jet.

basyah pasha.

bata, **batu-bata** brick; **atap bata** tiled roof; **bata-bata** in doubt; **kebata-bataan** perplexity.

batak, I **membatak** to rove as nomads; to rob.

batak II hill tribes in Sumatra.

batal to abolish, annul; ter-**batal** cancelled; **membatalkan** to abrogate; **dibatalkan** to repeal; **kuasa pembantal** right of veto.

batalion battalion.

batang stem (*of trees, flowers*); **batang kayu**; **batang pokok** tree stem; **batang hidung**

bridge of the nose; **batang tubuh** trunk of the body; **batang hari** river; **menjadi batang** to die; numeral coefficient, **rokok sebatang** one cigarette.

batara title for Hindu Gods and Rulers of Majapahit.

batas limit; bank (*round wet rice plots*); **berbatas** limited; **pembatasan** curtailment.

batel two-masted sailing ship.

bati, sebati united; milk and water mixed.

batik Javanese patterned cloth; **membatik** process of making such cloth.

batil metal bowl

batin *pagan* proto-Malay headman; esoteric, inner, hidden.

batir, batir-batir cord fastening a keris scabbard to its belt.

batrik patriarch.

batu stone, rock; milestone, mile; **batu api** flint; **batu arang** coal; **batu asah** whetstone; **batu bata** brick; **batu berani** magnet; **batu besi** granitic rock; **batu canai** grindstone; **batu dacing** the weight on a balance; **batu duga** plummet; **batu kepala** crown of the head; **batu merah** laterite; **batu sauh** anchor; **batu sempadan** boundary stone; **air batu** ice.

batuk cough; **batuk bertahun** chronic cough; **batuk darah** to cough with spitting of blood; **batuk kering** pulmonary tuberculosis.

batung, siput **batung** mollusc.

bau smell, scent; sebau alike, suited; of the same type; **berbau** to exude smell; **membau** to smell (*sth*).

bauk beard, whiskers.

baulu, kuih baulu sponge cake.

baung curved like a banana; flat gong.

baur, campur baur mixed up, complicated.

bawa to bring, carry, exhort, drive; **bawa pergi** to take away; **pergi bawa** to go and fetch; **bawa keluar** to take outside; **bawa masuk** to bring in.

bawah I doorkeeper.

bawah II below; the underneath; **kebawah** downwards; **di bawah** under; **bawahnya** bottom of things, the underneath.

bawal, ikan **bawal** pomfret.

ba wang bulbs; leeks, onions; **bawang putih** garlic.

bawasir piles, haemorrhoids; also **wasir**.

bawat drooping; **mata bawat** drooping eyelids, sleepiness; **payung bawat** longhandled state umbrella.

bawel tiresome; chatterbox.

baya, sebaya of the same age; **bahaya** danger.

bayak big-bellied, bulky.

bayam spinach.

bayan, burung bayan paroquet.

bayang shadow, reflection, vague outline; **berbayang** in vague outline; **membayangkan** to suggest, foreshadow.

bayar, membayar to pay.

bayas small wild palm.

bayat allegiance; homage to religious leader.

bayi baby.

bayu wind, breeze; **bayu berpuput** the wind blows.

bayuh plurality of wives.

bayung small chopper.

bayur genus of trees with useful timber.

bazar bazaar; = **pasar**.

bea dues; taxes, toll; **membea** to tax; **pebean** customs station.

bebal stupid, dull, dense; **kebebalan** stupidity.

beban I burden, load; **membebankan** to put a burden on.

beban II naughty (*of child*).

bebang stoppage (*in mid-*

wifery); **kebebangan** stoppage; mati **kebebangan** stillborn.

bebar rushing here and there; to scatter.

bebas free, familiar; **kebebasan** liberty, liberation; **membebaskan** to absolve; free.

bebat, membebat wrapping round; **bebat luka** ligature.

bebek duck; **membebek** to play the duck (follow blindly).

bebeksan dance.

beber, membeberkan to open rolled umbrella *or* sail; to unfold.

beberas, ikan beberas drummer fish.

bebesaran mulberry.

beca rickshaw; **beca roda tiga** cycle-rickshaw, tri-shaw.

becak muddy; slushy.

becang, becang-becok sound of quarrelling.

becek = becak slushy.

becok parrot wrasse.

becus, tak becus unable, not in a state to, incompetent.

beda, beza different (*from daripada*); **bezanya** difference; **membezakan** to differentiate; **pembezaan** to discriminate.

bedah, membedah to operate; **ahli bedah** surgeon.

bedak I division into equal parts; **berbedak** to divide.

bedak II cosmetic powder *esp* rice powder; **berbedak** powdered with cosmetic.

bedal, membedal to hit, swish.

bedama chopper.

bedan, bedan-bedan heat-spots, nettle rash.

bedar large cargo boat.

bedara name of several trees.

Bedawi Bedouin.

bedaya court dancers.

bedebah ill-starred, accursed.

bedegap strong.

bedegong unmannerly; self-fish.

bedek to take aim.

bedel to operate; = **bedah**.

bedeng shed, barracks.

bedia spangles.

bedil gun; **bedil selamat** salute of guns; **ubat bedil** gunpowder; **membedil** to shoot.

beduk large mosque drum.

bedukang, ikan bedukang fresh water catfish.

bedung swaddling cloth for a child.

bedurai, bizurai viceroy.

bega, membega pointing at, aiming at.

begahak, ikan begahak a large river fish.

begak smart, dandified.

begal robber; **membegal** to rob.

begap compact; sturdy, robust.

begar I stiff; hard; proud.

begar II, legar, berbegar to wheel in a circle; wheelround.

begawan holy, blessed.

begini = bagai ini in this way; so.

begitu = bagai itu in that way; thus.

begu forest demon.

begudu tadpoles.

beguk neck glands; **sakit beguk** mumps.

bejar out of humour.

bejat spoilt (*of plaiting*).

beka, berbeka to gossip; to discuss.

bekah cracked (*as dry soil*).

bekal, bekalan rations; supplies, stores, provisions.

bekam, membekam cup (*for bleeding*); **berbekam** suffused (*of blood under the skin*).

bekang I opened out (*of fish hook*).

bekang II kind of cake; *also* **bingka.**

bekas trace, impression; receptacle; former; **bekas jari** fingermarks; **bekas penghulu**

ex-headman; **bekas air basin** for retaining water.

bekat, penuh bekat chock-full.

bekil, ikan bekil a fish.

bekot, membekot boycott.

beku, membeku to clot, coagulate, freeze.

bekuk to bend double, break a neck.

bekukung, ikan bekukung sea bream.

bel bel fruit tree.

bela, membela to bring up (child); pembela rearer, nurse; pembelaan rearing.

bela atonement by blood to champion; to uphold; membela to avenge; pembela avenger; bela sungkawa condolence.

belacak abundant (of fruit); ikan belacak goby.

belacan paste of fish or prawns.

belacu unbleached cotton.

beladau tiny curved dagger.

belah, membelah to split; retak menanti belah the crack awaits the split; bagai pinang dibelah dua like an areca nut split in two (a perfect match (of lovers)); sebelah one of a pair; sebelah barat towards the west; sebelah-menyebelah on both sides.

belahak, terbelahak belching.

belai coaxing, caresses; cumbu belai.

belak I mottled (of wood, diseased skin).

belak II opening out of folds or crease, holding the fold open.

belaka altogether; quite; all; perempuan belaka all of them women.

belakang rear, back; di belakang in rear; membelakang to have one's back turned to; gaji kebelakangan backpay.

belakin blacking, shoe polish.

belalah guzzle.

belalai trunk (of elephant).

belalak staring.

belalang grasshopper; belalang ranting stick insect.

belam, celum-belam over-familiarity; berbelam-belam indistinct.

belambang truss; lath; belambang nibung flooring.

belan to put a crossbar to the door.

belanak, ikan belanak grey mullet.

Belanda Dutch; orang Belanda Dutchman; ayam belanda turkey; kucing belanda rabbit.

belandong too loose, floppy, baggy (of garments).

belang stripes (of tigers, snakes); kuda belang zebra; berbelang striped; harimau mati tinggal belangnya dead tigers leave behind their stripes.

belanga earthenware cooking pot.

belangkas king crab.

belanja outlay expenditure; membelanjakan to expend; belanja hidup cost of living; belanjawan budget.

belantan club, cudgel, truncheon.

belantara, hutan belantara forest.

belantik spring trap; belantik sembat where the noose catches the game; belantik pesawat where a gun shoots.

belar, selar-belar mischievous (of children).

belaram, balgham mucus.

belas I word used in forming the numerals from 11–19; eg sebelas eleven; dua belas twelve.

belas II compassion, pity.

belasah, membelasah to cane; swish, belabour.

belat large screen of bamboo or bertam used in fish traps.

belati European (of knives, string, tobacco etc).

belatuk woodpecker.

belau, belau-belau blinking, shimmering, trying to the eyes.

beldu velvet.

belebas lath laid horizontally.

belebat sweetmeat of steamed yams.

belebau belabouring; swishing.

beleda gruel of kacang hijau.

beledok, cengkok-beledok zigzagging of river or road.

belek, membelek to scrutinize closely; examining carefully.

belekok heron.

belelang poet; staring (of eyes).

belen rolling pin.

belencas = lencas, ulat belencas hairy caterpillar.

belencong lamp used at shadow play.

beleng, tunggal beleng quite alone; without relatives.

belenggu fetters, shackles; **terbelenggu** enchained (of legs, hearts).

belengket linked together.

belengkok sharp bend in a river's course.

belengkong, yu belengkong dogfish.

belengset lower eyelid turned inside out.

belera weaver's sword.

belerang sulphur; **belerang bang** arsenic.

belewar, buah belewar passion fruit.

beli, membeli to buy; **membelikan** to buy for; **pembeli** purchaser; **belian** purchase; **berjual beli** to buy and sell.

belia young; youth; fresh; muda belia young and fresh.

beliak, terbeliak protruding eyes.

belian, hantu belian spirit.

beliau he, she (respectful); semalam beliau belayar yesterday the gentleman just mentioned sailed.

belibas, ikan belibas food fish (of genus Siganus).

belibat double-bladed paddle.

belibis, burung belibis whistling teal.

belida, ikan belida a large river fish.

belidang, ikan belidang eel.

beligu wax gourd = kundur.

belikat, tulang belikat shoulder blade.

beliku sharp bend in a river's course.

belilah retching; muntah belilah vomiting and retching.

belimbing, buah belimbing well-known fruit; leathery turtle.

belin small edible eel.

beling porcelain or glass crushed fine.

belingkang, terbelingkang sprawling.

belingut, terbelingut sprained (of ankle).

belinjau tree with edible fruit.

belintang, kayu belintang crossbars (of fences).

belit coiling round; **membelit** to coil round.

Belitong Billiton.

belitung, siput belitung a shell.

beliung small hatchet; **puting beliung** waterspout.

beliut bent.

belodok prominent (of eyes); ikan belodok goby.

beloh to plough; kerat belob to cross-plough.

belok I pulley-block.

belok II to bend; tack (of boat); turn wheel right or left (of person); **membelokkan** to change course (of water, boat).

belolok fruit of sugar palm.

belon not yet;=belum.

belongkang river boat.

belongkeng small edible snail.

belongsong wrapper;=kelongsong.

belontok, ikan belontok a fish.

belorong white-legged.

belotah harvest time; threshing feast.

belu, belu-belai to chatter, gossip.

beluam monk's collecting bag.

belubur round rice bin; piled up, heaped.

beludak black cobra.

beludal dough cake.

beluduh looking large (of house).

belukang, ikan belukang edible fish.

belukap mangrove.

belukar secondary jungle; belukar muda new secondary jungle.

beluku plough.

belulang hide, untanned leather.

belum not yet; not; belum pernah never yet; sebelum before.

belumpai not yet;=belum sampai.

belun balloon; dirigible.

belung overgrown.

belungkang butt end of palm leaf stalk.

belungkur, ikan belungkur Queensland smelt.

belunjur to stretch o.s., stretch one's leg.

beluntas seashore shrub.

belur crystal;=hablur.

beluru, akar beluru a big climber.

belus slipping off easily, loose (of rings).

belut I swamp eel.

belut II, membelut to desert to the enemy; pembelut deserter, traitor.

beman tax for royal band.

bembam to roast in hot ash.

bemban shrubs used in basketry.

bembeng lifting a light object in the hand.

bembereng, ikan bembereng a fish.

bena I tidal bore; orang bena commoner: the child of a raja father and commoner mother.

bena II, membena to construct.

bena III important; unusual; putih bena remarkably fair; bena tak bena not caring, unconcerned.

benah insect pest; blight.

benak dull, slow of apprehension; marrow; brains.

benalu tree parasite.

benam, terbenam buried, immersed; **membenamkan** to immerse.

benang thread, yarn; threadlike line; benang emas gold thread; benang arang charcoal guideline drawn by carpenters; benang putus boleh dihubung, patah arang sudah sekali broken thread can be joined, charcoal broken is done for (some quarrels can be patched up, others never).

benangsari style.

benar right, accurate, true; truly, really; jahat benar really wicked; sebenarnya in fact; membenarkan to approve, confirm; kebenaran approval, assent.

benara washerman, dhobi.

bencah swamp, marsh.

bencana, bencana alam disaster, misfortune: bencanakan to cause trouble.

bencang visibly unfinished (of house).

bencar, memancar dazzling.

benci hatred; to hate; **membencikan** to loathe; **pembenci** hater; charm to cause lover to hate a rival; **kebencian** object of hate; hatred.

benda thing, article, object, material; **harta benda** property; **mata benda** treasures; **nama benda** noun; **kebendaan** materialism.

bendahara title of State Official; rank next to the heir apparent; **perbendaharaan** treasury.

bendahari Treasury Officer.

bendala bandolier.

bendalu mistletoe shrub.

bendang wet rice field.

bendari ship's cook.

bendawat stay, lashing, cordage in a ship.

bende small gong; to hawk.

bendelam covered vessel cut out of coconut shell.

bendera flag; **tiang bendera** flagstaff.

benderang I, **terang-benderang** very bright, brilliant.

benderang II, **tombak benderang** spear with a tuft of horse hair attached to it; spear of state.

benderung passage between two palace buildings.

bendi I carriage on two wheels.

bendi II, kacang bendi, sayur bendi 'Ladies fingers.'

bendir gong used by hawkers.

bendo chopper, woodknife.

bendong dyke; **membendong** to dam; **terbendong** dammed; weir.

benduan transported convict.

bendul crossbeam; **bendul pintu** threshold beam.

benet bayonet.

bengah conceited, stuck up.

bengak to boast, lie.

bengal temporarily deaf (*from a blow, after flying*).

bengang buzzing of ears;

terbengang wide open; **tercengang-bengang** gaping with astonishment.

bengap artificially dull of hearing; ring dull (*as bad coin*).

bengawan river; lake.

bengek asthmatic wheezing.

benggal, **benggal-benggil** covered with lumps and bumps.

Benggala Bengal; **Benggali** one from Northern India.

benggol two and a half cents.

benggul large bump *or* lump.

bengis cruel, nasty; **kebengisan** cruelty.

bengkah, **membengkah** to strike opponent's top with one's own.

bengkak swollen; **bengkak-bengkil** covered with bumps.

bengkal, mengkal hard, unripe.

bengkalai incomplete (*of work eg plaited mat, sewing*).

bengkalis kind of fish.

bengkang, **bengkang-bengkok** zigzagging of road; blocked up.

bengkar to open out (*of bud, fruit*).

bengkarak unfinished work; skeleton, bare bones.

bengkarong skink, large green lizard.

bengkawan, **mengkawan** lath; numeral coefficient for ataps.

bengkayang gorged, glutted.

bengkel plant; machinery; workshop.

bengkeng irritable; bullying (*children and inferiors*).

bengkerap bankrupt.

bengkil small swelling; **terbengkil-bengkil** struggling.

bengkok bent, crooked; **bengkang-bengkok** zigzag.

bengkong I girdle; **bengkong, leher scarf**; **membengkong** to carry a load.

bengkong II, tukang bengkong circumciser.

bengku, bengku-bengku crutches to support boat's awning.

bengkunang dwarf musk deer.

benguk, sakit benguk goitre, mumps; terbenguk sunk in dejection.

bengut twisted, awry.

benian coffer; trader, merchant.

benih seeds, grain for use as seed.

bening clear, limpid; *also* hening.

benjil bumpy.

benk bank.

benta sore, boil; rumput benta rice grass.

bentala the earth.

bentan relapse, return of sickness.

bentang, membentang to spread out; bring forward; terbentang unrolled.

bentangan traces for draught buffalo.

bentangur name of trees yielding good timber.

bentar, sebentar a moment.

bentara court; herald (*generally two*); ie bentara kanan, bentara kiri.

bentas to tear up and dash down.

bentoh, bentes to wrestle; trip up.

benteng fort; parapet, breastwork; = baluarti; dykes.

bentet cracked, burst open.

bentok, bentrok colliding (*of cars*).

bentuk bend, curve; shape, form; numeral coefficient for curved objects; sebentuk 'cincin ring.

bentulu fish.

bentur, membentur bending; terbentur in collision; frustrated.

benturung the bearcat, weasel.

bentus, terbentus colliding.

benua continent; benua China China; benua Eropah Europe.

benuang, rusa benuang variety of deer.

benum untrodden (*as distant jungle*); mountain.

benyai insipid (*of badly cooked rice*).

benyek sodden (*of boiled rice, pudding*).

benzin benzene.

bera changing colour; red; pale; inflamed (*of brown faces*); red, blushing; pale and swollen.

berabe difficult, complicated (*of work*).

beragi, burung beragi painted snipe.

berah, berah lolok to guzzle.

berahi amorous; love; lustful; berahikan to be in love with.

Berahman Brahmin.

berai, cerai-berai scattered; broken-up.

beraja planet.

berak I, terberak to suck down in mud.

berak II to defecate, ease o.s.

berakah self-important, stuck-up; daring.

beraksa, kuda beraksa winged steed; winged dragon; buah beraksa bullock heart's fruit.

beram generic name for liquors made of fermented rice spirit; = peram.

berambang onion, shallot.

beramin, bakul beramin openwork in basketry.

beranda veranda.

berandal rogue, gangster.

berandang conspicuous; not shut in.

berang I, berang-berang otter.

berang II angry; wrath.

berangai, mati berangai apparently dead.

berangan, buah berangan chestnut; **buah berangan babi** acorn; **warangan berangan putih** white arsenical oxide.

berangas barnacles.

berani brave, bold; bravery; **berani mati** fearless of death; **batu berani, besi berani** magnetic iron.

beranta Malay river boat.

berantah, antah-berantah fairy.

berapa how much; *see* apa.

beras raw husked rice; **beras petas** rice of all sorts; **beras belanda** pearl barley; **beras berteh** parched rice.

berat heavy, weighty; **beratnya** weight; **keberatan** weight; **memberatkan** to burden.

berata Hindu idol.

berau, teberau crashing of rotten trees.

bercak pockpitted.

bercat, ikan bercat murrel.

berdus pot-bellied.

berek–berek, burung berek-berek bay-headed bee eater.

beremban padi barn; crossbar (*for dam, door*).

berembang seaside tree.

beremi a vegetable.

berenang to swim; *see* renang.

bereng, bereng-bereng flat knobless Chinese gong.

berenga maggots.

berengau kind of trumpet.

berenggil serrated (*of mountain range*).

berengos moustache.

berengut surly, snarling.

berentang to tug to get away.

beres in good order (*of work*); **membereskan** to arrange; settle; repair.

beret, ceret-beret streaming (*of diarrhoea*).

berewok shaggy (*of hair*).

berguk long veil for women pilgrims.

berhala idol, image.

beri, memberi to give, bestow; allow; **memberi tahu** to give information of; **pemberian** gift.

beria very; **sakit beria** very ill.

beriang large monitor lizard.

berida veteran; experienced.

beringin, pokok beringin waringin tree.

beringis grinning.

beris, tanah beris sandy accretion.

berisik tumultuous (*of cries*).

berita news; information; **warta berita** news; **pemberita** journalist, newsman.

berkas tied bundle; to round up (*as criminals*).

berkat blessing; blessed; **dengan berkat tuan** with your blessing.

berkik, burung berkik snipe; *also* burung tiruk-tiruk.

berkil, ikan berkil sea perch.

berkuk, burung berkuk large green pigeon.

berlian diamond, brilliant.

Berma Brahma; Burma.

berma red (*Brahma's colour*).

bermat, sampan bermat one-masted undecked sailing boat.

bernas full (*of grain*); plump (*of infants*); spirited (*of speech*).

bernis varnish.

beroga, ayam beroga jungle fowl.

berohi arrowroot.

beroker broker, pimp.

berondong shoot; **berondongan** rattling of salvoes.

berong askew (*of mouth*); swollen cheek.

berongan edible gastropod.

berongis ajar (*of doors*).

berongsang, memberongsang angry; to flare up (*of anger*).

beronok sea slug.

berontak, memberontak to rebel, resist; **pemberontakan** mutiny, rebellion; **pemberontak** rebel.

beroti horizontal lath, rung.

bersat gone down the wrong way (*of food in gullet*).

bersih clean, pure; **membersihkan** to cleanse; **kebersihan** cleanliness.

bersil, tersersil emerging (*as snake from hole*).

bersin to sneeze.

bersut scowling; spitting (*of cats*); snarling (*of dogs*).

bertam well-known palm (*split for wattled house panels*).

bertih, beras bertih rice fried in the husk.

bertuh to collide, run up against.

beruang honey bear; **kutu beruang** insect rice pest.

beruas, pokok beruas wild mangosteen.

berudu tadpole; (*usually*) **anak berudu**; *also* **remudu**.

berui, yu berui sawfish.

berujul small coulter.

beruk pig-tailed monkey; **beruk hantar hasil** mumps; **turun beruk** rupture, hernia.

berumbun looming large.

berumbung cylinder; cylindrical.

berus brush.

besan relationship between parents whose children marry each other.

besar large, great; **besar hati** elated; **besar kepala** swollen-headed; **pembesar suara** loudspeaker; **membesarkan** to aggrandize, to magnify; **membesar diri** to boast; **kebesaran** greatness.

besek closed basket.

besengek curried chicken.

beser incontinence of urine.

beset, membeset to skin.

besi iron; **besi baja** steel; **besi berani** magnet; **batu besi** granite; **tukang besi** blacksmith.

besikal bicycle.

besikor, ikan besikor grunters.

besing whizzing.

Besisi, orang Besisi proto-Malay aborigines.

besit iron; to switch.

besok tomorrow; in the future; *also* **esok**.

bestari well born and well bred; accomplished.

besut, membesut to refine metals.

besuta fine silk fabric.

beta me; **beta semua** we all; **sahabat beta** you (*all terms used in letter writing*).

betah convalescent, better (*after illness*).

betak–betak skin disease, prickly heat.

betapa how?, in what manner?

Betara title given in old Java to major divinities and to reigning princes of great power.

betari sugar millet.

betas ripping open, splitting open (*as seam*).

Betawi Batavia (*now Djakarta*).

beteka water melon.

beti female slave; palace attendant.

betik, betik-betik prickly heat.

Betik, buah betik papaya fruit; **betik semangka** red-fleshed papaya; **timun betik** squash melon.

betina female (*of animals*).

beting bar, reef, sandbank; **membeting** (*of fish*) to dart along in the shoals near a reef; **berbeting** stranded.

betis calf; **tulang betis** shinbone.

betot, membetot to extract, pull out.

betuk, ikan betuk climbing perch; *also* **puyu**.

betul correct, true; straight; **betulkan** to correct; **kebetulan** by a coincidence.

betung large (of bamboo, cane); **buluh betung** large species with edible shoot; **katak betung** large species of frog; **membetung najis** sewerage.

betutu, ikan betutu edible fish.

bewah feast for the dead; also **berarwah**.

bewak = **biawak**.

beza, beda, bedza difference.

bi in; on; with.

bia, boa tolls, taxes; **siput bia** cowrie shell.

biadab disrespectful; discourtesy.

biah synagogue, temple.

biak prolific, reproductive; **membiakkan** to breed; **pembiakan** breeding.

biang on heat (of animals); lascivious (of women); **biangbiut** zigzag.

bianglala rainbow.

biaperi merchant, trader.

biar to permit, allow; may; no matter if; **biarlah** never mind; **biar putih tulang jangan putih mata** let the bones whiten, but not the eyes (better death than shame); **pembiaran** connivance.

biara convent, monastery.

bias deflected from their course.

biasa accustomed; customary, normal, usual; **perkataan yang biasa** the usual remark; **luar biasa** extraordinary, unusual; **membiasakan** to accustom; **kebiasaan** custom, practice.

biasiswa grant, scholarship.

biawak monitor lizard (and other large species).

biawas guava.

biaya cost, expenses; special allowance.

bibi lady; mistress; queen (in cards).

bibir lip (of person); edge, rim; **bibir mata** eyelids.

bibit, membibit to carry in fingers; also **bimbit**.

bibliografi bibliography.

bicana, tanah bicana fatherland.

bicara opinion, discussion, deliberation; judicial proceeding; **berbicara** to discuss.

bicokok small crocodile.

bicu screw-jack.

bida innovation in religion (opposite of sunna).

bidaah deceitful; lying; lie.

bidadari nymph, fairy; houri of Muslim paradise.

bidai chicks (of thin strips of bamboo or bertam).

bidak pawn (in chess).

bidal, bidalan maxim, proverb; thimble; (better) didal.

bidan midwife; **bidan terjun** midwife summoned without previous notice.

bidang broad (of chest, cloth, mats); numeral coefficient for lands, mats etc; **sebidang tanah** piece of land.

bidar large boat.

bidari goal (in game).

bidas, membidas to spring back (of frogs); react (of persons); **bidasan** reaction.

biduan musician, singer.

biduanda royal musician; pagan Malay tribe.

biduk river boat for fishing or cargo; **Bintang Biduk Ursa Major**.

bighair separate, distinct from.

bija honorific title.

bijak learned; prudent; tactful; clever at talking.

bijaksana learned; prudent; chaste.

bijan sesame, ginjili yielding oil.

bijana, tanah bijana fatherland.

biji seed, pip, stone of fruit; numeral coefficient for small objects; biji mata eyeball.

bijih unsmelted tin ore; bijih besi tungsten.

bijirin cereal.

bikin to do; make; bikin betul to put right.

bikir virginity.

biku narrow lace edging; zigzag pattern; Buddhist monk, Lama.

bil bill.

bila when; apabila when; barang bila, bila-bila whenever.

bilah thin strap or lath; numeral coefficient for needles, chisels, knives etc; sebilah pisau knife.

bilai weal; fringe, hem.

bilal muezzin.

bilang, membilang to count, enumerate; bilang kali any number of times; bilangan enumeration; tale; terbilang famous, talked about.

bilar myopia.

bilas washing in fresh or scented water (after a bath in common water).

bilau, kacau-bilau in confusion, topsy-turvy.

bil–hak in truth.

bilik room, apartment; bilik tidur bedroom; bilik darjah classroom; bilik mutalaah study.

bilis bleary-eyed; ikan bilis anchovies.

billahi by God.

biludak, ular biludak venomous snake.

bilur weal, wale from caning.

bimbang anxious, worried, nervous; membimbangkan to worry.

bimbing protruding (of ears).

bimbit = bibit

bin son of; Hassan bin Rahmat Hassan son of Rahmat.

bina structure, building; membina to erect, create, build.

binal, binal-binalan self-willed, troublesome (of children).

binasa ruined, destruction; membinasakan to destroy; kebinasaan destruction.

binatang animal, creature; binatang yang liar wild animals; binatang yang jinak domestic animals.

binatu laundryman.

bincang, berbincang to debate; membincangkan to discuss; perbincangan discussion.

bincul, **bincut** bumpy (of forehead from knock).

bindu turning lathe; mata bindu cord working a lathe.

bingal obstinate, disobedient; buat bingal to pretend deafness.

bingas growling; menacing; quick-tempered.

bingit uneasy; fussy; deafening.

bingka, kuih bingka cake of rice flower, coconut milk and sugar; see bengkang.

bingkah clod; sebingkah tanah clod of earth.

bingkai rim, edging, frame.

bingkas to spring back; trigger; bingkas bedil to pull a trigger; membingkaskan to be released.

bingkis complimentary gift accompanying a letter; eg surat serta bingkisan letter and gift.

bingung bewildered; stupid, dull; membingungkan to bewilder, muddle, confuse.

bini wife; anak bini family; laki bini man and wife; berbini married; memperbinikan to take a wife; bini-binian polygamous.

binjai tree yielding fruit used in mixing a dish of 'sambal'.

bint, **binti** daughter; Bedah

binti Abdul Rahman Bedah daughter of Abdul Rahman.

bintang star, medal; **bintang berekor** comet.

bintat heatspot; **mosquito** bite.

bintik, bintik-bintik covered with small spots.

bintil stye in the eye.

bintit small swelling such as caused by a mosquito.

biografi biography.

biokimia biochemistry.

biola violin.

biong curved (of cutting edge of betel nut scissors).

bipang sweetmeat of sweet rice.

birah herbs with swollen stems that irritate the skin.

birai sharp edge; frame; gunwale; parapet.

biram elephant; **biram berjuang** war elephant.

biras husband of a wife's sister, wife of a husband's brother (when two men marry sisters or two women brothers).

birat scar on the mouth; marks from a caning.

biri, kambing biri-biri sheep.

birih = birai.

biring, sakit biring inflammation of the eyelids.

birit buttocks.

birsam pleurisy.

biru blue; **lebam biru blue (as bruise); kebiru-biruan** bluish.

bisa I venom, venomous.

bisa II can, be able to; = **boleh.**

bisai smart, dainty.

bisan = besan.

bisat, tiada bisat not to care.

bisi fast; unchaste.

bisik, berbisik to whisper.

bising chatter, tiresome noise.

Bismillah in the name of God.

Bisnu Vishnu.

bisu dumb, mute.

bisul boil; **bisul api, bisul lada** small scattered boils.

bitamin vitamin.

biting bamboo splinter for pinning a leaf rice wrapper.

biuku water tortoise; **mata biuku** languorous eyes.

bius stupefied; **kena bius** anaesthetized; **ubat bius** anaesthetic.

biut disobedient; hanging badly; **biang-biut** zigzag.

bizurai viceroy.

blokade blockade.

bobok to bore a hole; **membobok** submerged in water.

bobos gaping; **membobos** to be leaking.

bobot weighty, important.

bobotok titbit in banana leaf.

bobrok ruined (of building).

bocah child.

bocok mosquito net awning for cradles.

bocong lidless water-kettle.

bocor leaking; **mulut bocor** babbling mouth; **bocor-bacir** leaking everywhere.

bodek testicles; **sakit bodek** hydrocele.

bodoh dense, silly; **orang bodoh** fool.

bodok leprosy early stage.

bodong squall of wind.

boga pleasure; **anta-boga** fabulous serpent.

begam tinsel spangles on a head ornament.

bogang, telanjang bogang stark naked.

bogi buggy.

bogil, telanjang bogil stark naked.

bogok fat.

bogol handcuffs.

bogot horrid; ugly; **hitam bogot** hideously black.

bohok goitre, mumps; puddle.

bohong lie, lying, false.

boikut boycott.

bojing hair brushed with a parting.

bojot entangled; **terbojot** escaped from its place.

bok mattress; **bok tilam** mother; = **embuk**.

bokca bag, wallet.

bokek weak.

bokong inside out; upside down.

bokop, bakup closed by inflammation of the eyes; crab.

bokor flat-rimmed metal plate.

bokos miserable, rueful.

bokot veiling, wrapping up.

bol anus; **jambu bol** tree with fruit eaten raw.

bola ball; **main bola** to play football.

bolak, bolak-balik to and fro; vaciliating; **cakap bolak-balik** to prevaricate.

boleh can, able to; **boleh jadi** may be; **boleh juga** yes, all right; **apa boleh buat** what can be done; **seberapa boleh** as much as possible; **dengan sebolah-bolehnya** to the best of one's ability; **kebolehan** ability.

bolok swollen (of eyes).

bolong, membolong to paint in one colour esp black or dark blue.

bolos pierced through; stripped (of hair, leaves, clothes); to break rank.

bolot, membolot to wrap up; bundle together.

bolsa clothes bag.

bolsak mattress.

bolu sponge cake; also **baulu**.

bom shaft of a carriage; boom of a ship; bomb; **bom lempar** hand grenade.

bomantara firmament.

bomba pump; fire station; **pejabat bomba** fire brigade.

bomoh, bomor village doctor, magician.

bonang Javanese orchestra.

bonas bonus.

bonceng, tukang bonceng sponger.

boncol, bonjol swollen. bumpy (esp of forehead).

bonda mother; **ayah bonda** parents; **bonda saudara** aunts.

bondok hump on animal's back.

bondol Java sparrow.

boneka doll, puppet; **bonekakan** to treat as a puppet.

bonet bonnet.

bong ring for animal fights.

bongak conceited, bumptious.

bonggol hump (of camel, cattle); protuberance on tree; knob.

bongkah large piece.

bongkak arrogant, conceited.

bongkal measure of weight for precious article; also **bungkal**.

bongkam, azmat pembongkam amulet to silence; **membongkam** to silence.

bongkang, terbongkang left sprawling or afloat (of corpse).

bongkar, membongkar to heave up (of anchor); turn over or out (contents of boxes); **terbongkar** upheaved, turned over.

bongkas upturned of roots.

bongkil refuse of beans after the extraction of oil.

bongking sprawling face downwards with posterior raised.

bongkok humpbacked.

bongkol, bonggol hump.

bongkong parasitic clump on tree trunk.

bongkot stem, trunk.

bonglai ginger, in medicine.

bongok heavily built; clumsy.

bongsang basket for fruit.

bongsu, busu youngest, last of children; **pak busu** youngest uncle; **anak tangga bongsu** lowest step.

bonjol = **boncol**.

bonyor soft and bad (of fruit).

fish, meat); sloppy; *also* **bonyok.**

bopeng, *also* **mopeng** pock-marked.

bor auger.

borak unravelled, untied; loose (*of tobacco*); berborak to chatter.

borang form (*stationery*).

bordu gunwale.

boreh yellow cosmetic.

borek spotted; ayam borek spotted fowl; bapanya borek anak rintik it the father is spotted, the offspring will be speckled (like father like son).

boria bands of musicians that serenaded houses in the month of Muharram especially in Penang.

boriah, sampan boriah a boat.

boroh, memboroh to bail.

borok suppurating skin disease.

borong, memborong to buy *or* sell wholesale; undertake entire job o.s.; beli borong to buy wholesale.

boros prodigal; extravagant.

bortel carrot.

bosa, tali bosa rope attached to a ship's cable to stop it when sufficiently run out.

bosan bored, fed up; mem-bosankan to satiate.

boseh, boseh perut fat (*of paunch*).

boseta small box.

bosor gluttonous; holed, broken through.

bota goblin, evil spirit.

botak bald; burung botak adjutant bird.

botan rose peony.

botoh gambler, cockfighter.

botok fish steamed with herbs.

botol bottle.

botor, kacang botor edible bean.

boya buoy.

boyak fat and flabby; flavourless (*of tobacco*).

Boyan isle of Bawean; orang Boyan native of Bawean.

boyas pot-bellied.

boyong to move house; pem-boyongan colonization.

bu, ibu mother.

buah fruit; numeral coefficient; rumah sebuah a house; kampung dua buah two villages; buah-buahan fruit of all sorts; berbuah to fruit.

buai, berbuai to rock in a cradle, swing; buaian swinging cot.

buak bubbling up, surging up.

bual, berbual to chatter; bualan to gossip.

buana universe; teri buana the three worlds.

buang, membuang to throw away, discard, banish; buang air besar to defecate; buang air kecil to urinate; orang buangan exile; terbuang discarded.

buapak head of a descent group in Negri Sembilan.

buar lavish, extravagant.

buas savage (*of beasts*); naughty (*of children*); tough and vicious (*of old men*).

buat, membuat to do; make, manufacture; buat-buat to feign, pretend, sham; buatan manufactured; perbuatan act, deed.

buaya crocodile; buaya tembaga, buaya katak the common crocodile; lidah buaya aloe; buaya darat womanizer, wolf; buaya mangap gaping; membuaya to crawl on one's belly; Burung buaya stork-billed kingfisher.

bubar disperse (*of meetings, crowd*); membubarkan to break up (*meeting*).

bubu river fish trap; bubu jantung heart-shaped; bubu batang long; = lukah.

bubuh, membubuh to put (away) (in box, cupboard); affix (seal, fitting); bubuh cap, membubuh to affix a seal.

bubuk weevil, woodmaggot; dimakan bubuk worm-eaten.

bubul, penyakit bubul bubul sore on soles of feet; membubul to repair nets.

bubung = **bumbung**.

bubur rice broth, gruel.

bubus bald (through illness).

bubut, burung bubut Malaysian crow pheasant; layar bubut staysail; membubut to turn (on lathe); pembubut turner.

bucing queue, pigtail.

bucu corner, angle; raised chip pattern in basketry.

budak young boy or girl.

budaya cultured; kebudayaan culture.

budek, surat budek anonymous letter.

budi sense, intelligence; kindness, character; akal budi, budi bicara common sense; budi bahasa character and breeding; budi pekerti character, disposition; balas budi to return a kindness; hutang budi debt of gratitude.

budiman clever; discreet.

budu pickled anchovy = peda.

buduk mutilation of the nose due to leprosy.

budur prominent (of eyes).

bugar, sihat bugar sound and well.

bugil stark (of person); telanjang bugil stark naked.

Bugis name of a people from Celebes.

buhul knot; membuhul to tie in a knot; terbuhul knotted.

bui gaol.

buih foam, froth; berbuih to froth.

bujal projecting outward (of navel).

bujam plaited envelope-shaped bag (for betel or tobacco).

bujang single, unmarried (of either sex); duduk membujang to lead a single life.

bujangga Hindu sage; court poet; dragon; perahu perbujangan dragon boat.

bujuk, membujuk to coax, persuade, flatter, calm; ikan bujuk kurrel.

bujur lengthwise, longitudinal; oval (of faces); oblong; bujur bulat elliptical; bujur telur oval; membujur to stretch out diagonally; bujur lalu lintang patah held lengthwise it passes, crosswise it breaks (one must follow customary procedure).

bujut tangled (as a top's string).

buk book.

buka, membuka to open (book, door, mouth, shop, conference, new land); buka daun to show one's cards at play; buka kasut to take off shoes; buka rahsia to reveal a secret.

bukan no, not (implying an alternative); bukan dia yang buat it was not he (but another) who did it; bukan sengaja not on purpose; dia marah bukan? he is angry, isn't he?; bukan main very, remarkably; bukan buatan genuine, real; bukan-bukan absurd, lacking reason.

bukat troubled, disturbed (of water).

bukau wide gorge, valley.

bukit hill; anak bukit hillock; kaki bukit foot of a hill; orang bukit aboriginal tribe; bukit pasir dune.

bukti evidence, proof; membuktikan to prove, verify.

buku book; joint, knot; gist; core; buku jari knuckles;

buku kaki, buku sila reef knot; buku tunai cash book; buku bicara gist of a discussion; buku karangan gist of an essay; berbuku in lumps.

bukut, membukut to cover up, conceal; pembukut cover.

bulai albino.

bulan moon; month; sehari bulan first day of the month; empat belas hari bulan fourteenth day of the moon = bulan pernama; bulan timbul next month; bulan terang moonlight.

bulang, membulang to wrap (band round waist, fastening of spur round legs of fighting cock); bulang ulu prince's headkerchief; bulang-baling whizzing vane; berbulang to wrap round.

bular whitish discolouration of the eye; buta bular blind with such discolouration.

bulat round (as a ball); circular (as a wheel); bulat bumi globe; bulat bujur, bulat bun-tar, bulat telur oval, elliptical; telanjang bulat wholly naked; dengan sebulat suara unanimously; kebulatan unanimity.

buldan city, town.

buldozer bulldozer.

buletin bulletin.

buli, buli-buli small flask or bottle.

bulir ear of grain, panicle.

bulu wool, feathers; hair of the body; bulu kening eyebrows; bulu roma fine body hair; berbulu hairy.

buluh bamboo, generic name for many bamboos; buluh bangsi reed pipe; seperdu buluh clump of bamboo.

bulukan musty, mouldy.

bulur starving; kebuluran starvation.

bumban wreath (of victor).

bumbu curry spices.

bumbun hunter's tree hut for watching game bird; to heap up.

bumbung roof; tulang bum-bung ridge pole; bumbung atap palm leaf roof; membum-bung to describe a curve.

bumi earth, world; bumiputera patriots, sons of the soil; ibnu bumi geography; geology; dikebumikan buried; Bumi mana yang tak kena hujan where is earth that escapes rain? (who is without sin?); kajibumi geology.

bun small brass box.

buncah confused, bewildered.

buncis, kacang buncis kidney bean.

buncit distended (of belly).

bundar rounded, globular.

bundung cattle disease; liver fluke.

bunga flower; flowery pattern; bunga api sparks, fireworks; bunga air mawar rose; bunga karang coralline sponge; bunga wang interest on money.

bungar, bungaran first fruit, first crop; ayam bungar pullet; bajak bungar first ploughing.

bungkah solid.

bungkal one ounce (gold-smith's) = 16 mayam.

bungkus bundle, package: bungkusan package.

bunglon chameleon.

bungsil very young coconut.

bungur tree with purple flowers and useful timber.

bunian, orang-bunian invisible forest elves.

buntak stumpy, beamy; blobber; gemuk buntak fat and broad.

buntal puffers, globe fish; buntal batu, buntal katak boxfish.

buntang, terbuntang staring (as the eyes of a choking or dying person).

buntar round, domed, roughly hemispherical; **buntar bayang-bayang** round (*of one's shadow at noon*).

buntat bezoar stone; **buntat nyior** bezoar found in a coconut.

buntil bag (*generally of cloth*).

bunting pregnant, in foal, swollen (*of grain*); **bunting sarat** advanced pregnancy.

buntu blocked (*of road, well*); at a dead end.

buntuk short.

buntung maimed; amputated.

buntur glutted.

buntut posterior, tail end, stern; bottom (*of pot*); **ber-buntut** in a queue.

bunuh, **membunuh** to kill; erase; put an end to; **mati dibunuh** murdered; **pembunuhan** killing, slaughter.

bunut, **hujan bunut** heavy rain.

bunyi sound, noise, meaning, accent, intonation; **bunyi-bunyian** music; **berbunyi** sound; **membunyikan** to enunciate, read.

bupala prince.

bupati Javanese title—lord of the earth.

bura, **membura** to spit (*as snake or dragon*); **ular naga bura** vipers.

burai, **terburai** gushing out (*as entrails*).

buram sketch, draft.

burang model (*of boat*); schedule, form.

buras, **memburas** to chatter, discuss; to delete, wipe out.

burhan proof, evidence.

buri rear, back, stern.

burit posterior; **di buritan** astern.

burju fort; sign of the zodiac.

burkak veil of female pilgrim.

buru, **memburu** to hunt; **berburu** to hunt in company;

terburu-buru quickly, hurriedly; **pemburu** hunter; **perburuan** the game hunted.

buradai, **buradai mani** jewelled sari.

buruh, **buroh** labourer; labour (*political*); **kaum buruh** Labour Party.

buruj fort; sign of the zodiac.

buruk plain (*of faces*); shabby (*of clothes, building, conduct*); **baik buruknya** quality (*the good and bad of it*); **memburukkan nama** to defame.

burun, **gurun**, **kambing burun** serow.

burung bird (*always prefixed to bird names*); **burung pipit** sparrow.

burut hernia, rupture, hydrocele.

busa foam, lather; **berbusa** to froth.

busana raiment.

busar bow, arc; bow for cleaning cotton; **seperti kapas dibusar** like cotton after cleaning.

buseh pot-bellied.

busi rice bran; sparking plug.

bustan flower garden.

busuk putrid (*of fish, meat*); foul (*of smell*); **busuk hati** vicious, bad; **membusukkan nama** to defame.

busung dropsical inflammation; **penyakit busung air** dropsy; **busung darah** aneurism, large varicose vein; **busung pasir** mound of sand, dune.

busut ant-hill.

but, **terbut-but** quietly (*of a lone traveller through forest*); boot.

buta blind; **buta tuli** blind and deaf; **pukul buta tuli** striking recklessly; **membuta** to sleep soundly; **makan gaji buta** to have a soft job.

butala the earth.

butang button; **butang dasi** stud.

butek turbid.

butir data; grain; numeral coefficient for coconuts, eggs, bananas, small round objects; **butir-butir** details, items.

butuh penis; **membutuhkan** to need, require; **kebutuhan** requirements, importance.

butuk fish steamed with herbs.

butul side (*of doors, roads*).

butut worn out, threadbare.

buyar, **kertas buyar** blotting paper; = kertas sap.

buyung round-bottomed earthenware water jar; **Buyung** proper name = youngster.

buyut flabby (*of flesh*); **perut membuyut** flabby obesity, *also* in pregnancy.

C

ca tea.

cabai Indian long pepper; chilli; **cabai burung**, **cabai rawit** bird pepper.

cabak, **burung cabak** a night bird.

cabang fork; main branches of a tree; junction; **bercabang forked**; **besi cabang tiga** trident.

cabar timid; **mencabar** to discourage; to challenge; impatient; careless.

cabi linch pin.

cabik torn, rent; **cobak-cabik** tattered; **mencabikkan** to tear in strips.

cabir torn to pieces; **cabar-cabir** torn about all over.

cabuh uproar, disturbance.

cabuk sloughing ulcer on the lower leg; **ikan cabuk** herring.

cabul outrageous behaviour; licentious violence; **berbuat cabul** to commit an outrage (*esp rape*); **mencabuli** outrage against (*person or place*).

cabur, **kecaburan** disorder, terror.

cabus, **bercabus** empty (*of talk*).

cabut, **mencabut** to pull out, drag out; to uproot; to draw; **tercabut** pulled out, drawn (*of knife*).

caca salad.

cacah, **mencacah** to prick; to tattoo; to vaccinate; **bercacah** tattooed.

cacak, **mencacak** to stick (*pole*) into ground, erect; **tercacak** implanted; **mencacak lari** to bolt, run.

cacap hair wash.

cacar smallpox; **cacar air** chickenpox; **tanam cacar** to vaccinate.

cacat blemish, flaw; **bercacat** having a flaw; **mencacatkan** to criticize, find fault with.

cacau to confuse; disorder.

caci reeling gear; **mencaci maki** to abuse, vilify.

cacil feeling too small or light for its purpose.

cacing worms; **cacing gulung** earthworm; **cacing kerawit** threadworm; **cacing rambu** maggots in sores.

cadak differing at all; **sama tak cadak alike**, with no difference

cadang, **mendadangkan** to earmark (*money against emergencies*); suggest; **cadangan** proposal, suggestion.

cadar, **kain cadar** bedsheet; tablecloth.

cadas sandstone, rock.

cadik outrigger.

caduk curling up.

cadum to snatch up (*a child*).

cadung, **bercadung** sprouting.

cagak forked stick or rest, easel; **tercagak** stuck on a rest, stand; **mencagak** to mount on a stand.

cagar, mencagarkan to give (sth) as security for payment, surety for bail; cagaran pledge, deposit, surety.

cagat, tercagat hard, obstinate.

cagu, penyakit cagu disease of the toes.

cagul, tercagul projecting from a hole.

cagut chin; mencagut to bite with long beak (as bird, fish).

cah interjection (col: for Esah).

cahar lax (of stools); pencahar aperient; mencahar to purge.

cahaya light, gleam; bercahaya shining.

caing picked to pieces.

caipau hat, soldier's cap.

cair watery (of food, soil); to melt.

cais rein, bridle.

cak Malay pipit; cak padi munia; cak raya weaver bird.

cakah at an obtuse angle; mencakah to walk with legs wide apart; obtuse.

cakal–bakal founder of a village.

cakang = cakah.

cakap to undertake to; competent to; speak; cakap angin to talk rot; bercakap to have one's say, converse; percakapan conversation, talk.

cakar, mencakar to scratch; cakar-balar badly scratched; pencakar rake; pencakar langit skyscraper.

cakara joint earnings of ma and wife.

cakawari ancestors of the fifth generation.

cakela, rumah cakela brothel.

cakera discus, quoit.

cakerawala vault of heaven; selagi ada peredaran cakerawala as long as the heavens revolve.

cako shako.

caku, pisau caku pocket knife.

cakuk, mencakuk to hook with pole; crook; hit with elephant goad; golok cakuk bill hook.

cakup catching in the open mouth.

cakus, mencakus to carry a burden suspended from a stick that rests on the shoulder.

cal shawl.

calak smart (at work, of look); pencalak pestle of betel nut pounder.

calang leafless, bare.

calar scratch (of skin); calarbalar scratched all over; bercalar scratched.

caling tusk; canine tooth.

calit, mencalit to smudge (with ink, dirt); colloquial.

calu steamer's run; habit, routine.

calun, colon candidate (for post, election); mencalunkan to choose as a candidate.

calung bamboo water vessel, bamboo dipper; tin for latex.

cam, camkan, mengecam to recognize (by sight).

camang seesaw yoke (in loom).

camar, burung camar tern.

camat head of a sub-district.

cambah seed bud in coconut; bercambah germinating, budding.

cambai coarse leaf used as interior sireh.

cambang whiskers; cambang bauk side whiskers and beard; bercambang whiskered; also jambang.

cambus to whip, flagellate.

cambung large bowl, large basin.

camca spoon.

camdik to tease, get at.

campah flavourless (of food).

campak, mencampakkan to throw down; discarded; campak bunga children's game;

tercampak to throw down; discarded; measles.

campang to paddle vigorously.

campin speed; clever, competent.

camping in rags; compang-camping tattered at the edges.

campung broken at the tip; destroyed at one blow.

campur to add, mix up; mencampuri to mingle; bahasa campuran mixed dialects; bercampur to mix (with people, in an affair); campur-baur well-mixed; mencampurkan to mix up; mencampuri to meddle in.

camuk, mencamuk, to stab strike.

camur to scatter about, throw here and there.

canai to whet; mencanai to sharpen (knives); to grind (gems); batu canai whetstone; papan canai pastry board.

canang small gong; men-canangkan to announce with beat of gong.

canar climbing shrubs from which sarsaparilla is made.

cancang, tercancang to erect.

cancut, bercancut to pull up one's sleeves (to fight).

canda, canda, peti box (for keeping gold, jewellery); skittish.

candak to shorten a fishing line.

candakia tricky, slanderous.

candan black aloes wood.

candang, berani candang dauntless.

candat grapnel anchor.

candi Hindu monument; mausoleum; skittish (of ponies, women).

candik prince's concubine.

candit barb of a Malay anchor.

candu prepared opium.

candung, parang candung chopper in which the handle and blade are in one piece.

cang clanging; kuih cang pulut rice wrapped in bamboo leaves.

cangak, mencangak looking up startled.

cangam, mencangam to catch in the mouth.

cangap having a triangular notch (of pole).

cangerai ill luck; buang cangerai to circumcise.

canggah, bercanggah pronged (of spear, fork); mencanggah to point with two fingers levelled (at person).

canggal metal sheath (for long finger nails worn by Malay makyong dancers and brides).

canggek, conggang-canggek up and down bobbing motion; see-saw.

canggung inharmonious (of sound); clumsy; snag in the river; tercanggung left desolate, deserted.

cangip, cungap-cangip panting, out of breath.

cangkat low hill; shoal; shallow.

cangkih uneven, irregular; congkah-cangkih all ups and downs.

cangking, mencangking to lift in both hands; holding a person's arm to his side.

cangkir cup of porcelain or glass; spur, hind claw of bird.

cangkis irregular (of handwriting); scrawl.

cangkriman riddle.

cangku broker.

cangkuk large hook; ber-cangkuk hook-shaped; di-cangkuk caught in a hook.

cangkul hoe; mencangkul to hoe.

cangkum to embrace.

cangkung squatting on the haunches.

canguk, mencanguk to sit with head peering down.

cangut project of creese hilt from waist belt.

cantas, mencantas to sever by a single blow from a heavy cutting instrument; lopping, pruning.

cantel safety pin.

cantengan whitlow.

cantik pretty, good-looking; **bercantik** beautified.

cantil triangular sail.

canting coconut dipper; weight to prevent anchor from dragging; **canting-canting** scribbled over.

cantis, mencantis to cut off an extremity by accident or design.

cantol, mencantol to hook (as thorn).

cantum, bercantum joined together (as bird's ruffled feathers).

cap stamp or seal; bubuh cap to affix seal; **capkan** to print.

capa game of heads or tails; Ngai camphor plant.

capah unpainted platter; wide (of stride).

capai, mencapai to achieve; grasp extending the arms upward; attain one's desire; **tercapai** grasped, attained.

capak, mencapak to underrate (advice, foe); be indifferent to country; slight deliberately.

capal sandals.

capang wide-spreading (of ears, nostrils).

capgome 15th day of Chinese new year.

capik lame; limping; **capik riuk** suffering from a fracture badly set.

capil sun hat.

caping (metal or coconut shell) modesty piece for infant girls.

capjiki game with twelve dice.

caplak dog tick.

caplok, mencaplok to snap (at chicken bait, by crocodile).

capras brass plate on orderly's shoulder scarf; driver's badge.

capuk to insult by exposing the private parts; pockmarked; **bercapuk-capuk** notched (of badly-cut hair).

capung dragonfly.

cara way, fashion, style, method; **secara** like, resembling; **acara** programme.

carah, bercarah in scraps, small pieces.

carak clear, visible; = **cerah.**

carang leaf-bearing twigs; **mencarang panas** to grow hot (of day).

carbi grease used for lubrication.

cari, mencari to hunt for (person, thing); to seek a livelihood; cari jalan, cari ikhtiar to search for a means or course of action; **pencarian** means of livelihood; harta **sepencarian** joint earnings of husband and wife.

carik tearing; rent; **corak-carik** in shreds; **mencarik** to tear bits off; **carik-carikan** to tear to shreds.

caruk runnel, ditch; creek.

carum, bercarum to subscribe to a club fund; **caruman** gratuity.

carut obscene language; **mencarut** to use obscene language.

cas bill, charge, account; **mencaskan** to charge at; butt opponent at football.

cat paint; **mengecat** to paint; **bercat** painted.

catak horsefly; = **pikat.**

catang rattan basket cosy.

catar to charter.

catat, mencatat to make a

note; catatan memorandum; also **catit.**

catu, catuan ration, dole; **mencatukan** to dole out, distribute.

catuk, mencatuk to peck (of bird); bite (of snake); perch; **ceratuk; tercatuk** sticking up.

catur chess; **buah catur** chessmen; **main catur, bercatur** to play chess.

catut pincer; **pencatut** dealer in black market.

cauk dimple from laughter; **lesung pipit.**

caul, kain caul cloth from the Indian port, Chaul.

caung hollow in cheeks through loss of teeth.

caus thin from emaciation.

cawak dimple; **bercawak** dimpled.

cawan cup; **alas cawan** saucer.

cawang forking of boughs; **bercawang** forked, branching off; **cawangan** branch organization; river's tributary.

cawas, mencawas to use a punt pole as an oar in deep water.

cawat loincloth, suspensory bandage; (fig) **sepuluh jong datang; anjing bercawat ekor juga** ten junks may arrive but a dog's only cloth is his tail.

cawi, burung cawi drongo.

cawis ready.

cebak to excavate (in quarry work); digging out by sidelong blows.

cebar—cebur splashing (of bathers).

cebek to carry in the hand (as a suitcase).

cebet to pick and carry in the fingers.

cebik pouting, making a wry face.

cebis chipped, torn at the edge; **secebis** scrap.

cebok I ladle, coconut scoop;

mencebok to scoop water; **bercebok** to cleanse the body after defecation or urination.

cebok II to walk through puddles or floods.

cebol dwarf.

cebong tadpole.

cebur plump (sound); to plunge into water; **menceburkan diri** to plunge o.s. into; **tercebur** ruined.

cecah, cicah dipping (pen into ink); **sececah** moment.

cecak, cicak freckled; tabby; **belang cecak** spotted (of shells, leopards).

cecap, mencecap to taste; **burung cecap** sunbird.

cecar, mencecar to bother, bully; cross-examine.

cecaru, ikan cecaru horse mackerel.

ceceng, menceceng to run off with tail up.

cecer, cicir, berceceran dribbling away (as money from a pocket).

cecereh freshwater carp.

cecewe, burung cecewe plover.

cedak to erect; palm leaf hood.

cedas to smooth a plait by passing a rattan over it; nimble, active.

cedera flaw, defect; **mendatangkan cedera** to injure s.o.'s reputation; **kecederaan** damage or losses in war.

ceding too thin (of children); small (of plants, fruits).

cedok to ladle up; baling.

ceduk sunken (of cheeks, eyes).

cedungan, padi cedungan wet padi; **mencedung** to plant wet padi.

cega, mencega wary, cautious (of birds, fish, people).

cegah=tegah.

cegak strong; strong and active (after sickness).

cegar shallow rapids, race.

cegat, tercegat erect, stiff.

ceguk, seceguk gulp; = **seteguk.**

cegung severed, cut.

ceh fie!, for shame!, faugh!

cek, encek cheque.

cekah to split open; splitting under pressure.

cekak holding between the thumb and forefinger; **secekak** pinch; **bercekak pinggang** with arms akimbo; **bercekak** to quarrel.

cekal stout-hearted; strength; **mencekal** to grasp neck; arrest.

cekam sharp pointed stick used in making holes for planting hill paddy; **sakit cekam** sore under a toe nail; **tilam cekam** mattress stuffed and sewn.

cekang tight; tightly stretched, taut.

cekap skilful, expert, competent.

cekar to put steering wheel hard over.

cekatan quick, adroit.

cekau, mencekau to seize (in one's clutches, talons); grab.

cekawari remote descendants; also **cengkawari.**

cekel, cikil, kekel miserly, stingy.

ceki small Chinese playing cards.

cekih, tercekih open and showing contents (of fruits).

cekik, mencekik leher to seize by the throat; **mati tercekik** death by choking.

cekit, mencekit, bercekit to peck at, take a little at a time.

ceku denting with the finger nail.

cekuh to pick up with the finger and thumb.

cekuk, mencekuk to feed an infant forcibly; administer medicine to an unwilling child;

cekuk-cekek choking (of a drowning man).

cekung concave.

cekup, mencekup to cover with palm; catch under the hand; pick up food with finger tips.

cekur creeping weed much used in children's medicine; name of a shrub the leaves of which are eaten as vegetables.

cekut, secekut pinch; **mencekut** to take a pinch of.

cela defect; **tiada celanya** flawless; **bercela** damage; **mencelakan** to blame; to criticize; **celaan** blame, criticism; **kecelaan** defective; criticized.

celadang square rice basket.

celaga soot; handle of tiller.

celah interspace, cleavage, cleft; **celah bukit** pass between hills; **celah batu** space between two boulders; **celah jari** space between two fingers.

celak I antimony powder (used to darken the fringe of the eye).

celak II, tercelak clean, bright.

celaka accursed; **nasib celaka** accursed fate; **orang celaka** confounded person; **celakanya** what damnable luck.

celakuti betel nut scissors; = **kacip.**

celam-celum tramping (in and out of a house without ceremony).

celana trousers.

celang, mencelang staring (of eyes).

celangak open (of doors).

celangap agape (of mouth).

celapah soiling, dishonouring.

celapak astride, sitting on the fork, sitting astride; **jatuh tercelapak** to fall astride with legs parted.

celar, mencelar to open eyes wide.

celari, kain celari silk with gold thread.

celaru disorderly; confused, untidy.

celas–celus passing in and out without ceremony.

celat, mencelat leap high or far.

celatu flying ant; (better) **kelekatu**.

celatuk, bercelatuk to joke.

cele, kain cele chequered fabric.

celebuk having a cavity, undercut (of river bank).

celebur to plunge into water.

celedang–celedok swaggering, rolling gait.

celekati betel nut scissors.

celekut to swindle, cheat.

celempung musical instrument, set of gongs.

celeng hog, pig; = babi.

celengap agape, openmouthed.

celengkang–celengkok meandering, zigzagging.

celepa watch-shaped tobacco box suspended by chain from belt or kerchief.

celepih to fold over an edge.

celepik sound of flicking; sound of small object dropping on floor.

celepuk to bake in embers.

celepuk sound of a splash.

celi keen-eyed.

celici greedy; prevaricating.

celih idle, lazy, sluggish.

celik, mencelikkan mata to open eyes; (fig) si buta baharu celik blind man who sees for the first time (beggar on horseback).

celika cunning; false.

celis unsatisfied; tercelis-celis lidah with one's tongue hanging out; mencelis to chop up, mince.

celomis filthy; talkative; sickly.

celonet upturning; projecting; = ceronet.

celoteh, berceloteh to chatter.

celum–celam tramping, stamping.

celung stall for an elephant or buffalo.

celungap greedy (of children).

celup steeping in; dyeing; dicelup merah dyed red.

celupak small saucer for an opium smoker's lamp.

celupar chattering, talkative; also mulut celupar.

celur, mencelurkan to dip in boiling water.

celurut musk shrew; = cencurut.

celus fitting easily (of rings, clothes); big enough (of any aperture).

celut, pencelut thief; cry of children when playing hide-and-seek.

celutong big black wormlike millipede.

cema, tanda cema to lay an accusation.

cemabai tattered.

cemahang illness (caused by offending forest tree or elephant).

cemamping tattered.

cenami black throughout.

cemar dirt, filth; dirty (of persons, words, reputation); mencemari to defile; dicemar polluted; bercemar kaki to soil the feet.

cemara false hair; tuft of horse hair under spear blade; pokok cemara casuarina tree.

cemas apprehensive, anxious, nervous; dengan cemas anxiously; kecemasan emergency; pertolongan cemas first aid; cemas-cemas narrowly escaping; cemas mati barely escaping death.

cemat to warp a ship; tali cemat towrope.

cembul casket, small box; laksana cembul dengan tutupnya casket and its cover (exactly suited one to another).

cembung, bulat cembung convex.

cemburu suspicious (of infidelity, crime); jealous.

cemek, mencemek to show disgust; make a wry face.

oemengkian, cěngkian purging croton.

cemer extremely dimsighted, nearly blind.

cemerkap rough; slipshod (of workmanship).

cemerlang radiant, glittering.

cemeti horsewhip.

cemidu nervous, self-conscious.

cemiduk shy, reluctant to meet people.

cemongkah, **cemangkeh** projecting unevenly (as teeth).

cempa, bunga cempa cempaka flower.

cempaka campak tree; cempaka biru frangipani.

cempala stick used by the manager (dalang) of the shadow play; quarrelsome; cempala mulut quick in speech; cempala tangan quick to strike.

cempana, jempana litter.

cempedak jackfruit; = nangka.

cempelik pitch and toss (game).

cempelung sound of a heavy body falling into water.

cempera, bercempera scattering, helter-skelter.

cemperai name of several low-country shrubs.

cemperas, ikan cemperas freshwater carp.

cemperling tree starling; mata cemperling very red eyes; also perling.

cempiang armed and open gang robbery or piracy.

cemping, secemping very small bit, morsel.

cempiras red jungle tick.

cempung to lift (person, load) in one's embrace.

cempurit sticks by which the leather figures in shadow play are manipulated.

cemuas dirty (of lips from food); greasy.

cemucup love grass.

cemuk pod, pod-shaped beads; to quarrel; to hit out at in fun with a stick.

cemus sated = jemu.

cena mark, scar (on fighting cock, evidence of his prowess); kecenaan scarred.

cenaku weretiger.

cenangau malodorous flying bug very destructive to padi = pianggang.

cenangga congenitally deformed; tangan cenangga deformed hand.

cenangkas long cutlass.

cenayang shaman (with the powers of a medium to consult the spirit world).

cencada mantis.

cencadu fruit bats, mantis.

cencala fantail flycatcher.

cencaluk prawn pickle.

cencang, cincang, mencencang to mince (up), cut fine; bercencang slashed.

cencawan joint cavity of the knee.

cencawi, burung cencawi King crow.

cenceng, mencenceng scamper off (as child, deer).

cencodak garpike, swordfish = todak.

concurut musk shrew.

cenda kind, sort.

cendala pariah (in caste); low (of conduct).

cendana sandalwood.

cendarik orchid.

cendawan fungus, mushroom, mould; **cendawan mabuk** poisoned by fungi; **bercendawan** mouldy.

cendayam fair, beautiful.

cendera moon fairy; deep (*of sleep*); **cendera mata** gift; darling; delight of the eye; souvenir.

cenderai small trees.

cenderawasih moonbird; bird of paradise.

cenderung sloping, declivitous; **cenderung hati** inclining to.

cenderus, mencenderuskan to remove rancidity from ghee.

cenduai, minyak cenduai oil made from a flower and used for enticing women by magic.

cendul kind of thin broth with cakes of dough floating in it.

cenela slipper.

cenerul, bercenerul to scream with laughter.

cengai, cengal large tree with very hard commercial timber.

cengam, mencengam to seize in the mouth.

cengang, tercengang dumbfounded, amazed; **tercengang-cengang** agape with astonishment.

cengeng whining, querulous (*of infants*).

cenggek, bercenggek to perch.

cengi talking with a nasal twang.

cengil captious, hypercritical; talking vehemently; strict (*of employer, teacher*).

cengir to twitch the nose angrily.

cengris stinking (*of strong scent, fruit*).

cengkadak, cengkaduk praying mantis.

cengkal measure of length 12 feet.

cengkam gripping between finger and thumb.

cengkang wakeful, sleepless; barring the passage; = **sengkang**.

cengkaruk sweetmeat made of boiled rice.

cengkau broker, middleman.

cengkedi malignant, ghostly.

cengkek to limp on one side of the foot.

cengkek tight at the waist, narrow-waisted.

cengkenit tick infesting dogs and pigs.

cengkera hollow-cheeked, sunken-faced.

cengkeram part payment in advance.

cengkerama talk (*of lovers*); to amuse o.s.; be spread (*of news*).

cengkerek cricket.

cengkereng, cengkering chickenpox.

cengkerung hollow-eyed.

cengkiak bulldog ant; kiak-kiak.

cengkih, buah cengkih the clove-spice.

cengking emaciated; **cengking-mengking**.

cengkir very young coconut.

cengkolong withdrawing a small amount from a large, drawing on a deposit.

cengkuak, burung cengkuai blue-grey flycatcher.

cengkuas shaggy, unkempt; to carry off over the shoulder.

cengkuk leaf monkey; zig-zagging (*of road, river*).

cengkul deformed, bent (*of arm*); twisted (*of leg*).

cengkung I deformed, bent, twisted.

cengkung II hollow-eyed, sunken (*of the eyes, cheeks*).

cengkurai, kain cengkurai

mottled silk fabric; **bereng-kurai** crumbling to fragments, breaking up into pieces.

cengkus-mengkis bickering.

cengkuyung, siput cengkuyung large cowrie shell.

cengup-cengap sound of eating.

cenok, burung cenok lesser green-billed malkoha.

cenonot, cenonot ayam 'parson's nose', rump of cooked fowl.

centadu green leaf caterpillar; *also* sentadu, mentadu.

centayu king of the vultures.

centeng subordinate customs officer.

centung cockatoo's crest.

centut stunted.

cenung, tercenung contemplative.

cenuram declivitous, steep; *also* curam.

cepak I, mencepak dribble.

cepak II sound of lapping.

cepaka = cempaka.

cepat quick; cepat lari to run fast; bercepat-cepat to hurry; kecepatan speed.

cepeh limp and hanging (*of buffalo horn*).

cepelok ornamental pillowend.

ceper flat-edged metal plate (*commonly put under water vessels*); small salver.

cepu round (*metal or wooden or china*) box with convex lid for betel requisites.

cepua blush of shame, guilty look.

cepuh club-footed.

cepuk small (*wooden or metal*) box for food.

cerabah ugly (*of child*).

ceracak many-spiked.

ceracap bamboo castanets.

cerah clear (*of weather, daylight, complexion*); cuaca cerah clear daylight.

cerai severance; separation, divorce; bercerai to separate from; to be divorced from; ceraikan to separate (*one person from another*); ceraiberai broken up, scattered; ceraian separation; paragraph.

cerak certain, definite.

cerakin portable chest with trays for medicinal herbs; analyse.

ceramah conversable, garrulous; talk; ramah.

cerana salver holding vessels for betel requisites.

cerancang bristling, spiky.

cerang thin mountaintop forest; clearing.

ceranggah branching into points.

cerap to take note of; be cognizant; cerap luar extroversion.

cerapung foaming (*of waves*).

cerat spout, nozzle; mencerat to broach, drain off, tap.

ceratuk, berceratuk sitting or squatting in a row.

cerau sound of pouring water.

cerawat arrow of fire, rocket.

cerbak gluttonous.

cerbis slip (*of bank*).

cerca slander, abuse, insult; mencerca to revile.

cercak slightly pock-marked.

cercap, mencercap to leap out of the water.

cercek, ikan seluang cercek freshwater carp.

cerdas smart (*of wits*); crafty, clever, alert in body; kecerdasan development, advancement; intelligence; buffalo whip.

cerdik cunning, sharp-witted, bright, intelligence; kecerdikan cleverness, craftiness.

cere, padi cere quick ripening strain of rice.

cerek kettle, kettle-shaped water vessel.

cerewet to bicker; nagging; fussing, grumbling; **burung cerewet** Burmese wattled lapwing.

cergas, kecergasan energetic.

ceri, gelang ceri bangle.

ceria clean, clear; menceriakan diri to purify o.s.; baca ceria to read an address of loyalty to a ruler on his accession.

ceridau noise of people (arguing or quarreling); noise of birds; flying round, swarming.

ceriga being on one's guard, wary, watchful = curiga.

cering, cering-cering feverish, indisposed.

cerita tale, false report, fiction; bercerita telling a tale; menceritakan to narrate.

cerkau to keep grabbing at; also cekau.

cerlang bright, glorious = cemerlang.

cerlih, tupai cerlih type of squirrel.

cermai tree with small acid fruit.

cermat conscientious; painstaking; neat; neatness in appearance or dress.

cermin mirror; glass spangles; shining examples; cermin mata spectacles.

cerna digested; mencernakan to digest; kecernaan digestion.

ceroboh rough, unseemly; aggressive; menceroboh to trespass; pencerobohan outrages, breaches of a treaty.

cerobong ship's funnel; factory chimney.

ceronggah projecting untidily.

ceronggok sitting in crowds.

ceropong chimney, funnel.

cerotok arranged in a sitting row.

cerpelai mongoose.

cerpen short story.

cerpu sandals.

ceruak to throw away slops (out of window etc).

cerubah weapon.

cerucah ship.

cerucup love-grass, burr; also kemuncup.

ceruh second pounding of rice to whiten it; menceruh to mill twice.

ceruk corner, nook; blind alley; diceruk gunung ravine; ceruk-menceruk to hunt in every nook; menceruk to reap.

cerul crumbling (of soil).

cerun sloping (of hill, roof).

cerung source of a river, cerung-cerang tinkling of anklets.

cerup, cerup-cerap sound of lapping or eating.

cerut, mencerut to squeeze, constrict, compress on all sides; cigar; sickle.

cerutu cheroot, cigar.

cetai, bercetai-cetai torn to ribbons.

cetak, mencetak to print; to mould a steel article; cetakan printed edition; pencetak printer.

cetas crack of a whip.

cetek shallow (of water, knowledge).

ceteng lift or carry with one.

cetera story = cerita; payung cetera state umbrella.

ceteri tent, awning, canopy.

ceteria member of the princely or warrior caste; warrior.

ceti chetty; moneylender.

cetok, bank; mencetok to peck with beak.

cetus, cetus api flint for making fire; mencetus to strike flint.

cewe, pawang name for fourfooted animals and snakes esp at sea; cewe mengaum tiger; cewe panjang crocodile.

China Chinese; **Negeri China** China; **bunga cina** gardenia.

china buta intermediate husband a thrice-divorced Muslim woman must have before remarriage to her original husband; = **muhallil.**

ci measure of weight used in weighing opium.

ciak twitter of small birds; sparrows; **ciak uban** white-headed Munia; **ciak raya** weaver bird.

ciang swollen (of udders with milk).

ciap, menciap cheeping of chickens, twittering, squeaking.

ciar, terciar-ciar squalling (of infant).

cias impatience; **tunjuk cias** to display temper.

ciau, menciau to row boat standing; **terciau** worn in a careless and indecent way.

cicak house lizard, gecko; **cicak terbang** flying lizard.

cicih penis.

cicik to feel repugnance.

cicil, mencicil to pay instalments; **cicilan** instalments.

cicinda great-grandchild.

cicit great-grandchild; **mencicit** squeak of mice; twitter of birds; **mencicit lari** to make a bolt.

cida, tercida to dislocate (shoulder).

cigak monkey.

oik form of **encik,** polite form of address; **Oik Ahmad** Mister Ahmad.

cika severe colic.

cikar waggon.

cikerak refuse basket.

ciku sapodilla.

oikutan hiccup.

cilat trick, dodge.

cilawagi ancestors of the fifth generation back.

cili chilli, red pepper.

cilik small.

cilok, mencilok to steal; **pencilok** thief.

cimcili, burung cimcili resident paradise flycatcher.

cimpur soft (of durian).

cincang to mince.

cincau tubers of a climber, jelly made from them.

cincin finger ring; **cincin sebentuk** one ring; **cincin tanda betrothal ring.**

cincu owner's agent on a Chinese ship.

cinda great-grandson; polite form of **cicit.**

cindai, kain cindai silk fabric of Sind origin once popular as waist sashes.

cingam mangrove shrub with very hard wood used for fences.

cinta loving; desire; regret; longing; **bercinta** to have a lover; be sad, anxious; **bercintakan** to be in love with; mourn for the dead; **mencinta** to conjure up.

cintamani wish gem, philosopher's stone; **ular cintamani** legendary snake possessing this stone.

cinting = **centeng.**

cipai Sumatran monkey.

cipan battle axe; young tapir.

cipta, menciptakan to conjure up; create, invent; **ciptaan** invention; **pencipta** inventor; **tercipta** created.

circir small bell.

ciri address to Malay ruler at his installation.

cirit diarrhoea; **cirit-birit** running continuously.

cis = **ceh.**

cita feeling; **sukacita** feeling joy, glad; **dukacita** sad; to fix one's thought upon a talisman in order to get its magical aid; **kain cita** chintz.

ciu ceremonial sitting mat of three layers.

cium, mencium to sniff, smell; kiss; **mencium** to kiss with noses; **pencium** organ for smelling; **tercium** caught the smell of.

ciut short, thin (*as hair*).

coang, bercoang-coang sticking up (*as spears*).

coba, mencoba attempting, trying, testing; (*col*) please; **coba tengok, coba-coba** to try half-heartedly, not seriously; **mencobakan** to test, try; **cobaan** test; **percobaan** effort, attempt, experiment.

cobak, cobak-cabik tattered and torn.

coban needle of horn *or* bamboo used in making fishing nets and sails, small shuttle for gold thread.

cobar, cobar-cabir tattered and torn.

cobek saucer for crushing spices; **secobek** pinch.

cobis, secobis splinter, fragment from the edge.

cocok, mencocok to pierce, prick, inject, make holes; **cocok sanggul** hairpin; **perut mencocok** to have stabbing abdominal pain; **bercocok** strung (*of beads*); **secocok** in agreement.

cocol, mencocol to dip.

codak, mencodak to raise the head; **tercodak** lifted up.

codot fruit vat.

cogah robust, strong, vigorous.

cogan sign in the sky; state emblem; **cogan kata** motto, slogan.

cogat, cegat standing up in an empty place.

cogok, tercogok prominent.

cok ornamental hairpin.

cokar draughts (*game*).

cokek singing and dancing.

cokelat, warna cokelat chocolate brown colour.

cokera servant, boy.

coket, mencoket to take a little.

cokin, kain cokin short bathing cloth.

coking, tercoking projecting; **tercoking-coking** swaggering.

cokmar bludgeon, mace.

cokoh, tercokoh brooding.

cokok to splash water in fun; **mencokok** to startle; **pak pecokok** old rogue.

cokol, bercokol sitting still for long.

colak, colak-caling in disorder.

colar-calar scratched all over.

colek, colet, mencolek to kidnap; pick out with a pin *or* tip of a finger; strike a match; **mencolek hati** to tickle, cause laughter; **pencolek gigi** toothpick.

coli tight short bodice.

colok match for fuse; **colok mata in** the limelight; **mencolok mata** to strike the eye.

colong, mencolong to steal.

colot, mencolot to spring (*like frogs*).

comberan drain, ditch.

comblang pimp, go-between.

combol door knob.

comek imperial beard; small cuttlefish.

comel dainty, pretty; **mencomel** to grouse.

comot dirty (*of body, writing*).

compang-camping torn, tattered at the edge, frayed.

compis chipped at the edge.

compok, harimau compok golden cat.

conderong inclining, leaning; **conderong hati** mental leaning; *also* **enderong condong**.

condong sloping, inclined; **matahari condong** setting sun; **hati condong** biased; **condong kepada** favouring; oblique; **kecondongan** inclination.

conet pointed and upturning.

congak, mencongak to raise head and chin; do mental arithmetic in class; **congakkan** to tilt up a person's head.

congeh gaping (of wounds).

congek purulent running from the ear.

conggah, conggah-cemangkeh projecting unevenly, sticking out every direction; also **congkah.**

conggang–congget to keep bending forward and then straightening (as a hill-climber).

conggeng sticking out (as a thorn).

congget bobbing up and down.

conggok to put upright.

congkah projecting unevenly, out of line; **congkah-mangkeh** not properly piled up or arranged.

congkak proud, conceited; cowrie shell, game played with this shell; **papan congkak** board used for playing this game.

congkar–cangkir projecting spikily.

congkelang to gallop.

congkong guardhouse.

congo pickpocket.

congok, mencongok to stand erect.

congol to protrude.

congong foolish, stupid, silly, idiotic.

contang, menconteng to smear smirch; **terconteng** smudged.

contoh specimen; pattern; model; **ambil contoh** to take as a model or example.

contong leaf or paper screwed into a cone and inverted to form a bag or wrapper for sweets etc.

cop spade; as you were!; it won't do!

copet, mencopet to pilfer; **pencopet** pickpocket.

copot loose (of knots, teeth, nail).

corak coloured pattern on cloth; **bercorak** having a pattern; **corak-corek** tattered.

corang cheating at games; **pencorang** cheat.

corat–caret scrawl (of drawing); scrawled.

corek striped (of pattern); scratched.

coreng to besmear; stripes, streaks; **coreng-moreng** streaked all over; **bercoreng** streaked; scrawled over; tattooed.

coret stripes.

coro cockroach = lipas.

corong funnel (for bottle or cask); chimney (of lamp); **corong radio** loudspeaker; **mencorong** to belch forth.

corot left behind, rearmost, last; **pencorot** lastcomer.

cota police baton.

cotet very little; small at the end.

cotok beak; **mencotok** to peck, tap.

cu = bongsu youngest of brothers or sisters.

cuaca weather; **terang cuaca** clear bright weather; **ramalan cuaca** weatherforecast.

cuai inferior, unimportant; **mencuaikan** to treat lightly, underrate.

cuak timid, nervous.

cual to let drop through careless handling; cloth in the first stage of its manufacture.

cuali independent; **kaum cuali** independent; **kecuali** except; **kecuali kalau dia lambat** unless they are late.

cuani kind of cloth.

cuar, tercuar sticking up high.

cuat, tercuat sticking up (of short object).

cuba=coba.

cubih to let drop.

cubit, mencubit to pinch between thumb and finger; mencubit to pinch.

cubung larvae of flies.

cuca spell to silence *or* confuse an enemy; mencuca to so silence *or* confuse.

cuci, mencuci to cleanse; develop a film; cuci tangan to wash the hands.

cucu, cucunda grandchild(ren).

cucuh, mencucuh to set fire to, light; cucuh meriam ten fire a cannon.

cucuk=cocok.

cucup, mencucup to sip; kiss (*with the lips*); *also* kucup.

cucur, mencucur to flow, trickle; mencucuri to let liquid fall on; mencucurkan to sprinkle liquid on; cucuran atap eaves of the roof; kuih cucur Malay cake.

cucut shark; mencucut to suck, lap.

cugat, cegat to erect.

cuh! on! (*cry to hunting dogs*).

cuik saucer; ikan cuik fish steamed and salted.

cuit, mencuit to poke a person with one's finger; tercuit-cuit gesticulating with the fingers.

cuk mosquito larvae.

cuka vinegar; makan cuka to get a taste of vinegar; cuka belanda acetic acid.

cukai tax, customs, duty; cukai pendapatan income tax.

cukil game like draughts.

cukit fork.

cuku dried gambier root.

cukup enough, full; dengan secukupnya sufficiently; mencukupi to make up; complete.

cukur, mencukur to shave; bercukur to shave (*o.s.*).

cula horn (*of dragon, rhinoceros*); cula tupai aphrodisiac talisman.

culan, bunga culan plant whose flowers are used to scent tea and clothes.

culas lazy, born tired, inert, sluggish.

Culia Muslim traders from Malabar.

culik, culik-culik female cuckoo; penculik kidnapper; *also* colek.

culim pipeful (*of tobacco, opium*); menculim to fill a pipe.

cuma in vain; only; mati percuma dead to no purpose; cuma sepuluh sen only ten cents.

cumbu to coax; flirt with; cumbuan endearment; bercumbu-cumbuan flirting, exchanging endearments.

cun Chinese inch.

cunam long delicate pincers for extracting wax from the ear; prepared lime used in the betel quid.

cunda grandchild.

cundang, mencundang to conquer by magic (*esp women*); kecundang conquest; position of the defeated relative to the victor; *also* kundang.

cungap, tercungap, mencungap to pant; panting; cungap-cangip.

cungkil, mencungkil to gouge out; vaccinate; pick teeth; pencungkil gigi toothpick.

cungkup grave cover.

cunglit plover.

cupak measure of capacity; quarter of a gantang, half a coconut shellful.

cupar to sneer at, deride.

cupet short, inadequate.

cupil too near an edge; about to fall.

cuping ear-lobe; cuping hidung curve of nostrils.

cupis to break away (*of cliff*).

cuplik, mencuplik to borrow; cite; cuplikan quotation.

cupul, tercupul too short cord; untidy, loose.

cupur extreme edge.

cur to sizzle (*as food fried*).

cura to babble; joke.

curah emptying out; curahkan to pour out.

curai loose; mencuraikan to unravel; explain.

curam sloping, steep.

curang deceitful; mencurang to cheat; pencurang sharper; cheat.

curat, mencurat to pour down, gush out.

curi, mencuri to steal; pencuri thief; kecurian stolen; curi-curi stealthily.

curiah friendly.

curiga knife; suspicion, distrust.

curut = corot.

cus fizz! buzz off!; fie!

cutam black and gilt niello.

outap waist buckle of shiny black material.

cuti furlough, holiday; ber-outi to be on leave.

D

daawa accusation, indictment, claim; kena daawa to be sued, charged; mendaawa atas to accuse; Pendaawa Raya Public Prosecutor.

daayah propaganda.

daba foul air, strong smell; leather belt pouch for cartridges.

dabir clerk, scribe.

dabung, mendabung to file the teeth level.

dabus broad round shaft of wood with a short spike set like a spearhead at its end; main dabus self-stabbing dervish dance.

dacing steelyard; scales; anak dacing, batu dacing, buah dacing weight on steelyard.

dada chest, breast; mendada, berdada to fight breast to breast = hand to hand.

dadah drugs, medicines.

dadak stone-deaf; kedadak suddenly; cekik kedadak may you choke suddenly; mendadak bustle.

dadap metal shield.

dadar thin pancake; mendadar to distribute charity.

dadih curdled milk; air dadih whey; buffalo milk.

dadu, buah dadu dice; main dadu to play with dice; berdadu to gossip.

daduk, menduduk to beg, solicit for alms.

dadung, mendadung to sing to sleep.

daerah district, region; bahasa daerah dialect.

dafnah laurel.

daftar list, catalogue; daftar alamat directory; pendaftar registrar; mendaftarkan to list; to enrol; register; pendaftaran registration.

daga, mendaga to breast (*hill, current*); make an effort; daga-dagi insubordination; pendagi agitator; mendagi to resist authority.

dagang alien, stranger, foreigner; dagangan articles of commerce; perdagangan commerce; berdagang to go abroad, travel.

dagel, tukang dagel clown.

dagi covetousness.

daging flesh, meat; daging babi pork; daging kambing mutton; daging lembu beef; daging darah one's own flesh and blood; mendaging fleshy, plump.

dagu chin.

dah = sudah get on! (*cry to cattle*).

dahaga thirst; thirsty; lapar dahaga hunger and thirst; resistance to authority; dahaga-dahagi all sorts of contempt of authority.

dahagi extreme covetousness.

dahak phlegm; berdahak to hawk up phlegm.

daham, berdaham to clear the throat to attract attention; to hum and haw.

dahan large bough, branch; harimau dahan large tiger cat; pendahan javelin.

dahana, mendahana to beg for alms.

dahi forehead.

dahlia dahlia (*flower*).

dahriah, kaum dahriah free-thinker.

dahsyat panic; awful, fearful; memberi dahsyat to terrify.

dahu, burung dahu the adjutant bird.

dahuk covetous.

dahulu before; zaman dahulu past age; bulan dahulu last month; lebih dahulu ahead; dahulu daripada itu before that; mendahulukan to do first, prefer; berdahulu-dahulu-an hurrying to get ahead of another.

dai muezzin; propagandist.

daif *guon* weak, feeble.

daieram diaphragm.

dailog dialogue.

daim eternal, lasting.

daing dried fish; Bugis title; minta darah pada daing to ask for blood from dried fish (trying to get blood out of a stone).

Dajal antichrist; liar, deceiver.

dak = tidak no, not; buat dak to pretend not to know.

daka, tiang daka wooden supports upon which rest the planks in a Muslim's grave.

dakaik subtle question.

dakap, mendakap embracing;

berdakap-dakapan embracing one another.

dakar = dangkar stubborn, obstinate.

dakhil trusty.

daki dirt; dry sweat; mendaki to ascend, climb up.

daksina south.

daku me (*form from the word* aku *after* akan, —kan, dengan).

dal, kacang dal pulse; split peas.

dalal broker, intermediary, go-between.

dalalah exegesis of the Koran; *see* dalil.

dalam interior; inside; in; while, during; dalam rumah in the house; bahasa dalam court language; dalamnya depth; mendalamkan, memperdalamkan to deepen.

dalang reciter of shadow play; secret leader of revolt.

dali, berdali to descend (*of a spirit on to the ear posy of a raja on installation*).

dalih evasion; berdalih equivocate.

dalik, dolak-dalik shilly-shallying.

dalil proof (*esp by citation of the Koran*); memberi dalil to produce proof.

dalu, berdalu mistletoe.

dalung pedestal tray with a number of dishes.

dam draughts (*game*); buah dam draughts (*pieces*); religious penalty; (*of cloth*) check.

damai conciliation, agreement; damaikan to effect a settlement; berdamai to be at peace; perdamaian settlement of a difference; perdamaian sementara armistice.

damak, anak damak dart for a blow pipe.

damal slow to move; difficult to sail or row (*of boat*).

daman sheet of a large sail.

damar resin from various Malayan trees; torch made of resin.

damba to desire, wish to possess.

dambal slow (of boats).

dambin fat as an ox.

dambun, berdambun boom of a drum.

damdam, dam check (of patterns); see dendam.

damik to strike with the palm of the hand, slap.

dampak, mendampak to strike, knock.

dampar, terdampar beached, stranded, driven ashore.

dampil, berdampil-dampil rubbing shoulders (in crowds).

damping, berdamping dengan close to; side by side.

dan and, furthermore; time to do; **dankah** pergi is there time to go?; **tak dan** there is no time.

dana alms; see dahana.

danam yoke beam for draught.

danau lake also danu.

danawa giant demon.

dandan decoration (of person or ship); **mendandani** to decorate; quip; cable for ship; thick rattan rope for tethering cattle.

dandang large copper boiler.

dandi lute; speckled (of deer, plant).

dang honorific for ladies of birth; = dayang.

dangai sweetmeat of glutinous rice and coconut.

dangak, mendangak to hold the head up; also dongak.

dangau watcher's hut in rice field or orchard.

dangir, mendangir to dig and throw earth in a heap.

dangka, terdangka-dangka to go inshore; skirt.

dangkal dry, lacking in juiciness; shallow (of water).

dangkar, dongkor-dangkar bundled out, expelled.

dangking, dongkang-dangking extremely emaciated.

dangkung leprosy in the mutilating stage.

danguk, mendanguk to have the head thrust forward; **terdanguk** aground with bows on reef and stern in water.

dangut, mendangut to call at a house (remaining on the ladder).

dansanak blood relations on one's mother's side.

danta ivory; **asmara danta** beautiful white teeth.

danu pool; **ular danu** rainbow.

danur archer.

danur putrefaction from a corpse.

dap tabur, drum; long-handled sword.

dapan, di hadapan in front; also, depan.

dapat, mendapat to obtain; incur; contrive; be able; discover; meet; **dapat wang** to get money; **dapat rahsia** to discover a secret; **mendapatkan orang** to go to find a person; **pendapat** finding; opinion; **pendapatan** earnings; **tak dapat tidak** it must be; **kedapatan** found; **terdapat** found; got.

dapra ship's rope or rattan fender.

dapur stove; kitchen; **rumah dapur** cookhouse, kitchen; **dapur tanah** mud-oven; **dapur-dapur susu** outer portion of the breast, **dapur-dapur kubur** enclosure, border planks of a grave.

dar abode; **dar al-fanak** transitory abode, the world; **dar-al** Islam abode of the Muslim faith, Muslim world.

dara maiden; hymen; **anak dara** virgin; **perdaraan** court damsels.

darab to multiply arithmetically.

darah blood; daging darah one's own flesh and blood; berdarah bleeding, suffused with blood.

darai impotent (*of males*).

darapata silk skirt.

daras, mendaras to recite the Koran; study.

darat dry land; interior of a country; angin darat land breeze, offshore wind; mendarat, naik darat to disembark; daratan large tract of dry land.

dargah shrine.

dari from, out of; about; than; dari kampung from the village; dari mana? from where?; dari sini from here; dari hal itu about that matter; daripada from, out of; regarding; than.

dari-dari tortoise.

darjah, darjat grade, rank, standard, degree; darjah penghidupan standard of living; naik darjah to get promotion.

darmasiswa scholarship, grant to a student.

darmawisata school trip.

daru, pokok daru tree with commercial timber.

daruk, ikan daruk carp.

darurat necessity, serious trouble, time of stress, emergency.

darwis dervish.

darya sea.

das boom of gun; lima das salute of five guns.

dasa ten; sedasa batch of ten.

dasar principle; bed of river, floor of sea; basis of a system, foundation, policy; pada dasarnya fundamentally; berdasar having a basis of.

dasi necktie.

dastur, layar dastur studding sail.

dasun garlic.

dasus, berdasus whispering.

datang to come, approach; datangnya coming, arrival; bulan datang coming month; mendatangi to attack; mendatangkan to cause to come about.

datar flat (*of ground*); dataran plain; datar tinggi plateau.

datia giant ogre.

datin female form of datuk.

datuk, datok, datu grandfather, grandsire; title of distinction; datuk perempuan grandmother; datuk nenek ancestors.

datung—datuk my grandsire.

Daud David.

dauk grey (*of horses*).

daulat majesty, ruler's divinity; daulat tuanku your majesty; daulat sovereign; negeri yang berdaulat sovereign state.

daun leaf, blade of grass; lobe of ear; daun pokok leaf of tree; daun pakau playing card; berdaun leafy; mendaun kayu as the leaves of the forest in number; burung daun green leaf bird.

daup beamy and heavy (*of boat*); heavy (*of features*).

daur cycle of years.

dawa, daawa lawsuit; kena dawa to be sued.

dawai wire; dawai berduri barbed wire.

dawas faded; exhausted (*of soil*).

dawat ink; berdawat inky; inked.

daya force; resource; stratagem; daya upaya resources, means; apakah daya? what can one do?; memperdayakan to trick, deceive; barat-daya south-west.

dayah foster mother, wet-nurse.

Dayak Dyak.

dayang damsel, young girl; **awang dan dayang** young men and maidens; **dayang-dayang** attendants in a court.

dayu, mendayu-dayu to rumble softly.

dayuh, terdayuh hati worried, depressed.

dayuk, terdayuk pinggang swaying the hips.

dayung oar; **anak dayung** rower; **berdayung** to row, scull; **mendayungkan** to propel by rowing.

dayus despicable coward; unmanly (*esp as a cuckold or a henpecked husband*).

debak-debuk sound (*of flop, smacking*).

debam sound of heavy fall.

debap sound of light fall.

debar beating of the heart; **berdebar-debar hatinya** he felt his heart throb.

debet debit.

debik bleat (*of goats*); sound of tap, rap.

debing sound of a light thump.

debri debris.

debu dust, powder; **berdebu** desquamating; powdery, dusty, hazy; **cakap mendebu** to talk rubbish.

debuk, berdebuk-debuk gurgling (*as bottle*).

debum thumping sound.

debung thud (*of drum, coconuts, durians falling*).

debup sound of flopping down.

debur sound (*of a plunge, surf, falling earth*).

debus, debus-debus rustling of birds in leaves; to miss the top aimed at (*in contest*).

decak to hop.

decing chinking sound.

decit twittering *or* squeaky sound.

decuh, decuh-decah bubbling.

dedah, terdedah open (*of door*); left uncovered; exposed (*of person*).

dedai, berdedai-dedai in long straggling and disorderly lines.

dedak rice polishings, fine bran; **berdedak** crowded together, massed.

dedal thimble; *also* bidal.

dedalu mistletoe; *also* bendalu.

dedam, berdedam crowded together.

dedap generic name given to a number of trees that bear very bright scarlet flowers.

dedar feverish, out of sorts.

dedas to cut.

dedau, mendedau to shout, cry out in distress.

dedel, mendedel to undo (*sewing, hem*).

dedes musk; civet cat; to slice thinly.

definisi definition.

degam, berdegam thundering blows.

degan young coconut.

degap, berdegap-degap tapping of blows on floor; beating of the heart.

degar, berdegar-degar slamming of a door; **cakap berdegar-degar** to boast, brag.

degil stiff-necked, obstinate, unyielding, insistent.

Degul, Pulau Degul East Indian island used by the Dutch as penal settlement.

degum booming sound; mumps.

dek, dek kapal deck (*of ship*).

dekah, berdekah-dekah guffawing.

dekak, dekak-dekak abacus.

dekam, mendekam to sit crouched (*as tiger*).

dekan bamboo rat.

Dekan Dean of a Faculty.

dekar I lucky; effective.

dekar II artful, clever (*esp at a game*); **pendekar** fencing master, swashbuckler, gang leader.

dekat near, hard by; **dekat ke darat** near the shore; **rumah dekat** adjacent house; **dekat habis** nearly finished; **mendekati** to approach; **mendekatkan** to bring close.

dekih caked with dirt.

deklarasi declaration.

deku, berdeku to kneel.

dekunci cultivated ginger.

dekung sound of a gong.

dekus, mendekus to snarl (*of cat, tiger*); blow (*of porpoise*).

dekut, mendekut to coo; calling pigeons; **buluh dekut** bamboo instrument used to call pigeons for snaring.

delah, ikan delah sea bream.

delaki=laki-laki.

delamak embroidered cloth put over dish covers.

delan snag in a river.

delap shameless.

delapan eight; the number eight; **delapan belas** eighteen; **delapan puluh** eighty; *also* **lapan.**

delik, mendelik to stare at (*fixedly, sternly*).

delima, buah delima pomegranate; **delima merekah** bursting pomegranate (ruby lips); **batu delima** ruby.

delta delta.

dema they all = dia semua.

demah, mendemah to apply warm compress in sickness (*by heated stone ashes, hotwater bottle*).

demak stumpy, not tapering.

demam fever; **demam gigil** fever with ague; **demam kepialu** any violent fever; **demam selesema** influenza; **demam kura** fever with enlarged spleen.

demang headman.

demap greedy, gluttonous.

dembai, berdembai-dembai slouching (*of children*).

dembuduk, ikan dembuduk horse-mackerel.

demek damp.

demen eager for, fond of.

demes big and flat (*of nose*).

demi by, with, on, at; **seorang demi seorang** one by one; **demi Allah!** by God! **demi dilihatnya dia bertanya** as soon as it was seen by him he inquired.

demikian so, thus, in this way; **demikian itu** in that way; **demikian halnya** so it is, that is the position *or* the situation.

demit forest elves; spirit; I, your little one (*in invocations*).

demokrasi democracy.

demokratik democratic.

dempak broad, beamy, blunted, squared.

dempang, dempang-dempang clanging of hollow things; **cakap berdempang-dempang** to make empty boasts.

dempet, berdempet sticking together (*of two bananas, sweets*); jammed together (*of houses*).

dempir cracked-sounding (*of gong*).

dempok, terdempok to approach very near; collide with.

dempul caulking for boats.

demukut broken pieces of rice husk; chaff;=lemukut, melukut.

demut, terdemut-demut agog; throbbing.

den I. me (*of superiors familiarly to inferiors*).

denah, penyakit denah disease of the feet (*ascribed to an evil spirit*).

denai wild beast track; **denai gajah lalu** track of elephants passing.

denak decoy bird or animal; ayam denak jungle fowl.

dencang clank of a scabbard; small bird.

dencing chink of a coin.

dencong to hop (as in hop-scotch).

denda fine; kena denda to incur a fine, be fined; dendakan to fine.

dendam longing; rindu dendam loving, longing; grudge = dandan.

dendan order, arrangement; plaiting, design, style; berdendan to plait; awan dendan plait ornament.

dendang I, burung dendang, si dendang name given to the crow; timun dendang bitter inedible gourd.

dendang II, berdendang to sing at work, drone a chorus or lullaby or pantun.

deneh to run (as colour); warna turun terdeneh the colour is running.

dengan with, along with, by means of, by; berjalan dengan dia to walk with him; potong dengan pisau to cut with a knife; dengan seorang diri by o.s.; dengan tiada sepertinya inadequate.

dengar to listen to, hear; sekali dengar, dengarlah to listen; dengar khabar to hear news; terdengar heard; perdengaran sense of hearing.

dengih, terdengih-dengih panting.

denging, mendenging to buzz slightly.

dengkang croak (of frog); terdengkang-dengkang croaking laugh; dengkang-dengkang crooked (of arm).

dengkek thin; shallow (water, learning).

dengkel juiceless and sparse (of the flesh of durians).

dengki envious hatred, spite; menaruh dengki to nurse a grudge; berasa dengki to feel spiteful.

dengking, berdengking to yelp (of dogs).

dengkol short and round, bent, twisted.

dengkong, berdengkong to bay (of dogs); berdengkong-dengkong clang (as beaten metal).

dengkul kneel; mendengkul to kneel.

dengkur, berdengkur to snore.

dengkus whinny (of horse).

dengkut halt; lame.

dengu foolish, stupid; berdengu sniff, snort.

dengung humming; berdengung to give out a humming sound.

dengus, mendengus to snort, sniff.

dengut, mendengut, berdengut to murmur (of quails); hitam berdengut-dengut very black.

dening yoke; sedening a pair.

dentam—dentum slamming sound.

dentang, berdentang-dentang clanging.

denyut, berdenyut throbbing (of pulse, tooth, boil); denyutan throbbing.

depa span of arms out-stretched; fathom, six feet.

depa=dia apa they all (the number being uncertain).

depak, berdepak-depak clattering of a horse's hooves.

depan front; di hadapan, di depan in front.

depang to stretch out the arms, bar the way.

departemen department.

depu, ikan depu small catfish.

depun lining of garment.

dera corporal punishment; mendera to flog.

derai, berderai-derai straggling (of crowds); berderai loose (of earth); streaming (of tears).

derak, derak-deruk sound of rending cloth, breaking branch.

deram, menderam rumbling of thunder, tiger's roar, dog's growl.

derama drama.

derang, derung-derang chink of coins; terang-benderang clear; benderang siang dawn.

derap, berderap rattling noise; sound of fire arms; tramping of troops.

deras rapid (of motion); speedy; terlalu deras larinya he ran away fast; penderas accelerator; menderas to revise one's study of the Koran.

derau, berderau sound of rustling; approach of rain; to work in cooperation (esp in rice fields).

derawa syrup; gula derawa.

derebar driver.

deres, menderes to tap palm for toddy; = sadap.

deret row, series, long line; berderet-deret in long straggling lines.

derhaka traitorous; treason, betrayal; menderhaka, berbuat derhaka to turn traitor, betray.

derham gold or silver Arab coin.

deria sense.

derik, berderik slight rending noise of cloth; slight crackle of breaking twigs.

dering, berdering ringing sound; trumpeting of an elephant.

deris, menderis rustle of grass; ripping sound of cloth.

derita, menderita to endure, suffer; tiada terderita insupportable.

derji tailor.

derma alms, gifts; berderma giving alms, donations; penderma donor, benefactor; penderma darah blood donor; orang dermawan benefactor.

dermaga mole, wharf.

dermasiswa financial assistance.

dermawan charitable.

derni threshold or sill of a door; pintu derni light screen door.

deru, menderu to roar (of storm, waves).

derum to kneel (of elephants); derumkan gajah to cause an elephant to kneel; sound of a falling tree.

derun, berderun-derun going in shoals (of people, beasts, fish); sederun together.

derung, derung-derang clanging of a bell.

derus sound of rubbing; scraping.

derut dull scraping sound.

desa district, country (as opposed to town); bertandang desa to go wandering from place to place.

desah sound of brushing.

desak to harass, urge, press; terdesak crowded out; desakan strong pressure.

desar swishing of rain; hissing (as water falling on hot iron).

desas-desus sound of whispering; rumour.

desau, berdesau rustling of tall grass.

desik rustling of leaves.

desing, berdesing whistling of wind; whizzing of bullets.

desir, berdesir sound of sand driven by the wind.

desit sound of anything dragged along fast.

desor deep rustling.

destar turban; detar headkerchief.

detak sound of nicking wood.

detar, berdetar sound of violent shivering.

detas, detus-detas crackling (as of fire crackers).

detektif detective.

detik noise of breaking twig.

deting twang of a stretched string when struck.

detis sound of quiet oozing.

detus sound of dripping water.

dewa Hindu demigod; fairy.

dewana courtly, royal.

dewangga rich cloth (often mentioned in romance); damask.

dewasa time, date, era; adult, fully grown.

dewata godhead, deity, divinity; **dewata mulia raya** greatest of gods; **burung dewata** bird of paradise.

dewek self.

dewi goddess; fairy; **Maha Dewi** wife of Shiva; **Dewi Pertiwi** mother earth.

di in, at, on; **di sini** here; **di sana** there; **di dalam** inside; **di luar** outside; **di bandar in a town; **di kepala** at the head; **di atas** on the top; **di mana?** where?; **di suatu kedai at a certain shop; prefix forming the passive; **di = adi** noble.

dia he, she, it, they, him, her, them; **akan dia** to him; also **emphatic for ia.**

diagram diagram.

dialek dialect; see **loghat.**

diam being silent quiet, still; to live, dwell; **diam-diam** silently; **mendiamkan** to silence; **terdiam** silent, still; **pendiam** person given to silence; **mendiami** to inhabit a place, live at; **tempat kediaman** place of abode; **kediaman** accommodation.

dian candle; **kaki dian** candlestick; **lilin dian** wax of a candle; **burung kaki dian** redshank.

diang toasting, heating before a fire; **berdiang** to warm o.s. over a fire (custom for Malay women newly confined); **mendiang** to become a spirit, die; the deceased.

diat, diat, pendiat blood money, compensation for killing or wounding; **mendiatkan** to pay blood money for; earthwork trap for elephant.

dibaj a Persian silk.

didal thimble; also **bidal, lidal.**

didih, mendidih to boil, effervesce; **air mendidih** boiling water.

didik, mendidik nurturing, fostering, bringing up; **pendidik** educator; **didikan** rearing, educating; **pendidikan** to nurture; education.

didis, mendidis to hash.

dikau form of **engkau**; you, thou, thee.

dikir, zikir to chant verses, religious verses.

dikit, sedikit a little; **sedikit-sedikit** very little; **berdikit-dikit** sparingly.

diktator dictator.

dil, main di kind of hockey.

din the Muslim religion; common in man's name eg **Kamaruddin.**

dina poor, mean, humble.

dinamis dynamics.

dinamit dynamite.

dinamo dynamo.

dinar gold coin.

dinda, adinda corrupt honorific in titles.

dinding screening, light partition, wall generally; **mendindingkan** to screen, partition off; **pendinding** charm to ward off enemies.

dingin cold, chilly; **dinginkan** to chill.

dingkis, ikan dingkis small food fish.

dini, dinihari dawn.

diploma diploma.

diplomasi diplomacy.

diplomat diplomat.

diraja, angkatan raja, diraja royal hearse; honorific (in title).

dirgahayu long life (to your highness).

diri self; **seorang diri** all by o.s.; **diriku I**, myself; **dirinya** himself, herself, itself, themselves; **di dalam diri** to o.s. (mentally); **bawa diri** to run away; **minta diri** to beg leave; depart; **berdiri** to stand erect; **terdiri** set erect; **mendirikan** to set upright, build, found; **pendiri** founder; **pendirian** erection, establishment, foundation; attitude.

dirus, mendirus to irrigate, water plants.

disiplin discipline.

diskusi discussion.

dito ditto.

diwal stone wall, thick outer wall of a palace or fortress.

diwan, dewan royal audience hall, council of state, high court; board, committee; **Dewan Tunku Abdul Rahman T. Abdul Rahman Hall**; **Dewan, Bahasa dan Pustaka** Language and Literature Agencies; **Dewan Pertuanan House of Lords**; **Dewan Orang Ramai House of Commons**; **Dewan Rendah Lower House**; **Dewan Tinggi Upper House**; **Dewan Senate Senate House**; **Dewan Rakyat House of Representatives**.

Diwani official, authorized (of currency).

doa prayer, incantation; **doa selamat** benediction; **berdoa** to pray, hope; **mendoakan** to pray for.

doang only, merely.

dobi washerman.

dobrak to break (door, fence).

dobol holed (of sack).

dodet, mendodet to cut open.

dodol, kuih dodol cake made from glutinous rice with coconut milk and sugar.

dodor loose (of clothes).

dodos, mendodos to plane.

dodot, mendodot to beg; to smoke cigarette or opium.

dogang, tali dogang support by a rope, rope to prevent a tree from falling on its fellers.

dogel, togel tailless (of fowls).

dogol hornless, combless (of cocks); bald (of men).

dohok, terdohok stumbling, ready to fall.

dok dock (for ships).

dokok breast ornaments (worn at marriages and ceremonies).

doktor doctor.

dokumen document.

dola litter, dhooly.

dolak-dalik vacillating (of talk).

dom personal property of husband or wife, property owned before marriage; dome.

domah, pendomah gift presented by a ruler's envoy.

doman, pedoman a compass; **hantu doman** dog-faced spirit.

domba fat-tailed sheep.

domol snout; = **moncong**.

dompak, mendompak to prance (of horse); clustered (as houses).

dompet purse.

doncang, mendoncang to jump.

dondang lullabies; **berdondang** to croon lullabies.

dondon pattern or colour; **kain sedondon** suit of one pattern.

dong, dom meaningless word at the end of a sentence.

dongak, mengdongak with head up.

dongeng tale for chanting.

legend; **mendongeng** to keep asking (of children).

dongkol hornless or with drooping horns; combless; **mendongkol** to nurse anger.

dongkor-dangkar bundled out, expelled.

dongkrak screw jack.

dongok disproportionately broad, badly proportioned.

donia lady.

donor boggy (as land after rain).

doran, joran fishing rod.

dorong to stimulate, urge, drive; **terdorong** fallen forward, tripped up; **pendorong** driver; **pendorongan** advancement.

dos carton, cardboard box.

dosa sin; **berdosa** sinful.

dosen dozen.

doyak octopus; also **loyak**.

doyan I, me; **tak doyan** don't care; octopus.

dua two; **angka dua** reduplication sign; **dua belas** twelve; **dua puluh** twenty; **kedua** both; **yang kedua** second; **mendua-kan** to have two of; **berdua** in a party of two; **pendua** duplicate (of letter, keris); **pedua-kan** mortgage giving half the yearly crop as interest.

duai, ipar duai brother-in-law, sister-in-law.

dubur anus; also **jubur**.

duda widower, wifeless divorce of **janda**.

dudor a wild palm.

dudu, mendudu pressing forward in shoals, keeping straight on; also **dudun**.

duduk to sit down, be seated; be located; **duduknya** site, position; **penduduk** inhabitant; **kedudukan** position; **tempat kedudukan** residence.

duga probing, fathoming, sounding; **salah duga** guessing wrong; **dugaan** guess; conjecturing; **batu penduga** sounding lead; **temu duga** interview.

dugal nausea; squeamish; **mendugal** to feel seasick.

duit cent; small change; **duit sen** small currency; **berduit** to have money; **cari duit** to look for a livelihood.

duk short form of **duduk**.

duka grief, sadness; **dukacita** sorrow, mourning.

dukan booth, shop.

dukat ducat.

duku popular buff-skinned fruit (a variety of the langsat); **to rap with the knuckles**.

dukuh hamlet.

dukun Malay medicine man or woman.

dukung, mendukung to carry on the hip or back; carry in a scarf or cloth; **berdukung** so carried.

dulang wooden platter or tray; **mendulang** to wash for ore.

dulapan eight; also **delapan**, **lapan**.

duli dust; **sembah ke bawah duli** to offer at the feet of royalty; **menjunjung duli** to do homage; **duli baginda** his highness; **Duli Baginda Seri Paduka Yang Di Pertuan Agung** His Majesty The King.

dumung black venomous snake.

dunak large basket.

dungkal, berdungkal to start off; **berdungkal-dungkal trudging**.

dungu stupid; also **dengu**.

dunia, duniawi the world; **dunia akhirat** the world hereafter; **peredaran dunia** life's ups and downs.

dupa incense; **bakar dupa** to burn incense.

dur pearl.

dura anxiety; berhati dura worried, anxious.

Durga consort of Shiva, goddess of death.

durhaka treason.

duri thorn, quill, sting; berduri thorny, barbed; kawat berduri barbed wire; adakah duri dipertajamkan does one sharpen thorns?

durian thorny fruit (very greatly prized); durian belanda soursop.

durias muslin.

durja countenance, face.

durjana evil, wicked, treacherous; menteri durjana traitorous minister.

dusi, mendusi drowsy but restless, suffering from colic.

dusta lie, false report; berdusta to lie; mendusta false.

dusun orchard, fruitgrove without a dwelling house; kepala dusun village headman.

duta envoy, ambassador.

duyung dugong; ekor duyung tail of the dugong; forked; treacherous; air mata duyung tears of the dugong (potent love philtre); menduyung to hover.

duyun, berduyun-duyun pressing (as in crowds).

E

ebam lidded porcelain pot.

eban to fling aside.

ebek awning (on ship or over a window).

ebeng, mengebeng to sway the body as a dancing girl.

ebonit ebonite.

ecek outward, apparently, on the surface.

eceran retail.

edah speaking across a distance.

edan infatuated; edan kesmaran madly in love.

edar to move; peredaran movements, revolution; also idar.

egah, mengegah to waddle (of old women); teregah-egah wobbling (as a stake in a stream).

egak capture.

egos, mengegos to dodge, evade.

eh interjection of wonder.

eja, mengeja to spell; ejaan spelling.

ejek, ejit, mengejek to tease, mock at, scoff at.

ekar acre.

ekor tail, extremity; numeral coefficient for animals; ekor mata corner of the eye; burung seekor one bird; ekor belangkas king crab's tail; hairstyle; bintang berekor comet; berekor-ekor one behind the other.

ekseima eczema.

ekspot export.

ekspres express.

ela yard.

elah deception, trickery; olah-elah all sorts of dodges; mengelah to cheat; mengelah daun to cheat at cards; pengalah trickster.

elak evasion; getting out of the way; mengelakkan to dodge (blow); mengelak diri to evade a promise.

elat cheat.

elektron, letron electron.

elemen, unsur element.

elok handsome (of person); fine (of things); keelokan beauty, excellence.

elon, mengeloni to take the part of, favour (esp a child).

emas gold; emas kahwin dowry given to brides; emas kerajang tinsel; emas muda alloyed gold; emas tua pure gold; emas putih platinum;

keemasan golden; ikan emas goldfish.

embacang horse mango; *also* macang, bacang.

embah grandparent.

embak disturbance, riot; rioh embak occasion, time; seembak on two occasions.

embal half-cooked; soft and damp.

embalau shellac, sealing wax, resin for fixing handles, solder.

emban arrangement of ropes enabling a porter to secure a burden carried on the back.

embarau wooden *or* stone embankment by river *or* shore.

embas like, resembling.

embat, mengembat to cane; ular kena embat whipped snake; rattan basket trap for river fish; belantik embat spring trap.

embek sunsail; *also* ebek.

embel grass-covered swamp.

embel—embel small additions.

ember bucket.

embih form of address to girls.

embik, mengembik to bleat.

embuh to want, wish, yearn; hidup segan, mati tak embuh reluctant to live, reluctant to die.

embuk mother.

embuli embulism.

embun dew, haze; embun betina light dew; embun jantan heavy morning dew; mengembun falling of dew; berembun bedewed, in the dew.

embus, hembus to blow, snort (*from nostril*); angin berembus lalu jua the wind blows all the while; mengembuskan nafas yang akhir to die; embusan bellows; current.

embut, mengembut to throb;

terembut-embut flickering (*of lamps*); dying (*of trees*).

empang, mengempang to bar, dam, stop the course *or* flow of anything; dam; empangan air dam; terempang stopped; barah empang large internal abscess; eccentric.

empap, mengempap to press down, hit with a flat object; drop down on; strike with palm; sepelempap hand's breadth.

empar, mengempar to drift from its course; walk in splay-footed way.

empat four; empat kaki four feet; empat persegi quadrilateral; empat sama segi square; berempat making four in all; keempatnya all the four; seperempat quarter.

empedal gizzard.

empedu gall; pundi-pundi empedu gall-bladder; batu empedu gallstone.

empek to long for.

empenak to pet, coddle.

emper pent roof, verandah.

emping rice plucked, crushed and cooked before it has attained maturity.

empis wings of hidden fencing guiding pig *or* rat into a noose trap.

empoyan reel on fishing-rod.

empu master craftsman; empu jari thumb; empu kaki big toe.

empuan lady = perempuan in titles; tengku empuan, tengku puan queen; datuk empuan, tuk puan wife of a major commoner chief.

empuh overflow of a river *or* pot; mengempuhkan to inundate; empuhan inundation, flood; keempuhan flooded.

empuk tender (*of cooked food*); mengempukkan to make soft, cook till tender; mellow.

empul, mengempul to beat

about against adverse wind (*of ships*).

empulur, mempulur pith; core; empulur rimba.

empunya, yang empunya whose is; mempunyai to possess, own.

empuyan reel on fishing rod.

emrat water pot.

emul, mengemul to be impudently officious; intrude, butt in.

enak delightful, enjoyable.

enam six; beranam making six, six in all; keenam sixthly; set of six; yang keenam sixth; seperenam a sixth.

enap, enapan sediment; mengenap to settle (*of soil*).

enau sugar palm.

enca—benca in pieces; drifting.

encik Mr, Mrs, Miss; encik-encik dan tuan-tuan ladies and gentlemen.

encir thin (*of gruel etc*).

encok rheumatic.

encot lame; aslant, lopsided.

endal, mengendal elastic, resilient; to cram, stuff.

endang nun of Hindu times.

endap, mengendap to crouch, waylay, spy on; play hide and seek; terendap stooping to watch; sediment.

endas head; mengendas to bang the head against.

endasan chopping block; = landasan.

enderia organs of sense.

endong I, mengendong to console, soothe a child.

endong II, indung mother; = induk.

endul swing support, hammock, cradle; sling for an injured arm.

endus, mengendus to smell; get wind of.

engah, terengah-engah panting; = mengah.

engak stupid, bewildered.

enggak no; not; plaited bird-shaped receptacle for sweet rice.

enggal, enggok-enggal swaying, bobbing up and down.

enggan I unwilling, reluctant.

enggan II up to, as far as.

enggang rhinoceros hornbill.

enggat as far as, up to.

engget, mengengget to hook down (*fruit, branches*).

enggil, berenggil serrated (*as mountains*).

engkah, engkah-engkah half-ripe.

engkak crow.

engkang, mengengkang to walk with legs apart.

engkap flue for smoke; terengkap-angkap going up and down.

engkau thou, thee, you.

engkil, terengkil having small excrescences (*of tree bark*).

engku title of high rank, style higher than tengku.

engkung grandfather.

engor, ikan engor-engor river catish.

engsang to blow the nose with the fingers.

engsel hinge.

engsut edging away; see esut, kesot.

enjak, mengenjak to tread down; pengenjak sole of the foot; jalan mengenjak to walk in a springing manner.

enjal to be forced down on one's seat; to be pushed back (*as a restless child*).

enjelai cereal; Job's tears; also jelai.

enjen engine.

enjet affected, capricious.

enjima, enzim enzyme.

enjut I to bob up and down; mengenjut to tug (*as fish tugs at a line*).

enjut II bent, out of true.

ensiklopedia encyclopaedia.

entah expression of doubt and interrogation; perhaps, I do not know; **entahlah** I do not know; **entah ya entah tidak** unknown whether the answer is yes or no.

entak to ram down, pound down; **mengentak kaki** to stamp the feet; **pengentak** pounder, pestle; **entak** enti up and down.

entang to heed; **tak entang** not care a jot; **entangkan** even if; *see* **sementang**.

entar moment.

entek, mengentek to winnow rice by shaking it in a sieve and giving occasional forward and backward jerks.

enten, mengenten to graft.

enteng light, easy.

entimun cucumber.

enum young.

enyah be off; **mengenyahkan** to kick out, shoo off.

enyak, mengenyak to press down.

epah, mengepah to lease, farm; **mengepahkan** to give a lease, let.

epeh to chatter; **orang epeh** chatterbox.

epek outer posts used to keep the screens in position against the framework of a large fish trap.

epok envelope-shaped plaited bag for betel requisites; **epok-epok** sweetmeat, pastry.

epolet epaulette.

erak, bererak, mengerak to get free, edging away.

eram, ram, mengeram to sit on an egg; sit brooding (*of persons*); **mengeramkan** to hatch.

erang I, **mengerang** to groan from pain.

erang II dark blue, black, dark; **erang-erut** askew, awry.

erat tight, close; **mengerat** to compress, fasten.

erau, derau visiting for the purpose of condoling and assisting.

ereh, mengereh to rule, direct.

erek, mengerek to neigh (*of horse*); trumpet (*of elephant*).

ereng I, **hering, burung ereng** vulture.

ereng II awry; **mengereng** sideways.

eret, heret, mengeret to drag forcibly along the ground.

erong teacup; slanting; — **serong**.

Eropah Europe.

erti meaning; **ertinya** the meaning of it is; **bererti** having a meaning; **mengertikan** to explain, impart a meaning; **pengertian** concept.

eru, ru, pokok ru casuarina tree.

erut, herut twisted, awry; **erang-erut** askew; zigzag.

esa one, sole; **Tuhan yang esa** the one God; **esa-esaan** alone; loneliness; **yang esa** the one. the only.

esah, sah, mengesahkan to validate, confirm, approve; **minit mesyuarat disahkan** the minutes of the meeting are approved.

esak to sob; **teresak-esak** sobbing.

esang, mengesang to blow the nose.

esek disease causing the skin to become dry and scaly.

esok, besok tomorrow, some time; **esok lusa** tomorrow or the next day; **setelah keesokan harinya** when the next day came.

esrar, tanda esrar evidence of religion, sacraments.

esut edging off; = **engsut**.

etek aunt.

eter ether.
ewa reluctant, averse.

F

faal deed, good work; function.
fabrik factory.
fadihat disgrace, shame.
fadil eminent, excellent.
fadul meddling, violent.
faedah benefit, profit, interest on money; berfaedah profitable.
faham to understand; concept, comprehension; salah faham misunderstanding.
fahrasat index of book.
faidah=faedah.
failasuf philosopher.
fajar dawn; fajar sidik the true dawn; fajar menyinsing naik dawn broke.
fakar, zul-fakar famous sword belonging to Ali.
fakih expert in.
fakir religious mendicant; needy person.
faktor factor.
falak vault of heaven; ilmu falak astronomy.
falsafat philosophy.
falsu false, counterfeit.
fanak transitory; negeri yang fanak the perishable world.
fanam small Indian coin.
fanatik fanatic.
fantasi fantasy.
faraid Muslim law of inheritance.
faraj pudendum muliebre.
farak separation, difference.
fardu, perlu obligatory.
Farsi Persian.
fasal paragraph, section; concerning, about; apa fasal? why?; fasal itu as for that.
fasih fluent; berlidah fasih eloquent.
fasis, faham fasis fascism.
fatihah confession of Islamic faith; chapter one of the Koran.
fatwa legal ruling by a Muslim jurist.
fauna fauna.
Februari February.
federal federal.
federasi federation.
feduli, fazuli to care, bother, heed.
feel act; good works; conduct, character.
feguam=peguam.
fellah agriculturist, farmer.
feri ferry.
Feringgi Portuguese.
festa feast, festival.
fesyen fashion.
fich law based on Muslim theology.
fikir, berfikir to think to o.s., reflect; memikirkan to think about; fikiran thought, reflection.
filem film.
firasat horoscope; second sight.
firdaus paradise.
firman decree of God; berfirman to decree; commandment.
fitnah slander, libel; memfitnahkan to libel.
fitrah tithe.
fizik physic.
folio folio.
fomula formula.
fonetik phonetic.
fonim phoneme.
fonology phonology.
foram forum.
fosfat, posfat phosphate.
fosfor, posforus phosphorus.
foto photo.
fuad heart; fuad alzakiah sincere heart.
fulan so-and-so; si fulan (usually pronounced si polan).
fulus money.
fungsi function.
furkan scriptures (Old and New Testament and Koran).

fusta Portuguese ship.

G

gaba palm fronds used as decoration.

gabah unhusked rice; dome.

gabak overcast, dull.

gabal coarse (*of work*); rough.

gabenor governor.

gabuk bulky; besar gabuk big without strength; biawak gabuk monitor lizard.

gabung, bergabung to be bundled up; to be affiliated with; menggabungkan to unite; pergabungan union, association.

gabus, kayu gabus spongy wood; gabus kayu imported cork; parang gabus sharp wood knife.

gacung mantis.

gada cudgel, club for fighting, cosh; gada-gada pennon.

gadah cylinder (*for sweetmeats*).

gadai mortgage, pawn; pajak gadai pawnshop; bergadai to pawn; tebus gadai to redeem from pawn; gadaian pledge.

gadang big, large.

gadi handcart.

gading tusk of elephant, ivory; ulu gading ivory hilt; nyior gading coconut palm with ivory-coloured nuts; buluh gading the large bamboo; gading-gading ribs of boats.

gadis maiden, unmarried girl.

gado-gado spiced vegetable salad.

gaduh quarrel, row; bergaduh to quarrel; pergaduhan altercation.

gadum boat.

gadung climbing plant from whose tubers a narcotic is made; mabuk gadung intoxicated (*by eating the tubers*).

gadungan false, were; harimau gadungan weretiger.

gaek old man.

gaeng wooden fin keel.

gagah forceful; vigorous; big and strong; gagah berani, gagah perkasa brave, dauntless; menggagahi to exert force on.

gagai to hang, be suspended (*of climbers*).

gagak large-billed crow; gagak pulang ke benua; hitam pergi, hitam balik the crow came home as black as when he went (none the better for travel).

gagal to fail, be abortive, be frustrated; kegagalan failure; menggagalkan to frustrate.

gagang stalk or stem of a flower or leaf.

gagap to stammer; orang gagap stammerer.

gagau to grope about, search with the hand; tergagau-gagau fumbling with hands out.

gaget afraid.

gagu dumb; = bisu.

gah renown; famous.

gahar, menggahar to clean, scrub.

gahara of royal parentage on both sides; anak gahara princeling so born.

gahari = ugahari.

gaharu aloes' wood, fragrant eagle wood.

gahing, tergahing craving.

gahir longing, desire.

gain askew.

gaing rough (*of edge of blade*).

gairah passion.

gajah elephant; gajah tunggal solitary rogue elephant; gajah meta rutting elephant; gajah mina walrus; gajah menyusu kitchen annexe; penthouse; burung gembala gajah whitewinged black jay; sakit gajah-gajahan elephantiasis.

gajak posture, carriage.

gaji salary; makan gaji to work for wages; orang gaji employees; menggajikan to employ on wages.

gajus, buah gajus cashew.

gak = agak.

gala, gala-gala caulking, pitch; tiada bergala unlimited, unbounded; segala all; segala-galanya all of them.

galagasi spider.

galah pole for knocking down fruit; punt pole; pole for clothes line; bergalah using a pole; punting.

galak bellicose, fiery, aggressive; galakan stimulus; menggalakkan to encourage, urge; penggalak powder in the touch-hole of a gun; galak kali often.

galang transverse bar; galang perahu rollers for hauling up boats; bantal galang bolster; menggalang to bar, obstruct; tergalang aground (of boats).

galar crushed-bamboo floormat.

galas shoulder-pole; burden; wares; menggalas carrying over the shoulder on pole; to trade, vend; penggalas petty trader; penggalasan wares, trading.

galau, bergalau bustle of crowd; to be in confusion.

galgal hurried and rough (of behaviour).

gali, menggali to dig; penggali spade; barang galian minerals dug up.

galias large three-masted galley.

galingan bunds in rice fields.

galir slipping loose, not fitted or fixed properly; perkataan yang galir fluent but foolish talk.

galis pair of braces.

galuh princess.

galur furrow, channel; = alur; susur galur pedigree; menggalur-galur trace source.

galut, bergalut to wrestle; = gelut.

gam gum.

gamak, menggamak to appraise the size or weight; guess, reckon, think; tidak tergamak incalculable; gamak-gamak at a guess, approximately; gamakan assumption.

gamam, tergamam flustered; tergamam-gamam speculating, considering.

gamang nervous (at heights).

gamat, bergamat to be lively.

gambang xylophone; balai gambang houseboat.

gambar picture, photo; statue; wayang gambar cinema; gambarajah diagram; gambar timbul bas-relief; tukang gambar photographer, painter, sculptor; bergambar to have picture taken; menggambarkan to make a picture; imagine.

gambir gambier.

gambuh Javanese dance; male character dancer.

gambus Arab lute.

gambut, tanah gambut fibrous, peaty soil.

gamelan Javanese orchestra.

gamgam, naik gamgam to get excited, flare up.

gamis Arab shirt, chemise.

gamit, menggamit to beckon, invite to come.

gampang easy; light (of weight); anak gampang bastard; menggampangkan treat as easy.

gamuh a necked water jar.

gan to put off paying.

Gana, Sang Gana Hindu elephant-god Ganesha.

ganal nearly; ganal-ganal mati as good as dead.

ganang, gunung-ganang mountains.

ganas fierce (*of animals*); **harimau ganas** man-eating tiger; **mengganas** to be fierce; **pengganas** terrorist.

gancang nimble, agile.

gancaran prose.

gancu long crook for pulling down fruit *or* branches.

ganda fold; **lima kali ganda** five-fold; **sekali ganda** two-fold, as much again; **berlipat ganda** doubled; **ganda-berganda** compound (*of interest*); **harga ganda-berganda** price many times increased; **pergandaan** reduplication; **perkataan berganda** reduplicated words.

gandala obstacle = gendala.

gandam black (*of teeth from betel chewing*).

gandan, gebar gandan silk coverlet.

gandapura plant whose seeds smell of musk and are an article of trade.

gandar lever for rice pounder; **menggandar** to pound with the lever; **gandar cincin** claws (*in a ring*) which hold the gem in position.

gandariah plant with edible fruit.

gandarukam plant (*yielding a gum used for soldering*).

gandarusa medicinal plant.

gandasuli medicinal herb with fragrant flowers.

gandewa archer's bow.

gandi bow; **main gandi** archery.

gandik gold frontlet decorating a bride's fringe.

gandin large mallet.

ganding, berganding close to one another; **berganding tangan** hand in hand.

gandu black bean used for a marble.

gandul, menggandul to hang, be suspended; *see* kandul.

gandum wheat.

gandung light logs attached as outriggers to a native boat to give it greater steadiness.

gang brazier's chisel.

Gangga Ganges.

ganggang, berganggang to warm o.s.; **mengganggang** to toast (*bread*) over a fire; *see* panggang.

ganggu, mengganggu to interfere with (*other's work*); importune (*as a beggar*); intrude and bother, threaten, molest; **gangguan** annoyance, interference; **terganggu** interfered with.

ganggut to graze; grazing.

gangsa bell metal; bronze.

gangsi, menggangsi to perfume cloth with incense.

gangsir mole cricket; **menggangsir** to tunnel, make a hole.

ganih white (*of cloth*).

ganja I Indian hemp, hashish.

ganja II guard at the top of a keris blade; **keris ganja iras** keris with such a guard.

ganjak, berganjak to shift one's seat, move slightly; **menganjak** to shift, move; **tidak berganjak** irremovable.

ganjal odd (*of numbers*); anything used as a wedge; **menganjal** to wedge.

ganjapuri = kaca-puri.

ganjar, menganjar to reward; **ganjaran** reward, present.

ganjat abnormal; tangled.

ganjil odd (*of numbers*); abnormal (*of dress, conduct*); **pakaian ganjil** fancy dress.

ganju ordeal to divine a criminal.

ganjur pike, lance; to keep advancing; = anjur.

gantang measure of capacity = 4 *cupak*.

ganti substitute; replacement; instead; **ganti rugi** compensation for injury, reparation; **menggantikan** to substitute, replace; **berganti** in place of; **berganti-ganti** in turns; **ganti nama** pronoun.

gantih bulging, bulbous; = antih to spin thread.

gantung to hang up; hung up; **gantungkan** to hang up; **bergantung** to depend; **tempat boleh bergantung** place which one can depend on.

ganyah, mengganyah to scrub, rub vigorously.

ganyang to destroy.

ganyut hard (of cooked potatoes, yams).

gapah, gopoh-gapah scurrying.

gapai, menggapai to hold up the hand to grasp, clutch at, wave a hand.

gapil, menggapil to carry off absent-mindedly; **gapil mulut** obtrusive; **gapil tangan** prone to hold.

gapis flowering tree.

gapit pincers, clamp; **menggapit** to nip.

gapura main gate to palace.

gar = degar to reverberate; slam.

gara, gahara, gara-gara omen.

garak, guling-garak rolling from side to side.

garam salt; **garam cium** smelling salts; **garam jantan** coarse salt; **kurang garam** insipid; **bergaram** salted; **bagai asam dengan garam** like salt and acid (perfect match).

garang fierce, hot-tempered, bold; **menggarang** to rage.

garau hoarse, deep (of voice).

garfu table fork.

gari handcuffs; **menggari** to handcuff; sealing wax.

garing crisp (of toast); to grill; kind of satchel or basket.

garis scratch; drawn line;

garisan line; **garisan lintang** latitudinal lines; **garisan bujur** longitudinal lines; **bergaris** scratched; **menggaris** to scratch; **garis besar** important.

garu, menggaru to scratch less hard than garuk.

Garuda Vishnu's eagle.

garuk, menggaruk scratch hard with the nails; **penggaruk** rake.

garung to groan from pain.

garut, bergarut to scrape together; become abraded; **menggarut** to scratch hard.

gas gas; **minyak gas** kerosene, oil; **gas pemedah mata** tear gas.

gasa ell (about 33 inches).

gasak to act with vigour; to eat gluttonously; **gasak lari** abscond.

gasal odd (of numbers).

gasang lustful, passionate.

gasing spinning top; main **gasing** to spin a top.

gasir mole-cricket; = keridik.

gatak, menggatak to sway (of spinning top).

gatal itchy; lustful; **sakit gatal** itch; **gatal miang** extremely itchy; lascivious.

gatik I, me; see patik too, also.

gauk, menggauk to croak.

gaul, menggaul to mix ingredients; **bergaul** mixing; **campur gaul** completely mixed; **pergaulan** society.

gaun gown.

gaung ravine; to hollow out, excavate; **bergaung** to echo, reverberate.

gauris cowrie shell.

gawa, pergawa strong.

gawai work, activities, services; **pengawai** officer.

gawal erring; social error; mistaken.

gawang pounding young rice in rhythmic time; **tergawang-gawang** with arms waving in the air.

gawar, gawar-gawar, gegawar coconut fronds hung on a line in to denote quarantine or bar access.

gawat dangerous.

gaya bearing; manner, style, tone; **rupa gaya** appearance and ways; **bergaya** affected; **tidak bergaya** unconscious.

gayah, bergayah-gayah to munch, masticate.

gayal elastic (of ball).

gayam Otaheite chestnut.

gayan, menggayan to thrust down net over river fish.

gayang, tergayang-gayang unsteady, swaying (of the body from dizziness, intoxication).

gayat giddy, dizzy (from looking down from height).

gayu old (of persons, trees).

gayuh, menggayuh to clutch at.

gayung coconut ladle with a long handle; to play at single stick.

gayut, bergayut hanging from a rope or bough (as a monkey).

gaz ell (about 33 inches).

gebang I tall palm with huge leaves.

gebang II to yarn, chat.

gebar rug, blanket; **bergebar** blanketed.

gebeng cabin; **perahu gebeng** boat with a small cabin and palm leaf awning.

geberau sad, anxious.

gebu delicate in texture; loose; **gebu cantik** daintily pretty.

gebuk, menggebuk to strike, hit, drub.

gebur floury, crumbling (as boiled potato).

geoar to water (of mouth).

geda, bergeda-geda smeared (of face, nose).

gedabak clumsy, heavy (of tread).

gedabir loose folds of skin; dewlap of an ox; gills of a cock; also **gelambir**.

gedak-geduk thudding (of bands); rattling (of carts).

gedang big; **menggedangkan** to enlarge.

gede big.

gedebak-gedebuk thudding (of falling fruit); trampling (of feet); thumping (of heart).

gedebung bamboo box, envelope-shaped bag.

gedebus sound of loose shoes.

gedegap thudding sound.

gedegar coarse (of fabrics).

gedegum thud (of falling on a wooden floor).

gedek, menggedek-gedek to exhibit an article for sale.

Gedembai, Kelembai giant that turns all to stone.

gedempong, gemuk gedempong corpulent, very fat.

gedombak small makyung drum.

gedubang short heavy Achinese cutlass.

gedubil, meka gedubil brazenfaced.

gedubur too long (of coats, gowns).

geduk, beduk mosque drum.

godumpas shameless trickster.

gedung store, large shop, godown; = **gudang**.

gedut puckered, crumpled.

gegaba, gaba-gegaba decorated gate.

gegabah daring, reckless.

gegadan seemly, proper.

gegai loose (of fittings of house).

gegak loud, noisy (of laughter, crowds); **gegak gempita** extreme uproar.

gegala, gala-gala caulking.

gegaman hand weapons.

gegana rainbow.

gegancung, belalang gancung mantis.

gegap, tergegap-gegap faltering (in speech, from shyness).

gegapi malodorous bug.

gegar, menggegar quivering, shaking; reverberation; **tergegar** jarred, concussed.

gegas, bergegas-gegas to hurry; **tergegas** hurried, spurred.

gegat moth, silver fish (that destroys books and clothes).

gegau, tergegau startled (into leaping up or crying out).

gegak to like.

geger panic; **menggeger** to be panic-stricken; **bergeger** to tremble (as a man on a narrow bridge); **menggegerkan** to create panic.

gegerak scarecrow made of bamboo or tins.

gegetar tinsel flowers on wire for headdress of bride or actress; rattled in trees by cords.

gela, bergela leaky (of boats).

gelabir dewlap, cock's wattles; **menggelabir** to hang in folds; = gedabir gelambir.

gelabur, menggelabur to plunge into water.

geladah to search a suspected person.

geladak ship's deck; **penumpang geladak** deck passenger.

geladir slime, mucus; large plank in a ship's side removed for handling cargo.

gelagah wild sugar cane.

gelagak guffaw.

gelak laugh; **tertawa gelak-gelak** to laugh loud and long.

gelakak chuckling laugh, guffaw.

gelalar resisting (of a goat or dog being dragged on a leash).

gelam, pokok gelam tree (with papery bark growing near the

coast); name of a tribe of Orang Laut.

gelama, ikan gelama generic name given to a number of jew fish.

gelambir dewlap of an ox; gills of a cock; also gelabir.

gelancah choppy (of sea).

gelancar to slip down; see gelincir

gelang bracelet, anklet; **gelang pintal** bracelet of twisted strands; **gelang pucuk rebung** with chevron pattern; **gelang kaki** anklets.

gelanggang, gelangang, ayam cockpit, arena; **gelanggang susu** dark circle round the teat.

gelang-gelang, gelanggelang raya tapeworm.

gelangsar, menggelangsar to slip up, slide.

gelanting dangling.

gelap dark; obscure; illegal; **gelap katup** pitch dark; **gelap gulita; pasar gelap** black market; **mata-mata gelap** detective.

gelar title (of honour); familiar nickname; **gelaran, gelaran pusaka; bergelar** titled; **menggelari** to confer title on.

gelas glass, tumbler; **bergelas** to make kites fight (with powdered glass on kite strings).

gelasar, menggelasar to slip, slide (as man on slippery ground).

gelatah hopping about.

gelatuk, menggelatuk to chatter (of teeth from cold).

gelebak open (of wound).

gelebar to flap continuously.

geleca light feather mattress.

gelecek to skid, slip; (sport) dribble.

gelecok, tergelecok sprained.

geledang, menggeledang to stretch out the arm at right angles to the body.

geledek thunderclap.

geleding, menggeleding to become warped (*of wood*).

geledoh seething; = beluduh.

gelegak, menggelegak boiling up, bubbling (*of hot water*).

gelegar girder on which floor joists rest.

gelegata nettle rash, prickly heat.

gelegut = gelugut.

gelek to roll over (*as a wheel of a vehicle over a man*); to roll from side to side; kena gelek, tergelek to be run over.

gelekak, menggelekak to crumble away (*as plaster*).

gelekek, menggelekek to giggle.

gelema mucus, phlegm.

geleman, geli geleman wincing (*at sound or sight*); nauseated.

gelemat decking over the bows and stern of a boat.

gelemayar = kelemayar.

gelembung bubble; menggelembung to form bubbles.

gelembur to hang in folds (*of old person's creased skin*).

gelempang, bergelempangan, tergelempang sprawling (*as dead or tired men*).

gelempok, gelempok-gemuk extremely fat.

gelempung sound of drums, lint for bandages.

gelen gallon.

geleng, menggeleng to shake the head in refusal.

gelenggang, daun gelenggang medicinal plant,

gelentang, guling-gelentang rolling over and over.

gelentar, menggelentar to quiver, tremble; *see* ketar gemetar.

gelenyar, menggelenyar itching, tingling; restless.

gelepek, tergelepek made slack; flopping down.

gelepok muddied.

gelepung sound of a heavy splash into water.

geletak, menggeletak lying down, sprawling.

geletar, menggeletar to keep shivering, trembling.

geletek, menggeletek to wriggle, hop (*as fish, prawns*); be skittish; hati menggeletek fluttering of heart.

geleting tinkle.

geletis, menggeletis to writhe, wriggle.

geletuk, menggeletuk tick loudly.

geli ticklish; amused, wishing to laugh; on edge; geli hati tickled, amused; geli geleman on edge; menggelikan hati to tickle; penggeli hati amusing (*of talk, book*).

geliang=geliat to writhe, wriggle (*as snake*); convolution.

geliat, menggeliat to stretch o.s.; tergeliat sprained, dislocated.

gelibas marine food fish.

gelibat double-bladed paddle; fish; glimpse; nampak segelibat seen for a moment.

gelicau, menggelicau chirping (*of birds*).

gelicik, tergelicik skidded, sliding.

geligin rod with white cord for holding the warp to each interlocking heddle in a loom.

geligis, menggeligis to shudder.

geligit, menggeligit to keep biting.

gelimbir pendulous (*of aged or fat cheeks*).

gelincat, tergelincat ricocheting.

gelincir, tergelincir slipping, becoming derailed *or* detached from a rotating wheel.

gelincoh to stumble.

gelinding wheel; **menggelinding** to revolve.

gelindung reel for thread; roller for rice field.

gelinggam red lead; red dye.

gelingsir, menggelingsir to glide; go down (of sun).

gelinjang, menggelinjang to prance about, cut capers.

gelintang, tergelintang sprawling, lying.

gelintar, menggelintar to search all round.

gelisah, menggelisah to be restless.

geliserin glycerine.

gelitak, menggelitak to tickle.

gelitik, menggelitik to tickle.

geliung galleon.

geliut, geliang-geliut wriggling.

gelob globe.

gelobok, menggelobok to gurgle (as water when a bottle is filled).

gelocak, menggelocak suppurating; swishing about, disturbed (of water).

gelodar, menggelodar to struggle for safety in water.

gelohok, tergelohok having gaps (as seam); broken for some distance but not continuously.

gelojoh, gelujuh gluttonous; hasty and rough.

gelokak peeled off (of dry bark, plaster).

gelombang waves, rollers; radio wavelength; **hempasan gelombang** breakers; **gelombang sederhana** medium wave.

geloneng small gong.

gelonggong, bergelonggong perforated (as a gnawed coconut).

gelongsor, menggelongsor to slide down, slip down.

gelopak = kelopak.

gelora stormy (of sea); squally; **gelora semangat** strongly moved; also **gelorah**.

gelosang, menggelosang to drive (workers); hurry.

gelosok to rub clothes vigorously when being washed.

gelotak, menggelotak to split a coconut husk.

geluduk thunder.

geluga red dye; **kayu geluga** tree from which the red dye is obtained.

gelugur, asam gelugur yellow-orange fluted fruit.

gelugut, menggelugut to shiver (from cold, fear).

geluh, mengeluh to sigh; **geluh leher** cut-throat.

geluk water dipper of coconut shell.

gelulur to fall down (as at football).

gelumang, gelamang smeared with dirt.

gelumur, bergelumur to dirty, besmear.

geluncur, menggeluncur to slide down.

gelung (of rope, rattan, snake) coil; **bergelung** coiled; **menggelung** to wind into coil.

geluntur red earthworm.

gelup to fall out (of teeth).

gelupar, menggelupar to jump up and down and flap wings in pain; also **gelepor**.

gelupas, menggelupas to peel off (of skin, paint).

gelut, bergelut to struggle, wrestle, romp; **menggelut** to embrace in wrestling.

gema echo, reverberation; repercussion.

gemak to undertake to;= **gamak**.

gemal, segemal handful of rice (newly reaped with the stalk); **bergemal-gemal** in handfuls.

gemala bezoar stone found in snakes, talisman.

gemalai, lemah gemalai extremely weak.

geman, geli geman feeling repulsion at sights or sounds.

gemang thick, barrel-shaped.

gemap, tergemap thunderstruck dumbfounded.

gemar to like; be pleased; **gemar minum susu** to like drinking milk; menggemari to like (food); **kegemaran** pleasure, hobby.

gemas anger, envy, annoyance.

gemaung echoing, reverberating, humming.

gemawan flying clouds.

gembak tuft of grass; lock of hair.

gembala herdsman; gembala gajah mahout; gembala singa lion tamer; menggembalakan to herd, rear (animals); to lead (people); burung gembala kerbau buffalo mynah.

gembel dewlap.

gembereng cymbal.

gembira agog; excited; enthusiasm; naik gembira to become excited; bergembira lively; menggembirakan to excite, enliven.

gembleng, bergembleng to unite; mengembleng to weld iron.

gembuk, menggembuk to stir up sediment.

gembul raised knob, boss, hump.

gembung = kembung.

gembur loose (of earth); menggemburkan to loosen (earth).

gembut hollow (of made soil); springy (of turf); menggembut to pulsate, go up and down.

gemelatuk chattering of teeth with cold or fear.

gemeletap tapping noise.

gemelugut continuous shivering and trembling.

gementam crashing sound.

gementar trembling all over: also gemetar, gentar, ketar.

gemercak noise of splashing.

gemerencak sound of clashing (swords).

gemerencang sound of clanging (of swords, bell).

gemerencing sound of tinkling.

gemerincik crackle.

gemerisik rustling noise.

gemerlap glittering, shimmering.

gemertak sound (pattering of rain, chattering of teeth, tapping of feet).

gemertuk chattering (of teeth).

gemetar, gementar trembling all over.

gemi, ikan gemi sucking fish.

gemilang, gilang-gemilang resplendent.

gemilap lustrous.

gemoyap flapping.

gempa, gempa bumi earthquake; bergempa quaking (of the earth); gerak gempa tremor.

gempal medium (of build); sturdy.

gempar alarm, noise, clamour; bergempar to be excited.

gempita noise; gegak gempita extreme uproar.

gempur, menggempur to storm, attack and destroy; penggempur storming party.

gemuk adipose, fat, plump; gemuk gedempung rolling in fat; menggemukkan to fatten.

gemuruh roll of thunder; roar of water; murmur of an angry crowd.

genahar furnace for sugar boiling; smelting metals; genahar gunung crater.

genaling vengeful influence from his victim that can kill a hunter.

genang I, genang-genang sweetmeat.

genang II, tergenang stand in floods (of water).

genap complete, full; even; **sepuluh ringgit genap** the full ten dollars; **segenap** every; **setelah genap** on completion; **penggenap** complementary.

gencat, menggencat to restrain; frustrate, stop; **gencatan senjata** ceasefire.

gencet, menggencet to press, squeeze; **tergencet** in a fix.

gencu lipstick; **gencu pipi** rouge.

gencuk to twist the pestle in pounding grain; shake a leg; dance.

gendala hindrance, obstruction, difficulty; also **kendala.**

gendali Palembang type of shoe.

gendang drum; **gendang raya** large drum; **segendang kertas** roll of paper.

gendap, juru **gendap** leading drummer in a Malay band.

gendeng to heel over; = **sendeng.**

genderang war drum.

gendi, kendi clay water pot.

gendir Javanese musical instrument.

gendit, kendit hanging belt (of chain or coin).

gendung, kendung, meng= **gendung** to carry (in a fold of sarung or waistbelt); **gendungan** bundle, parcel.

gendut distended (of stomach).

geneh teeth of a cow elephant.

geneng fine, beautiful.

generato generator.

genggam to grasp in fist, claw; **segenggam** handful; **genggaman** clutch, grasping.

genggang I striped fabric.

genggang II cranny.

genggeng to carry an object by seizing a small portion of it between the teeth; **siput genggeng** shell.

genggong sort of Jew's harp made of bamboo.

genggulang bamboo stake split at the end to serve as altar for Malay pawang.

genggulong millipede.

gengsi relatives, family.

genit coquettish, sexy.

genjah, padi **genjah** rice plant that ripens quickly.

genjala lampblack, soot; also **jelaga.**

genjang awry, crooked, a-slant, out of line.

genjur stiff (of hair); **keras genjur** hard and unyielding.

genjut aslant, awry.

genta bell; **anak genta** clapper; = **loceng.**

gentala magic wheeled car.

gentang, gentang-gentang sinuous and tapering.

gentar quivering, shaking, trembling.

gentas, menggentas to pluck (flower) breaking a stalk.

gentat shrunken, dented.

genteh, genteh susu sweet-meat.

gentel pill, pellet; **menggentel** to roll in the fingertips.

genting extremely slender, critical gap (pass between hills); **pinggang genting** wasp-waisted; **kegentingan** tension.

gentis wasp-waisted.

gentung large open jar.

genuak packed closely.

genyang-genyut uneven, wobbling.

genyeh to rub roughly.

genyi revolted (at dirt, smell of wounds).

genyit, tergenyit winking.

genyut awry (of lines).

geografi geography.

gepeng flat; = **pipih.**

gepuh padlock.

gepuk small watch-shaped tobacco box.

gera, menggera frighten.

gerabak railway truck *or* coach.

gerabang perforated; **meng-gerabang** in strips.

geradi grille.

geraf graph.

geragai hook for catching crocodile.

geragas, menggeragas claw-ing, pawing; scrambling.

geragau to claw wildly; small shrimps.

gerai bridal dais; bed; market stall; **tergerai** loosened (*of hair*).

gerak motion, movement; **gerak-geri twitch; gerak hati** impulse; **bergerak** to move, start up; **menggerakkan** to cause to move; **penggerakan** movement.

geram eager, agog; **geram hati** excited; **menggeram** to get excited.

gerambi curved dagger.

geramsut cloth from which Arab zouave jackets are made.

geran grant (*for land*); **geran mati** freehold; **geran hidup** leasehold.

gerang I keen, eager, en-raptured; **bergerang hati, menggerangkan** to stimulate; excited.

gerang II oily cosmetic.

gerangan possibly, maybe.

geranggang bamboo spear.

geranyam, menggeranyam quivering (*of heat haze*).

gerapah, menggerapah to hack skin off animal.

gerapai, menggerapai to fum-ble with the hand, feel about.

gerapak to bluff (attempting to frighten).

gerapu, bergerapu rough to the touch.

geratak to seek everywhere, hunt for.

gerau chef, cook.

gerayak loot; **menggerayak** to loot.

gerayang, menggerayang to go about picking up odds and ends.

gerbak, menggerbak spread (*of scent*).

gerbang spread open; **pintu gerbang** main gate; **tergerbang** dishevelled; **menggerbangkan** to loosen, spread out.

gerbas-gerbus rustling.

gerbek noisy clapper used to frighten squirrels and birds from fruit trees.

gerebek, menggerebek aslant.

gerecek, menggerecek to tease.

gerecok, menggerecok to plague, worry with talk.

geredak noise of collision, thud, bang.

geredam thudding.

geregak I boil up; = **gelegak**.

geregak II bamboo scare-crow.

geregau, menggeregau to seize in talons.

gereja church; **burung gereja** sparrow.

gerek, menggerek to bore, drill hole; **penggerek** cobbler's awl; **senggerek** auger; unicorn's horn

gereluh, menggereluh to snore; = **reluh, keruh.**

geremang hairs on end.

geremut, menggeremut to throb (*of boil*); to crowd (*of persons*).

gerencang, menggerencang continually repeated clanging noise.

gerendek I small fitting; **bergerendek** full of gadgets.

gerendek II tremulous and low (*of voice*).

gerendeng to adopt a threatening attitude (*of fighting cock or animal*).

gereng to bluff (*of fighting cock or fishes*).

gerengau clawing, scratching.

gerengseng large brass cooking pan.

gerentam noise of a heavy fall or stamping.

gerenyam, menggerenyam itch from prickly heat.

gerenyau restless (of children).

geresah = gelisah restless.

gergaji saw.

gergasi tusked cannibal demon.

gerham molar tooth; **gerham bongsu** wisdom tooth.

gerhana eclipse (of sun, moon); **kena gerhana** to suffer eclipse.

geri, gerak-geri involuntary movement.

geriak, menggeriak swarming, abundant (of insects).

geriang iguana, monitor lizard.

gericau, menggericau twitter (of birds).

gerigi(s) tooth-edged, serrated; jagged.

gerila guerilla.

gerim, kain gerim flannel.

gerimis, hujan gerimis drizzling rain, drizzle.

gerinda, batu gerinda whetstone used for filing teeth.

gerindam = gurindam.

gering sick (of royalty); **gering ulu** suffering from headache; **gering tengah** stomachache.

gerinjam ear cleaner.

gerit wild rubber vines; to scrape; **geritan api** matches.

gerlap = kerlap.

gerling = kerling.

germang, menggermang to bristle up.

germit auger, drill; = **gerodi.**

germut, menggermut to swarm (as ants, people).

gernyut, menggernyut to throb (of boil); **gernyut-gernyut bagai kambing berulat** squirming like a goat with maggoty sores.

gerobak railway truck or coach; also **gerabak.**

gerobok crockery chest, cupboard; **menggerobok** to bubble up.

Geroda, Burung Geroda Vishnu's eagle.

gerodak, menggerodak to rummage in a box.

gerodek, menggerodek to rattle (as a stone in a box).

gerodi auger.

gerogoh barrel-like trap for prawns.

gerogol house on raft.

gerogot to gnaw all over.

gerombol, bergerombol to assemble in clusters.

gerombong group, party.

gerompak, menggerompak to swarm over in clusters.

gerondong goitre; **siput gerondong** mollusc.

gerongga = rongga hollow.

geronggang hollow inside (of cylinders, pipes, trees, caves); handle for the small knife (tuai).

geronggong hollow; = **geronggang.**

geronyot, menggeronyot giving a twinge of pain.

geropis, menggeropis to do fine delicate work.

geropok, tergeropok stumbling and falling (into mud, water).

geros gross.

gersak sound of dry leaves trodden upon.

gersik gravel, coarse sand; also **kersik.**

gertak narrow bridge; **menggertakkan** to spur (a horse); urge on; intimidate, bully.

gertang hard; = **keras.**

geru, menggeru trumpet (of elephant).

geruai weak (of the overgrown).

geruduh bumping (in collision).

gerugul, hantu gerugul evil spirit of the forest.

gerugut deeply wrinkled.

geruh ill-luck, mischance; geruh luka, ajal mati if I am unlucky I shall be wounded, if my hour has come I shall die.

geruit, menggeruit to wriggle weakly (of insect); squirm.

geruk palm leaf wrapper for jackfruit on the tree.

gerun panic, alarm; penggerun formidable in appearance or manner; kambing gerun Malay serow.

gerundang tadpole.

gerunding large lizard.

gerung, menggerung to trumpet (of elephant); roar (of tigers).

gerup portion of a Malay loom in which the sisir is fixed.

gerus sandpapering, polishing.

gerut, ikan gerut-gerut a fish.

gerutu rough (of skin, bark); menggerutu to grumble.

gerutup, menggerutup noise of artillery fire.

gesa, bergesa to hasten; tergesa-gesa hurried; in a hurry.

gesek rubbing, scraping; menggesek to scrape (match, violin).

gesel, menggesel to rub (two sticks together to make fire); bergesel brushing together.

geseng to rub; tergesenggeseng bagai anak tidak diaku rubbing against one like a child snubbed.

geser, menggeser to close up, move a little.

geta dais, sleeping platform, broad sofa or couch; geta peraduan sleeping dais.

getah sap, latex (esp of rubber trees); pokok getah rubber tree; getah tiruan synthetic rubber; menggetah to lime birds; bergetah sappy, sticky.

getak to fall (of blossom); fall out (of hair, teeth).

getang taut (as a parchment lid); menggetang to tie tight.

getas brittle; getas tangan heavy-handed; getas-getas a cake.

getek I to pick out; getek puru dibibir to pick at a sore lip (advertise a family scandal); to bite (as ant); hate, be revolted.

getek II immodest (in talk, conduct of women); menggetek to flaunt.

geti-geti a plant; a Malay cake.

getik to loathe.

getil pinching, nipping between thumb and forefinger; belut digetil ekor an eel with tail nipped (symbol of slippery speed).

getis brittle; to break a stalk, pluck flowers.

getu, menggetu to nip (flea, bug); kill; pinch between thumb and forefinger.

gewang mother-of-pearl used for button; tergewang-gewang with hands waving.

ghabra alarmed.

ghafor very forgiving, all merciful.

ghaib invisible; vanished; mysterious; ilmu ghaib mysticism.

ghali galley.

ghalias large galley.

ghalib victorious, successful; normal; pada ghalibnya usually.

gharib foreign; stranger.

ghasal ritual ablution.

ghaza victorious.

ghina to be rich (in God, mystics).

ghulam servant, slave.

ghuluf,—kulup prepuce.

gi dripping, clarified buttermilk.

giai, menggiai to swagger.

giam hardwood tree.

gian penniless, bankrupt.

giang lewd; on heat.

giap irresolute.

giat active, enthusiastic; **menggiat** to taunt, tease; **kegiatan** activity; **menggiatkan** to encourage; **penggiat** incentive.

giau, menggiau to cut the rice with a sickle set opposite to a wooden hook for gathering the sheaves; **pisau penggiau.**

gibang, bergibang brag; *also* **gebang.**

gibas, kambing gibas fat-tailed sheep; = **kibas.**

gidik, bergidik to shudder.

gigi tooth; serrated edge; **gigi anjing, gigi asu** canine teeth.

gigih, gigil obstinate.

gigil, menggigil to chatter (*of teeth*); shiver (*from cold*); **demam gigil** ague.

gigit, menggigit to bite, nip.

gila mad, insane; infatuated; **anjing gila** mad dog; **gila babi** epilepsy; **gila bahasa** slightly mad, eccentric; **gila berahi** madly in love; **gila isim** religious madness; **gila ekor, gila urat** amative, salacious; **mengkuang murai gila fantail** fly-catcher.

gilang shining; **gilang-gemilang** glittering, radiant, resplendent.

gilap lustrous (*of polished surface*); **menggilap** burnish; **gilap-gemilap** glittering.

gilas, menggilas to grind fine; knead.

gilau = kilau

gili—gili bank, towpath.

giling to roll into a spherical *or* cylindrical shape; roll up a cigarette; grind curry stuffs with roller; **batu giling** roller for grinding spices; **gilingan** axle of waterwheel.

gilir, bergilir to happen in turn; **bergilir-gilir** in succession, in turn; **giliran** one's turn; **gilir singgah pada dia** it is his turn; **tunggu gilir** to await one's turn.

gilis rattan fastening oar to thole pin.

gimbal, menggimbul to stick out (*of a cheek from food*).

gimpai large gold *or* silver pendant.

gincah = kincah.

gincu rouge.

gingging standing on one leg clasping the other.

ginjal kidneys; *also* **kerinjal.**

ginjat, teginjat-ginjat walking on tiptoe.

girap to quicken the stroke when rowing.

giras, kain giras coarse linen.

giri mountain (*in place names*).

girik, girik-girik betel nut pounder.

giring, menggiring to drive wild elephants; **giring-giring** sort of bell made out of sea shell.

gisal, menggisal to rub (*eg seed pod or powder in the palms of the hands*).

gisar, menggisar to twist, spin; *also* **kisar.**

giung, menggiung to interrupt (*talk*).

giwah shoe.

goa cave; **kelawar goa** bat; **kambing goa** Malayan serow.

gobar gloomy, sombre, overcast; **gobar hati** depressed, worried; **spreading** (*of rumour*).

gobek areca nut pounder; **gobek api** fire syringe.

gocoh, menggocoh to pummel with closed fists; **bergocoh** to box spar, cuff.

goda spurring on, harassing; **menggoda** to urge on.

godak, menggodak to stir; **nasi godak** medicinal mixture of rice and herbs.

godam, menggodam to strike a heavy blow (*eg with club*); penggodam club, knuckle-duster.

godek to waggle a stick in a hole; tergodek-godek wagging (*of a dog's tail*).

godok base of skull, nape of neck.

gogoh, menggogoh to shiver (*from fever*).

gogok necklace; menggogok to gulp down water with lifted chin.

gogol long-handled chisel used by braziers.

gok hump on Indian cattle; jail, prison cage.

gol goal.

golak, golak-golek topsy-turvy, to and fro, up and down; bergolak to bubble, boil up.

golang—golek swaying (*of ball, pendulum*).

golek, bergolek to roll over and over (*as a ball*); to wobble (*of boats*); menggolekkan to trundle a wheel; spin (*coin, marble*); bantal golek bolster.

goleng, menggoleng to touch, nudge; = guling.

golf golf.

golok wood knife, chopper; golok-galor covered with scratches.

golong, gulong, menggolong-longkan from into a party; tergolong included (*in party, group*); golongan group.

golot, bergolot-golot with fussy energy.

gomba frontlet for elephant.

gombak, bergombak wear-ing a sarung with no garment under it; marine pursenet tied to stake; large water jar.

gomit, menggomit to tickle (*of palms*).

gomol, menggomol to em brace and try to throw; bergomol to wrestle.

gompang clump of bushes.

goncang, guncang to cause anything to rock or sway, shake.

gondah anxious, distracted, depressed; gondah gulana.

gondang, siput gondang gen-eric name for several marine shells of the genus Dolium; gondang bukit land shell.

gondek drooping.

gondok goitre; gondok thy-roid gland; short and thick (*of buffalo horns*).

gondol bare-headed; bald; treeless; stripped of all posses-sions.

gondong goitre.

gong large gong with a boss.

gonggong seizing and carry-ing off in the mouth (*as a dog*); generic name for a number of shells.

goni, guni sack, bag.

gonjak, menggonjak to ridi-cule; kena gonjak to be made ridiculous.

gonjing, bergonjing to wran-gle (*of children*).

gonjong high-pitched (*of roof*); steep and pointed (*of hill*); high.

gontai slow, slowly.

gonyeh, menggonyeh to munch (*of toothless*).

gonyoh, menggonyoh to scrub hard; gonyoh-ganyah rubbing and scrubbing.

gopoh, bergopoh to hasten; tergopoh in a hurry; gopoh-gapah hurriedly.

gopong coconut shell bowl in a rattan holder; = sekul.

gorab, gorap dhow, Arab ship.

gorek, korek, gorek api matches.

goreng fried; ikan goreng

fried fish; **nasi goreng** fried rice; **menggoreng** fry with oil; to flatter.

goris, menggoris to scratch; **goris api** matches; **tergoris** scratched.

gosok to abrade; **menggosok** to scrub, clean; **bergosok** cleaned; **penggosok** scrubbing brush.

gosong sandbank, shoal.

gotong, gotong-royong co-operating; **menggotong** to carry a heavy load (of two or more persons together).

goyang to shake; **bergoyang** to sway; **menggoyang-goyang** to keep waving.

grafik graph, graphic.

gu double yoke of a bullock cart; **segu** a pair.

gua, goa cave.

guai-gali shaky, loose.

guam thrush in children; **peguam** lawyer, pleader.

guar hillock.

gubah, menggubah to compose; cut and arrange flowers; **timun digubah** cucumber slice; **tergubah** to cut and arrange; **gubahan** posy; **penggubah** composer.

gubal alburnum, sapwood, portion of a tree trunk immediately under the bark; **nyior gubal** coconut with the husk off.

gubang one-masted seagoing perahu of a Bugis type; notch cut in tree trunk climbing.

gubermen government.

gubuk hut, shack.

guci vessel of glazed earthenware.

gudang store house, godown; **gudang ubat** dispensary.

gudo, gudu-gudu hookah.

gugah, menggugah to waken, rouse.

gugat, menggugat to charge, sue (person in court).

gugup noise.

gugur to drop (of fruit, miscarriage, hair); abortion.

gugus cluster; **bergugus** in bunches (of fruit); in groups (of men, stars); **gugusan pulau-pulau** archipelago.

guit, kuit gentle sidelong push with the foot.

gula sugar; **gula batu** lump sugar; **gula melaka** coconut sugar; **gula pasir** granular sugar **gula merah.**

gulai currying, curried food; **menggulai** to prepare curry.

gulana, gondah-gulana brooding, melancholy, sad.

gulat to wrestle, have a tussle.

guli marbles.

guliga bezoar stone used as talisman.

guling to roll; revolving; **guling-gantang** rolling over and over; **berguling** to roll; **menggulingkan** to topple over.

gulita, gelap gulita pitch dark.

gulung, menggulung rolling up; **kawat segulung** roll of wire; **bergulung** rolled; **gulungan, golongan** social circle, a group.

gumpal clod, lump; **bergumpal** lumpy; **bergumpal-gumpal** in many lumps.

gumpung copse, thicket.

gun comb in a loom.

guna benefit, use; **mengguna-kan** to use; **apa gunanya?** what's the use of it?; **balas guna** repay; **berguna** useful; magical; **ubat guna** philtre; **guna-guna** philtres of all sorts.

gunam trumpet (of elephant).

gunawan skilled in magic arts.

guncang, berguncang to quake violently; **mengguncang** to shake.

gundal knob (eg on stick).

gundi decorated with coloured paper; **kembal gundi** baskets so decorated and used at weddings.

gundik secondary wife of a prince; concubine.

gunggang hollow; = **gerong-gang**.

guni sack.

gunjai fringe (of scarf, curtain).

gunjang, menggunjang to poke with a stick at objects above (eg fruit).

guntak rattle of pips in a dry fruit.

guntang ship's officer.

guntil small sack.

gunting scissors, shears; to cut with scissors; **tukang gunting** babber, tailor's cutter; **menggunting** to cut with scissors.

guntung hill-girt valley; shortened; to cut down (of house pillars).

guntur thunder.

gunung mountain; **gunung berapi** volcano; **gunung-ganang** ranges of mountains.

gup thudding sound.

gurah, menggurah to clean the mouth by rinsing; **pokok gurah** coastal tree.

gurami, ikan gurami freshwater carp.

gurau sporting, jesting, flirting; **gurau jenaka** quips and cranks; **gurau senda** flirtation; **bergurau** to flirt; sport.

gurdi, gerodi gimlet.

guri small vessel of earthenware (larger than takar).

gurindam proverbial verse.

gurita, ikan gurita octopus; also **kurita**.

guru teacher; **guru besar** headmaster; **mak guru** school mistress.

guruh thunder; **guruh-gemuruh** thunderbolt; beating loudly.

gurun jungle; desert.

gurus piastre.

gus together, all at a time, collectively; **tiga kali gus** three volleys.

gusar taking offence, angry; **menggusarkan** to anger; cause anxiety.

gusi gums of the mouth.

gustan to go astern; reverse (car).

gusti title of some distinction, master, lord; **bergusti** to wrestle; instalments of loan with interest.

gusur, menggusur to pull, drag.

gutgut large crow, pheasant; also **bubut**.

gutik to touch; take in the fingers.

H

haba heat, warmth of fire; **berhaba** hot.

habah jot, little.

habat way, manner.

habib friend; form of address for sayids.

habis done, finished; entirely; the end of; **belum habis** not yet finished; **sehabis-habis** utterly, completely; **penghabisan** termination, end; **yang penghabisan** the last.

habitat habitat.

habluk piebald.

hablur rock crystal.

Habsyi Abyssinian, Ethiopian, Negro.

habuan share, portion.

habuk dust, chaff, powder; **habuk gergaji** sawdust; **habuk tanah** silt.

had limit, boundary; as far as; **had ini** up to here; **terhad, berhad** limited; **had laju** speed limit.

hadam digested (of food).

hadap in front (of); **hadapan** front, portion in front; **di hadapan** in the presence of; in front of; **ke hadapan** to the front, forward; **hadapi, meng-hadapi** to face; **terhadap** relative to, regarding.

hadar, mati hadar dead to no purpose.

hadas, mandi hadas ablution after defilement.

hadiah gift, present; **hadiah-kan** to give.

hadir present, in attendance; **menghadiri** to attend (meeting).

hadis traditions about the Prophet.

hadrat presence; **ke hadrat** into the presence of.

hafal well versed in the Koran; knowing by heart.

haf bek half-back.

hai ho, there!

haibat, hebat awe-inspiring, terrible; **haibat nampaknya** looks grand.

haid menstruation.

haiderit hydrate.

haiderojan hydrogen.

haiderokarbon hydrocarbon.

hairan astonished, surprised; **tidak hairan** no wonder!; **menghairankan** amazed; consternation.

haiwan fauna, beasts.

hajat wish, intention; **berhajat** intending.

haji pilgrim to Mecca; **naik haji** to do the pilgrimage; **hari raya haji** feast of the Pilgrims, on 10 Zulhijah.

hajrat, hijrat the flight of Prophet Muhammad to Medinah in A.D. 622; the Muslim calendar year reckoned from then.

hak truth; **al-Hak** the Truth, the Real, the Absolute, ie God; **Hak al-Yakin** the Absol-

ute Truth; right; **hak mutlak** natural right; **hakcipta** copyright; **berhak** possessing a right.

hakikat truth, especially divine truth.

hakim judge, judge of the supreme court.

hakisan erosion.

hakmilik ownership.

hal affair; circumstances; case; position; **mengadukan hal** to lay one's case (*before any person*); **darihal** concerning, regarding; **itu lain hal** that's another matter; **dengan hal yang demikian so accordingly**; **pada halnya** actually.

hala direction; **menghala ke timur** in an easterly direction; **tidak tentu hala** aimlessly.

halai, halai-balai confused, disorderly.

halaju speed-limit; **had laju.**

halal legitimate, permissible according to Muslim law; **halal dimakan** permissible to be eaten.

halaman courtyard.

halang, alang to obstruct, handicap.

halau, menghalaukan to drive away, expel.

halba aromatic plant (*foenum graecum*).

halban, kayu halban, *also* leban tree.

halia ginger (*Zingiber officinale*).

halilintar lightning; **batu halilintar** celt, neolith.

halimunan dark, invisible; magic art of making o.s. invisible.

halintah, lintah horse leech.

halipan centipede; **jari hali-pan** pattern made by cutting trailers diagonally from the mid-rib of a palm leaf.

halkah horse collar.

halkum throat, gullet.

haloba, loba covetousness, greed.

haluan bows (of boat, ship); beralih haluan change course (of ship); sehaluan steering the same course; agreeing.

halus fine in texture; delicate; minute; invisible (of elves); orang halus invisible elves; kerja halus office job; menghalusi to inquire tactfully into.

halwa fruit in syrup, preserved fruits.

hama gnat, very small insect, microbe.

hamak surly.

hamba slave; hamba berhutang debt slave; hamba tebusan bought slave; hamba sahaya field and domestic slaves; hamba Allah slave of God; diperhamba I, me, we, us; memperhambakan to make o.s. the servant of (a girl).

hambal rug; also ambal.

hambar tasteless; also ambar.

hambat, menghambat to pursue, chase; run.

hambur, menghamburkan to scatter; terhambur scattered; berhamburan scattered everywhere; to leap, prance; jump over; menghamburkan to scatter; shed (tears).

hambus to blow; hambus lari to drive away.

hamil pregnant (more polite than bunting).

hamis rank, stinking (of meat, fish).

hamlar clownish.

hampa lacking content, empty; hampa sahaja dia ke situ his errand there was fruitless; tangan hampa empty-handed.

hampagas vacuum.

hampar to be spread out flat; batu hampar bedrock; hamparan carpet, mat; menghamparkan to spread out.

hampas dregs, dross; hampas tebu megass; hampas sutera silk dross.

hampir near; nearly, almost; hampir dapat nearly obtained; hampir serupa nearly identical; hampir-hampir very nearly; hampir kepada near; berhampiran in close touch with; menghampiri to approach.

hampus = **hapus.**

hamun, menghamun to abuse, revile.

hamzah Arabic letter representing final glottal stop.

hancing rank, foul (of urine).

hancur crushed; melted, dissolved; hancur hati brokenhearted; hancur luluh crushed to pieces; menghancurkan to crush, dissolve.

handai comrade; sahabat handai friend and pal.

handal trusty, reliable; successful; also handalan.

hang you, thou; obsolete Malay title, **Hang Tuah.**

hangat hot, warm; hangat hati angry, heated; menghangatkan to heat.

hangga suited to, fitting; hangga sahaya suitable for me.

hangit scorching; bau hangit the smell of burning.

hangus burnt to cinders; hanguskan to consume by burning; belanja hangus sum given by a bridegroom's family towards his wedding feast.

hantar to convey; conduct; send in a person's charge; menghantarkan to send under escort; terhantar stretched out, prone.

hantu ghost, evil spirit; informer, secret agent; hantu bungkus, hantu bangkit sheeted death; hantu belian tiger spirit; hantu jamuan familiar spirit; hantu tanah gnomes of the soil, garden gnomes;

burung hantu Malayan orchard owl; **jari hantu** middle finger; **rumah hantu** Masonic Lodge; **berhantu** to hold a seance.

Hanuman monkey god of Ramayana.

hanya only; except; **hanya dia yang berani** there was no one courageous except him; **hanya seorang** there was only one person; **buah hanya sedikit** only a little fruit.

hanyir stinking (of uncooked fish, meat).

hanyut drifting, floating; **hanyutkan to set adrift; berhanyut** adrift; **berhanyut-hanyut** drifting about; **orang hanyut** vagrant; **menghanyutkan** to set adrift.

hap Chinese purse.

hapal well versed in the Koran; also **hafal.**

hapus to abolish, wipe out, erase; **terhapus** expunged, obliterated.

hara, huru-hara uproar; also **hiru-hara, haru-hara.**

haram unlawful, forbidden by religious law; **anak haram, haram zadah** bastard; **Masjid Al-haram** mosque forbidden to all but Muslims; **haram!** never!, God forbid!; **mengharamkan** to declare unlawful, forbid.

harap to hope, expect; confidence, trust; **putus harap** disappointed; **berharap** to hope, trust; **mengharapkan** to hope for; **pecah harapan** to embezzle.

harau to haul a line; also **arau.**

hardik, menghardik to scold, snarl at.

harga price; **harga mati** fixed price; **berharga** priced; valuable; **mengharga kan** to prize, respect.

hargari, gari handcuffs.

hari day; **siang hari** daylight; **tengahari** midday; **malam hari** night-time; **sepanjang hari** all day; **keesokan hari** the following day; **hari besar, hari raya** holiday; **sehari-hari, tiap-tiap hari** daily, everyday; **harian haribulan** day of the month, date.

harimau tiger, leopard; also **rimau; harimau akar, harimau bintang, harimau belang** common leopard; **harimau kumbang, harimau puntung perun, harimau tarum** black leopard; **harimau jadi-jadian** were-tiger; **kecil-kecil anak harimau** though tiny, a tiger cub.

harmoni harmony.

harmonika harmonica.

haris I watchman.

haris II farmer.

harisah, bubur harisah broth of wheat and meat.

harpus resin used by violinists.

harta assets, property; **harta benda** possessions in general; **harta pusaka** heirlooms, inherited property.

hartal yellow face powder; general strike.

hartawan wealthy.

haru, haru-haru, haru-biru uproar, tumult; **mengharu** to annoy, pester; **terharu** plagued.

harum fragrant, perfumed.

harus current (of stream); tide; proper, fitting; right; probable; **seharusnya** properly.

hasad envy, jealousy, spite.

hasil product; revenue, rent, tax; **hasil bumi** crops; **hasil mahsul** various products of a country; **hasil negeri** state revenue; **hasil pintu** house rates; **menghasilkan** to bring to pass; **berhasil** successful.

hasrat longing, keen desire; **menyampaikan hasrat** to realize a desire.

hasta length from elbow to fingertips.

hasud envy, jealousy.

hasyarat insects.

hat, had as far as.

hata, hatta next (word introducing new paragraph).

hatam to end, finish; termination; sudah hatam it is finished (used esp of the completion of religious studies); also khatam.

hati heart and liver; the interior portion of anything; seat of feelings; ambil dihati to store up a grudge; membaca di dalam hati to read to o.s.; belas hati compassion; berdebar hati beat of the heart from excitement; besar hati elated; buah hati term of endearment; haneur hati heart-broken; jauh hati feeling melancholy; kecil hati hurt; lembut hati soft-hearted; makan hati to brood; puas hati satisfied; putih hati sincere; putus hati in despair; tersangkut hati lovingly attached; sedap hati complacent; suci hati pure of motive; tawar hati disinclined; terang hati clear-sighted; memperhatikan to notice, heed; pemerhati observer.

haup dead.

haus thirsty; worn by friction; to abrade.

hawa air, climate, temperature; hawa panas hot climate.

hawar pestilence, epidemic.

haya, hundang-haya swaying from side to side.

hayat life; kajihayat biology.

hebah gift (esp of land); to announce; juru hebah announcer.

hebat, haibat terrible, awe-inspiring, grand.

hela, menghela to draw over the ground, drag; penghela puller, drawer.

helai numeral coefficient for cloth, grass, leaves, paper;

sehelai kain one cloth; sehelai rambut a single hair.

helat, lat alternate, intervening.

helikopter helicopter.

heman affection, interest, care, devotion to.

hemat careful; attention; ambition, aspiration; tinggal hemat ambitious.

hembalang to hurl violently.

hembaling to whirl.

hembus=embus.

hemispiar hemisphere.

hemogelobin haemoglobin.

hempas, menghempas to hurl down; terhempas to dash down; hempas pulas dashing wildly about.

hempedal=pedal.

hempedu bile, gall; pundi-pundi hempedu gall-bladder.

himpit, menghimpit to squeeze; terhimpit squeezed; penghimpit press.

hendak wish, intention, purpose; hendakkan to desire; kehendak desire, wish; berkehendak to wish for; sekehendak in accordance with one's wishes.

hening clear, transparent.

hentam, menghentam to hit hard, bang on, punch, stamp on.

henti, berhenti to come to a stop; berhentikan to put a stop to; perhentian ending.

hep pretext, excuse for quarrel; mencari hep to seek to pick a quarrel.

herek to shriek, cry out with pain.

heret to drag along, lead (animal).

hero hero.

heroin heroine.

herti=erti.

hias, berhias to beautify o.s.; menghiasi to adorn; perhiasan decoration.

hibuh noise, uproar; to make a big fuss.

hibur, menghibur comfort, solace; to console; **taman hiburan** amusement park; **penghibur** comforter.

hidang, menghidang to serve up (food); present (radio programme); **sehidang** course; **makan sehidangan** to eat from the same dish.

hidayat right guidance in religion.

hidrat hydrate.

hidrojen hydrogen.

hidrokarbon hydrocarbon.

hidu, menghidu to sniff, smell, scent.

hidung nose; **hidung mancung** sharp-cut nose; **batang hidung** ridge of the nose; **liang hidung** nostril cavity.

hidup animate, live, alive; to live, get a livelihood; **seumur hidup** as long as I live; **sehidup semati** in life and in death; **matahari hidup** the rising sun; **menghidupkan** to bring to life; **kehidupan** life; means of livelihood; **hidupan** organism; **taraf kehidupan** standard of living; **susu hidup** fresh milk.

hijab curtain, veil.

hijau green.

hijrat the Hegira; **tahun hijrat A.H.** (anno Hejirae: Muslim calendar year reckoned from the Hegira).

hikayat story; romance; autobiography; **menghikayatkan** to tell a tale, write a tale; **sahib al-hikayat** narrator, writer.

hikmat wisdom, knowledge, magic art; **gemala hikmat** wonder-working talisman.

hilang lost; to disappear; to die; **hilang ingatan** forgetful; **hilang semangat** to faint; lose heart; **menghilangkan** to cause to disappear; **kehilangan** lost, dead.

hilap, khilaf error.

hilir to go downstream; lower reaches of a river; **hulu hilir** top and bottom, beginning and end; **menghilirkan** to let drift downstream.

himpun, berhimpun to meet together; **himpunkan** to bring together; **perhimpunan** gathering, meeting.

hina mean, humble, degraded (of persons); **hina dina** the poor and lowly; **menghinakan** to insult humiliate; **kehinaan** degradation; **penghinaan** to scorn.

hincit be off!, go away!; to chase off.

hindar, menghindarkan to avert; **terhindar** averted, avoided.

hindik, menghindik to use a (foot) lever; **lesung hindik** rice mortar whose pestle is worked with the foot.

Hindu Hindu.

hingga up to, as far as, until; **hingga pada masa ini** up to the present time; **sehingga** until; **perhinggaan** boundary, limit; **tiada terhingga** boundless; **menghinggakan** to fix limit.

hinggap to perch; settle, alight (of bird); **dihinggap penyakit** visited by sickness; **terhinggap api** caught fire, alight.

hiperbol hyperbola.

hipotisis hypothesis.

hirap, menghirap to disappear, vanish.

hirau, menghiraukan to heed, care, trouble about.

hiris, menghiris slicing, slitting, ripping up; **sehiris roti** slice of bread.

hiruk-pikuk uproar, din.

his for shame; also **is**.

hisab computation, calculation; **ilmu hisab** mathematics; **tidak terhisab** incalculable.

histori history; **historilki** historian.

hitam black, very dark in coloration; **hitam bogot** hideously black; **hitam legam** pitch black; **hitam manis** dark brown.

hitung, menghitung calculation; to reckon, count; **hitungan** reckoning; **hitung-panjang** average.

hobi hobby.

hodoh ugly, unsightly.

hogoh to mimic.

hohok miserly.

hoi hey!, what ho!

hokah hookah.

hoki hockey.

Hokian Fuhkien (*the province*).

Holanda Hollander, Dutch; *also* **Belanda**.

holi Hind, feast of Krishna; main holi dance then by children.

homa burnt sacrifice.

homam burnt sacrifice.

hon horn.

honar fraud; subject of reproach; **khabar berhonar** scandal; **membuat honar** to perpetrate fraud.

hongah, hongah-hongah to push straight on.

hongkar—hangkar higgledy-piggledy.

hong, om! Malay magician opening appeal to the Hindu trinity.

honorarium honorarium.

horizontal horizontal.

horloji clock, watch.

hormat honour, respect; **memberi hormat** to pay respect to; **yang berhormat** the Honourable (*member of legislative Councils*); **yang kehormat** the honorary.

hormon hormone.

hospital hospital.

hostel hostel.

hotel hotel.

Hua He, God (*for Islamic mystic*).

hubaya–hubaya by all means; above all things; **hubaya-hubaya jangan** don't on any account.

hubung, menghubung to join, unite, combine; **hubungan** join, connection; **berhubung** connected; **perhubungan** liaison.

Hudai, orang Hudai name of a tribe of aborigines in the Malay Peninsula.

hudak, menghudak to pursue; **penghudak** persecutor.

hudang = udang.

hudar, menghudar to bolt, clear off.

hudud hoopoe.

hui interjection of astonishment.

hujah calumny; **menghujah** to slander; **berhujah** to wrangle; proof, evidence.

hujan rain; **hujan batu, hujan beku** hail; **hujan panas** rain with sunshine; **hujan lebat** heavy rain; **hujan renyai-renyai, rintik** drizzle; **musim hujan** wet season; **menghujani** to rain (*bullets*); **burung hujan** broad bill.

hujung end, point, extremity; **hujung tanah** cape, promontory; **tahu hujung pangkalnya** to know from beginning to end, know inside out.

hukah hookah.

hukama *plural of* **hakim**; learned men, authorities (*on law, theology*).

huknah lavement.

hukum judge's decree, judgment; **hukum Allah** God's decree (*esp of death*); system of law (*esp Islamic*); **jatuhkan hukum** to pass sentence; **kena hukum** to incur the penalty; **hukuman** decrees;

punishment; **menghukumkan** to punish; to convict.

hulam vegetable condiments.

hulu head, upper portion; beginning; hilt; handle; upper waters of a river; interior of a country; **hulu hati** pit of the stomach; **hulu keris** handle of a keris; **orang hulu** dwellers upcountry; **dahulu** before; **penghulu** headman.

hulubalang leader in war, captain; (*Acheh, Perak*) territorial chief.

hulur, menghulurkan to extend a hand, pay out rope; **terhulur** extended.

huma dry rice field; **berhuma** owing a dry rice field; **padi huma** rice from a hill clearing; **perhumaan** dry rice clearings.

humanisme humanism.

humban, menghumban to hurl far; bolt, run.

humbas, menghumbas (*sl*) to scarper.

hun share, one hundredth of a tahil.

huna temple.

hundang–hanya to stagger to and fro.

hungap, terhungap-hungap panting.

hunggah to run, rush.

hunjam, menghunjam to force into the ground, whip a top from a distance.

hunjur, hunjurkan to stretch out (*hand, foot*).

hunus, menghunus to draw (*weapon from scabbard*); **terhunus** drawn.

hurai to analyse.

huru, huru-hara uproar, tumult.

huruf letters of the alphabet; **huruf besar** capital; **huruf pangkal** initials; **huruf Jawi** Malayan-Arabic lettering; **huruf Rumi** romanized characters; **buta huruf** illiterate.

hurung = urung.

hursus special.

hutan jungle; **hutan simpan** forest reserve; **hutan bakau** mangrove forest; **hutan rimba** primaeval jungle; **menghutan** afforestation.

hutang debt; owing; due; **hutang piutang** debts; **berhutang** to owe; **orang berhutang** debtor; **orang hutangan** debt slave.

huyung unsteady.

I

ia he, she, it; **iaitu, ialah** namely; **mengiakan** to approve; agree.

iau, mengiau to mew.

iba yearning, passionate regret; loving, longing; **mengiba-(hati) win pity**; *also* **hiba.**

ibadat acts of devotion; **beribadat** pious, devout.

ibarat metaphor, parallel, analogous case; **ambil ibarat** to give an example, illustrate a point by a parable.

ibar–ibar dug-out.

ibau mussel.

Iblis Satan, the devil, Belial.

ibni, ibnu son of (*formal*) of rulers; (*usually* **bin**).

Ibrahim Abraham.

Ibrani Hebrew.

ibtidak beginning, exordium; **huruf al-ibtidak** introductory words of a chapter.

ibu mother; **ibubapa** parents; **ibu jari** royal mother; **kaum ibu** mothers' society; **ibu jari** thumb; **ibu kaki** big toe; **ibu negeri** capital of a country; **ibu kejahatan** source of wickedness.

ibul palm used for matmaking.

id feast day; **id ulfitri** feast on

the first day of the breaking of the fast.

idam, mengidam to have pregnant longings; **idam-idaman** things so longed for.

idap, mengidap to suffer from a chronic disease; **idap sakit** from disease.

idar, beridar to revolve, travel round; **mengidari** to go round; **peridaran** revolution (of planet).

iddah period wherein a Muslim widow or divorcee may not remarry.

ide idea.

idealis idealism.

idealogi ideology.

idzin, izin permission.

igal, mengigal to spread the tail (of peacock).

igama religion; also agama, ugama.

igap to catch, arrest.

igau, mengigau to talk in a nightmare, delirium; to have a nightmare; muttering or crying in sleep; **igau-igauan** delirious, suffering from nightmare.

igu, gu double yoke (of bullock cart).

ihram ritual consecration; conduct and clothing enjoined on pilgrims to Mecca.

ihsan good works; benevolence; kindness.

ihtikar to hoard grain to sell it at higher price.

ihtilam seminal pollution in dreams.

ihtimal to order to take.

ihwal = hal ahwal.

ija, mengija to buy rice before the harvest; giving an advance.

ijab answer to a prayer; **ijab kabul** to accept a proposal of marriage.

ijabat granting of prayer.

ijas prune (fruit).

ijau green.

ijazah diploma, certificate.

ijmak consensus of Muslim theological opinion; common accord.

ijtihad zeal; diligence; perfection; legal ruling or interpretation of the Koran and hadis.

ijuk sugar palm fibre; **tali ijuk** rope made of this fibre.

ikal curl; curly (of hair).

ikamat bilal's second call for prayer.

ikan generic name for fish; **ikan air tawar, ikan sungai** freshwater fish; **ikan kering** dried fish; **ikan-ikan** ship's log.

ikat binding, fastening; **ikat pinggang** belt; **ikatan** bonds, fastenings; **mengikatkan** to fasten, put together; **perikatan** league, alliance.

ikhlas sincerity; sincere; **surat tulus ikhlas** the letter is sincere.

ikhtiar free choice; initiative; plan, course; **dengan ikhtiarnya sendiri** by his own choice; **mencari ikhtiar** to think out a plan; **tidak berikhtiar** unable to choose a way.

ikhtilaf wrong; inconsistent; contradiction.

ikhtisar summary; definition; outline.

ikhwan brothers.

iklim climate; **iklim sederhana** temperate climate; **iklim panas** tropical climate.

ikonomi economy.

ikrab intimate, close (of friends); near (of relatives).

ikrar, ikral promise, pledge, attestation; **surat ikrar** affidavit; **mengikrarkan** to acknowledge; **ikrar janji** to acknowledge an agreement.

iktibar example; lesson; **menjadi iktibar** to serve as an example.

iktidal symmetry.

iktikad will, purpose; **berik-tikad** believing firmly.

iktikaf agreement (between persons, scholars).

iktirad to criticize, stand out against.

iktiraf to recognize (government etc).

iktisab lawful profit.

iktisad economy; **iktisad negeri** state economy.

iktisar compendium, epitome.

ikut, mengikut to follow (person, wish, custom, example); obey (orders); seperti berikut as follows.

ilah God; **ilahat** divinity; ya Ilahi O God.

ilai, mengilai to roar with laughter; whoop (of gibbons); **ilam, ilam-ilam** dimly visible, vague.

ilau to glisten (of light on water); see kilau.

ilegal illegal.

ilham divine inspiration; mendapat ilham receiving inspiration.

ilmu knowledge; scholarship; science; ilmu akhirat eschatology; ilmu adab ethics; ilmu ugama theology; ilmu bahasa philology; ilmu bintang astronomy; ilmu hayat biology; ilmu kesihatan hygiene; ilmu hisab mathematics; ilmu tumbuh-tumbuhan botany; ilmu tata-rakyat civics.

ilustrasi illustration.

imaginesi imagination.

imam leader (of congregation at prayer in a mosque); imam perang leader in war; imamal leadership.

iman faith, creed, belief, religion; membawa iman to accept the true faith; beriman religious.

imbai lukewarm (of cooked rice).

imbal one-sided; unsteady (of furniture); unequal (of chair legs, of affected gait); one-sided (of judge's decision).

imbang reluctant but prepared to fight; wavering (of breeze); lopsided; matched, equal; balance; offset (of price etc); **imbangan** compensation; tidak seimbang imbalance.

imbas glimpse; crossing of a spirit causing illness; imbas mengimbas sway (of ship's mast).

imbau, mengimbau to throw or swing a heavy object with both hands; call, summon, mention (person's name); terimbau called.

imbuh to make up the balance, make additional payment; contribute; rial imbuh money paid above the assessed value in compensation for land taken over by the state.

imej image.

imigrasi, imigresen immigration.

imitasi imitation.

imkan to support; make possible.

imlak dictation.

impas paid off (of debts).

imperialis imperialistic.

imperialisma imperialism.

impi, rimpi utopia, dreamland.

impot to import.

imtihan test, examination.

inai henna; red dye obtained locally from a shrub; malam berinai the night on which the bride's fingers are stained with henna; pokok inai henna tree.

inang nurse, duenna, chamberwoman to a princess.

inanganda (polite) = **inang**.

inap, menginap to spend a night; rumah penginapan hotel, inn.

inas humming apparatus on a

Malay humming kite; **pekong inas** malignant tumour.

inayat help (*of God*); bounty.

incang, incang-incut zigzag, askew.

incar to drill, bore.

incat, terincat dwarfed (*of men, trees*).

inci inch.

incik = **encik**.

incit be off!, go away!; **incitkan** to shoo away.

incung, incung perlis large tree.

incut awry; **terincut-incut** limping.

indah precious, important, fine, handsome; **indah khabar, dari rupa** the report was finer than the reality; **indahkan** to heed, attach importance to (*person, thing*).

indang, mengindang to winnow rice with a sidewards jerk.

indarus defeated (*of a fighting cook and forfeit to the winner*).

indas all but, nearly.

indasteri industry.

indayang frond of coconut palm.

Indera god of Mahameru, the Hindu Olympus (**keinderaan**) name given to class of minor divinities inhabiting Indra's heaven; **mengindera** royal.

Inderaloka Indra's heaven.

indik to lever by pressure with the foot; **lesung indik** padi-pounder worked with the foot.

inding, menginding to watch expectantly; listen attentively.

individu individual; **individualis** individualist.

induk dam; **induk ayam** laying hen; **induk kerbau** milch buffalo; **perindukan brood** of chickens; **induk semang** landlady.

indung mother; **indung madu** honeycomb; **indung mutiara** mother of pearl.

industeri industry.

inflasi inflation.

inga, teringa-inga agape, at a loss.

ingar brawling; noisy disturbance; **ingar-bangar** very great uproar.

ingat to recollect, remember; **ingat-ingat** to take care, look out; **ingatan** attention to one's surroundings; recollection; **ingati** to remember; **ingatkan** to remind, recall (*to mind*); **peringatan** reminder.

ingau, ingau-ingau dozing, half awake.

Inggeris English.

inggih yes.

inggu Asafoetida, smelly coral fish.

ingin to long, desire, yearn.

ingka, gelak ingka to break into laughter, burst out laughing.

ingkar to deny; be reluctant; **ingkar akan** breaking a pledge.

ingsang = **insang**.

ingsun I, (the royal) we; poet; darling.

ingus mucus from the nose; **buang ingus** to blow one's nose.

ini this, these (here); **ini dia** here it is; **serupa ini** like this one.

inisiatif initiative.

injak, menginjak to step on (*soil, ladder*); **menginjak-injaki** to trample on (*person*); to disregard (*law*); **injakan pedal** (*of cycle, sewing machine*).

injap inturning mouth of trap with thorn or bamboo spikes to prevent escape of fish caught.

injekshan injection.

Injil Bible, New Testament, Gospel.

inkar = **ingkar.**

inna verily; **inna lillahi wa inna ilaihi raji un** verily we come from God and return to God (*said on hearing of a death*).

inni verily.

insaf fairness, true justice; sympathy; consideration; **ber-insaf akan diri** conscious of one's own position *or* conduct; to judge o.s.; **menginsaf** to be aware of.

insan mortal man; **insani** human; **roh insan** the human intelligent spirit.

insang = **isang** gills (*of fish*).

inspektor inspector.

insinuasi insinuation.

inspirasi inspiration.

institusi institution.

insulin insulin.

insuran, insurin insurance.

insyak Allah if God wills it.

inta you.

intaha end, conclusion.

intai, mengintai to peer, pry; **mengintai-intaikan** to keep an eye on; **pengintai** scout, sniper.

intan diamond; jewel (*darling*); **intan mentah** uncut diamond.

integrasi integration.

intelek intellect; **intelektual** intellectual.

intensip intensive.

interbiu interview.

interim interim.

internasional international.

inti stuffing of sugar in Malay dumplings; **inti sari** the best, cream (*of book, instruction*).

intikad criticism.

intil, mengintil to follow behind.

intip, mengintip espionage; to pry, reconnoitre; **pengintip** scout, informer.

intu, mengintu to revive (*a dead fire*).

intuisi intuition.

inu young (*title,* **Radin Inu-Raja Muda**).

inulangan flag, banner.

invalide invalid.

inverterberit invertebrate.

inya duenna; = **inang.**

ipar brother- *or* sister-in-law; **abang ipar** husband of elder sister; brother-in-law older than o.s.; **adik ipar** younger brother-in-law.

ipil tree.

ipuh poison tree, upas (*Anitiaris toxicaria*); getah ipuh vegetable poison obtained from this tree; **beripuh** poisoned (*of darts, arrows*).

ipung snake.

ira section, segment (*of orange, lemon, durian*); resin in wood; sinews in meat.

irab declension of verbs.

iradat will of God.

iram, payung iram ceremonial umbrella with flounced edge; to blush, change colour.

irama tempo, rhythm, measure in music; **berirama** rhythmical.

Iran Persia.

irap colour; **seirap** of the same colour, alike; = **kirap.**

iras, seiras of one and the same piece (*of steel, wood*); of the same stock *or* family; **keris ganja iras** creese with blade and cross piece out of one length of steel; **mengiras** to form one piece.

iri, iri hati spiteful, jealous, envious.

irigasi irrigation.

irik, mengirik to thresh rice by trampling the stalks; twist vermicelli.

iring, mengiring to follow in procession, in Indian file, one after another; **beriring-iringan** in long succession; **mengiring jalan** to line the road; **peng-iring** attendant, follower.

iris = **hiris**.

irung cup, small glass.

irup, mengirup to lap liquid loudly from spoon *or* cup.

Isa, nabi Isa Jesus.

Isahak Isaac.

isak, terisak-isak sobbing; asthmatic coughing.

isang gills (*of fish*).

isap, mengisap sucking; drawing in one's breath; **mengisap rokok** to smoke.

isar humility as a stage in the progress of a Muslim mystic.

isbat ratification; **mengisbatkan** to confirm, ratify, corroborate; **isbatkan** to affirm.

isi contents; **isi negeri** inhabitants of a country; **isi rumah** inmates of a house; **isipadu** cube root; volume; **berisi** having contents; **mengisikan** to fill (*cart, car, cup*); **pengisi** factor.

isim name; **bismillah in the name of God.**

ising to kill time (*rather than be idle*); **ising-ising** time-killing.

isit, isit mulut gums (*of mouth*).

Iskandar Alexander; **Iskandar Zul-Karnain** Alexander the Great; **Iskandariah** Alexandria.

Islam Islam; peace in God; **ugama Islam** Islamic religion; **mengislamkan** convert to Islam.

isnad chain of authorities for a Muslim tradition.

Isnain, Isnin Monday.

Ispanyol Spanish.

Israfil Archangel who will sound the Last Trump.

Istambul Constantinople.

istana ruler's palace; **beristana** to reside in a palace.

isteri wife (*more formal and polite than bini*); **beristeri** married; **beristerikan** to take a wife, marry (a wife).

istiadat customary ceremonial.

istibrak I woman's abstinence from sexual intercourse for three months after divorce *or* widowhood.

istibrak II shot silk.

istifaham investigation, inquiry.

istighfar to ask pardon (*from God*); **baca istighfar** to pray for pardon.

istihsan approval (*for an unlawful action*).

istikharat, sembahyang istikharat to pray for right guidance.

istikmal use; **mengistikmalkan** to use, utilize.

istilah technical term, terminology.

istimewa special; specially; apart from; **istimewa pula** how much the more; **keistimewaan** difference, speciality.

istinggar matchlock (*gun*).

istinggi I clew on sail.

istinggi II incense; **istinggi ladan joss stick**; *also* **setanggi**.

istinja cleansing the body with water after defecating.

istirahat pause, rest, recess; **beristirahat** to rest.

istislam acceptance of the Islamic creed.

istiwa, khat al-istiwa equator.

istrika iron.

isya, waktu isya hour of evening prayer.

isyarat sign, signal; **beri isyarat** to signal (*by nod, wink*); **mengisyaratkan** to give a signal; **isyarat pertanyaan** question mark.

isyk love, mystic love wherein lover and beloved are one.

isytihar to publish, notify; **perisytiharan** proclamation; **mengisytiharkan** to publicize.

itah, itah besi climber.

Ithnain Monday; *also* **Isnain.**

itik duck; **itik air** grebe, masked finfoot; **itik surati, itik nila** Muscovy duck; **berdiri itik** to stand on one leg; *also* **bebek.**

itu the, that, those (there); **itu dia** that is he; **itulah** precisely; **lepas itu, setelah itu** after that, then; **sebab itu** because of that, therefore; **itu pun** in spite of that.

Izazil Azaziel; Satan before the Fall.

izin permission, consent; **surat izin** licence; **mengizinkan** to permit, allow.

Izrail Azrael.

izzat honour, distinction.

J

jabal mountain; **menjabal** to rob.

jabar almighty (*of God*); **Malik ul-jabar** the Almighty King, God.

jabarut, alam jabarut the sphere attained by the mystic.

jabat grasping in the hand, holding; **jabatan** sense of touch; occupation, profession; = **jawatan; berjabat** to hold; **jabat tangan, jabat salam** to shake hands; **pejabat** Government Department; **Pejabat Kerja Raya** Public Works Department.

jabhati determination.

jabil slip-knot cloth purse.

jabing prominent (*of ears*).

jabra, jibra, al-jabra algebra; = **aljibra.**

jabu, berjabu billowing (*of ashes, dust, smoke, powder, cloud*).

jabun, berjabun-jabun billowy (*of dense foliage, smoke, cloud*).

jabung resin, glue.

jabur mixed up = **jabur;** psalm = **zabur.**

jadah, zadah son, born of; **haram jadah** bastard; illbegotten.

jadam bitter aloes imported for use as an aperient, tonic; silver-ware with blue-black filling in the low relief; coarse brass-ware for buckles with a filling of pitch in the low relief.

jadi I, menjadi be born; **harijadi** birthday; become; **jadi fitnah** become slandered; function as; **jadi kerani** be a clerk; adds up to; **2 dengan 2 jadi 4,** 2+2=4; serves as; **jadi tuladan** serves as example; **jadi orang lain** becomes different person; **kejadian** creation, incident; **terjadi** created, come to pass; **menjadikan** to create, appoint (*person as*); **dijadikan** is (*was, were*) created; (*as conjunction*) and so, therefore.

jadi II, bintang jadi Capricorn.

jadual schedule, list; **jadua waktu** time-table.

jaga to be alert, be awake, be watchful, beware; **orang jaga** watchman; **berjaga-jaga** to celebrate nightly festivities; **terjaga** awakened, alert; **menjaga** to watch; **penjaga** watchman, guard; **penjagaan** watch, supervision.

jagad = **jagat.**

jagal, berjagal to deal in small wares; **jagalan** small wares, goods; **menjagal** to slaughter; **penjagalan** abattoir.

jagang trestles, stand; = **jegang** moat.

jagat the world; freckles; **berjagat** freckled.

jagla amusing.

jago fighting cock; (*fig*) champion, political candidate; business boss.

jagung maize, Indian corn; **menjagung** sprouting of rice, pustules, breasts.

jaguni spirit presiding over lucky and unlucky times.

jagur burly; = **janggur**.

jagut chin; = **dagu**; *also* **jang-gut.**

jah dignity, rank, greatness.

jahad holy war.

jahan cat-fish; world; = **johan.**

jahanam hell, gehenna; gone to hell, damned (*of persons*); destroyed (*of things*); **sudah jahanam** it's ruined *or* spoilt.

jahang fiery (*of colour*); crimson; **menjahang** to abuse violently.

jahar aloud (*of the chanting of the* zikir).

jaharu pariah, low scoundrel.

jahat naughty (*of child*); wicked, evil, immoral; **dengan jahat** with evil intent; **men-jahatkan** find (*acts*) evil, defame (*person*); **kejahatan** naughtiness, wickedness; **per-jahat** evil-doer, criminal, bandit.

jahi ginger.

jahil ignorant of religion; **orang jahil** layman; **kejahilan** ignorance; **jahiliat** the ignorance of pre-Islamic days.

jahim blazing (*of hell*).

jahit, menjahit to sew; **tukang jahit** tailor, seamstress; **jarum penjahit** needle; **jahitan** sewing, style of sewing.

Jahudi Jew, Jewish.

jail, penjail rod with noose of fibre (*for catching pigeons, prawns*).

jais, kalis jais very unreceptive *or* inattentive.

jaiz lawful of Muslims; possible.

jaja, menjaja, berjaja to hawk; **penjaja** hawker.

jajah, menjajah to travel; **menjajahi** to traverse, tour; **jajahan** territories, district;

penjajahan imperialism, colonization; **tanah jajahan** colony.

jajak, menjajak to sound (out), fathom, appraise.

jajal, menjajal to try, test.

jajan, jajanan, wang jajan pocket money.

jajar line, row; **menjajar** to form a line; **menjajarkan** to arrange in line; **berjajar, sejajar** in line, in a row; **ja-jaran line, range.**

jajat, menjajat to mimic.

jaka young bachelor.

jakan playing marbles.

jakal jackal.

jakas a screw-pipe; = **pandan.**

jakat, zakat tithe.

jaksa judicial officer; **Jaksa Pen-gaman** Justice of the Peace.

Jakun proto-Malay nomads of Pahang and Negri Sembilan.

jakun(g), jakum Adam's apple.

jala casting-net; **menjala** throw a casting-net; **jala-jala** trellis-work; **penjala** fisherman with net.

jalad executioner.

jalak starling; **ayam jalak** cock marked like a starling; **one or two-masted open sailing-vessel**; = **galak** combative of fighting cocks.

jalal exalted (*of God*); **abdal jalal** servant of the Exalted.

jalalah majesty (*of God*).

jalan path road, course to take, movement; to continue, walk; **jalan raya** high-road; **jalan bahasa** way of speech; idiom; **jalan darat** to travel by land; **menjalankan** to set moving; **berjalan** to go on one's way; **perjalanan** journey.

jalang wild (*of animals*); **perempuan jalang** loose woman; **menjalang** to pay formal visit to one's mother-in-law after marriage.

jalar, menjalar to spread (of plants); creep (of snakes).

jali, terjali clear, revealed; sounded; **zikir jali** chanted (praise of God).

jalia galley.

jalibut galley-boat, rowboat; also **galibut**.

jalil sublime (of God); **Abdul Jalil** Muslim personal name.

jalin, menjalin to tie bamboo or rattan strips parallel to make screens or blinds; braid hair, twine, cord; **berjalin** tied side by side, entwined.

jaling = jaring.

Jalinus, Jalinus Hakim Galen the Wise.

jalis sitting in company; **sejalis** in company.

jalla exalted (of God).

jaloi murrel (freshwater).

jalu cock's natural spur; male; **=jantan** to sleepwalk.

jalur large dug-out canoe; strip of land; stripe; **berjalur** striped.

Jalut Goliath.

jam clock, watch; meter; hour; **satu jam** one hour; **jam satu** one o'clock; **sebuah jam** watch, clock; **jam tangan** wrist watch; **tukang jam** watch-maker.

jam' union (of the mystic with God).

jamaah, jamaat, jumaat assembly, congregation.

jamah physical contact; to handle (articles); enjoy a woman; **jamah-jamahan** casual concubine.

jamak usual.

jamal beauty, elegance; beautiful; **Jamaluddin** Muslim male name.

jaman time, age; **=zaman**.

jamang gold or silver frontlet worn by a woman.

jamar tern; **=camar**.

jambak tuft of hair; crest (of plant, fruit); cluster (of fruit); bunch (of keys); rose-apple.

jamban river bathing-place; latrine; **bunga jamban** water hyacinth.

jambang flower-tub; **jambangan** side-whiskers.

jambar jungle hut; **sejambar nasi** helping of rice.

jambat = jabat.

jambatan quay, pier, bridge with rail.

jambi Sumatran state.

jambiah curved dagger.

jamboree jamboree.

jambret, menjambret to grab at.

jambu name for various fruit and other trees; **jambu air mawar** rose-apple.

jambua, limau jambua pomelo.

jambul crest (of birds); tuft (of hair) on horse's forehead; **burung berjambul** crested jay.

jamik principal; **masjid jamik** chief mosque, Friday's mosque-service; **=masjid jumaat**.

jamin bail; **orang jamin, penjamin** guarantor, surety; **menjaminkan** bail out, answer for; **jaminan** guarantee.

jamjam, zamzam water from Hagar's well at Mecca; water; **jamjam durja** complexion.

jampal weight or coin of varying value.

jampang, jampangkan to make light of; **=gampang**.

jampi incantation; **menjampi** to practise magic by incantation.

jampuk the scops owl; **menjampuk** to interrupt, break into a conversation.

jampul light boat.

jamrud emerald; **=zamrud**.

jamu, menjamu to entertain, treat; keep (familiar spirit); **hantu jamuan** familiar spirit; **perjamuan** entertainment.

dinner; **jamuan teh** a tea party; **jamu-jamu** plant.

jamung torch of dry fronds.

jamur mushroom, fungus.

Jan father of all djinns.

jan = **jangan**.

jana, jana-bejana birth-place.

janabah major ritual impurity after coitus.

janah, janat paradise.

janakuasa generator.

janda widow, divorcee; **janda berhias** childless **janda** entitled to bridal dress on re-marriage.

jangak abandoned, profligate; **penjangak** sneak-thief, petty criminal.

jangan don't; lest; **janganlah do not; supaya jangan** lest; **jangankan** so far from; not to mention.

jangat, menjangat to strip skin of, split (*rattan or palm-fronds for mat-making*).

janggal discordant to the ear, unpleasant to the eye; **men-janggalkan** to botch, spoil.

janggar cashew-nut.

Janggi Zanzibari, Negro; **pauh janggi** mythical tree in the middle of the ocean; **buah pauh janggi** double coconut of the Seychelles.

janggur big, burly; = **jagur**.

janggus, buah janggus cashew-nut; = **gajus**.

janggut the beard; **berjang-gut** bearded; **janggut bauk** full beard.

jangka callipers, compasses; **sampai jangka** just right; **jangkanya** I reckon; **jangka-jangka** approximate reckoning; **menjangkakan** to anticipate; **jangkatekatan** barometer; **jangkangin** anemometer; **jangkasuhu** thermometer.

jangkah, menjangkah to overstep obstacle; = **langkah**.

jangkang, menjangkang to walk straddling; **terjangkang** wide open (*of legs, doors*); see **kangkang** name for trees with stilt roots.

jangkar anchor; roots of mangrove and bracken; legs of craw-fish; **menari jangkar** a dervish dance.

jangkat shoulder-basket; shallow; watering-place; = **cangkat**.

jangkau = **jengkau**.

jangkerek ground cricket.

jangki basket, wicker knapsack.

jangkih—mangkih projecting irregularly (*as spikes*).

jangkil irritable.

jangking, jongkang-jang-king sticking up irregularly.

jangkit, menjangkit to infect; **berjangkit** infectious, spreading (*of disease, war*); **jangkitan** infection, epidemic, contamination.

jangku chin.

jangkung tall (*of persons*).

jangla wild, untamable.

jani numb and faint from cold; **peluh jani** in a cold sweat.

janik sea-urchin; **ringgit janik** the Mexican dollar.

janin foetus.

janjang house-ladder.

janjar row, line; *also* **jajar**.

janji agreement, contract, stipulation; **minta janji** to request the fulfilment of an agreement; **pegang janji** to observe an agreement; **per-janjian** contract.

jannah, jannat paradise, heaven.

jantan male (*usually of animals*), masculine; **anak jantan** manly person; **embun jantan** dew in heavy drops; **ketam jantan** plane (*carpenter's*).

jantang feller's scaffold round big tree; distinct, visible.

jantina sex.

jantung anatomical heart, heart-shaped core; **jantung betis** calf; **jantung paha** fleshy part of the thigh; **jantung tangan** triceps; **jantung pisang** heart-shaped and coloured spadix of the banana; **jantung hati** (*heart and liver*) my life, darling.

jantur sorcery; **terjantur** bewitched.

Januari January.

janubi, kutub janubi South Pole.

jap come together, collected; **sudah jap** it is complete, it has come about; **sejap-jap** each and every.

jara borer, drill, instrument for cleaning coarse cotton-wool; churn; **kepala jara** buttermilk.

jarah, **menjarah** to plunder, raid; **penjarah** slave carried off by raiders; mite; atom; **bom jarah** atom bomb; *also* **zarah**.

jarak apart, distance between; **jaraknya** inter-space; **menjarakkan** move apart, separate; **berjarak** give space, spaced out; castor-oil plant; **minyak jarak** castor oil; **padang jarak** desolate place.

jaram, **menjaram** to use a head lotion of cold water and leaves; **penjaram** the lotion.

jaran horse.

jarang wide apart (*of houses, trees, teeth*); separated by wide interval; seldom; **jarang dia datang** he seldom comes.

jaras a rough creel; a bunch (*of flowers, fruits with stalk*); **sejaras manggis** bunch of mangosteens; **menjaras** to arrange in a bunch; **berjaras** arranged in a bunch *or* skein.

jari fingers, toes; **anak jari** fingers; **jari hantu** middle finger; **jari kelingking** little finger; **jari manis** ring finger; **jari telunjuk** index-finger; **berjari-jari** trailing (*as roots, tentacles*); **jari-jari** spoke of wheel; radius of circle.

jariah, **amal jariah** charitable work of permanent utility; slave-girl.

jaring net (*fishing, tennis*); **menjaring** to net (*fish, birds*); **jaring-jaring** trellis-work.

jaru, **ikan jaru** fish; *also* **cencaru**.

jarum needle, hand (*of clock*); **jarum cucuk** bodkin; **lubang jarum** eye of a needle.

jas coat.

jasa duty, loyal service; **berbuat jasa** to do one's duty; **lupakan jasa** to fail in one's duty.

jasad the physical body (*as opposed to the soul*).

jasmani corporeal, physical; **roh jasmani** the spirit animating the body.

jati genuine (*of article*); real thoroughbred (*of men, animals*); **kayu jati** teak (wood).

jatuh to fall, happen, occur; **jatuh sakit** to fall ill; **jatuh hati** to fall in love; **jatuhan**, **menjatuhkan** to let drop; **kejatuhan** fall.

Jaudi a Jew, Jewish.

jauh distant, far away, far advanced (*of time*); **jauh malam** late at night; **jauhmenjauhi** to keep off (*at a distance*); **jauhnya** as far away as possible; **kejauhan** distance.

jauhar gem; embryo; **jauhari** jeweller; poet; clever; expert, specialist.

jauk small tortoise.

jauza Gemini (*in the Zodiac*); walnut.

Jawa Javanese; **tanah Jawa** Java; **asam jawa** tamarind.

jawab reply, retort; **menjawab** to make a reply; **ber-**

jawab to retort, (give one's) reply; **tanggungjawab** to have to answer for one's act, be responsible for.

jawat, menjawat seize, hold (**jabat** is commoner); **jawatan** occupation; **jawatankuasa** committee; **jawatankuasa tadbir** Central or Executive Committee.

Jawi Malayan, Sumatran and Javan; **huruf Jawi** Arabic script; **Jawi peranakan, Jawi Pekan** townsmen of mixed Malay and Indian blood; **jawi-jawi, jejawi** fig tree.

jaya victorious; **menjaya** to succeed (in work); win (in game, battle); **berjaya** successful; **kejayaan** victory, success, achievement.

jayeng victorious over.

jazirah peninsula.

jebah I broad, full (of face).

jebah II assorted (of goods).

jebai, berjebai scattered.

jebak cage trap for birds; **menjebak** to trap.

jebang long shield; prominent (of ears).

jebat civet; **musang jebat** civet cat.

jebek muddy after rain; to curl the lip in disdain.

jebuh, ikan jebuh fish.

jebung fish, leatherjacket.

jeda moment, pause (in rain, storm, fighting); **tak berjeda** ceaseless, incessant.

jeding water-tank (of masonry); curled up (of lip).

jegang stiff (of corpse, muscle from exertion); also **jenkang**; = **tegang**.

jegela, orang jegela juggler, clown.

jegil, terjegil bulging (of eyes).

jegung ship's chest, sternlocker.

jejak, jijak smart, trim, in order (of situation).

jejaka youth.

jejal, menjejal to close a crack, stuff (child's mouth with food); **berjejal-jejal** crowded.

jejas abraded, scratched; rubbed (of fabrics); **jejasnya** scratch, mark.

jejeh slightly spilling, slopping.

jejek erect, firm; fixed (of price) settled.

jejer, jijer row, line, file; **berjejer** in rows.

jel gaol, jail.

jela, berjela-jela trailing (of strings, ribbons).

jelabak, terjelabak to collapse (as a building).

jelabas, mulut jelabas babbling; = **elampus**.

jelabir slobbering.

jeladak to creep, crawl.

jeladan bird.

jeladeri ocean.

jelaga soot; = **celaga**.

jelah I clear; **kejelahan** clearness; = **cerah**.

jelah II, menjelah to trap birds by using a sticky substance.

jelai millet.

jelajah, menjelajah cruise; **kapal penjelajah** cruiser.

jelak sated, disgusted; **jemu jelak** sick of.

jelan to put out the tongue (rudely); **terjelan** stuck out.

jelanak, menjelanak to advance under cover, stalk (under cover of grass).

jelang exactly before; **jelang siang** just at daybreak; **wide-awake**, quick-witted; **menjelang** to look for the new moon that ends Ramadan.

jolangak, menjelangak to throw back the head (as one nearly blind).

jelantah rice half cooked (with grains left hard); coconut oil left after frying; uneven (of crop).

jelantik, jelatik Java sparrow, rice-bird.

jelantur big black millipede.

jelapak, terjelapak flopped down from fatigue.

jelapang rice-barn on posts.

jelar, menjelar to creep (of snake, plant); protruding (of tongue).

jelas settled, wound up, made plain; **jelaskan** to settle account; **jelasnya** to sum up.

jelat, terjelat carelessly thrown down.

jelata, rakyat jelata proletariat.

jelatang stinging-nettle; **sea-flea**.

jelatik = **jelantik**.

jelatin gelatine.

jelau, jenguk-jelau to peer at anything.

jelawai tree.

jelawat fish.

jelebau kind of river-turtle.

jelebu, laut jelebu the distant hazy sea; = **selebu-lebu**.

jelebut = **kelebut**.

jeleh, menjeleh stick out the tongue; = **jelir**.

jelejeh, jelejeis, berjelejeis dribble (of infants); trickle (of viscous fluid).

jelek ugly, bad (of unpleasant words, condition).

jeleket adhering (as gummy surface).

jelempah general rotting of fruit on tree; scattered.

jelepak, putih menjelepak pure white.

jelepang criss-cross.

jelepet = **jeleket**.

jelepo to fall with legs huddled.

jeli ravishing.

jelimpat, menjelimpat to go out of one's way; drop in for a short call.

jelinap, menjelinap to shoot ahead (of boat, race-horse); slip along furtively.

jeling sidelong, languishing look; **menjeling** to look at s.o. out of the corner of one's eye.

je.ingar, menjelingar to glance all round; be inattentive.

jelir = **jelar**.

jelita pretty, attractive; herb.

jelma, menjelma to take human form (of gods); change o.s.; **menjelmakan** to create; embody; **penjelmaan** incarnation, embodiment.

jelojoh = **gelojoh**.

jelok deep (of bowl, basin).

jelu, jelu masak pisang weasel.

jeluak, menjeluak to retch.

jeluang thin paper (for kites etc).

jeluat, jeling-jeluat to give a long sidelong look; see **jeling**.

jeludu, menjeludu to glide (as duck boat).

jelujur, menjelujur to tack; **jelujuran** tacking, temporary sewing; horizontal bars shot into sockets to close a cattle-pen.

jelum to wet or wash without actual immersion; **ubat jelum** lotion.

jelungkap, menjelungkap to rebound (of elastic body released from strain).

jeluntung chicken-pox.

jelunut viscous (of lime, glue); **menjelunut** to adhere.

jelurai fried cake.

jelutung leaf-monkey; kind of wild rubber tree (its rubber is used in making chewing-gum, the timber is valuable).

jemaah = **jumaah**.

jemah future, about to come; = **kelak**.

jemala crown of head, skull.

jemang, sejemang moment.

jemawa conceit, pride.

jemba measure of length (3.6 metres); **menjemba** to grasp at, reach for; come.

jembak, **terjembak-jembak** flapping (*as long hair etc*).

jembalang evil spirit of the soil.

jembatan = **jambatan**.

jembel poor (*of people*); shabby (*of clothes*).

jembiah = **jambiah**.

jemeki spangles.

jemekian purging croton.

jemerlang = **cemerlang**.

jemerung fish, freshwater Cyprinoid.

jemertas grass.

jemertek eight (*in games*).

jemur, **menjemur** to put to dry in the sun; **berjemur** to sun o.s.; **jemuran** open veranda.

jempana sedan, litter.

jemparing arrow.

jempul thumb; prime, superfine; **jempulan** champion; ikan **jempul** grey mullet.

jemput, **menjemput** to take in the fingertips; invite (*to accompany, to feast*); **jemputan** invitation; **jomput-jemput** sweet-meat of fried banana.

jemu sated, disgusted, nauseated; = **jemu-jelak**.

jemuan wicked.

jemuas dirty (*as child's face or hands*) from food.

jemuju caraway seed.

jeneha(r), **jenehak**, ikan **jeneha** red snapper.

jenak, **sejenak** moment.

jenaka tricky, wily; farcical; **berjenaka** to make farcical jokes, play the fool.

jenalit familiar, acquainted with.

jenang uprights of door or window; chief assistant to a Batin *or* headman of a Jakun tribe.

jenangau = **cenangau**.

jenawi, **pedang jenawi** long sword.

jenayah crime; **penjenayah** criminal.

jenazah bier, royal hearse; (*fig*) the body of a deceased prince.

jendala = **cendala**.

jendal-jendul bumpy (*of roads*).

jendela window.

jendera fast asleep; = **cendera**.

jenderal general.

jendul bumpy (*of roads*); prominent (*of forehead*).

jenehak = **jenehar**.

jenela = **jendela**.

jengah I, **menjengah** to crane the neck to see, peer.

jenga(h) II bashful, ashamed.

jengat hide, skin; *see* **jangat**.

jengek, **menjengeki** to mock, ridicule; **jengekan** mockery; *see* **ejek**.

jenggal-jenggul bumpy.

jenggala jungle; savage, wild.

jenggar-jenggur fast growing, overgrown.

jengger cockscomb.

jenggi forest spirits that deceive hunters.

jenggut = **janggut**.

jengit, **berjengit** to be startled, spring up (*from pain*); lift and lower (*tail, head*).

jengkal span between thumb and finger; **jengka!** telunjuk span between the thumb and index finger; **jengkal kelengkeng** the span between the thumb and little finger.

jengkang, **menjengkang** to draw out a leg, extend a leg; = **kengkang**.

jengkang-jengkung limping.

jengkau, **menjengkau** to stretch out arm to clutch, reach out.

jengkek to hop, limp; *see* **jingkat**.

jengkel malicious, embittered; **kejengkelan** envy, bitterness; **menjengkelkan** to embitter.

jengkeng, **menjengkeng** to

walk on tiptoe; **jengkeng-jengkut** limping; **berjengkeng-an** spiky.

jengkerik mole-cricket; = **cengkerek.**

jengket, terjengket-jengket to walk on tiptoe.

jengking raising the tail aloft; **kala jengking** common house scorpion.

jengkit to curve upwards.

jengkol = **kokol** = **jering.**

jengkolet upside down, capsized, turned turtle.

jenguk, menjenguk to peer from cover, peep, crane.

jengul, menjengul to emerge above the surface, poke out.

jenis kind, species; **berjenis-jenis** of all kinds, various; **menjeniskan** to classify.

jenjala babbling; *also* **cencala.**

jenjang I ladder, steps.

jenjang II long, slender; = **jinjang.**

jenjarum Ixora and other plants.

jenjuang = **lenjuang.**

jenohong = **senohong.**

jentaka ill-luck.

jentat, menjentat to leap (*of flea*).

jentayu fabulous bird (*believed to have the power of calling down rain and dew*).

jentelmen gentlemen.

jentera wheel, machine; **berjentera** to revolve; **pesawat berjentera** machinery.

jentik to trap with the nails, flick (marble); **jentik-jentik** caddis mosquito larvae.

jenting short in one leg.

jenu = **tuba.**

jenuh full, satiated; **makan jenuh** to eat one's fill; **jenuh bekerja** to have had enough of work; **menjenuhkan** to make satisfied or bored.

jenut salt-lick; *see* **sira.**

jepang sea-weed jelly.

jepit = **sepit.**

Jepun Japan(ese); **bunga jepun** oleander; **kacang jepun** soya-bean.

jeput = **jemput; sejeput hari** all day.

jera deterred by experience; **menjerakan** to deter, put off.

jerabai, berjerabai frayed, in fringes, tattered; shabby.

jerabun = **jerembun.**

jerabut covered with fibrous hairs *or* feathers.

jeragur tree with yellow flowers.

jerah plentiful, abundant (*of crops*); prevalent (*of disease*); **jerah-jerih** extremely tired.

jerahak unfinished, abandoned (*of work*); to push sprawling.

jerahap, terjerahap to fall prostrate (*with limbs outstretched*).

jerait, berjeraitan interlinked (*as the links of chain, strands of net*).

jeram rapid, cataract.

jeramah to seize with claws and teeth.

jerambah platform outside a Malay house for kitchen purposes; **menjerambah** to treat a person without respect.

jerambai hanging in fringes, frayed, tattered.

jerambang will o' the wisp.

jerami straw, stubble.

jeran = **jera.**

jerang, menjerang to put pots *or* pans on a fire to heat.

jerangau medicinal plant.

jerangkak to crawl on hands and knees.

jerangkang, terjerangkang to fall with legs in the air; **berjerangkangan** projecting (*as ribs*).

jerangkap tilted.

jerangkau coarse (*of sewing*).

jerangkung human skeleton; spook.

jerap, menjerap saturate, permeate; see **serap**.

jerat noose, snare, lasso; **menjerat** to snare (birds, mouse-deer etc).

jerau dark-red.

jeraus nimble.

jerawat pimple on the face.

jerbak, menjerbak to pervade; = **menjerbak**.

jerbu = **selebu** hazy or distant open sea.

jereba, menjereba to spring at; tilt a boat.

jeregang; berjeregang stretched in the air (as telegraph wires).

jereket adhering (of gummy or sticky surface).

jeremak, berjeremak, jerempak suddenly face to face.

jeremang = **jermang** short prop to steady boat.

jeremba to reach out for (sth).

jerembab, jerembab to fall headlong; **terjerembab** prone.

jerembeh drooping; untidy (of skirt); = **rembah-rembeh**.

jerembet interlinked, intertwined; = **jerait**.

jerembun stacked, heaped up.

jerempak, terjerempak to meet unexpectedly.

jerendap to fall sprawling.

jereng squinting.

jerengkek very thin, emaciated.

jerepet interlocked; untidy.

jeri afraid, hesitant.

jeriau split laths just below the floor of Malay house; small raft.

jerih exhausted, exhausting; **batuk jerih** whooping-cough.

jeriji trellis; finger.

jering tree with strong-smelling pods.

jeringai, menjeringai grin, showing the gums.

jeringkai thin, emaciated.

jerinjing, berjerinjingan protruding (of skinny ribs).

jerit, menjerit shriek, scream; **jeritan** shriek; crying.

jerjak bars (on window), railing; thin perpendicular laths.

jerkah, menjerkah to menace, intimidate, shout.

jerkat, pinang jerkat unripe betel-nut.

jermal large trap (ending in a large net).

Jerman German; **negeri Jerman** Germany.

jermang props (for boat).

jermin, pokok jermin fragrant shrub.

jernang dragon's blood (red resin from the fruit of a rattan).

jernih clear, limpid (of fluids, hearts).

jeru, menjeru to visit (a house).

jeruang–jeruit rickety (of floors).

jerubung awning for deck-cargo.

jeruh steep (of roof).

jeruhuk stumbling into a hole concealed by long grass.

jeruji lattice; also **jeriji**.

jeruju tidal shrub with white or mauve flowers.

jerujuk, menjerujuk to crawl in and out.

jerujul, menjerujul poke the head out (of hole, cage).

jeruk generic name for fruits of the citron class and for acid pickles preserved in salt; **menjerukkan** to pickle.

jerukup, menjerukup over-arching of branches.

jerumat, menjerumat to darn (stockings, clothes).

jerumbai dangling (of fringes).

jerumbun lair of wild sow; but; heaped up, full (of measure).

jerumus, terjerumus to sprawl on one's face.

jerun medicinal mallow of yellow flowers.

jerung man-eating shark.

jerungkah, menjerungkah uneven, jagged (of teeth).

jerungkau, menjerungkau to over-arch (of trees); hang over face (of hair).

jerungkis, terjerungkis aslant, bent upwards (as post on rapid).

jerungkung knocked on one's back.

jerungkup, menjerungkup to cover o.s. (with blanket, veil).

jerunyas tattered (of fabric, paper); rough (of wood).

jerupih heeling over; men- jerupih to add band or layer to increase height.

jerupik upper (deepwater) screen in the wings (sayap) of a (belat) fish-trap.

jerut, menjerut to compress neck, strangle; = cerut.

jet jet.

jibilah nature, disposition.

Jibrail the angel Gabriel.

jidar line round printed page; ruler; menjidari to draw a line with a ruler.

jidat forehead.

jih, jir target.

jijak to trail footsteps; im- pression; berjijak to tread; steep.

jijas scratched but not pierced.

jijik to feel nausea, disgust.

jika, jikalau, kalau if.

jilak ship's lockers.

jilat, menjilat to lick, lap up.

jilid volume; binding; men- jilid to bind; tukang jilid, penjilid book-binder.

jimak coition; berjimak to have coitus.

jimat careful, economical; = azimat.

jimbil to lift an object with the fingers.

jimnastic gymnastic.

jin genie.

jinak tame, docile, familiar; berjinak-jinakan familiar with; menjinakkan to tame.

jingga dark yellow, reddish yellow.

jinggang slender, thin.

jinggi tutelary spirit (as of cave).

jingkat, berjingkat to limp, having one leg too short.

jingkik, berjingkik-jingkik to shop on one leg.

jingkir warming platform (for a woman newly confined).

jingkrak, berjingkrak to hop with glee, kick up a row, storm.

jinias genius.

jinjal hardship, trouble.

jinjang long and slender (of neck); native dance; attach- ment of a spirit to a man; polong tak berjinjang familiar spirit that has not found a master.

jinjing, menjinjing to carry (light article dangling in the hand).

jinjit, menjinjit to carry in the fingers.

jintan caraway seed; jintan hitam cummin; jintan putih white cummin; jintan manis aniseed.

jintih trees with edible fruits.

jintik jerking so as to propel.

jiografi geography.

jip jeep.

jipan = cipan.

jir target, point aimed at in a game.

jirai, sejirai strip; small quantity.

jirak tree.

jiran neighbour; negeri-negeri yang berjiran neighbouring countries.

jirat grave (esp non-Muslim).

jirim matter; **jirim-kelebu** grey matter.

jirjir olives.

jirus irrigating; **=dirus**.

jism (physical) body; **jismani** corporeal, bodily.

jitu precise (of answer); exact; home (of blows).

jiwa life, breath of individual life, soul; **serahkan jiwa** to give up one's life; **utama jiwa** breath of life.

jobong prostitute.

jodo(h) match; **sejodoh** pair; **jodohan** twin-soul; **perjodohan** match marriage; **menjodohkan** to make a match, marry off.

jogan standard with metallic emblem.

jogar draughts; **main tujuh papan jogar** to play (games of) draughts.

joget dancing girl.

jogi yogi ascetic.

johan champion; **johan pahlawan** warrior, champion.

johar, **johari=jauhar**, **jauhari**.

johong, **menjohong** to exercise a charm making a girl fall sick.

jojol, **menjojol** to project upwards; **terjojol** protruding.

jolok, **menjolok** to knock with a pole to bring down (fruit, nests etc).

jolong, **menjolong** to project (as beak, snout); **ikan jolongjolong** garfish; **jolong-jolong** for the first time.

jombang pretty, handsome.

jometri geometry.

jompak, **menjompak** to prance (of horse).

jompo old, defective.

jong junk, sea-going ship.

jongah, **jongang** projecting (of teeth).

jongit up-curling (of lip).

jongkang projecting; **jong-**

kang-jongking sticking out **jongkang-jongkit** see-sawing (of children, rickety floor).

jongkar-jangkir with tips sticking out; spiky.

jongkat-jongkit see-sawing (of floor); **jambatan jungkatan** drawbridge.

jongkir end, tip; **jongkir, terjongkir** upside down.

jongkit tilt up (of plank, tail); **jongkang-jongkit** unsteady (of flooring).

jongkok, **berjongkok** to squat.

jongkol tin coin.

jongkong dinghy, short beamy boat; **sampan jongkong**, **tampang jongkong** tin slab.

jongor snout; beak of warboat; sword of swordfish; **menjongor** to shoot forward (as head of a tortoise).

jongos boy servant.

jonjot to pick with the fingers, pluck out (hairs).

joran fishing-rod.

jorang narrow channel, watercourse, gully.

jori pair of horses.

joring shred; **tanah sejoring** small patch (of land, of cloth).

jorok, **menjorok** to protect; dirty; **penjorok** dirty blackguard.

jorong metal vase for sirih leaf; section, division, corner; conical funnel or tube.

jose shining silk.

jotor medical drug.

jotos boxing; **berjotos** to box.

J.P. Jaksa Pendamai Justice of the Peace; also **Jaksa Pengaman**.

jua=juga also; and yet; all the same; for all that; still; to some extent.

juadah cake, sweetmeat.

juah, **menjuah** to pout (of spoilt child); **=juar**.

juak, juak-juak court pages; menjuakkan to push as far as will reach, stretch out; berjuak to compete, engage in contest; menjuakkan incite (*cocks*) to fight.

jual, menjual to sell; jual-janji to sell subject to a condition; berjual-beli trading; jualan thing for sale; penjualan sale.

juandang=juara, bujang juandang lucky spirit.

juang, berjuang to fight (of *large animal*); biram berjuang fighting elephant; perjuangan battle, heavy fighting; pejuang fighter.

juar hardwood shade tree.

juara trainer of fighting animals; champion; ikan juara river catfish.

juaran=joran.

jubah Haji's gown, dalmatic.

jubin, batu jubin floor tiles.

jubli jubilee.

jubung=jerubung.

jubur anus.

judi gambling; main judi, berjudi to gamble; penjudi gambler.

juga, jugak=jua.

jugi yogi, ascetic.

juih pouting of the lower lip.

juita charming; precious, rare.

jujat slander; = hujah, hujat.

juju, tuju mahout's 'picks up' to elephant.

jujuh, berjujuh flowing continuously (of *water*); rain from eaves; in unbroken line (of *marching ants, crowds, etc*).

jujur price of brides; kejujuran offers, terms offered; berjujuran protruding of several objects; honest.

jujus, berjujus to stop; tiada berjujus continuous.

jujut=jonjot.

juku-juku hard-shelled water tortoise.

julai projecting, overhanging (as *branches*); July; julai-julita neat, pretty, graceful.

julang, menjulang lifting up aloft; to carry on the shoulder; julangan seat on the shoulders; penjulang nurse.

julap aperient.

julat, menjulat to dart up (of *tongues of flame*); go to limit of, reach; sepenjulat lembing as far as a spear can reach.

juli dhooly, litter.

julik wrapped in a single petal (as a *very young bud*).

juling squinting, cockeyed, cross-eyed; juling air squinting slightly; menjulingi to squint at.

julir fish spear, harpoon.

julita, julai-julita pretty, graceful.

juluk=jolok.

julung unlucky from childhood; kejulungan mishap.

julur, menjulurkan to stick out (*tongue*); menjulur to stretch out; terjulur extended.

jumaat, hari Jumaat Friday.

Jumadilakhir sixth Muslim Month.

Jumadilawal fifth Muslim month.

jumah, jumaah assembly; jumah menteri Cabinet Ministers.

jumantara firmament.

jumantin emerald.

jumawa conceited, arrogant.

jumbai, berjumbai dangling (of *hair*);=rumbai.

jumbil dewlap.

jumburiah republic.

jumjumah skull.

jumlah total; jumlahnya total sum; berjumlah to total, add up; menjumlahkan to add up.

jumpa to meet (*person*); come across (*thing*); berjumpa to meet; perjumpaan meeting.

jumpalit to turn a somersault.

jumpul grey mullet; = **jempul**.

jumpung, ikan jumpung parrot fish.

Jun June.

junam, menjunam to dive down (of hawk, kite).

jundai, (si-) magic charm to cause madness.

jungat, menjungat to tilt up.

junggang-jungkit to tilt, wobble; see-saw.

jungkil, terjungkil fallen headlong, toppled head over heels.

jungkir, menjungkir to turn a somersault.

jungur=jongor.

jungut spur (of mountain, river-bank).

junjung, menjunjung to carry on the head; **junjung titah** to execute a royal command; **junjungan** prop (for a vine); synonym for the Prophet.

juntai, berjuntai dangling (of feet); **duduk berjuntai** to sit with the feet dangling in the air.

junterung method; **tidak junterung** haphazard.

junub major ablution (after coition, seminal discharge, childbirth).

junun possessed, frenzied, eccentric.

jurai, berjurai hanging down loosely in tatters or a fringe; **sejurai** strip (of grass, fish); slice.

juram=curam.

jurang canyon, glen.

jurangan master of the native perahu.

juri jury.

jurik spook, ghost.

juring(an) section of fruit.

jurit, penjurit warrior, raider.

juru expert in; **juru bahasa** interpreter; **jurucakap** spokes-man; **juruhebah** radio announcer; **jurumudi** steersman; **jurutera** engineer; **kejuruteraan** engineering; **penjuru** corner; **juruodit** auditor.

jurung corner; = **penjuru.**

jurus, sejurus moment; dragging, pulling; = **dirus; berjurus** good, successful.

justa = dusta.

justisia court of justice.

jut snare of expanding loops for wild pig; riverine fishtrap; fishbasket.

juta a million; **berjuta-juta** millions.

juz section of the Koran (which is divided into thirty such sections).

juzuk constituent.

K

kaabah the Caaba inside the Great Mosque at Mecca.

kabab small lumps of meat roasted on a spit, **kebab.**

kabak spinach.

kabal invulnerable; = **kebal.**

kabang-kabang spider's web.

kabar = khabar; dregs of coconut milk; also **kebar.**

kabaret cabaret.

kabau name of several trees.

kabeh all.

Kabil Cain.

kabil = kebil; berkabilan to be cautious.

kabinet cabinet.

kabir great (of God, rulers); **mengabir** to paddle from the bows; draw a boat in to the bank.

kabisat, tahun kabisat leap year.

kabit pickpocket, thief.

kabohiderat, karbohidrat carbohydrate.

kabu-kabu, kekabu, ka-puk tree cotton (*for pillows, mattresses*).

kabul approval; dikabulkan to approve; mengkabulkan to concede; kabuli rice mixed with other dishes.

kabun, berkabun-kabun to rise in columns (*of smoke*).

kabung sugar palm; white mourning headband; berka-bung in mourning; sekabung= measurement (1.88 metres); mengapung to chop up; seka-bung piece.

kabur dim (*of sight*); faint, indistinct (*of distant scene*); kabur-kabur coconut beetle; mengaburkan to obscure.

kabureta carburettor.

kabus dimly visible, obscure (*as object in smoke, haze, twilight*).

kabut mist; dark; kelam-kabut gloomy, dark; in a commotion; berkabut vague, hazy (*of ideas*).

kaca glass (*material*); kaca muka mirror; kaca mata eye-glass; berkaca-kaca eyes filling with tears; kaca piring gar-denia; kaca-puri sort of mausoleum; type of hole in Malay grave.

kacak smart, dandified; arro-gant; terkacak-kacak step-ping gingerly along; mengacak to lift (to assess the weight).

kacang generic name for beans; kacang-kacang ball bearings; kacang tanah, ka-cang goreng groundnut, mon-key nut, peanut; kacang buncis kidney bean.

kacar, siput kacar shell; fussy; bustle.

kacat unripe; areca nut (pinang) used for cleaning teeth.

kacau confused, chaotic; ka-cau-bilau extremely confused;

mengacau to stir, mix, confuse, disturb; pengacau disturber, agitator; kekacauan disturb-ance.

kaci cutch; tungsten, wolfram; kain kaci white cotton.

kacih, kocah-kacih fiddling about with things; in a hurry.

kacip areca nut scissors.

kacir = **kocar**.

kacit = **kacip**; mengacit(kan) to fasten.

kacu extract of areca nuts boiled with lime; handkerchief.

kacuak cockroach.

kacukan impure (*of race*); unidiomatic (*of language*); mix-ture.

kacung, belalang kacung man-tis, youngster, errand boy.

kad card.

kadak fate, destiny; to fulfil, satisfy.

kadal skink, grass lizard;= bengkarung.

kadam sole (*of foot*); di bawah kadam below the sole of the (*prince's*) foot (ie *the position of the subject*).

kadang, kadang-kadang, ter-kadang, terkadang-kadang at times, occasionally.

kadar power, ability; pro-portion; rate; sekadar as far as one can, as far as one's ability goes; approximately; kadar dua bulan about two months; mengadar to sleep outside the house.

kadet cadet.

kadha= **kadak**.

kadi registrar of Muslim marriages and divorces.

kadim eternal, ageless; seka-dim full *or* half brothers and sisters; mengdimkan to anti-cipate; forecast.

kadir mighty, powerful.

kaduk a vine the leaves of which resemble those of the sirih vine; Pak Kaduk empty-headed fool of Malay folk-lore.

kadut, kain kadut sacking.

kaedah aim, object, method, procedure.

kaf the Arabic and Jawi 'k', in Malay often representing a glottal check, *eg* encik.

kafan shroud; **berkafan** shrouded.

kafilah caravan.

kafir non-Muslim, infidel; **mengkafirkan** to accuse a Moslem of unbelief.

kafsigar shoemaker.

kagak no, not.

kaget terrified, startled.

kagum amazed; surprised; **mengkagumkan** amazing, surprising; **kekaguman** amazement.

–kah interrogative suffix; **benarkah?** is it true?

kahak phlegm; **berkahak** to clear one's throat.

kahang, terkahang empty, unfinished (*of house*).

kahar all-powerful (*of God*).

kahat scarce; scarcity, famine.

kahin astrologer; magician.

Kahira Cairo.

kahwa coffee.

kahwin marriage; **berkahwin** to marry; **emas kahwin** dowry; = mahar; *also* **kawin**.

kaidah = kaedah.

kaifiat manner; special way, mode (*of doing things*).

kail, mata kail fish hook; **mengail** to fish; **pengail** fisherman; **kail-kailan** tonsilitis.

kain cloth; skirt, sarung; **kain baju** clothing; **kain batik** Javanese painted sarung.

kais, mengais to scratch up (*food; of chickens*); **kais pagi makan pagi** living from hand to mouth.

kaisar Caesar; kaiser, emperor.

kait hook; **berkait** hooked; **dikait onak** caught by thorns;

pengait hook; **mengait(kan)** to hook; **berkait tangan** arm in arm; **kaitan** connection, relation.

kajai, tali kajai halter for a horse.

kajang palm-frond roofing (*for boats, carts etc*); double sheet of paper; **tekajang** roofed, under shelter; **kertas kajang** foolscap paper.

kajangan bin.

kajau, mengajau to headhunt.

kaji I, kajibumi geology; **kajicuaca** meteorology; **kajidaya** mechanics; **kajigerak** thermodynamics; **kajihaiwan** zoology; **kajihayat** biology; **kajilembaga** embryology; **kajilogam** metallurgy; **kajipenyakit** pathology; **kajipurba** archeology.

kaji II, mengaji to learn to recite the Koran, study religion; **mengkaji** to examine, study (*any subject*); **pengajian** studies; **kajian** study.

kak = kakak.

kakah, terkakah-kakah guffawing.

kakak elder sister; **adik kakak** younger and elder brothers and sisters; near relatives; **mengkak** to quack (*of ducks*); cackle (*of hen*).

kakanda elder brother *or* sister (*politer variant of* kakak).

kakang = kakak.

kakap, mengakap to stalk; work (*field etc*); **pengakap** scout; **budak pengakap** Boy Scout, Cub; **perahu kakap** river boat.

kakas I = karkas.

kakas II, perkakas instrument, appliances.

kakatua cockatoo; pincers; fish.

kakek grandfather; old man.

kaki foot, leg; base, lower extremity; **kaki bukit** foot of the hill; bekas kaki footprint; jalan kaki to go on foot; tapak kaki sole of the foot; kaki langit horizon; kaki is used as numerical classifier of such things as flowers, umbrellas.

kako-kakoi to fidget; meddle.

kaku stiff (from cold, death); hard (of frozen meat); hard.

kakus latrine, privy; = karkus.

kal half a cupak.

kala time age, period; scorpion; dahulu kala in ancient times; apakala when; kadangkala sometimes; berkala at intervals, periodic.

kalah defeated, worsted; kalahkan, mengalahkan to defeat; = alah; kekalahan defeat; mengalah to give in.

kalai to scrape a pot; water hornet.

kalak, songsang kalak upside down, topsy-turvy.

kalakian moreover, further; then, and then next.

kalam pen; word, saying, speech; kind of black sand; panjangkan kalam to talk at length.

kalamkari painted calico.

kalandar religious mendicant; = kalender.

kalang support, base, prop; kalang ayam hen roost; piratical tribe of Orang Laut; shipyard; kalangan group, circle (of people).

kalas thole loop, rattan rowlock; habis kalas, mengkalas ended; cleaned out.

kalau if supposing that; = jikalau.

kalbu heart.

kaldai donkey, ass.

kaldu broth.

kaleidoskop kaleidoscope; position.

kalender calendar.

kali times, occasion, instance;

barangkali perhaps; berapa kali? how often?; sekali once; sekali-kali most, exceedingly; sekalipun even; sekalian all.

kalian open cast, alluvial mine; = galian; all, you all; = sekalian.

kaliber calibre.

kalifah = khalifah.

kalih shifting; to change position; = alih.

kalik, kolak-kalik backwards and forwards.

kalikausar pool in paradise.

kalimah, **kalimat** clause, sentence; anak kalimah subordinate clause; induk kalimah main sentence; kalimah majemuk compound sentence; dua kalimah syahadat the two statements of the Muslim confession of faith.

kalimantang streak of light, beam, fluorescence.

kaling, **kaleng** tinplate, sheet iron coated with tin; tukang kaling tinsmith.

kalip mad, bewitched.

kalis pure; matt, dull; impervious (to water); immune (from infection), impermanent; dendam tak kalis imperishable longing (love).

kalkir, kertas kalkir tracing paper.

kalo sieve.

kalpat caulking.

kalsium calcium.

kalu, kalok kalung fine sieve.

kalui, ikan kalui kind of carp.

kaluk curl; crook (of stick, handle); berkaluk curved (of handle).

kalung ornamental gold neckchain; fruit bat; = keluang; akar kalung wild pepper; mengalungkan to hang around the neck.

kalut, berkalut confused disturbed; in turmoil; mengalutkan to confuse.

Kama, Betara Kama Hindu God of Love.

kamal perfect (of God).

kaman labour line, shed.

kamar chamber, room, ship's cabin; moon; **mengamar** to stay overnight.

kamarban kind of belt, cummerbund.

kamariah, tahun kamariah lunar year.

kamat call to begin prayer.

kamban, mengamban to lash, tie.

kambang, mengambang to float (on water, in the air); = **ambang**.

kambar, kambau large sea turtle.

kambeli woollen cloth, blanket, rug.

kambi frame for wall panels; **pintu kambi** swing door with a wooden frame.

kambing goat, sheep; **kambing biri-biri** sheep; **kambing gunung, kambing hutan** serow.

kambu block at the end of a piston rod; **to fall sick again, worse than before.**

kambus, mengambuskan to close a hole with earth; **terkambus** blocked.

kambut open-mouthed plaited bag for rice.

kamera camera.

kami we (excluding the person addressed).

kamik, komak-kamik to move the lips, mumble.

kamil perfect; fulfilled.

kamir leaven, fermentation.

Kamis Thursday; = **Khamis**.

kamis shirt; **kamisah** shirt, chemise.

kamit, komak-kamik = kamek.

kampa(h) lettuce tree.

kampai to lie back, lean; **terkampai** leant.

kampil small matting sack (for flour, rice).

kampilan broad sword.

kampit = kampil pouch, bag (for money).

kampret (animal) bat.

kampuh linked strip; numeral classifier for things in pairs; **telur ikan sekampuh** one pair of fish roes; **kain berkampuh** skirt of two widths sewn together.

kampung village; homestead, house and garden; **berkampung** to assemble; **kampungkan** to bring together, collect.

kamu you; **kamu sekalian** you all.

kamus dictionary.

kan = akan suffix to verbs; type of teapot.

kana, gelang kana gold armlets.

kanak, kanak-kanak young child, infant.

kanan on the right hand; senior (in rank); **kaki kanan** right leg; **sebelah kanan** on the right; **terkanan** leading, outstanding.

kancah large pot for cooking rice.

kancap level with; brimful.

kancil mouse deer; **Tragulus ravus; Sang Kancil** the Brer Rabbit of Malay folklore.

kancing button, fastener, bolt; **kancingkan to** bolt (door); **terkancing** secure, fastened up.

kanoung long and large section of bamboo for carrying water.

kancut loincloth.

kanda elder playmate of royal infant; = **kakanda.**

kandang stall, pen, stye, kennel; **mengandang** to pen, confine; **terkandang** enclosed, penned; **kandang kuda** stable.

kandar, mengandar to carry on each end of a pole over the shoulder.

kandas, mengandas to beach, run ashore; **terkandas** aground, beached, stranded; **kekandasan** failure.

kandi wallet, small bag.

kandil branched candlestick, chandelier.

kandis wild mangosteen.

kandul folding up in a cloth, curtain or net; bunt of a net.

kandung carrying in a sack; mengandung to be pregnant (of women and animals); containing; terkandung included.

kandut lap, pocket.

kang horse's bit; tali kang reins; =kekang; =kakang = kakak; large water-jar.

kangar, lang kangar eagle.

kangcu owner of a kangka.

kanggaru kangaroo.

kangka old form of land concession in Johore.

kangkang wide apart (of legs); celah kangkang crotch; mengangkang to ..it or walk with legs apart; terkangkang straddling; wide open (of door, box).

kangkung white or pink flowered herb eaten like spinach

kangsa bell metal; =gangsa.

kangsar tall tree; belalang kangsar house cricket.

kangsin mischief-maker, agitator, troublemaker.

kanguk fish eagle.

kanigara sunflower.

kanisah synagogue.

kanjai, kanjaikan to fool, deceive.

kanjal deceived unexpectedly (as clever person by fool).

kanjar broad dagger; tearing at anything; tugging and running.

kanji rice gruel; starch; menganji to starch.

kanjing high, honourable (in royal titles).

kanjus lock-up (at police-station); gaol.

kanta lens.

kantan wild ginger (whose flowers are used in salads).

kantang mudbank at a river mouth.

kantih = antih.

kantil, kontal-kantil pendulous and swaying; = anting, kanting.

kantin canteen.

kanting, kotang-kanting dagnling and swinging; = anting, kantil.

kantu stiff, hard.

kantuk sleepiness; terkantuk asleep, dozing; = antuk.

kantung I the Canton province.

kantung II pouch, pocket.

kantur office; kantur pusat central office.

kanun Muslim administrative law (not revealed law); terkanun statutory, legal.

kanyon canyon.

kap roof, cover; challenge cup; tali kap ship's cable; challenge cup.

kapa nervous trembling; terkapa-kapa quivering, gasping.

kapada see ke, pada; = kepada.

kapai, terkapai-kapai groping, flailing arms, flapping arms; desperate, at one's witsend.

kapak axe; gigi kapak large front teeth; ular kapak viper.

kapal ship; kapal api steamship; kapal layar sailing ship; kapal muatan merchant ship; kapalterbang aeroplane; kapal perang warship; kapal selam submarine.

kapalan callosity, corn.

kapan = kaïan when.

kapang pile worm; berkapang dirty smeared, mouldy, rotten.

kapangan, bulan kapangan eclipse of the moon.

kapar I moth.

kapar II, **terkapar** outstretched; **berkaparan** littered; **kaparan** wrecked; grass and weeds cut and hoed.

kapas cotton wool; **kapas hantu** musk mallow; **ikan kapas-kapas** small seafish; **limau kapas** common lime.

kapi pulley; accomplished, complete.

kapik, **kopak-kapik** very limp and pendulous.

kapir infidel; non-Muslim; *also* **kafir**.

kapiran unsuccessful; ploughed (*in examination*).

kapis scallop.

kapista wicked.

kapit to stand close beside, support; **pengapit** best man (*at wedding*); assessor (*at trial*).

kapital capital; **kapitalisma** capitalism.

kapitan naval *or* army captain; headman of racial division of population.

Kapri Caffre, Negro.

kapu-kapu water lettuce.

kapuk tree cotton; **berkapuk** to clasp grab (*person from behind*).

kapur lime, chalk chewed with a betel quid; **kapur tulis** blackboard chalk; **kapur barus** camphor; **kapur masak** plaster; **kapur tohor** whitewash; **mengapur** to granulate; heal up; **mengapuri** to whitewash.

kara, **sebatang kara** alone in the world; **kacang kara** plant; **udang kara** large crab *or* lobster.

karah spotted, variegated; **kulit kara** tortoise shell; **penyu karah** turtle yielding the best shell.

karak, **berkarak** to fight (*of cats, dogs*); torch made of coconut fronds.

karam to be wrecked at sea; sink, founder (*of ship*).

karan current (*electric*).

karang coral reef; **bunga karang** sponge; **penyakit karang** gravel (*med*); literary composition; ordered garden; **karangan** composition, essay; **pengarang** writer, author; **pengarang akhbar** editor.

karantina quarantine.

karap weaver's comb.

karar peaceful, stable.

karas, **karas-karas,** **kekaras** Malay sweet cake.

karat corrosion, rust; deterioration; **karat di hati** malice; **berkarat** to rust, corrode.

karau, **mengarau(kan)** disturb; stir up; **kardus** cardboard.

kari curry; person learned in Koran.

karib near (*of relation*); intimate (*of friends*); **sahabat karib** close friend.

karih, **mengarih** to stir (*rice*); **pengarih** spoon.

karim generous, merciful.

karing, **ikan karing gajah** river fish.

karipap curry puffs.

karis = **karih.**

karkas, **karkas ayam** scratching of a chicken; (*fig*) scrawl.

karkus latrine, privy.

karma karma.

karna, **kerana** because, because of, owing to.

karpet carpet.

karpus nightcap, beret.

kartu playing card; **kartu pos** postcard.

kartus cartridge.

karuk torch of dry fronds; **pisang karuk** plant.

karun Korah (*Jew famous for riches*); **harta karun** treasuretrove.

karung matting sack.

karut involved, obscure; false;

mengarut to lie; rambling story; (**karut** *is also used as an expletive = nonsense*).

karya work of art.

kas cash.

kasa = khasah brass stand, pedestal dish; = gangsa.

kasab = kasap.

kasad intention, plan.

kasai cosmetic face powder; weevil.

kasam grudge; revenge.

kasang = kersang.

kasap rough to the touch, coarse; sailor whose duty is to attend to the lamps and stores.

kasar rough (*of texture, manners*); **kekasaran** roughness; **berkasar** to be rough.

kasau rafters; **kasau jantan** main rafters; **kasau betina** lesser rafters.

kasi coil; to give; castrated; **ayam kasi** capon.

kasih love; **kekasih** lover; **terimakasih** thank you; **kasihan** pity.

kasik, kosak-kasik sound of a restless man; fidgeting.

kasip too late.

kaskas poppy seeds.

kaspe, ubi kaspe cassava.

kasrah vowel point indicating **e** *or* **i.**

kastam customs.

kastila Castile (*Spain*); **papaya; ubi kastila** sweet potato.

kasteria a kshatriya, member of the Hindu warrior caste; knight.

kasur mattress.

kasus case.

kasut shoe, boot; **kasut kayu** clogs; **pakai kasut** to wear shoes.

kata saying, utterance; **berkata** to say; **berkata-kata** to keep talking; **mengatakan** to utter, mention; **perkataan** words; **kata-dua** ultimatum; **kata sifat** adjective; **kata keterang-**

an adverb; **kata berlawan** antonym; **katemajmuk** compound-word.

katagori category.

katak frog, toad; **katak betung** bullfrog.

katalog catalogue.

katam short section (*of sugar cane*).

katang, katang-katang small mengkuang pouch; rattan runners on the posts of jermal fish traps.

katar kind of cloth; heavy cargo boat with Chinese sail.

kates papaya; cactus.

Kat(h)olik Roman Catholic.

kati 0.60 kilograms, 16 tahil.

katib scribe; writer.

katihan rug, carpet.

katik stunted, dwarf (*cock, person*).

katil charpoy, bedstead.

katimumul corn.

katimuna = sakti – muna magic serpent of Malay folklore.

katir outrigger.

katlum bastion.

katuk, mengatuk to hit, rap hard; = ketuk.

katul rice bran.

katung king turtle; **terkatung-katung** bobbing up and down.

katup, mengatup to shut, close; **terkatup** closed.

katwal constable.

kau you, thou; = engkau.

kauk, berkauk to cry out, scream.

kaul vow; **berkaul** to vow; **bayar kaul** to fulfil a vow.

kaum, kaum kerabat, kaum keluarga family; **kaum buruh** labour party.

kaung, ikan kaung a river carp.

kaup to scrape up.

kaus shoe; **kaus kaki** sock; **kaus tangan** glove; couch, sofa; bow.

kaut, mengaut to scrape up.

kawaad drill; **berkawaad** to drill.

kawah cauldron; crater of a volcano.

kawa-kawa spider.

kawal, berkawal to keep guard; **mengawali** to watch, control, discipline; **pengawal** watchman.

kawan friend; herd; **sekawan gajah** herd of elephants.

kawang, minyak kawang vegetable oil.

kawar chief.

kawasan region, area, district; **kawasan teropika** tropics.

kawat wire, cables; **kawat berduri** barbed wire; **surat kawat** telegram.

kawi, bahasa kawi old poetic language; **adat kawi** ancient custom; **batu kawi** magnet.

kawin=kahwin.

kaya rich, wealthy; **menjadi kaya** to become rich; **Orang Kaya** great chief; **seri kaya** sweet pastry; **kekayaan** richness.

kayak like; **=seperti.**

kayal=khayal.

kayan see **kayu.**

kayap eruptive disease.

kayau, mengayau Dyak head-hunting; inundating; snag.

kayu wood, timber; **kayu api** firewood; **kayu-kayuan, kayu-kayan** timbers of different kinds; **pokok kayu** tree.

kayuh oar, paddle; **berkayuh** to paddle; **pedal** (*cycle*); row (*boat*).

ke to (*a place*); at (*a date*); **ke suatu tempat** to (*a certain place*); **kepada** to (*a person*); at (*a date*); **ke sana** thither; **ke dalam** into; **ke mana** whither?; **ke bawah** below; **ke luar=keluar.**

kebab=kabab.

kebabal young jackfruit eaten as a vegetable.

kebah breaking into perspira-tion during fever.

kebal impenetrable of the flesh; invulnerable; **kereta kebal** military tank.

kebam to suck (*as a sweet*); suck in the lips till they cease to be visible.

kebambam mango.

keban workbasket.

kebas benumbed; shaking out a cloth vigorously; deadened; paralysed temporarily.

kebasi kind of fish.

kebat wrap (*puttees, scarf*); **=bebat.**

kebat-kebit restless with beating heart.

kebaya kind of long garment worn by Malay woman.

kebayan, nenek kebayan fairy godmother of Malay romance.

kebek to have one's tongue in one's cheek.

kebel cable.

kebelai hungry.

kebil blinking in a stupid, absentminded way.

kebiri=kembiri.

kebuk cylinder for making vermicelli.

kebun plantation, garden, estate; **berkebun** owning garden or estate; **tukang kebun** gardener; **pekebun kecil** (rubber) smallholder.

kebur I, mengebur to stir up (*water*).

kebur II to clean a well by agitating the water.

kebus, kebas-kebus rustling.

kecah, berkecah scattered; topsy-turvy.

kecai, mengecaikan to tear into tiny pieces; **berkecai** torn to pieces.

kecam, mengecam to criti-cize; **kecaman** criticism.

kecambah seed-bud; **berkecambah** to sprout.

kecamuk furious (of combat); littered.

kecap I, mengecap to smack the lips; enjoy; terkecap to taste (of food).

kecap II, ketcup soya bean sauce.

kecapi lute with four strings.

kecar large poisonous snail.

kecau, terkecau convulsed and drawn up (of limbs).

keceh to light matches.

kecek, mengecek to chatter, talk; wheedle and cheat.

kecele discomfited, crestfallen.

keceng to close one's eye.

kecepung to be involved in.

kecewa disappointed.

keci ketch, small tonnage sailing boat.

kecicak, berkecicak to trample round.

kecil, kecik small; dari kecil from when I was tiny; kecil hati hurt (of feelings); mengecilkan to make small, belittle, underestimate.

kecimpung splashing (of bathers etc); berkercimpung to be involved in.

kecindan joking.

kecipak to splash.

kecoh I cheating at cards, swindling.

kecoh II, kecoh-kecah fussing about, fidgeting.

kecok lame owing to injury.

kecong swindling by denying a debt incurred.

kecu gang robber.

kecuali to except, exclude; not count; mengkecualikan to except; dikecualikan with the exception of.

kecubung poisonous herb (datura); mabuk kecubung intoxicated by datura poisoning; = ketopong.

kecundang see **cundang.**

kecung afraid; bulu kecung neck feathers of cocks.

kecup, mengecup to kiss with the mouth (and not in the Malay way: see cium).

kecura = Zuhara.

kecut shrunken, shrivelled up; kecutkan to shrink; pengecut coward.

kedada = pedada.

kedadak suddenly; cekek-kedadak may you choke at once; very deaf.

kedah = dedah open, exposed.

kedai booth, stall; (retail) shop; berkedai to keep a shop; pekedai shopkeeper.

kedak, lintang kedak lying across each other confusedly; kedak-kedak noise made by a rickety cart on a bad road.

kedal disease causing peeling of the skin.

kedali = kendali.

kedam staunch, weather-proof.

kedampas = kedumpas.

kedang stretched out, with limbs extended.

kedangking three.

kedangsa, limau kedangsa cultivated lime.

kedap close, almost water-proof (of sail cloth, meshing); kedap udara airtight.

kedari = dari-dari.

kedarung large tree.

kedayan servants, followers of a prince.

kedeh dwarf, stunted (of men, trees); mengedeh to grow less (of sickness).

kedek bent backward; ter-kedek-kedek waddling; min-cing (of gait).

kedekit, kedekut stingy, miserly.

kedelai, kacang kedelai soya bean.

kedemi sucking-fish.

kedempung plop; plump (sound); worm-eaten (of fruit).

kedemut, ikan kedemut horse mackerel.

kedengkang-kedeng-kung sound of clanging or banging.

kedengkek scraggy, emaciated.

kedengking clinking.

kedepung worm-eaten.

keder afraid, trembling; confused.

kedera, ikan kedera small sea fish.

kedera-kedera stool.

kederang spiny shrub.

kedewas, bawal kedewas white pomfrey.

kedi hermaphrodite.

kedidi, burung kedidi plover.

kediri self; = sendiri.

kedondong, pokok kedon-dong hog plum.

kedu, terkedu slight stoop (as of writer at desk).

keduduk generic name for a number o. plants with pink flowers (*Melastoma*).

keduk mask; to ladle.

kedumpas cheat, trickster.

kedung pool; centre to which one can refer.

kedut crease; wrinkle; ber-kedut crumpled (of a dress); wrinkled.

kehel, kihil, terkehel dislocated (of joint, muscle); not fitting into place; off course (of ships).

kehendak desire, wish; see hendak.

kejai rubber; mengejai to stretch (things).

kejal hard, firm (of flesh, stone).

kejam cruel; closing the eye for some time; keeping the eyes shut; kejamkan, menge-jamkan to close the eye; kekejaman brutality; cruelty, aggressiveness.

kejan, mengejan to hurry a

person to do urge to do quickly.

kejang stiff (as a corpse); berkejang convulsed (of limbs); kekejangan to have cramp.

kejap flick of an eye; sekejap moment, second.

kejar, mengejar to chase, pursue.

kejat firmly fixed (things embedded); definitely settled.

keji discreditable, disgraceful, infamous; pengejian contempt.

kejip wink; mengejip to deplore, criticize.

kejora planet Venus; = zuhrah.

keju cheese.

kejur stiff (of leaves); unpliable.

kejut stiff startled; terkejut startled; mengejutkan to startle.

kek = akek loom.

kekabu = kabu-kabu.

kekah leaf monkey.

kekal permanent; mengekalkan to make permanent.

kekam = kekat.

kekang, kang horse's bit; bridle; mengekang to adjust a bit; to curb.

kekapas, burung kekapas leaf bird.

kekar opening of blossoms; mengekar to separate rice grains.

kekasih sweet-heart, darling; see kasih.

kekat scum (of water); balik kekat tide has turned; also kekam.

kekau to have a nightmare; awake suddenly.

kekawin epic narrative (Javanese)

kekeh, terkekeh-kekeh guffawing.

kekek, mengekek to giggle; hornbill; ikan kekek small fishes.

kekek stingy, miserly.

keker telescope.

kekoa chrysanthemum.

kekok awkward, clumsy.

kekunyit, burung kekunyit oriole.

kelab club.

kelabakan to flounder, sprawl; be confused.

kelabang centipede; **mengelabang** to plait.

kelabat seed.

kelabau tree; **ikan kelabau** carp.

kelabu grey, ash-coloured; **mata kelabu** film over the eye.

kelabung higgledy-piggledy.

keladak dregs, refuse, the last and worst of anything.

keladau to divide up goods found whose owner is unknown; **mengeladau** to keep an eye open.

keladi calladium, aroid.

kelah I river fish; accusation, charge.

kelah II, berkelah to picnic; **perkelahan** picnic.

kelahi, berkelahi to quarrel; **perkelahian** quarrel.

kelak presently, in the future; **kemudian hari kelak** hereafter, anon

kelakar droll, farcical; comic (*of persons*); course, plan.

kelalang decanter, earthen waterjug with a small neck.

kelam dull, overcast; **kelam-kabut** confused, chaotic; *also* **kerabut**.

kelama, kelama ijau weed sold as vegetable.

kelamarin = kelmarin.

kelambir dewlap; coconut.

kelambit fruit bat, flying fox.

kelambu mosquito net.

kelambur wrinkled furrowed.

kelamin, sekelamin married pair couple; family; sex, gender.

kelamkari coloured cotton cloth

kelampung floating.

kelana wanderer, rover; **papa kelana** poor vagrant.

kelang I, kelang-kelok winding, meandering; **kelang-kabut, kelam-kabut** in a commotion.

kelang II mill; press; factory; **kelang ubi tapioca** mill; **kilang**.

kelangkang crotch · *see* kangkang.

kelanit to take to pieces; **mengelanit** to unsew, undo sewing.

kelantang, mengelantang to set to dry in the sun.

kelapa coconut; **pokok kelapa** coconut palm; **kelapa kering** copra.

kelar, mengelar to slash transversely; **berkelar-kelar** slashed

kelara, ikan kelara young sembilang fish.

kelarah fruit worm.

kelarai diamond-shaped pattern (*in plaited mat*).

kelari, ikan kelari river fish.

kelas class standard, rank; classroom.

kelasa hump (*on camel*).

kelasak door-mat; shield.

kelasau species of bat.

kelasi sailor.

kelasik classic.

kelat I tart; astringent; **tali kelat** sheet of a small boat.

kelat II generic name for a number of trees (*Eugenia species*).

kelati areca nut scissors.

kelau, kelip-kelau glistening (*as the surface of the sea*).

kolawa, kelalawar cave bat; clubs suit in cards.

kelayak = khalayak.

kelayu large tree.

kelebah upturned sod.

kelebak = kelebok.

kelebang—kelebut going to and fro.

kelebas, pari kelebas electric ray flash.

kelebat *see* **kelibat.**

kelebek, kelebet, mengelebet to turn back (*corner of page*); turn up (*cuffs*).

kelebok, kelebok-kelebak falling with thud.

kelebong, kelebam stumbling (*of orator, reader*).

kelebu water-logged, foundered.

kelebut I hat rest; **kelebut kasut** shoe last.

kelebut II = **kelebang.**

kelecek to dribble (at football).

keledang large tree with valuable timber.

keledar course, plan; careful measure; **mengeledarkan** to contrive, devise a course; **topi keledar** crash helmet.

keledek sweet potato; **loyar keledek** hedge lawyer.

keledut crumpled.

keleh, mengeleh to notice, look.

kelek I armpit; **mengelek** to carry under the arm.

kelek II = **balik.**

kelekati, kelekatu flying ants.

kelelap submerged, sunk.

kelelawar = kelawar.

kelelut broken (*of dying speech*); **berkelelut** to stick out one's tongue.

kelemata, kumbang kelemata coconut beetle.

kelemayar luminous millipede.

kelemayuh sort of gangrene.

kelembahang aroid causing skin irritation.

Kelembai invisible giantess who petrifies people.

kelembak best sort of aloes wood.

kelembuai, siput **kelembuai** large dark-shelled snail.

kelembubu = selembubu.

kelembung inflated.

kelemek, terkelemek opened out (*of soft steel fish hook*).

kelemoyang medicinal herbs; **kelemoyang air** black lily.

kelemping pendulous (*of breast, belly*).

kelempung sound of splash, plump.

kelemumur scaly scurf, dandruff.

kelemunting rose myrtle.

kelencung, kelenkung, block of wood with holes at each end to keep two ropes apart.

kelendara ring attaching yard to mast.

kelengar unconscious; faint; **kelengar matahari** sunstroke.

kelenggara cherish; *see* **lenggara.**

kelengkang key-ring; *also* **gelang-kunci.**

kelengkeng little finger; **burung kelengkeng** hornbill; **kurung kelengkeng** innermost chamber in fish trap.

kelengkiak large black ant; *also* **kongkiak.**

kelengkok = kelongkong.

kelengkung = kerengkung.

kelenjar gland.

kelening tinkling.

kelentang clanging.

kelenteng I, **kelenting** Chinese temple.

kelenteng II tinkling.

kelentit clitoris; **kelentit puteri** cockle.

kelentung wooden cattlebell; hawker's rattle.

kelenyar restless, anxious.

kelenyuk strained, almost dislocated.

kelepai, terkelepai dangling (*as fractured arm, branch*).

kelepak I sound of slaps or noisy flapping.

kelepak II hanging limp; baju kelepak coat open at neck.

kelepat, kalpat caulking; mengelepatkan to caulk.

kelepek, terkelepek dangling (of broken branch).

kelepet dangling (of broken horn, branch, wing).

kelepir testicle; flick, shaking arm or leg.

kelepit limp (of elephant's, dog's ear).

kelepuk flopping.

kelepung sound of plumping into water; sweetmeat; see ondeh-ondeh, buah Melaka.

kelepur = **gelupar**.

keleput to squat with legs bent to the side.

keletreng marbles; main kelereng to play marbles.

kelesa I lazy, slovenly.

kelesa II river fish; lazy and unenthusiastic type of character.

kelesek dry skin of banana stem.

keletak I sound of rapping or tapping.

keletak II to lie down without bedding.

keletang banging unceasingly.

keletar shivering.

keletik ticking continuously, tapping sound.

keletuk sound of knocking.

kelewah, tekelewah sagging (of a pocket, collar).

kelewang short one-edged sabre.

keli edible river catfish.

kelian alluvial mine; you, thou; also kalian.

keliar, berkeliaran to loaf about, stroll around.

keliat, mengeliat to wriggle (away).

kelibat double-headed paddle; mengelibat to paddle; sekelibat fish; moment; glance.

kelicap name applied to various small birds (esp sunbird).

kelici climber of medicinal value.

kelicu to pilfer.

keliding potter's wheel.

kelik, mengelik to sway the body so as to dodge.

keliki(h) papaya.

kelikir rattan nose ring for buffaloes; batu kelikir gravel.

keliling position round, part around; berkeliling around, encircling; mengelilingi to encircle; alam sekeliling environment; pekeliling circular.

kelilip grit in the eye.

kelim seam; kelim pipeh hem.

kelinci rabbit, hare.

kelincir = **gelincir**.

kelincung to take a short cut, take a side path.

kelindan I thread (for spinning); berpilin bagai kelindan twined like strands of thread; terkelindan discontented, disappointed.

kelindan II lorry attendant; (bas) bus conductor.

Keling Tamil, Telugu (from the old kingdom of Kalinga).

kelingkam gold or silver tinsel for embroidering velvet.

kelingking see **kelengkeng**.

kelingsir, mengelingsir to slip, slide.

kelinik clinic.

kelintang, buah kelintang fruit of the horseradish tree.

kelintung wooden cattle bell; = kelentung.

kelinyar fast; to gad about.

kelip, berkelip-kelip twinkling (of stars); terkelip-kelip flickering; kelip-kelip fireflies; berkerlipan glittering.

kelipuk = telipuk blue waterlily.

kelir screen (*for shadow play*); colour.

keliru puzzled; **terkeliru** confused; **mengelirukan** to puzzle, confuse; **kekeliruan** confusion, bewilderment.

kelis = mengelis = kelit.

kelit, **mengelit** to dart aside; **berkelit-kelit** dodging behind cover.

kelitah affected, capricious; style (*of writer*).

kelitek, **wayang kelitek** show with wooden puppets.

keliti thole pin, rowlock.

keliut, **burung keliut** golden plover.

kelmarin yesterday; some time ago; **kelmarin dahulu** the day before yesterday.

kelocak choppy (*o; water*); abraded (*of skin*).

kelodak silt, tailings.

kelodan thunder; **panah kelodan** thunderbolt.

keloh *see* **keluh.**

kelok, **berkelok** curving, sinuous (*of pattern, road*).

kelola, **mengelola** to superintend (*business*); **pengelola** organizer; **pengelolaan** management.

keloloh casual (*of work*).

kelompang empty egg-shell after the chick is hatched; moist sweetmeat: also **kelumpang.**

kelompok, **sekelompok** group (*of people, houses*); **berkelompok** to be in a group.

kelonek, **kelonit** a little, a bit.

kelong large marine fish trap.

kelongkang hobble for cattle.

kelongkong, **nyior kelongkong** coconut so young that the shell is soft.

kelongsong wrapper; sloughed skin of snake: leaf or paper twisted into an inverted cone for a container.

kelongsor = gelongsor, **menggelongsor.**

kelontang noisy clapper, scarecrow.

kelontong = kelentung.

kelonyor, air kelonyor eau de cologne.

kelopak thin cover *or* sheath; **kelopak bunga** sepal; **kelopak mata** eyelid; **burung kelopak pinang** nuthatch.

kelopek peeling (*of skin*); *see* **kopek.**

kelor tree.

kclorak, rumput **kelorak** grass.

keloran chlorine.

kelorek mean, stingy.

kelorid chloride.

kelorofil chlorophyll.

keloroiom chloroform.

kelosok = gelosok.

kelosong = kelongsong.

kelotak = gelotak.

kcloyak torn, peeled (*of skin*) but not severed.

kcloyang, burung **keloyang** a bird.

keloyor, **berkeloyor** to saunter, lounge.

kelu dumb, speechless; **terkelu** struck dumb; bisu kelu deaf and dumb.

keluai, **musang keluai** palm civet.

keluak, buah **keluak** nut of a fruit (**kepayang**).

keluan buffalo's nose rope.

keluang fruit-eating flying fox.

keluar motion outwards; to go out; **keluarkan**, **mengeluarkan** to expel, reveal; utter; **pengeluaran** product; production.

keluarga family, kinsfolk; **kaum keluarga** circle of relations.

kelubak torn; *see* **kobak.**

kelubi, asam kelubi stemless palm with edible fruit.

kelubung veiling, to veil; see selubung veiling (so as to cover both shoulders).

keluh, keloh, mengeluh to sigh; keluh-kesah anxious, restless, worried.

kelui, rumput kelui a grass.

keluih breadfruit.

kelukur scraped, abraded.

keluli steel.

kelulu properly arranged; tak kelulu muddled; excessive, extreme.

kelulus galley (ship).

kelulut bee.

kelum turned inward.

kelumbung = kelubung.

kelumit, sekelumit tiny bit, a little.

kelumpang = kelompang.

kelumpuk = kelompok.

kelumpung cluster; = kelompok.

kelumun cover, wrapper; berkelumun to be covered.

kelun, berkelun wreathing; rising in a spiral.

keluna, ikan keluna a fish.

kelunak, ubi kelunak tubers.

kelung coil of rattan; rambuk kelung style of coiffure.

kelupas, mengelupas to peel off, come off.

kelupur = gelupar.

kelur I to call; see kur.

kelur II = kelor.

keluron miscarriage.

kelurut whitlow.

kelus peeled, stripped off.

kemabal young jackfruit.

kemal, berkemal damp, clammy, dingy.

kemalai, lemah kemalai very weak; also gemalai.

kemam, mengemam hold in mouth (of sweet, food).

kemamam weak after illness.

kemamar dizzy and blinking.

keman sensitive plant.

kemanakan niece, nephew.

kemandalam water jug; also kendelam.

kemang evil spirit affecting new-born children.

kemanga tree.

kemangi plant used to flavour fish.

kemantin = pengantin.

kemarau dry; drought; musim kemarau dry season; kemarau kontang absolute drought.

kemari = ke mari = mari.

kemarin see kelmarin.

kemaruk ravenous (esp after illness).

kemas tidy (of bedding, rooms); dengan kemas neatly; berkemas tidied up; mengemaskan to pack (luggage); tidy up.

kematu, kembatu corn, hard skin.

kemayuh see kayuh.

kembal round-lidded basket of screw pine.

kembala = gembala.

kembali to go back, return; kembalikan, mengembalikan to give back.

kembam to fasten tightly.

kemban, berkemban to wear a cloth tied above the bosom.

kembang to open (of blossoms); expand; kembang biak prolific; kembang kuncup opening and shutting; kembang hati elated; berkembang to blossom out; develop; mengembangkan to open; terkembang opened, spread.

kembar twin; anak kembar twins; mengembari to match, duplicate.

kembara, mengembara to wander.

kembatu see kematu.

Kembayat Cambay (port in India).

kembera helter-skelter; = cempara.

kembering weretiger.

kembili tuber.

kembiri gelded, castrated; ayam kembiri capon; kembirikan to castrate.

kemboja frangipani.

Kemboja Cambodia.

kembokan fingerbowl.

kembu fisherman's wickerwork basket with narrow neck.

kembung inflated; perut kembung bloated stomach; kembungan to inflate.

kembur, berkembur to chatter, drivel till the mouth froths.

kemburan bones of the hand.

kemburu = cemburu.

kemeh, berkemeh to urinate.

kemeja shirt.

kemejan, yu kemejan shark; also kemeyan.

kemek dented (of metal).

kemeling, kemeling telur water-hyacinth.

kemelut crisis in a disease; crucial.

kemendalu mistletoe, tree parasite; also bendalu.

kemendikai water melon; = mendikai.

kemendit = kendit, gendit.

kemeniran shrub; also meniran.

Kemenjaya = Kama–jaya.

kementam thundering.

kemenyan incense, benzoin; kayu kemenyan the tree; bakar kemenyan to burn benzoin.

kemera = kembera.

kemering = kembering.

kemetut stunted, dwarfed; orang kemetut dwarf.

kemi sucking fish; see gemi.

kemia = kimia.

kemik dented (metal).

kemila to plait a fourth strand in a rope.

kemilap = gemilap.

kemilau flash of lightning; see kilau.

kemin, berkemin close-set (of joinery).

kemirau unripe, hard (of fruit).

kemis = kemeh = khamis, berkemis to beg; pengemis beggar.

kemit, kemit tubuh garment or ornament given as a love token.

kemuk, kemuk-kemek with many dents.

kemung gong.

kempa, cap kempa seal of state.

kempal = gempal.

kempang river dug-out.

kempang–kempis see kembang, kembung.

kempas large tree with commercial timber; kempas-kempis panting.

kempelang, mengempelang to hit hard.

kempen campaign.

kemperas river fish.

kempik sirih bag.

kempis, kempih shrunken, empty, deflated; kempis perut flat (of the abdomen in sick person).

kempit = kepit earthenware water jar (carried under arm).

kempu large lidded round lacquer box with handle and trays.

kempul, terkempul-kempul panting for breath.

kempun = kepun.

kempun, terkempun-kempun pinched (as a tight skirt between the thighs).

kempunan to desire, want; be gravely disappointed, unsatisfied; tanggung kempunan go unsatisfied, be disappointed.

kempung shrunken (of cheek from loss of teeth).

kempungan bladder; *see* kembung.

kemucut = kemuncup.

kemudi rudder; **berkemudi** to steer; **mengemudikan** to steer; **pengemudi** steersman.

kemudian, **kemudian daripada itu** after that; then; **hari yang kemudian** day to come.

kemukus cubebs; **addled** (*of eggs*).

kemumu seaweed.

kemuncak top, apex, crest (*of hill*).

kemungkus = kemukus.

kemuning tree yielding a veined yellow wood.

kemunting shrub with edible fruit.

kemuruk rotten (*of eggs*).

kemut, **terkemut-kemut** throb (*of pulse*).

Ken Javanese female title.

kena to contact, touch, hit; experience; suffer, incur; have to, must; **kena denda** to incur a fine; **kena sakit** to fall ill; **kena**, **mengenakan** to affix, put on; deceive; **terkena** deceived; **kena-mengena** (people) related.

kenahang malignant disease.

kenal, **mengenal** to recognize at sight; **kenalkan**, **mengenalkan** to introduce to persons; **berkenal-kenalan** to become acquainted; **perkenalan** acquaintance.

kenaling shaking with fear.

kenan I, **berkenan** to find favour with, appeal to; take kindly to something; **memperkenankan** to approve.

kenan II congenital deformity or weakness.

kenang, **kenangkan**, **mengenangkan** to recall with longing, remember fondly; **kenangan** fond memories.

kenanga tree with scented green flowers.

kenantan white (*of fighting cocks*).

kenap servant, waiter.

kenapa why?, for what reason?; = **kena apa.**

kenari canary-seed; **burung kenari** canary.

kenas pickle (*of shellfish*).

kencana gold.

kencang stiff (*of rope, breeze*); strong (*of tide*); fast; guide; **kencang-kencung** to jingle, clank.

kencar, **terkencar** flurried, agitated.

kenceng bowdrill; copper cooking pan.

kencing urine; to urinate; **terkencing** to urinate accidentally; **air kencing** urine.

kencit slight diarrhoea.

kencung aslant; **kasut kencung** slipper with upturned toe.

kencup bud-shaped; closing (*of flowers*).

kendaga shell-encrusted ornamental box.

kendak illicit lover (*of either sex*); **berkendak** to commit adultery.

kendala = gendala.

kendali bridle; to curb; **tali kendali** reins; **mengendalikan** to bridle, guide, control, organize; **peluru kendali** guided missile.

kendang drum; = **gendang.**

kendara, **kendaraan** vehicle; **mengendarai** to ride.

kendalam = kemandalam.

kenderap large river catfish.

kenderi pea half red, half black; goldsmith's weight.

kendi water-kettle; **burung kendi** curlew; **nila kendi** sapphire.

kendil pot for boiling rice.

kendiri = sendiri.

kendit narrow belt (*often of coins*); *also* **gendit.**

kendong carrying in small fold or wrapper.

kendur slack, relaxed, easy (of rope, chain); **kendurkan** to slacken.

kenduri feast (esp on religious occasions); **berkenduri** to hold a feast.

kenek servants, chauffeur's assistant.

keng to bark, howl, yelp.

kengkalong = **kalong**.

kengkang, terkengkang walking (as one bow-legged with knees apart).

kengkarong = **bengkarong**.

kengkeng I, terkengkang-kengkeng with legs apart (as of running dog or disabled man).

kengkeng II, mengengkeng to yelp, squeal (of dog).

kengkiak = **kelengkiak**.

kengkiang = **rengkiang**.

kengkunang = **kunang**.

kenidai tree.

kening forehead; bulu kening eyebrow.

kenining to whirl wildly and irregularly (of tops).

kenjah, berkenjah-kenjah littered (of fruit).

kenjang, mengenjang to dig.

kenjar taut; jerking; berkenjar-kenjar to dance a Bugis war dance.

kenjas to snatch (from person's hands).

kenjur erect, stiff.

kenop collar stud; knob; truncheon.

kensol cancel.

kental thick (of fluid); close, thick (of friends); **pengentalan** condensation.

kentala, burung kentala heron.

kentang, ubi kentang potato.

kentar goldsmith's weight.

kentara = **ketara**.

kentas = **gentas**.

kenting reverberant sound.

kentung sounding block that serves as a gong.

kentut fart; terkentut to fart. break wind.

kenung gong.

kenya maiden.

kenyal pliable to the touch. resilient, elastic.

kenyam, mengenyam to taste. try with the lips.

kenyang satisfied (after food). replete; mengenyangkan to satisfy.

kenyi sickly, poorly.

kenyir to long for, desire.

kenyit lifted (of eyebrows).

kenyuk–kenyek spoilt (of butter, cream).

kenyup got in, entered; = termasuk

kenyut sucking movement.

kep cap.

kepada = **kapada**.

kepah generic name for a number of shells, conch.

kepai tired and stiff; dirty white shrimp.

kepak I wings of birds that do not fly; mengepak-ngepak to flap; berkepak to have wings.

kepak II, mengepak to carry across the hip; bend and break.

kepal lump, fistful, morsel.

kepala head (of person, animal); leader; pancung kepala beheaded; ringan kepala flighty, quick-witted; kepala kampung village headman; kepala negeri capital of country; kepala surat heading of Malay letter; kepala tahun beginning of the year; berkepala having a head; mengepala to be headman; mengepalai to lead, be head of.

kepalang insufficient, of little account; bukan kepalang out of the common; also alang kepalang.

kepam musty (*of clothes*).

kepang watch (on a ship); mengepang to plait twine.

kepar perch-like river fish.

keparat unbelieving; infidel (*esp as abuse*).

kepari, pokok kepari mint.

kepau, kepau laut coral fish.

kepaya papaya.

kepayang big tree with poisonous seeds; (*fig*) mabok kepayang madly in love by o.s.

kepayat small river fish.

kepek = kemek betel pouch; dent.

kepeng half cent.

kepepet in difficulties, broke, hard pressed.

kepet unwashed (after excretion).

kepiah = kopiah

kepialu, demam kepialu malaria; kepialu radang severe fever with delirium.

kepiat coconut husk drained of milk.

kepik, kepik merah insect harmful to crops.

kepil, mengepil to go alongside; berkepil-kepil set or brought alongside.

kepinding bug.

keping piece (*of bread, meat, paper, wood etc*); berkeping-keping in pieces.

kepingin = ingin.

kepinis = tempinis.

kepinjai flea.

kepir sprinkle with the fingers.

kepiran neglected, slighted, abandoned.

kepis fish basket.

kepit, mengepit to press between arm and ribs; terkepit to be sandwiched.

kepiting large edible sea crab.

kepompong chrysalis, cocoon.

keponakan = kemanakan nephew, niece.

kepruk, limau kepruk tangerine, orange.

kepuh, mengepuh bellying of sails; layar mengepuh royal sail.

kepuk round rice bin of bark.

kepul cloud; berkepul thick (*of smoke*); mengepul to be thick.

kepulaga, buah kepulaga cardamom seeds.

kepum hollow (*of cheeks*); *also* kempum.

kepundan lava; lubang kepundan crater.

kepung, mengepung to encircle, surround, besiege; terkepung surrounded.

kepur large tree.

kepurun broth made from sago meal.

kepuyu freshwater climbing fish.

kepuyuk small flying cockroach.

kera common long-tailed monkey; (*fig*) kera sumbang unsociable person.

kerabat to climb up, swarm up; family relations; kaum kerabat family; berkerabat to be related.

kerabek to pick off, tear out.

kerabu ear-stud; fish *or* prawn salad.

kerabut = kelam kabut.

keracak jumping for joy; ripples on the water.

keracang = kerajang.

keracap wooden musical instrument in menora performance.

keradan swelling at tip of elephant's trunk.

keradang, mengeradang to crash (*of crockery*).

keraeng Bugis royal title.

kerah, mengerah(kan) to call (*people*) together, call up.

conscript; conscription, general call-up.

kerahi melon.

kerai sunblind, chicks; **rotan kerai, ikan kerai** large fish.

kerajang, emas kerajang gold leaf.

kerak scorched rice adhering to the inside of the pot; cracking sound.

kerakah carrack.

kerakal stones, road metal; **mengerakali** to metal roads.

kerakap old dry sirih leaves.

keram, mengeram to lock up, imprison.

kerama, kerma curse, calamity.

keramas, bedak keramas rice flour cosmetic.

keramat holy, miraculous; holy place.

kerambil coconut.

kerambit narrow-bladed curved dagger.

kerampang fork of the body, crotch.

keran tap; portable brazier.

kerana because.

kerancang = kerajang.

keranda (three plank) coffin.

kerandang, buah kerandang pinky white fruit.

kerang I generic name for shellfish *esp* cockles; **kerang-kerong** clanging noise; **kerang-kerangan** stepping stones over mud.

kerang II, kerang-kerut uneven, irregular.

kerangka = rangka.

kerangkap = keram-pang.

kerangkengan iron cage *(for prisoners, wild beasts).*

kerani clerk.

keranjang rough basket; **tali keranjang** specious ruse.

keranjat = peranjat.

keranji generic name for a number of trees.

keranta louse *(in putrid bodies).*

kerantin quarantine.

keranting = belalang ranting.

kerantung bamboo musical instrument.

keranyah leavings *(on plates);* **makan keranyah** ravenous.

kerap frequent; close *(of texture);* **kerap-kali** often; **mengerapi** to do repeatedly.

kerapai = gerapai.

kerapak = gerapak.

kerapis, keropas-kerapis oddments, trifles picked up.

kerapu, ikan kerapu kind of sea perch; **berkerapu** rough.

keras hard, stiff, obstinate, rigid; **keras hati** obstinate; **perentah keras** harsh rule; **kekerasan** hardness; force; **mengeraskan** to harden; **berkeras** to insist, refuse to yield.

kerat to sever, cut off; **se-kerat, keratan** portion cut off; **mengerat** to amputate, cut, sever; **carat,** measure of weight for diamonds.

keratun palace and grounds in Java.

kerau unripe, hard *(of fruit).*

kerawak, tupai kerawak large squirrel.

kerawang openwork, lace, fretwork; **berkerawang** fretted.

kerawat rattan binding; **kera-wat beliung** rattan binding for an adzehead.

kerawi large underground wasp.

kerawit, cacing kerawit threadworm.

kerayang = rayang, ga-yang.

kerayung tree with medicinal bark.

kerbang = gerbang.

kerbas sound of articles dropped.

kerbat, mengerbat to fasten.

kerbau water buffalo; **kerbau jalang** wild buffalo.

kerbuk to bore hole; = **tebuk**.

kercap–kercip smacking; noise of splashing.

kercau sound of splashing in water; stiff, cramped (of limbs).

kercut common sedge used in mat-making and for sails.

kerda curry comb; also **keruk**.

kerdam–kerdum thudding (as rice pounders).

kerdan, aras kerdan fritters, puffs.

kerdas leguminous trees.

kerdau sealing wax palm.

kerdil dwarf; stunted.

kerdum see **kerdam**.

kerdut, keredut = **kedut**.

keredak filthy, caked with filth.

keredit credit.

kereh, kerih scratching hard.

kerejut puckered (of clothes).

kerek pulley; **mengerek** to hoist.

kerekeh industrious at moneymaking.

kerekek, berkerekek dengan kudis covered with scabies.

kereket bragging loudly.

kerekot stingy; bent, uneven; **mengerekot** to curl or coil up.

keremut puckered (of face); creased.

keren forceful, loud (of voice).

kerenah caprice, whim.

kerencat to stop suddenly.

kerencing, kerencang, kerencong chinking (of money).

kereng gruff, surly.

kerengga red ant.

kerenggamunggu cardamon spice.

kerengkam see **rengkam**.

kerengkiang = **rengkiang**.

kerengkung gullet, throat.

kerengseng = **gerengseng**.

kerenyeh = **terkerenyeh** smiling broadly.

kerepas, mengerepas to fidget; grope; also **kerepes**.

kerepek crisp sweetmeat, dried slice of tapioca for frying.

kerepas, mengerepas to grope after tiny objects.

kerepot, mengerepot to shrivel; shrunk (of skin round boil); also **keriput**.

keresek dry old banana frond.

kereseng just revealing the interior.

keresut wrinkled (of forehead).

kereta carriage, car, coach; **keretapi** train; **kereta kebal** tank; **kereta lembu** bullock cart; **berkereta** riding in car.

keretan, keretan api matches.

keretut uneven, crinkled.

keri tiny sickle for weeding.

keria, kuih keria sweetmeat of yams and sugar.

keriang, keriang–keriut creaking of doors.

keriat–kerut = kering–keriut.

keriau, berkeriau to shout, curse.

keribas sound of shaking out.

kerical humblest slave.

kericau chirrup of birds.

kericek, tupai kericek dwarf squirrel.

keridik mole cricket.

keridu din, confusion.

kerik sound of scraping or creaking; **mengerik** to scratch, scrape.

kerikal large (brass) pedestal tray.

keriket cricket.

kerikil, batu kerikil gravel, pebbles.

kerikit, mengerikiti to gnaw.

keriling bent (but not broken).

kerim cream.

Kerimun, Pulau Kerimun Carimons.

kerimut = keremut.

kerincing clinking, chinking.

kering dry (*of season, surface*); dried up (*of well*); keringkan, mengeringkan to make dry; kekeringan dryness; dried out; on dry land; (*fig*) penniless.

keringat sweat; berkeringat to be sweaty.

kerinjal kidneys.

kerintil hanging in thick clusters.

kerinting = keriting.

kerinyut, kerenyut knitted.

kerion crayon.

kerip, mengerip to make a gnawing sound; pengerip thing that gnaws.

keris creese, Malay dagger; keris picit the oldest type of keris; berkeris wearing or holding a keris.

kerisi, ikan kerisi sea bream.

kerisis crisis.

keristian Christian.

kerit, mengerit to gnaw (*of mice*).

keritik I, berkeritik to crackle, sputter.

keritik II criticism; critical, dangerous; mengeritik to criticize; pengeritik critic; keritikus, kritikus critic.

keriting, rambut keriting woolly or frizzled hair; curly.

keriuk, berkeriuk cackle (*of chicken*).

keriut, berkeriut to creak (*of oars, hinges*).

kerjaya career

kerkah, kerkak, kerkap to crunch (*as a dog a bone*).

kerkas to scratch (*of fowls*).

kerkau claw-shaped (*of de-*

formed fingers); mengerkau to claw.

kerketa crab.

kerki blinds of sedan chair.

kerkup, kerkap-kerkup crunching.

kerkut chain on a door.

kerlap, mengerlap glittering (*as a gem*); terkerlap to fall asleep momentarily.

kerling, mengerling give a sidelong glance.

kerlip, mengerlip flickering (*of light*); sekerlip mata in the twinkle of an eye; kerlipan glittering, twinkling.

kerlok feeling with fingers (*for bones in the throat etc*).

kerma curse; jatuh kerma falling of curse; Betara Kerma Hindu Cupid.

kermah, siput kermah univalve mollusc with ornamental shell.

kermak weed eaten as vegetable.

kermangka large tree.

kermanici chop, cutlet.

kermi, cacing kermi threadworms.

kermunting = kemunting.

kermut throb, twitch; *see* **kemut.**

kerna = karna; *also* **kerana.**

kernai, mengernai to chop into small pieces (*as meat*).

kernap, padi kernap patches of seedlings planted here and there.

kernu powder horn.

kernyam, mengernyam itching, smarting; to fidget, itch; be lustful.

kernyat-kernyut creaking (*of shoes*).

kernyau creaking, grating.

kernyih grinning, grimacing; mengernyih to grin.

kernying snarling.

kernyit, kernyut furrowed; frowning; curled (*of lips*).

kernyuk, mengernyuk to stuff away.

kernyut twitch (*of the mouth from pain*); **bekernyut** to twitch.

kerobak full of holes; torn; scarred, pock-marked.

kerobek, mengerobek to pick out pieces; poke *or* dig with finger.

kerobok hamper.

kerocok rattle; **berkerocok** to rattle.

kerodong veil; **berkerodong** to veil.

keroket croquette.

kerokot sort of porcelain.

keromiam chromium.

keromong set of gongs in Javanese orchestra.

keroncor king crab.

kerongcang gold foil.

kerongcong large tinkling anklet; rough bell.

kerong-kerong small sea perch.

kerongkong throat, gullet.

kerongsang = **kerosang**.

kerongsong = **kelong-song**.

kerontang, kering keron-tang parched.

keropak palm leaf for writing.

keropas, keropas-kerapis oddments.

keropok composition of tapi-oca flour and prawn fried as a crisp biscuit.

kerosang brooch (*worn in sets of three*); also **kerongsang**.

kerosek see **kosek**.

kerosok rustling; tembakau kerosok dried tobacco leaves.

kerosong sloughed snake skin.

kerotok wooden buffalo bell.

kerotot knobbly; rough as a file.

keroyok, mengeroyok to attack in mob.

kerpai powder horn.

kerpak noise of tapping, cracking.

kerpas, **kerpis**, **kerpus** rustling sound.

kerpik, **kerpuk** sounds of cracking.

kerpus = karpus ridge of roof; rustling.

kersai cooked with each grain separate (*of rice*).

kersak crackling, rustling.

kersang stiff and dry.

kersau frizzy (*of hair*).

kersik sand, gravel; rustling of leaves.

kersip blink.

kersuk heavy rustle.

kersut shrivelled, puckered.

kertah kind of land crab.

kertak creak, sound of rap-ping.

kertakuk, ikan kertakuk small spiny mudfish.

kertang caked with dirt.

kertap, kertap-kertup sound of crunching.

kertas paper; playing card; kertas pasir sandpaper.

kertau mulberry tree; small insect destructive to cloth.

kertik sound of crackling, cracking, ticking, clicking.

ke(r)tika, bintang kertika the Seven Sisters, Pleiades.

kerting tinkling sound.

kertip tapping sound.

kertis to nibble, tug lightly.

kertuk tapping, knocking sound.

kertup sound of crunching.

kertus cartridge; rustling sound.

keruan ascertainable; certain; tidak keruan in utter confu-sion.

kerubung swarm (*of bees*).

kerubut plant with huge crimson flowers.

kerucul, kerucut conical leaf *or* paper bag.

kerudung veil; lampshade.

kerudut wrinkled, furrowed.

keruh turbid, thick, muddy (of water); impure; confused; **mengeruh** to become turbid; snore; **kekeruhan** confusion.

keruing tree yielding wood oil and good timber.

keruit, mengeruit to wag the tail; **burung keruit** the Eastern golden plover.

keruk to scratch; **mengeruk** to burrow.

kerukut curled, shrivelled (of leaves).

kerul curly; **berkerul** to make the hair wavy; make hair neat.

kerulit twinkling.

keruma itch mite; = **kuman**.

kerumit moving the mouth; munch; speak.

kerumuk, berkurumuk crumpled up.

kerumun, berkerumun to assemble in crowds; **mengerumuni** to mob.

kerumus, berkerumus kissing wildly, hugging

kerun, berkerun-kerun in long lines.

kerunas to keep taking pieces out of a store of food.

kerung, kerung-kerang rattling.

keruntil abundant (of hanging fruit).

kerunting wooden cattle bell.

keruntul hanging in many branches.

keruntung fish basket; bamboo money box.

kerup, kerup-kerap sound of eating (raw cucumber etc).

keruping scab (over wound).

kerusi chair; seat (in Parliament); **pengerusi** chairman; **mengerusikan** to chair, preside over.

kerusut tangled (of string, hair etc).

kerut I creasing up, puckering up, frowning.

kerut II = **erut**.

kerutu rough to the touch (of skin).

kerutup cracking sound; assault by a mob.

keruyuk to crow.

keruyup uxorious.

kesa firstly; **yang kesa** the first.

kesah I, **keluh-kesah** anxious, restless.

kesah II story; **al-kesah** the story is.

kesai butcher.

kesak edging about, shifting uneasily in one seat.

kesal disappointed, cross; **kekesalan** disappointment; **mengesali** to feel disappointment or regret about.

kesan, berkesan mark, impression, trail, footprint; **beri kesan** to make an impression; **berkesan** bearing a mark.

kesang to blow the nose with the fingers.

kesangka large earthenware cooking pot.

kesap-kesip blinking (of eyes).

kesasar astray.

kesat rough to the touch; to wipe off; **pengesat** wiper.

kesbih, pokok kesbih canna.

kesek to scrub, rub = **gesek**; **mengesek** to scrub, rub.

kesel = **gesel**.

keselak choking.

keseng, berdiri keseng to stand nervously expectant without being heeded.

kesetan doormat.

kesiap, terkesiap startled.

kesima, terkesima dumb with amazement.

kesimbukan = **simbuk** washbasin.

kesing dull grey landbug.

kesip, mengesip to suck.

nibble; lacking kernel (*of fruit*); buta kesip blind with the eye-ball affected.

keskul beggar's bowl.

kesmak dried fruit imported from China.

kesmaran, edan kesmaran passionately in love, enam-oured.

Kesna, Betara Kesna Hindu divinity Krishna.

kesomplok to hit; done out of one's money; penniless.

kesot, mengesot to move by sliding.

kesterian zenana for wives (isteri).

kestila Castile (*Spain*).

kestul pistol.

kesturi musk; glandular se-cretion of the male (Asian) deer; musang kesturi civet cat; tikus kesturi musk shrew.

kesuari, burung kesuari cas-sowary.

kesuh, kesuh-keseh panting, gasping.

kesuir hairy in the nostrils.

kesuk, kesuk-kesek sound of whispering.

kesuma flower; beautiful woman (*of noble family*).

kesumba anatto, red dye; red, dyed red; burung kesumba trogon.

kesup sound of sucking.

kesur to shove; = sorong.

kesusasteraan literature.

kesusu harassed, flurried.

ketabahan cross-piece of paddle-rudder.

ketageh to crave, be addicted to (*drink, cigarettes etc*).

ketah = kutaha interrogative particle.

ketai, berketai-ketai to crum-ble, disintegrate (*of clothes, wood*).

ketak sound of rapping, tapping; crease, fold, wrinkle.

ketakung pitcher plant.

ketam crab; plane; planing. harvesting; mengetam to har-vest.

ketambak, bawal ketambak pomfrey.

ketampi, ikan ketampi owl.

ketan dry pulut rice.

ketang taut, stretched, tight.

ketap, mengetap to shut tight (*lips*).

ketapak foundation.

ketapang Indian almond.

ketar to quiver; terketar-ketar agog with fear or excitement.

ketara conspicuous, visible, obvious.

ketarap, ikan ketarap parrot wrasse.

ketas cracking sound (*of whip*).

ketat tight (*as cork, shoes*); strict (*rules, regulations*); me-ngetat to tighten.

ketawa = tertawa.

ketaya torch holder.

ketayap small white skullcap worn under turban; sweet-meat.

ketegar obstinate; hati ke-tegar stubborn.

ketek small, little.

ketel I thick (*of foliage*); crowded (*of persons*).

ketel II drop (*of water*).

ketela, ubi ketela sweet potato.

ketelum bastion.

keteng half cent; mengeteng to buy retail (*singly*).

ketengga tree with black-veined yellow wood used for walking sticks.

ketepeng ornamental shrub.

ketering, cincin ketering ring with a removable stone.

ketes drop (*of water*).

keti hundred thousand; ber-keti-keti in hundreds of thousands.

ketiak armpit.

ketial stuck fast (*as cork in*

bottle); slow to move because fat.

ketiap, perahu ketiap house boat used in rivers.

ketiau a large tree.

ketiding, kiding large basket for storing rice *or* fruit.

ketik long legs of insects; baketik to make ticking sound.

ketika time, division of time, period, moment; pada ketika itu at that time.

ketil pinch; nipping.

ketilang blackbird.

ketimbul breadfruit.

ketimbung making a splashing noise.

ketimun = timun.

keting, urat keting Achilles' tendon; mengeting to hamstring; to appeal.

ketip nip, bite; small coin; mengetip to nip, bite (*of sand flies, mosquitoes*); silver piece.

ketipung small drum; — ketimpung.

ketirah red-leaved shrub.

ketiri cashew.

ketis grasshopper's long legs.

ketit, seketit pinch (*of salt*).

ketitir, burung ketitir barred ground dove; = merbuk.

ketola pumpkin, gourd, musk melon.

keton, ringgit keton ducatoon; tree.

ketopong Persian high crown; ketopong besi military helmet.

ketoprak popular Javanese song and dance.

ketoyong upside down (*of spinning top*).

ketua elder, minor headman; mengetuai (majlis) preside over (meeting).

ketuat, ketuit wart.

ketuban foetal membranes.

ketubung = kerubung.

ketuir shrub with medicinal seed.

ketuk cluck; tapping, rapping, note of certain birds; small sounding block; pengetuk knocker, hammer.

ketul thick piece, clot, hard lump; loaf.

ketulul receiver of stolen goods

ketumang, ikan ketumang freshwater murrel.

ketumbak fish.

ketumbar coriander.

ketumbe scurf; dandruff; = kelemumur.

ketumbi last (*dregs*); (*fig*) ketumbi tahi ayam social outcast.

ketumbit stye in the eye.

ketumbu lidded basket.

ketumbuhan smallpox.

ketung, mengetung to cut; break.

ketungging large scorpion.

ketuntung thudding of drum.

ketup, ketup-ketup noise of tapping.

ketupat coconut leaf square *or* polygonal packet in which rice is boiled.

ketupuk fish owl.

ketur vase-shaped spittoon; ketur air small pool.

ketus sound of splitting.

keweh with drooping horns (*of water buffalo*).

keyangan fairyland; home of the gods.

khabar news; suratkhabar newspaper; khabar angin rumour; apa khabar? what is your news?, how do you do?; mengkhabarkan to report, tell.

khabith impurity, wickedness.

khadam household servant.

khafi concealed.

Khair good.

khakan emperor.

khalaik, khalayak God's creatures; khalayak ramai the public.

khali to be silent *or* inactive, stop.

khalifah caliph, religious head of the state; *also* **kalifah**.

khalik creator.

khalil friend; khalil Allah friend of God.

khalis pure, unspotted.

khalkah creation of the world.

khalwat retirement from the world; close proximity; **berkhalwat** to go into retreat.

khamar spirit, alcohol.

khamiri leavened.

khamis fifth day of the week, Thursday.

khanah storehouse; kutub-khanah library; perpustakaan.

khandak moat.

khanjar large dagger.

kharab ruined, destroyed.

kharajat tax, revenue.

khas special, exclusive; khas bagi dia specially for him.

khasah gauze, muslin.

khasiat special properties (*of herbs, drugs*).

khat line; handwriting.

khatalistiwa = khatulis-tiwa.

khatam ended, concluded; khatam Koran to complete reading the Kuran.

khatan circumcision; ber-khatan to be circumcised.

khatib reader and preacher in the mosque.

khatifah rug, carpet.

khatulistiwa equator.

khayal, khayalan vision, dream, fantasy; imagination; engrossed, enthusiastic.

khemah tent; berkhemah to camp.

kheranda = keranda.

Khersani from Khorassan.

khianat treachery; berkhia-nat to be treacherous; commit sabotage.

khiar optional; of a duty.

khidmat service; perkhid-

matan service; berkhidmat to be loyal, serve one's country.

khilaf error, mistake; kekhila-fan mistaken.

khizanah treasury, strong-room.

khoja title for Muslim mer-chant.

khuatir fearful, apprehensive, nervous; khuatirkan to be nervous about.

khuduk humility.

khulak divorce granted to a woman by her husband in return for the restoration of her dowry; = tebus talak.

khuldi, buah khuldi Adam's apple.

khuluk ature, character.

khurafat fable, fiction.

khurma date palm.

khusmat enmity; berkhusmat to make enemy of.

Khusrau Cyrus.

khusus special, exclusive; khususnya in particular.

khusyuk engrossed, concen-trating; humble.

khutbah address, cermon; khutbah nikah marriage ser-vice.

kia lock stitch, chain stitch; jahit bekia to sew with that stitch; kia kia to be happy, enjoy o.s.; yu kia kia shark.

kiah to strain, stretch apart; pengiah shoehorn.

kiai title of honour for reli-gious leaders and teachers.

kiak-kiak large black biting ant; *also* kengkiak.

kial, terkial-kial to exert o.s., struggle.

kiam to stand erect during prayer.

kiamat the last day; hari kiamat day of judgement.

kiambang water lettuce.

kian so many, so much; sepuluh kian ten times as much; kian ... kian ... the more . . . the more . . .; **sekian this much**, that is all; **sekian-sekian** such and such (a number, date *etc*); **kian ke mari** hither and thither.

kiang-kiut sound of creaking.

kiani royal.

kiap two upright pieces of wood propping a mast.

kias allusion, hint, allegory, analogy; **mengiaskan** to talk in parables; **kiasan** deduction by analogy, hint.

kiat stiff; **terkiat** sprained, dislocated.

kibang-kibut topsy-turvy.

kibar, **berkibar** to flap, wave; **mengibarkan** to cause to wave, flag.

kibas, **mengibas** to flap (*ears, fan*); **mengibaskan** to shake off; **kambing kibas** fat-tailed sheep.

kiblat direction of Mecca; **mengadap kiblat** to face the kaabah in Mecca.

kibriah pride; grand (*of God*).

kicak, **kicak-kicau** to twitter; person lacking in self-respect.

kicap, **kicap-kicau** twitter of robin; soya bean sauce.

kicau, **berkicau** to twitter.

kicuh = keocoh.

kicu(h) to cheat, swindle; **mengicu** to swindle.

kida-kida spangles.

kidal left-handed.

kidang = kijang.

kidap rubbish.

kidek, **terkidek-kidek** strutting.

kiding night line with a rod that springs up when there is a bite and lifts the fish out of the water.

kidul south.

kidung song, hymn; **mengidung** to chant verses.

kifayat, **fardu-kifayat** collective religious obligations.

kijai, **terkijai-kijai** quivering.

kijang barking deer.

kijing edible mussel.

kik loom; *also* **akik**, **kek**.

kikih, **terkikih-kikih** to laugh uproariously.

kikir file; miserly; **mengikir** to file smooth.

kikis, **mengikiskan** to scrape; **terkikis** vanished.

kilah ruse; shellfish; **berkilah** to be deceptive, devious.

kilai reels to keep the strands apart in string making.

kilan, **terkilan** dissatisfied, aggrieved; span.

kilang press, mill, factory; **kilang getah** rubber factory; **kilang papan** sawmill.

kilap flash, shine; **sekilap mata** in the twinkling of an eye.

kilas rattan noose (*for binding man or beast*).

kilat lightning, flash; **kilat sabung-menyabung** there is forked lightning; **berkilat** to flash, shine.

kilau sheet-lightning; **kilau-kilauan** flashing at intervals; lustre.

kili seam; nun.

kilik, **mengilik-ngilik** to tickle, egg on, incite; carry on the hip.

kilir, **mengilir** to whet, sharpen; **kiliran** whetstone; **kiliran budi** sharpener of the wits.

kilogram kilogram.

kilometer kilometre.

kilowat kilowatt.

kima giant clam.

kimah price, value.

kimbah to clean with sand and water, scoop up.

kimbang, **terkimbang-kimbang** hovering; hesitating.

kimbul outboard platform at ship's stern.

kimia chemistry; *also* kemia.

kimkha gold brocade, damask.

kimpa(l) welded, solid; nugget.

kina, pokok kina cinchona.

kinang betel quid.

kinantan milk-white (*of cocks*).

kinca syrup.

kincah, mengincah to rinse; dress (*fowl*).

kincak, terkincak-kincak gesticulating with head, arms and legs.

kincang, kecoh kincang tricks, ruses.

ki(n)cang to swindle; kincang-kicoh swindling and trickery.

kincau, mengincau to stir, mix.

kincir water-wheel for irrigating rice-fields.

kindang, kindang-kindang cross-belt of cloth worn by bridegrooms.

kindergarten kindergarten.

kingkap gold brocade.

kini now, this moment.

kinja, terkinja-kinja to hop about and stamp.

kintal bull-frog; quintal; 100 kilograms.

kinyang rock crystal.

kios kiosk.

kipa lame (*of one-legged person*).

kipai partially paralysed.

kipan young tapir; = cipan.

kipas fan (*hand or ceiling*); propeller (*of ship, aeroplane*); berkipas equipped with a fan; mengipas to fan.

kipsiau earthenware tea-kettle.

kira to calculate, reckon, conclude; accounts, reckoning; sekiranya if, perhaps; kira-kira accounts; approximately; ilmu kira-kira arithmetic;

mengira to reckon, estimate; jurukira accountant.

kirai, mengirai to shake (dust, water) out of cloth.

kirana ray of light; beautiful, lovely.

kirap, mengirap to flap; disappear; parry.

kirau half-ripe.

kirbat wineskin.

kiri on the left hand, left.

kirik creepy (*from fear*); shuddering; mengirik to stamp on, trample.

kirim, mengirim(kan) to send, despatch (*letter, article*); mengirim surat to send a letter; si pengirim consignor, sender.

kirip, siput kirip edible shellfish.

kisa small drag net.

kisah = kesah.

kisai, mengisai to sift (*rice*).

kisar, berkisar to change (*of wind*), revolve; mengisarkan to grind (*knife, grain*); change, alter (*watch*); pengisar mill.

kisas vengeance; kisaskan to exact an eye for an eye, punish in kind.

kisi-kisi trellis, lattice.

kisil = gesel.

kisip shrunk (*of fruit*); almost missing.

kismis raisins, currants.

kisut crinkled.

kita we (*including person addressed*).

kitab scripture, any book.

kitai, terkitai-kitai quivering; mengitaikan to shake the hand or foot to allay pain.

kitang, ikan kitang butterfish.

kitar, sekitar around; berkitar to revolve round.

kitik, mengitik to tickle.

kitil a little; kusut kitil-kitil a little crumpled.

kitiran windmill.

kiuk cluck (*of frightened fowl*); terkiuk sprained.

kiung land snails; = **gondang**.
kiwi supercargo in a Malay perahu.
kizib false, lying.
klinik clinic.
koa card game.
kobah kettle-drum; mallet.
kobak, **kobakkan** to peel (husk); gaping (as wound).
kobalt cobalt.
kobar, **berkobar** to flare up (of fire, temper).
kobis cabbage; **bunga kobis** cauliflower.
koboi cowboy.
kobok group, body; **berkobok-kobok** in groups.
kocah scatter seed, disturb water.
kocak, **mengocak** to disturb liquid till it ripples; **berkocak** to shake (bottle of liquid).
kocar-kacir higgledy-piggledy.
kocek pocket.
Koci Cochin-China.
kocoh, **terkocoh-kocoh** bustling; hurriedly.
kocok, **mengocok** to shuffle (cards); shake.
kocong white cloth put over the head of corpse or man who is about to be executed.
kod code.
kodak, **cucur kodak** round balls of banana and flour fried.
kodek to hop about; **terkodek-kodek** wagging of dog's tail.
kodi score, twenty.
kodisil codicil.
kodok frog, toad; **kuih kodok** sweetmeat.
kohong stinking (of decomposed flesh).
kohor slowly.
koi slowly! (to elephant).
koja water-jug with handles and narrow neck.
kojoh flooded (of rice fields).
kojol stiff (as corpse).
kok single beamless yoke.

kokak to gnaw.
kokila mynah; = **tiung**.
kokoh = **kukuh**.
kokok, **berkokok** to crow.
kokol, **mengokol** to draw up the knees, huddle; **batok kokol** cough that doubles one up.
kokong claw-like, incurving (of hands).
kokot bent hook; **kokot betina** gudgeon (on gate etc); **kokot jantan** pintle of rudder or gate-post; **terkokot** twisted.
kol cabbage.
kolah stone or cement water tank.
kolak banana or yam boiled with sugar and coconut milk.
kolam pool, reservoir.
kolang-kalek to and fro, up and down.
kolang-kaling fruit of the sugar-palm peeled.
koleh, **koleh-koleh** tapioca starch; **koleh-koleh** sweetmeat of flour in granules.
kolej college.
kolek small sea-going sailing boat; **berkolek-kolek** bobbing about.
kolesum Chinese tonic; ginseng.
koleksi collection.
kolektif collective.
kolera cholera.
kolijiah college.
koloh, **air koloh** slops of water that has dyed cloth.
kolokan spoilt, troublesome.
kolonel colonel.
kolong space under (house, table); **rumah kolong** house on piles.
koloran waistband, belt.
kolot old fashioned, conservative.
kolui slow! (to elephants).
koma comma; **koma bernoktah** semicolon.
komak-kamek = **komat-kamit**.

komandan commandant.

komando commando.

komanwel commonwealth.

komat-kamit munching; mumbling.

komel, mengomel to chatter.

komen comment.

komeng small (of the head); undeveloped.

komet comet.

komidi comedy.

komodor commodore.

kompas compass, theodolite.

kompelot plot; accomplice.

kompeni company; East India Company.

kompensasi compensation.

komperang long, very loose trousers.

komperes compress.

kompes to keep cross-examining, intimidate.

kompleks complex.

kompol, mengompol bed-wetting.

komponen component.

kompong=rompong.

kompor brazier.

komposisi composition.

kompot docked (of tail); short (of stump).

kompromi to compromise.

komunis communist.

koncah rough, choppy (of water).

koncet pigtail.

konco comrade, supporter.

koncor king crab.

kondangan visitor to a feast.

kondensar condensor.

kondoran hernia, hydrocele.

konek child's penis.

konfrantasi confrontation.

konflik conflict.

kong to bark (of dogs); rib of Malay or Chinese vessel.

konggres congress.

kongkalingkong intriguing, deceitful; main kongkalingkong to intrigue.

kongkang slow loris.

kongkiak bulldog ant.

kongkong shackles, stocks.

kongsi partner; kongsi gelap secret society; rumah kongsi communal house; perkongsian partnership.

konkerit concrete.

konklusi conclusion.

kono old-fashioned.

konon report says; memperkonon deceive, dupe.

konperensi conference.

konsep concept.

konservatif conservative.

konservator conservator.

konsesi concession.

konset concert.

konsol consul.

konsolat consulate.

konstitusi constitution.

konstruksi construction.

konstruktif constructive.

konta story, scandal.

kontak contact.

kontal-kontil swinging (of long ear-rings as one walks).

kontan cash down.

kontang, kontang-kanting dry, parched.

konterek contract.

konterekter contractor.

kontijen contingent.

kontor contour.

kontot docked (of tails).

kontra contra.

kontradiksi contradiction.

kontrol control.

konvenshen convention.

konyol misbehaving; half-witted.

konyong, sekonyong-konyong suddenly.

kooperasi cooperation.

koordinesi coordination.

kop Indo-chinese cycle of twelve years.

kopah, berkopah-kopah in clots (as blood).

kopak, mengopak to open (orange or other fruit); senapang kopak breech loader.

kopan coupon.

kopek, mengopek to peel fruit; pendulous, flaccid (of breasts); **emak kopek raja's** foster mother; **mengopek** to suck (breast).

koperak bamboo clapper, scarecrow.

kopet narrow (of path, hole).

kopi coffee.

kopiah beret, untasselled fez.

kopok musical instrument.

kopor trunk.

kopral corporal.

korah ball.

korapsi corruption.

korban sacrifice; victim.

korek, mengorek to make a hole; **korek api** match; **kapal korek** dredger.

koreksi correction.

koreng streaked by nature or dirt.

koresponden correspondent.

koret dregs; **nomor koret** last on the list.

kormak spiced stew.

korok long hole or tunnel; **mengorok** to tunnel.

korong, korong kampung area round hamlet or household.

koros chorus.

kos cost.

kosa elephant goad; **mengosai** to goad.

kosain cosine.

kosak-kasek rustling.

kosek to wash (rice, fish etc).

kosekan cosecant.

kosel, terkosel-kosel hesitating (over eating, work etc).

kosmopolit cosmopolitan.

kosong empty (of box etc); vacant (of post).

kot home! (to elephant).

kota fort, city town; **mengotai** to ortify; **berkota** fortified.

kotah, sekotah all, the whole.

kotai old and dry (of areca-nut, coconut); dangling.

kotak locker, drawer small box (for matches, cosmetics etc).

kotek tail; **bintang kotek** star with a tail, comet; **terkotek-kotek** wagging.

koteng, parang koteng chopper without handle; **terkoteng-koteng** alone, solitary.

koterok corkscrew.

kotos to pick with the fingers.

kotong, kuntong short (of drawers, shorts); sleeveless (of coat).

kotong-katang itching all over.

kotor dirty, foul (of persons, clothes, utensils etc); **cakap kotor** to talk smut; **datang kotor** to menstruate; **mengotorkan** to dirty.

koyak torn (of clothes, paper); **koyak-koyak** all torn; **mengoyakkan** to tear.

koyam, bubur koyam broth made from pulut rice.

koyan measure of weight, 40 pikuls.

koyok medical plaster.

ku = **aku** I, me.

krisis crisis.

kuah sauce, gravy.

kuak, terkuak, berkuak parted. separated.

kual, terkual rolling (of ship); **terkual-kapai** rolling (as one swimming on his back).

kuala estuary, mouth of main river, confluence.

kualat misfortune.

kuali open iron cooking pan, frying-pan.

kualiti quality.

kuang, burung kuang pheasant. Argus Pheasant.

kuang-kuit, burung kuang-kuit cuckoo shrike.

kuangwong coconut beetle.

kuantiti quantity.

Kuantung, orang Kuantung Muslim Yunnanese.

kuap, menguap to yawn; **terkuap** stuffy (*of room*).

kuar, menguarkan to make a way (*as a blind man with stick*).

kuarik Bugis breast-shield ornament of metal.

kuas painter's brush.

kuasa power, authority; **kuasa mati** probate; **surat kuasa** power of attorney; **berkuasa** empowered; **maha kuasa** almighty.

kuat strong (*of body, voice, fittings*).

kuatir = khuatir

kuau pheasant.

kuayah name for several climbing plants.

kubah dome, cupola; **berkubah** vaulted.

kubang buffalo wallow; **berkubang** wallowing.

kubik cubic.

kubin, cicak kubin flying lizard.

kuboid cuboid.

kubra abortive, frustrated.

kubti Coptic.

kubu stockade for war.

kubung flying lemur.

kubur tomb, grave.

kubus cube.

kucai leek, Chinese chives.

kucam pale, wan.

kucandan dalliance, flirtation.

kucar—kacir pell-mell (*of fugitives*); in disorder, scattered; in a mess.

kucek, mengucek to rub (*eyes*); to launder

Kuci = Koci.

kucil, terkucil slipped off; **mengucilkan** to let slip off, remove.

kucing cat; **kucing hutan** wild cat; **mata kucing** fruit popular with Malays; stone.

kucir queue (*of hair*).

kuda horse; **kuda lumba** race-horse; **kuda pacu** horse for riding; **anak kuda** colt; **kuda-kuda** trestle, easel, roof truss.

kudai small matwork box for tobacco.

kudal filthy.

kudangan wish *or* request by fiancée which her future husband must fulfil.

kudap snack sweetmeat.

kudeta coup d'état.

kudi woodknife (*parang*).

kudis scurf, scabies; **kudis buta** scabies all over the body; **kudis api** shingles; **kudis cengkering** dermatitis.

kudrat power (*esp of God*).

kuda Hindu processional idol; bud of flower.

kuduk nape of neck; *also* **kodok, godok.**

kudung maimed (*without finger or limb*); **mengudungkan** to amputate (*arm, leg*).

kudus holy, pure; **ruh al kudus** the Holy Ghost.

kueng headman.

kufu, kupu, sekufu of equal rank.

kufur unbeliever.

kui goldsmith's crucible; **rice bin**; partitioned space.

kuih cake.

kuil temple.

kuilu rabbi.

kuini Malay mango.

kuinin quinine.

kuis, menguis to push aside *or* towards o.s. with foot *or* hand.

kuit, menguit to beckon (with finger); **kuit kapai** to scrabble after.

kuiz quiz.

kujau jug.

kujur fish spear; **sekujur badan** all over (the body).

kujut, mengujut .o garrotte, strangle; **berkujut** strangled.

kuki cook.

kuku finger *or* toe nail, claw.

kukuh strong, firm; **mengu-kuhkan** to strengthen.

kukuk to overripe (*of rice*).

kukup alluvial flats at an estuary.

kukur, **mengukur** to scrape (*flesh of coconut*); **kukuran** scraper.

kukuran to coo.

kukus, **mengukus** to steam (glutinous rice); **kukusan** steamer.

kul cabbage.

kula I, we; = **patik**.

kulah Kabuli headgear; mango tree.

kulai, **terkulai** dangling (*of broken arm, branch*).

kulak half-coconut-full; to buy for resale.

kulakasar luggage, baggage.

kulan, pokok kulan trees which produce gutta-percha.

kulang, rumput kulang pulut weed eaten as vegetable.

kulansing small packet of sirih sent to invite a person to a feast.

kulasentana family of prince.

kulat mushroom, fungus; ber-kulat mildewed, mouldy.

kulawangsa family.

kuli coolie, unskilled labourer.

kuliah lecture; = **kuliiah**.

kulim tree with useful timber.

kulir trowel.

kulit skin, pelt, dried hide, husk, leather, shell (*of egg*).

kulkulah quavering of the voice.

kulliah = **kuliah**.

kultur culture.

kulum, **mengulum** to suck, hold in the mouth; **mengulum senyum** to smile with closed lips.

kulup foreskin prepuce.

kulur breadfruit.

kulzum, Laut Kulzum Re Sea.

kumai beading (*on ship's side, furniture*).

kuma–kuma saffron; = koma-koma.

kumal slightly soiled, with pattern or lettering defaced (*of clothes, lettering*).

kuman itch-mite; parasite; bacillus; germ; **kajikuman** bacteriology.

kumandang echo.

kumara Hindu god of war.

kumat relapsing (*of the sick*).

kumba water-pot; kumba mayang pot decorated with palm-blossom.

kumbah, **mengumbah** wash (*rice, dishes etc*); air **kumbahan** water in which creese or charm has been washed.

kumbakara potter.

kumbang black flying borer beetle; kumbang **bertanduk** stag beetle.

kumbar palm with short thick stem and acid fruit.

kumbik, pokok kumbik candlenut tree.

kumbuh, rumput kumbuh sedges used for mat-making.

kumi (please) eat.

kumin, sekumin particle.

kumiuke communiqué.

kumis moustache; berkumis moustached.

kumkuma saffron.

kumpai, rumput kumpai swamp-grass used for wicks.

kumpar, **mengumpar** to wind thread on a reel.

kumpeni company.

kumpul, berkumpul to gather together, assemble; terkumpul assembled; **mengumpulkan** to amass, collect; **kumpulan** collection.

kumuh dirty.

kumur, berkumur-kumur gargle, gargling.

kumus large timber tree.

kun, kun-fa yakun be and it

was (*the words of Allah when he created the world*); cone.

kuna, kuno old-fashioned; primitive (*of persons*).

kunang, kunang-kunang fireflies; berkunang-kunang to glitter.

kunani, si kunani name of legendary white champion fighting cock.

kunapa corpse.

kunau large clam.

kunca small basket; bale of straw; measure.

kunci, ibu kunci lock, keyhole; anak kunci key; kunci mangga padlock; menguncikan to lock; terkunci locked, concluded.

kuncung tuft, crest.

kuncup closed (*of flowers*); menguncup to curl up; kuncupkan to close; furl; penguncup constrictor.

kundai bun (*of hair*).

kundang, budak kundang pages serving Malay royalty; mengundang to take everywhere with one; to invite.

kundur wax gourd.

kungkang = kongkang.

kungkum folded (*of bird's wing*).

kuning yellow; putih kuning creamy; kuning emas deep yellow; kuning langsat beige; kekuning-kuningan yellowish.

kunjung, mengunjungi, berkunjung to pay visit to person or place; kunjungan visit.

kuntau (Chinese) art of self-defence; berkuntau to employ this art.

kuntit, menguntit to follow (at a person's back).

kuntuan satin-like silk.

kuntul tailless (*of fowls*); penis; egret.

kuntum bud; numeral coefficient for flowers; sekuntum bunga one flower; menguntum to bud; terkuntum in bud.

kunun = konon.

kunut, doa kunut prayer said during subuh (*early morning*).

kunyah, mengunyah to chew, masticate.

kunyam pinched (*of cheeks*); shrunken.

kunyit turmeric.

kunyuk monkey; = kera.

kunyung = konyong.

kuorum quorum.

kupak, mengupak to break open (*box, room*).

kupang sea-mussels; a tencent coin; daun kupang herb used for skin complaints.

kupas to peel (*skin, fruit, bark*); mengupas to peel, skin.

kupat-kapit swishing (*of ail*); flapping (*as empty sack*).

kuping ear; scab.

kupu I, sekupu equal in rank.

kupu II, kupu-kupu butterfly, moth; kupu-kupu malam prostitute.

kupui, kupoi tree with edible fruit.

kupur = kupor, akar kupur brambles.

kur koo (*of the ring dove (tekukur)*); call to birds and the bird-soul; kur semangat expression of encouragement and surprise.

kura spleen; demam kura malaria; kura-kura tortoise.

kurai, berkurai veined (*of wood*).

Kuran Muslim sacred book; mengaji Kuran to learn to read the Kuran.

kurang less, fewer, lacking, too little, minus; kurang baik inferior; kurang ajar unmannerly; lebih kurang more or less; mengurangkan to decrease; kekurangan to be short of; shortage; sekurang-kurangnya at the least.

kurap ringworm.

kuras quire of paper; **menguras** to wash out, clean.
kurator curator.
kurau fish; **rumput kurau** (*fodder*) sedge.
kurbal crowbar.
kurban = korban.
kurik speckled (*of cocks*); see borek.
kurita octopus; *also* gurita.
kurnia gift, bounty (*of God, king*); **dengan kurnia Allah** by God's grace; **mengurniakan** to give, bestow.
kurrat radiance, light.
kursus course.
kurun cycle of years; century.
kurung prison, internment, confinement; compartment; **kena kurung** to be interned; **tanda kurung** bracket (*in writing*); **berkurung** to be confined to the house; **perintah berkurung** curfew.
kurus thin (*of person*), emaciated; **kurus kering** thin and wasted; **menguruskan** to make thin.
kus puss!puss!
kusa, rumput kusa fodder-grass.
kusal, mengusal to rub, roll.
kusam dull, tarnished, faded.
kusar = gusar.
kusau, berkusau-kusau tangled.
kusi, pinang kusi dried areca nut.
kusik to stir slightly.
kusir driver (*of carriage*).
kusta leprosy; **kusta bangau** with white patches on the skin; **kusta bunga** with the initial discoloured patches.
Kustantiniah Constantinople.
kusti, berkusti to box; = gusti.
kusu, berkusu-kusu in knots, clusters (*of people*).
kusuk = gosok.
kusut tangled (*of hair, thread*

etc); **kusut masai** much tangled; **mengusutkan** to tangle; perplex.
kutaha an interrogative;=tah, kah.
kutai = kotai to dangle by a thread.
kutak, mengutak to shake violently; **kutak-katik** upset.
kutang, baju kutang bodice, sleeveless vest.
kutat pimply.
kutat-kutit hesitating, wavering.
kuteri berth in ship.
kuti, menguti to tear into small pieces.
kutil, kotil wart; sekutil tiny piece; **mengutil** to pick a tiny piece.
kutip, mengutip to pick up (*things*); **wang kutipan** subscription, collection.
kutu I louse.
kutu II, sekutu ally; **persekutuan** federation.
kutub pole; **kutub utara** north pole.
kutuk condemn; **mengutuk** to condemn.
kutur egret; *see* bangau.
kutut, kutut-kutut rough (*of surface*).
kuyu heavy (*of eyes*); low-spirited.
kuyung tree.
kuyup, basah kuyup dripping wet.
kuyut moping; = kuyu.

L

la is not; **la-ilaha illa'llah** there is no God but Allah.
laal ruby.
laanat *see* laknat.
laba I profit; **laba rugi** profit and loss; **berlaba** making a profit.

laba II, laba-laba spider.

labang I deaf.

labang II, melabang to wander aimlessly.

laberak to beat, thrash; attack, charge.

laberang shrouds from ship's side to masthead.

labi-labi freshwater turtle.

labu bottle gourd, calabash; labu kendi kettle-shaped; labu-labu pottery water vessel modelled on the gourd.

labuci spangle.

labuh trailing, too long; melabuhkan let down; berlabuh anchored moored; pelabuhan port.

labun, berlabun to chatter, gossip.

labur, melabur to whitewash; laburan, pelabur provisions (for labourers, sailors); investment; investor.

lacak, berlacak, melacak abundant.

lacar, melacar to be abraded.

laci drawer.

lacur frustrated, unsuccessful; mistaken; perempuan lacur prostitute.

lacut, melacut to whip.

lada pepper (white or black); lada hitam black pepper; tumbuk lada small one-edged dagger.

ladaian riverine fish trap.

ladam horse shoe; pukul ladam to shoe horses.

ladan resin used for caulking or joss sticks; setanggi ladan joss sticks.

ladang dry (not irrigated); clearing; ladang getah rubber estate; peladang farmer; berladang to farm.

laden, meladeni to wait on, serve; stand up to, pay attention to; answer.

lading long curved chopper with blade narrow near hilt;

perahu lading long narrow dug-out canoe.

ladu rice dumplings in syrup.

ladun singing (in Malay opera).

ladung, batu ladung plummet (for sounding lead); berladung weighted.

lafath, lafaz correct pronunciation of the Kuran; spoken words; satu lafath dua makna one word with two meanings.

laga, berlaga to collide, crash (as car in collision); melagakan to set (animal) to fight; ikan pelaga fighting fish.

lagak manner, conduct; melagak to boast; browbeat (the poor); lagak-pura pose; lagak bahasa style.

lagam horse's bit; berlagam bitted.

lagang, melagang to set the thread or leaves (in weaving etc); take initial steps (in work plans).

lageh to talk or question endlessly.

lagi more, still more; still, moreover, besides; tambahan lagi moreover; selagi as long as; satu lagi another.

lagu tune, intoning; song; bawa lagu to start off a tune; berlagu intoning, chanting; melagukan to chant, intone.

lagun lagoon.

lagut occupied, absorbed.

lah particle suffixed to the emphatic word in a sentence.

lahad, lahat niche for the body in a Muslim grave.

lahak rotting (of piles of food).

lahan = perlahan.

lahang palm sap.

lahar lava.

lahir to appear; be born; external; **melahirkan** to give birth to.

lahu, lau, ikan lahu jew fish.

lai = helai.

lailah, lailat night; **Alfu lailah, wa lailah the** 1001 Nights.

lain other, another, different; **yang lain** the other one(s); **berlainan** different; **melainkan** except (that).

lais, ikan lais glass catfish; **pohon lais** screwpine used for mat making; **melais** to back water (rowing).

lajak, melajak to go too far, overshoot one's mark; **terlajak** skidded.

lajang, orang lajang unmarried person.

laju fast, rapid (of walking).

lajur long strip of land; stripe, column; **melajur** to extend (as furrow).

lak, batu lak sealing wax.

laka big liana with red heartwood used for joss sticks; lacquer.

lakab descriptive name (for dead rulers).

lakak, melakak to hit (with stick).

lakar unfinished; **lakaran** model (of boat); pattern, sketch.

laken woollen cloth.

laki husband; **laki bini** husband and wife; **berlaki** married; **laki-laki, lelaki** man.

lakin still, yet; **wa lakin** and yet.

laklakan gullet, throat.

laknat curse; accursed.

lakri sealing wax.

laksa ten thousand; mixture of vermicelli and fish paste; **berlaksa-laksa** tens of thousands.

Laksamana high native official corresponding to a minister of marine or admiral.

laksana like, resembling; **seperti** or **bagai; melaksanakan** to compare, be like; give form to; realize; carry out.

laktus lactose.

laku manner, behaviour; to act or behave; take effect; sell well, be in demand; **seperti laku orang gila** like the conduct of a mad man; **ringgit ini tiada laku** this dollar is not legal tender; **kelakuan** conduct; **tidak laku** not selling well, 'on the shelf'; **berlaku** to happen.

lakum, pokok lakum wild vines.

lakun stage play; **lakunkan** to represent a play on the stage; **pelakun** actor.

lakur, lakur baur mixed, fused; **melakurkan** to fuse an alloy of metal.

lala, siput lala marine mollusc; **melala** to swim on one's back.

lalab cold vegetables eaten with curry; =**ulam.**

lalah, melalah gluttonous; **melalah** to chase; **terlalah** pursued.

lalai dawdling, careless, dreamy; **melalaikan** to be careless about, forget; **kelalaian** apathy.

lalak, melalak to howl (of children).

lalang long coarse grass; **lalu lalang** passing to and fro.

lalar touch hole (of cannon); **melalar** wander about restlessly.

lalat housefly; **lalat hijau** bluebottle; **lalat kuda** horsefly; **tahi lalat** freckles.

lalau, melalau to hinder; ward off (trespassers); **hikmat lalau** charm to prevent a girl from marrying another; **pelalau.**

lali insensitive (from disease or habit); unconscious (from anaesthetics); **buku lali** anklebone.

lalu past, after, afterwards; elapsed; **tahun lalu** last year; **berdiri lalu berkata** stood up and then spoke; **melalui** to pass through (*town etc*); **terlalu** very; **lalu lalang** to pass to and fro; **yang lalu ago**.

lam sea-worm yielding a medicinal oil.

lama long (*of time*); ancient, former; **berapa lama?** how long?; **lama-lama, lama-kelamaan** after a long time, finally; **selama as long as; selama-lamanya** for ever.

lamai, ipar lamai brother *or* sister-in-law.

laman = halaman.

lamang cutlass.

lamar, melamar to ask (*girl*) in marriage; **lamaran** request (*for girl's hand*).

lamat, matalamat bull's eye, target; **lamat-lamat** hazy.

lambai, melambai to wave, beckon; **melambai** to wave one's hand.

lambak heap; **melambak, berlambak-lambak** to lie in heaps.

lambang mark, sign, emblem, symbol; **= tanda.**

lambaran mat.

lambat slow, late; (*fig*) **biar lambat asal selamat** let him (*it*) be slow provided that it makes for safety; **kelambatan** slowness; to be overdue.

lambing pricked up (*of ears*).

lambir = gelambir.

lambuk, melambuk to loosen earth; **celana lambuk** loose (*of trousers*).

lambung side flank; **kapal roda lambung** paddle steamer; **melambung** to go up (*as wave*); bouncing up (*as ball*).

lambur large jellyfish.

lambut, melambut to bulge (*of pocket*).

lamin, melamin to decorate bridal dais; **pelamin** bridal dais; bridal bedroom; **kelamin** couple (*married male and female*).

lamina, baju lamina coat of mail.

lampai slender, graceful; **panjang lampai** tall and slim; **melampai** to droop (*of branches, leaves*); sway.

lampam, ikan lampam freshwater carp.

lampan, melampan wash for tin with a wooden tray.

lampang, melampang tap, slap.

lampar, berlampar scattered (*as leaves*); sprawling (*of bodies of men asleep*).

lampas, melampas to polish (*knives*), sandpaper; **pelampas** akal sharpener of wits.

lampau too much; **terlampau** very; **melampau** to overdo it; **pelampau** extremist.

lampias to flow, gush.

lampin baby's napkin; **berlampin** swaddled.

lampir, lampiran enclosure to letter, annex; **terlampir** enclosed.

lampit rattan mat.

lampu lamp; **lampu duduk** table lamp; **lampu picit** electric torch.

lampung floating; **kayu lampung** touchwood; **jambatan lampung** pontoon; **pelampung** float for net *or* line.

lampus dead; **= mampus.**

lamu sea-weed for making jelly.

lamun provided that, if.

lamur short-sighted.

lan nauseated (*by food*).

lanang man, manly; **melanang** to twist strands to make cord.

lanar, lanau ooze, slime, alluvium; **berlanau** slimy.

lanas = nanas.

lanca ship's launch, sailing boat; rickshaw.

lancang swift sailing yacht; model ship (*set adrift with offerings for spirits*).

lancap tapering and smooth; melancap to masturbate; terlancap slipped out (of remark).

lancar fluent (of speech); swift (of boats); melancar to glide; melancarkan to hurl (spear etc); launch, expedite; pelancar kapalterbang catapult for planes; pelancarasuk beams supporting the girders.

lancing Javanese trousers.

lancip tapering and sharp.

lancuk large puddle.

lancung counterfeit, debased (of currency); false (of friends); melancungkan to counterfeit; melancung to tour go sightseeing; pelancung tourist

lancur, melancur to gush (out of pipe); = pancur.

lancut, melancut to squirt out noisily.

landa to wash for gold; constantly worn.

landai shelving.

landaian large hilt to creese.

landak porcupine; landak raya large porcupine; landak batu, landak kelubi, landak ubi brush-tailed porcupine.

landasan anvil; chopping block; landasan terbang air strip; landasan keretapi railway track.

landuh, melanduh long, trailing.

landung, melandung trailing, long (of rope); loose (of clothes).

landur, melandur to hang low; drag along.

landut, melandut to sag (of pocket from contents).

lang generic name for hawks, kites and eagles; lang rajawali generic name for small hawks.

langah, terlangah opened wide, agape; terpelangah left open on purpose.

langau horse-fly; (fig) seperti langau di pantat gajah like a fly on the haunch of an elephant (toady).

langgai triangular push-net (worked by one man); belat langgai purse-net anchored in estuary; = ambai.

langgaian platform for drying fish.

langgam style, habit; melody; = lagu.

langgan, berlanggan to subscribe, club together to buy; langganan subscription; subscriber; pelanggan regular customer; client.

langgang, tunggang-langgang head over heels.

langgar, berlanggar to collide; melanggar to attack, ram; infringe; perlanggaran collision, attack.

langgas free, without ties.

langgeng eternal, lasting.

langguk proud, grand.

langir material used as soap esp for cleaning the hair.

langis, tumpas langis completely destroyed.

langit sky; kaki langit horizon; langit-langit canopy, ceiling; roof of the mouth; melangit to soar.

langkah pace, stride, step; langkah kanan good fortune; melangkah to stride, set out.

langkai slim, graceful.

langkan latticed verandah; railing of bridge.

langkap = lengkap.

langkapura Ceylon, Sri Lanka.

langkas spirited, swift (of horses); tangkas over (of fruit season).

langkat three days from now; tikar berlangkat (sitting mat) of several thicknesses.

langkau, melangkau to skip, omit, pass over; langkau sehari every other day.

langkitang edible fresh-water molluscs.

langkup, terlangkup bottom upwards, capsized (*of a boat*); =tangkup.

langlai, lemah langlai lissom and graceful.

langlang, melanglang to patrol; langlang buana wandering over the earth.

langling, burung langling hornbill.

langsai settled (*of debt, business*); =selesai.

langsar tall and slim (*of person*); lucky, successful.

langsat fruit with buff-coloured rind; fawn-coloured (*of dogs*).

langsi, melangsi to give out a shrill note.

langsing, melangsing=melangsi log brake of bullock cart.

langsir curtain, hangings; see langsi.

langsuir whining female banshee hostile to pregnant women.

langsung forthwith directly; impetuous, excessive; berjalan-langsung ke pekan they went straight to the market; melangsungkan to settle a deal; hari langsung last day of a wedding.

langu unpleasant (*of smell*), disagreeable (*of taste*).

languk, melanguk to peer with head curved down; =canguk.

langut, melangut to look upwards; long for.

lanja, melanja to go visiting.

lanjai, melanjai slender, fragile.

lanjam ploughshare.

lanjang slender; see telanjang.

lanjar and forthwith; next; =langsung; melanjar to trail; lanjaran props.

lanji, perempuan lanji prostitute.

lanjung tall and slender.

lanjur, telanjur protracted; dragging; gone too far; irrevocable (*of words*).

lanjut too long (*of breasts, tale*); melanjutkan to lengthen; lanjutan continuation.

lanolin lanolin.

lantah =jelantah.

lantai floor, decking; besi lantai sheet iron; basuh lantai cleansing ceremony after child is born.

lantak, melantak to ram down; luluh lantak crushed under heavy blows or weight; pelantak ramrod; pestle of betel-nut pounder.

lantam loud (*of voice*); conceited.

lantang distinct (*of sound*); spacious (*of view*).

lantar I, terlantar outstretched; stranded; neglected; pelantaran unroofed gangway.

lantar II, melantar to cause (*loss etc*); present (*request*); lantaran cause; because; lantaran itu therefore; pelantar intermediary.

lantas forthwith, and immediately; to go right into, go right across.

lantik, melantik to instal (*ruler, chief*); appoint; belantik spring gun for big game.

lantin payment to a judge in addition to a fine.

lanting, burung selanting long-billed partridge; small raft; back basket; melanting to hurl, throw; bounce.

lantul, melantul to rebound.

lantung strong (*of smell*), putrid; melantung to knock.

lantur, melantur stray (*of thoughts*).

lanun, Ilanun sea pirates.

lanyah muddy; *see* lanyau.

lanyak, melanyak to trample down (*as buffaloes to prepare rice fields for cultivation*).

lanyau mud with hard crust.

lap, mengelap to dab with cloth or blotting paper; kain lap dish cloth; kertas lap blotting paper.

lapah, melapah to skin animals.

lapan eight; = delapan.

lapang empty, vacant, open; tanah lapang open country; kelapangan leisure, ease; lapangan terbang airport.

lapar hungry; lapar dahaga hunger and thirst; kelaparan hunger.

lapat—lapat barely audible or visible.

lapih, berlapih to plait (*hair*).

lapik mat, pad, base, the surface on which a thing rests; lapik kaki sandals; lapik duduk mat for sitting on.

lapis layer, fold; berlapis in folds; lapisan layer, stratum.

lapuk mildew; berlapuk mouldy.

lapun net, trap.

lapur, melapurkan to report; lapuran report.

lara anxiety, cares of love.

larah, berlarah-larahan one after another, in succession.

larak fleshiness (*of pips in fruit*).

larang, melarang to forbid; larangan forbidden; hutan larangan forest reserve.

larap readily saleable; melarapkan to undo a knot, separate strands of a rope.

laras smooth and cylindrical; senapang dua laras double-barrelled gun; clef; selaras concordant; menyelaraskan to harmonize, coordinate.

larat dragging on slowly, lengthy; tiada larat unable to,

lacking power to; **melarat** to spread.

larau annoyance; melarau to become worried.

lari, berlari to run, run away, abscond; berlari-larian to run in a hurry; aimlessly; melarikan to make (*engine*) run; orang pelarian refugee; garisan selari parallel lines; ulasan selari running commentary.

larih, melarih to pour into a glass.

larik, melarik to turn on a lathe, polish (*wood, ivory*).

laris in demand (*of goods*).

lar—lar glittering.

laron flying-ants; = kelekatu.

laru yeast *etc* put into toddy.

larung coffin.

larut I farther than intended; dragging (*of anchors*); larut malam late at night.

larut II to dissolve.

las batu las whetstone.

lasa, lesa numbed (*of limbs*).

lasah energetic; memperlasah to work s.o. hard; belasah to switch.

lasak energetic, restless, meddlesome; tahan lasak to endure rough wear, wear well; rugged.

lasam place in Java famous for its batik work.

lasi afraid, scared.

lastik catapult.

lasu stale, musty (*of food kept too long*).

lasykar soldier.

lat intervening (*of time, things*); lat sehari every second day; berlat intermittent.

lata, melata to creep; pokok melata creeper (*plant*).

latah suffering from hysteria.

latak dregs of oil.

latam, melatam to stamp down (*soil*); roll earth, prepare rice fields by making buffaloes trample them.

latang, jelatang nettle.

latar surface, level; colour background; **pelataran** platform.

latif fine, delicate, gentle.

latih, melatih to train (*teachers etc*); latihan training, trained; pelatih trainee.

latu, lelatu spark.

latuk edible seaweed.

latuk, parang latuk chopper (*the tip of which turns down*).

latung, minyak latung crude petroleum.

latur blistered (*of skin*).

lau if; coop; walau and if, although; jikalau if.

lauk materials cooked for consumption with rice; lauk pauk all kinds of such food.

laun slow, protracted, dragging on; lambat laun eventually; berlaun to dawdle.

laung, berlaung call, shout; melaungkan to call to (*person*); sepelaung as far as a shout is audible shouting distance.

laut sea; laut lepas high seas, open sea; Orang Laut coastal Proto-Malay tribes; melaut to go to sea; spacious; lautan seas, ocean.

lawa I, melawa, mempelawa to invite; pelawa crossbar.

lawa II smart, attractive.

lawah unobstructed (*of view*), open; lawah-lawah spider.

lawai thread.

lawak, berlawak to clown, speak and act comically; pelawak clown, comedian.

lawamah vicious.

lawan antagonist, opponent, rival; contrary, opposite; against, versus; berlawan having a contest; melawan to oppose; perlawanan opposition, contest.

lawang large outer gate; bunga lawang mace, clove flowers; ikan lawang catfish.

lawar preparation of minced fish.

lawas empty, vacant (*of land*); clear (*of view*); melawas not fruiting any more.

lawat, melawat to visit; pelawat visitor; lawatan visit.

lawi bird's curving tail feather; lawi ayam tiny curved dagger carried by women.

layah veil; melayah to bend over; fly low.

layak fitting, proper; fitted; qualified; kelayakan qualification.

layam, melayam to brandish a sword in a dance.

layan, melayankan to serve guest with food; melayani to wait upon, attend to; pelayan attendant, waiter; layanan attention, treatment.

layang, melayang to fly, soar in the air; layang-layang child's kite; swallow, swifts.

layap, melayap to skim close to (*sea, earth*); berlayap-layapan skimming along.

layar sail; belayar to sail; pelayaran voyage; layar apit lug sail; layar dastur spinnaker; layar topang foresail; ilmu pe'ayaran navigation.

layu faded (*of flowers*), drooping (*of plants*).

layuh paralysis.

layunan prince's remains; royal bier.

layur, melayurkan to parch (*of sun*); make crisp by heating, scorch.

lazat delicious.

lazim usual, traditional, ordinary; lazimnya usually; kelaziman usage, custom.

lazuardi lapis lazuli.

lebah bee; kawan lebah swarm of bees; sarang lebah bees' nest.

lebai pious elder.

lebak sound of slap.

lebal label.

lebam black and blue (of bruise); contusion.

leban name of several kinds of trees.

lebang weak (esp before childbirth).

lebap thump (of fruit falling).

lebar I sound of heavy splash.

lebar II broad, wide; melebarkan to widen.

lebaran, hari raya lebaran feast on 1 Syawal (after fasting month).

lebas, melebas to whip, lash.

lebat dense (of fruit, hair, leaves); hujan lebat heavy rain; bulu keningnya lebat his eyebrows were bushy.

lebih more, superior, greater; lebihnya remainder; lebih kurang more or less; melebihkan to augment; berlebih-lebihan going on increasingly.

lebir, melebir to hang limp (as collar, hat brim).

lebu dust; lebu duli dust below the royal feet (ie humble way of indirectly addressing a prince).

lebuhraya broad highway.

lebuk sound of thud.

lebum thud (of coconut falling).

lebur I molten (of metal); dissolved; destroyed; meleburkan to smelt, dissolve; terlebur crushed; leburan smelting.

lebur II, keluburan abyss.

leca necklet of beads or gems.

lecah muddy and wet.

lecak, lecak-lecuk squelching sound.

lecam, ikan lecam sea bream.

lecap saturated (of towel etc).

lecat licked clean (of plate); smooth.

leceh sticky and adhesive; worthless (of person, article etc); melecehkan to belittle, neglect; troublesome (of persons).

lecek I crumpled (of cloth, paper); melecek to blow the nose.

lecek II soft and pulpy; melecek to break up (by grinding, crushing or rubbing).

lecer idling; = leceh.

lecet, melecet to be abraded, suppurate; berlecet moistened.

lecing to whizz.

lecit, melecit to blow nose with fingers; be squirted out.

lecuh, melecuh to soak rice or vegetable in water; withered.

lecuk shiny, oily; to coax, flatter; mix, knead with hands or feet.

lecur, melecur scalded by ho water, withered by heat.

lecus sound of squirting out.

lecut, melecut to squirt out (of pips, juice); melecutkan to squeeze out; to hurl a stick.

ledak, meledak to explode (of dynamite); ledakan explosion, eruption.

ledang to tread on.

ledang II shimmering in the sun.

ledat, meledat to claim, ask for.

ledes red and raw (of eyelids).

leding, meleding sag (of plank under weight).

ledos burst (of sack); collapse.

leftenan lieutenant.

lega spacious, roomy; easy (of circumstances); comfortable after illness; kelegaan to ease, comfort; melegakan to afford relief.

legar—leguk bumpy (of roads); = lekak-lekok.

legam, hitam legam pitch-black; legum-legam sound of bangs.

legar, berlegar to revolve, circle round.

legas to spin.

legat, melegat to keep on the same course (of ships); keep up for a long while (*laughter or weeping*).

legeh watershed.

legek to play with (*child*).

leger cask; floor beam.

legislatif legislative.

legit sweet, nice.

legoh—legah rumbling.

legojo executioner.

legu, melegu to plait the selvage (*of mats*).

legum boom; **legum-legam** bang after bang.

legundi a shrub.

legung boom (*noise*).

lehar open, unobstructed.

leher (*anat*) neck; **leher** column of the neck; **leher baju** coat collar; **berleher** with neck or collar.

leka absorbed in, lingering over, dwelling on; dawdling over; **leka bermain** lingering over play.

lekah split, broken.

lekak, melekak to circle round.

lekak—lekok full of hollows, bumpy (*of ground*).

lekam, melekam to grasp with thumb and first finger.

lekang not adhering (*of flesh, fruit*); **rambutan lekang** rambutan fruit whose flesh is separable from the pip; cracked.

lekap, melekap to stick; come close to; **melekapkan** to affix, gum, press.

lekar I rattan holder or stand for cooking pots.

lekar II reading stand for Kuran, lectern.

lekas quickly; **selekasnya as quickly as possible; melekaskan** to accelerate.

lekat, melekat to adhere (*of gum*); **lekatkan** to stick a thing on; **terlekat** stuck on.

lekeh filthy (*of person*); **berlekeh** fouled.

lekir streaky; **panau lekir** disease discolouring the skin; **ular sawa lekir** streaky mottled snake.

lekit beginning to stick; insecurely stuck.

lekor, likur twenty (*added to digits*); **satu lekor** twenty-one; **lima lekor** twenty-five.

lektor lecture.

lektrik, lekterik, letrik electric.

leku, meleku to lean on elbows.

lekuk dent (*in metal*); hollow, puddle; **hearts suit in cards.**

lekum gullet; = **halkum.**

lekup-lekap rattling.

lela, melela to wave a staff or drawn weapon in Malay fencing; swagger; **melelakan** to brandish (*staff, weapon*); swivel gun; **Maharajalela** title of chamberlain at Malay court; **bermaharajalela** to act arrogantly; **gendang melela** drum.

lelabah=labah-labah.

lelah tired, fatigued; **penat lelah, letih lelah** extremely tired; **berhenti lelah** to rest; **sakit lelah** asthma; **kelelahan** exhaustion.

lelai, melelai to droop (*of branch*); **lelaikan** to pull down end of a branch.

lelak in bits, broken.

lelaki=laki-laki.

lelan, terlelan oblivious of one's surroundings.

lelancur young cock; youth.

lelang=lelong.

lelangon park, garden;=**taman.**

lelap deep (*of sleep*); forfeited (*of pledges*); **pajak lelap** shop for sale of forfeited pledges.

lelar, memperlelar to use or drag about continually; **melelarkan** to keep urging a person to work.

lelas, melelas scraped, trimmed, abraded, smoothed.

lelat, sirih lelat sirih presented by groom to bride at weddings.

lelatu = latu.

lele, ikan lele river fish.

leleh, meleleh to trickle slowly; berkelelehan trickling; lelehan trickle.

lelep, melelepkan to submerge.

leler = leleh careless; keleleran neglected, slovenly.

lelewa, berlelewa to show off.

lelong I, melelong stagger with body erect but legs failing.

lelong II sale by auction; to auction; tukang lelong auctioneer; tangkap lelong to buy at auction.

lelucun low farce.

lemah weak in body, not rigid; lemah lembut gentle; lemah hati soft-hearted; melemahkan to weaken; kelemahan weakness.

lemak fat (o, meat); grease; nasi lemak rice cooked in coconut milk; rich, savoury

leman elephant.

lemang glutinous rice cooked with coconut milk in green bamboo lined with banana leaf.

lemari = almari.

lemas asphyxiated (by gas, smoke, drowning); mati lemas dead from suffocation; drowned; melemaskan to stifle, suffocate.

lemau not crisp, soft and tough.

lemba low (of stature).

lembab = lembap.

lembaga original form, embryo; seed (of plants); statue, model, pattern; Lembaga Perniagaan Board of Trade; adat lembaga primitive custom; perlembagaan political constitution.

lembah low-lying land, meadows.

lembak, melembak to spill over from fullness; boil over (of water).

lembam nerveless, languid, inert.

lembang trodden into ruts, dented (of soft ground etc); low, tender (of voice).

lembap moist damp (of cloth, sheets etc).

lembar strands (of hair, thread etc); tali yang tiga lembar cord of three strands; numeral coefficient for thread, paper etc; melembarkan to fasten paper together.

lembata coconut beetle; kumbang kelemata.

lembayung I, merah lembayung crimson; Ceylon spinach; = remayung.

lembayung II water hyacinth.

lembega medicinal shrub; also rembega.

lembek I too soft (of rice, or what should be firm); nasi lembek.

lembek II thin mattress.

lembesu = tembesu.

lembidang flat rim (of plate, saucer).

lembing spear; lembing buang dart, light javelin; lembing tikam pari spear with three barbs.

lemboyan, orang lemboyan elves.

lembu bull, cow, ox; lembu betina cow; lembu jantan lembu hutan smaller wild ox; ikan lembu leather jacket.

lembuara state spear; giant sea fish.

lembugai horseradish tree; also rembugai.

lembung, melembung to be blown or puffed out; see kembung, gelembung.

lembur night work, overtime work.

lembusir shoulder (of ox).
lembut I tender (of meat); soft (of voice); gentle (of character); lemah lembut amiable; berhati lembut docile; melembutkan to soften.
lembut II = limbat.
lemek small-scaled silvery Cyprinid.
Lemender Armenian.
lemes soft, weak, refined.
lemon lime.
lempah affluent; melempah to overflow; see limpah.
lempai, melempai to curve down (of leaves, branches); terlempai curved down drooping.
lempam damp (of squibs); inactive.
lempang straight; melempangkan to straighten, put parallel; apit lempang ship's planking.
lempap, melempap to beat cotton.
lempar, melempar to throw, cast; lemparkan, melemparkan to throw (anything).
lempata blue-flowered plant.
lempedai = empedal.
lempek, berlempek-lempek in layers, plastered.
lempeng plug (of tobacco).
lemper glutinous rice steamed in banana leaf with meat.
lemping light, flat cakes; melemping thin and flat.
lempoyan reel on fishing-rod.
lempoyang wild ginger plants.
lempuk durians cooked with sugar; melempuk to so cook.
lempung soft, friable, light (of wood); lempung-lempung splashing.
lemuas, berlemuas dirty (esp of face).
lemuju = jemuju.
lemukut rice bran; see melukut.

lena deep (of sleep); terlena fast asleep; melenakan to put to sleep; berlena-lena dawdling.
lenat trampled (of crops).
lencam, ikan lencam sea bream.
lencana ribbon or badge (worn to indicate membership).
lencas, belencas hairy caterpillar; melencas to wriggle.
lencet = lecet.
lencit, melencit to squirt out, slip out.
lencong, melencong to swerve, deviate ricochet.
lencun, basah lencun dripping wet.
lendat, melendat to beat, scrub; pursue debtor for payment; to trample, crush.
lendeh, melendeh to snuggle.
lendip stilted, affected (of person's gait); neat (of phrase).
lendir mucus, sticky discharge, thin pus; kacang lendir lady's finger.
lendung, melendung to bend, sag.
lendut, melendut bend, yield (of plank, floor).
leng measure for grain.
lenga sesame, til, ginjili; = bijan.
lengah to dawdle, waste time; melengahkan to delay; kelengahan dawdling, state of inactivity.
lengai inattentive, neglectful, dawdling.
lengak to throw back the head and look up; lengok-lengak sound of slapping.
lengan (of animal) arm, foreleg; sleeve; pangkal lengan upper arm; hujung lengan lower arm.
lengang sparse (of population or attendance at a show etc).
lengar, terlengar knocked dizzy.

lengas I moist (of sweets, sweaty hand); pengukur lengas hygrometer.

lengas II to look turning round.

lengat cook in steamer;=kukus.

lenggak, pelenggak garden seat.

lenggana unwilling, reluctant.

lenggang I at leisure; pausing (to think).

lenggang, II melenggang to sway head and body; lenggang yang lemah lembut slow and undulating motion; lenggang janda small curved knife; mandi lenggang perut to bathe ceremonially in seventh month of pregnancy; berlenggang to roll (of boats).

lenggara, melenggarakan to look after, cherish, protect;=pelihara.

lenggek storey floor.

lenggok, melenggok to bridle, toss up head, sway head and body from side to side.

lengguak, burung lengguak large thick-billed green pigeon.

lenggundi small tree with violet flowers.

lenggung, melenggung to reflect, pause to think; see lengung.

lenggut, melenggut to doze (with head nodding).

lengit beaten badly at a game.

lengkang I opened (of anklets, rings).

lengkang II round, band, circlet; lengkangnya circumference (of a garment round the waist).

lengkap full, complete, ready; salengkap pakaian complete suit of clothes; lengkap senjata fully armed; kelengkapan equipment.

lengkara fabulous.

lengkayan tree platform for guns in stockade.

lengket, berlengket sticking (as eyelids).

lengkiak=kelengkiak.

lengkok, melengkok to wind (of roads etc); meanderings (of walkers); arc.

lengkong I, lengkong-lengkang clanging (of metal).

lengkong II bow-shaped, curved, circular, encircling; melengkong in a circle; belat lengkong screen fish trap; selengkong all round; lengkongan circle.

lengkor, melengkor to be slightly bowed or bent.

lengkoyan fishing reel.

lengkuas kind of wild ginger.

lengos, melengos to turn one's head away.

lengsan fickle.

lengsar tapering.

lengser, melengser to slip down (of skirt, sun etc); make slippery, grease.

lengset, belengset everted, turned out (of diseased eyelid); membelengset to sleep.

lenguh, melenguh to feel weak and tired; lenguh lumpuh stiff all over.

lengung I, melengung to reflect, brood.

lengung II, melengung to look back at;=toleh.

lening tinkling of little bell.

lenja I, melenja to take liberties=manja; berlenja to dribble at the mouth, salivate.

lenja II, melenja to sulk.

lenjang to level ground by trampling of cattle, trample on.

lenjar, biji kelenjar glands; sakit kelenjaran glandular swellings.

lenjuang red-leaved garden shrub.

¹**enjun**—lencun.

¹**ens** lens.

¹**entam**—lentum sound (*of crash, stamping*).

lentang, telentang lying on one's back; **lentang-lentung** clanging of metal.

lenteh, perlenteh lustful, lascivious.

lentek curling back, concave (*of hair, teeth filed so as to give a concave surface, nostrils, roofs etc*).

lentera lantern.

lenting, melenting springy (*of planks*); curling (*of paper*); to leap; **belenting** stretched to bursting point.

lentok, terlentok inclined to one side (*as a head*); **melentok** to incline the head to one side; **lentang-lentok** swaying from side to side.

lentong=**lantong** stinking; sound of clashing; **pelentong** measles.

lentuk, melentuk to be flexible (*of rattan, wire*); **melentukkan** to bend.

lentul, melentul to feel empty (*from hunger*).

lentum booming (*sound of a gun*).

lentur, melentur to bend down (*of branches etc*); be flexible (*as a cane*).

lenung booming of a gong.

lenyah muddy.

lenyai=lunyai.

lenyak fast asleep.

lenyap vanished; **melenyapkan** to cause to vanish.

lenyar restless; see gelenyar.

lenyau crusted mud; =lanyau.

lenyeh, melenyeh to knead flour.

lenyek to rub, squash (*with hands or feet*); mash (*potatoes etc*).

lenyet squashy (*as overripe fruit*).

lepa I careless, negligence; *see* alpa; **lepa-lepa** lowest part of palm cabbage.

lepa II, terlepa sprawling (*of tired person*); trailing (*of clothes*); **melepakan** to plaster (*walls*).

lepak I, melepak, putih melepak white; thudding noise; slap; = sepak.

lepak II, berlepak thrown down; scattered (*of soft things*).

lepan meadows, low land (*uncultivated*).

lepang cucumber; **ombak bunga lepang** foam-tipped waves.

lepap, terlepap prone (*of person*); flat-bottomed boat.

lepar banisters, rails; **lepar kajang** roof pole for palm leaf awning.

lepas escaped, free; past, ago, since; **lepas sembahyang** after prayers; **lepas dari penjara** released from gaol; **kain lepas** loose scarf; **berlepas** to depart; **terlepas** escaped; **melepaskan** to free, let go, release; **kelepasan** freedom; **lepas itu** after that, then; **seorang lepas seorang** one after another.

lepat, kuih lepat generic name for sweetmeats cooked in leaves.

lepau eating house or stall; kitchen verandah.

lepehkan to fold over (*the corner of a page or cloth*).

lepek I, burung lepek-lepek broad bill; **melepek** squelching sound.

lepek II drenched, wet; layer (*of dirt, paint*); **melepek** to drop (*of person, from fatigue*).

leper broad and shallow (*of boats, dishes*); not rounded (*of rims*); **leper-leper** gunwale.

lepet, melepet folded back; — **kelepet**.

lepoh, terlepoh twisted (*of limb from a fall*).

lepu, ikan lepu angler fish.

lepuh, melepuh blistered.

lepuk to beat one another with their wings (of fighting cocks).

lepung thumping sound.

lepur, mati lepur suffocated in mud.

lepus slow, slack; limp (of invalids); sound of air escaping.

lerah, melerah to drop; broken off (as fruit blown down by a storm).

lerai, meleraikan to separate (as persons fighting).

lerak broken open (of house); tree the fruit of which is used as soap.

lerang strip, width of cloth; **lerang-lerang** bier.

lerap coin used for playing pitch-and-toss.

lerek, melerek to bore through; **terlerek** to run over by car.

lereng edge, contour; lower slopes of hill; **jalan lereng** sloping road; **kereta lereng** bicycle; **melereng bukit** to follow hill path.

leret line, file; **berleret-leret** straggling in long line; **leretan gunung** chain of mountains; **meleret** to trail on (of tale).

leroi, meleroi to strip maize seed off central pith.

lerok to go off on another tack; =**belok** concave (as a bay).

les reins; =**ras** lesson; list; picture frame.

lesa=**lasa** paddle rudder for raft.

lesah swishing sound.

lesak rustling (as rain).

lesap vanished; see **resap, lenyap**.

lesar to put down (dish etc with no mat, doily or saucer).

lesau, melesau to idle, slack; **pelesau** slacker.

leser to drag; **pukul leser** to dribble a ball along the ground; **meleser** to draggle (of clothes, skirts).

lesi, pucat lesi very pale, anaemic.

lesing to hurl from sling; whistle, whizz.

lesir, tawar lesir quite flavourless, insipid; **lesirkan** to whizz stone along surface of water; **bermain lesir** sword dance.

lesit, melesit to hum (of angry wasps, cricket etc); squirt out; blow the nose.

leson licence.

lestaka thick centre of archer's bow.

lestari eternal, lasting.

lesterung=**restung**.

lesu utterly tired out, completely exhausted; **letih lesu** worn out; **melesukan** to tire.

lesuk, 'esuk pipit dimple.

lesung mortar (for pounding); **lesung indik** pounder worked by foot; **lesung tangan** pounder worked by hand.

lesut I swish of cane or whip.

lesut II shrunken, shrivelled, withered but not dry.

leta mean, low, base, despicable.

letai exhausted, weak.

letak I, **letaknya** site position, place; **terletak** placed, laid down; **meletakkan** to put down, place; resign; appoint.

letak II weak (from illness).

letam sound of slamming.

letang sound of clanging.

letap sound of snapping.

letas=**letus** to crackle quietly (of burning grass).

leteh I tired, weary.

leteh II, **leteh-leteh** cargo boat.

letek to tick (as a clock); crack.

leter, berleter to chatter incessantly; **peleter** chatterer, gossip.

leterek electric; *also* **letrik**.

leting tinkling, clinking; **mc-leting** to hop (*as fish in basket*).

letis lip-smacking noise.

letos to open up.

letrik electric.

letron electron.

letuk knocking sound.

letum—letam thudding (*of tread*).

letung clanging sound.

letup, **meletup** to go off with a bang; **meletupkan** to fire, explode; **letupan** explosion; **letup-letup** herb whose pods pop.

letur, **meletur** to be blistered; keep burning.

letus sound of detonation; **letusan** burst of explosions, guns; **meletus** to burst (*of boils*); explode (*of gunpowder etc*).

lewa, **melewa** to dawdle waste time.

lewah, **melewah** abundant (*of fruit, wares*).

lewar, **melewar** to go in shoals; fly in swarms.

lewat, **melawati** to pass by; behind time; **lewat pukul 4** after 4 o'clock; **selewat-lewatnya** at the **very** latest; **kelewatan** failure to keep an appointment.

leweh, **meleweh** open (*of lips*); sagging (*of lower lip*); careless.

liang aperture; **liang hidung** nostril; **liang jarum** eye of needle; **liang luka** gash of wound; **liang mata** eye socket.

liar undomesticated (*of animals*); wild (*of nomads*); **orang liar** aboriginal tribesmen.

lias, **pelias** charm to divert enemy's weapon.

liat tough (*of meat*); clayey (*of soil*); elastic (*of rubber*), flexible, pliant; **meliat** to become tough; **liat-liut** twisting (*as snake*)

liau, **meliau** to fester, run.

libat, **melibat** to bind up, bandage (*foot etc*); **terlibat** to involve (*in matter*).

liberal liberal.

libur, **hari libur** holiday; berlibur on holiday.

libut, **kayu libut** spongy wood.

licak flattened, trodden flat (*as fruit in one spot*).

licau oiled, glossy (*of hair*); **licin licau** smooth and glossy.

licek false, sly, tricky.

licin smooth, slippery; **licin licau** quite finished; **minyak pelicin** lubricating oil.

lidah tongue; spokesman; interpreter; **lidah bercabang** double-faced; **lidah tidak bertulang** rash (*in talk*); **keras lidah** mispronouncing; **patah lidah** broken (*of speech*); **lidah buaya** aloe; **lidah pengarang** editorial.

lidal thimble; **=lidal**.

lidas itching; smarting (*esp around mouth*).

lidi veins of coconut palm frond; **panyapu lidi** broom of lidi; **ular lidi** thin snake.

ligan, **peligan** to chase away.

ligas to amble (*of horses etc*).

ligat, **meligat** to spin very rapidly.

ligi, **meligi** to pierce; *see* **seligi**.

lihat, **melihat** to see, look at, behold; **melihati** to study, inspect; **terlihat** coming into sight; **kelihatan** visible; **penglihatan** view, opinion.

likas reel.

likat thick and sticky; **bukat likat** turbid.

likau tree used for firewood.

liku bend (*in river, road*); **berliku-liku** winding; *see* **siku**; to meander.

likung to surround.

likur=lekor.

lil large spheroidal riverine basket trap.

lilahi to God; al-hamdu lillahi praise be to God.

lilang shrub.

lilau, melilau to totter (*as a sick man*).

lilin wax; candle, taper; **lilin lebah** bees' wax; **kain lilin** waxed sarung; **burung lilin** small southern hornbill.

lilis to trim slightly; **selilis** thin slice.

lilit turn, twist; girth; **tali tiga lilit** three twists of string round (*an article*); **selilit** all round; **lilitan** circumference; **melilit** to coil round.

lima five; **lima belas** fifteen; **lima puluh** fifty; **lima ratus** five hundred; **lima ribu** five thousand; **kelima** set of five; **yang kelima** fifth.

limar silk cloth.

limas pyramidal (*of roofs*); **rumah limas** house where four sides of roof run up to one point; **candi limas** pyramid.

limau citrus fruit; **limau kapas, limau nipis** common lime; **limau manis** orange; **limau kesturi** musky orange; **mandi berlimau** to wash with lime juice.

limbah cesspool, drain; **limbahan pelimbah.**

limbai, melimbai to sway arms when walking *or* dancing.

limbang to wash (*ore, rice*); **loiter after; limbang tengah hari** just after midday; =**rembang** *also* **lembang.**

limbat, ikan limbat edible catfish; **to** hurl; **berlimbat-limbat** to flutter (*of torn clothes*).

limbing large (*of ears*); bent and thick at edge.

limbubu whirlwind; =**selembubu.**

limbuk emerald dove; = **punai tanah.**

limbungan dock, slipway;

kusta **limbungan** leprosy with mutilation.

limbur, sambur-limbur dusk; in wild confusion; *also* **saburlimbur.**

limpa liver; **limpa kecil** spleen; **anak limpa** pancreas.

limpah overflowing; **limpah mewah** abundant; **limpah kurnia** abundant generosity; **melimpah** to overflow (*of wells, population etc*); **melimpahkan** to bestow in abundance.

limpapas moth, butterfly.

limpas, melimpas to wet.

limpit layer.

limpuk heap, pile; **ikan limpuk** catfish.

limun=**halimunan.**

linan linen.

linang, berlinang-linang to trickle, flow (*of tears, sweat*); still, calm (*of water*).

linau, pinang linau sealing wax palm; **nibung linau** tall, tufted palm.

lincah, melincah to move restlessly, fidget, be active; **lincah-lincah** to be always changing one's job, house *etc*.

lincam, melincam flash (*of lightning*); moment.

lincin=**licin.**

lincir slippery; **minyak lincir** machine oil.

lincun=**lencun.**

lincung, melincung to go off at a tangent; *see* **kelincung.**

lindang completely finished.

lindap abating (*of heat*); decreasing (*of fever*).

lindeh, berlindeh to lean against with slack body; to press firmly; *also* **lindih.**

lindu earthquake.

lindung shelter, protection; veil; **berlindung** taking cover; **perlindungan** shelter, protection; **terlindung** under shelter, protected; **melindungkan, melindungi** to protect.

ling half a cupak, one eigth of a gantang; ikan ling common carp.

lingar, melingar to keep looking around

lingga pillar erected as mark.

linggam red lead.

linggayuran tall and slender.

linggi covered decking at stem and stern of Malay boat.

linggis crowbar; long hoe; linggisan dayung long pole fixed alongside boat's gunwale as rest for oars.

linguistik linguistics.

lingkap to fold back.

lingkar, melingkar to coil (rope etc); berlingkar in coils; lingkaran concentric ring.

lingking, buah lingking ly-chee.

lingkup folded back; teling-kup overturned (of cup); melingkupi cover, veil.

lintabung a grass.

lintadu mantis.

lintah leech; (fig) bloodsucker, sponger; telinga lintah ears alert for gossip.

lintang barrier across; lin-tangnya width; garisan lintang the latitude; lintang pukang topsy-turvy; melintang lying across; melintangkan to put across; terlintang placed across.

lintar lightning; = halilintar.

lintas, melintas to cut across; dash past, flash by; jin lintasan evil spirit darting across in front of man.

lintuh unconscious; weak, flaccid.

linyak trodden flat; berlinyak quarrel; revolving on one spot (of a top).

lio brick kiln.

lipan centipede; = halipan.

lipas cockroach; lipas kudung quick worker; ekor lipas curls at nape of neck.

lipat fold; lipat dua folded

double; lipat ganda manifold; dua kali lipat twice as much; pisau lipat pocket knife; ber-lipat folded; lipatan fold.

lipit small fold, hem; kala lipit house scorpion.

lipstik lipstick.

lipur, melipurkan calming; to console; penglipur lara com-orter; chanter of folk tales.

liput flooding, swamping over-coming; terliput flooded, overcome.

lir like; sang lir-sari flower-like goddess.

lira, melira smooth, level.

lirek, melirek to glance aside.

liring = lereng.

lis list; line (in mouldings).

lisah restless; menggelisah to fidget.

lisan tongue; oral.

listerik electric.

lisut = lesut.

litah I, litah mulut garrulous.

litah II, selitar all round, around.

litenan lieutenant.

litup, melitupi cover and conceal.

liu, liu-liu stern paddle.

liuk, meliuk-liuk to twist and turn; movement of fencer or dancing girl; terliuk-liuk sway-ing.

liung, ali liung sort of belt for carrying a keris.

liur, air liur saliva; air liur basi unpleasant saliva common on waking.

liut supple; liat-liut twisting waist; terbelit twisted.

liwat sodomy; bestiality; = lowat.

loak rubbish basket; tukang loak dealer in secondhand wares.

loba greedy, covetous.

lobak radish.

loban resin; gum benjamin; ikan loban fish.

locak, melocak to be abraded; ripple of sea; abundant (of fruit).

loceng bell, handbell, wall bell; **loceng gila** alarm bell.

locok, melocok to masturbate; press pestle up and down; push (a cue) forward; **pelocok** piston.

locot blister from a burn.

lodak silt, mud; = **kelodak**.

lodan, ikan lodan whale.

lodeh, sayur lodeh mixed vegetables cooked to pulp.

lodoh soft overripe, over-boiled.

lodong large section of bamboo for cooking.

loga abode, place; **syurga-loga** heaven; also **loka**.

logam metal, mineral; **pan-calogam** alloy of five minerals; **bermalogam** red talismanic stone.

loghat dialect; word for word translation (of the Kuran); **ilmu loghat** philology; **kitab loghat** vocabulary.

logic logic.

logu, ikan logu sea fish.

loh tablet; **papan loh** school slate; now; **loh-loh** at once.

loha forenoon; **sembahyang loha** forenoon prayer.

lohoh decayed and stinking.

lohor noon; **sembahyang lohor** midday prayer; also **zohor**.

loji lodge; factory of East India Company.

lojik logic.

lok curve in creese blade; **berlok** curved.

lokan edible bivalve found in muddy estuaries and mangrove swamps.

lokap lock-up.

lokar locker; sailor's quarters.

lokat loose (as wallpaper, plaster).

lokcuan silk crepe.

lokek stingy, mean, miserly.

loket locket.

loki Chinese prostitute.

loklek mincing (of walk); dawdle.

loklok I trochus shell (from which buttons are made).

loklok II pearl.

lokoh hard (of durians); shabby, not smart.

lokos, melokos spattered (with mud, wet flour etc).

loksun consumptive with spitting of blood.

loktong prostitute.

lolong Chinese lantern.

loloh, meloloh to stuff, feed up (animals for slaughter).

lolok, melolok to spy on; scout; eddying; air **lolok** eddies.

lolong, melolong to howl (of dogs); shrieking (of women).

lolor, lolor-lolor quickly.

lolos slipping off (as a finger ring); see **lulus**.

loma, ikan loma carp.

lomba, berlomba-lomba to compete, race (of horses, cars); complete; play of porpoise; **tempat berlomba kuda** race-course; **lomba-lomba** porpoise, dolphin; **pelomba** contestant; = **lumba**.

lombar, melombar to pay out rope; = **hulur**.

lombok capsicum; = **cabai**.

lombong deep mine (of tin, gold); alluvial mine; **melombong** to mine; chasm left after volcanic explosion.

lomis—lomis wheedling.

lompat leaping; **melompat** to spring; **lompat bergalah** pole vault; **terlompat-lompat** jumping up and down; **berlompatan** jumping in turn; **lompat katak** leapfrog.

lompi completely.

lompok, berlompok-lompok in lumps (of dirt).

lompong empty; **kuih lompong** cake.

loncat, meloncat to leap (of fish, frogs); **terloncat-loncat** hopping about.

lonceng=loceng.

loncer loose (as nail).

lonco, melonco to saunter, stroll.

loncong tapering upwards (as roof).

loncos tapering upwards, coming to a point; stripped (of clothes); **telanjang loncos** stark naked.

londang shallow stagnant pool; rice swamp.

londar, londar naga tailings, silt from mines; locus.

londeh, terlondeh loose and slipping (of sarung).

loneng railing, balustrade.

long Malay coffin; **sulung** eldest.

longgak looking upwards with head bent right back.

longgar too big (of hole); loose (of clothes); **melonggarkan** to loosen.

longgor grown up quickly, strapping (of children).

longkah easily separated (as fruit from rind); loosened.

longkai, berlongkai-longkai long and graceful.

longkang drain, ditch, cesspool; row of plants in hill rice-field.

longlai, lemah longlai drooping, graceful.

longlang, longlang burung Jawa child's game.

longok, melongok to go to see, stare.

longong, melongong agape, open-mouthed.

longsen dozen.

longsong, terlongsong gone too far, rash.

longsor, melongsor to slide down, slide off.

lonjak, melonjak to leap, skip; **cakap melonjak** to boast.

lonjong long and straight (of trees); oval shape.

lonjor stick; numeral coefficient for long things.

lonta, terlonta-lonta always struggling (of the poor).

lontar, daun lontar leaf of Palmyra palm used for writing before paper; **melontarkan** to hurl, throw overhand; **pelontar** missile.

lonteh prostitute; also **pelonteh.**

lontok short and thick; **tua lontok** old and stumpy.

lontos straight (as plain pillar).

lop name for eldest son; =**Kulup.**

lopak puddle; sections of wet ricefield; **lopak-lopak** pouch of pine leaf; **lopak-lopek** confused in disorder.

lopis confection of glutinous rice, palm sugar and coconut.

lopong muddied.

lor north; **achi lor** hide and seek.

lorah=lurah.

lorat worried, confused.

lorek fretted (of earrings), patterned; **berlorek-lorek** so marked; running of ear; also **torek.**

loreng=coreng striped.

lori lorry.

lorong alley, lane, path; corridor; **melorongkan** to open a way.

los almond.

losen dozen.

loseng, belah loseng split bamboos.

losi reserved seat (at cinema etc).

losment hotel, cafe.

loso, meloso to move on one's belly (as snake).

losong, kurap losong ringworm with peeling of skin; =**kosong** empty.

iota small metal water jar.

lotar = lontar.

loteng upper storey of house.

loteri lottery.

lotong black long-tailed monkeys; **ekor lotong** swivel gun with tail piece.

loya, meloya feeling squeamish, ready to vomit.

loyak soft, overboiled.

loyang brass; cake mould; large tray.

loyar lawyer; **loyar keledek** lawyer with small practice; **pinang loyar** cudgel from **pinang liar**

loyong, meloyong to walk stooping and tottering.

lu you; **raga lu** rice basket.

luah, meluah to eject food from mouth; feel sick.

luak, meluak to feel squeamish at sight of food; territory ruled by a tribal **penghulu**; to have decreased in quantity.

luan = haluan.

luang Thai title; abating (*of storms*); vacant space (*of time*); **peluang** opportunity.

luap, meluap to boil over.

luar outer portion, part beyond *or* outside; **di luar** outside; **ko luar** outward; **datang dari luar** came from outside; **orang luar** strangers, foreigners; **luar biasa** unusual.

luas ample, broad, wide; **keluasan, luasnya** area; **meluaskan** widen.

luasa = leluasa widespread.

luat, meluat to hate; feel nausea at (*seeing, hearing*).

lubang hole, pit, gap, aperture; **berlubang-lubang** full of holes; **pukul lubang** to be a broker.

luber to overflow.

lubok deep pool in river *or* sea; *also* **lubuk.**

lucah low, shameless; filthy (*of language*).

lucas missing (*target*).

lucu dainty, pretty; funny; **dilucu** ridiculed.

lucup, melucup to dive.

lucur, perempuan lucur, pelucur harlot; *also* **lacur.**

lucut slipped (*off, down or away*); dropped and lost; **senang terlucut** easily undone; **melucutkan jawatan** to resign a post; **lucut senjata** to disarm; **melucut** abraded.

ludah spittle; **berludah** to spit; **ludahkan** to eject from mouth.

ludang, perahu ludang narrow rowing boat.

ludes finished (*of money*).

luding, tenggiri luding mackerel.

luek, meluek to retch hard and vomit.

lugas, melugas to feel about, to hiccup.

lugat = loghat.

lugu willing.

lugut needles of bamboo; **= miang**

lui = balut quits, a draw.

luih I more.

luih II, meluih to retch slightly, feel nausea.

luka wound, scratch; **mata luka** orifice of wound; **melukai** to wound.

lukah generic name for small riverine fish trap.; **melukah** to expose one's person.

lukis, melukis to draw, paint; **lukisan** drawing; **pelukis** draughtsman.

luku, meluku scratch; to harm with nails.

luli, meluli to wind cotton on to .pindle.

luluh crushed to powder.

lulur, melulur to swallow whole (*as snake*).

lulus just slipping through, getting through; passing (*an examination*); **meluluskan** to bring to pass; **kelulusan** accomplishment.

lulut cosmetic; **melulut** to rub person; **pelulut** shampooer.

lum, masak lum overripe.

lumak oily.

lumang, berlumang smeared with mud; **mengelumang** to wallow in mud.

lumar dirt; berlumar dirtied, smeared.

lumas, melumas to smear (with oil).

lumat fine (from mincing); padi lumat well-ripened rice.

lumayan enough but not too much; = sedang.

lumba = lomba.

lumban, ikan lumban small fish.

lumbung rice barn; = lombong.

lumer to liquefy.

lumpang vacancy, open space; cannon's mouth; berapa lumpang how many cannons.

lumpuh paralysed (esp of the eg); lame from beri-beri.

lumpur mud.

lumur, berlumur soiled (with paint etc); besmeared.

lumus soiled (esp of face); tungkus lumus in a mess, in trouble.

lumut alga; moss, lichen, seaweed; berlumut covered with lichen.

lunak sweet and juicy (of fruit); too soft (of rice).

lunar alluvium.

lunas keel (of boat); bottom (of pot); settled (of debts); **melunaskan** to pay a debt, execute a plan.

lunau mud; see lanar.

luncung snout; = muncung.

luncur, meluncur to slip down slide; forfeited (of pledges pawned); luncurkan to launch a ship; pesawat peluncur glider.

lundu river catfish.

lunggam to guzzle (of children).

lungguh, melungguh to sit at ease; lungguhan land enjoyed free by officials in lieu of pay.

lungkum convex; high at the sides; domed; see mungkum.

lungkup, terlungkup inverted (of cups); capsized (of boats).

lungsur = longsor.

lunjur, berlunjur kaki to stretch out one's legs.

lunsing warp in loom.

lunta = lonta.

luntang, peluntang fisherman's float that drifts with baited line.

luntur fading, not fast (of colours); peluntur purgative.

lunyah, melunyah treading down swampy soil for rice planting.

lunyai soft and crumpled (of worn cloth).

lupa I rod through which threads pass in weaving.

lupa II to forget; lupakan to forget; pelupa forgetful person; lupa-lupa fish bladder.

lupas, melupas; = kelupas.

lupat, siput lupat shell fish.

lupi, papan lupi fore and aft decking of Malay ship.

lupuh, melupuh to flatten out bamboos for flooring; pelupuh flattened bamboos.

luput left behind, loose, free; luput dari mata gone from sight.

lurah valley between hills; groove, slot in joinery; lurah hidung furrow in upper lip; kelurahan district.

luru, meluru to dash up, charge (of persons, beasts).

luruh to fall (of flowers leaves); be shed; seluruh all over, throughout; also seluroh.

lurup, susup lurup helter-skelter.

lurus straight and smooth; **meluruskan** straighter; **kelurusan** straightness, honesty.

lurut, melurut to run chain through fingers; **pelurut** wooden smoother of screwpine for plaiting; **kelurut** whitlow; to flow (*of stream*); decline.

lusa day after tomorrow; **esok lusa** in a day or two.

lusuh crumpled; comfortably soft (*of shoes etc*); a bit shabby.

lut penetrating, effective; **tiada lut** it did not penetrate (*of a bullet, weapon*).

luti, meluti to crumple in the hand (*of cloth*).

lutsinar transparent.

lutu, melutu to attack in swarms (*of wasps, bees*).

lutut knee; **kepala lutut** fore-part of knee; **tempurung lutut** knee cap; **berlutut** to be on one's knees; **betemu lutut** to sit side by side.

luyu, mata luyu tired and drooping (*of eyes*).

luyut, meluyut hanging (*of fruits on boughs*).

M

ma plural pronominal suffix; **sahaya-ma** we; **dia ma, dema** they.

ma' = mak.

maa water; **maa'l hayat** water of life.

maab place of return.

maaf forgiveness; **minta maaf** to apologize; **maafkan** to pardon.

maalumat information; = **maklumat.**

maamal laboratory; = **makmal.**

mabir, tabir-mabir all sorts of curtains.

mabuk intoxicated; sea-sick; **mabuk bunga selasih** drunk and swaying; love-sick; **memabukkan** to intoxicate; **pemabuk** drunkard.

mabur to fly; run.

Mac March.

macam kind, sort, quality; like; **macam ini** like this; **macam mana?** in what way?; **bermacam-macam** of various types.

macan tiger; **macan-macanan** a child's game.

macang horse mango; **sakit macang** suffering from a bubo.

macat stuck fast.

macis matches.

mada must (*of elephants*); = **meta.**

madah speech, praise; **bermadah** to speak, talk; **madahkan** to relate, tell.

madali musical instruments.

madam I melancholy, doleful.

madam II lady.

madang always; = **semedang.**

madat opium; ammunition for guns.

madi = mazi.

madinat city.

madrasah school (*esp religious*).

madu honey; rival wife *or* mistress; **bermadu** having a co-wife.

madukara bee; silk with pattern in gold thread.

mafhum understanding; **telah mafhum** to have understood.

magang ripe and rotten (*of fruit*); turned sour (*of fermented liquor*).

magel half-ripe; *see* **mangkal.**

magersari lodgers on a rich man's ground.

maghlub conquered, defeated.

Maghrabi Moroccan, Moorish.

maghrib west; sunset.

magnesia magnesia.

magnesium magnesium.

magnet magnet.

magun compartment aft for steersman; kajang magun fixed awning.

mah is it not so? surely.

maha very, most; meha besar, maha kuasa descriptive of God; maha mulia most illustrious; Hi: Highness; maha guru professor.

Mahabiru = Mahameru.

Mahadewa Siva, the Supreme God.

Mahadewi wife of Siva.

mahaduta minister, plenipotentiary.

mahajana important person; proletariat.

mahal expensive, dear; hard to find.

mahaligai = maligai.

Mahameru fabulous mountain, the heaven of Indra.

mahang generic name for softwood trees.

mahar bridegroom's settlement on Muslim bride.

maharaja great raja, title once royal; = seri maharaja one of the titles of the Bendahara of mediaeval Malacca.

maharana the great war (of the Mahabharata).

maharani great queen.

maharupa supremely lovely.

mahasiswa undergraduate.

mahator junior queen in ancient Java.

mahbub beloved (of men).

mahdi, imam mahdi the leader who Muslims believe will come to the earth before the Last Day.

Maheswara Supreme Lord; = Siva.

mahfuz learnt by heart; Loh Mahfuz Muslim tablet of fate; **mahfuzkan** learn by heart.

mahir expert, skilled; mahirkan to train; kemahiran skill.

mahisa buffalo.

mahkamah Muslim court, Supreme Court.

mahkota crown; mahkota alam royal title in Acheh; Tengku Mahkota Crown Prince.

mahmud praised, lauded.

mahsul products (of a country); hasil mahsul products, exports.

mahsyar, padang mahsyar place where the dead assemble on Judgement Day.

Mahtab moonbeam.

mahu = mau.

mai = mari title of male and female issue between Ea a and Syarifah.

maikcrub microbe.

mail mile; = Ismail; steel pencil for applying kohl to the eyes.

maimun fortunate.

main, bermain to play; main silat to fence; main wayang to be an actor; pemain player; permainan game, amusement.

maja generic name for a number of plants.

majakani oak galls imported for medicinal use.

majal blunt (of knives); majal selera poor (of appetite); sial majal unlucky.

majallah journal, magazine, periodical.

majapada the earth.

majapahit sacred belfruit tree of the Hindus; famous 13th century Javanese kingdom.

majemuk complex; compound (of sentence); miscellaneous (of a book's contents).

majerin margarine.

majikan employer.

majir childless, barren.

majisteret magistrate.

majlis official assembly, social gathering; **majlis undangan** legislative council.

majmuk anthology, compendium, composite.

majnun mad, possessed.

maju progressive, prosperous, successful; **memajukan** to advance (*of country*); **kemajuan** development.

Majuj Magog.

majung oakum

Majusi Magian; Fire-worshipper.

majzub drawn to God; wrapped in devotion.

mak mother; **mak bapa** parents; **mak tiri** stepmother; **mak angkat** adoptive mother; **mak mehtua** mother-in-law; a term of polite address to all women of the generation of one's mother.

maka then, next (*used in writing as a punctuation word*).

makalah newspaper article.

makam grave with a small pavilion over it, grave shrine; **makamkan** to entomb, enshrine.

makan to eat, consume, wear away; **makan angin** to get some fresh air; **makan besar** feast; **makan gaji** to work for wages; **makanan** food; **termakan** devoured.

makar hard, stony (*of fruit*); trick; resourceful, wily.

makas, keras makas very hard.

makbul approved; heard (*of prayers*).

makelar broker.

makenah white veil worn by women at prayers.

makhdum honorific for Muslim pundits.

makhluk mankind, God's creatures.

maki, memaki abuse, revile; **kena maki** to suffer abuse.

Maki, sena Maki Meccan senna.

makin the more; **makin lama makin sakit** the more time passes the more sick (*he is*).

makjizat miracle.

makjun compounded medicine.

makkul intelligible, reasonable.

maklap convert to Islam.

maklum known; **tuan lebih maklum** you will know better sir; **maklumakan** to inform; **maklumat** announcement, communiqué.

makmal laboratory.

makmum congregation who repeat prayers after their *imam.*

makmur prosperous and populous; **kemakmuran** peace and plenty.

makna meaning; **bermakna** having a meaning.

maknawi esoteric, spiritual.

maknit magnet.

makota = mahkota.

makrifat wisdom, knowledge.

makroni macaroni.

makruf well-known.

makruh improper; reprehensible (*but not forbidden*).

maksiat wickedness, sin.

maksima maximum.

maksud wish; intention; **bermaksud** wishing; intending.

maksyuk beloved.

maktab college.

makyung dramatic performance popular in northern Malaya.

makzul deposed (*of ruler*); **makzulkan** to depose.

mal property; **baitul-mal** state treasury; **bicara mal** civil suit.

mala accursed, unlucky; **mala pestaka** extreme ill luck.

malah nay, rather, furthermore; *also* **malahan**.

malai flower worn in hair.

malaikat angel; soul (of dead).

malak angel; malak al-maut angel of death.

malakat market, mart.

malakut, alam malakut world of angels and spirits.

malam I dark, night (from sunset); malam sabtu Friday evening; malam hari night-time; malam tadi, semalam last night; malam sekarang tonight; bermalaman to pass the night; semalaman all night.

malam II a little intoxicated; overripe and spoilt.

malang thwarting, crossed by fortune, unlucky; kemalangan to be unlucky; bad luck; accident.

malap flickering, dim (of lamp); smouldering (of fire).

malar constantly; malar pucat always pale.

malas lazy, idle; pemalas idler.

malau=embalau.

malaun cursed by God, wicked.

mali, mali-mali, memali shrubs.

maligai princess's bower in the upper storey of a palace.

malik lord, king.

malim one learned in religion; navigator, pilot.

maling steal; pintu maling back or side door; maling curi pilfering and thieving.

malis faint (of colour, smell).

malu shy, reluctant, nervous, humble, ashamed; beri malu to shame; dapat malu to be put to shame; kemaluan pudenda (of either sex); pemalu shy person; rumput si malu sensitive plant.

malung, ikan malung eel.

mam to chew; feed (of infants).

mamah to masticate, chew;

mamah biak to chew the cud.

mamai wandering (of the aged); talking in one's sleep.

mamak maternal uncle.

mamalia mammal.

mamam=mam.

mamanda court form of mamak.

mamang absent-minded; gopoh mamang extreme haste.

mambang ghost, spirit; sakit mambang kuning jaundice.

mambu, daun mambu leaf of a tree.

mambung empty of contents (of jackfruit).

mamek gone bad in taste (of food); tasteless.

mami aunt; dish of vermicelli.

mamlakat sovereignty.

mamluk slave.

mampal blunted (of end of stick).

mampat densely packed (of earth); choked (of pipe).

mampir to call at, visit.

mampu having power or money to do.

mampung spongy, light (of bread).

mampus dead (of beasts).

mamung fixed; dazed; horse mackerel.

mana where?; yang mana? which?; orang mana? who?; rumah mana? which house?; datang dari mana? whence?

manah heirloom, prized (as an heirloom); esteemed.

manai, pucat manai pale from loss of blood.

manan gracious (of God).

manau, rotan manau largest of the rattans.

manca manifold; manca warna multi-coloured.

mancak thick coconut milk got by a second squeezing of the pulp.

mancit, tikus mancit rat.

mancung high and shorp (of

nose); dried sheath of coconut palm blossom.

manda = mamanda, mandi-manda all sorts of ablutions.

mandah rice barn; **tongkat mandah** ears of rice of a lucky shape.

Mandakini heavenly Ganges.

mandalika monkey-jack tree with edible fruit.

mandam dizzy, intoxicated.

mandat mandate.

mandeh maternal aunt.

mandek to stop, halt, get stuck.

mandi bathe; **memandikan** to bathe; **tempat mandi** bathing place.

nandika post (*in outer compartment of fish trap*).

mandolin mandoline.

mandom quiet (*of horse*).

manduk shy, retiring.

mandul barren (*of women*).

mandung cock, fowl.

mandur overseer, foreman.

manfaat profit, gain.

mangap agape.

mangar firm (*of fruits, breasts*).

mangau, termangau-mangau agape with amazement.

mangga mango; **kunci mangga** padlock; **sakit mangga** suffering from bubo.

manggap unsuccessful; stupid; unfit, inactive.

manggar fallen palm blossom; **ular mangga** nyior a snake.

manggis mangosteen.

manggul mound, knoll, hillock.

mangkal, mangkar hard (*of fruit, esp durians*).

mangkas hard (*of rice*).

mangkat dead (*of prince*).

mangkeh sticking out in all directions.

mangkin = makin dregs (*of tea*).

mangku upholding; nursing; **mangku bumi** regent.

mangkuk bowl; cup; **pinggan mangkuk** crockery.

mangkus efficacious; = **mustajab**.

mangmang challenge by gesture or words.

mangsa prey (*of beasts*).

mangsai = masai; **masak mangsai** overcooked.

mangsi (*cuttle fish*) ink; **ikan mangsi** cuttle fish.

mangut day dreaming, dazed.

mani semen; **pancaran mani** emission of sperm.

Maniaka nymph of Indra's heaven.

manifesto manifesto.

manik bead; **bermanik** wearing beads.

manikam gem, jewel.

manipulasi manipulation.

manira, manera I, we.

manis sweet (*of sugar*); **hitam manis** light brown; **jari manis** fourth finger; **kencing manis** diabetes; **muka manis** pleasant face; **manisan** honey, sweets.

manja spoilt (*as child*); spoilt darling; **manjakan** to spoil.

manjakani = majakani.

manjan, bermanjan to rove in quest of girls (*of youths*).

manjung torch; **manjungan prow** (*of ship*).

manjur efficacious (*of drugs*); potent (*of poison*).

mansukh annulled; **memansukhkan** to cancel.

mantap stolid, calm, steady.

mantera magic spell.

manteri = menteri minister.

mantik, ilmu mantik logic.

mantil topping lift.

mantu = menantu.

manuk bird, fowl; **manuk dewata** bird of paradise.

manus smell of dead bodies, of cemetery.

manusia human being, mortal; mankind; **kemanusiaan** humanity.

manuskrip manuscript.

manyau to talk in one's sleep *or* when very sleepy.

manzil halting place, resthouse.

manzum threaded.

mar check to the queen (*chess*).

mara advance, progress; peril; **mara bahaya, bermara** endangered; **saudara mara** relatives of all degrees.

marah wrathful; **naik marah** to get angry; **memarahkan** enraged; **pemarah** hothead.

marak to flare up; **naik marak** to come into the limelight.

maras afraid.

marbut marabout; caretaker and drumbeater at a mosque.

mardan men.

marem satisfied, comfortable.

marga wild; **marga satwa** wild beasts.

marghub pleasant.

marhain, kaum marhain proletariat.

marhum deceased.

mari come here!, here!; **ke mari** hither, come.

Marikh Mars (*planet*).

marin = kelmarin.

marine marine.

marjerin margarine.

marjik return (*to God*).

markah (*school*) marks; stripes (*denoting rank of soldiers*).

markas military headquarters.

market market.

marmar, batu marmar marble.

marmut guinea pig.

martabat rank, grade; prestige.

martil hammer, police truncheon.

maruas small hand drum.

marut, carut-carut all sorts of obscene remarks.

mas measure of weight; 16 mas = 1 tahil.

masa time, era, epoch; tense.

masaalah, masaalah enigma, problem.

masai, kusut masai much entangled (*of hair*).

masak ripe (*of fruit*); cooked (*of food*); **memasak** to cook; **masakan** style of cooking, food.

masakan how can it be?; is it possible?

masala praying mat.

masam sour (*of taste, looks*); **masam muka** sour-faced; **rasa masam** acerbity.

masebuk to butt in (*in prayers*).

Maseh Messiah, Jesus; **Masehi** Christian; **tahun Maseh Anno Domini.**

masih still; **masih tidur lagi** still sleeping.

masin salty; effective; **lidahnya masin** his speech is effective.

masing-masing severally, each (*of persons*).

Masir Egypt.

masjid mosque.

maskapai limited company.

mastautin, bermastautin to reside.

mastul headcloth.

mastuli thick silk fabric heavy with gold thread.

mastur veiled.

masya Allah God forbid; cheer up.

masyaikh elders.

masyakat difficult, troublesome.

masyarakat society; **balai masyarakat** community centre.

masyghul sad.

masyhur famous; **masyhurkan** to spread fame of; **pemasyhuran** proclamation.

masyrik east.

mat check of king (*chess*);
Mat = Muhammad.

mata eye, score; biji mata eyeball; mata sasaran bull's eye;
mata jarum eye of needle;
mata luka opening in wound;
mata ikan wart; mata kayu
knot in wood; mata air spring,
source of river; mata pisau
blade of knife; mata gelap
detective; mata-mata policeman.

matab fireworks.

matahari sun; matahari hidup
rising sun; matahari naik
sunrise; matahari mati sunset;
bunga matahari sunflower.

mata-mata police(man); mata
gelap detective.

matang sand dune, mound;
= permataaa mature; kematangan mature, cooked.

mateng cooked.

materi to solder; fixed.

material material.

materialis materialist.

maeros sailor.

mati dead (*of living things*);
stopped (*of cars, watches etc*);
extinguished (*of lamps etc*);
mati lemas drowned; kematian
death; mematikan to kill,
extinguish.

matlamat, matalamat
objective target.

matra dimension.

matran metropolitan bishop.

mau wish, intention, will;
mau tak mau whether willing
or not; dia mau pergi he is
willing to go; kemauan desire,
craving.

mauduk title (*of a talk*).

maujud existent, concrete.

maulai Lord (of God).

maulana my lord, master
(*term applied to eminent
Muslim scholar*).

maulud Prophet's birthday.

maung bitter and smelling.

maut death, hour of death;

malik-ul maut angel of death.

mauz banana.

mawa leaf monkey (*believed
by Malays to live on dew*).

mawar, air mawar rosewater;
bunga air mawar rose.

mawas orang-utan; tulang
mawas prehistoric iron tools.

mawin, kawin-mawin all
kinds of wedding festivities.

maya unsubstantial, illusory;
maya pada this transitory
earth; alive; spirit of life.

mayam a goldsmith's weight.

mayan absent-minded.

mayang palm blossom; panicle; mayang mengurai unfolding palm blossom; putu
mayang sweetmeat.

mayat corpse; peti mayat
coffin.

mayung, ikan mayung marine catfish.

mayur, sayur-mayur all sorts
of vegetables.

mazhab I altar for sacrificing.

mazhab II religious sect.

mazi transparent element in
semen.

mazkur, termazkur written,
recorded.

mazmur hymn.

mecrat to die; fall in a trance.

medak soft but not stinking
(*of fish*).

medali flute.

medan field (*esp of battle*).

medang trees of moderate
size with timber used in minor
construction; batu medang
sela gypsum, hydrous calcium
sulphate imported from China.

medit mean, stingy.

medium medium.

medok full of holes; dirty.

medu squeamish, feeling sick.

mega cloud; mega berarak
driving clouds.

megah famous, renowned;
kemegahan greatness, renown.

megak bold, saucy.

megan sweetmeat; sort of cabobs.

megari = **nampak**.

megat hereditary title borne by men of royal descent on the mother's side.

megrek sickly, wasted.

megun still and contemplative, brooding, sulking.

meja table.

mejam apparently motionless.

mejan dysentery.

mejana whilst.

mejelis pretty, beautiful; = **majlis**.

mek form of address to girls of good family.

mekanik mechanic.

mekanikal mechanical.

mekap make-up.

mekar unfolding (of palm blossom).

mekmulong dramatic performance.

meksimam maximum.

mekteng, cabuk **mekteng** suppurating ulcer.

mekula lotus.

mel, kapal mel mail steamer; mel udara airmail.

melainkan but, still, nevertheless, except; see lain.

melaka tree (with edible fruits and used for tanning); gula melaka palm sugar.

Melaka port.

melambang large dug-out boat.

melar extendable, elastic.

melarat, **mudarat** difficulty, loss, injury; see larat.

melas not fitting well; not coinciding.

melati name for jasmine (usually melur).

Melayu Malayan, Malay; anak Melayu, orang Melayu Malays; Melayu jati a true Malay.

melek to keep awake; melek huruf to know how to read and write.

melela = **lela**.

melik envy, greed.

melimum = **halimun**.

meling to turn away, look in another direction; memelingkan orang to turn eyes away and not notice people.

melion million.

melir to break (of skin round a boil).

melit inquisitive; melitnya curiosity.

melkiwi supercargo.

melodi melody.

melong overgrown (of children for their age); large scented lily.

melongo agape with wonder.

meluh to plough a rice field for the first time.

melukut broken rice grains; also lemukut, temukut.

melulu only, wholly.

melur jasmine; also melati.

mem English lady.

memang I to keep repeating or dragging up.

memang II naturally; as a matter of fact; of course; memang jahat notoriously wicked; memang begitu of course that is the case.

memar soft, bruised (of fruit from fall).

membacang = **embacang**.

membal rebound.

memberang = **berang-berang** otter.

membiang, ikan membiang herring.

memek whining, fretting (as a young child); soft (of lyre).

memerang = **berang** otter.

memo memo.

memorandam memorandum.

mempan to incur injury (from shot).

memparang, ikan memparang herring, dorab; see parang.

mempedal = **empedal**.

mempelai bridegroom; bride; naik mempelai to ascend the bridal dais.

mempelam = empelam.

memper almost, resembling.

mempinang, ikan mempinang coral fish; also pinang-pinang.

mempoyan shrub popular for fences.

mempulur = empulur.

mempurung, ikan mempurung herring.

mena calculation; tidak se-mena-mena for no reason, without motive; tidak terpemenai innumerable.

menahagu to ask to borrow.

menahun all the year; see tahun.

menak noble.

menampun = minta ampun to ask leave (of royalty) to retire from the presence.

menang to win, succeed; menangkan to give victory to; favour; kemenangan victory.

menantu son- or daughter-in-law.

menara minaret; church spire.

menasabah congruous, proper, credible.

menatu washerman.

menceng askew.

mencing crammed full, stretched tight.

mencit mouse; rat.

mencok perch.

mencong much askew; pencong-mencong criss-cross.

mendak bowed, stooping hiding; silenced; to settle (o silt in water).

mendalu mistletoe; = bendalu.

mendam drunk; mendam berahi drunk with love.

mendap silt; to settle (of silt).

mendapa kiosk; = pendapa.

mendeleka tree yielding a kind of breadfruit.

mendelikai watermelon.

mendera, manis mendera gentle and sweet (of women).

menderang brilliant; = benderang.

menderung sedges used for mat making.

mendiang deceased, dead.

mendikai = mendelikai.

mendonan strangers, visitors.

mendora Malayo-Siamese dramatic performance

mendung lowering (of clouds).

mengah panting puffing; sakit mengah asthma.

mengap agape.

mengapa why?; tidak mengapa never mind.

mengeh puffing (from over-eating).

mengelai, tikar mengelai fine sleeping mat.

mengerna coloured, gay; beloved.

mengetin to lodge a claim; pengetingan claim.

mengga, semengga-mengga individually, singly.

menggul knots on tree; menggul-menggul gnarled.

mengiang radiant; ular mengiang rainbow.

mengindera royal.

mengkal half-ripe (of fruit).

mengkala when

mengkalai = bengkalai.

mengkalas, cuci mengkalas cleaned out (of gamblers).

mengkam gripe, colic.

mengkapas, ikan mengkapas small carnivorous fish.

mengkara, udang mengkara crawfish.

mengkaring, ikan mengkaring fighting fish.

mengkarung = bengkarung.

Mengkasar Macassar.

mengkawan = bengkawan.

mengkelan stuck in one's throat (of food).

mengkeret to shrink, huddle up; afraid.

mengkis to defy, challenge.

mengkona tuskless (*of male elephants*).

mengkong, cengkung-mengkung hollow of cheeks.

mengkuang screw pine whose leaves are used for plaiting mats.

mengkudu shrub whose root bark furnishes red *or* purple dye.

mengkunang mousedeer; = bengkunang.

mengok awry (*of lines*); = bengut.

mengong = menung pensive, brooding.

mengset to fall fast asleep.

mengsol slanting.

mengsu, bulu mengsu fine hair on the forehead.

meniaga to trade; *also* berniaga.

menila, rantai menila long neck-chain of gold links.

meninggal die; *see* tinggal.

meniran = kemeniran.

menjak, semenjak since (*of time*).

menjama medium, average.

menjelai cereal.

menjelis = mejelis pretty.

mensiang triangular rush in rice fields.

menta rutting (*of elephant*); = meta.

mentadak praying mantis; *also* cengkadak.

mentadu green caterpillar; *also* sentadu.

mentah uncooked (*of flesh*); unripe (*of fruits*); kain mentah unbleached cotton; crude (*of oil*).

mental resilient.

mentang although; *also* sementang.

mentara = sementara while; boundary.

mentat shrunken.

mentega butter; mentega tiruan margarine.

menteri minister, vizier; perdana menteri prime minister; menteri pertahanan minister of defence; menteri pelajaran minister of education; menteri kewangan minister of finance; menteri buruh minister of labour.

mentibang millipede.

mentimun generic name for gourds, pumpkins, cucumbers *etc*; *also* timun.

mentora, balai mentora reception room in palace.

mentua father- *or* mother-in-law; mentua taya sister *or* brother of one's in-laws; burung tebang mentua hornbill.

mentung dull-witted; to go straight on without turning.

menturong bearcat; = benturong.

menung, termenung pensive, contemplative.

menunggal cent.

menyawak monitor lizard; = biyawak.

menyeroka to open up and irrigate rice fields.

mepas to fly-fish.

meragi, burung meragi painted snipe.

Merah old Sumatran title.

merah red; merah tua dark red; merah perang bright red; merah muda light red; merah padam crimson (*as from anger*); memerahkan to redden.

merak peacock; merak pongsu peacock pheasant.

merakap, jahil merakap extremely ignorant (*esp of religion*).

merang, merah merang bright red.

merangu musical instrument now obsolete.

meranti large trees with timber in great demand for boards *etc.*

merawan timber tree; **ikan merawan** red sea perch.

merbah yellow-vented bulbul; **merbah jambul, merbah telinga merah** red-whiskered bulbul; **merbah sampah** red-winged babbler.

merbak = semerbak.

merbang flowing (*of hair*); *see* **gerbang.**

merbau Malacca teak (*valuable hard wood*).

merbuk spotted dove.

merca swooning, faint; **merca pada the earth.**

mercu top (*of mountain*); crest.

mercun cracker, fireworks.

merdangga long drum.

merdeheka, merdeka free (*of person*); **merdehekakan** to free; **kemerdehekaan** freedom.

merdesa urbane, cultured.

merdu melodious (*of music, voice*).

merebu bristling.

mereh, urat mereh windpipe.

mereka they; them; their; **mereka itu** those persons.

merekah split; *see* **rekah.**

merem to shut the eyes.

mereng to heel over (*of boat*); oblique.

merguk pilgrim's veil (*showing only the eyes*).

Meriam Mary; **Siti Meriam** the Virgin Mary.

meriam cannon; **pedati meriam** gun carriage; **meriam penangkis** anti-aircraft gun; **pasukan meriam** gun crew.

merica pepper; = **lada.**

merinyu police inspector, overseer, bailiff.

merjan coral (*beads*); large gold beads.

merkubang tree.

merkunyit, akar merkunyit plant.

merlilin, burung merlilin hornbill; *also* **burung lilin.**

merlimau, akar merlimau thorny wild orange.

merlokan plant.

merombong small tree.

merosot decrease.

meroyan, sakit meroyan disease of women; generic name for a number of plants.

merpadi plant.

merpati domestic pigeon.

merpisang palm.

merpuing plant.

mersek shrill, piercing (*of voice, sound*).

mersiul, burung mersiul crested green woodpartridge.

mersuji, ikan mersuji food fish.

merta, serta-merta immediately; **air merta jiwa** water of life.

mertabak meat *or* eggs fried in bread.

mertabat = martabat.

Meru a fabulous mountain; *also* **Mahameru.**

meruah self-respect.

merual long oblong flag.

meruap to boil over, boil up.

meruar to call out.

meruas small two-headed drum.

merubi, keris merubi creese with a knobby potato-shaped hilt.

merunggai horseradish tree.

merus, tanah merus landslide.

merut, kerut-merut wrinkled.

mesan grave-stone; = **nisan.**

mesara allowance; = **sara.**

mesarung, siput mesarung shell.

mesem to smile; **bermesem mesem** to keep smiling

mesera = mesra.

mesikur, ikan mesikur food fish.

mesin machine; *also* **mesen.**

mesiu saltpetre used for making gun powder.

meski, meskipun even if, although.

mesra absorbed (*of sugar in liquid*); **mesrakan** to absorb.

mesta mangosteen.

mestari skilled workman.

mesti must, needs must.

mestika, mustika bezoar, talismanic stone.

Mesuara, Maheswara Siva.

mesui tree with fragrant bark.

mesum dirty (*of clothes, persons*).

meta rutting, mad (*of elephants*).

metah, putih metah snow-white.

metai cushion, mat.

meteor meteor.

meteoroloji meteorology; **kajicuaca.**

meter meter.

meterai to seal; *also* **meteri.**

methil methyl.

metren matron.

metu sad; = **mutu.**

mewah abundant (*of food*); **kemewahan** abundance prosperity.

mewek pouting, ready to cry.

miang fine hairlike pieces of bamboo seen when a bamboo is split; itching.

miap, ciap-miap twittering of birds.

midar, mengidar *from* idar.

mihrab niche in mosque indicating the direction in which Mecca lies.

mika you (*to intimates*).

mikro micro.

mikrofon microphone.

mikroskop microscope.

mil, mel mile; mail; **keretapi** mel mail train.

milam old dame.

miligram milligram.

milik property, ownership;

milik saya my property; **milik negara** nationalized; memiliki own; **pemilik** owner.

mimbar pulpit *or* lectern in mosque.

mimi king crab; = **belangkas.**

mimis small shot.

mimisan nosebleeding.

mimpi dream; **bermimpi-mimpi** continually seeing in dream.

min from, of.

mina, gajah mina whale; walrus.

minantu = menantu.

minat desire, craving, interest; **berminat** having a liking for.

minduk, tok minduk assistants at seance (*main puteri*).

minggat to run away.

minggir to skirt; *see* pinggir.

minggu week; hari **Minggu** Sunday; **minggu bahasa** language week.

minhaj path, way.

minit minute (*sixty seconds*).

minta, meminta to ask for; **minta ampun** to beg pardon; **minta diri** to take one's leave; **minta damai** to ask for armistice; **permintaan** request.

mintak girdle.

mintal plump.

minum to drink; makan dan minum eating and drinking; **minuman** drink; **peminuman** man given to drink.

minyak oil, grease, fat; **minyak gas** kerosene; **minyak kelapa** coconut oil; **minyak sapi** suet; **minyak benzen** petrol bermingak oiled, greased.

mipat to take the wrong turning.

mir, amir (mior) children of a female descendant of the Prophet (Syarifah) by a commoner.

mirah, batu mirah ruby, carbuncle (*gem*).

mirat mirror.

miring to lie on one side (of persons); swerve aside; to heel (of boats); otak miring eccentric.

mirip to resemble, be similarly directed.

miris, tiris-miris leaking badly.

misa buffalo; ancient Javanese title; =mahisa.

misai moustache; misai lebat heavy moustache.

misal, mithal example; misalnya for instance; misalan emblem, symbol.

misan honey; =manisan; tombstone; =nisan.

misbah lamp.

mising ptomaine poisoning from shellfish.

Misir, Mesir Egyptian.

miskal, mithkal shekel, goldsmith's weight.

miskin poor; kemiskinan poverty.

misoa vermicelli.

misoh revile, abuse; =maki.

misru fabric of silk and cotton mixed.

mistar ruler, ruled line.

misteri mystery.

mistik mystic.

mitai sweetmeat.

mitoloji mythology.

mizan Libra in the zodiac; scales.

moa eel; =belut.

mobil motorcar.

modal capital; modal tetap fixed capital; pemodal capitalist.

modan modern; also moden.

modar, mati modar to die an unholy death (of beasts dead without having the throat cut as Islam enjoins).

mode mode.

model model.

moden modern; also moderen.

modin muezzin; circumciser; also mudin.

modus mood.

moga, semoga, moga-moga would that, may it happen that; sa-moga if only; thing, article.

mogah adultery; also mukah.

mogok to strike (of men from work); pemogok striker; pemogokan strike.

moh come along; willing; =embuh.

mohon to apply for; ask to be excused; bermohon to take one's leave (from a superior); permohonan to request.

mohor seal; cap mohor royal seal. royal initials on coin.

mokmit moving of the mouth while speaking or eating.

molek charming, pretty; kecil molek dainty (of girl).

moler prostitute.

molikul molecule.

molong, buah molong sweetmeat resembling buah Melaka.

molor sleepy.

momok bogey; blunt.

momot, comot-momot dirty (from ashes).

mompong used up (of clumps of nipah etc).

moncol to project, put out.

moncong snout (of fish, dog); beak (of birds); moncong cerek spout of kettle; to put out.

mondok short and thick, stumpy; see montok.

monel pretty, fair (of child).

mong sound of gong.

monggek, muntah monggek sick from guzzling.

monggok I mound-shaped; ulat monggok millipede.

monggok II stoop; also membongkok.

monggol gnarled (of trees); =bonggol.

mongkor sedan chair; mongkor kaca carrying chair with glass windows.

mongkos miserable, rueful.

mongmong small gong.

monir, licin monir stripped quite bare.

monogami monogamy.

monogram monogram.

monopoli monopoly.

monsun monsoon.

montel plump.

montok short in proportion to its length, stumpy; *see* mondok.

monumen monument.

monyeh, termonyeh-monyeh ashamed, bashful.

monyet monkey, ape; rumah monyet sentry box.

mopeng pockmarked; = bopeng.

moral moral.

moralis moralist.

moreng, coreng-moreng streaked with dirt in all directions.

morfoloji morphology; kaji-bentuk.

mori fine white cotton for making batik cloth.

morong glum, dejected, despondent.

mota flowering sedge (*used to make sacking*).

motif motive.

motor, motor sangkut outboard motor for boats.

moyang great-grandparents (*father or mother*); nenek moyang ancestors.

moyong pitcher plant.

moyot parent of moyang.

mozah slippers.

mu you, thou; = kamu.

muafakat agreement, conspiracy; bermuafakat to confer, conspire; sepakat in agreement.

muak satiety, disgust, physical nausea.

mual to swell (*of rice when boiled*); feel queasy.

mualamat science.

mualap convert to Islam.

mualif editor.

mualim expert in religion.

muara estuary; = kuala.

muat to contain, hold, accommodate; muatan cargo; bermuat having as cargo.

muazam great, exalted (*of rulers*).

nubah neither good nor wicked.

mubarak blessed.

mubazir redundant, unused; extravagant.

mubtadi beginner.

mubut fragile, weak.

muda young, unripe; light (*of colouring*); muda belia young and fresh; orang muda young people; pemuda youth; pemudi girl; emas muda inferior gold.

mudah easy (*to do, get*); dengan mudah easily; memudahkan to make easy; mudah-mudahan one hopes that.

mudarat loss, detriment, injury, harm.

mudi, juru mudi steersman.

mudik, **mudek** to go upstream.

mufarik separated.

mufasal separated, detailed.

mufasir commentator (*esp of the Kuran*).

muflis bankrupt; muflisi insolvency.

mufti Muslim consultant jurist.

mughayat supreme (*in titles*).

muhabbat love, affection; utusan muhabbat goodwill mission; *also* mnhibbah.

muhajir exile.

muhalil—cinabuta intermediate husband a thrice divorced Muslim woman must have before remarriage to her original husband.

Muharram first month of the Muslim year.

muhit, al-muhit the all-embracing (God); laut muhit ocean circling the world.

muhrim too closely related to marry.

muhsin honest, virtuous.

mujahadat holy war.

mujallah journal, periodical.

mujammal summarized, collected.

mujarrab tested, efficacious (of drugs etc).

mujarrad abstract; hati mujarrad naked heart.

mujtahid founders of schools of Muslim law.

mujur fortunate, lucky; kemujuran.

muka face, countenance; muka manis pleasant looking; muka surat page; air muka expression, look; muka-muka feigned feelings; beri muka to encourage; mengemukakan to bring forward; terkemuka prominent.

mukaddam first, leading.

mukaddas holy; Baitalmukaddas Jerusalem.

mukah fornication; paramour.

mukammal perfected, excellent.

mukarram revered.

mukim parish, territorial division, area served by one mosque.

mukjizat miracle.

mukmin faithful, devout (of Muslims).

muktabar honoured, respected.

muktamad final.

muktamar congress, conference.

mukun lidded bowl or cup.

mukuti Indian woman's nose ring.

mula beginning; mulanya its origin; pada mulanya originally; mula-mula first of all; semula over again; sebermula

to begin with; permulaan commencement.

mulas, perut mulas colic, gripe.

mulia noble, illustrious, glorious; yang maha mulia His Highness; memuliakan to honour; kemuliaan mark of honour.

muluk kings.

mulur extendable, elastic.

mulut mouth; mulut manis soft spoken; mulut jahat malicious tongue; buah mulut people's talk; mulut sungai mouth of river; bermulut having a mouth.

mumbang green unripe coconut.

mumbung piled high (of plate, measure).

mumkin possible, feasible; = mungkin.

mumut mouldering, worn away.

munafik hypocritical (in religion).

munajat private devotion.

munasabah probable; credible, consistent.

muncak = kemuncak.

muncih residue of goods; balance left (of money).

muncikari pimp, procuress.

muncis defeated.

muncul to appear above the surface.

muncung = moncong.

muncup = kemuncup love-grass.

mundam lidded bowl for water made of metal.

mundar-mandir to go up and down, move to and fro.

mundur to retreat withdraw; backward, underdeveloped.

mungil nice, sweet, dainty.

mungkin = mumkin.

mungkir to break a promise; mungkir janji to repudiate an agreement.

mungkum deep (of bowls); dome-shaped, convex.

Munkar and **Nakir** the Angel inquisitors of Muslim newly de..d.

munsyi teacher of a language.

muntah vomit; **muntahkan** to vomit.

muntaha end, final.

muntil short and fat; sleek.

mur myrrh.

mura, ular mura venomous spitting snake.

murad aim, purpose.

murah generous; good-hearted; liberal; cheap; **maha murah** all-generous (of God); **kemurahan** generosity, clemency.

murai magpie robin; murai gajah fairy bluebird; murai gila fantail fly-catcher; badak murai tapir.

murakkab compound composite; jahil murakkab dense ignorance.

muram gloomy (of face); dull (of moon).

murang fuse, match for cannon.

murba common, ordinary.

muri metal flute.

murid pupil.

muring grumbling, irritable.

muris fabric.

murka wrath (of God or ruler); **memurikakan** to make angry; dimurkai to incur anger of; **kemurkaan** wrathfulness.

murni pure (of ideals).

mursal apostle.

murshid pious; spiritual guide.

murtad apostate, renegade; agnostic.

murti form; Teri-murti triple form, Hindu triad.

muru sour milk.

murup fiery red.

Musa Moses.

musafir traveller, tourist.

musakat trouble, torment.

musalla praying mat.

musang civetcat, polecat.

musara salary, allowance.

musibat disastrous, unlucky.

musim season; musim hujan wet season; musim kemarau dry season; musim tengkujuh monsoon season.

musium = muzium.

muslihat plan, policy; muslihat perang military tactics.

musnah destroyed, damaged; **memusnahkan** to destroy.

musuh enemy, foe, opponent; bermusuh to be at enmity; **permusuhan** hostilities.

mustaed ready, prepared.

mustahak important.

mustahil incredible, ridiculous, impossible.

mustajab efficacious.

mustakim upright, honest.

musyarakat society.

musykil difficult (to solve), musykil hati worried.

musyrik polytheists.

musytari Jupiter (astr).

mutakadim former, ancestral.

mutakhir of latter days, modern.

mutalaah study, reading.

mutia pearl, mother-of-pearl.

mutiara pearl; ayam mutiara guinea-fowl.

mutlak absolute, unlimited; hak mutlak natural rights; wakil mutlak plenipotentiary.

mutu carat; emas sepuluh mutu twenty-four carat gold; quality of goods; mutu manikam gems.

muwahid monotheist.

muwakal agent.

muzik music.

muzium museum.

N

naam yes, certainly, so it is.

naas = **nahas**.

nabatah, alam nabatah the vegetable world.

nabi prophet; **nabi Isa** Jesus; **nabi-nabi** starfish of seven points.

nada tone; musical note; **nada utama** ground tone.

nadi pulse; **urat nadi** artery.

nadir rare, curious; Malacca boat.

nafas breath; **bernafas to** breathe.

nafi denial, rejection, negative; **menafikan** to reject, deny.

nafiri long trumpet.

nafkah sustenance; alimony; **mencari nafkah** to seek a livelihood.

nafsi oneself; **nafsi-nafsi** to put oneself first.

nafsu lust, appetite; **bernafsu** to have lust, appetite.

naga dragon, snake of supernatural size; **gemala naga** luminous bezoar with which a dragon lights its way; **naga berjuang** type of pattern in carving.

nagara = **negara**.

nagasari ironwood, Indian rose chestnut.

nah there, take it.

nahak, ternahak overcome by desire, roused (of feelings).

nahas accident, misfortune.

nahi forbidden (by Islam).

nahu grammar; **ilmu nahu** syntax.

naib deputy; **naib kadi** a Kadi's deputy; **naib yang di pertua** vice-president.

naik to ascend; **naik kereta** to mount up into a carriage; **tengah naik** half-grown; **kenaikan** mount, rise.

nailon nylon.

naim delightful.

najam star.

najis filthy, defiling (from religious viewpoint); to excrete; **najis besar** faeces; **najis kecil** urine.

nak = **hendak** to desire to, wish to; = **na'**.

naka part singing, singing in alternation.

nakal mischievous, naughty; **menakal** to be mischievous.

nakhoda captain, skipper of trading ship.

Nakir one of the angels who interrogate the dead in the grave.

nal wad (in gun).

nalan five (in children's games).

nalar regularly.

naleh measure of capacity = 16 gantang.

nali turn (in game); innings.

naluri instinct.

nam = **enam** six.

nama name, designation, renown; **menamakan** to name; **bernama** by name; to be named; **ternama** famous; **nama samaran** alias.

nambi ulcerating disease of feet.

namnam fruit tree.

nampak to see; to be visible.

nampal marl.

nan who, which, that; = **yang**.

nana elder brother.

nanah pus, matter; **menanah** to suppurate.

nanai monkey (in language of magic).

nanap staring (of eyes).

nanar dazed (from drink, injury).

nanas, nenas pineapple.

nang = **yang** who, which.

nanggal plough; = **tenggala**.

nangka jackfruit.

nangui rare pig of great size.

naning large wasp; **tupai naning** squirrel.

nanjak to climb (*hills*).

nanti I later.

nanti II, **menanti** to wait, stay; **ternanti-nanti** to be kept waiting a long time.

nantiasa = sentiasa, **nentiasa** always.

nap, **ternap-nap** quietly.

napas breath, respiration.

napi = nafi.

napuh larger chevrotin *or* mouse deer.

nara man, hero (*in titles*).

naraka hell; **api ˜ raka** hell-fire.

narwastu spikenard, frankincense.

nas authoritative quotation from the Kuran or the Traditions.

nasab family, lineage.

nasabah relation, connection; **nasabahkan** to classify.

nasak, **ikan nasak** goby.

nasar vulture.

nasi cooked rice; **nasi goreng** fried rice; **nasi kuning** rice cooked with saffron; **nasi lemak** rice cooked in coconut milk; **nasi minyak** rice cooked in oil.

nasib fate, destiny; **nasib buruk** bad luck; **membawa nasib** to travel in search of fortune.

nasihat advice; **penasihat** adviser.

nasional national.

nasionalis nationalist.

nasionalisasi nationalize.

naskhah original manuscript.

Nasrani Nazarene; Christian; Eurasian; *also* **Serani**.

nasut mankind.

nasyid antiphonal singing.

nata prince, king.

natal, **hari natal** Christmas.

natang small window.

natar smooth, level; **= rata**;

background (*of a batik pattern*).

nati fool, blockhead.

natijah result, conclusion.

nau sugar palm; **= enau**.

naung shade, shelter; **bernaung** sheltered; **shelter o.s.**; **menaungi** to protect; **penaung** patron.

nayam ploughshare.

nayub dance.

nazam composition.

nazar vow, promise; **bernazar** to vow.

nazim poet, composer.

nazir inspector.

nebeng village headman.

negara state, country; **negara bukit** hilltop; **kettledrum**.

negatip negative.

negeri country; **ibu negeri** capital.

nek titular prefix indicating high rank in a commoner; **= nenek**; nauseated.

neka species; **serbaneka** of various kinds; **= aneka**.

nekara royal kettledrum.

nekat fixed determination.

nekmat delight, pleasure; delicious, pleasant.

nelayan fisherman.

nenda (*court and lit*) **= nenek**.

nenek great-grandparent (*male or female*).

nenenda (*court and lit*) **= nenek**.

nenes, **bernenes** to ooze out.

neng dear (*esp to daughters*).

nentiasa = sentiasa.

neraca scales, balance; **daun neraca** pan of scales.

nesan gravestone.

nescaya certainly, inevitably.

nesta = nista.

nestapa sad, sorrowful.

ngacau to be delirious.

ngacir to scurry, run fast.

ngada, **mengada-ngada** to give o.s. airs.

ngadah, **tengadah** to look skyward.

ngah = tengah middle one of a family; ngah-ngah panting.

nganga open, agape (of mouth); **mengangakan mulut** to open the mouth wide; **ternganga** agape.

ngangut, mengangut to mutter inaudibly, mumble.

ngap, ngap-ngap tired, panting.

ngapa why?; = **mengapa**

ngarai ravine, gorge; = **jurang**.

ngaum, mengaum to roar (as tigers).

ngaung, mengaung to reverberate (as an empty house).

ngek-ngek sickly.

ngelu aching (of head).

ngeng worthless.

ngeong, mengeong mew (of cat).

ngeram = geram.

ngeran angry, annoyed.

ngerang, mengerang to groan from pain.

ngeri fearful, alarmed; creepy.

ngeriap to crawl, swarm.

ngorong-ngering clashing, clanging.

ngiang, mengiang to whizz, whistle (of sound).

ngiau, mengiau to mew (of cats).

ngibing advance to girl to dance.

ngih, mengih to blow the nose.

ngilu having one's teeth on edge.

ngit its no go!, it won't do!

ngok-ngok to go straight ahead.

ngongak agape and doddering.

ngungap, mengungap to pant.

ngung-nging buzzing (of bees).

ngut-ngit scrubbing sound; sound of quail.

ngut-ngut mumbling (from age).

ni abbr of **ini**.

nian excessively, very, truly; benar nian very true.

niat wish, intention, vow, hope; bayar niat to fulfil a vow; **berniat-niat** to keep hoping.

nibung tall tufted palm.

nidera sleepy, fast asleep.

nifas childbirth.

nikah wedding, marriage ceremony; **menikahkan** to marry off (son or daughter).

nikal nickel.

nikmat = nekmat = neemat.

nikotin nicotine.

Nil Nile.

Nila, Nila Utama first king of Singapore.

nila blue (dye); indigo; **permata nila** sapphire.

nilai, menilaikan to appraise, value; **tiada ternilai** priceless; **penilaian** valuation; **bernilai** valuable.

nilakandi sapphire; patchouli.

nilong slow loris.

nilur, perisai nilur shield.

ning tinkle.

ningrat, kaum ningrat aristocracy.

nini grandmother, old lady.

nipah palm used for thatching.

nipis thin (of planks, cloth etc).

nira juice of sugar and coconut palm.

nirai row, line; = **baris**.

nirmala pure, clean.

niru = nyiru.

nisa women.

nisab family, lineage; = **nasab**.

nisan = nesan.

nisang Japanese brothel keeper.

nisbah ratio; Arab names denoting descent.

nisbi relative, comparative.

niskala immaterial; abstract.

nista abuse; **menista** to use insulting language.

nistapa = nestapa.
niterid nitride; nitrid.
niterit nitrate; nitrat.
nitrojan nitrogen; nitrojen.
nobat royal band; **menobatkan** to instal a ruler.
nobel novel.
nobelis novelist.
noda speck of dirt.
noga gastropod mollusc.
Noh Noah.
nokreng vulture.
noktah dot, vowel point; **noktah bertindih** colon; **koma bernoktah** semi-colon.
nomad nomads.
nombor number.
nona unmarried foreign girl; **buah nona** custard apple; **nona kapri** bullock's heart fruit.
nongkrong to squat.
noni little girl, small nona.
nonok mons Veneris of young girl.
nonong, menonong to hurry straight ahead without looking back.
nonsen nonsense.
normal normal.
not knot.
nota note.
notaris notary.
notis notice.
nu, nun yonder.
nubuat gift of prophecy.
nujum astrological tables, horoscope; **ahli nujum** astrologer.
nukil, menukilkan to cite; **nukilan** quotation.
nun yonder!
nur light (*of sun, truth*); **Nur-slain** light of my eyes (*letter heading*).
nurani bright (*of (woman's face*); **hati nurani** enlightened heart.
nurbisa antidote to venom.
nuri, burung nuri parrot, lory.
nurmala pure, clean.

nus sepia *or* cuttlefish; **nus kurita** octopus.
nusus refusing to cohabit (*of wife*).
nusyadar sal ammoniac.
nutfah sperm seed of life; **se-perma**.
nya him; his, her; it; its; third person pronoun.
nyah be off!, get away!; **nyahkan** to drive away.
nyai mistress; form of address.
nyak mother; **nyakkan** to push down (*goods into trunk etc*).
nyala, bernyala to glow; flare up (*of fire*); **bernyala-nyala** to keep blazing; **menyalakan** to set alight.
nyalang wide open (*of eyes*); **menyalangkan** to open eyes wide.
nyam to eat (*of children*).
nyaman fit; pleasant; contented.
nyamuk mosquito; **nyamuk tiruk** anopheles mosquito.
nyampang perhaps; just in case.
nyana, menyana to think, conjecture.
nyang = **moyang** great-grandparent; = **yang**.
nyanyah, menyanyah to babble nonsense.
nyanyar overripe, bruised; crumbling.
nyanyi, menyanyi to sing; **bernyanyi** to sing to o.s.; **penyanyi** singer; **nyanyian** song.
nyanyuk senile, in one's dotage.
nyap-nyap to cheep (*of birds*); chatter.
nyarap to plug (*bottle, hole*).
nyaring shrill (*of voice*).
nyaris nearly, almost.
nyata plain, clear, obvious; **menyatakan** to explain; **ke-nyataan** explanation; notification; **penyata** report.

nyatuh timber-tree.

nyawa soul, life, spirit; me-nyawa to breathe heavily; ny-awa ikan more dead than alive.

nyedar deep (of sleep).

nyenyai coarse, loosely woven.

nyenyak deep (of sleep).

nyenyeh, menyenyeh to pester, chatter.

nyenyen, menyenyen to mimic with the lips, tease.

nyeri pain, ache.

nyinyir to chatter; orang tua nyinyir old bore.

nyirih mangrove tree.

nyiru winnowing tray.

nyiur coconut; pokok nyiur coconut tree.

nyolo censer.

nyolong to pilfer; = colong.

nyongkom, menyongkom to snuggle against.

nyonya married Chinese lady.

nyonyeh mumbling; orang tua nyonyeh mumbling dotard.

nyonyong, menyonyong to stick out.

nyonyot, menyonyot to suck (breast).

nyut, nyut-nyut to throb (as boil).

O

oak = uak.

oasis oasis.

obam ovum.

obari ovary.

objektif objective.

obor torch; = suluh.

obrak, mengobrak to turn over.

obral, mengobral to sell off, expend.

obrol, mengobrol to chatter.

ocak, ocak-ocak source (of stream).

oceh, mengoceh to twitter; chatter, babble.

ocok, mengocok to incite, provoke.

odoh ugly.

ofis, opis office.

ogah hookah; reluctant, unwilling.

ogak, berogak-ogak to clown, joke.

ogam, mengogam to urge on to frenzy.

ogoh, mengogoh to shake (of branch).

ogok, mengogok to limp.

Ogos August.

oi hi!

oja, mengoja to excite (cocks, animals).

ojok, mengojok to grope one's way slowly.

okok stingy.

oksid oxide.

oksijan oxygen.

Oktober October.

olah attitude, manner, whim; mengolah to give trouble; to process, work.

olahraga sports.

olak eddy (of wind, water); berolak eddying; olak-alek to and fro.

Olanda = **Belanda** Dutch.

oleh by (person, agent); through the medium of, owing to; olehnya by him; beroleh to obtain.

olek = ulit.

oleng to rock (of boat); to waver (of mind).

oles, mengoles to smear.

olimpiad olympiad.

Olimpik Olympic.

olok, olok-olok joking, jesting; mengolok-olok to tease, make fun of.

ombak wave (of sea); mabuk ombak seasick; berombak to surge; surging; ombak-ombak tabir folds in curtain.

ombang – **ambing** rocked.

omboh piston (of Malay bellows, engine).

omel, mengomel to grouse, grumble.

omong, beromong to babble, chatter.

ompang, ompang-ompang traders' gifts.

ompok border to embroidery; **berompok** having a border.

ompol, mengompol to wet the bed.

ompong toothless.

onak thorny rattan, barbed thorn.

onang-aning descendants in the seventh generation.

onar = honar commotion, brawl.

ondeh, ondeh-ondeh sweet dumplings of flour and coconut.

oneng-oneng great-great-great-grandchildren.

ong address to Hindu trinity; *also* hong.

ongah-angih wobbling.

onggok-onggol pitching of ships.

ongji licence, permit.

ongkah to totter along.

ongleak bitts for anchor cable.

ongkas, terongkas slipped down.

ongkos expenditure, outlay, cost.

onyak-anyik loose (*as post, tooth*).

onyas-anyis in disorder (*of articles*).

onyong pouting.

onyot = nyonyot to suck the breast.

opak-opak cake; **opak-apek** untidy (*of parcel*).

opau bead purse worn on belt.

open, mengopen to notice; pick up anything dropped.

operasi operation.

opereter operator.

opor roast chicken *or* duck.

oportunis opportunist.

oposisi opposition.

optimis optimist.

optimistik optimistic

opu Bugis title.

orak, mengorak to uncoil (*of snakes*); unwind a coil; **mengorak langkah** to get a move on.

orang human being, man *or* woman; **orang Melayu** Malay; **kata orang** people say.

orbit orbit.

ordi order, command.

ordinit ordinate.

organ organ.

organik organic.

organisasi organization.

orientalis orientalist.

orientasi orientation.

orkes orchestra.

orlit stud earring.

orlong = relung.

orlop hawse hole on ships.

orna = warna.

ornamen ornament.

orong, orong-orong vent where the match is applied to a cannon.

otak physical brain; (*fig*) tajam **otaknya** he has a quick brain.

otar, otar-otar small round metal shield with bells.

otek, ikan otek catfish.

otomatik automatic.

otot muscle; **mengotot** to be tough.

oyak, mengoyak to shake, jolt.

ozon ozone.

P

pabean customs.

paberik factory.

pablisiti publicity.

pacai sandalwood scraped and sprinkled over corpse.

pacak, pacak tunggal hairpin; **memacak** to stick; **terpacak** planted.

pacal I, me (*when addressing ruler*); **ikan pacal** large herring.

pacang, memacang to engage.

pacar sitting mat of five layers of fine screw-pine.

pacat jungle leech.

pacau talisman hung on fruit trees to cause sickness to pilferers.

paceli mango cooked in sugar.

pacih kind of draughts game.

pacomberan cesspool; drain.

pacu spur; **memacu** to spur on; **kuda pacuan** racehorse.

pacul hoe; = **cangkul**; **terpacul** squeezed out.

pada, seri pada foot (*of royalty*); royal title; sufficient; **dalam pada itu** in those circumstances; **by, at, near, in; according to; kepada** to; **daripada** from.

padah I result; (*fig*) **mulut terdorong emas padahnya** slip of the tongue and a fine is the consequence.

padah II, **pedah** ill omen, warning.

padah III, **memadahkan** to invite (*guests*).

padam extinguished, put out (*a light, fire etc*); **memadamkan** to put out; **pemadam** extinguisher; **merah padam** blazing red (*of angry face*).

padan fitting, adequate; harmonizing; matching.

padang plain, playing field; **padang terbang** airfield; **padang ternakan** ranch.

padat crammed, full, packed; **memadatkan** to cram full, ram down (*earth*); **kepadatan** density.

padau, layar padau storm sail.

paderi Christian priests, missionaries.

padi rice in the husk; **padi sanah, padi bendang** wet rice; **padi bukit, padi huma, padi ladang** hill rice; **burung laki padi** tailor birds.

padma lotus.

padsyah ruler.

padu solid, massive; **isi padu** cube root; **berpadu** coagulated, welded; **tarpadu** firmly welded; **perpaduan** unity, amalgamation.

paduh to invite; = **padah**.

paduk starting place for games.

paduka (*lit*) foot; (*in titles*) **Seri Paduka** Sultan His Highness the Sultan; **paduka tuan** esquire.

padung tendril of vines; **burung padung** hornbill.

padusi woman, wife.

paduta Head of Chancery at an embassy.

paedah = **faedah**.

pagai, nyiur pagai dwarf coconut palm with small pale green nuts; = **nyiur puyuh**.

pagan sturdy, big and strong.

pagar fence, palisade, railings; **pagar buluh** bamboo hedge; **memagar** to make a fence.

pagas = **pangkas**.

pageri puggaree; band round sun hat.

pagi morning; **pagi-pagi** early in the morning.

pagoda pagoda.

pagu ceiling; shelf above kitchen fireplace.

pagut, memagut to peck (*of birds*); to bite (*of fish*); embrace; **pagutan** peck, bite.

paha thigh, quarter, ham (*of animal*); **pangkal paha** hip; **tulang paha** femur; **diberi betis hendak paha** given the calf he wants the thigh—he is never satisfied.

pahala reward for good works (*rel*).

paham, faham to understand; **kurang paham** not quite understood; **salah paham** misunderstand.

pahar large metal pedestal tray; coulter (*of plough*).

pahat chisel; **pahat bulat** round; **pahat jantan** narrow and thick; **memahat** to carve; **berpahat** chiselled.

pahi, mata pahi iron tip of ploughshare.

pahit bitter to taste.

pahlawan hero, champion; heroic.

paip pipe; tobacco pipe.

pais, ikan pais fish spiced and baked in a banana leaf.

pajak monopoly; tax; shop; **pajak candu** monopoly of selling opium; **pajak gadai** pawnbroker's shop; **pajak pendapatan** income tax; **pajak tanah** land tax.

pajang, memajang to decorate with flowers and leaves; **pemajangan** bridal apartment.

pajuh gluttonous; **pemajuh** to guzzle.

paka, puru-paka yaws.

pakai using or wearing anything, assuming, adopting, employing; **memakai** to wear, to use; **pakaian seragam** uniform.

pakal, memakal to caulk.

pakam effective (*of brakes*).

pakan woof; **tirai yang berpakankan emas** curtain shot with gold.

pakar expert.

pakaram to catch fish.

pakarangan fishing vessel.

pakat, berpakat to confer, agree on a plan or action; **sepakat** in concert, in collusion.

pakau, daun pakau playing cards; handle of bucket; frame.

paket parcel.

pakir = **fakir.**

pakis fern.

pakma parasite with flowers to which magic qualities are ascribed.

pakpui fortune telling by sticks in Chinese temple.

paksa force, compulsion, coercion; **memaksa** to compel; **terpaksa** compelled; opportune moment; **paksa belayar** favourable time to start a voyage.

paksi bird; peg of top; **paksi dewata** bird of paradise; axis; **paksi bindu** iron pegs holding wood to be turned.

paksina the north; = **utara.**

paktur = **faktor.**

paku peg, nail, pip on uniform; fern; **paku besi** iron nail; **paku mati** a nail which cannot be extracted; **pakukan** to nail; **terpaku** nailed, embedded.

pakuh hornbill.

pakuk, memakuk to hack.

pakum vacuum = **hampagas.**

pakus store house.

pakyung young prince in *makyung* performance.

pal, buang pal to tack (*in sailing*).

pala, buah pala nutmeg; **halwa pala** nutmegs in syrup; **pala-pala** genuinely, properly; **sepala-pala** as thoroughly as possible; **burung pala** crane.

palak hot (*of body*); **pemalak** hot-tempered person.

palam, memalam plughole; **pemalam** plug.

palama palm tree.

palang crossbar (*on door*); cross-strip in plaiting.

palar, berpalar unattended; **memalar** to grasp at; put up with smaller profit than was expected; **tak palar** unwanted.

palas, pokok palas small fan palms; **palas-palas** rail, clothes rack; **palas lintang** bridge of a ship.

palat, kayu palat stocks for holding up a boy's feet for caning.

palau scar, mark on person.

paldu side awnings on ship.

paleh, memaleh to bring into good condition (of horses).

paling, berpaling to turn head to one side, look round; extremely; most; **paling haluan** to change a ship's course; **palingkan, memalingkan** to turn the head; **paling murah** cheapest.

palis, memalis to glance out of the corner of one's eye, cast a sideiong glance.

palit, memalit to smear or smudge; **terpalit** smeared.

palka hatch of ship.

paluh pool (after tide); puddle.

palung trough used for watering or feeding animals.

palsu false, forged, counterfeit.

paltu depty, working partner.

palu, memalu to hit with stick.

palut, memalut to wrap up; **berpalut** enwrapped.

pam pump.

pamah low ground, meadows; low (of ground).

paman maternai uncle.

pameo saying, proverb, slogan.

pamer, mempamerkan show off; **pameran** exhibition.

pamflet pamphlet.

pamit ask leave to depart.

pamong teacher, educator.

pampang, terpampang stretching out before one's eyes.

pampas customary restitution for wounding.

pamur damascening on a creese; **berpamur** damascened.

pan grandmother.

panah archer's bow; **anak panah** arrow; **panah petir** thunderbolt; **panah lintar** lightning.

panakawan court pages.

panai = **fanak**.

panar amazed, agape.

panas hot (of fire, weather); **panas terik** torrid (of weather);

memanaskan to heat food etc; **kepanasan** heat.

panasaran inquisitive, eager to know.

panatik fanatic.

panau discoloured patches on skin.

panca five; multiple, varied; **panca indera** the five senses; **panca logam** alloy of several metals.

pancaka funeral pyre.

pancang stake; pile; **memancang** to drive in stakes.

pancar flowing out violently, gushing out; **kilat memancar** lightning flashing; **tempat pancaran** broadcasting station.

pancaragam orchestra.

pancaroba ill-wind.

pancarona multicolour.

panci little pan.

pancing, memancing to angle (for fish).

pancit I, memancit to emit a thin stream; **pancitkan** to inject.

pancit II punctured, leaking (of tyre).

pancung cutting off a projection; **memancung** to lop off; **pancungkan kepala** to behead.

pancuran pipe, hollow bamboo.

pancut, memancut to squirt out (of water); **pemancut** squirt.

pandai clever, skilled, versed in; craftsman; **pandai emas** goldsmith; **kepandaian** skill, cleverness.

pandak short; = **pendek**.

pandam to fix a gold or silver plate or vessel on a block of resin for engraving.

pandan generic name for fragrant screw-pine (used for basket or mat-making).

pandang, memandang to stare at, look at, heed; **selayang pandang** at a glance;

pandangan observation; view; **pemandangan** scene.

pandir, Pak Pandir old fool of Malay folklore.

pandita Hindu sage, scholar; *also* **pendita**.

pandu guide; **memandu** to guide; **pemandu** guide, pilot, driver; **panduan** reference; guidance.

panen harvest.

pangan tract of forest.

pangeran title for princes and nobles.

pangestu blessing.

panggak proud; to display (*to neighbours*); **pemanggak** things worn *or* put out for show.

panggang, memanggang roast on a spit; **roti panggang** toasted bread.

panggar platform for drying fish.

panggas frame with two up-rights for stocking firewood.

panggil, memanggil to call, summon, invite; **panggilan** summons, call.

panggu portion, share.

pangguk to prop.

panggul pelvis; hip; **memanggul** to shoulder arms,

panggung platform; stage; theatre; **seri panggung** star, leading actress; **bersila panggung** to sit cross-legged.

pangkah mark of a cross; caste mark; **punkah**; to defeat, trump.

pangkal start, origin, beginning, commencement; **pangkal lengan** upper arm; **pangkalan** pier.

pangkas, memangkas to trim to a level; **berpangkas** trimmed.

pangkat rank, standard; to run **pangkat** to lose rank; **berpangkat** possessed of rank, important.

pangking sleeping platform.

pangku, memangku to hold on lap; **pangkuan** lap; **pemangku** deputy.

pangkung to club, batter.

pangkur hoe.

panglima, panglima commander, executive officer, military leader; **Panglima Agung** Supreme Commander.

pangling to forget, fail to recognize.

panglong (*Chinese*) logging station.

pangok to raise the head.

pangonan pasture land.

pangsa compartment; segment of fruit; **rumah pangsa** block of flats; **berpangsa** in sections.

pangsai to defecate.

pangsi peg of top; = **paksi**.

pangur scraper.

pangus, memangus to breathe, spout (*of whales*).

pani, nibung pani tufts on a maize cob.

panik panic.

panir cheese.

panitia committee; = **jawatan-kuasa**.

panja figure of bloody hand carried in procession at Hassan-Husain celebrations.

panjak drummer in *makyong* troupe; *gamelan* player.

panjang long, lengthy; **umur panjang** long life; **sepanjang** all along; **panjangkan** to lengthen; **panjang lebar** in detail; **berpanjangan** continuous.

panjar payment in advance.

panjat, memanjat to climb (*tree, mast, ladders, but not hills*).

panji, panji-panji small triangular flag; ancient Javanese military grade.

panjut rough torch; illuminations; **panjut-panjut** long loose trousers.

pankerias pancreas.

pantai shore, beach.

pantak, memantak to drive in.

pantang prohibited thing; tabu; berpantang to abstain; berpantang daging not to eat meat; pantangan forbidden thing.

pantas active; pantas akal quick-witted; pantas tangan deft.

pantat posterior (of person); buttocks; main pantat to commit sodomy; pantat periuk bottom of pot.

pantau river fish; memantau to see, look at.

panti house, dwelling.

pantik, memantik to strike matches.

pantis, berpantis to use kohl or lipstick.

pantomim pantomime.

pantul, memantul to ricochet.

pantun rhyming quatrain with inner assonance; pantun berikat set of quatrains.

panus candle holder.

papa evil; destitute; kepapaan poverty.

papah, memapah to support a man walking; berpapah to be supported.

papak smooth; ayam papak combless cock without tail feathers.

papan plank; papan catur chessboard; papan batu school slate; muka papan shameless (fig).

papar flat (as hedge top); level; paparkan to set forth; recount, consider.

papas, memapas to remove or take off (clothes, mats); papas angin make headway against wind.

para shelf, rack; attic or framework raised above flooring; word introducing plurals; para pendengar (all) listeners.

paradoks paradox.

parafin paraffin.

paragraf paragraph.

parah serious (of wounds); critical (of illness).

parak separation; berparak divided; porak-parak to run off stumbling and tripping.

param—param medical embrocation used by women after confinement.

paramasastera grammar; = nahu.

paran direction; memarani to make for (place).

parang cleaver, chopper; memarang to chop, cut; ikan parang-parang wolf herring.

parap, memarap to strike hard.

paras looks, face; level; memaras to smooth out, plane (wood).

parasait parasite.

parau hoarse; see serak.

parewa rioter, Bohemian.

pari generic name for fish of the skate and ray type; sengat pari sting of the ray; ekor pari used for 'cat-o'-nine-tails': pari-pari fairy = peri.

parih, memarih to deal cards; cast dice.

paris—porak.

paris white cloth.

parit ditch, drain, canal; parit lindungan dug-out, shelter.

pariti parity.

pariwarta news.

parlimen parliament.

Parsi Persian.

parti party.

partikelir particular.

paruh beak, bill of bird; separuh half; separuh mati half-dead.

parun anvil.

parung—sari, keris parung sari wavy snake-like creese.

paru—paru lungs, gills.

parut scar; **berparut** scarred; **memarut** to scrape, rasp (*coconuts*).

parwah care, anxiety; **ambil parwah** to heed.

pas pass, licence; **to pass** (*examination*).

pasah, pasah nikah to annul marriage on wife's complaint.

pasak wooden peg, bolt, nail, wedge; axis; **pasak negeri** the old families, 'back-bone' of the country.

pasal=fasal.

pasalewa multicolour trousers.

pasang, air **pasang** incoming tide; **memasang** to adjust, fasten; light (*lamp*); fire (*gun*); **sepasang** pair; **sakit pasang-pasang** hernia.

pasanggerahan government rest house.

pasar market, bazaar; **bahasa pasar** bazaar Malay.

pasara=pasar market; *also* pusara.

pasat, terpasat, augin pasat trade winds.

pasi, pucat pasi very pale.

Pasifik Pacific Ocean.

pasin, sepasin caterpillar.

pasir sand; sandy beach; **busung pasir** dune, sandhill; **gula pasir** granular sugar.

pasisir, pesisir sands, shore.

paska Easter; Passover.

pasmat Spanish dollar.

pasmen gold *or* silver braid.

paspet passport.

passif,pasib passive.

pasti certainly.

pasu vase, flowerpot, wash-basin.

pasukan troop (*of soldiers etc*).

pasung, memasung to hand-cuff, fetter; **rumah pasung** lock-up; **pasungan** handcuffs.

patah broken fractured, snapped (*of rigid things only*); numerical coefficient for say-

ings, words; **patah lidah** speechless; **patah riuk** compound fracture; **mematahkan** to break.

patam ornamental edging.

patar rasp; **mematar** to smoothe with rasp.

patarwali plant.

pateri solder; **paterikan** to solder.

pati concentrated; cream of coconut milk; **gist** (*of news*).

patih obedient, docile.

patihah=fatihah.

patik I, me (*used by Malay to Ruler*).

patil small adze for planing *also* **kepatil.**

patin, ikan patin a large cat-fish.

pating large peg used for climbing trees.

patma, padma lotus.

patpat, main **patpat boys** game.

patuh, berpatuh obedient subservient; **mematuhi** to influence; **tidak berpatuh** un-manageable.

patuk, mematuk to peck.

patung image, statue, dummy; **belalang patung** dragon-fly; **ikan patung** a fresh water fish; **anak patung** doll.

patut proper, seemly; **fair** (*of decisions*); acceptable (*of views*); **dengan patut** properly; fairly; **mematutkan** to adjust fairly.

pauh wild mango.

pauk to hook; **lauk-pauk** all sorts of curried dishes.

paun pound, pen for cattle; pound sterling; pound of weight.

paung bread, Chinese biscuits.

paur sprout of young bamboo shoot.

paus I, ikan **paus** whale.

paus II pope.

paut to hook down, pull towards o.s.; **mamaut** to seize in both hands and pull; **berpaut pada** to cling to.

pavilion pavilion.

pawah, rempah pawah all sorts of spices; **pawahkan tanah** to give usufruct of land in return for part of crop.

pawai cortege, suite, train of raja.

pawaka fire.

pawana wind.

pawang magician (*expert in spells, talismans, drugs*).

pawat, payung pawat state umbrella on tall stick.

pawitra, air pawitra lustral water.

paya swamp, marsh; **paya kumbuh** reedy marsh.

payah difficult (*of work*); severe (*of illness*).

payang a type of fishing boat.

payar, perahu payar, pemayar patrol boat; **memayari** to patrol, cruise.

payau brackish; flavourless

payon roof, shed.

payu price, value; valuable; in demand.

payung umbrella; **payung cetera** canopy; **payung paku** head of nail; **memayungkan** to protect, shelter.

pebahu yardarm.

pebin octagonal top for gambling.

Februari = Februari.

pecah I smashed (*of crockery, eggs, glass etc*); broken open; **pecah belah** scattered; **berpecah** divided; **pecahan** broken piece, fraction, rupture; **memecahkan** to smash; solve.

pecah II kale.

pecak dented (*of ball, fruit*); destroyed (*of one eye*).

pecakari syringe.

pecal, memecal to massage; vegetable dish.

pecat, memecat to dismiss; **pecat diri** to resign.

pecok lame.

pecomberan cesspool.

pecun Chinese dragon festival.

pecus good, able, efficient.

pecut, memecut to whip up.

peda, anchovies pickled in brine.

pedada = berembang.

pedaka collar with pendants.

pedal, pedal ayam padlock.

pedanda Brahmin priest in Bali.

pedang sword, scythe; **memedang** to fight with swords; scythe grass.

pedap to absorb; **kertas pedap** blotting paper.

pedar rancid (*of oil*).

pedas hot (*as chillies*).

pedati cart, sledge; **pedati meriam** gun carriage.

pedato = pidatu.

pedeh smarting (*of cut, speech etc*).

pedena vat, urn.

pedendang gold *or* silver braid; **burung pedendang** masked finfoot.

pedengan screen, curtain, mask.

pedewak Bugis ship.

pedoman compass of ship; **ambil pedoman** to set a course; **berpedoman** to use a compass.

pedor lame (*from deformed shinbone*).

pedu, empedu gall.

pedukang, ikan pedukang valuable catfish.

peduli, feduli to care, heed.

podusi woman; **= padusi**.

peduta envoy, ambassador.

pegaga, daun pegaga creeping herb put to many medicinal uses.

pegal stiff (*of limbs*).

pegan, terpegan silent and bewildered.

pegang, memegang to grasp, hold (person, things, words); berpegang kepada to hold to; pemegang handrail.

pegar, ayam pegar crested pheasant.

pegas spring (of clock).

pegat, memegat to intercept (enemy); = mengadang.

pegawai official; pegawai daerah district officer.

peguam lawyer; see guam.

pegun, terpegun speechless, silent for a moment.

pehak = pihak.

pejajaran evil spirit, devil, villain.

pejal firm (of flesh); hard (of stone); pejalkan to press earth down tight.

pejalwapan condensation.

pejam, memejamkan to close the eye.

pejar incessant (of rain).

pejera sights on gun.

pejuh = pejar.

peka responsive, sensitive; memeka to heed.

pekaca lotus; ratna pekaca jewel of the lotus (term of endearment).

pekak I deaf; not ringing (of coins); pekak badak, stone-deaf.

pekak II knave in cards; anise.

pekaka, burung pekaka kingfisher; guru pekaka, assistant teacher.

pekam safety brake.

pekan a small town; market; week; bunga pekan jasmin(e).

pekap to cover (mouth or ear) with hand.

pekapur tiny box for lime.

pekarangan compound of house.

pekasam fish, shellfish or meat pickled in brine.

pekat thick (of gravy etc); concentrated; (of coffee) strong; dark.

pekatu, bedil pekatu cannon.

pekatul flour from broken grains of rice.

pekau, terpekau yelling, screaming.

pekek, memekek to scream; terpekek-pekek screaming without stopping.

pekerja worker.

pekerma honorific in titles.

pekerti character, disposition.

pekin, terpekin thoughtful, pondering.

peking, memeking to whine.

pekis angry, irritable.

pekiwan urinal, privy.

pekojan quarter of town for Indian merchants.

pekong joss; idol.

pekpa cancer; kayap pekpa carbuncle on back or neck.

peku a thousand (cents, men).

pekuk malformed (of limb).

pekula lotus.

pekulun your highness, sire.

pekung foul ulcer.

pekup claw-shaped from rheumatism (of hand).

pekur = tefekur.

pel mop; pill.

pelabur investor.

peladang farmer; see ladang.

pelaga, buah pelaga cardamom; ikan pelaga fighting fish.

pelahan, terpelahang wide open (as door).

pelahap gluttonous.

pelajar student, learner; pelajaran learning, education, lesson.

pelak I mottled.

pelak II evil spirit, evil influence.

pelakun actor, actress.

pelalah ravenous.

pelalauan notice to trespassers.

pelaling, ikan pelaling horse mackerel.

pelamin bridal dais, marriagebed.

pelampang shed for a feast.

pelampung float (for line, net).

pelana saddle; **berpelana** saddled.

pelancar joist (for floors); launcher.

pelancit, terpelancit squirting (out of pipe).

pelancung tourist.

pelanduk mouse deer.

pelang I coloured stripe in sarung; **berpelang** striped.

pelang II old type of boat.

pelangah, terpelangah set wide open.

pelangi rainbow.

pelangking litter.

pelantar gangway; platform; staging; bench.

pelantik = belantik.

pelanting, terpelanting sent rolling (of coconuts, footballs); **terpelanting** rolling.

pelapah skinner; = pelepah.

pelas, memelas to splice (ropes).

pelasari climbing plant with scent.

pelastik plastic.

pelasuh idler.

pelat I gramophone record.

pelat II faulty of pronunciation, of dialect (as a child).

pelata, ikan pelata mackerel.

pelatinam platinum.

pelatuk = belatuk.

pelatut idler.

pelau vain, unsuccessful, unrewarded.

pelbagai of various kinds; **mempelbagaikan** to diversify.

pelbaya executioner.

peleceh flatterer.

pelecet, terpelecet squirting out.

pelecok, terpelecok sprained (of ankle, wrist).

pelekat I placard; gum.

pelekat II, kain pelekat sarung from Pulicat.

pelekuh, terpelekuh humped (of back).

pelekuk, terpelekuk bent; sprained (of ankle).

pelembap, sepelembap breadth of hand.

pelengak, terpelengak dumbfounded.

pelengan temples (of forehead).

pelepah palm frond.

peles, pelis tiny (scent) bottle.

pelesat, terpelesat rolling some distance.

peleset, terpeleset slipping; = gelincir.

pelesit woman's familiar spirit in shape of vampire cricket.

pelet = pelat; bird-line.

peleting weaver's spool; pilfer.

peletok, terpeletok twisted (of neck).

pelihara, memelihara to breed animals; bring up child, look after; **pemelihara** breeder; **pemeliharaan** breeding, maintenance.

pelik remarkable, difficult, abnormal (of person).

pelimbahan cesspool.

pelindis roller.

pelindung shelterer, protector.

pelinggam, batu pelinggam alabaster; marble.

pelinteng catapult.

pelipatan, pelipatan lutut hollow behind knee.

pelipir kitchen.

pelipis temples (of forehead).

pelipit seam.

pelir penis.

pelisau slovenly.

peliser ribbon.

pelit stingy.

pelita lamp; pelita duduk standing lamp.

pelitik screw.

pelohong having large hole, gaping.

pelojok corner (*of room*).

pelomok to break fowl's neck.

pelonggol stake, stump.

pelontang any float to hold up line *or* net in water.

pelopor leader, pioneer.

pelor = peluru bullet.

pelosok corner, nook.

pelosot, terpelosot fallen (*of prices*).

pelowap condense.

pelu impotent (*of male*).

peluang lull after storm; chance, opportunity.

pelubong concealed pit trap for beast.

pelubor rice bin.

peluh sweat; **berpeluh** to perspire.

peluit siren, whistle.

peluk, memeluk to embrace; **berpeluk tubuh** to fold one's arms; **sepemeluk** armful.

peluncur glider.

pelung bent, warped, dented; **ikan pelung** grey mullet.

pelupuh bamboo wattlework; **melupuh** to beat bamboo flat and split for flooring.

pemabuk drunkard.

pemadat opium addict.

pemajangan bridal bed.

pemajikan = majikan.

pemakal caulking.

pemalam plug for leak, cork for bottle.

pemali tabu (*of forbidden act*).

pemalut wrapper; *see* **pembalut**.

pemanas hot-tempered person.

pemancar radio transmitter.

pemangku in an acting capacity, deputy.

pemanis spell for beauty.

pemara second compartment in fish trap.

pemarip singer of lullabies for royal infants.

pemarit grapnel (*to recover sunken object*).

pematah proverb; **=pepatah**.

pematang raised path, causeway, embankment; **=permatang**.

pematung bamboo conduit.

pemayang large fishing boat; drag net.

pembabar screen to drive fish.

pembakal initiator; embryo.

pembarep eldest born.

pembaris ruler (*for drawing lines*).

pembayan brother- *or* sister-in-law.

pembesar official, dignitary.

pembohong liar.

pemborong contractor; wholesaler.

pemelak clown, buffoon.

pemengkul post at outer angles of compartment in fish trap.

pemerentis surveyor's trace.

pemerhati observer.

pemidang frame for stretching cloth for embroidery.

pemilik owner.

pemimpin guide, leader.

pemimpit whistle to decoy deer.

peminang money *or* present clinching engagement to marry.

peminggir boundary.

pemirah timid person.

pemodal capitalist.

pemparang, ikan pemparang herring.

pemuka leader (*of party*).

pemukat fisherman using net.

pemulas corkscrew.

pemulih restoring; restorative.

pemungut collector.

pemuntal headcloth.

pemuras blunderbuss, muzzle loader.

pemutar screwdriver; winch.

pena I, tali pena breast rope in elephant harness.

pena II pen.

penabur pellets, shot.

penadah bamboo shute trap fixed in weir.

penaga ironwood, Indian rose chestnut.

penagak lasting (of goods).

penagan gambler's stake.

penahap corner; quarter of globe.

penaja starter of any movement or work (esp weaving); sponsor.

penajur line of stakes to drive fish into trap.

penak, anak penak children and grandchildren; = pinak.

penaka if, supposing; like, resembling.

penakan, anak penakan nephew, niece; bapa penakan uncle.

penakawan raja's suite.

penal panel.

penala tuning fork.

penalu mistletoe; = bendalu.

penambak bund, buttress.

penampan tray.

penampang transverse section.

penanak, sepenanak as long as it takes rice to boil.

penangan bruise from blow with fist.

penanggahan palace kitchen; temporary kitchen house.

penanggalan calendar; vampire consisting of head and entrails.

penara, penara bukit plateau.

penaram fish or prawn paste.

penasaran resentful.

penat tired, fatigued; berpenat-penat to take pains.

penatu laundryman.

penawar antidote.

pencak art of self-defence; memencak to practise art of self-defence; = silat.

pencalak steel pounder of betel nut crusher.

pencalang Bugis trading ship.

pencang askew; pencang-pencut all awry.

pencar, berpencar-pencar to scatter (of troops); diverge.

pencaus hotel.

pencerut tight band.

pencil, terpencil isolated, segregated; memencilkan to isolate, avoid.

penda, penda-memenda to amend (bill in council); right; **pendaan** amendment; also pinda

pendahan javelin.

pendam to plant, bury, conceal; terpendam buried, concealed.

pendap, memendapkan to keep concealed.

pendapa hall.

pendapur frame of wood round Malay grave.

pendar I phosphorescence; light of fireflies; berpendar shimmering; seeing stars before eyes.

pendar II, berpendar to whirl, rotate, be giddy.

pendaram prawns or fish fried in flour.

pendaringan large rice jar.

pendek short; pendeknya in short; pendekkan to shorten; abridge.

pendekar expert at the art of self-defence (Malay); champion.

pendendang, burung pendendang masked finfoot.

penderah magical (of creeses).

pendiat elephant corral.

pending large waist-buckle.

pendipun, baju pendipun coat decorated with design in gold leaf or gilt paper.

pendua duplicate; keris pendua second creese.

penduk metal casing of creese sheath.

penembahan ruler to whom homage (*sembah*) is paid.

pengantin bride *or* bridegroom.

pengap shut up, stuffy; to conceal (*in one's heart*); bottle (*fish*).

pengapuh, layar pengapuh topsail.

pengar dizzy (*from blow*).

pengaruh influence, authority; **berpengaruh** influential.

pengasam acid cleaner.

pengat fruit cooked in coconut milk and sugar.

pengatu, bedil pengatu cannon.

pengawinan spearmen.

pengembar wide-meshed screen to frighten fish into net.

pengemis beggar, mendicant.

pengeran title of nobility in Java and Brunei; = **pangeran**.

pengeras present to a *pawang*.

pengerek awl.

penggaga creeper whose leaves are eaten as vegetables.

penggal part of book; school term; **berpenggal-penggal** in sections; **memenggalkan** to cut off; cut into sections.

penggawa, Dato' Penggawa Kelantan headman.

penghulu headman of small district; **balai penghulu** headman's court.

pengilir basket fish trap.

pengit, hangit-pengit smelling musty, sweaty, scorched; loud noise in ears.

pengkalan jetty; *see* pangkal; (*military*) base.

pengkar bow-legged.

pengkul curved, crooked; **memengkul** to turn aside; to wind (*road*).

pengsan unconscious; = **pingsan**; **terpengsan** to faint.

penguin penguin.

pengulun His Highness.

pening giddy, dizzy.

penisilin penicillin.

peniti pin.

penjahit seamstress.

penjajap Bugis warship.

penjalin strip of bamboo for making screens.

penjan tubers *or* bananas dipped in boiling sugar.

penjara prison; **penjarakan** to imprison.

penjong to project.

penjul balance in smal' change.

penjurit raider, robber, warrior.

penjuru angle, corner; **pepenjuru** diagonal.

penomah bridegroom's contribution to his bride's parents towards cost of wedding feast.

penoman gun sight; = **pedoman**.

pensil pencil.

penta, berpenta-penta in numbers, quantities.

pental, terpental to fall sprawling.

pentar weak (*of voice*).

pentas platform on posts; broad hanging wall-shelf.

pentil to twang guitar.

penting important.

pentul knob; **pentulan** party leader.

pentung club; **mementong** to club.

penuh full, complete; **penuh sesak** chock-full, congested; **memenuhi** to fill.

penyangak pilferer, sneak thief.

penyangku broken.

penyanyi singer.

penyap to conceal; vanished.

penyauk angler's landing scoop.

penyek flattened, snub (*of nose*).

penyelam diver.

penyengat wasp.

penyu green turtle; **penyu karah** hawksbill turtle.

peon, piun orderly, errand boy.

pepah, memepah to lash out.

pepak, penuh pepak chockful; masticate.

pepaku, burung pepaku red-wattled lapwing.

pepas, memepas to fly-fish; **pepas dibelanga** fish in one's cooking pot.

pepat cut level (of teeth); **memepat** pollarded (of trees); **penuh pepat** chockfull.

pepatah adage, maxim, saying.

pepaya papaya.

pepe sweetmeat of banana and flour.

pepek to have side bet at game.

peper, memeper to edge away; be blown off its course.

pepes fish spiced and roasted.

pepet the mark over 'e': taling.

pepuah frizzy-haired; Papuan.

pepuju womb.

peputut disciple of Hindu ascetic.

pepuyu, ikan pepuyu climbing perch.

per spring of watch; electric lamp.

perabu prince; **perabuan** majesty; palace.

perabung ridge of Malay house.

perabut appurtenances, furniture.

peracut large boil; parachute.

perada gold or silver tinsel.

peraga, memperagakan to show off (clothes); see **raga**.

peragawati fashion model.

perah, memerah to squeeze (juice out of fruit); **kambing**

perah milch goat; **pemerahan** milking.

perahu boat, ship; **berperahu** by boat, on ship.

perai, berperai-perai scattering (of crowds); crumbling (of bread).

perajurit warrior; see **penjurit**.

perak I startled (of cattle, deer); **perak siang** daybreak.

perak II silver; **perak asam** alloyed silver.

peraka hatch of ship.

peraktis practice.

peram, memeram to keep fruit till ripe; **berperam** fermented, cooped up.

perambut, tali perambut catgut between fishing line and hook.

peran clown (eg in makyung and menora shows); **peranan** role, function.

perancah skeleton framework of wooden house.

perancang programme, plan, design, draft.

Perancis French.

perancit to skim stone along surface of water; **terperancit** spattered (of water).

perancut spattered.

perang I war, fighting; **berperang** to be at war; **perang-an** warfare, state of war.

perang II brown (tea-colour) (of hair).

perangai disposition; **berperangai jahat** having bad character.

peranggang, ayam peranggang tender chicken big enough to roast.

Peranggi European.

peranggu, seperanggu set of buttons; suit of clothes.

perangkap trap (for birds, small animals).

perangko postage stamp; franked, post-free.

peranja tiered benches in theatre.

peranjar platform for big game hunter in jungle, scaffolding.

peranjat, terperanjat startled.

peranti apparatus, machine.

peranyak, terperanyak flopping down from astonishment.

perap, memerap to dart and peck; nag and intrude; keep article shut up.

perapatan crossroads.

perapus breaker of crockery.

peras, memeras to squeeze out (juice, fruit); **perasan** extraction; **pemeras** extortioner; **pemerasan** extortion.

perasejarah prehistoric.

perat rancid (of oil); = **tengik**.

perata pastry; = **roti canai**.

perawan maiden, virgin.

perawas plant with aromatic leaves.

perawis ingredient, component.

perbahasa, peribahasa idiomatic saying, maxim.

perbani, bulan perbani waxing moon.

perca, perca kain rag; **getah perca** gutta percha.

percaya to trust, believe; **kepercayaan** trusty, reliable; **surat kepercayaan** credentials.

percik drop; drops; **memercik** to be sprinkled; **memercikkan** to sprinkle; **percikan** drops.

percit spurting out (of water).

percul, tepercul protruding (of animal's head).

percuma in vain; gratis.

perdah handle of adze; large adze for planing.

perdana, perdana menteri prime minister.

perdata cautious, accurate.

perdi to deal cards.

perdu base of tree trunk; **seperdu** clump.

perdus, teperdus pot-bellied, big.

pereh, terpereh 'done in', staggering.

perekat gum, glue, cement.

perem frame.

pereman civilian; = **periman**.

perempuan woman, wife.

perencah, buat perencah to clarify soup etc by boiling prawn shells in it.

pereng stinking.

perengau gaping (as wound).

perenggan boundary.

perentah order, direction; **memerentah** to rule; **pemerentah** government; controller; **pemerentahan** administration, government.

perepat tall mangrove swamp tree.

perewah spices, ingredients.

pergam Green Imperial Pigeon.

perganda propaganda.

pergar serow.

pergat frigate.

pergedel meat pie.

pergi to go; **pemergian** journey.

pergok, memergok to come across.

pergul gilding.

peri I situation; **perihal** concerning.

peri II word; **tiada terperi** beyond words.

peri III fairy.

peria edible gourd.

periai nobleman.

perian large section of bamboo used as water vessel.

periang auspicious moment or season.

periap deceitful.

peridi prolific (of animals).

perigi well; **perigi buta** disused well.

perih = **pedeh** severe, smarting (of wound).

periksa examination; **me-**

meriksa to examine; **kena periksa** to be examined.

periman civilian; **pakaian periman** mufti; = **pereman**.

perimbon astrological tables.

perimpin bolt-rope, rope edging to sail.

perimitih, perimitif, primitif primitive.

perincat, burung **perincat** finch.

perincip principle.

perincis to allocate small portions.

perincit sun-bird.

perindu, buluh **perindu** bamboo with slits cut in it, emitting musical notes.

Peringgi Portuguese.

peringkat grade level, rank; **peringkat awal** primary.

perinsip principle.

perisa delicious.

perisai shield, armour; **kereta perisai** armoured car.

periskop periscope.

peristiwa historical fact; episode.

perit I pricking; panas perit **tingling** (of heat).

perit II finch; also peret.

periuk earthenware pot for cooking; **periuk api** bomb; **periuk kera** pitcher-plant.

perizam prism.

perkakas apparatus, equipment; **perkakas perang** munitions of war.

perkara affair, matter.

perkasa valiant, gallant.

perkuku, ikan **perkuku sea** bream.

perkuku barred grounddove.

perlahan slow, quiet, gentle.

perlak varnished.

perlan to swallow greedily.

perlang glittering; = **cemerlang**.

perlenteh fast, profligate; idle.

perli to tease, mimic.

perling sparkling (of eyes).

perlip enamoured.

perlu obligatory (for Muslims), necessary; **keperluan** necessity.

perlus slipping through; **memperluskan** to slip finger.

perlut slipping (of knot).

permai pretty, beautiful.

permaidani carpet.

permaisura king of lower rank than his consort.

permaisuri queen of lower rank than her lord, any queen.

permana, tidak terpermanai incalculable (of numbers).

permanen permanent.

permata jewel, gem.

permatang dune, sandhill, bund, ridge.

permen peppermint.

permisi permission to depart.

pernah at one time, ever; tidak pernah never.

pernama full (of moon); bulan pernama full moon.

peras glass or earthenware bowl.

perofail profile.

perogram programme.

perogresib progressive.

perohong, terperohong gaping (of wound).

perojek project.

peroksid peroxide.

perompak pirate.

peronggah to use filthy language.

peronyok to crumple; terperonyok crumpled.

perosok, terperosok to slip, fall into hole; be sunken (of eyes).

perotin protein; protin.

perpatih chief legendary founder of Minangkabau law.

persaah (newspaper) article.

persangga parasang (about 3½ miles).

persegi = **segi**.

persekot advance of money.

persen per cent; *also* peratus.

persero partner, shareholder.

persetua, sekali persetua once upon a time.

persih clean, bright; = bersih.

persik peach.

persil, terpersil to protrude (*of eyes*).

perspektip perspective.

pertala magic steed.

pertama first; **yang pertama** first; **pertama-tama** at the very first.

pertanda executioner.

pertiwi the earth.

peruak, terperuak agape (*of wounds*).

peruan yard of mast *or* flagpole.

peruang to cleanse corpse for burial; **cincin peruang** ring given to cleanser.

perui dry and crumbling (*as flour*).

peruk to stuff into.

perum sounding lead; **buang perum** to leave lead.

perumah proper, seemly.

perun, puntung perun charred wood; **memerun** to collect and burn trunks and branches left charred after previous burn.

perunggu bronze.

perunjung, seperunjung distance from fingers with arms stretched high above head down to toes.

perus surly, crusty.

perusa domineering; **memerusa** to compel, force.

perusuh grumbler; bad-tempered; rioter.

perut stomach, womb; **perut kapal** ship's hold.

perwara court damsels, ladies.

perwira heroic warrior, officer.

pesa beam in loom for woven cloth.

pesai, berpesai-pesai crumbling, scaling off.

pesak gusset (*to widen skirt or coat* &c).

pesaka = pusaka.

pesam warm; **pesam-pesam kuku** tepid, lukewarm.

pesan commission, order, message; **memesan** to order (*articles*).

pesanggerahan government rest house.

pesantren house for students of religion

pesara market; = pasar.

pesat quick, quickly prospering.

pesawat apparatus, tool, machinery; **pesawat terbang** aeroplane.

peseban passage round dais in palace audience hall; **verandah** to palace audience hall.

pesek pug (*of noses*).

peser half a cent.

peshen fashion.

pesiar, besiar to stroll.

pesimis pessimist.

pesing stinking (*as urinals*).

pesirah Palembang tribal headman.

pesisir sands, shore.

pesolot creek.

pesona slander, calumny; enchantment; **kena pesona** spellbound.

pesong, terpesong to change direction, alter course.

pespektib perspective.

pessimis pessimist.

pesta feast, festival; **berpesta** to feast.

pestaka = pustaka.

pesti sure, convincing; = pasti.

pesuk perforated; **berpesuk-pesuk** having holes.

peta chart, map; **peta angin** weather chart; **petakan** to draw, sketch.

petah eloquent (*of speech*).

petai, buah petai stinking edible bean.

petak section (*of area or cube*); plot.

petala stratum; one of the seven tiers of heaven and of earth in Muslim cosmology.

petaling small hardwood tree.

petam bridal headband.

petamari fast ship with one or two masts.

petang afternoon, evening.

petani farmer, agriculturist.

petar, memetar to train gun on.

petaram large fishing net.

petarang fishing net.

petas fire crackers.

petek I, memetek to pluck, play (*guitar*); switch on.

petek II, ikan petek-petek sea perches.

petong, kepetengan village guard.

peterana platform for princes in ruler's audience chamber.

peteras arrogant conceit.

peteri=pateri solder.

peterum, ubat peterum cartridge powder.

peti box; peti besi iron safe.

petia to mark down, take notice of.

petiban, petiban sampir bridal gift.

petiman steamer for rice.

peting to flick small object with thumb; terpeting-peting swaggering.

petinggi headman.

petir thunderclap; memetir crashing of thunder.

petis thick extract from juice of boiled prawns.

petitih maxim, saying.

petola, petola ular snake gourd; petola manis dish-rag gourd.

petolul procuress.

petor factory agent.

petua=fatwa.

petung, petung-petung carnivorous freshwater fish.

peturun, harimau peturun black panther.

petut lame.

petutu, ikan petutu carp.

pi=pergi to go; counter for Chinese gambling.

piagam record; Piagam Atlantic Atlantic Charter.

piak strip (*of paper*).

pial cock's wattle; gills of hen; memial to twist ear.

piala glass phial, goblet, prize cup.

pialang to buy through agent whom one repays.

pialing, burung pialing little Malay parrot.

piama rice planting season.

pianggang green rice bug.

piano piano.

piantan auspicious or usual time; piantan hujan usual time for rain.

piari, kuntum piari clitoris.

piarit flash spear with double barb.

pias strip (*of cloth, land*).

piat, memiat to twist (*ear*); descendant of fifth and sixth generation.

piatu parentless; motherless; anak piatu orphan.

piawai correct; gantang yang piawai bushel measure that is true.

pica, terpica dawdling, careless.

picik too small (*of space, room*).

picin to close eye; terpicin-picin blinking.

picit, memicit to massage by squeezing.

picu trigger of gun.

pidana, hukum pidana criminal law.

pidatu, pidato speech; harangue.

pidi, memidi to throw (*marbles*).

pigmen pigment.

pigura picture, portrait.

pihak, pehak side, party, direction; **bagi pihak** on behalf of.

pijak, pijak-pijak pedal, treadle; **memijak** to trample; **terpijak** accidentally step on.

pijar borax (used by goldsmith for melting solder); **merah pijar** fiery red; **memijar** glow green and blue (of flames).

pijat bed bug; **ikan pijat-pijat** sea bream.

pikat stinging horsefly; **memikat** snare birds; **pemikat** fowler; **terpikat** snared.

pikau, terpikau dazed from sleep, shouting from nightmare; **blue-breasted quail.**

piket picket.

pikul, sepikul 100 katis; **memikul** to carry heavy burden over shoulder.

pilek cold, catarrh.

pili, pili air water tap, standpipe, hydrant.

pilih, memilih to choose; **pemilih** chooser; **pilihan** picked (of person); **pilihanraya** election.

pilin, memilin to twist (fibre into cord); **berpilin** twisted.

pilis mark smeared or stuck on forehead to cure headache.

pilong blind.

pilu sorrowful, anxious; **memilukan** to move, affect; ship; also **pilau**.

pilus sweetmeat of glutinous rice eaten with syrup.

pimpin, berpimpin tangan going hand in hand; **memimpin** to guide; **pimpinan** guidance; **pemimpin** leader.

pimping grass.

pimpong pingpong.

pinak, anak pinak descendant.

pinang areca nut palm; **pinang raja** sealing wax palm; **meminang** to send areca nut to ask in marriage, court; **meminangkan** to betroth daugh-

ter; **ikan pinang-pinang** sea bream.

pinar, pinar emas embroidered with gold thread.

pinas cargo boat.

pincang lame temporarily; unequal (of undertakings).

pincuk fruit or vegetable cooked in sugar and fish paste.

pindah, berpindah to remove oneself; **memindahkan** darah to transfuse blood; **pindahkan** to transport, transfer; **pemindahan** removal, transfer.

pindai, memindai to gaze at.

pindang fish cooked as soup.

pinga, terpinga-pinga dumbfounded, bewildered.

pingai cream-coloured, white; **burung pingai** bird of life.

pingat medal.

pinggan porcelain plate; **pinggan mangkuk** crockery.

pinggang waist; **buah pinggang** kidneys; **tali pinggang** waist belt; **dayung pinggang** oars amidship.

pinggir border (of country); **edge** (of cloth).

pinggul buttock.

pingit, berpingit to be secluded; **memingit** to confine, sequester.

pingkal, terpingkal-pingkal to laugh uproariously.

pingkir beggared, without money.

pinjam, meminjam to borrow; **beri pinjam, pinjamkan** to lend; **pinjaman** loan.

pinjul small change left out of bigger sum paid over; swollen, bumpy.

pinta request; to request; **meminta** to ask for; **permintaan** request.

pintal, berpintal twisted (of strands); **memintal** to twist; **pemintal** spinning wheel.

pintang, hilang pintang completely lost.

pintar clever, sharp; **kepintaran** cleverness; **burung pintar** weaverbird; *also* **pintar pintau.**

pintas at a glance; **memintas** to take a short cut; **pintasan** short cut.

pintau, burung pintau weaverbird; = **tempua.**

pintu doorway, door; **pintu air** sluice-gate; **pintu gerbang** gate.

pinuh bin used in rice field

pionir pioneer.

pipi cheek; **lesung pipi** dimple.

pipih thin and flat; **cacing pipih** tapeworm.

pipis to grind (*curry stuffs*); **burung terbang** dipipiskan **lada** while the bird is on the wing the pepper is being crushed.

pipit finch, sparrow; **pipit padang** Malay pipit; **pipit pinang** spotted munia; **pipit uban** white-headed munia.

pirai, penyakit angin pirai gout, rheumatism.

piramid pyramid.

pirau grey; **berpirau-pirau** to zigzag, make detour

Piraun, Firaun Pharaoh.

pirih severe (*of illness*).

pirik, memirik to crush fine (*of spices*).

piring saucer.

piru, ayam piru guinea fowl.

pirus turquoise; = **perus.**

pisah, berpisah to part from one another, separate; **pisahkan** to put asunder, segregate.

pisang banana; **pisang sesikat** row of bananas; **ikan pisang-pisang** sun bream.

pisau knife; **pisau cukur** razor; **pisau lipat** clasp knife; **burung pisau raut** heron.

pisik = **fizik** physics.

pisit, memisit to interrogate; **pisit-pisit** to keep cross-examining.

piskal sheriff.

pistol pistol.

pit Chinese brush pen; **pit-pit** chirp.

pita tape, ribbon.

pitah = **petah.**

pitam vertigo; **pitam babi** epilepsy; **naik pitam** to become dizzy.

piting = **kepiting** crab.

pitis very small coin with hole in centre.

pitpit, burung pipit brain-fever bird.

pitrah = **fitrah.**

pitu seven.

piuh, terpiuh knotted (*of coils, roots, problems*); **piuh pilin** twisted and knotted; to contort.

piun, peon office boy, errand boy.

piut descendant of fourth generation.

piutang money due to one, credit; **hutang piutang** debts and credits.

planit planet.

plasma plasm.

plastik plastic.

plot plot.

po Chinese dice box; **tikam po** stake when dicing with it.

pocok corner.

poho peppermint.

pohon tree; stem; origin, source; **pohon kayu** tree; **pohonkan** to ask for, solicit.

pokah broken; **memokah** to break.

pokeng tailless (*of fowls*).

pokeri blackguard, rogue.

pokok tree; stem; origin; cause; principal; **pokok nyior** coconut tree; **pokok cerita** plot of tale; **harga pokok** cost price; **wang pokok** capital.

pokrol advocate.

pokta peerless, pre-eminent.

polang-paling veering.

poleng check (*pattern*).

polis police; **badan polis** constabulary.

polisi policy; police.

politik politic.

politikus politician.

polok, memolok to guzzle, gorge.

polong familiar spirit in form of cricket.

polos plain, unpatterned (*of fabric*).

pompa squirt, syringe, hose; *see* **bomba**.

pompang Chinese purse net for small fish.

pompong small inedible cuttlefish; **kepompong** chrysalis, cocoon.

pondar short and stout.

pondik conceited.

pondok hut, shed; school and lodgings for students of religion.

pondong shelter to protect young plants; = **pondok**.

ponen hermaphrodite who passes as female.

pongah cocky.

pongkang large piece of cut wood; upside down (*of curtain*).

pongking lifted (*of posterior*).

pongkis flat open basket for carrying earth.

pongoh conceited.

pongpong, burung pongpong fluffy-backed babbler.

pongsu anthill; = **busut pusu**.

ponok hump (*of Indian bull*).

pontang-panting to run helter-skelter; **berpontang-panting** tumbling down.

pontianak vampire ghosts of women dead in childbed.

ponting to bilk, cheat, play truant.

pontoh royal ceremonial armlets; **pontoh naga** large armlet for prince; **pontoh ular lidi** narrow armlet for his consort.

ponu bride.

popi dolls, images.

popok, kain popok baby's napkin, diaper.

popor butt of gun.

populer popular.

porak, porak-parik scattered (*of goods*); in disorder.

porok half coconut shell used in child's game.

poros axle of wheel.

pos sound of air escaping from hole *or* nostril; post, mail.

positip positive.

potensi potential.

potlot pencil.

potong to slice, cut; **memotong** to cut off; **ikan sepotong** slice of fish; **potongan** cut; **berpotong-potong** in slices.

potret portrait, photograph.

poyang great-grandfather *or* -mother; **pupu poyang** distant cousins.

poyot great-great-grandparents.

pramugari air hostess.

pramuka scout; *also* **pengakap**.

prasangka prejudice.

premium premium.

presiden president.

prosa prose.

prospektus prospectus.

protokol protocol.

puadai cloth spread for ruler *or* bride *or* bridegroom to walk on.

puak family, group, party; **berpuak-puak** in parties.

puaka nature spirit of place; **berpuaka** haunted.

pual, berpual to eddy (*of smoke*); bubble up (*of water*).

pualam marble, alabaster.

puan large silver *or* wooden betel caddy carried for rulers *or* bridegrooms; = **perempuan** (*in titles*) lady.

puar wild ginger; **berpuar** to fight mimic battle in rice fields with **puar** stems to expel evil spirits.

puas satisfied, sated; **puas hati** content; **sepuas-puasnya** to one's heart's content; **memuaskan** to satisfy.

puasa fast; **bulan puasa** Ramadan; **berpuasa** to fast.

puasara = **pasara**.

pucang areca nut palm; = **pinang**.

pucat pale; **pucat lesi pale and sickly; **memucat** to turn pale.

puci teapot.

pucik two main posts at entrance to large marine fish traps.

pucuk shoot (of plant); top twigs; **pucuk rebung** bamboo shoot; classifier for needles, letters etc, eg **jarum sepucuk** one needle.

pucung, **burung pucung** dusky-grey heron; **pucung hitam** black bittern.

pudar dim, obscure.

pudi, podi tiny gems; **intan pudi** tiny diamonds.

pudina, daun pudina mint.

puding, **pokok puding** garden croton; pudding.

pudur to extinguish (of fire).

pugar fit; hard; taut; well; recovered; **memugar** to rehabilitate.

puing ruin of house.

puja, **memuja** to worship idols; **pujaan** Hindu rituals.

pujang blind man's buff played in dark.

pujangga author, scholar, thinker.

puji, **memuji** to praise, commend; **memuji-muji** to flatter; **terpuji** commendable; famous; **puji-pujian** compliments.

pujuk = **bujuk** to coax.

pujut, **memujut** to strangle.

pukal solid (of metal); **bayar pukal** to pay lump sum; **emas pukal** solid gold.

pukang fork (of body); **memukang** to cut up joints; **lari lintang-pukang** to run headlong.

pukas vulva; **berpukas** to talk obscenities; **berpukas-pukasan** to bathe nude.

pukat large fishing net, seine net; **pukat cina** seine with pocket; **memukat** to fish with seine; **pemukat** fisherman.

pukau narcotic burnt by burglars to drug to sleep the inmates of house; **kena pukau** to be so drugged.

pukul vulva, pudendum muliebre.

pukul, **memukul** to hit, beat, hammer; **pukul gambar** to photograph; **pukul taligeram** to telegraph; **pukul rata** to strike an average; **pukul berapa?** what is the time?

pula also, likewise, again; **demikian pula** and so once more; **siapa pula?** who then?; **mengapa pula?** why then?

pulai large tree with milky sap.

pulan well-cooked but not soft (of rice).

pulang to return, go home, go back; **memulangkan** to give back, restore.

pulas, **memulaskan** to twist, wring; **pemulas** corkscrew.

pulasan fruit closely resembling the rambutan.

pulasari = **pelasari**.

pulau island, isolated piece of rising ground (in sea, river, swamp); **pulaukan** to boycott, isolate.

puli, **berpuli-puli** rubbing legs together.

pulih restored to original condition; **pulang pulih** to be back to normal health; **memulihkan** to restore to original state.

pulpa pulp.

puluh ten; **tiga puluh** thirty; **perpuluhan** decimal.

pulun, **memulun** to crumple or bunch up; **kain berpulun-**

pulun, memulun sarung gathered up in folds.

pulung, memulung to roll (cigarette).

pulur pith; =empulur.

pulut, padi pulut sweet glutinous rice.

pumpun marine worm used as bait; pumpunkan to gather together, collect; terpumpun collected.

pun even, also, too; itu pun that also; even so; sekalipun although; adapun now, also, too.

punah, terpunah utterly destroyed, lost, vanished; memunah wasted.

punai pigeon, dove.

punat core of boil.

punca outer end (of rope etc); punca pengetahuan first stage knowledge, primer.

puncak acme, top (of hill); memuncak to rise steeply, climax.

punci what luck!

pundak shoulder.

pundi, pundi-pundi purse; pundi-pundi kecing urinary bladder.

punding tangled (of string etc).

pung plump, plop.

pungah conceited.

punggah, memunggah to unload; tukang punggah stevedore.

punggal, memunggal to hurl stone.

pungguk, burung pungguk Malayan hawk owl.

punggung buttocks; punggung pisau back of knife.

punggur dead tree stump.

pungkah large piece cut off.

pungkur=punggung buttocks; tulang pungkur pubic bone.

pungut, anak pungut adopted child; memungut to adopt,

pick, collect; pungutan collection; pemungut collector.

puni small iron bucket.

punjung arbour, summerhouse.

punjut to gather up and tie (at top of bundle etc); memunjut to swell to head.

puntal, berpuntal-puntal coiled, wound (as ropes).

puntang-panting topsyturvy (of things).

punti banana; ular punti snake.

puntianak=pontianak.

puntul blunt.

puntung stump (of candle, cigar); half-burnt log; si puntung eunuch.

punya to possess; mempunyai to own, possess; dia punya he owns; his; kepunyaan property.

pupa pupa.

pupu, sepupu first cousin; dua pupu second cousin.

pupuh, berpupuh to fly at each other (of cocks).

pupuk plaster, poultice; manure; memupuk to apply (poultice, manure); memupuk to manure; pupuk muka facecream.

pupul reel on fishing rods.

pupur rice powder; cosmetic; berpupur powdered.

pupus blighted (of plants); without relations; extinct.

puput reed whistle; memuput to blow flute; berpuput (of wind) to blow; dipuput angin blown by wind; puputan pair of bellows.

pura city, town; Singapura Lion City, ie Singapore; purapura feignedly, pretending.

purba ancient; purba kala old times.

puri ruler's private apartments in palace.

puris veins in palm fronds; =lidi.

puru (*med*) yaws; **puru ibu** biggest sore in secondary yaws.

purun rushes used for basketry.

purus, **memurus** to suffer from diarrhoea.

purut rough (*of skin*); **limau purut** lime.

purwa, **wayang purwa** shadow play.

pus, **buah pus** testicles.

pusa urge, impulse.

pusaka heirloom; **harta pusaka** hereditary property.

pusang, **pusang hati** worried, anxious.

pusar, **pusar-pusar** whorl in finger print; hair; **pusaran air** whirlpool.

pusat navel; centre; **sama pusat** concentric.

pusing, **berpusing** to rotate, whirl; **pusingan** cycle; **pusingkan** to turn (*a thing*) round.

puspa flower.

pusparagam multicolour.

pusta small fast Portuguese ship.

pustaka book of astrology, horoscope; **perpustakaan** library.

pusu ant hill; = **busut**.

pusut pricker.

putar, **berputar** to rotate, change direction, tack; **memutar** to twist; **pemutar** screwdriver.

putarwali woody climber with medicinal uses.

putera prince (*son*); **bumi putera** son of the soil, native.

puteri princess (*daughter*).

putih white; **orang putih** European; **memutih** to turn white.

putik fruit as it shows when the bloom has just dropped.

puting piece of blade inserted into hilt or handle; **puting beliung** tornado.

putu cakes of rice flour or nuts.

putus broken (*of cord, rope, hope*); **putus bicara** settled (*of discussion*); **putus harga** fixed (*of price*); **keputusan** decision.

puyan grime; **berpuyan** grimy.

puyu, **angin puyu** whirlwind; **puyu-puyu** climbing perch.

puyuh barred bustard quail.

R

ra'ayat = **rakyat** subjects, people, citizens; **kerakyatan** nationality; **rakyat jelata** the masses.

raba, **meraba** to grope; fondle.

rabak badly torn (*of cloth*); gash, rent.

raban, **meraban** to rave, be delirious; stray along zig-zagging aimlessly.

rabas to fall (*of tears*); drip.

rabbani Divine; **Tuhan rabbani** Lord God.

Rabbi Lord (*of God*); **Rabbi al-alamin** God of all worlds.

rabik, **robak-rabik** torn at edge, tattered; to grasp, reach; = **capai**.

rabit torn at edge, torn; **bibir rabit** harelip; **merabit** to tear.

rabu lungs; **kembang rabu** exulting; **hari Rabu** Wednesday.

rabuk tinder, touchwood.

rabun fumigation; **merabun** to send smoke into house so as to drive away mosquitoes or evil spirits; **mata rabun** dim (*of sight*).

rabung ridge thatch in Malay roof; **air naik merabung** very high tide.

rabut, **merabut** to tear out forcibly.

racau, **meracau** delirious, raving (*of persons in fever*).

racik, meracik snare of hanging nooses for catching birds; to slice coconut; seracik thin slice.

racun poison (*esp stomach poison*); meracun to poison.

radai fin (*of fish*); gutter under eaves; to ask alms; take idol in procession.

radak, meradak to stab (*with spear or from below*); shoot (*of pain*); to guzzle (*sl*).

radam blind; meradam to sleep blind to the world.

radang, meradang, naik meradang to get angry, flare up; heated; fevered (*of body*).

radar radar.

rada-rada a little; rada-rada gila a little mad.

radas apparatus.

radi grace of God; radi Allah anhu may God be pleased with him (*exclamatory remark when names of early Caliphs are mentioned*).

radical radical.

radio radio.

radiogram radiogram.

radium radium.

radup hem stitch.

rafidi 'forsakers' (*name used by Sunnites for Syiah sect*).

raga coarsely plaited creel; basket; buah raga kind of football or basketwork; sepak raga primitive Malay football; meraga to show off; peraga dandy.

ragah strong, sturdy.

ragam tune, melody; whim, caprice; style (*of dress, writing*); panca ragam musical band; pakaian seragam uniform clothing; meragam to show temperament.

ragan seven.

ragang, meragang to climb, scale (*ladder*); scramble; ragangan framework.

ragas, meragas to tug at

(*grass, hair*); to pull about; leap up on (*as hen about to lay*).

ragi yeast; colour; batu ragi faded (*of pattern*); burung meragi painted snipe.

ragu dubious, uncertain; ragu hati; ragu-ragu wavering; tidak ragu-ragu lagi it is certain.

ragum clamp, pincers, vice.

ragung, teragung bumped, knocked.

ragus, meragus to pluck forcibly (*at grass, hair*); gluttonous; = rakus.

ragut, meragut to tug (*at grass, hair*).

rahak hard work.

raham womb; *see* rahim.

rahang jaw; tulang rahang jawbone; tali rahang bridle; merahang to shout, yell.

rahap, kain rahap funeral pall; collapsed (*of building*); fallen (*of durians*); alighted (*of birds*).

rahasia = rahsia.

rahat I spinning wheel for winding thread.

rahat II break, rest, pause.

rahib Christian monk, nun.

rahim merciful (*of God*); womb; = raham.

rahman compassionate.

rahmat mercy; pulang ke rahmatu 'llah to return to the mercy of God, die.

rahsia, rahasia secret; menaruh rahsia to keep a secret.

Rahu dragon that is believed to attempt to swallow the moon at eclipse; bulan dimakan rahu eclipse.

rai, raikan to entertain guests publicly.

raib vanished; = ghaib.

raih to draw to o.s., grab; buy (*commodity*) to sell again; peraih middleman.

rais to sweep off (*as one sweeps crumbs off table*).

raja king, queen, prince or

princess; **raja berasal** prince by descent; **Raja Muda** heir apparent; **raja sehari** bridegroom; **budak raja** courtiers; **hamba raja** menials about court.

Rajab seventh Muslim month.

rajah blueprint, diagram, chart, outline sketch, tattoo marks; **rajah empat segi** square; **rajah tiga segi** triangle.

rajang, merajang to slice up (*tobacco*) finely.

rajau rice stalks left at reaping as unripe.

rajawali kite, sparrowhawk.

raji, rajikan to digest.

rajin stoned (*of criminals*); = rejan.

rajin diligent, industrious; **barang kerajinan tangan** handmade goods.

rajister register.

rajuk, merajuk to sulk; **perajuk** sulker.

rajut, merajut to make nets; knit.

rak scrub, small jungle; physically able, fit.

raka having defect making it fragile; ready to break.

rakaat standing position in Muslim prayer; **sembahyang empat rakaat** four prayers.

rakah, merakah gelak split with laughing.

rakak, merakak = rangkak.

rakam, merakam to stamp, print, paint, record (*on tape or disc*); **rakaman** printing, recording.

rakan comrade, colleague, partner in business; **rakanan** partnership.

rakap, merakap to crawl (*as beggar*); to eke out livelihood.

rakas, merakas to feel one's way (*as burglar*).

rakat scarlet pea (*also known as buah saga*).

raket racquet.

rakit bamboo raft, floating bamboo (*bath house*); **berakit** on raft; **merakit** to make a raft.

raksa mercury, quicksilver.

raksamala fragrant resin used as incense.

raksasa ogre, giant; **rapat raksasa** large meeting.

raksi yielding fragrance; **meraksi** to perfume; **peraksi** scent made from leaves of flowers; astrological 'star'; **seraksi** born under same star; suited (*of wedded pair*).

rakus greedy.

rakut, merakut to deceive; set a snare; weave a web (*of spider*).

rakyat subject of country; **orang rakyat** aborigines; see **ra'yat.**

ralat (*print*) error, errata.

ralip half-asleep; accustomed to; **ralipnya** their practice, habit; = ghalib.

ram, mengeram brooding, sitting on eggs; = eram, **tingkap ram** louvres.

rama father; **rama-rama** butterfly, moth.

Ramadan fast month; = bulan puasa.

ramah friendly, familiar, cordial; **dengan ramah-tamah** with great affability; **peramah** affable person.

ramai populous, crowded, busy (*of place*); crowded, numerous, noisy (*of persons*); **orang ramai** the public; **suara ramai** public voice; **meramaikan** to make numerous, noisy.

ramak to grab, seize.

ramal I horoscope, forecast; **meramalkan** to forecast.

ramal II kerchief.

ramang = remang.

ramas, meramas to knead (*clay, dough, coconut pulp*).

rambah moist (*of soil*); to collide (*of two spinning tops*); chop down trees; **rambahan** brushwood chopped down.

rambai, pohon rambai common fruit tree; saddle hackles of cock; beard of goat; rambai ayam=lawi rambai small curved dagger.

rambak, **merambak** to increase (*in wealth, in number*); spread (*of creepers*).

rambanan grass and herbs for feeding goats.

rambang, **merambang** to take a random aim with a gun; jala rambang wide-meshed casting net; rambang mata to have a roving eye; tengah hari rambang noon.

rambas, **merambas** to exorcize evil spirit.

rambat to creep up (*as snake up tree*).

rambih, **merambih** to go on a religious pilgrimage with many comrades.

rambu fringe (*on cloth, curtain*); berambu fringed.

rambun tangled undergrowth, roots, climbers, creepers.

rambung, getah rambung Indian rubber.

rambut hair (*of head*); rambut ikal curly hair; perambut gut at end of fishing line.

rambutan fruit.

rambuti woolly (*of cloth*).

ramek-ramek titbits of buffalo meat.

rami rhea grass; tali rami string made of it.

ramin loop work in basketry; beramin loops; looped.

rampai mixed, various; rampai-rampaian miscellany of writings; bunga rampai posy.

rampak, **merampak** to be thick and spread laterally (*of foliage of shrubs*).

rampang, pinang rampang juiceless areca nut.

rampas, **merampas** to take by force (*of robbers by law*); to confiscate (*by court*); rampasan loot, booty.

rampat, **merampat** to cut down (*plants*) indiscriminately; abuse indiscriminately.

rampeh, **merampeh** to haul in (*line; branch of fruit tree*).

ramping slender (*of waists*); rompang-ramping tattered.

rampok, **merampok** to housebreak, burgle.

rampung mutilated (*of ear or nose*).

rampus, **merampus** to flounce in a rage, be abusive.

ramsum=**rangsum**.

ramu, **meramu** to collect odds and ends; ramuan building materials; peramu collector of scraps.

ramus, beramus hairy (*of faces*); shaggy.

ran tree hut of aborigines.

rana long ailings (*of persons*); wasting from age.

ranah utterly destroyed; meadows.

ranak to arise; ranak terbit trill of voice; beranak-ranak trilling.

ranap levelled to the ground (*of house*); meranapkan to level by stamping or pressing.

rancah=**rencah**.

rancak fine, smart, lively; merancak to hack, cut off.

rancana mixture.

rancang vertical (*of pointed stake*); merancang to plan, arrange ahead; rancangan plan, project, scheme, programme; perancang drafter of programme.

rancap sharp, pointed; merancap to masturbate (*of males*); merancapkan to sharpen.

rancu to mix dialects.

rancung sharp-pointed; **me-rancung** to cut at an angle, sharpen.

randa = janda (*but includes widowers*).

randah, berpindah-randah to keep moving about; nomads.

randai I, merandai to wade through (*water, grass*).

randai II Minangkabau dance; **berandai-randai** continuously in succession.

randau, merandau to mix by hand (*spices to improve curry*).

randek to stop, halt.

randi, kain randi Siamese silk coverlet.

randu cotton tree; to stir liquid by hand.

randuk, kambing randuk bearded old billy goat; **me-randuk** to wade through.

randung, merandung to trample.

rang draft (*of laws*); **tanah rang** rice field (*banked and previously cultivated, but now fallow*).

rangah, merangah to be bumptious, swagger.

rangai, merangai to clear weeds from a field purposely flooded.

rangak gastropod mollusc with ornamental shells.

rangas white ant; **merangas** certain to succeed; spoilt.

rangga official title; dry and stiff (*of hair*); **ranggu-rangga** sticking out, untidy; **berangga** branching.

ranggah, meranggahkan to strip a tree of fruit breaking the branches.

ranggak, meranggakkan to haul a boat ashore.

ranggas dead, leafless; fallen branches.

ranggeh, meranggeh to reach for.

ranggi smart; affected; conceited.

ranggit, teranggit-ranggit making convulsive movement.

ranggoi, meranggoi to scrape thorn off a nibung palm.

ranggu puzzling (*from variety*).

ranggung, meranggung to squat with knees apart; work laboriously on all fours.

rangin long shield used in war dances; to steal.

rangka framework (*of house, kite*).

rangkai, serangkai cluster; **berangkai** strung together; **merangkaikan** to string together (*flowers, beads*); **rang-kaian** link; chain.

rangkak, merangkak to crawl on hands and knees; **merang-kak-rangkak** stumbling (*as learner*).

rangkap, merangkap to link lines of verse; **serangkap** couplets (*of verses*); **bunyi rangkap** diphthong; **perangkap** trap.

rangket, merangket to cane.

rangkik univalve predatory mollusc with ornamental shell.

rangkok, burung rangkok rhinoceros hornbill.

rangkul, merangkul to embrace, clasp.

rangkum to grasp in both hands (*bundle*); cuddle; **se-rangkum** as much as can be carried in two hands.

rangkup, merangkup to form a space by putting hands together for drinking.

rangrang red ant.

rangsang stimulant; stimulating; **perangsang** exciting (*of drink*); stimulus; **merang-sang** to stimulate.

rangsum rations for soldiers.

rangum, merangum to snatch away.

rangup crisp (*as dry leaves*).

rani queen.

ranjah, meranjah to rob by violence.

ranjak, peranjak garden seat.

ranjang couch; iron bedstead.

ranjau caltrop (*of iron, bamboo to trap enemies*).

Ranjuna Arjuna, famous archer in the Mahabhrata.

rantai chain; **rantai tangan** bangle; **mata rantai** link of chain; **merantaikan** to chain.

rantam, berantam to subscribe to a project, club together; co-operate in work; **rantaman** contribution.

rantang hamper, foodbasket.

rantau reach of a river, stretch of coast; **teluk rantau** inlets and stretches of coasts; **merantau** travel abroad.

ranting twig; **belalang ranting** stick-insect; **kuang ranting** peacock-pheasant.

rantus contagious.

ranum quite ripe (*of fruit*).

ranyah, meranyah to help o.s. first to food; pick tit-bits out of a dish.

ranyau, meranyau to cleanse a well.

rap, tanah rap land cleared for planting; to well together (*of choir*); = **derap**.

rapah, merapah to trample through scrub.

rapai, merapai to fondle (*bosom*); fumble with.

rapang, ikan rapang mullet.

rapat close (*of joinery, stitches*); closed; assembled; meeting; **merapat** to come together; **merapatkan** to bring together.

rapi tidy (*of clothes*); accurate; strong (*of guards*).

rapih I, merapih chipped at the edge; = **serpeh**.

rapih II natty.

rapik to talk inconsequently in semi-delirium.

rapu, merapu to pick up odds and ends.

rapuh fragile, friable, brittle.

rapung, merapung drift.

rapus, merapus to tug forcibly; throw a buffalo for slaughter.

rarai reins (*for horses*).

rasa taste, feeling, sensation; **rasanya** it feels, tastes; **berasa, merasa** to feel; **terasa** felt; **perasaan** feeling, sensation, emotion.

rasai, merasai to undergo, endure.

rasau, pandan rasau screwpine.

rasian ominous dream.

rasional rational.

rasit = **resit** receipt.

rasuk larger floor crossbeam; **merasuk** to harry; **dirasuk polong** plagued by a bottle-imp.

rasul messenger, apostle; **Rasul Allah** God's Apostle; Muhammad.

rasyid orthodox.

rasywah gift, bribe; = **tumbuk rusuk**; *also* **raswah**.

rata level; common; flat (*of ground*); **hitung rata** to strike an average; **serata dunia** throughout the world; **rata-rata** all over; **meratakan** to level.

ratah, meratah to eat (*fish, meat without rice*).

ratap wailing; **ratap tangis** weeping and wailing; **meratapi** bemoan, wail.

ratib to repeat a sentence acknowledging Allah.

ratna jewel; **ratna mutu manikam** jewels of all kinds.

ratu king; queen.

ratus hundred; **seratus** a hundred; **beratus-ratus** hundreds.

rau swish of heavy rain; *also* **derau**.

raun rounds (*of police, sentry*).

raung, meraung roar (from pain); roar (of tigers).

raup, seraup as much as two hands can hold; meraup to scoop (earth) with joined hands.

raut, meraut to whittle, pare (stick); pisau raut small sharp knife for whittling a stick.

rawa, burung rawa pied imperial pigeon; march; shrimp net of a triangular sack propelled by two poles; fen, marsh.
Rawa district in Sumatra; kain rawa bright tie-and-dye mantilla.

rawah=rawa partnership where one supplies capital; telinga rawah one deaf to advice.

rawai, merawal moor lines of unbaited hooks across an estuary to entangle fish.

rawak, merawak to fire in the air to frighten thieves; random.

rawan emotion (esp tenderness); memberi rawan to stir emotions; numeral coefficient for string; serawan jala one casting net.

rawang marsh;=kerawang fretted (of woodwork, metalwork); merawang to wash a dead body for burial;=meruang.

rawat, merawati to attend to; jururawat nurse; rawatan first aid.

rawi narrator, author; merawikan to narrate.

rawit, cabai rawit cayenne pepper;=rabit, babit to implicate.

raya great, large; bunga raya hibiscus; jalan raya high road; Jabatan Kerja Raya J.K.R.; beraya to be on holiday; merayakan celebration.

rayah, merayah to raid and rob.

rayang, merayang to be in a whirl; see gayang.

rayan—rayan nightmare; delirium.

rayap, merayap to crawl, creep (of insects, plants).

rayau, merayau to roam.

rayon rayon.

rayu sad and melancholy; merayu hati to sadden, move; rayuan coaxing, persuasion; surat rayuan petition.

reaksi reaction.

realisme realism.

realistik realistic.

realiti reality.

reba thicket at waterside; dry felled timber ready for burning.

rebab viol.

rebah to flop down; rebah pengsan to fall in a faint; merebahkan to let down, cause to recline.

rebak, merebak to spread (of fire, news); deep (of wound).

reban I pen for poultry; rebankan to pen.

reban II broken and dropped; merebankan to break and drop.

reban III to hurl aside.

rebana tambourine.

rebang to let tresses loose.

rebat, merebat to bar (gate, river) with brushwood.

rebeh torn, broken or hanging; down on one side (of an ear, wing); hanging unevenly.

rebolusi revolution.

rebuk, merebuk to suppurate (of a sore).

rebung young edible shoots of bamboo.

rebus boiled; telur rebus boiled egg; merebus to boil.

rebut, merebut to snatch (as thief); win (prize in game); berebut snatch and tearing.

recak slightly pockmarked; merecak kuda to ride a horse.

receh oddments; wang receh small change.

recik, merecik to sprinkle.

recok tumult, hubbub.

recup, merecup to come to the surface (of sprouting plant).

reda decreasing (of rain, fire, epidemics, storm).

redah, meredah to take a direct way through the bush.

redam crushed to pieces, ie remuk redam faintly visible, faintly audible.

redan large tree.

redang deep swamp, marsh.

redap small drum; meredap to spread (as tumour, rash).

redas, meredas to cut with scissors.

redi hammock.

redih, meredih to transplant rice seedlings in thick bunches (redihan) from the nursery to the field.

redik to scold; = hardik.

redum gloomy, dull; = redup; meredum to bar a road.

redup overcast and still (before storm); obscure (of sun).

referendum referendum.

refleksi reflection.

rega = harga.

regang taut (of rope); meregangkan to tighten (cord, net); beregang-regang to stiffen one's body; peregang seluar trouser stretcher.

regas to cut with a saw.

regat, meregat to cut off = kerat; to take a short direct cut.

reges leafless.

register register.

registrasi registration.

regol main gate.

regu gang, party.

rehan consciousness that travels in dreams (during sleep).

rehat = rihat.

reja leavings; scraps (of cloth).

rejah, merejah to charge forward heedless of others, intrude; perejah intruder; thruster.

rejam to stone to death; execute by pressing into mud.

rejan intense physical strain (of childbirth, cough etc); batuk rejan whooping cough; sakit rejan dysentery.

rejang divination from days of the month as symbolized by different animals; to break up soil with a crowbar; perejang.

rejasa tin.

rejeh bloodshot (of eyes).

rejim regime.

reju to attack, charge (as fighting fish).

rejuk, merejuk to prance, jump.

rejul, merejul to protrude from hole or crevice; fish through mesh of net.

rek, rek-rek to drip (of rain).

reka composition, invention; rekaan fiction; merekakan to plan, design.

reka bentok graphic arts.

rekah, merekah cracked (as lips, soil); to split open, burst open (of buds).

rekam, hati merekam sullen; = rakam.

rekemen, **rekomen** to recommend.

reket not growing properly (of plants).

rekod record.

rekomen = rekemen.

rekut lashing of rattan for adze blade.

rel rail.

rela, **reda** willing (to be, or do); consent; dengan suka rela gladly; merelai to consent to; kerelaan consent, permission.

relah torn (of seams); merelahkan to split (seams).

relai crumbling (of wood); pearl shell.

relang, merelang to glitter; ring of rattan or wire; dog collar.

relap, merelap to flash, glitter (of gems); gemerlapan flashing (of stars).

relas, merelas abraded (of skin).

relau furnace for smelting tin.

reluh, mereluh to snore.

relung coil of rattan; 1½ acres; merelung to cover (with dish cover).

remah left over (of rice).

remaja adolescent, marriageable.

remak better, preferable; remak saya mati better that I should die.

reman cord or stick releasing traps.

remang, meremang bristling (of neck hair).

remat lashing of adze.

remayung Ceylon spinach.

remba, beremba-remba in lines (of walkers).

rembah, merembah to trickle down (of tears); rembah-rembeh to keep trickling

remban swipe (legs with knife).

rembang zenith; tengahari rembang high noon; merembang to aim at a target.

rembas utterly (broken, disappeared); rembas kena full (of blow).

rembat trap, snare.

rembatan crossbeam (of house); crossbar (of door).

rembek, berembek to wobble (of punt pole).

rembes I, merembes to trickle (of liquid).

rembes II red and watering (of eyes).

rembet hampered (by work); merembet spread (of epidemic, fire).

rembia sago palm; = rumbia.

rembuk advice, discussion.

rembunai average (of person's size or height).

remeh-temeh unimportant, trifling.

remis small edible shellfish.

rempah I spices for curry.

rempah II, rebah-rempah to fall and roll (of persons); topple over.

rempak, serempak all at once, concurrently; serempak hari on the same day.

rempang, rempang bahasa eccentric.

rempat blown on to a lee-shore; merempat to drift.

rempit to cane, whip.

rempoh exhausted (of energy).

rempong pinioned (of legs); merempong to pinion the legs.

rempuh, merempuh to rush against, force a way, charge.

remudu tadpole; = berudu.

remuk smashed; remuk-redam crushed to atoms.

remunia tree with acid fruit.

remut, meremut to throb, pulsate; = kemut.

renak, pepak renak littered (of articles).

renang, berenang to swim; terenang-renang swimming about.

rencah, perencah flavouring of prawns; to clarify and flavour dishes; condiments.

rencak cauldron.

rencam confusing, puzzling; merencam to confuse by their number; rencaman confusion.

rencana programme; article; minutes draft; plan; merencanakan to narrate; compose, draft, plan.

rencang clanging; loud-voiced and talkative.

rencat, terencat dwarfed; = genjat.

renceh small (in names of fishes, of money).

rencek to give o.s. airs.

renceng slender (of body); serenceng string of beads.

rencet hopping about.

rencis = renjis.

rencong a dagger; = tumbuk lada.

renda lace; merenda to make lace.

rendah low in stature; merendahkan lower in height; merendahkan diri to abase o.s.; riuh-rendah loud uproar.

rendam, berendam to wallow, soak o.s.; terendam submerged, flooded; merendamkan to immerse.

rendang I spiced meat cooked till dry; merendang to make rendang.

rendang II umbrageous (of trees).

rendap, merendap sink (as stone in water).

rendeng I the rainy season.

rendeng II, berendeng-rendeng one behind the other; dandified.

renduh, merenduh to be laden with fruit.

renek small (of person); fine (of rain).

reng king vulture; also hereng.

renga larvae; berenga flyblown.

rengak, merengak to be strong (of smell).

rengap, merengap to puff and blow; to blow away.

rengas trees with prettily veined timber and irritant sap.

rengat colic; crack; rengat hati torn with anger; merengat to perspire.

rengau, terperengau wide open (of door).

rengeh, merengeh to neigh, whinny.

rengek, merengek whine, wheedle (of children).

renget linked, closely joined.

renggam small knife for reaping grain.

renggang apart, parted (of joinery); distant (of relations); berenggang to go apart.

renggat corrugations (on horns).

renggis stripped (of fruit, leaves); almost bare (of feathers).

renggut, merenggut to tug at (animal); renggutan tug; tugging.

rengit gnat.

rengka saddle for howdah.

rengkam growth on coral reefs.

rengkas, ringkas concise, abbreviated; rengkasnya briefly, in short; rengkasan summary, abbreviation; merengkaskan to make a digest.

rengkat lame from having one leg too short.

rengkau, merengkau to sob.

rengkeh to totter under a burden; bend.

rengkek poor (of plant growth).

rengkesa goblin that spoils crops.

rengkiang rice granary on four posts.

rengkuh, merengkuh to drag (boughs); tug (at oars).

rengkung gullet; = kerengkung; merengkung coiled, in a circle.

rengrengan draft, scheme.

rengsa, merengsa obstinate (of long illness); to be listless.

rengus surly; perengus gruff person.

rengut, merengut to grumble; perengut grumbler.

rening, merening swollen from abscess, tight (of skin) from swelling.

renjana love, longing.

renjar ranger.

renjas, merenjas to jump with rage.

renjis, merenjiskan to sprinkle with water; direnjis basted.

renjong, merenjong to raise; ketam renjong land crab.

rensa = rengsa.

renta, tua renta very old; merenta-renta to stamp the foot, look or appear angry.

rentaka iron swivel gun.

rentak–rentaknya beat of accented syllables in verse; merentak to stamp the feet (esp in anger).

rentan susceptible to illness; tired.

rentang, merentangkan to stretch tight (cord etc); direntang tightened.

rentap to pull with a jerk, wrench at; stamp.

rentas, merentas to cut a path through jungle; garisan rentas cross-section; perentas transversal.

renteng, serenteng string (of fireworks).

rentis, merentis to cut a narrow path through jungle, mark out the way; perentis jalan pioneer.

renung to stare, contemplate.

renut, tali renut bell band in elephant's harness.

renyah intricate; troublesome; merenyah to take trouble.

renyai drizzling (of rain).

renyak to tread down (grass); press down (goods into trunk etc).

renyap, merenyap to hit (esp on the mouth).

renyau crusted mud.

renyeh I, merenyeh to flounce in anger; berenyeh slippery after rain.

renyeh II protracted (of illness).

renyek crumpled.

renyuh to poke with finger.

renyuk crumpled; renyuk-renyek crumpled all over; to sulk; do with a bad grace.

repang level (of hedges); even (teeth); merepangkan to cut level; perepang diameter of sawn trunk.

repas fragile; rotten (of fences, wood).

repeh fragile (as biscuits); merepeh to break a bit off (biscuit, flowers).

repek, merepek to talk nonsense, chatter.

repes, merepes to fidget with small objects.

repet, merepet to talk drivel; repetan idle chatter.

repih to crumble.

repis, serepis to chip off the edge of crockery.

repor strong rope for tethering buffaloes.

repot report.

repu, merepu to heap up piles of rubbish for burning to smoke out mosquitoes.

republik republic.

repuh, repuhan overgrown clearing; merepuh in full bloom (of durians).

repui friable; crumbling (of clods).

reput decayed and crumbling.

resa expulsive contractions in labour pains; pulse.

resah nervous, fidgety, restless.

resak a tree with good timber.

resam customary usage; natural habit; large ferns.

resan, meresan to resent undeserved slur; almost musty (of food).

resap, meresap absorbed (of dew, sweat); to vanish; enter (into heart).

resdung = restung.

resek, meresek shrill (of voice); piercing (of violins).

resemi = resmi.

resepi recipe.

resi, reshi Hindu hermit.

residu residue.

resiko risk.

resin turtle.

resit, meresit to disappear from one place and appear elsewhere (*of pains*).

resmi custom, habit; official; surat resmi official letter.

restu blessing; influence.

restung syphilis of the nose; restung jahat cancer of the nose.

resuk, meresuk to enter blindly into a hole.

resume résumé.

reta, mereta to talk nonsense, drivel.

retak crack (*in porcelain, wood, wall*); lines on the palm, creases; beretak cracked.

retas split (*of seam*).

reteh, meretah to vesiculate from white pustules and swell up; mereteh to hop (*of spinning tops*).

retek, meretek to shiver.

retin diamonds (*in cards*).

retina retina.

revolusi revolution.

rewang, merewang to act at random (*as wild shot*).

rewel voluble, garrulous; uncertain, halting.

rezeki food, livelihood, earnings, income; rezeki murah income easily earned.

ria I, suka ria enjoyment.

ria II proud, arrogant.

riak ripple on water; riak ikan ripples caused by fish; beriak-riak to ripple.

riaksi = reaksi.

rial Spanish real, dollar.

riam rapid shallow cataract.

rian skein of thread.

riang elated, in high spirits; shivering from fever.

riap, meriap to spread (*of weeds*).

rias pith of banana stem.

riau, meriau to wash (*in streams*) for gold ore.

riazat self-mortification.

riba, meriba to hold in lap; ribaan lap; moneylender's interest.

ribu one thousand; tiga ribu three thousand; beribu-ribu thousands; daun ribu-ribu climbing fern.

ribut hurricane; turun ribut a storm descended.

ricau, merican to twitter (*of birds*).

ridip dorsal fin of sharks; ridge of crocodile backbone.

ridwan grace; darul-ridwan land of God's grace, State of Perak.

rigap smart, active.

rihal bookrest (*esp for the Kuran*).

rihat rest (*in the middle of work*); also rehat, rahat.

rijal al-ghaib invisible spirits of saints who protect mankind.

rijim rejim.

rimah crumbs of food dropped on floor.

rimas to break out (*of sweat*); get hot with rash.

rimau = harimau tiger.

rimba primeval forest; rimba raya great virgin forest.

rimbas rice planter's adze-shaped weeder.

rimbun lofty and thick (*of foliage*); heap.

rimis half cent.

rimpang, rempang trailing roots of ginger; serimpang shred of ginger; berimpang trailing.

rimpi bananas dried in the sun or over a fire.

rimping, perimping last in row.

rincih petty; perniagaan rincih petty trading; harga rincih retail price; belanja rincih-rincih petty disbursements; merincih to slice, mince.

rincik to slice, mince; petty.

rindu to long for (child, lover); rindu dendam passionate yearning; buluh perindu bamboo with slits which emits musical notes.

ring long basket.

ringan light in weight; unimportant; meringankan to treat lightly, lighten; ringan kepala quick-witted, flighty.

ringga untidy (of hair).

ringgit dollar.

ringin, sapu-sapu ringin game where children squat, hop and sing.

ringis, meringis to grin; = meringai.

ringit joined, linked.

ringkai emaciated.

ringkik to neigh, whinny.

ringkuk, meringkuk to crouch, sit or sleep hunched up; meringkukkan to imprison.

rintang, merintang to bar, stop; merintangkan kayu to put timber to bar; rintangan obstacle.

rintas, merintas crossing.

rintau, berintau-rintau flickering, shimmering.

rintih, merintih to groan.

rintik drop, dot, speckle; berintik-rintik speckled, dotted; to fall in drops.

rintis jungle path.

rinyau, ikan rinyau sand smelts.

ripai subscription to newspaper; meripai to collect (money); teripai-ripai projecting (of fractured bones).

ripu embarrassed by poverty; in a whirl.

ripuk broken, crushed.

risa cyst, wen; nuchal thickening.

risalat letter; tract; thesis.

risau, risau hati anxious, troubled; merisau to fret, worry.

risik I, merisik to make inoffensive inquiries; perisik spy.

risik II rustling; merisik to rustle.

riu, ikan riu catfish.

riuh din of fighters; hubbub of children at play; riuhrendah extremely noisy.

riuk, patah riuk having a compound fracture.

riang curved, convex.

riwayat story, account; beriwayat to narrate, state.

rizab reserve.

robak-rabik torn; holed (of basket)

robek torn (of mats, cloth).

roboh to collapse (of house, tree); batu roboh avalanche, landslide; merobohkan to bring crashing down.

robok, merobok to gurgle, bubble; hati robok boiling with anger.

rocah dirty, unwashed.

rocoh to prod from below with a stick.

roda wheel; anak roda spokes; anak roda lambung paddle wheel.

rodak = gerodak; rodak hati rattled, agitated.

rodan agonising, painful.

rodi order.

rodok, merodok to stab from below.

rodong friend; chance acquaintance; husband; merodong to come across, encounter.

rogoh, merogoh to insert hand into pocket.

rogol, merogol to rape; perogol rapist.

roh spirit of life; terbang roh life flew away; fainted; rohani spiritual.

rojak vinegar salad; **anak rojak** pestle of betel nut pounder; **merojak** to pound betel nut.

roji daily bread.

rojok to return (*esp to wife after annullable divorce*); refer to; reference.

rojol, merojol to emerge (*of head from hole*).

roket rocket.

rokok cigarette; **merokok** to smoke cigarette.

rokyat sight, observation; **rokyat al hilal** sight of new moon that fixes beginning and end of Ramadan fast.

roma, bulu roma fine body hair; liang roma pores.

roman appearance, look (*of persons*); paku roman tufted fern; roman panas prickly heat.

romantik romantic.

romba fisherman's mark, beacon.

rombak, merombak to undo; untie; dismantle; **rombakan** undoing.

rombang–rambing tattered.

rombeng tattered (*of clothes*); **rombengkan** to sell old clothes.

rombong nest of small round fancy lidded baskets of screw-pine; **rombongan** (*political*) group; ikan rombong sea perch.

romen romance.

romok, meromok to look poorly (*of chicken*); depressed (*of persons*).

rompak, merompak to commit piracy; **perompak** pirate.

rompang–ramping tattered at the edge (*of fabrics*).

romping chipped at the edge (*of teeth*); gnawed away (*of fruits by birds*).

rompis jagged (*as edge of ear*).

rompok edging of cloth to embroidery; **merompok** to make border.

rompong mutilated (*of ear, nose, by accident or disease*); **merompongkan** to mutilate.

rona colour; = warna.

ronda rounds; kapal peronda patrol ship.

rondah–randeh in confusion, disordered.

rondoh–randah piled in disorder (*of luggage etc*).

rong, balairong palace hall.

rongak with gaps (*of teeth, fence*); bergigi rongak gaptoothed.

rongga hole (*of ear, in trees*); berongga hollow.

ronggah, peronggah to use filthy language.

ronggeng dance with singing in pairs.

ronggok, meronggok to stoop (*of old*); **beronggok-ronggok** in groups of persons seated on floor.

rongkok, merongkok to stoop.

rongkol cluster (*of fruits*); bunch (*of keys*).

rongkong, kerongkong gullet.

rongos, merongos to be short-tempered; **perongos** touchy person.

rongrong, merongrong importune; to worry for money, sponge for food.

ronta, meronta-ronta to struggle to free o.s. from arrest.

rontek pennoned lance.

rontok to fall (*of hair, flowers*).

ronyeh, menyonyehkan to damage flowers; babble.

ronyoh overripe, soft.

ronyok crumpled; **peronyok** to crumple paper.

ropak untidy; ropak-rapek topsy-turvy; jagged at edge; **meropak** to perpetrate gang robbery by night.

ropol frill; **bantal beropol** pillow with frilled edge.

rosak damaged, not working, broken (*of things*); **rosak mata** having injured sight; **rosak tanam-tanaman** crops spoilt; **merosakkan** to damage; **kerosakan** injury.

rosok dismantled; **rosokan** rubbish; **merosok** to grope in pocket.

rosot, merosot to slip (*of garment*); to fall away (*of prestige*).

rotan cane, rattan; **rotan semambu** Malacca cane.

roti bread; **roti panggang** toast.

rotok, merotok crack of rifles.

royak, meroyak to spread (*of skin disease, news*).

royal extravagant.

royalti royalty.

royan, meroyan to suffer loss of blood consequent on childbirth.

royat to tell, inform; = **riwayat**.

royong reeling, staggering.

ru, eru casuarina tree.

rua street.

ruadat homage, honour.

ruah, meruahkan to empty (*grain*); defecate; **lempah ruah** poured out; **meruah** to call, hail; **diruah** called; **bulan ruah Syaaban** 8th Muslim month (*of all souls*).

ruai loose (*of fitting, rope*); weak, shaky.

ruak, meruak to spread (*of cobra's hood*); expand, be scattered.

ruak-ruak, burung ruak-ruak white-breasted water hen.

ruam whitish spots of thrush; **ruam panas** prickly heat.

ruan murrel.

ruang hollow, space between; room; **ilmu ukur ruang** method of calculating cube root; **ruangan (warta)** column in newspaper.

ruap, meruap to boil over;

meruap hati to boil with rage.

ruas sections between joints of bamboo.

ruat uprooted (*but not broken*) (*of tree, tooth*).

rubah jackal.

rubai quatrain.

ruban scum on coconut oil; **meruban** to remove scum.

ruba-ruba gift made by ship's captain to port officials.

rubban Christian monk; **rubbanat** Christian nun.

rubiah female hermit and religious teacher.

rubin, batu rubin paving stones, floor tiles.

rubing temporary top strake in Malay sailing ship.

rubu, merubu-rubu to stray aimlessly; fumble (*in search*).

rucah common, ordinary.

rudu drooping (*of eyelids from fatigue*); **merudu** to glide (*as boat*).

rudus heavy sword broadening at tip.

rugi to suffer loss, damages, diminution of property or profits; **ganti rugi** compensation; **kerugian** loss.

ruing square frame for serving thread to spool connected with winder.

ruit, capik ruit lame from badly set fracture.

rujah dirty, smeared; **merujah** to stab downwards.

rujuk to revert, refer; = **rojok**.

rukam small trees with edible berries.

rukh castle, rook (*chess*).

rukiah sorcery.

ruku, ruku-ruku basil; = **selaseh**; **burung ruku** common sandpiper.

rukuk to bow in prayer.

rukun article of faith; corner stone, basis; **rukun Islam** the five obligatory Muslim duties.

Rum Byzantium, Rome.

rumah house, dwelling; **rumah atap** house walled and roofed with palm fronds; **rumah batu** brick house; **berumah** owning *or* living in a house.

Rumawi = Rumi.

rumbai, **berumbai-rumbai** tasselled, fringed; **terumbai** dangling.

rumbia sago palm.

rumbing, ikan rumbing coral fish.

rumbu fish trap.

rumbun, merumbunkan to pile brushwood on fire.

Rumi Roman; Byzantine; **huruf Rumi** romanized letters.

rumi, ikan rumi-rumi sucking fish.

rumit complicated, ticklish; **kerumitan** trouble, difficulty, complexity.

rumpair algae.

rumpun numeral coefficient for plants that grow from one root in clumps; **berumpun-rumpun** in clumps.

rumput grass, weed; **berumput** covered with grass; **merumput** to weed grass.

rumrum to coax a girl with flattery.

rumus abbreviation; formula; **merumuskan** to abbreviate, summarize.

runas, merunas to graze.

runcing sharp-pointed, tapering; **meruncing** to sharpen, point.

runding reckoning, calculation; **berunding** to deliberate, debate; **merundingkan** to discuss; **rundingan** proposal, plan.

runduk, merunduk to bow the head.

rundung, merundung to pester (*of beggars, ills*); **merundungkan** to cause to slant; crash down on.

rundu-randa following in crowds.

rungguh pledge, thing pawned.

runggu-rangga spiky.

rungkap, merungkap to speak rudely.

rungkup, merungkup to overhang (*as eaves*); overarch, overspread.

rungut, merungut to mumble complaints, grumble.

runjang, merunjang to poke into a hole; fumble in business.

runjau, merunjau to be tall and lanky.

runjung, merunjung piled high and cone-shaped.

runtai, meruntai trailing, dangling; **seruntai** cluster of fruit.

runtas, meruntas to pull with a jerk.

runti, merunti to remove rough skin off canes, polish canes.

runtih, meruntih to pluck (*flower, leaf*).

runting worn thin, fragile.

runtuh to topple, fall down (*as house*); **meruntuhkan** to bring toppling down; **keruntuhan** collapse.

runtun, meruntunkan to pull down, tug down (*branch, rope*).

runut to grumble; trail, track (*of beasts*).

runyas frayed, tattered.

runyis dirty, littered.

rupa appearance, look; **rupanya** apparently; **serupa** alike; **menyerupai** to resemble; **berupa** having the look of; **merupa** to assume a form; **keserupaan** identity.

rupabumi landscape.

rupiah Indonesian unit of currency = 100 cents.

rusa sambhur deer; **rusa senggirek** unicorn.

rusam pivot for teaching children to walk.

rusing, merusing to be peevish, grumble; *also* **runsing**.

rusuh, kerusuhan disturbance; **merusuh** to riot; **perusuh** rioter, anarchist.

rusuk side of body, house; rib; **rusuk surat** margin of letter; **dirusuk abeam; tumbuk rusuk** to bribe; **merusuk** approach from the side.

rusut to decrease.

rut able to endure.

rutuk, merutuk to grumble.

rutup, terutup crackle of food frying.

ruyung thick outer bark of palms.

ruyup to droop with fatigue (*of eyes*); to go to sleep (*of sun*).

S

sa = se I one; **setengah** one half; **budak seorang** one youth; **sesuatu** something; **seseorang** person.

saadat majesty; **Baginda sa-adat HM** the King.

saat moment, time; **saat ini** here and now; **saat itu then**, immediately.

Saba Sheba, Sabaea.

saba, bersaba to mix with, be acquainted with; **menyaba** to visit, frequent.

sabak baker's oven; vat for boiling palm sugar; **menyabak** boiling palm sugar; to weep.

saban each, every; **saban hari** daily.

sabang to muzzle a dog; **layar sabang** small jib used in small boats.

sabar patient; **sabarkan** to be patient with.

sabasani, pohon sabasani snake-like tree.

sabda, bersabda to speak, say (*of the Prophet*).

Sabi Sabaan; heretical.

sabil path; **perang sabil Allah** holy war; **mati sabil** dead in the course of duty.

sabit sickle; **bintang sabit** star and crescent; **bulan sabit** new crescent moon; **menyabit** to cut with sickle.

sabjek subject.

sabjektib subjective.

sabotaj sabotage.

Sabtu Saturday, Sabbath.

sabuk waist belt, sash with fringed ends.

sabun soap; albino (*of men*).

sabung, menyabung to dart at each other (*of fighting cocks*); **kilat sabung-menyabung** flashing lightning.

sabur uproar (*of crowds*); shouting, singing; **sabur-limur** wild confusion.

sabut fibre, husk of coconut; **tali sabut coir rope; bongkok sabut** round-backed.

sadah lime for betel chewing.

sadai, tersadai beached (*of boats*); prone (*of crocodiles*); **menyadaikan** to beach.

sadak leaning (*of pillars*); raking (*of masts*); **menyadak** to poke at from below.

sadang, pintu sadang-sading curtained entrance to bridal couch.

sadap, menyadap to tap toddy palms; **pisau penyadap** tapping knife.

sadar I aware, conscious; = **sedar**.

sadar II breast, front.

sadariah, baju sadariah Haji's waistcoat.

sadau I, menyadau to knock down a bee's nest.

sadau II to row with long oar.

sadaya all.

sadik straight, honest; **fajar sadik** true dawn; = **siddik**.

sadikit = sedikit a little; **sedikit-sedikit** very little.

sado two-wheeled pony trap.

sadu pre-eminent.

sadung, tersadung tripped up.

sadur plating, plated; **menyadur** to plate.

saf line, row; **bersaf-saf** in lines (of troops).

Safar second Muslim month.

safar journey.

safi pure, noble.

safir traveller; = musafir.

saga, biji saga red and black seed of tree; goldsmith's weight.

sagai, ikan sagai horse mackerel.

sagang, tersagang propped at an angle, leaning against a rock.

sagar sugar; = sakar.

sagat, menyagat to rasp coconut pulp, scrape out sago pith; **penyagat** scraper.

sagu sago; **sagu pisang** pith of banana stem; **sagu tepung** tapioca; **sagu hati** compensation, consolation prize.

sagun dish of rice flour and coconut pulp fried.

sagur river boat, dug-out.

sah legal, valid, authentic; **mengesahkan** to legalize.

sahabat friend, comrade; **bersahabat** on friendly terms.

sahaja, saja only, merely; **bersahaja** empty-handed.

saham to share.

sahan platter.

sahang pepper.

sahap cover of cooking pot; **bersahap** covered.

saharah large chest, box.

sahaya household slave; **hamba sahaya** serfs and slaves; I, me; also saya.

sahi careless, thoughtless; strong tea.

sahib master; **sahib ulhikayat** storyteller.

sahifah epistle, letter.

sahih valid, certain, proved.

sahir sorcerer.

sahur meal taken between midnight and dawn in fasting month Ramadan.

sahut, menyahut to reply.

Said name given to boys born on Friday.

saidani two lords Hassan and Husain.

Saidi, Ya Saidi! O Lord!

saidina master, title of the Prophet Muhammad and his four Companions.

saif sword.

saikoloji psychology.

Sailan Ceylon.

sain signature; to sign.

saing, bersaing side by side; **menyaingi** to accompany.

sains science.

saintifik scientific.

sair hell fire.

sais groom, chauffeur, coachman.

saiyid male descendant of Prophet Muhammad.

sajadah praying mat.

sajak rhyme, harmony, poetry; **bersajak dengan** to rhyme with.

sajang spirits, arrack.

saji food served; **tudung saji** dish cover; **menyajikan** to dish up food.

saka female ancestry; **saka-baka** ancestry on both sides.

sakai aborigines; subject (of chiefs).

sakal contrary (of winds); **angin sakal** headwind; to rap with knuckles.

sakalian all together; also sekelian.

sakan big and sturdy.

sakar sugar; hell fire.

sakarin saccharine.

sakat, pokok sakat orchids; **suku sakat** one's family (including all of common ancestry); **menyakat** to annoy (of people); **penyakat** tease.

sakhawat bounty, generosity.

sakhlat, kain sakhlat woollen cloth.

saki comrade; **saki-baki** remainder, balance.

sakinat at peace, peaceful.

saking because of, on account of.

sakit ache, agony; ill; unwell, sick, in pain; **sakit hati** annoyed; **menyakiti** to injure; **penyakit** illness, disease; **kesakitan** in pain.

sakratul—maut the death agony.

saksama careful inquiry, justice.

saksi witness (person); **huruf saksi** vowels in romanized spelling.

sakti supernatural power (of Hindu deities); **kesaktian** having supernatural power.

saktimuna monstrous serpent.

saku bag, pocket (of coat etc); **menyakukan** to separate; **ternaku**.

sal shawl, puggaree.

salad lettuce.

salah mistaken, at fault, guilty; **salah faham** to misunderstand; **bersalah** to commit a fault; **menyalahkan** to blame, denounce as wrong; **kesalahan** fault, crime.

salai, menyalai to heat over a fire, smoke fish; **salaian** rack over fire for smoking; **penyalai** platform for drying fish.

salak I thorny palms with edible fruit.

salak II, menyalak to bark.

salam peace; **salam alaikum** peace be with you (usual Muslim greeting); **bersalam-salaman** greeting one another.

salang I, menyalang to execute by driving a long creese through the shoulder to the heart.

salang II net or cane receptacle for food that can be raised or lowered from ceiling; **kayu salang** tripod-shaped frame.

salap salve, ointment.

salasal diabetes.

salasilah genealogy of princes; pedigree on male side as opposed to matrilineal (teromba); also **silasilah**.

salat prayer.

salatin sultans.

salawat prayer, invocation.

saleh I pious.

saleh II throwbacks (of animals); freak; motion to or from; **saleh kembali** to revert.

salek traveller.

sali strong, firm; **sama sali** equal in strength; **berhati sali** honest, steadfast.

salib cross for crucifixion; **perang salib** crusade; **menyalibkan** to crucify.

salim, hati salim sound heart of a mystic free from idolatry and hypocrisy.

salin, menyalin to change clothes; **bersalin warna** to change its colour; **persalinan** present of raiment.

saling one another; **saling membantu** helping each other.

salji, salju snow; = **thalji**.

salla blessing.

salui, ikan tulang salui horse mackerel.

saluk, destar **saluk** twined headkerchief; **bersaluk** wearing a headkerchief.

salung flute; = **suling** lamp glass.

saluran conduit, gutter, pipe; **saluran letrik** electric wires.

salut, menyalut to case, cover, enwrap; **bersalut emas** goldplated.

sama same, alike, equal; **sama besarnya** of equal size; **sama juga** it's all the same;

bersama-sama together; menyamakan to treat as equal; persamaan equality, similarity.

samad the supporter (God).

samak I sky, heaven.

samak II, pokok samak trees like mangrove whose bark is used for tanning; menyamak to tan.

Saman, ratib Saman ritual named after 18th century founder of mystic order.

saman legal summons.

samang, anak samang child adopted into matrilineal tribe; induk samang women adopting such a child.

samar dim, vague; hari samar muka it has become dusk; tersamar disguised, concealed; samaran to camouflage; disguised; nama samaran penname; menyamarkan diri to disguise o.s. as.

sambal condiments eaten with curry; menyambal to prepare condiments.

sambalewa half-hearted (of workers); slack.

sambang deserted bee's nest; empty (of nests); half-filled (of grain); bersambang to go round; menyambangi to visit.

sambar, menyambar to pounce and seize; sambaran prey; pouncing; penyambar snatch thief.

sambas pattern in basketry.

sambat, bersambat joined with; menyambat to tie, join; menyambat to ask for co-operation.

sambau, rumput sambau a hardy grass.

sambil simultaneously (of action); sambil lalu sambil ia berteriak he shouted as he passed; sambilan accessory.

sambit, menyambit to hurl; = lempar.

sambuk whip; dinghy; coconut husk.

sambung, menyambung to join on lengthen; bersambung to be joined on, continue; sambungan additional.

sambut, menyambut to receive, greet; sambutan response, reception, welcome; sambut-menyambut exchange visit.

sementara = sementara.

sami Hindu idol; Buddhist monk.

samin, nasi samin rice cooked in butter.

samir rough sheets of palm fronds stitched for temporary roofing.

sampah rubbish; sampah sarap refuse of all sorts; bakul sampah wastepaper basket.

sampai to arrive (of persons, trains etc); to reach (of hands); surat belum sampai the letters have not yet come; tangan tidak sampai my hands won't reach.

sampak metal collar to prevent tang of blade splitting a wooden handle; seluar sampak shorts, drawers.

sampan I harbour boat propelled by sweeps, canoe.

sampan II shuttle of sewing machine.

sampang wood varnish; menyampang to paddle from the bows.

sampar epidemics (among birds); pest; sampar haiwan rinderpest.

sampat, balai sampat ceremonial bathing pyramid used on third day after marriage; mandi sampat to so bathe.

sampil leg of slaughtered beast; husk at base of palm fronds.

samping side, flank; pintu

samping side door; **bersampingan** side by side; **bersamping** wearing a sarung to the knees.

sampir cross-piece of creese sheath; **sampiran** clothes rack or line; *also* (s)**ampaian**.

sampu to hit away; *also* **sampuk**; **demam sampu** tuberculosis.

sampuk, menyampuk to butt in (*on conversation, in work*); **tersampuk** crossed by a spirit and so ill.

sampul wrapper; envelope; cover; pillowcase; **menyampul** to wrap.

sampun to cut short (*of grass, hair*).

sampur sash held behind their backs by dancers.

Samsam Siamese-speaking Muslims.

samsing rowdy, rough.

samsir = shamsir scimitar.

samsu Chinese rice spirit.

samudra ocean.

samum simoom, Arabian dust storm.

samun, menyamun to rob on highway; **penyamun** robber; **semak samun** thick undergrowth, scrub.

samunsur isotope.

samurai class of Japanese nobility.

sana over there, somewhere there; **ke sana** thither; **sebelah sana** in that direction.

sanad authorities for a Tradition (*Hadis*).

sanak, sanak saudara akin; relatives, relatives on the maternal side; **anak sanak ibu** nephew, niece.

sanan = sana.

sanat year of the Hegira.

sanbal spikenard.

sanda = sandar pawn.

sandai one (*in children's game*).

sandak to draw in part of the line when fishing.

sanda malam the nightflowering tuberose.

sandang shoulder sash, cordon of an order; **menyandang** to wear hung over the shoulder.

sandar, bersandar leaning against; **bersandarkan** to have for support; **sandar menyandar** to support mutually; **tersandar** supported.

sandera debt slave, hostage.

sanding, bersanding to sit ceremonially side by side on a dais (*of bride and groom*); **bersanding** having sharp corners.

sandiwara play, comedy, concert.

sandung heddles of a loom; **sandungan** cradle.

sang = si honorific for Hindu deities, kings and animals in folklore; **Sang Kancil Mr** Mousedeer.

sanga dross on smelted metal.

sangai palm leaf dish cover; to keep heated.

sangap to yawn.

sangar reeking (*as onions*).

sangat very, excessively; **tersangat** most, exceedingly; **kesangatan** excess.

sangga prop of boom; catch on anklet; **penyangga** prop; catch; **menyangga** to prop; hold fast (*of catch*).

sanggah, menyanggah to oppose, contest, protest at; **sanggahan** protest.

sanggam, menyanggam to borrow for one occasion; borrow with no intention of returning.

sanggama union, confederation.

sanggan low pedestal stand; saucer on feet.

sanggar family altar.

sanggat, tersanggat partly aground.

sanggerah to bleed.

sanggit scraping, rubbing (as branches); **menyanggit gigi** to grind teeth.

sanggul coiffure; **bersanggul** coiffured; **menyanggul** to do one's coiffure.

sanggup, menyanggup to affirm readiness or ability to accept responsibility for.

sanggurdi stirrup.

sangir tusk, dog-tooth of mouse-deer; **tersangir** with dog-tooth exposed.

sangka opinion; expectation; suspicion; **pada sangka saya** to my mind; **tiada dia sangka** they never suspected.

sangkak, menyangkak to stand in the way of, impede; **penyangkak obstructive; menyangkak** to bristle (of hair from fright).

sangkal, menyangkal to deny, refuse request; **bersangkal** to make one's denial.

sangkala date, time; also **sengkala.**

sangkang many.

sangkar cage, coop, hen's nest.

sangkau, menyangkau to reach for without rising.

sangkih inflated with food.

sangkil hitting the mark (of blows); leaving a balance over; fulfilling a purpose well.

sangku brass washbasin.

sangkur bayonet.

sangkut, bersangkut cohesion; stick-in-the-mud; **tersangkut** stuck; **menyangkut** to hang firmly on a rack; **bersangkut-paut** implicated in an affair.

sangling, menyangling to polish metal, burnish.

sanglok miscarry (of animals).

sangluat stall for refractory buffalo.

sangsai agony, pain, torture.

Sangsakerta Sanskrit.

sangsang, menyangsang to hinder.

sang-serok, burung sangserok chestnut-breasted tree partridge.

sangsi doubt, anxiety; **menyangsikan** to be doubtful about.

sangu seaweed that produces gelatine.

sang-ulun majesty (title).

sanjai tall and well-built.

sanjung, menyanjung to praise, flatter.

sanok, burung sanok greenbilled malkoha.

Sanskerit Sanskrit.

santa, santa rasul=sunnat al-Rasul public admission to Muslim faith after circumcision.

santak, menyantak to lunge and hit.

santan coconut milk; **kepala santan** cream of it.

santap, bersantap to eat and drink (of princes); **santapan** royal food.

santau deadly mixture of poisons.

santing beautiful, fine.

santiran similar; likeness (in mirror).

santun dignified, stately; **sopan santun** quiet and dignified.

santung, santung pelalai spell to prevent girl from marrying rival.

sanubari, hati sanubari innermost, secret (of heart's feeling).

sap inkpad; **kertas sap** blotting paper.

sapa, menyapa to greet (person).

sapar jungle shelter; **bersapar** to encamp.

sapat broken-off (of blades of grass).

sapeh, menyapeh to wean.

sapi bull, cow, ox; **minyak sapi** ghee.

sapir sapper.

sapta seven.

sapu, menyapu to brush on (*paint*); stroke; wipe (*eyes*); sweep away; **penyapu** broom; **tersapu** to wipe off; **saputangan** handkerchief.

saput filmy cover; **disaput awan** clouded over.

sara sustenance, allowance, pension; **bersara** pensioned; **menyara** to support, bring up.

saraf, ilmu **saraf** science of inflexion; **urat saraf** nerve; **penyakit saraf** neurosis.

sarah wooden chest.

sarak spiced shellfish baked in the shell; clouds; **bersarak** parted; **menyarak** to wean.

saran, menyaran to suggest; **saranan** suggestion.

sarang nest (*for birds*); **sarang lebah** bee's nest; **sarang laba-laba** spider's web; **bersarang** possessed (*of a nest*).

sarap infantile rash; sampah **sarap** litter; **menyarap** to line with leaves; **sarapan** breakfast.

sarat heavily laden (*of cart, ship etc*).

sarau hanging kitchen rack; creel for collector of seaweed; unlucky.

sardi glanders.

sarhad boundary.

sari flower; **taman sari** flower garden; **raja sari** bridegroom (*royal for a day*); **sari** or **saree**.

saring, menyaring to strain; **saringan** filter.

Sarip = Shariff.

saripati quintessence; *also* **inti pati.**

sarit difficult, poor; **sarit-sarit** seldom.

sarjan sergeant.

sarjana expert, doctor.

sarkas circus.

sarsar confused, bewildered.

sartan Cancer in the Zodiac.

saru dim (*of sight*); **menyaru** to disguise.

saruk tripped up (*by creeper*); **menyaruk** to step into.

sarung covering (*for chair*); skirt; sheath (*of knife*); **sarung kaki** socks; **bersarung** having a sheath.

sarut scrape; = **garut** tangled.

sarwa all; **sarwa sekelian alam** whole world.

sarwal trousers; *also* **seluar.**

sas crupper of saddle.

sasa, tegap sasa strong, sturdy (*of men, beasts*).

sasak wattled (*of bamboo fence*).

sasap, susup-sasap helter-skelter; to weed.

sasar, sasau eccentric, odd; **sasar bahasa** slightly queer; **sasaran** target; **menyasar** to aim.

sasian, anak sasian student, pupil.

sastera Hindu sacred book; **kesusasteraan** literature.

sasterawan literary man.

sasteria knight; = **kesatria.**

sasul, tersasul gone past one's objective, overshot.

sat ace (*in cards*); **sat lekuk** ace of hearts; = **saat.**

satah, sembah satah kowtow.

satai cabobs served on skewer.

satang punt pole.

satar line (*of writing, print*).

satelit satellite.

satir, sumpah satir to swear an irrevocable oath.

satu one; **satu pun tidak not** even **one; bersatu** united; **persatuan** unity; association; **kesatuan** union; **kesatuan peniaga** guild.

satwa wild beast; **marga satwa** fauna; *also* **mergastua.**

sau soughing noise, rustle, hiss (*of steam*).

saudagar wholesale dealer, merchant.

saudara brother, sister, cousin, any collateral relative; **anak saudara** nephew, niece; **sanak saudara** kinsfolk; **bersaudara** related.

sauh anchor; **sauh terbang** flying grapnel.

saujana, padang saujana plain stretching to the horizon; **saujana mata memandang** as far as the eye can see.

sauk scoop; to scoop up (drinking water to one's mouth); landing net for fish; **menyauk** to net; **pak sauk** pilferer.

sauku whip.

saum fasting.

saung cave, cavern.

saur=sahur, bersaur caught (of feet); **menyaur** to lasso the feet of beasts; **tersaur** entangled.

saus sauce.

sawa python; snakes; **buah sawa** sapodilla, ciku.

sawah irrigated ricefields; **bersawah** owning or cultivating ricefields.

sawan fits, convulsions; **sawan babi** epilepsy; **sawan bangkai** apoplexy.

sawang cobweb; space between earth and sky; vast and uninhabited; **punai sawang** green pigeon.

sawar fence for trapping animals; **tali sawar** cords hung with fronds to quarantine house.

sawat belt; **sawat sandang** shoulder belt.

sawi, sawi-sawi Indian mustard.

sawit, kelapa sawit oil palm; **sawitan** suit of one pattern.

saya=sahaya I, me.

sayak white pleated cloth worn under the front of a woman's jacket.

sayang affection (of parents, lovers); **sayangnya** the pity of it; **penyayang** lover; one who pities.

sayap wing (of bird, army); mudguard; **sayap ikan** fin; **bersayap** winged.

sayat, menyayat to cut off bits of skin or flesh.

sayembara contest of suitors for a bride.

sayid title of descendants of the Prophet.

sayip born of royal father and royal mother; =gahara.

sayu melancholic, sad; **kesayuan** melancholy.

sayung, menyayung to cut on the skew (esp in paring rattans); **sayung tirus** tapering unevenly.

sayup hardly visible or audible; far away; **sayup mata memandang** almost out of sight.

sayur vegetable; **sayur-sayuran** all sorts of vegetables.

se II=sama sa; sebesar ini as big as this; **sepanjang jalan** all along the road.

seba to have audience of a ruler.

sebab cause, motive, incentive; **apa sebab?** why?, what is the motive?; **oleh sebab** because; **bersebab** having a reason; **menyebabkan** to cause.

sebai shawl worn over the shoulders, scarf.

sebak flooding (of rivers, tears); **air sebak** floodwater; **penyakit sebak** tightness of the chest with difficult breathing.

sebal resentful, disillusioned, mortified; **menyebal** to sulk.

sebam tarnished (of lustre); dull (of colour).

sebar, beri-beri numb (of limbs); **menyebar** to scatter, sow.

sebarau, ikan sebarau carp.

sebat, menyebat to swish; cane, whip away; filch; choked (of throat, nostril).

sebawa beautiful.

sebek to pout (of infant about to cry).

sebekah, ikan sebekah sea perches.

sebeng, layar sebeng movable stage curtain.

seberang opposite side (of river, road, etc); menyeberang to cross (road, river).

seberhana, pakaian seberhana full dress.

seberot, menyeberot to snatch, steal.

sebit, menyebit to tear into thin strips.

sebok, menyebok, masuk sebok to intrude on a company, butt into.

sebong internode of bamboo.

sebu choked (of nose); sebukan to fill up.

sebun blind (of boil); to fill a hole.

seburut shrub with large purple flowers.

sebut, menyebutkan to mention, cite; pronounce (word); tersebut cited; sebutan pronunciation; jadi sebut to get talked about.

sedak I, tersedak choking from swallowing, hiccuping.

sedak II, menyedak to tauten; parchment of drum.

sedakang, ikan sedakang silver bream.

sedal, menyedalkan to hang up clothes to dry.

sedam, sedam-sedam booming (of cannon).

sedan, tersedan-sedan sobbing.

sedang medium in size; just right; in the middle of; sedang masak just ripe; sedangkan although.

sedap delicious to taste; comfortable.

sedar conscious, aware, awake to; tiada sedar unaware.

sedat slow-witted.

sedau striped (of mousedeer).

sedawa belch.

sedeh tearful; tersedeh-sedeh quietly sobbing; sedeh hati grieving.

sedek, tersedek di hati flashed on the mind.

sedekah alms, freewill offering.

sedekala, sediakala former, past; continual.

sedelinggam red lead.

sederhana moderate, average, medium.

sedia ready, prepared; bersedia to prepare o.s.; menyediakan to prepare (food); persediaan preparation.

sedikit = sadikit.

sedingin life plant used in medicine.

sedu, tersedu-sedu hiccoughing.

seduh, **menyeduh** to soak in warm water.

sedut, menyedut to sniff up, inhale.

seduyah shrub.

sega smooth, polished; rotan sega best rattan.

segah replete, distended with flatulence.

segak I hot; menyegak to flare up.

segak II smart, chic.

segala all, whole.

segan reluctant, shy; jangan segan don't hesitate.

seganda fragrant.

segani helmsman.

segar fit, healthy (of people); segarkan to invigorate; segar kabung spiky twig of the sugar palm.

segara ocean.

segeh, bersegeh tidy; tidied.

segel seal; **menyegel** to seal.

segenting isthmus.

segera quickly; **dengan segera, menyegerakan** to speed up.

segi side, facet; **segi tiga** triangle; **bersegi-segi** with many facets.

segok inconvenient (of clothes).

seguro to frank (letters).

seh clan.

sehat, sihat healthy; **ilmu kesihatan** hygiene.

seher sorcery; also **sihir**.

sejahtera peace, safety; **kesejahteraan** to enjoy tranquillity.

sejajar in line.

sejak = **semenjak**.

sejarah genealogy; annals.

sejat dried; evaporated (of water).

sejonak while.

sejuk cold, cool, shivery; **sejukkan** to cool, pacify.

sejurus moment.

sek rustling.

seka, berseka to wash o.s.; **menyeka** to wipe (face, table).

sekah I broken and dangling.

sekah II nimble (of body); stamp on coin.

sekak chess.

sekakar miser.

sekala hitherto.

sekali once; **sekalipun** although.

sekam rice husk.

sekang, menyekang to plug.

sekap, menyekap to keep fruit in bin to ripen.

sekara flower.

sekarang now, immediately; presently.

sekat, menyekat to hinder, obstruct; **sekatan** obstruction; **bersekat** restricted.

sekati royal musical instrument.

sekeduduk Singapore rhododendron (actually Melastoma); to live as man and wife.

sekedup camel's saddle.

sekeh to rap head with one's knuckles; also **sekel**.

sekelian = **sakalian**.

sekendi, burung sekendi white ibis.

sekerba full.

sekerup screw.

sekian, sekian banyak so many as this; **sekian lama** so long as I have caid.

sekim scheme.

sekin knife.

sekip bull's eye, target.

sekitar neighbourhood.

sekoci ship's cutter, sloop.

sekoi millet.

sekolah school; **sekolah gambar** museum.

sekolarship scholarship.

sekongkol gangster.

sekopong spades (in cards).

sekotah all of it, all over; **sekotah Tanah Melayu** all over Malaya.

sekretari secretary.

seksa torment, pain; **menyeksakan** to torture, oppress.

seksyen section.

sekul bowl of three-quarters of a coconut shell.

sekunin little.

sekunar two-masted schooner.

sekut miserly, niggardly.

sekutu = **kutu**.

sela I interstice; slit; fork; **bersela** at intervals; **tidak bersela** continuous; **menyela** to interplant.

sela II saddle; cross-eyed.

selada salad.

seladang Malaya's wild ox; on the same level.

seladeri celery.

selak I bar, bolt (of door); **menyelak** to bar.

selak II, **menyelak** to lift up (skirt); **terselak** raised.

selaka rack for censing clothes.

selalu always, continually.

selam, menyelam to dive; juru selam, penyelam diver; kapal selam submarine.

selamat safety; selamat jalan good-bye (to s.o. going); selamat tinggal good-bye (to s.o. staying); selamatkan, menyelamatkan to save rescue.

selamba shameless, bare-faced; menyelamba to behave with effrontery.

selambu stubble after harvest.

selampai, menyelampai to wear cloth over shoulder; kain selampai handkerchief.

selampit flat braid or plait; berselampit to wear cloth between thighs as loincloth; reciter of folk tales.

selang passage between two buildings; intervening (in space or time); selang berapa hari after an interval of some days; berselang intervening; alternate; selangkan = sedangkan although.

selangat, ikan selangat shad.

selangin = senangin.

selangka, tulang selangka collarbone.

selangkan perineum.

selanting, burung selanting long-billed partridge.

selap, terselap unconscious or hysterical from attack of spirit.

selapan eight.

selaput membrane, film over eye; tarnish on brass; selaput mata cataract; dirty, untidy.

selar, tanda selar brand on horse; menyelarkan to brand; selar-belar rummaging, turning topsy-turvy; horse mackerel.

selara, ikan selara poison-spined edible fish; also sembilang.

selarak crossbar for doors.

selaroh on the same plane, level.

selarung track made by elephants.

Selasa Tuesday; see Thalatha.

selasar front verandah level with house floor balcony passage.

selaseh basil; ayam selaseh black-boned fowl; buah selaseh passion-fruit.

selat strait; interspace, crevice.

selatan south; bawal selatan pomfret.

selawat prayer; berselawat to invoke God's blessing.

selawe twenty-five.

selayar, ikan selayar food fish.

selayun scarecrow.

selayur hairtail or scabbard (fish).

selderi celery.

sele jam jelly.

selebu, laut selebu distant, hazy ocean.

seleder lazybones

seleguri yellow-flowered mallow.

selekeh, berselekeh smeared with sticky dirt.

selekoh twisting; bend (of road).

selekor, ikan selekor horse mackerel.

seleler, berseleler trickle of blood.

selemah, ikan selemah milk-fish.

selembada, semut selembada large biting ant.

selembana, menyelembana to lie head to wind.

selembayong crossbar for ship's pennant.

selembubu, angin selembubu whirlwind.

selempada = selembada.

selempai I anxious, worried.

selempang II, terselempang

astride, with legs apart;—
selepang.

selempukau oriole;—burung
kunyit.

selendang shoulder scarf
used as veil.

selendar cylinder;—kebuk.

selengar strong (of scent).

selenggara, menyelenggara-
kan to organize; tend, look
after; penyelenggara organizer.

selentek, menyelentek to nip,
flick with the nails.

selenyap, angin selenyap
double hydrocele, scrotal hernia.

selepa watch-shaped tobacco
box;—celepa.

selepang, berselepang to wear
a sash over one shoulder and
under the other.

selepat, berselepat caked with
sticky substance.

selepe gold or silver waist-
buckle.

selepong, berselepong smeared
with mud.

selepur, berselepur immersed
in mud.

selera appetite; zest for life;
patah selera without appetite.

selerak scattered (of clothes
etc).

selerang outer skin.

selesa leisure; having time;
comfortable; tidak selesa not
free, engaged in work; uncomfortable.

selesai ended; settled (of
business, debt); menyelesaikan
to settle, wind up; penyelesaian disposal; settlement.

selesema cold in head;
demam selesema influenza.

seletar all round.

seleweng dirty, untidy (of
person); orang seleweng busybody.

selia, menyeliakan to inspect
carefully; solve; penyelia super-

visor; selia handsome, dainty.

seliap, ikan seliap marine
horse mackerel.

seliar to wander (as ghost).

seliat to flay, skin (animal).

selicin, ikan selicin parrotfish.

selidik, menyelidik to investigate; penyelidikan inquiry, investigation.

seligi dart, wooden javelin,
sharpened bamboo or nibung
palm.

seligit straggling (of crowds),
winding about.

selimang, ikan selimang batu
small carp.

selimbu rice stalks that grow
after harvest.

selimpat braided-ribbon pattern in lace, mat-making;
ular selimpat sea snakes with
flattened tails.

selimut, kain selimut rug,
blanket; berselimut covered;
menyelimutkan to enwrap.

selinap, menyelinap to strip
off the outer skin (of bamboo);
tear off the skin of a fowl for
cooking; move fast in order to
escape.

selindung, berselindung to
take cover, hide.

seling small silver, five, ten,
twenty cents; **papan seling**
ceiling.

seliok sound (as siren).

seliput, menyeliputi to cover
(as barnacles).

selir secondary wife; coverlet;
rustle.

selirat, berselirat to reticulate.

selisih, selisihnya difference;
berselisih to fail to meet (of
joinery); disagree; perselisihan
disagreement.

selisik, menyelisik to hunt for
fleas on dog.

selisir to walk round the
edge of (cliff etc).

selit, menyelitkan to insert;
terselit inserted into crevice.

selogan slogan.

seloka quatrains of four rhyming lines.

selomor slough (of snake); **menyelomor** to slough.

selompot mace (spice).

selompret trumpet.

selongkar to rummage for contraband; steal food off plate.

selongsong wrapper; dog muzzle.

selop slipper.

seloroh comical (as clown); farcical, teasing.

seluang, ikan seluang small carp.

seluar trousers; **berseluar** trousered.

selubung veil; **berselubung** to wrap up; veil o.s.

seludang sheath of the palm blossom.

seludip palm spathe; = **seludang.**

seludu catfish.

seluduk, **menyeluduk** to crawl crouching.

seludup, **menyeludup** to crawl quietly; duck; cause a search; smuggle.

seluit, burung seluit green broadbill.

seluk, **menyeluk** to grope (in hole, pocket); examine; **seluk-beluk** intricacies of problem; **berseluk** twisting.

selulup, **berselulup** to plunge into water.

selulus incontinence of the bladder.

selumbar long thorn; splinter of glass.

selumbir moss; rough (of timber); **terselumbir** to cut off.

selumbu slough (of snakes); = **selomor.**

selunput short-tempered.

seludup contraband.

selungkang bad (of coin).

selungkap loose (of nails).

selup sloop.

selupat membrane, skin of egg under shell.

selurai, tepung selurai macaroni; vermicelli.

selusuh medicine to hasten or ease childbirth.

selusur handrail of bridge; **menyelusur** to slip down tree.

selut slush, mud, puddle.

semah sacrifice, offerings; **menyemah** to sacrifice.

semai, **menyemaikan** to plant rice seedlings in nursery.

semak I undergrowth; semak samun undergrowth of all kinds.

semak II, **menyemak** to revise script or proof; **penyemak** proof reader, checker.

semalu sensitive plant.

semambu, rotan semambu Malacca cane.

semampai dangling loosely.

seman spoilt (of yeast); relapse in measles.

semanar salamander.

semang negritos of Upper Perak.

semangat vital force (of men, plants); spirit; lemah semangat faint, weak; **bersemangat** energetic, full of vitality; lively (of tunes).

semangka water melon.

semangkuk, kembang semangkuk tree whose seeds are used medicinally.

semantan young coconut.

semantung thunder without rain.

semar clown in shadow play.

semaram, ikan semaram sca peroh.

semasema catarrh; see **selesema.**

semat, **menyematkan** to pin together; **penyemat** fastener; jarum penyemat pins; **tersemat** pinned.

semata altogether, utterly.

semawa to invite.

semawat heavens, sky.

semayam, bersemayam to reside (of Rulers).

semayan clerk.

sembada proper, just.

sembah obeisance, respectful address; **menyembahkan** to present gift respectfully; **persembahan** gift or address.

sembahyang = sembah yang to pray; **sembahyang wajib** Muslim's obligatory prayer.

sembai tailings (mining); silt.

sembak, ikan sembak tunny.

sembam, tersembam falling headlong on one's face.

sembang to chatter, gossip.

sembap swollen (esp of cheek from toothache).

sembat, menyembat to cane, whip away; **jahit sembat** hemstitch.

sembawa to offer; invite to feast.

sembeleh, menyembeleh to slaughter beast by cutting throat as Islam ordains.

sembelit constipation.

sembelu metal vase for sirih.

sember cracked (of voice).

semberani, kuda semberani flying steed.

semberap betel box.

semberip small pedestal tray.

semberono nonchalant, casual.

sembeta props to keep a boat steady on beach.

sembiang small fish spear.

sembilan nine.

sembilang catfish with poisonous spine.

sembilek, puru sembilek haemorrhoids.

sembilu bamboo splinter.

sembir edge (of tray etc); ridge of belimbing fruit.

semboyan alarm gong; signals (morse etc); motto.

sembuang tray of offerings to spirits cast into jungle.

sembuh healed, cured; **sembuhkan** to cure.

sembul, tersembul protruding (of eyes, breasts).

sembulu rough, unplaned.

sembung plant much used in medicine and magic.

sembunyi, bersembunyi to hide o.s.; to conceal; **tersembunyi** hidden.

sembur, menyemburkan to eject from mouth; **bersemburan** spurting; **tersembur** spurted.

semburit sodomy.

semburna golden (of colour).

semedang all the time.

semelit = sembelit

sememeh smeared, dirty (of mouth).

semena, tidak semena-mena without good reason.

semenanjung peninsula.

semenda, bersemenda related by marriage to matrilineal tribe.

semendal mica.

semenderasa = cempaka.

semenderasa wilis frangipani.

semenggah proper, becoming.

semenjak, semenjak itu ever since.

semenjana average, medium.

sementang although supposing.

sementara while, as long as; **sementara itu** meanwhile.

sementelah, sementelahan moreover.

sementung dull, stupid.

semerbak pervasive (of scent).

semerdanta white and fragrant.

semesta whole, all over; **semesta alam** throughout the universe.

semi sprout; **musim semi** spring.

seminar seminar.

semoga may it happen that!

semor, masak semor to stew.

sempada, ketam sempada crab.

sempadan boundary (of plot); frontier; side of figure (triangle etc).

sempak splintered (of wall).

sempal, tersempal protruding; menyempal to cram mouth.

sempalai prostrate from fatigue.

sempana blessed, luck-bringing; sempanakan to bless.

sempang I hyphen.

sempang II =simpang.

sempang—sempung swaying about (of an old boat).

sempat having the time to do; tiada sempat aku pergi I had no time to go.

sempelah refuse, rubbish, dregs.

sempelat, bersempelat caked with dirt.

semperong kitchen chimney.

sempil exposed (as tooth).

sempilai fighting fish.

sempit narrow, cramping; kesempitan narrowness (of means).

sempoa abacus.

sempok to gore.

sempok to hit a sidelong blow.

sempolong little girl's hairbun.

sempoyongan staggering.

semprot squirt, spray.

sempudal, bersempudal filthy (of person, clothes).

sempuras, bersempuras untidy, dirty.

sempurna perfect (of men, work); menyempurnakan to accomplish, fulfil (vow, intention); complete (work).

semput short of breath.

semsem keen; passionately in love.

semu deceit, ruse, pretence; tersemu cheated.

semua, kesemuanya all of them.

semudera ocean; = samudra.

Senujong = Sang Yang Ujong Holyhead.

semurup lean-to hut.

semut ant; semut api long black stinging ant.

sen cent; =duit.

sena I yellow-flowered shade tree; also angsana.

sena II army.

senai, bersenai to rest (of medium at Malay magician's seance).

senak gripes due to flatulence; menyenak flood and overflow of tide; tersenak over-filled, choked.

senalau always.

senam, bersenam to stretch o.s., do physical exercises; senaman drill, exercise; material under plating.

senamaki senna of Mecca, purgative.

senandika soliloquy.

senandung, bersenandung to sing to o.s., hum, croon.

senang easy (of work); at leisure (of persons); comfortable, well-to-do; kesenangan comfort, ease, convenience.

senangin, ikan senangin edible threadfish.

senantan white (of fighting cocks).

senapang gun; senapang angin airgun.

senapati war chief.

Senara = Seri Nara (title).

senarai list; =daftar.

senawat plaited rattan buffalo whip with bamboo handle.

senawi ship's passenger who works his passage.

senda, gurau senda dalliance; flirt; sport; joke; mempersendakan to tease, joke.

sendal, menyendalkan to insert wedge; sendalan insertion.

sendalu moderate (of breeze); =bendalu mistletoe.

sendang spring (water).

sendar, bersendar to snore, snuffle.

sendarat, ikan sendarat sea perch.

sendat, tersendat close-fitting (of clo'hes).

sendawa saltpetre, nitre.

sendayan several sedges; grass used for mat-making.

sende one (in children's game).

sendel to lean against.

sendeng, tersendeng at a slant, heeling over.

senderung, ikan senderung sea perch.

sendi joint (of body, joinery), hinge; bersendi jointed, hinged.

sendiri self; dengan sendirinya of its own accord.

sendorong to slip forward.

sendu sad, grieved.

senduk spoon; menyenduk to ladle.

sendung pen for buffalo.

senebang–senebu trial of strength game.

senentiasa always, incessantly.

senet senate.

sengaja on purpose.

sengal rheumatic, sciatic.

sengam, menyengam to gorge.

sengap silent; menyengap to keep silent.

sengaring, ikan sengaring freshwater fish.

sengat sting (of bee, wasp etc); penyengat wasp.

sengau to talk through nose.

sengeh, tersengeh-sengeh grinning.

sengelat artful dodger.

senget, tersenget aslant.

senggagai clinging (to branch).

senggak to sing, roar in chorus.

senggam, menyenggam to guzzle.

senggan as far as here; also sehingga ini.

senggang at leisure; waktu senggang free time.

senggat as far as, up to.

senggau, menyenggau to reach up for; reach up (of flames).

senggayut, bersenggayut dangling.

senggoh long of tooth.

senggeruk snuff.

sengget to knock down fruit with pole.

senggirek anger.

senggol, bersenggol to butt against.

senggugu shrimp; also udang geragau.

sengguk, tersengguk-sengguk nodding with sleep.

senggulung large tropical centipede.

sengir turpentine smell.

sengiring catfish.

sengit pungent (of smell).

sengkak suffering from the fullness of indigestion; menyengkak to massage the stomach.

sengkal thwart.

sengkalan wooden board on which spices are crushed.

sengkang I cross (as illiterate's mark); tersengkang stuck (as bone in throat).

sengkang II, menyengkang to walk with one leg lifted; zigzag.

sengkar athwart.

sengkarut, bersengkarut tangled (of ropes).

sengkat, singkat too short, concise; sengkat akal not sufficiently intelligent; sengkat umur short-lived.

sengkayan waterspout.

sengkek, menyengkek to show off (of cocks); beggar.

sengkela hobbies for elephants.

sengkelang, bersengkelang having a cross; **sengkelang** crossed (of arms); scabies of the scrotum.

sengkelat, bersengkelat unwashed, filthy.

sengkeling crossed (of hands behind back).

sengkelit rattan loop in which tree climbers put their feet.

sengkenit small jungle tick.

sengker to confine, shut up.

sengketa, bersengketa to quarrel; bear a grudge.

sengkil, tersengkil exposed.

sengkokol curled up (with cold).

sengkol difficulty in swallowing from sore throat.

sengkuang, ubi sengkuang yam-bean.

sengkuap lean-to serving as verandah of house.

sengkul doubled up with cold.

sengsara agony, torture.

sengsat rolled up (of trousers etc.).

sengse Chinese medicine man.

sengsurit, burung sengsurit woodpartridge.

seni thin and fine; shrill (of voice); art; **senilukis** art of drawing; **seni pahat** art of sculpture; **seni rong** studio; ilmu kesinian fine arts; **seniman** artist.

senin = Isnin Monday.

sening, bunting sening beginning to swell (of rice ears).

seniwati artist (female).

senja sunset, evening.

senjak since; = semenjak.

senjang wanting symmetry.

senjata weapon of war of any kind; **alat senjata** munitions.

senjung beam holding scales for weighing.

senohong, ikan senohong thread-fin (fish).

senok tapir.

senonggang head downwards; main senonggang balik to turn somersault.

senonggeng bottom upwards, inverted.

senonoh proper, seemly, becoming.

senotol upside down (of top).

sensasi sensation.

sensitif sensitive.

sensor censor.

senta rowers' seats in boat.

sentada, ketam sentada crustacean; semut sentada white ant.

sentadu, belalang sentadu grasshopper; **ulat** sentadu green caterpillar.

sentak I to snarl at, scold.

sentak II, menyentakkan to pull at or out with a jerk; **tersentak** jerking involuntarily.

sental to scrub vigorously.

sentali, burung sentali coppersmith barbet (bird).

sentana family (of prince); perhaps; also sekiranya.

sentap, menyentap to tug, drag; **bersentap** to shrink (of fabrics).

senteri wanderer; **dagang** senteri stranger and wanderer.

sentiabu bayonet.

sentiasa always, perpetually.

sentil, tersentil stuck and partly visible.

sentimen sentiment.

sentimeter centimetre.

senting high, too short (of skirt); also sinting.

sentiong Chinese cemetery.

sentosa tranquillity, safety; **aman sentosa** peace and security; **kesentosaan** to be secure.

sentuh to touch, bump; effect; **tersentuh** accidentally brushing; **garisan sentuh** tangent.

sentul I, pokok sentul tall tree with acid fruit.

sentul II plump.

sentung oval for buffalo fight; head opening.

senuh full after meals.

senuhun monarch; = baginda.

senyampang if, in case, although.

senyap silent (*of persons*); senyap sunyi deserted, lonely.

senyar tingling.

senyum smile; **tersenyum** breaking into a smile.

senyur sir; ikan senyur batfish.

sep, tersep-sep timid (*of children*).

sepa, saya apa we all.

sepada, siapa ada who is there? greeting (*on entering house*).

sepah I quid of betel; burung sepah raja crimson sunbird.

sepah II, bersepah-sepah littered; menyepah to make a litter.

sepai smashed to bits (*as crockery*).

sepak I, menyepak to slap with open palm.

sepak II, menyepak to kick aside; bola sepak football.

sepakat, pakat to agree.

sepan sponge.

sepanar spanner.

sepanduk banner.

sepang thorny tree with yellow flower whose wood is boiled to make dye for mats.

sepang–seput shy.

Sepanyol Spanish.

sepasin chrysalis of dragonfly.

sepat freshwater fish.

sepatu shoe; sepatu besi horseshoe.

sepatung dragonfly.

sepeda cycle.

sepedo dynamite.

sepekolasi speculation.

sepen larder.

sepera, orang gila sepera idiot.

seperai white sheet, table cloth.

sepering spring.

sperma sperm.

seperti like; lari seperti dikejar syaitan to run as if plagued by a devil; dengan sepertinya properly, in a seemly fashion.

sepesan venomous spider.

sepesial special.

sepet half-closed (*of eyes*); mata sepet almond-shaped eyes.

sepi quiet, deserted.

sepiar sphere.

sepirit spirit.

sepit, menyepit to pinch (*as crab*); tersepit nipped; makan bersepit to eat with chopsticks.

sepoa abacus.

September September.

sepuh red gloss; superficial polish of manner; menyepuh to give a gold-red colour.

sepui gentle (*of breeze*); angin sepui bahasa soft breeze.

sepuk, tersepuk left littered (*of clothes*).

sepuleh restorative (*name given to several plants*).

sepunai to treat lightly.

seput dull (*of metal*); keretapi seput fast train.

sera, bersera bustling; frantic (*of mind*).

serabai sort of pancake.

serabut fibrous, rough.

seraga, bantal seraga large round pillow with silver or gold endplates used at ceremonies.

seragam uniform.

serah, menyerahkan to deliver up, surrender; berserah to submit o.s. to God.

serahi glass bottle *or* flask.

serai I lemon grass; **minyak serai** citronella oil.

serai II, terserai scattered.

serak I hoarse from catarrh; **burung serak owl.**

serak II, berserak littered (*of clothes*); **menyerakkan** to strew about; **scatter** (*of seeds*).

serakah greedy.

seram creepy onset of fever.

serama in time, in tune; **gendang serama** drum beaten on one side by stick, on the other by hand.

serambi open verandah in the front of house.

serampak at the same moment.

serampang three-pronged fish spear; **menyerampang** to mow; swipe near the ground.

serampin mat used for collecting sago.

seran, berseran striped (*of fabrics*).

serana style; bearing.

seranah imprecation; **sumpah seranah** to curse, revile.

serancak, burung serancak Malay pipit.

serandang bamboo trestles.

serandau, burung serandau purple heron.

Serandib Ceylon.

serandung, terserandung stumbling, tripping.

serang I boatswain, captain of small launch; **menyerang** to assail; **serangan** to attack; **penyerangan** aggression.

serang II shimmering in the light.

serangga mountain peak; chrysalis, insect; **kaji serangga** entomology.

seranggut to squat on one's hams.

serangguh, menyerangguh to squat on hams with hands on chin.

seranggung to sit with elbows apart and on table.

serangkak belt of thorns round fruit tree to stop pilferers.

serangsang abusive.

Serani, Nasrani Nazarene; Roman Catholic; Eurasian.

seranta, menyeranta to advertise, proclaim; = isytihar.

serap I, menyerap to be absorbed (*as dew*).

serap II skirting board.

serapah curse (*that will fend off tiger*); **sumpah serapah** abuse; **menyerapah** to curse.

serasa betel vine.

serasah, kain serasah printed Coromandel cotton.

serat jammed (*as cork*).

serati mahout.

serau tissue of antlers.

serawa sweetmeat of banana.

serawak, batu serawak antimony.

serawam thrush (*in infants*).

seraya while, and at the same time; **menangis seraya berkata** wept and said; **menyeraya** to co-operate in work.

serba all; **serba salah** all wrong; **serba jenis** all sorts; **serba sedikit** a little of everything.

serbah–serbeh hanging down; slovenly (*of dress*).

serbak, menyerbak pervasive (*of scent*).

serban, turban feeling heavy.

serbaneka of all sorts.

serbang cosmetic of dyed coconut husk for brides.

serbasama equal in all respects.

serbat sherbet, cool drink.

serbi = serba.

serbu, menyerbu to charge, dash; **serbuan** charge.

serbuk powder; **serbuk gergaji** sawdust; **serbuk kopi** coffee powder.

serdadu soldier; **ikan serdadu** catfish.

serdak dust, crumbs.

serdam bamboo flute.

serdang fan palm.

serdawa belch; = **sedawa**.

serdeh prominent (of chest).

serek I deterred (by experience); taught a lesson.

serek II, **menyerek** to sweep off (of cock with drooping wings from hen).

seremban child's game played with shells or pebbles; wearing a **sarung** high in front and low behind.

serembap to fall prone on one's face.

serempak, serempak serentak doing at the same time; **terserempak** erratic (of execution of work); **ketika serempak** emergency.

serempet, **menyerempet** graze; shot missing target.

serempu dug-out; keel of boat.

serendah, **pisang serendah** small banana.

serendeng to heel over, be at an angle.

sereng arrow of fire, rocket.

serengam excessive (of hair, things out of place).

serenjang erect (of persons).

serenjong in tall piles.

serep, **menyerep** to ask as to the position of any matter.

seret, **menyeret** to trail branch along ground, drag.

sergah, **menyergah** to startle by sudden noise.

sergam, **tersergam** in bold relief.

sergap, **menyergap** to surprise, startle.

sergut scamped (of work).

seri charm (of face, place); **seri panggung** star actress; **seri balai** centre of palace audience hall; **berseri** resplendent.

seriak to abate (of rain).

seriap heron.

seriat fishing by a trailing screen that frightens small fry and shrimps to leap into boat.

seriau shuddering (from shock).

seriawan thrush (med.).

seribelum cerebellum.

seri-gading shrub with scented leaves.

serigala jackal; **anjing serigala** Malayan wild dog.

serikat, syarikat company.

serikaya sweetmeat of egg, sugar and coconut steamed.

serimala carpenter.

serimpi royal Javanese dancers.

serindit little Malay parrot.

sering to twist tight (as cord); stiff (as paper); **bersering** twisted; **menyering** to hum round, buzz round; always; **seringkali** always.

seringai, **menyeringai** to grin widely.

seringing, **terseringing** grinning widely.

serit fine comb for delousing.

serius serious.

serkah split (of fruit).

serkai, **menyerkai** sifting; rinsing.

serkap conical coop; **menyerkap** to catch with coop.

serkas, sarkas circus.

serkup, **menyerkup** to catch in serkap.

serlah, terserlah gleaming white against dark.

serlang bright and gleaming.

serling pit to trap large animals.

serlum to don by slipping veil over head.

sermangin musical instrument.

sero large marine fish trap; share in company.

serobeh, **berserobeh** uncombed and unbrushed.

seroda belt of thorns to stop pilferers from climbing fruit trees.

serodi, menyerodi to polish gems.

serodok to creep under.

seroja lotus.

serok incurving; **serokan** inlet from sea, bay.

seroka, menyeroka to open up new ricefields.

seroloh to sink through mud.

serombong chimney.

serondong to lower head and butt.

serong askew (of line); **serong hati** crooked (of morals); **menyerong** to go off at a tangent.

seronggong crossbeams in mines.

seronok pleasant, enjoyable.

seronot, menyeronot to sneak away.

seropot to suck up, lap.

serpa blessing or cursing.

serpai broken to pieces; remnants left over.

serpeh chipped, broken at the edge.

serta together, along with, and; as soon as; **bersérta dengan** together with; **sertamerta** with the utmost expedition, at once; **menyertai** to accompany; **disertasi** thesis.

sertipikat certificate.

sertu, menyertu to perform a sevenfold ablution.

seru, menyeru to cry loudly; **berseru-seru** to keep shouting; **seruan** exclamation; **tanda seru** exclamation mark (!).

seruak, menyeruak to part a way.

seruh shrunken (of swelling).

seruit one-barbed spear.

seruk rice bin holding ten gantangs.

serul inadhesive (of boiled rice).

seruling bamboo or wooden flute.

serum serum.

serun fowl house.

serunai clarinet; **bunga serunai** yellow button flower.

serunda, menyerunda to drag boats overland.

serunding rasped coconut pulp mixed with sugar spices and fried.

serunjung, menyerunjung to leap and clutch.

seruntun, akar seruntun climber.

serunyai ruffled (of plumage).

serut plane; **menyerut** to plane.

serutu, cerutu ceroot, cigar.

sesah to beat with cane.

sesak packed (of crowds); **penuh sesak** chock-full; **sesak dada** bronchial, asthmatic; **menyesakkan** to cramp, overwhelm with work.

sesal repentance, regret, compunction; **menyesal** to be penitent, regret; **menyesalkan** to repent over, be sorry about; **sesalan** contrition; also **kesal**.

sesap, menyesap lap; **sesapan** birds' drinking place, saltlick.

sesar, menyesar to shove aside, push one's way.

sesat astray (on road, in conduct); **sesat barat** all astray; **menyesatkan** to lead astray.

sesawi mustard.

sesema cold, catarrh; = **selesema**.

seseorang each person.

seser fish net.

sesorok Gymnegryllus elegans.

sesuai congruent.

sesuatu—suatu each.

set set.

seta=hasta.

setabal constable.

setabil stable.

setai dangling by a thread.

setak small fishing boat.

setal stall for horse.

setambun trees with edible fruits.

Setanbul Istanbul.

setan *satan*; = **syaitan.**

setar, pokok setar tree with fruit good to eat.

setatik static.

setatistik statistic.

setatur stature.

setawar name for several plants.

setel suit of clothes; **menyetel** to wind *or* set a clock.

seteleng exhibition, show.

setem voice (*of voter*); postage stamp.

setempel seal; signet ring; postmark.

setengah half.

setensil stencil.

seterap punishment.

seterika flat iron.

seteru enemy; **berseteru dengan** at enmity with; **perseteruan** animosity.

seterup, air seterup syrup.

setesen station (*rail*).

seti satin.

setia loyal; **setiausaha** secretary; **bersetia** loyal.

setiabu snake.

setiawan loyal.

setimbal balance.

setinggan squatters.

setinggi clew on sail.

setoka, ikan setoka small sting-tailed ray.

setolop wall *or* hurricane lamp.

setom lamp chimney.

seton water vessel.

setonggang, ikan setonggang knightfish.

setop stew (*of fruit*); stop.

setor pay to store; **menyetorkan** to invest in; **penyetor** investor.

setu change due to spell; **disetui** metamorphosed.

setua wild beasts; **mergasetua** fauna.

setul, pokok setul fast-growing shade tree.

sewa hire, rent; **kereta sewa** hired car; **rumah sewa** rented house; **menyewa** to hire, rent; **penyewa** hirer.

sewah, sewah tekukur lesser hawk-cukcoo

sewajah, wajar appropriate.

sewenang at pleasure.

sewu thousand; **candi sewu** the 1000 shrines.

si— prefix to names of persons and animals; Si-Ahmad Mr Ahmad; **siapa?** who?

sia, sia-sia useless, futile; **sia-sia dia bekerja itu** his work was futile.

siah, bersiah bustling; **menyiahkan** to brush aside.

siak caretaker of mosque; = noja.

siakap, ikan siakap sea perch.

sial ill-omened, unlucky.

sialang wild bee's nest; **pokok sialang** trees where wild bees nest.

siamang long-armed black gibbon.

siang daylight; **siang-siang in good time**; **pesiang** to cut up and clean meat *or* fish.

siap ready; **bersiap** prepared; **menyiapkan** to make ready.

siapa? who?, whose?; **siapa-siapa** whosoever.

siar, bersiar to stroll; **siarkan** to circulate.

siarah wandering; **bintang siarah** planet.

siasat, menyiasat to investigate; **penyiasatan** inquiry; **siasat dunia** world politics; **ahli siasat** politician.

siat, menyiatkan to cut *or* tear off skin *or* covering; tear into shreds.

siau cooled (*of liquids*).

sibak, menyibak to part hair; **bersibak** parted.

sibang-sibuk bustling, busy.

sibar, sibar-sibar border added to jacket; annexe to house; **menyibar** to add a border; **bersibar** splashing all about.

sibiran shred, tattered piece.

sibuk, bersibuk frantically busy; **menyibuk** to bustle; **sibang-sibuk** in a whirl.

sibur ladle of coconut shell; **menyibur** to ladle.

sibut, sibang-sibut bustling.

sida courtier; eunuch; **menyida** to castrate.

sidai, menyidai to dry on clothes-line; **tersidai** hung to dry.

sidang members; **sidang jumaat** members of congregation; **sidang mesyuarat** member of council; **sidang pengurus** board of directors.

sidat cloth *or* leather armlet to hold talisman.

siddik, fajar **siddik** daybreak.

sidek, sidek jari fingerprint; **sidek-midek** close investigation; **menyidek** to examine, investigate.

sidi efficacious.

siding long line of rattan nooses to catch deer; **menyiding** to lie on one's side.

sidip, bersidip clinker-built (*of boats*).

sidrat al-muntaha heavenly tree.

sifat zero.

sifat outward appearance; attribute, quality, property; **mensifatkan** to express, describe; **bersifat** having an attribute, look *etc*; **sifat** nama adjective.

sifir, sipir arithmetical tables.

sigai rough ladder for mounting trees.

sigar, kain sigar bridegroom's headkerchief.

sigasir molecricket.

sigi metal band round creese sheath; **menyigi** to make a light with torch.

sigir conical fish trap of one split bamboo.

signal signal.

sigung, menyigung to nudge with elbow.

sihir sorcery; **ahli sihir** sorcerer; *also* seher.

sijil certificate (*sch*).

sikang, ikan sikang fish.

sikap carriage, bearing, pose, attitude; **bersikap** to stand to attention; **sikap berani** to show a bold front.

sikat hair comb; field harrow; **pisang sesikat** row of bananas; **bersikat** to comb one's hair.

sikek harrow; = **sikat**.

sikin knife, dagger.

sikit a little; = **sedikit**.

siko close-fitting jacket.

siku elbow, angle (*of road, river*); **siku-siku** carpenter's square; **siku-siku perahu** ribs of boat; *also* **liku**.

sikudomba sea monster.

sikut, main sikut-sikutan to elbow one another; to swindle; **tukang sikut** swindler.

sila please!; **sila ke mari** please come here!; **bersila** sit cross-legged; **batu medang sila** gypsum.

silam dusk, gloaming; time past; **silam bana** false dawn; **tersilam** overtaken by dark.

silambara contest of suitors for bride.

silang to cross at right angles; **teka silang kata** crossword puzzle; **silang-menyilang** crossed.

silap error; **tersilap** in error; **main silap mata** to do conjuring tricks.

silat, bersilat to dance a sword dance.

silau to glitter (*on sea etc*); tersilau dazzled; menyilaukan to dazzle.

silih, silih mata eye wash, pretence; menyilih to give in exchange, indemnify; salah-silih all sorts of mistakes.

silik, menyilik peer.

siling ceiling; shilling, small silver.

silir, angin siliran gently moving breeze.

silok blinking (of eyes of one just wakened).

silor, tersilor-silor to peer, moving head from side to side.

silu shy modest.

siluman invisible elves.

simak, menyimak listen attentively.

simbah, bersimbah streaming (with sweat, water); menyimbah to sprinkle with water.

simbai smart, dandified.

simbang frigate bird; bersimbang uncertain; to chatter.

simbar, air simbar tide rips.

simbat hem stitch.

simbok wash basin.

simbong breaking; coming back (of wind).

simbul symbol.

simbur, menyimbur to sprinkle with water; drench.

simen cement.

simpai flexible band or hoop; muzzle (for animals); menyimpai to bind, muzzle.

simpan to keep (article, secret); store up; bersimpan to pack up; tempat simpan to place for keeping; penyimpan keeper.

simpang crossing; simpang tiga where three roads cross; simpang-siur criss-crossing; bersimpang branching of roads; menyimpang to turn off main road, deviate.

simpat, kesimpatan stuck in one's throat.

simpati sympathy.

simpir spread out its tail (of peacock).

simpuh, bersimpuh kneeling, squatting.

simpul knot; menyimpul knot; tersimpul knotted; menarek kesimpulan gist; summary; inference; to draw a conclusion.

simpur small trees with hard wood and yellow flowers.

Sina Sinai.

sinanaga herpes.

sinar radiance, gleam, ray; bersinar flashing.

sindap scurf, dandruff.

sindir, menyindir to tease, chaff; sindiran innuendo, insinuation, allusion.

sindura red lead.

sing zinc.

singa lion; singa pura lion city, Singapore.

singahak, tersingahak startled.

singar, musim singar dangerous time (for bandits, tigers etc).

singgah to visit, call at a place; persinggahan port of call.

singgam up to, until.

singgang boiled in salt and acid (of fish).

singgasana throne.

singgat up to, as far as.

singgi, main singgi to play marbles.

singgir, menyinggir to insist.

singgit, bersinggit to be on bad terms; singgitan rivalry.

singguh, menyingguh to elbow away.

singkap, menyingkap to part (curtain); open (front of jacket).

singkeh labourer newly come from China.

singkil on edge (of teeth); top of mosquito net; tali singkil cord supporting it.

singkir, menyingkir to get out of the way; tersingkir kept away.

singkur, sepak singkur to kick aside.

singlet singlet.

singsat to roll up (sleeves).

singse Chinese medicine man.

singsing to turn up sleeves; shells used for window panes; also **singkat**.

sintir dice.

sintisis synthesis.

sintuk climber with enormous pods; tree whose bark is used for hairwash; **menyintuk** to use this wash.

sinyo senhor.

sipahi sepoy.

sipat measure; **tali sipat** plumb; **menyipat** to measure.

sipi off centre; **menyipi** to miss its mark; **kena sipi** he got a glancing blow.

sipilis syphilis.

sipir, sifir cypher, arithmetical tables.

sipu, tersipu-sipu shy, abashed.

sipua abacus; also **sepoa**.

siput generic name for shells and shell-fish; coiffure.

sir physical passion; **tak sir** not like (work); sizzling noise.

sira salt lick; candy, icing for cakes; **menyira** to ice.

sirah red.

sirai bird.

siram, menyiram to water plants; **bersiram** to bathe (of princes); serum.

siranjana state umbrella.

sirap roof shingles; quiet, deserted.

sirat network; bridge; **mata sirat** mesh; **menyirat** to make netting; **siratal-mustakim** bridge to Muslim heaven.

siri serial.

sirih betel vine; **menyirih** to offer sirih to guests.

sirik envious.

siring to throw away or pick up water by turning a

vessel at its side; **siring damar** wrapper round torch.

sirip fin of fish; crest of crocodile.

sirkulasi circulation.

sirkuler circular.

sirna lost, vanished.

sisa remains (esp of food); **ikan sisa Nabi** sole (fish).

sisi abreast, beside (of person, house); **menyisi** to go to the side.

sisih, menyisih to move away.

sisik scale (of fish, pangolin); **bersisik** scaly.

sisil to pull up sleeves.

sisip, menyisip to insert; **tersisip** inserted; **sisipan** anything inserted.

sisir comb (in loom, for hair); **pisang sesisir** single row in a bunch of bananas.

sistem system.

siswa student.

siswazah graduate.

sita, surat sita writ, summons; **menyita** to confiscate.

sitak valise.

sitar guitar, mandolin.

siti police whistle; lady; **Siti Meriam** Our Lady, the Virgin Mary.

sitin satin.

situ there (definite place); **ke situ** thither.

situn black glazed earthenware pot.

siuh be off (to chickens).

siul, bersiul to whistle; **burung siul** crested green woodpartridge.

siuman fit, well, recovered from swoon.

siung tusk (of boar, ogre); **bersiung** tusked.

siut singe (hair, mosquito on net).

Siwa Siva.

siwalan Palmyra palm;—**lontar**.

siya tiffin carrier.

skuter scooter.

sobat friend.

sobek fret (*ivory*); to carve.

sobok, **bersobok** to collide with, meet.

sodium sodium; natrium.

sodok, **menyodok** to ladle up; penyodok ladle.

soek tear.

sogang sea front palisade o slanting posts.

sogek quid of tobacco; menyogek to chew a quid.

sogok to invite (*to eat, drink*); wang sogokan bribe.

soh cry to buffalo to turn left.

soja, tersoja-soja kowtowing before idol, bowing low.

sok, sok-sek rustling, whispering; yard measure.

sokan, sukan sports.

sokma the Hindu (*pantheist*) transmigrating soul.

sokom, bersokom smeared (*with paint, soot*); menyokomkan to daub, smear.

sokong prop; menyokong to support (*roof, cause, party*); penyokong support.

solak to care for (*person*); long for (*food*).

soldadu soldier.

solek fashion, style (*esp of wearing headdress*); bersolek smart, foppish; persolek dandy.

solo solo.

som marrow (*in bones*).

sombok loudspeaker (*for gramophone*).

sombol, menyombol to stuff (*food into child's mouth*).

sombong bumptious; menyombong to swagger.

someng offensive (*to eye, ear*).

sompek chipped at the edge.

sompoh, menyompoh to carry on the shoulder; = julang.

sompok, tersompok encountered; to run up against.

sonak sting (*of ray*).

sondang, menyondang to lift heavy weight on back, shoulder; pikul.

sondek, getah sondek guttapercha.

sondol to butt with lowered head (*of cattle*).

sondong shore net for shrimps.

song lift one leg! (*mahout to elephant*).

songar arrogant, haughty.

songel protruding (*of cheeks from a quid*).

songkok velvet cap, white skullcap.

songsang opposite each other.

songsong, menyongsong to struggle against (*tide, eagle against wind*); bersongsong colliding (*of people*).

sontak chipped, broken.

sopak piebald skin disease.

sopan respectful; disopani treated with respect.

sopi I gin, geneva; sopi pahit gin and bitters.

sopi II chauffeur.

sorak, bersorak to cheer; menyorakkan to cheer or hoot (*person*).

sore evening.

sorek bamboo.

sorok, menyorok to crouch, hide, get under cover.

sorong to push forward; kereta sorong barrow; menyorong pushing forward; penyorong that which pushes from behind.

sorot ray of light, gleam; lampu penyorot searchlight.

sosial social.

sosialis socialist.

sosialisma socialism.

sosiologi sociology.

sosoh, menyosoh to whiten (*rice, maize*); perang sosoh hand to hand battle.

sosok buttonhole, eye.

sotoh flat roof.

sotong cuttlefish.

spekulasi speculation.

spesifikasi specification.

spiker speaker.

stadium stadium.

statik static.

statistik statistic.

status status.

steno steno.

stenografi stenography.

strateji strategy.

stratejik strategic.

struktur structure.

studio studio.

sua, bersua dengan to meet with, encounter (*of cocks*); **menyuakan** to push faces together to frighten *or* excite laughter.

suai to adapt, adjust; **sesuai, bersuai** well-fitting (*of clothes*); agreeing with one; **sesuaikan** to adjust.

suak, suak rambut parting (*of hair*).

suaka retreat for hermits; **orang suaka** alms men.

sual query; **bersual** to put a question; **bersual-sual** to debate.

sualak to like, long for (*as pregnant woman*).

suam hot, fevered; **suam-suam kuku** hottish, lukewarm.

suami husband; **bersuami** married (*of woman*); **bersuamikan** to be married to.

suang, suang-suang putus easily broken.

suangi evil spirit.

suap mouthful; **makan suap** to take bribes.

suar beacon, torch, fire, flare.

suara voice; **bunyi suara** elocution; **dengan bulat suara** with one voice, unanimously.

suarang property acquired by man and wife together.

suari, bantal suari ornamental cube-shaped marriage pillow.

suasa alloy of gold and copper.

suasana atmosphere, climate; circumstances (*of persons*).

suatu, satu one; **sesuatu** each, every.

subahat doubt, suspicion.

subal rough, coarse; awkward (*of persons*).

subam dull (*of lustre*).

suban splinter of wood.

subang large ear stud.

subhana praise to; **subhana Allah** praise to Allah.

subjek subject.

subjektib subjective.

subsidi subsidy.

subuh dawn; **waktu subuh** early morning.

subur flourishing (*of plants*); **menyuburkan** to promote growth.

subversib subversive.

suci pure (*of persons*); **suci hati** pure in heart; **menyucikan** to cleanse.

suda caltrops of bamboo; to stab upwards.

sudah done, finished; ended; **sudahlah** enough; **menyudahkan** to complete; end; **kesudahan** conclusion.

sudi satisfied, content.

sudip wooden spoon for stirring rice.

sudit spoon; **menyudit** to smoothe (*clay*) (*of potters*).

sudra untouchable pariah caste.

sudu duck's bill; small spoon of porcelain; **menyudu** to eat (*of ducks*).

sudur, menyudur to stretch out horizontally (*as branches*).

sudut nook, corner; angle; point of view.

suf woollen cloth.

sufi, ahli sufi mystic.

sufrah tablecloth.

sugar, menyugar to comb hair with fingers.

sugi, menyugi to clean one's

teeth with fibre; **penyugi** fibre for cleaning teeth.

sugih rich.

suguh, menyuguh to invite as guest; **suguhan** fare.

sugul = masyghul.

sugun dishevelled (of hair).

suhu temperature of body.

suhut scriptures.

suit, bersuit to whistle.

sujana excellent; eminent.

suji, suji timbul embroidery in relief; **bersuji** embroidered; gruel of flour taken with curry.

sujud to prostrate o.s. in prayer.

suka delight, like; **suka hati** delighted; **suka sama suka** liking one another.

sukan athlete, sports; see **sokan.**

sukar difficult (to do); **kesukaran** difficulties; **mempersukarkan** to aggravate.

sukarela voluntary; **sukarelawan** male volunteer; **sukarelawati** female volunteer.

sukat, menyukat to measure (grain, capacity, area); **sukatan** measurement.

suli enough, abundant (of food).

sukses success.

suku quarter; **suku jam;** quarter of an hour; **suku-sakat** relations.

sukum loop to prevent buffalo calf from suckling.

sukun breadfruit.

sula impaling stake; **menyula** to impale.

sulah bald; **lada sulah** white pepper.

sulai impotent.

Sulaiman Soloman.

Sulalat lineage, ancestry.

sulam, menyulam to embroider; **bersulam emas** embroidered in gold; **penyulam** refill.

sulang, bersulang-sulangan sharing drinks.

sulap, main sulap to do conjuring tricks.

sulat quadrant.

sulat-sulit irregular (of teeth).

sulbi spinal column.

suldi, buah suldi thyroid cartilage.

sule crippled.

sulfar sulphur; **sulfat** sulphate; **sulfid** sulphide.

suli weak in the legs.

suling fife of bamboo, flageolet; **menyuling** to distil perfumes; **tersuing** inverted, upside down.

sulit abstruse, private, secret, secluded.

suliwatang high Bugis title.

suluh torch, flare; **bersuluh** carrying a torch; **menyuluh** to light up; spy, scout.

suluk retreat, seclusion; **ahli suluk** mystic; **ilmu suluk** mysticism.

sulung eldest child; **gigi sulung** first teeth.

sulur sprout from roots; **sulur-suluran** runners (from plants).

sultan ruler.

sumbang improper (of conduct); aid, contribution.

sumbangsel contribution, donation.

sumbar, bersumbar to boast.

sumbat cork, plug, stopper; **menyumbat** to cork.

sumber spring, well; source of knowledge.

sumbi repaired (of damaged teeth); **menyumbi** to crown; repair.

sumbing jagged (of edge of blade).

sumbu wick for lamp; **bersumbu** having wick or fuse; **sumbu badak** horn of rhinoceros.

sumbuk small boat.

sumbul lidded hemispherical cane basket with pedestal.

sumpah oath; **angkat sumpah** to lift hand and affirm; **bersumpah** to take an oath; **sumpah serapah** curses; **kena sumpah** to be under a curse.

sumpit small *mengkuang* bag; **menyumpit** to shoot with blowpipe; **ikan sumpit-sumpit** fish that shoots insect prey by sprouting water; **sumpitan** blowpipe.

sumsum (*of bone*) marrow.

sumur spring, well.

sunat commendable though not obligatory by Islamic law; **bersunat** circumcised; **ahli sunat** Sunnites.

sundai sloping (*of drains etc*).

sundak, menyundak to bump one's head against roof.

sundal prostitute; **sundal malam** tuberose; **sundal bolong** vampire.

sundang Bugis sword, often wavy.

Sundari Woman's name, the Fair.

sundusin silk interwoven with gold.

sundut pedigree; **sundut-bersundut** by descent; **menyundut** to carry in a litter.

sungai river; **anak sungai** rivulet, tributary; **hulu sungai** upper waters of river; **ke sungai** to go to relieve o.s.; **sungai air beku** glacier.

sungga caltrop, spur; **menyungga** to spur.

sunggi, menyunggi to carry on the head.

sungging to paint; **seni sungging** art of painting.

sungguh true, correct, genuine, real; **sakit sungguh** really sick; **sungguhpun** it may be true that, although.

sungkah, menyungkah to guzzle.

sungkai small tree used for hedges.

sungkal, menyungkal to turn up earth.

sungkan reluctant, unwilling.

sungkap, tersungkap pulled loose of toe *or* finger nail.

sungkawa sorry; regret.

sungkit, kain sungkit cloth shot with gold *or* silver thread; **menyungkit** to lever open (*cork, tin*); **penyungkit** bottle opener.

sungkuk, tersungkuk-sungkuk nodding; **sungkuk-sangkak** dragging hurriedly.

sungkum, menyungkum to prostrate o.s.; to hide one's face in a mother's lap.

sungkur, menyungkur to fall on one's face; **tersungkur** fallen forward; **sungkur-sangkar** sprawling on one's face.

sungkup, menyungkup to cover with (*hand, lid*).

sunglap, main sunglap to do conjuring tricks.

sungsang upside down, inverted, frontside turned to the back.

sungu horn of animal.

sungut, bersungut grumble; **sungut-sungut antennae**; **whiskers** (*of cat*).

sunjam, tersunjam hung up head down.

Sunnah Sunnite, orthodox Muslim.

sunti knobs (*on ginger*); small breasts; **anak dara sunti** young virgin.

suntih, menyuntih to cut pieces off.

suntik to inject, vaccinate.

sunting posy worn behind ear; nut behind earring in unbored ears; **disunting** worn as ear posy; **bersunting** wearing a posy.

suntuk too late, leaving no time (*to do*); very late.

suntut thick (of neck).

sunyi quiet, lonely (of places); **sunyi-senyap** utterly lonely.

supai sepoy.

supaya in order that; **supaya jangan** lest.

superior superior.

superlatif superlative.

suplemen supplement.

sura hero.

surah chapter of the Koran.

surai horse's mane; dressed hair; to disperse.

suralaya Hindu heaven on Mount Meru.

suraloka Hindu heaven on Mount Meru.

suram clouded, overcast, dull.

surat letter, epistle, writing, memorandum, testimonial; **surat jemputan** invitation; **suratkhabar** newspaper; **bersurat** having a letter; **tersurat** written.

Surati of Surat, the Indian port; **itik surati** Manila duck.

surau small Muslim chapel where there are too few for a mosque.

suraya, bintang suraya Pleiades.

suri queen; comb in the loom; **mati suri** apparently but not really dead.

suria sun.

Suriani Syrian.

surih trail (of slugs etc); **surih-surih** lineage, genealogy.

surmah kohl, collyrium for women's eyes; = celak.

suruh menyuruh to order, command to do; **suruhan** command; **pesuruhjaya** commissioner.

surup proper, suitable.

surut ebb (of tide); to shrink (of boil).

surya sun.

suryakanta lens.

susah difficult (of tasks); troubled, worried (of persons);

bersusah-susah to take trouble; **menyusahkan** to worry; **kesusahan** trouble.

susastera, kesusasteraan literature, literary knowledge.

susila modest, polite; moral.

suspensi suspension.

susu breast; udder; milk; **puting susu** nipple and areola; **kepala susu** susu cream; **menyusu** to suck (of infants).

susuh cock's natural spur.

susuhunan title of the emperor of Mataram in Java.

susuk build (of boat); bearing (of man); **bersusuk** to do work from the beginning; **menyusuk** to found (town).

susul, menyusul to follow after and overtake; follow up (correspondence).

susun layer (of bricks, books etc); **bersusun** in layers; **menyusun** to pile up, stock; **susunan** arrangements, order; **tersusun** piled, arranged.

susup, susup-sasap helter-skelter; **menyusup** to crawl under.

susur outer edge (of cushion, beach); **susuran tangga** handrails, bannister; **menyusur** to shave past one's nose; **susur galur** to trace (origin).

susut shrinking in size or quantity; **susutan** shrinkage.

sutan commoner's title.

suten, bersuten to toss etc (for who is to start a game).

sutera silk; **ulat sutera** silkworm; **baju sutera** silk coat.

sutli coarse thread, twine.

sutu, ikan sutu thin fish that moves vertically.

Syaaban eighth Muslim month.

syabasy excellent!, good!

syaer quatrain of four lines with one rhyme; **bersyaer** writing a poem.

syafaat intercession.

syafakat compassion.

syagar sugar.

syah king, ruler; **syah** is suffixed to personal names of Malay rulers.

syahada handsome, noble.

syahadah certificate.

syahadan moreover, furthermore.

syahadat testimony; **kalimat syahadat** Muslim confession of faith.

syahbandar habour master.

syahid witness (to Muslim faith); **mati syahid** martyred.

syahmat checkmate.

syahmura weapon.

syahr city; moon.

syahriar lord, monarch.

syahwat orgasm.

syaikh complimentary title for Arabs.

syair=**syaer.**

syaitan devils; also **setan.**

syajrat genealogy.

syak suspicion; **syak dan waham** suspicion and doubt; **syak hati** suspicious.

syakar sugar; also **syagar.**

syakduf camel's saddle.

syal shawl.

Syam, benua Syam Syria.

Syamsiah solar.

syamsu sun.

syamsyir scimitar.

syarab wine.

syarah lecture; **bersyarah** to give a talk; **pensyarah** lecturer.

syarak Islamic religious law.

syarat clause, section, condition, stipulation.

syarbat sherbet.

syariat Islamic religious law.

Syarif proper name.

syarifah female descendant of the Prophet.

syarik partner; **syarikat** partnership, corporation, company; **bersyarikat** united, associated; **persyarikatan** federation; **syarikat wakil** agency.

syauk ecstasy of mystic.

Syawal tenth Muslim month.

syir share; **syir modal** share capital.

syirik polytheism.

syor advice, recommendation, proposal.

syubahat suspicious.

syufaat intercession.

syuhada witnesses.

syukur thanks.

syurga heaven.

T

taajub astonished; consternation.

taakul reason.

taala most high (of God).

taalek contract (marriage).

taaluk under rule of.

taat obedient; **yang taat yours obediently**; **ketaatan** allegiance.

tabah bold, determined, strong-minded.

tabak tray of food covered with a cloth (telampan) presented by a Raja.

tabal drum beaten at a Ruler's installation; **tabalkan** to instal to the thud of the tabal.

taban, getah taban gutta-percha.

tabaraka may he receive God's blessing.

tabi follower.

tabiat character, way of acting.

tabib physician.

tabik greetings (from inferiors); **tabik kecuali** forgive me; **angkat tabik** salute.

tabir curtain, hangings.

tabuh long mosque drum; **tabuh larangan** royal drum beaten only on emergencies.

tabuk, menabuk kepala to box s.o.'s ears, smack.

tab 260 **tai**

tabun, tabun-menabun rise in clouds.

tabung cylinder of bamboo; quiver; **tabung kertas** cardboard cylinder; **tabung surat** pillar box.

tabur, menabur to scatter, sow (seed); **bertaburan** scattered; **penabur** sower; grapeshot; **taburan** sowing.

tabut ark carried in the Hassan-Husein procession; Hindu processional idol.

tadah, menadah to intercept (with outstretched palms, tray) falling objects; **tadah tangan** to lift up hands in Muslim prayer; **bubu tadah** riverine fish trap.

tadar, bertadar to yield up, deliver.

tadbir administration; **ilmu tadbir** statecraft; **tadbiran** Government administration; **mentadbirkan** to administer, manage.

tadi, tahadi just now; **malam tadi** last night; **pagi tadi** this very morning.

tafahus investigation; **menafahuskan** to investigate.

tafsir interpretation of Kuran; commentary; **mentafsirkan** to annotate; interpret.

taftah taffeta.

tagak, tertagak-tagak deferred (of work).

tagan gambling stakes; money earmarked to pay a debt.

tagar distant thunder; **bertagar** rumbling.

tagih, ketagih craving (for cigarettes, opium etc).

–tah interrogative suffix expressing doubt or wonder; **apatah salahnya?** what is the harm?

tahadi = tadi.

tahajud, sembahyang tahajud commendable (but not obligatory) night prayer.

tahak, bertahak = belahak.

tahallil to legalize remarriage to the original husband of a woman divorced thrice by her temporary marriage to an intermediary; **muhallil, china buta.**

tahan to hold out (of persons); last (of thing, money); endure; (of work, pain); **tahan jerat** to set snares; **menahan** to restrain; **tertahan** able to be restrained.

tahana dignity; **bertahana** to sit in state.

tahang tub; ravine.

tahar, bertahar to maintain one's course (in trouble); keep (boat) on its course.

tahbis consecrated (of clergy, water); to dedicate.

tahi ordure, manure; dregs; **tahi angin** rubbish (of talk); **tahi arak** drunkard; **tahi hidung** snot; **tahi lalat** freckles; **tahi telinga** earwax.

tahil 1⅓ oz.

tahir pure, unspotted.

tahkik truth, real.

tahlil praise to God by repeating 'La ilaha illallah'.

tahmid repetition of 'hamdu lillahi' — Praise be to God.

tahniah congratulation.

tahsil collection of rents.

tahu to know, understand, recognize, be aware of; **mengambil tahu** to get to know; **diketahui** be it known; **berketahuan** possessed of knowledge; **pemberitahu** notices.

tahun year; **tahun hijrat** year of the Hegira; **tahun Masehi** Christian year; **awal tahun** beginning of year; **menahun** that lasts a year; **tahunan** annual.

taijin protector of Chinese.

taiko leprosy.

tair bird.

tairoid thyroid.

tais dirty.

taiso to drill, do gymnastics.

taj crown; taj al-salatin 'Crown of Kings' (well-known book).

taja, menaja to begin (mat-making); tajaan commencement.

tajak rice planter's weedcutter; menajak to weed.

tajalli clear, evident.

tajam sharp (as knife); tajam mata keen (of sight); mempertajamkan to sharpen; sifat tajam acrimony.

tajau jar (esp of buried treasure).

taji steel spur for fighting cock; bulang taji to fasten on the spur.

tajin, tepung tajin starch for linen.

tajuk aigrette of real flowers or of gold or silver worn by bridegrooms; corolla; tajuk mahkota crown's aigrette; headings of leading article.

tajung silk sarong.

tajur large fishing rod, fixed and left; menajur to angle with a rod.

tajwid correct pronunciation of the Arabic of the Kuran.

tak I, ta', tidak not; taksa ambiguous; ketaksaan ambiguity.

tak II not; tak pergi not going; also ta'.

takada, ta' ada is not at all.

takah, kuku takah slow loris; appearance; handsome.

takai, berteku-takai diligent.

takak, bertakak woven in two pieces that are sewn and joined (of sarung); menakak to sew together.

takal tackle, pulley.

takar porcelain ginger jar, small-necked water jar.

takat up to, as far as.

takau, burung takau green broadbill.

takbir I repetition of 'Allahu Akbar' God is great.

takbir II interpretation of dreams.

takdim beginning of salat.

takdir divine decree, fate.

takhta throne; naik takhta singgasana to ascend a throne; bertakhta enthroned.

takhyul delusion; imaginary.

taki, bertaki to dispute, quarrel.

takik small notch; menakik to nick, tap rubber.

takir dipper made of banana leaves or palm fronds; bathing bucket.

takjub wondering, marvelling.

taklid investiture.

taklik, nikah bertaklik to marry with the stipulation of automatic divorce for husband's desertion.

taklimat briefings.

takluk subject, dependent; negeri takluk colony; menaklukkan to subject.

takrif, takrifkan to inform, declare, define.

takrim esteem, respect.

takrir repetition, reiteration.

taksir negligence, omission, fault; appraisal; mentaksir to value.

taksis purity.

taktuk notch (eg in head of screw); horizontal notch in palm trunk to help climbers.

takung, bertakung stagnant; menakung to collect (of water); bertakung stagnant.

takur, burung takur many-coloured barbet.

takut afraid; menakuti to frighten; penakut coward.

takwa = tekua.

takwil elucidation of dreams.

takwim almanac, calendar.

takziah mourning; bertakziah to visit the house of the dead.

takzim respect, honour.

takzir punishment.

tal palmyra palm; = lontar.

tala padlock, echo; time (mus); bertala in harmony; **penala** tuning fork; **menala** to hit with fiat of hand.

talah, bertalah-talah hurriedly.

talai to keep stopping, dawdle; menalaikan to dawdle over.

talak divorce (of wife by husband).

talam tray.

talang hamlet, village; broker; agent for another; **talang kuda** horse dealer; **menalangkan** to lend money.

talar to stay a course; persevere; bertalaran frank, outspoken.

talbiah to surrender o.s. to God.

talenan chopping-block.

tali rope, cord, string, line; **taliair** canal; **tali bahu** shoulder strap; **tali kail** fishing line; **tali kasut** shoelace; **mempertalikan** to tie, join; **pertalian** tie, connection; **tali temali** cordage.

talib earnest student of religion.

talibisyen television.

talibun set of eulogistics; verses of several lines all having the rhyme.

taligeram telegram.

taligerap telegraph.

talikom telecommunications.

talipun telephone; also talifun.

talkin whispered recitation of creed to the dead on interment.

talu, bertalu-talu continuous (of sound).

tam slam, bang; = dentam.

tamaddun culture, civilization; bertamaddun cultured, civilized.

tamah, ramah-tamah genial, affable.

tamahul tolerance

tamak I = tamah.

tamak II greed; to covet.

tamam ended (of book, prayer).

taman flower garden.

tamar date (fruit).

tamasya show, spectacle.

tamat, tammat ended (esp of book); tamatkan to conclude.

tambah to accumulate, increase, be increased; additional, extra; bertambah to increase, accrue; menambah to add to, increase, enlarge; **tambahan** accretion, addendum, addition; **penambah** affix; **penambahan** appendix.

tambak banked up; menambak to bank up.

tambal = tampal.

tamban, ikan tamban pilchard, sardine.

tambang fare; perahu tambang passenger boat, ferry; **menambang** to go by ferry; **penambang** passenger.

tambar prophylactic, cure.

tambat, tertambat tied, moored; **tambatan** moorings; ayam tambatan old retainer; **menambatkan** to tether, moor.

tambera bronze; agreement engraved on bronze.

tambi errand boy, messenger.

tambo annals.

tambuh additional rice; bertambuh to give more rice to guests.

tambuk swamp, mud.

tambul refreshment.

tambun, tembun plump.

tambung unmannerly.

tambur European drum.

tambus = timbus.

tameng shield.

tamin reaping knife.

tampa, salah tampa to misunderstand; mistaken; menampa to think, suppose.

tampah winnowing tray.

tampak visible; **tampaknya** by the look of it.

tampal, menampal to patch (*coal*); post up (*notices*); tampalan patch.

tampan handsome; creating the impression of a man of quality.

tampang, setampang flat lateral slice (*of bread etc*); penampang cross-cut; flat side (*of fort*); menampang to slice, cut transversely.

tampar, menampar to slap.

tampas to lop off a projection.

tampek to find fault with, criticize.

tampel, bola tampel tennis; bulu tampel badminton; menampel to parry.

tampi, menampi winnow by tossing in a triangular sieve.

tampil to come to the fore (*as champion*); tampilkan to take to the front.

tampin leaf or nipah spathe bag (*for rice, sago*); menampin taruh to counter a wager.

tampoi trees, some with edible fruit.

tampuk juncture of stem and fruit; corolla.

tampun to fold like an envelope.

tampung piebald; badak tampung adult tapir; menampung to patch (*of clothes*); bertampung patched.

tamsil simile, parable.

tamu, tetamu guest, visitor.

tamuk, ikan belanak tamuk grey mullet.

tan, tan kuda stable; honorific in a few titles; tun.

tanaffus breathing.

tanah earth, soil, land, territory; colour, background (*of fabrics*); tanahair territorial area; tanah tumpah darah birthplace; tanah gembur loam.

tanai to carry on the hand.

tanak, bertanak to boil one's rice; menanak to boil rice.

tanam to plant; cucuk tanam to plant; bertanam to plant for o.s.; menanam plant; tertanam buried; tanam-tanaman plants of all sorts; crops.

tanau, burung tanau little Malay parrot.

tanbiat prophecy.

tancang, menancang to tie, fasten.

tancap, menancap to stick into (*as claw into flesh*).

tanda sign, mark, evidence, symptom, signal; tandatangan thumbprint, signature; bertanda marked; menandai to make a mark; menandakan to signify, show; tanda tempat landmark.

tandak, bertandak to stepdance.

tandan bunch (*of bananas, coconut*).

tandang, bertandang to tour, travel about; bertandang desa to roam.

tandas privy (*over river or sea*); cleaned out (*as gambler*).

tandatangan signature; tandatanya question.

tandil foreman, ship's mate.

tanding peer, equal; bertanding to be a match, equal; peer; pertandingan match, competition.

tandu litter, dhooly.

tanduk horn; menanduk to butt; bertanduk horned.

tandun, zaman tandun remote past.

tandur, tali tandur cords for pulling up blinds.

tandus bare (*of land*).

tang, ventang direction; tang mana? in what direction?

tangan hand and forearm; bekas tangan handwriting; tapak tangan palm.

tangar to take care, beware.

tangas, bertangas to steam the body.

tangek nasal (*as twang*).

tangga house ladder, stairs, steps; **anak tangga** rung, step; **bertangga** having a ladder; **tetangga** neighbours.

tanggal dropped off (*as leaf*); **menanggalkan** stripped off.

tanggam rabbet; **bertanggam** rabbeted, mortised; **tertanggam** fixed firmly.

tanggang, menanggang to control (*wife, husband*); **bertanggang mata** to keep awake.

tanggap, tanggapan concept.

tanggar to carry a burden; **tanggaran** burden.

tangguh time (*for payment*); **minta tangguh** seminggu to ask for a week's time; **bertangguh** to postpone.

tangguk landing net; **menangguk** to scoop up; landed.

tanggung, menanggung to support a burden; endure; **tanggung hutang** to guarantee a debt; **tertanggung** endured; **bertanggungjawab** to be accountable, be responsible.

tangis weeping; **menangis** to weep.

tangkai stalk, stem, handle of cup, dinner.

tangkal amulet, talisman (*against illness and evil spirits*).

tangkap, menangkap to catch, arrest, grasp; **tangkap gambar** to photograph; **tertangkap** captured.

tangkas swift, fleet (*of horses*); agile.

tangki tank; **kapal tangki** tanker.

tangkil, menangkil to dodge.

tangkis, menangkiskan to parry a weapon; **meriam penangkis** anti-aircraft gun.

tangkueh pumpkin preserved in sugar.

tangkul fishing net in square frame hanging from rod.

tangkup, menangkup to cap-ture by covering with hand; **menangkup ke bantal** to bury one's face in pillow; **setangkup** symmetry.

tangkur sea horse.

tanglung Chinese paper lantern.

tangsel wedge, stopper.

tangsi catgut.

tangsten tungsten.

tani farming; **petani** crofter, farmer; **bertani** to farm; **pertanian** agriculture.

tanjak erect but at an angle; headkerchief; **bertanjak** to stand or dance on tiptoe; **menanjak** to rise, point up (*as headdress*).

tanji music; **tukang tanji** musician.

tanju wall lamp.

tanjul to fish with rod; lasso (*beast or man*).

tanjung cape, promontory; **menanjung** to project like a cape; **anak tanjung** spit.

tanjur coconut-shell ladle with handle.

tanpa without.

tanti, nanti wait!

tanur oven.

tanya, bertanya to ask; **bertanyakan** to ask about a matter; **pertanyaan** inquiry, query.

tanzil revelation (*from God*).

tapa Hindu austerities, yogism; **pertapa** anchoret; ascetic; **pertapaan** asceticism; **bertapa** to practise austerities.

tapah, ikan tapah giant river fish.

tapai fermented drink; cake of sweet rice; fermented; **kucing tapai** rabbit; **to play** the confidence trick.

tapak base; sole of foot, shoe, footprint; site (*of house*); **tapak besi** horseshoe; **tapak kaki** footprint.

tapang boundary.

tapi, tetapi but.

tapih long unsewn skirt.

tapioka tapioca.

tapis, menapis to filter; **tapisan** strainer, filter; **penapis suratan** censor.

taplak tablecloth.

taptibau, burung taptibau great-eared nightjar.

tapuk, bertapuk accumulated, piled up (of debts); scabby, pockmarked.

tara level (of rank); **setara dengan** of equal rank with.

taraf rank, position; **setaraf** equal (in rank, grade).

tarah, menarah to plane wood; level (land); **tarahan** planing; **penarah** plane.

tarak abstinence, austerity.

taram salt lick; to bear a grudge.

tarang, petarangan nest of a broody hen.

tarasul letter-writing.

tarbil catapult, pellet bow.

tarbin turbine.

tarbus fez.

tari dance, act of dancing; **menari** to dance.

tarik, menarikkan to pull (cart etc); haul (rope); drag (animal); **penarik** puller; **tariktarik** accordion.

tarikat mystic's path to the Real.

tarikh date (of day, month); **bertarikh** dated.

taring tusk (of boar); canine tooth; **bertaring** having tusks.

taris to cord the outside of a box.

tarjamah to translate, interpret; **pentarjamah** translator.

tarkash quiver for arrows.

taru, bertaru sound of a dragon or royal trumpet; **naga taru** scroll doubled back.

taruh, menaruh to put in a place, set; name; affix a seal; **bertaruh wang** to stake money;

taruhan stake; **petaruh thing** entrusted.

taruk shoot (from plant); **bertaruk** sprouting.

tarum indigo plant.

tarung, bertarung to collide, clash; quarrel (in law court).

tarup shed, lean-to.

tas, kayu tas small tree whose wood is deemed a protection against tigers; **tas tangan** handbag.

tasak, menasak to stop bleeding.

tasawuf, ilmu tasawuf Islamic mysticism.

tasbih extolling God; **buah tasbih** rosary beads.

tasdik confirmation, attestation.

tasik lake.

taslim salutation; **taslimkan** to convey a letter.

tasmak glasses (for eyes).

tasrif declension (of nouns); conjugation (of verbs).

tasydid diacritical mark in Arabic script to indicate the doubling of the sound of a letter.

tasyrikh, ilmu tasyrikh anatomy: anatomi, kajibinatubuh.

tata arrangement, order, system; **tata bahasa** grammar; **tata tertib** discipline; **tata cara** procedure.

tatah, bertatah inlaid, studded with gems.

tatai, bertatai-tatai in ordered rows.

tatakan base, pedestal of cup.

tatal wood shavings.

tatam, bertatam lying in rows.

tatang, menatang to carry on the palm; carry gingerly.

tatap, menatap to scrutinize inspect carefully.

tatatertib discipline.

tathlith Holy Trinity.

tatih, bertatih to toddle (of infants).

tating to lift up with both hands.

tatkala time, when; **pada tatkala itu** at that time; **tatkala dia tiba** when he arrived.

taubat repentant; **taubat daripada** to repent (of).

taucang long pigtail; queue.

taufan typhoon.

taufik help of God.

taugeh sprouts of the mung bean.

tauhid unity of God; **ilmu tauhid** doctrine of tauhid; **mentanhidkan** to acknowledge that God is one.

tauk bride's tiara.

taukeh 'towkay', employer; any Chinese above labouring class.

taul, menaul to make fast (oar, anchor).

tauladan (= **teladan**) = **tuladan**.

taulan associate, comrades.

tauliah letter of appointment, commission.

taun, penyakit taun cholera.

taung dust storm; **ditaungi** covered with clouds of dust.

taup, bertaup mended (of rifts); united (of wounds).

taurat Old Testament.

taut nightline for fishing.

tawa, tertawa to laugh; **tertawa-tawa** to keep laughing; **tertawa gelak-gelak** to laugh aloud.

tawadu humble, docile, obedient.

tawaf to walk praying round the Kaaba at Mecca.

tawak, tawak-tawak small gong.

tawakal, bertawakal to rely on God; trust to luck.

tawan, menawan to make a prisoner of war; **tawanan** captive.

tawar tasteless (of food); insipid; not salty (of water); **menawar** to haggle, bargain.

tawarikh annals, history.

tawaruk attitudes forbidden for worshippers in mosque.

tawas alum.

tawi, menawi redeem from pawn.

taya, mentua taya man's uncles- or aunts-in-law.

tayamum ritual ablution of Muslim with sand when there is no water.

tayang, tayangkan to hold up to the light; wave gun or knife threateningly.

tayar tyre (eg motor vehicle).

tazkirat licence, permit.

tebah, menebah to beat rugs with rattan beater; thresh.

tebak I crowbar for stone breaking; **menebak** to quarry earth.

tebak II to hack off; smooth (with axe).

tebakang, ikan tebakang freshwater climbing perches.

tebal thick (of materials, lines); **bermuka tebal** thick-skinned, shameless.

teban, meneban to stake, bet; **tebanan** bet; **tebankan** to pledge one's future crop for repayment of a loan.

tebang, menebang to fell large trees; **tebangan** felling; timber felled; **penebang** feller.

tebar, menebar to cast a net; scatter seed; **bertebaran** scattered.

tebas, menebas to cut down (scrub, bushes); **tebang tebas** to cut down trees, big and small.

tebat fishpond; dam; **menebat** to dam.

tebeng I to persist; **tebeng main** to persist in playing.

tebeng II, menebeng to open and display (cloth etc); **tebeng-**

kan dada to expose the breast.

tebera, ikan tebera river carp.

teberau white-plumed river-reed.

tebing bank of river; menebing gather in banks.

tebok, menebok to thrust with the horns.

tebu sugar-cane.

tebuan hornet; tebuan air venomous water-insect.

tebuk, menebuk to drill a hole, gnaw a hole.

tebus, menebus to redeem from pawn; tebusan purchase, redemption; tebus talak;= khula.

tedarus reading the Koran in Ramadan.

tedas clear; merah tedas bright red.

tedeng screen from sun.

teduh calm, spent (of storm, rain); berteduh shelter.

tedung, ular tedung cobra; ular tedung senduk black cobra.

tefekur plunged in thought.

tega indifferent, unfeeling.

tegah unlawful acts; menegahkan to prohibit, forbid.

tegak erect (of person, hair); vertical; berdiri tegak to stand erect; menegakkan to set erect.

tegal cause, reason.

tegang taut (of rope); stiff (of hair); bertegang to stand firm; tegangkan to tauten.

tegap sturdy; tegap sasa well-knit and strong.

tegar obstinate; ketegaran obstinacy.

tegarun, kain tegarun gold-threaded silk fabric.

tegas obvious, certain, firm; tegasnya clearly; menegaskan stress.

teguh firm (of knots, agreements); constant, reliable; te-guh setia loyal.

teguk, seteguk air the water one can swallow at a gulp; meneguk to gulp down.

tegun, tertegun hesitating, breaking down.

tegur to accost; tegur sapa polite greeting; menegur to greet (person).

teh tea; daun teh tea-leaf.

tehok throw away, discard.

teja red and yellow sunset clouds.

teji = tezi swift (of steed).

tek tick; mesen tek typewriter.

tekad resolute.

tekak gullet; anak tekak uvula; kering tekak thirsty; bertekak to quarrel till hoarse.

tekal, amang tekal tungsten.

tekan, menekan to press, push hard, cross-examine; tekanan pressure, force; penekan press.

tekang crossbeam in mine.

tekap, menekap to cover (mouth, ear) with light pressure of hand; kertas tekap blotting paper.

tekat embroidery; bertekat manik embroidered in beads.

teka-teki conundrum, riddle; teka silang kata crossword puzzle.

tekebur arrogant, presumptuous.

tekek gekko, house lizard.

tekelek clogs.

teket ticket.

tekis too near the edge (sewing).

teknik technical; teknoloji technology.

teko teakettle.

tekoh warehouse.

tekong captain of Chinese junk.

teks text.

teksi taxi.

tekua, baju tekua long sleeve-less vest.

tekuk, bertekuk to crumple.

tekukur, burung tekukur large cuckoo dove.

tekun, bertekun to be diligent at; concentrate on.

tekup, menekup to cover and catch under hand.

tekur deficient of cash; **menekur** to look down.

tela I uncovered well.

tela II pan (of gun).

telaah inquiry; **menelaah** to study.

teladan (= **tauladan**) = **tuladan**.

teladas shallow rapid.

telaga mere, lake; spring; well; **telaga minyak** oil well.

telah already; did; has; have; was; were; **telah mati** has died; was dead; **telah pergi** had gone.

telan, menelan to swallow; **tertelan** accidentally swallowed.

telancang, burung telancang mangrove brown babbler.

telang, bertelang streaky (of markings); **buluh telang** bamboo famous for the water it holds.

telangkai broker (esp marriage); **dalam telangkai** betrothed.

telanjang, bertelanjang nude, bare.

telanjur projecting, stretching out.

telankup upside down (of plate etc); **telungkup.**

telap to permeate, soak into, penetrate.

telapak sole (of foot).

telapakan, tanah telapakan sites allocated to territorial chiefs (Undang) when attending court ceremonies.

telatah behaviour, conduct.

telatat lid of rice bin; rattan blinds.

telatap small bamboo raft.

telaten neat, careful (over work).

telau, bertelau-telau shimmering (of sunlight in patches like light in open forest).

teledek dancing girl.

teledor lazy; sleepyhead; slack.

teledu otter.

telegram telegram.

telegrapi telegraph.

telekan, bertelekan to rest the hands (on stick, table).

telekap, ubat telekap to plaster; cover with the hand.

teleku, berteleku to rest on one's elbows.

telekung white praying veil for women.

telempap, setelempap hand's breadth; also **pelempap.**

teleng cocked (of ear, eye, head to look aside); heeling (of ship); **telentang** lying on the back.

telengkoh bastion; to swerve accidentally.

telepa small box, casket (for tobacco).

telepuk, kain telepuk glazed linen stamped with gilt pattern from wooden blocks.

telerang, batu telerang quartz.

telimpung xylophone of small gongs.

telinga ear; handle of pot; **cuping telinga** ear lobe; **tahi telinga** wax (in ear); **pasang telinga** to listen to news.

telingkah conduct, behaviour; **bertelingkah** to disagree.

telipuk, bunga telipuk lotus; **telipuk putih** rose-coloured or white water lily.

teliti care; **dengan teliti** carefully; **ketelitian** accuracy.

telor lisping mispronouncing; = **pelat.**

telotak tip of leaf, petal.

telu three (in plant names).

teluk bay (of sea); bight; curve (in rivers); **teluk rantau** bends and reaches; **teluk kecil** cove.

teluki, bunga teluki pink; carnation.

telukup upside down (of boat); overthrown (of ruler).

telun, setelun in accord.

telung millipede.

telunjuk index finger.

teluntang on the back.

telur egg (of bird); testicles; roe; **bertelur** to lay eggs.

telus forcing a passage (of water).

telut, bertelut to kneel; easily chewed.

temabur scattered (of stars).

temaga = tembaga.

temalang bark receptacle for collecting wild bees' nests.

temali, teli-temali cordage.

teman companion; **berteman dengan** friendly with; **teman karib** crony.

temandang clothes; general appearance.

temara lance, spear.

Temasek old name for Singapore.

temas–temas cure (of illness, from shock) by exorcism.

temat, sirih setemat quid of betel.

tembadau Bornean wild ox.

tembaga brass, copper; **tembaga perunggu** bronze, bellmetal; **tembaga merah** copper.

tembak, menembak to shoot; aim at; get at; **menembakkan meriam** to fire a cannon; **tembakan** shooting, firing.

tembakang, ikan tembakang freshwater perchlike fish.

tembakau tobacco.

tembakul, ikan tembakul goby that appears to walk on mud.

tembam plump, bulging (of cheeks).

tembang I to sing verses.

tembang II sardine.

tembar to fish by beating water and netting.

tembarong projecting attic.

tembatu hard (of corns, bad mangosteen etc).

tembek near (of shot at target).

tembel stye on the eyelid.

tembelah dart quiver.

tembelang addled (of eggs).

tembelian, ikan tembelian large fish.

tembeliung edible bivalve; dragonfly.

tembelok shipworm, pileworm.

tembera carp.

temberam river fish trap.

temberang ship's stays; bragging; **tukang temberang** boaster.

temberas, ikan temberas carp.

tembereh, ikan tembereh edible marine fish.

tembereng splinter of porcelain, broken segment; **tembereng tajam** sector.

tembesu hardwood tree.

tembi to thrust out and sideways.

tembikai watermelon.

tembikar crock, shards; glazed earthenware; laquer.

tembilang long-handled spade.

tembilar trap with spiky entrance.

tembok stonewall, embankment.

tembokor metal plate put under water jars.

tembolok bird's crop.

tembu to encourage; assist.

tembuk perforated (of cloth, paper); **tembukan** tunnel.

tembuku knob.

tembun plump.

tembung cudgel; **bertembung** to knock up against; meet (of persons).

tembuni afterbirth; caul; **tembuni kecil** placenta.

tembup spell thought to cause dropsy.

tembus perforated; **menembus** to perforate (as bullets).

tembusa, kuïh tembusa curry puff.

Temenggung Malay minister (formerly in charge of defence, police).

temenung pensive; **ikan temenung** horse mackerel.

temiang, buluh temiang tall bamboo used for making blow pipes.

Temiar Aborigines.

temin metal band for sheath of creese; ferrule.

temoleh, ikan temoleh freshwater carp.

tempa, menempa to forge, weld.

tempah, wang tempah retaining fee; **menempah** to retain midwife; **bertempah** to book o.s. (cabin, seat etc).

tempang lame (from shortness of one leg or permanent deformity).

tempap, setempap hand's breadth; **menempap** measure by hand's breadth.

tempat spot, place; home; **tempat kerja** workplace; **tempat tinggal** house, home; **menempatkan** to place.

tempaus whale.

tempawan hammered, beaten, wrought.

tempayak larvae (of ant, bee).

tempayan large big-bellied earthenware jar.

tempe cakes made of fermented parboiled soya beans.

tempek short loud cheer of encouragement.

tempel, menempel to stick on patch over crack.

tempelak, menempelak to humiliate in public.

tempeleng box on the ear.

temperas, bertemperasan scattered (of chickens, crowds).

tempiar, bertempiaran — tempéras.

tempias beating in (of rain); spray (into ship).

tempinis, kayu tempinis ironwood used for tops and tool handles.

tempiras sandtick.

tempiring earwig.

tempoh, menempoh to push way through; **tempohan** charge, rush.

tempolong spittoon.

temponek monkey jackfruit.

tempong, menempong to roll marble at mark.

tempoyak salted durian conserve.

tempua weaverbird.

tempuh era, extension of time; **minta tempuh** to ask for time (to do, pay etc).

tempuling barbed fish spear, harpoon.

tempur, bertempur colliding, beating of waves on reef; **menempur** to attack.

tempurung half coconut shell; **katak di bawah tempurung** narrow-minded; **tempurung lutut** kneecap.

temu, bertemu to meet (of persons); **menemukan** to join; **tempat pertemuan** place of meeting.

temucut lovegrass.

temuduga interview.

temukus cubebs.

temukut broken rice grains.

temurun, turun-temurun down the ages, by long descent.

temut, temut-temut throbbing.

tenaga strength, exertion, labour; **bertenaga** energetic.

tenahak dissatisfied over work undone.

tenaik east.

tenang I still (of sea); calm.

tenang II, menenang to take aim.

tenar uproar, disturbance.

tenat severe (*illness*).

tenda ship's awning.

tendang, menendang to kick (*as footballer*).

tendas, menendas to decapitate.

tender tender.

tendon tendon.

teng military tank.

tengadah to look up; **tunduk tengadah** to look up and down.

tengah middle; **di tengah** in the middle, amidst; **pertengahan** centre, mean; **tengahan** median.

tengahari midday.

tengar mangrove tree.

tengas river fish.

tenggal to swallow.

tenggala plough; **tanah tenggala** arable land; **menenggala** to plough.

tenggalung, musang **tenggalung** civet.

tenggan, bertenggan in rolls of flesh.

tenggang fixed time; **bertenggang** to seek a way.

tenggara south-east.

tenggarang portable kitchen store.

tenggat limit, boundary.

tenggek I to toss in round circular sieve; winnow.

tenggek II, bertenggek to squat, perch.

tenggelam to sink (*in liquid*); **tenggelamkan** to submerge.

tengger, bertengger to perch (*as ape*).

tenggiling scaly anteater, pangolin.

tenggiri large mackerels.

tenggorok gullet, larynx.

tenggul, bertenggul to kneel.

tenggulung pill millipede.

tengik rancid (*of oil*).

tengit rancid; = **tengik.**

tengka between; **menengka** to be a go-between.

tengkalak unbaited; conical river fish trap.

tengkalang small granary on posts.

tengkaluk unripe but edible fruit.

tengkam gold weight.

tengkar, bertengkar to quarrel; **pertengkaran** altercation.

tengkarap ruined, destroyed.

tengkawang tallow-like fat extricated from several trees.

tengkek, burung **tengkek** kingfisher.

tengkel round droppings (*of goats*); pill.

tengkes undeveloped (*of one foot*).

tengking snarling (*of persons*); **mengking** to snarl.

tengkolok headkerchief.

tengkorak skull.

tengku I form of address to important raja.

tengku II opium prepared for smoking.

tengkujuh wet monsoon season.

tengkuk nape of neck; **bulu tengkuk** mane.

tengkulak middleman who buys crops.

tengkurap prone.

tengkuyung cowrie shell.

tengok, menengok to look and see, visit and see.

tenguh to low.

tenguk to grunt (*of pigs*).

tenung-tenging mooning, absent-minded.

tenjak to limp with heel raised.

tenong lidded basket on stand.

tentang I direction; **tentang mana** in which direction; **bertentang dengan** facing (*enemies, place*); opposite.

tentang II half flap window of village stall.

tentera troops, army; **tentera darat** land army; **tentera laut** navy; **tentera udara** air force.

tenteram peaceful; **kenteraman** peace.

tentu sure, definite, certain; definitely; **belum tentu** it is still uncertain; **menentukan** to fix; **menentukan penyakit** to diagnose.

tentuban foetal membranes.

tenuk tapir; = **badak.**

tenun, bertenun to weave; **tenunan** style of weaving.

tenung, menenung to gaze fixedly; **bertenung** to divine; **petenung** diviner.

tenyeh to press and rub with finger.

teologi theology.

teoretikus theorist; **teori** theory.

tepah, tepah anu to make an offer of marriage.

tepak I, menepak to pat.

tepak II, tepak sirih oblong box.

tepala, ikan tepala fighting fish.

tepam, menepam to clap hand on person's shoulder.

tepas wickerwork for walls; full; **bertepas** chockfull.

tepat accurate; exact (of direction, time); full; precise; **tengahari tepat** exactly midday; **menepatkan** to make straight for.

tapaut different, discrepant.

tepeh mollusc.

tepek, setepek plug of tobacco, clod of mud; **bertepek-tepek** plastered with mud.

tepi I edge, margin, border; **menepi** to step aside; edge away; **bertepi** having an edge.

tepi II brass knuckleduster.

tepik, menepik to pat.

tepis, menepiskan to push aside with back of hand.

tepoh Chinese dicing game.

tepok paralysed in legs.

tepu brimful; full (of sail).

tepuk clapping of hands; **tepuk sorak** clapping and cheering.

tepung flour; **tepung gandum** wheat flour.

tepus wild ginger plants.

tera seal, stamp, impression; **jurutera** engineer; **bertera** officially sealed; **dimeterai** stamped, sealed.

teradisi tradition.

terafik traffic.

terajidi tragedy.

terajang to trample, stamp on.

teraju scales for weighing; kite string.

terak hen's permanent laying place.

teral, meneral to force (labourers) to work.

teran, meneran to strain (in child labour or evacuation).

terang bright (of light, day); clear (of atmosphere); **terangkan** to throw light on, explain; **penerang** illuminator; **keterangan** explanation, proof.

terangkek bamboo receptacle for liquids.

terangkera stockade; name of a place in Malacca.

teransformer transformer; **teransister** transistor.

terap big tree; **berterap** engraved.

terapang, keris terapang creese having gold or silver casing round stem of sheath.

teras hard heartwood; essentials.

terasi = **belacan.**

terasul, ilmu terasul art of letter writing.

terat boundary.

teratai lotus; **teratai kecil** blue waterlily.

teratak humble hut.

teratu torture.

terau, menerau to wind thread off reel.

terawih night prayers during month of Ramadan.

terban collapsed (*of earth*).

terbang to fly (*of birds, dust*); kapalterbang aeroplane; penerbangan flight; terbangkan to blow up; jeruterbang airman.

terbis collapsed.

terbit to issue from below *or* inside; terbit perang war arose; terbitkan to cause to rise; terbitan publication; penerbit publisher; penerbitan editorial.

terbul, ikan terbul edible river carp.

terbus fez.

terek tight (*of knots*); oppressive; menerik to tighten.

terektor tractor.

tereluh snoring.

terendak sun hat; terendak lampu lampshade.

teri triple, three; Teri-murti Hindu trinity.

teriak, berteriak to shout out, cry out; meneriakkan to cry.

teriang scarce (*of last fruits on tree*).

terigu wheat; tepung terigu flour.

terima, menerima to receive, accept; terimakasih thank you; penerima receiver.

tering tuberculosis.

teringkas shorthand writing.

teringket fore sail.

teripang dried sea slugs; sea cucumber.

teritek dripping (*of liquids*).

teriti treaty.

teritip barnacle.

terjak kicking out (*as horse*).

terjal steep, declivitous.

terjemah to translate; terjemahan translation; menterjemahkan to translate; penterjemah translator.

terjun to leap down; air terjun waterfall.

terka, menerka to guess; terkaan conjecture.

terkam, menerkam to rush at; terkaman to dash; grasp.

terkap, menerkap to cover under concave surface.

terkul, senapang terkul muzzle loading gun.

termasa show; *also* temasya.

terminoloji terminology.

ternah unusual (*esp of dress*).

ternak, orang ternak sons of the soil; berternak to breed livestock.

ternang squat big-bellied water jar.

teromba oral tradition (*esp matrilineal genealogies*).

terompak wooden clogs.

terompet trumpet.

terona — teruna.

terongko prison, cell.

teronok jellyfish.

teropong binocular, tube, telescope, microscope; meneropong to look through.

terowongan tunnel.

terpa, menerpa to spring forward.

terpal tarpaulin.

terpedo torpedo.

tertawa laugh; *also* ketawa.

tertib ritual, order of procedure, programme; tatatertib discipline.

terubin fishing trap with spring shutter.

terubuk herring; telur terubuk salted hilsa roes.

terubung bark rice bin.

terucuk stakes in sea.

terulu rabbit.

teruk acute (*of illness*); severe (*of pain*); kerja teruk heavy work.

teruka, meneruka to open new land for cultivation.

terum kneel (*command to elephant*).

terumbu reef visible at low tide.

teruna young (of males).

terung egg plant, brinjal.

terup, terop, main terup to play card games; = **main kartu.**

terus right through (of tunnel etc); cakap terus terang to talk plainly, say outright; **terusan** canal, cutting; **penerusan** continuity; **menerusi** through.

terusi hydrated sulphate of iron.

tesmak glasses, spectacles.

testamen testament.

tetabas to recover by making offerings at tree or spot responsible for illness.

tetaguk hawk, owl.

tetak, menetak to hack, nick; **bertetak** slashing at each other.

tetal close (of texture); to squeeze down; **menetalkan** to press, squeeze down.

tetampan embroidered yellow shoulder napkin worn by those serving royalty or carrying regalia.

tetamu guest.

tetangga neighbours.

tetap fixed, permanent; **menetapkan** to fix; **menetapi** to fulfil promise.

tetapi but.

tetar, menetar to arrange warp in looms.

tetarik accordion.

tetas, menetas to be hatched (of eggs); slit open; **menetaskan** to sit on eggs.

tetek teat; emak tetek fostermother; **menetek(kan)** to suckle; breastfeed.

tetel offal.

tetes drip.

tetirah to go for cure.

tetiruk, burung tetiruk pintail snipe.

tetkala = **tatkala.**

tetua freckles.

tetuhu owl.

tetungap fish preserved in salt.

tewas worsted in war; **menewaskan** to defeat.

teyan, berteyan to club together, subscribe to fund.

tezi swift (of steeds).

thabit fixed, assured of acts; berthabit dengan in connection with.

Thalatha, Selasa, hari Selasa Tuesday.

thalji snow; also salji, thalju; thalji beku frost.

thamrat blossom.

thani the second.

thema theme.

thuluth third portion.

thumma then, moreover.

tiada is not.

tiaga trade; = **niaga.**

tian uterus; dalam tian pregnant; mandi tian to bathe in seventh month of pregnancy.

tiang post, pillar, column, pole, mast; tiang agung main mast.

tiap, tiap-tiap, setiap every, each; tiap-tiap hari daily.

tiarap, tertiarap prone; **meniarap** to lie prone; **tiarapkan** to invert.

tib book of spells, divination.

tiba arrive (of person, ship); tiba-tiba suddenly, abruptly.

tidak no, not; kalau tidak unless; **menidakkan** to deny, disregard.

tidur sleep; pergi tidur to go to sleep; tempat tidur bed, bedstead; **menidurkan** to put a child to sleep.

tiga three; bertiga three together; ketiga thirdly; yang ketiga the third; tigasegi triangle.

tijak = **pijak.**

tik tick (of clocks).

tikai, bertikai to disagree (of

views); **pertikaian** difference, quarrel, dispute.

tikam, menikam to stab, spear, pierce; stabbing.

tikar plaited mat; **tikar hampar** floor mat; **tikar bantal** sleeping mat and pillow.

tikasan tidemarks.

tika-tika reel of thread.

tike prepared opium.

tikit ticket.

tikung, menikung to wind (of roads).

tikus mouse, rat; **tikus cen-curut** muskshrew.

tila round (of base of gourd).

tilam mattress; **bertilam** having a mattress.

tilan, ikan tilan spiny eels.

tilik gaze; **tukang tilik** fortune teller; **tilikan** gaze divination.

tim, nasi tim steamed rice.

timah tin; bijih timah tin ore.

timang to balance (spear); dandle infants; **nama timang-timangan** pet name.

timba small bucket, bather's dipper; **timba ruang baling** well amidships; **menimba** to bale.

timbal, setimbal in equilibrium, balanced; **bertimbal, timbalan** balancing each other.

timbang, menimbang to weigh on scales; **bertimbang** considerate; **pertimbangan** consideration.

timbangantara to mediate.

timbau, menimbau to add upper strakes to boats; **timbauan** addition.

timbil stye; =tembel.

timbuk, menimbuk to hit downwards.

timbul to rise to the surface (of water); **timbul tenggelam** to bob up and down.

timbun, setimbun heap (of stones etc); **bertimbun** piled up; **menimbunkan** to pile up; **timbunan** pile.

timbus, menimbus to fill in holes.

timpa, menimpa to fall down on; **menimpakan** to bring down upon.

timpas dead low (of tides).

timpuh, bertimpuh to squat with legs sideways.

timpuk, menimpuk to fling a stone at person.

timpus, menimpus to taper.

timu, timu-timu proper, correct (of action).

timun cucumber; =mentimun.

timur east; **timur-laut** north-east.

tin tinned; susu tin tinned milk.

tindak step, stride; **bertindak** to take steps; **tindakan** steps, action.

tindan, menindan to put one on top of another.

tindas, menindas to kill (of flea, bug) with one's finger-nails; to squeeze, oppress, crush; **penindas** oppressor.

tindih, bertindih one lying on another; **menindih** to put one thing on another.

tindik, menindik to pierce (ears for rings); **bertindik** telinga to have one's ears pierced.

tineh, menineh to boil, effervesce.

ting tinkle.

tinggal to live, dwell; stay behind; **tempat tinggal** home; **tertinggal** abandoned; **meninggal** to die; **meninggalkan** to abandon; **ketinggalan** abandonment.

tinggang catfish.

tinggi tall; **tinggikan** to heighten; **ketinggian** height, altitude.

tinggung, bertinggung to squat on one's heels.

tingkah behaviour (of man); **bertingkah** to play up (of _horse_); **meningkah** to keep time.

tingkal borax; solder.

tingkap window.

tingkas=**tangkas.**

tingkat storey of house; social grade; **bertingkat-tingkat** to mount up.

tingkil bunch of fruit; **bertingkil-tingkil** hanging in clusters.

tingkir, bertingkir to perch (_as birds_).

tingkis, tingkis hati sad.

tingting sweetmeat of sugared beans.

tinjau, meninjau to crane the neck to see; **tinjau-meninjau** to peer around; **peninjau** observer, spy.

tinju, bertinju to box.

tinta ink.

tinting, meninting to ring a coin to test it; **ciak tinting** hopping game.

Tiong Hoa Chinese.

tipak turn;=**giliran.**

tipar dry ricefield;=**huma.**

tipikal typical.

tipis=**nipis.**

tipu deception, fraud; **kena tipu** cheated; **menipu** to cheat, defraud; **penipu** swindler.

tir castle, rook (_in chess_).

tirah, petirahan sanatorium.

tirai curtain; **tirai kelambu** mosquito curtain.

tiram oyster.

tiras fringe (_of cloth_); edge.

tiri, anak tiri stepchild; bapa tiri stepfather; emak tiri stepmother.

tiris oozing from a small leak (_in roof etc_).

tiru, tiru tauladan to follow a copy; **meniru** to imitate.

tiruk rong unbarbed fish spear; **meniruk** to spear fish; **nyamuk tiruk** culex mosquito; **burung tetiruk** snipe.

tirus taper (_as pillar_); acute.

tis slightly; **panas tis** rather hot.

tisik, menisik to darn, mend.

tisis thesis.

titah speech, command (_of ruler_); **bertitah** to speak (_of ruler_); **menitahkan orang** to issue a royal command.

titang basket tea cosy.

titar, bertitar-titar to hurry here and there.

titi small bridge (_of palm trunk etc_); any bridge; **meniti** to walk on tree trunk as bridge.

titik drop (_of water etc_); **menitik** to fall in drops; **titikberat** importance.

titinada musical score.

titip, menitipkan to deposit money in bank; **titipan** pledge, security.

titir, menitir to beat drum as signal; **bertitir** t.hudding.

titis, titisan driblets;=**titek.**

tiub tube.

tiung grackle, mynah; **tiung batu** broadbill roller.

tiup, bertiup to blow (_of wind_); **meniup** to blow.

to' familiar abbreviation for the title _dato'_.

toalang=**tualang.**

tobak, bertobak trimmed (_of nails_).

toboh group; **bertoboh-toboh** in clusters (_of people_).

todak, ikan todak garfish.

tofan typhoon.

togan, menogan to throw marbles at mark.

togel tailless (_of fowls_).

togok tree trunk stripped of branches.

togong fat, squat, clumsy.

toh birthmark.

tohok harpoon with rope attached.

tohor shallow (_of water_); **kapor tohor** whitewash.

toilet toilet.

tojang, menojang to push or press with both feet.

tokak, penyakit tokak ulcerated sore on leg, abscess; *also* **tukak.**

tokek split areca nut; **menokek** to split.

tokin iron rod with brass ring in the Johol insignia.

tokkek gecko, house lizard.

toko shop; = **kedai.**

tokoh quality, style of cloth; **sekoh ini** of the same type as this.

tokoh to add a little.

tokong shaved (*of head*); Buddhist temple.

tolak, menolak to push away, reject; **bertolak** to push off, start; **menolakkan** to push on to another; **kereta tolak** barrow.

toleh, menoleh to look back *or* aside.

toleran tolerant.

tolok match, equal, peer; **tiada tolok-banding** unparalleled, incomparable, matchless; **menolok** to equal; **tolok bulat** rollers.

tolol = **tolu.**

tolong help; **minta tolong** to ask for help; **menolong** to help; **pertolongan** aid.

tolu stupid, foolish; idiot.

tom bridle; indigo plant.

toman, ikan toman murrel; *also* **tuman.**

tomato tomato.

tombak lance (*circular and not spatular at base of blade*).

tombok additional payment.

tombol bump, lump (*on person*); door knob.

tombong seed bud in old coconut.

tomong Malay mortar; cannon.

tompok, setompok heap; **bertompok-tompok** in stacks; massed (*of clouds*); **tompokkan** to pile up.

toncit long back hair of Hindu.

tondong, menondong to hound out of the house; expel by traducing.

tong barrel, tub; **tong sampah** dustbin.

tonggak erect fixed snag in sea *or* river.

tonggek projecting (*of buttocks*).

tonggeng to stick up the posterior; **menonggengkan** to turn a pot upside down.

tonggok, bertonggok heaped up; **setonggok** pile.

tonggong, tertonggong-tonggong piled up.

tonggos prominent (*of front upper teeth*).

tongkah, menongkah to lengthen trousers by adding piece to waist.

tongkan moveable trapdoor over hatch in bows of boat.

tongkang sea-going barge, lighter for transporting cargo from ships to shore.

tongkat walking stick; vertical prop; **menongkat** to prop; **bertongkat** with walking stick.

tongkeng rump; **tulang tongkeng** coccyx.

tongkol central pith of ear of maize; **setongkol jagung** one head of maize; **ikan tongkol** tuna fish.

tongkong chunk of cut wood.

tongong stupid, dense.

Tongsan, pulang Tongsan to return to China.

tongsit trefoil knot in women's hair.

tongtong bamboo clapper struck as alarm.

tonik tonic.

tonjok, menonjok to box, spar.

tonjol, bertonjol having knobs at the ends; **menonjolkan** to push fingers in man's face; push to the fore (*wares, self*); *also* **tunjal.**

tonsil tonsil.

tonyeh to keep on asking questions *or* talking.

tonyoh, menonyoh to push food into child's mouth.

top, perahu top Indo-chinese and Siamese cargo boats; barge; top-top suddenly; main top dice; gamble.

topang forked prop, crutch; bertopang propped; menopang to prop.

topek to slice meat thin for drying.

topekong joss; image in Chinese shrine.

topeng mask; topeng gas gasmask; bertopeng masked.

topes beetling and likely to collapse (*of rocks, cliffs etc*).

topi sun hat.

topografi topography.

topok, menopok to tap to attract mousedeer.

topong rough plaited bag for fish paste (belacan).

torak spool, rolling pin; anak torak thread on spool; torak-torak cylinder.

torang knot at lower end of casting net; harimau torang kasau rafter patterned tiger, tiger with broad stripes.

toreh, menoreh to tap (*rubber etc*); penoreh tapper.

torek deaf and discharging (*of ears*).

toro, baju toro long pull-over coat.

torpedo torpedo.

total total.

toteh very thin piece.

toti servant.

totok pure blooded.

toya physically weak.

toyak cudgel, lathi.

toyor, menoyor to slap in face.

tradisional traditional.

tragedi tragedy.

trajik tragic.

transaksi transaction.

transistor transistor.

trigonometri trigonometry.

trombosa thrombosis.

tropika tropics.

tu, itu that, those.

tua old, aged persons; tertua very old.

tuah luck; bertuah lucky.

tuai tiny reaping knife concealed in palm of hand; menuai to cut rice stalk with it, harvest.

tuak palm wine, toddy.

tual sections of cut logs; bertual in pieces.

tuala towel, napkin.

tualang changing homes (*as vagabond*); pokok tualang trees where wild bees nest; very large jungle tree; petualang opportunist.

tuam to apply hot compress; bertuam using hot compress.

tuan title applied to Europeans, Sayids, Hajis; tuan hakim judge; tuanrumah house owner; tuanku your highness; tuanpunya owner.

tuang, menuangkan to pour out liquids into receptacles; tuangan mould.

Tuanku Your Highness, His Highness (*form of address to ruler*).

tuap rattan splint.

tuar river fish trap of thorny sticks.

tuarang dry weather.

tuas, menuas to lever up.

tub, tub-tub suddenly.

tuba, akar tuba roots used to poison fish for catching *or* as an insecticide; menuba to catch fish by using tuba.

tubagus title of descendants of former sultans of Banten.

tuban, tuban-tuban, tetuban foetal membranes.

tubi, menubikan to do work without stopping; bertubi-tubi persistent.

tubin the fourth day hence.

tubing to hit down with hand.

tubir steep cliff; edge of crater.

tubruk, menubruk to spring on, leap at.

tubuh whole body; **batang tubuh** trunk; **nama tubuh** personal name; **menubuhkan** to embody; **pertubuhan** organization; **setubuh** coition.

tubul, ikan tubul carp.

tuding at an angle; **menudingkan** to pull a stroke at an angle.

tuduh, menuduh to accuse; **tuduhan** accusation.

tudung veil; lid; **tudung saji** dish cover; **bertudung** veiled, lidded; **menudungkan** to veil.

tufah apple.

tugal dibble for rice; **menugal** to plant seed directly in the dry field.

tugas stiff (of breeze); task; **bertugas** to travel like the wind; carry out task; **tugas hati** ardent, determined.

tugu boundary stone; memorial stone, monument.

Tuhan God; **ketuhanan** attributes of God.

tuhfah gift; **tuhfat al-ajnas** gifts of different kinds.

tui pool, sweepstake; to begin again (after misdeal).

tuil lever; **menuilkan** to lever up slightly.

tujah to thrust with elbow.

tuju, menuju to aim at; **setuju** in accord with; **tujuan** aim, purpose; **persetujuan** agreement, concord; **menyetujui** to accede to, agree.

tujuh seven; **bertujuh** with six others; **yang ketujuh** seventh.

tukak ulcer; = **tokak.**

tukal large skein of thread.

tukang craftsman, specialist in handwork; **tukang ayan** tinsmith; **tukang jahit** tailor; **tukang masak** cook; **pertu-**

kangan craft; **tukang pelan** draughtsman.

tukar, bertukar, menukar to exchange, change; change; **pertukaran** exchange.

tukas, menukas to accuse without evidence.

tukik, menukik to plunge down, fly downwards.

tukil bamboo cylinder for liquid.

tukul hammer; **menukul** to hammer; **penukul** hammer.

tukun submerged reef.

tul, main tul child's game.

tuladan pattern, example, model.

tulah calamity (esp due to violating taboo).

tulang bone; **bertulang** full of bones.

tular infectious, contagious; **menular** to infect.

tulat third day hence.

tuli stone deaf; **buta tuli** deaf and dumb.

tulin genuine, real, original.

tulis, menulis to write; sketch; paint; **tulis-menulis** to scribble; **tertulis** written; **tulisan** script, writing; **penulis** writer.

tulus sincere; **tulus ikhlas** sincere and frank.

tum, tali tum reins.

tuma louse, fowltick.

tuman, toman accustomed; wont; **ikan toman** murrel.

tumang peg for stays of tent or flagmast; mooring post; **menumang** to be afraid of person.

tumba, setumba second, moment.

tumbal charm against sickness.

tumbang to fall (of trees); collapse; **tumbangkan** to bring crashing down.

tumbesar growth.

tumbu lidded coarse basket for rice.

tumbuh, bertumbuh to sprout (*of plants*); patah tumbuh hilang berganti the broken grows, the lost is replaced.

tumbuk, menumbuk to pound (*rice*); tertumbuk pounded; ketumbukan troop, corps.

tumis, menumis to fry onions in oil for curries.

tumit heel (*of foot*).

tumpah to spill, be spilt; air tumpah spilt water; tempat tumpah darah birthplace.

tumpak group; mass (*of cloud*).

tumpang, menumpang to lodge, be a lodger; take a lift *or* passage; rumah tumpangan lodging house; penumpang lodger; passenger; tumpangkan to deposit temporarily.

tumpar dead, croaked.

tumpas crashing (*of person in fall*).

tumpat stopped up (*of holes*); chockfull (*of room*); menumpat to stop, plug; ketumpatan density.

tumpeng cone of steamed rice.

tumpu, bertumpu to have a footing on (*ground*); be established (*of power*); menumpu to take a firm stance (*for jump etc*); concentrate; tempat tumpuan taking off place, rallying point.

tumpul blunt (*of knives etc*); tumpulkan to blunt.

tumpur finished; ruined (*of people*); hard up.

tumu tall mangrove tree.

tumus, tertumus to face forward (*of one falling*).

Tun, Tan 15th century honorific of the Malacca overlord and other nobles, retained in Perak and Johor by their descendants.

tuna wound; tertuna wounded.

tunai, wang tunai ready money, cash; menunaikan to fulfil a vow.

tunak, bertunak absorbed, heedless of interruption; devoted to a person.

tunam match for firing cannons; bakar tunam to light it.

tunang, bertunang to be affianced, engaged, bethrothed; tunangan one's betrothed; menunangkan to arrange a marriage between a couple.

tunas young shoot sprouting from branch; bertunas sprouting, shooting up.

tunda, menunda to tow (*boat*); kapal tunda tug; tali tunda towrope; bertunda in tow; tertunda deferred.

tunduk, bertunduk to bow one's head, stoop; menundukkan kepala to incline the head.

tundra tundra.

tundun mons veneris.

tungap croaked; dead.

tungau mites (*infesting fowls and man*).

tunggak stump of felled tree; menunggak to remain to be paid (*of instalments*).

tunggal solitary; anak tunggal only child.

tunggang, tunggang balik to fall head over heels; topsy-turvy; tunggangkan to invert (*bottle etc*); menunggang to straddle; kuda tunggangan riding horse.

tungging fourth day hence.

tunggu, bertunggu to keep guard; menunggu to watch by *or* over; penunggu watchman, guardian.

tunggul tree stump; butt (*of counterfoil*); tunggul panji-panji standard ensign.

tungkap tongue-tied.

tungku trivet (*of stones*); brazier.

tungkul, menungkul bow, surrender.

tungkus, tungkus lumus overwhelmed with work.

tunjal, menunjal to spring hard on the feet (as jumper); poke finger in person's face.

tunjang, akar tunjang taproot; **menunjang** to buttress (tree); support (with money).

tunjing high (of coiffure).

tunjuk, menunjukkan to exhibit (articles); point out; **pertunjukan** exhibition, display; **penunjuk** pointer; **tunjuk langit** kingpost; fern (that is used as vegetable and medicine).

tunjung, lunjung emas whiteor rose-coloured water lily.

tunku = **tengku**.

tuntung point, tip of needle; tortoise common in rice fields; **menuntung** to invert and rap; pour out.

tuntun, menuntun to lead (with leash, rope); watch; **rumah tuntunan** exhibition gallery; **penuntun** spectators.

tuntut, menuntut to pursue (knowledge, studies); claim a debt, demand fulfilment; **tuntutan** claim.

tunu, menunukan to burn up (house, last logs in clearing); **bertunu** burnt up.

tupai squirrel.

tupang = **topang**.

tup-tup suddenly; also **tubtub**.

tur mountain; **Tur sina** Sinai.

tura, bertura-tura to rave (in delirium).

Turan Turkestan.

turap plaster; **berturap** plastered; **menurap** to plaster; paint.

turas, menuras to filter (dye) through cloth.

turis, menuris to tap (rubber); scratch (bark).

Turki Turkey.

turnamen tournament.

turun to descend, come down;

go down; **turunkan** lower; **keturunan** descent; pedigree.

turus main post (of house); mooring post; **turus negeri** pillar of state; **menurus** to rise in column.

turut to follow, imitate; **turut serta** to go along with, participate; **berturut-turut** continuously, in succession; consecutive; **menurut** to follow.

tus sound of gun; sound of dripping water; **tuskan** to drip-dry sth.

tusuk, menusuk to pierce, prick.

tut, tutkan to graft; **tutan** grafting (in horticulture).

tutuh, menutuh to lop; pollard; **tutuh lari** to cut and run; **bertutuh** to come to blows.

tutuk, tutuk ketampi to cross arms, hold ears and jump up and down (as school punishment).

tutul spotted; **harimau tutul** leopard.

tutup closed; **bertutup** lidded; **menutupkan** to shut (book, eyes etc); **penutup** shutter.

tutur utterance; **tuturnya** elocution; **bertutur bahasa Inggeris** to speak English.

tuwu, burung tuwu Malayan bird.

U

ua = **tua**.

uai mother.

uak polite address to elders; **menguak** to bellow (of buffaloes).

uanda polite form of **uak**, elder.

uang, wang, keuangan finance.

uap vapour; **menguap** to steam; yawn.

uba sago vat.

ubah, berubah to be altered; **berubah-ubah** to keep changing; **tak berubah** consistent; **mengubah** to alter; **perubahan** alteration, variation, modification.

ubahansur evolution.

uban grey (of hair); **beruban** turned grey; **pipit uban** white-headed munia.

ubang, mengubang to cut curved groove in log.

ubar, mengubar to unroll.

ubat medicine; **ubat bedil** gunpowder, ammunition; **mengubatkan** to treat medically; **perubatan** medical.

ubi yam; **ubi kayu** tapioca; **ubi keledek** sweet potato.

ubil–ubil turban.

ubin floor tile, flagstone; **batu ubin** granite.

ubir to chase, follow.

ububan bellows.

ubun, ubun-ubun soft throbbing spot on crown of baby's head.

ubur, ubur-ubur fringed umbrella.

ucap, mengucap to utter; **ucap syukur** thanks to God; **ucapan** speech.

ucu youngest; = bungsu.

uda young; **mak uda** aunt younger than one's father or mother.

udak, mengudak to chase, follow.

udam faded (of looks).

udang crayfish, lobster, prawn shrimp.

udani title.

udap, udap-udapan vegetable snacks; **mengudap** to hurry.

udar, mengudar to loosen, unfasten.

udara air, atmosphere; **ilmu udara** meteorology.

udi ill luck.

udik I, mengudik to stir up.

udik II upstream, hinterland.

udit waistband, sash.

uduk, nasi uduk rice cooked with coconut milk; = **nasi lemak.**

udut, mengudut to smoke cigarettes; **pengudut** smoker.

udzor = uzur.

uek, menguek to quack.

ufti tribute.

ugahari equal in rank; royal on both sides; even.

ugama religion; **berugama** religious.

ugut, mengugut to blackmail, menace, frighten; bluff; **ugutan** threat.

ujar remark.

uji, batu uji touchstone; **menguji** to test; **ujian** test, examination.

ujrat wages, pay; hire.

ujud, wujud intention, purpose; **kewujudan** existence.

ujung end, extremity; **ujung tanah** cape, promontory; **ujung bulan** end of month.

ukas sea shell.

ukik, main **ukik** child's game with berries or coins.

ukir, mengukir to carve; **berukir** carved; **tukang ukir** carver; **ukiran carving.**

ukup, mengukup to perfume clothes with incense; **perukup** perfumed.

ukur, mengukur to measure length; **ukuran** measurement.

ula–ula pennon; also **ular-ular.**

ulam vegetable taken raw.

ulama theologians.

ulan climber.

ulanda, Belanda Dutch.

ulang, berulang to return again; **ulang kali** frequently; **ulang kaji** revision; **mengulang** to repeat; **ulang tahun** anniversary.

ulap, ulap-ulap broth made of aroids with coconut milk.

ular snake; ular-ular pennon; ular-ularan cramp; ular senduk cobra.

ulas cover (of cushions etc); wrapper; berulas covered; seulas pip of durians; juru ulas commentator; mengulas to comment.

ulat worm, maggot.

uli, menguli to knead (bread).

ulir screw.

ulit, mengulit to croon; mengulitkan to sing a child to sleep.

ulun servant; I; me.

um mother.

uman, menguman to abuse, nag at.

umang-umang hermit crab.

umbalan freight.

umbang, mengumbang to pitch (of ships).

umbar, mengumbar to let loose (beast).

umbi bulb (root); root, corm; perkataan umbi root word.

umbih snot.

umbing, mengumbing to recover (of the sick).

umbu turn right (command to elephant).

umbuk, umbuk-umbai all sorts of blandishments; mengumbuk to wheedle.

umbul, to grow quickly; umbul-umbul long pennon.

umbut palm cabbage.

ummat people, crowd.

umpak base, foundation; mengumpak to flatter.

umpama model, example; seumpama resembling; umpamanya for instance.

umpan bait (for fish); mengumpan to use bait.

umpat, mengumpat to revile, abuse, grumble at (behind one's back).

umpil, mengumpil to lever up (with crowbar, stick); pengumpil lever.

umpit, mengumpit to hide.

umpuk share.

umrah visit (to Mecca).

umum complicated; in general; umumkan to make obscure; pada umumnya universally; mengumumkan to make public, publish; common.

umur life; seumur hidup all one's life; separuh umur middle age; berumur of a certain age.

unai moist and odorous.

uncang cloth slipknot purse; bayar uncang-uncang to pay by instalments.

uncat, menguncat-uncat to keep lifting and lowering bait.

uncu Chinese tobacco pipe.

undak, mengundak to make no headway; terundak-undak labouring (of ship).

undan, burung undan white pelican; cob; berundan-undan dawdling (as in traffic jam).

undang, undang-undang laws; Majlis Undangan Legislative Council.

undi lots, dice; buah undi dice; buang undi, mengundi to ballot, vote; cast lots; pengundi voter.

undil tin or wooden moneybox.

unduk, unduk-unduk sea horse.

undung-undung cloth veiling woman's head.

undur, berundur to retreat, give way; mengundur diri to retire, take leave.

ungap, mengungap to pant.

ungar, ikan ungar sea perch.

ungas to gallop away.

unggang-unggit to seesaw.

unggas bird; unggas dewata bird of paradise.

unggat-unggit to wobble (as chair).

unggis, mengunggis to nibble (of mice etc).

unggul idea; dominant.

unggun, berunggun banked (of fire, with slow burning logs).

ungka gibbon.

ungkai, mengungkai to loosen, undo; **terungkai** undone.

ungkal obstinate; to uproot trees.

ungkap, mengungkap gasp; **terungkap-ungkap** gasping; **ungkapan** utterance.

ungkat, mengungkat to drag up the past.

ungkit to lever with timber or crowbar.

ungkuk-ungkap up and down (as trodden grass).

ungkur, ungkur-ungkuran fleeing in all directions.

ungsi, mengungsi to flee for safety; **pengungsi** evacuee.

ungu purple.

unjam clump of branches anchored at sea in several spots to attract fish.

unjuk, mengunjukkan to offer, proffer, hold out hand.

unjun, mengunjun to fish lowering and pulling up live bait.

unjur, belunjur to stretch one's legs; **unjuran** projection.

unjut cloth folded like envelope.

unsur element, constituent.

unta camel; **burung unta** ostrich.

untai thread for beads; **beruntai** dangling.

untal, menguntal to roll into pill; **untal-antil** swaying and dangling.

untang-anting dangling and swaying.

until pill, pellet; **beruntil-until** bit by bit.

unting skein of thread; **unting-unting** reckoning, accounts.

untuk allotted share; for the purpose of; **untukkan** to allot a share; **teruntuk** allocated; **per-untukan** vote.

untung gain; **untung besar** large profits; **beruntung** lucky, profitable; **keuntungan** profit.

untut elephantiasis; beri-beri; **kaki untut** leg swollen from it.

unwan title page, heading.

unyak-anyek loose (of tooth).

unyas-anyas untidy.

upacara rite, ceremonial.

upaduta chancellor of embassy.

upah payment for work done.

upak-apik loose (of fastening).

upam, terupam polished (of metal); **mengupam** to polish.

upar, mengupar to roll between the palms (leaves, dough etc).

upas poison of upas tree.

upaya resources, plan; **dengan seberapa upaya** one's ability; **mengupayakan** to take steps, plan.

upeti tribute to a more powerful state; also **ufti**.

upih flower sheath of betel and nibung palms.

upik, si upik term of address for daughters.

ura estimates, accounts; **ber-ura-ura** to deliberate, debate.

urai loose; **mengurai** to unfold (of palm blossoms); **mengurai-kan** to undo (knots etc); solve (problems); **uraian** solution of equation; also **hurai**.

uranium uranium.

urap vegetable salad; **berurap** scented with perfumes.

uras liquid medicinal embrocation.

urat, urat darah artery, vein; **urat saraf** nerves.

urdi order.

urea urea.

uri placenta; **tali uri** umbilical cord.

urian nude gymnosophist.

uring vulture.

urip alive and well.

uritan ovary.

uruk, menguruk to fill up land with soil.

urung, emas urung iron pyrites; **to swarm over; di-urung lalat** fly-covered.

urup, mengurup to change money.

urus, mengurus to arrange, organize, manage; **pengurus** manager; **urusan** executive; **pihak pengurus** management.

urut, mengurut to rub with palm, massage.

usah never mind!; **tak usah** do not.

usaha diligence (in industry); effort; **berusaha** industrious; **perusahaan getah** rubber industry; **mengusahakan** to perform with diligence.

usai over (of war); exhausted (of money).

usam dull (of metals).

usang dry (of hair); empty, shrivelled; old; out-of-date.

usap, mengusap to wipe tears.

usia life, lifetime, age.

usik, mengusik to tease, chaff; molest; meddle with things; **pengusik** teaser.

usir, mengusir to chase away, pursue.

ustaz master, lord; teacher.

usuk rafter.

usul origin; usul-asal pedigree; **ilmu usul** knowledge of the tenets of Islam; **mengusulkan** to introduce a proposal; request.

usung, mengusung to carry in litter; **berusung** borne in litter; **usungan** hammocklike litter.

usus intestine.

usut, mengusut to investigate.

utama eminent; **terutama** especially; **Yang Terutama** His Excellency (Governor, Ambassador).

utan = hutan.

utang debt, money due; **utang piutang** debts and credits; **bayar utang** to pay debts; **berutang in debt;** also hutang.

utara north; **bintang utara** pole star.

utarid, bintang utarid Mercury (astr).

utar-utar small round shield.

utas craftsman; **utasan** craftsmanship; **tali seutas** one rope.

utau signal to be silent.

utih = putih.

utuk appeal to higher court.

utus, mengutus to send an envoy; **utusan** delegation, mission; envoy; **utusan muhibbah** goodwill mission.

uzur sick, weak; **keuzuran** debility.

V

vagina, faraj vagina.

van van.

variasi variation.

vaselin Vaseline (trademark).

volta volt.

W

wa I and; **wallahu alam** and God knows best.

wa II, wak uncle; aunt.

waad contract; **berwaad** to contract, pledge o.s.

wabadu and then, and after that.

wabah epidemic; **= wabak.**

wadah tray, plate, font.

wadas stony ground.

wadat celibate.

wadi desert stream.

waduk belly, paunch; **waduk air** reservoir.

wadun womanly.

wadzih clear, evident.

wafak written amulet.

wafat dead (of prophets).

wagon wagon.

wah expressing surprise.

wahab Giver, God.

wahadat unity.

wahai ah!, oh! (inviting s.o.'s attention).

waham doubt; **menaruh syak dan waham** to entertain suspicion and mistrust.

wahdat individuality.

wahi revelation through vision or dream.

wahid single, unique (esp of God).

wahiu vision, divine revelation, inspiration.

wai water, river.

waizuri crown prince.

waja steel; = **baja**.

wajad ecstasy of saint.

wajah face, countenance.

wajan frying pan; basin.

wajar natural, right.

wajib obligatory by religion; **kewajipan** obligation; necessity.

wajik cake of glutinous rice grains, coconut milk and sugar.

wakaf benefaction for religion; **wakafkan** to bequeath land for religious purpose; **perwakafan** consecration.

wakil agent, commissary, representative; **surat wakil** power of attorney; **wakil mutlak** plenipotentiary; **mewakili** to represent; **perwakilan** delegation.

waktu time, opportunity; **waktu itu** at that time.

wakwak = **ungka**.

walad son of, child of.

walakin although.

walang, walang hati troubled, uneasy, sad.

walasan lever (for lathe).

walau and if, though; walaupun although, even if.

walhal although.

wal-hasil with the result that.

wali I guardian of unmarried girl; **wali ullah** Muslim saint.

wali II, kain wali yellow stole worn on the shoulder or round the neck down to the waist by court pages.

wali III, pisau wali small knife

walimah marriage feast.

wallahi by God.

waluku plough.

walwi bangle.

wan courtesy title of descendants of important non-royal chiefs.

wang money; **wang tunai** cash; **wang kertas** paper money; **wang simpanan** savings; **kewangan** finance.

wangi fragrant; **minyak wangi** scent, perfume.

wangkang Chinese ship, junk.

wangsa dynasty.

wanita woman.

wanta pomegranate.

wanti-wanti repeatedly.

wap steam, vapour.

warak I abstinence from the unlawful.

warak II rhinoceros.

warangan arsenic.

waras healthy, well; rational.

wardi order, command.

warga family, household; **warganegara** citizen.

warid jugular vein.

warik to abstain from the unlawful.

warip alive; **warip waras** alive and well.

waris, warith heir to property or title; **waris negeri** potential inheritor of the throne upon the male side.

warkat letter, epistle.

warna colour; **berwarna** coloured; **mewarnakan** to colour.

warta news, report, newspaper; **kewartawanan** journalism.

wartawan journalist.

wasangka suspicious, dubious.

wasi executor of a will.

wasiat exhortation, verbal testament, injunction; **surat wasiat** will; **berwasiat** to make a testament.

wasik spacious; omnipresent (*of God*).

wasilkan to convey to recipient (*of letter*).

wasir = bawasir.

wasitah mediator, umpire.

waslah symbol of elision, alif (*eg* khalifatullah).

waspada cautious; accurate; guarded.

waswas anxious, worried.

wat Buddhist temple.

watak character, attitude.

watan, wataniah birthplace, fatherland.

wathik trusting.

wati firmament.

watu sewatu, suatu one.

wau paper kite; main wau to fly a kite.

wawanchara press interview.

wayang theatrical show, opera; **wayang gambar** cinema; **wayang kulit** shadow play.

wayuh having more than one wife.

wazir vizier.

wedana head of district in Java.

weduk invulnerable.

wegah unwilling.

weh! *ecci* expressing surprise.

wenang authorized, rightly.

wesel postal order.

wet paddle with kicking stroke of single oar.

wetan the east.

widuri tree.

wijata instruction, teaching.

wijaya victorious.

wijil door, exit.

wila belfruit tree.

wiladah, mandi wiladah ceremonial lustration of pregnant woman.

wilahar mere, pool.

wilang frantic, mad.

wilayah district, province.

wilis dark green; dark blue.

windu cycle of eight years.

wira hero.

wirama tempo.

wirang shame, disgrace.

wirid Muslim forms of prayer.

wisma house.

wiwaha marriage.

wizurai viceroy.

wokshop workshop.

Wolanda Holland; Dutch.

wuduk ablution before prayer.

wujud existence, being; **mewujudkan** to bring into being, create; **terwujud** realized, created.

Y

ya yes.

yaani that is, ie; *also* yakni.

yad hand; front paw.

Yahudi Judea; Jew; Jewish.

yahum, angin yahum following wind.

yajuj Gog; **Yajuj wa-Majuj** Gog and Magog.

yak, belacak yak abundant (*of fruit*).

yakin certain, confident; **me-yakinkan** to aver positively; **keyakinan** certainty, confidence.

yakut ruby.

yam tuan who is lord; **Yang Dipertuan** (*title of Malay ruler*).

yang who, which, that; **orang yang belajar** people who study.
yarkan jaundice.
yasin chapter of the Kuran which is read to the dying.
yatim orphan.
yaum, yaum al-kiamat Day of Judgement.
yayasan institute, foundation.
yayi younger brother or sister.
yogia, sayogia proper, fitting.
yojana measure of length.
yu, ikan yu shark; **pokok yu** tree.
yuda war.
Yunan Ionia, Greece; **Yunani** Ionian, Greek.
yunit unit.
yuran subscription (to club).
Yushaa Joshua.

Z

zabad civet.
Zabaniah angels who push the damned into hellfire.
zabarjad topaz.
zabib raisins.
zabur, al-zabur the Psalms.
zadah child of; **haram zadah** bastard.
zahid hermit, dervish.

zaitun olive tree.
zakat Muslim tithe payable after fasting month.
zakiah pure, sincere.
zalim cruel.
zaman epoch, time; **zaman dahulu** former ages; **zaman sekarang** nowadays; **sampai akhir zaman** for ever.
zamin land, country.
zamrud emerald.
zamzam water.
Zanggi Ethiopian, Negro.
zeng zinc.
ziadah addition; to affix.
ziarah visit to shrine or holy place.
zinah fornication, adultery; **berzinah** to commit adultery.
zindik heretic, atheist, fire worshippers.
zirafah giraffe.
zirah, baju zirah coat of mail.
zuadah sweetmeats.
zuhal, bintang zuhal Saturn (astr).
Zuhara, bintang Zuhara Venus (astr).
Zulhijjah twelfth Muslim month.
Zulikha Potiphar's wife.
Zulkaedah eleventh Muslim month.
zulmat darkness.

ENGLISH-BAHASA MALAYSIA

DICTIONARY

A

a, an suatu, salah satu, seorang, sebuah, se, sebiji; (*at*) di.

aback ke belakang; **taken —** tercengang, tergemap, terperanjat.

abacus dekak-dekak, sepoa, cempoa.

abandon, to — menyerahkan, meninggalkan; **—ed** terbangai, terbengkalai, tertinggal.

abandonment pembuangan, pengasingan.

abase, to — merendahkan, menghinakan.

abash, to — mempermalukan, memberi malu.

abate, to — berkurang, mengurangkan; (*of storm, rain*) reda.

abatement pengurangan.

abattoir pembantaian.

abbey pertapaan, gereja.

abbot kepala pertapaan laki-laki.

abbreviate, to — memendekkan, meringkaskan, memotong.

abbreviation kependekan, huruf ringkas, potongan.

abdicate, to — meninggalkan kerajaan, turun takhta.

abdication turun takhta.

abdomen perut, abdomen.

abdominal yang berkenaan dengan perut.

abduct, to — melarikan, menculik.

abduction penculikan.

abductor penculik.

aberrant yang menyimpang (dari hal biasa), sesat.

aberration penyimpangan.

abet, to — membantu dalam perkara yang jahat.

abeyance, in — sedang ditunda; tidak berlaku, tidak dipakai.

abhor, to — benci sekali akan.

abhorrence kebencian, perasaan tidak suka akan.

abidance ketetapan.

abide, to — tetap; **to — by** menetapi; abiding kekal.

ability kebolehan, kecakapan, kepandaian, kemampuan.

abject hina.

abjection keadaan hina, kehinaan.

abjure, to — mengingkar dengan sumpah, menolak dengan sumpah.

ablaze terbakar; **to set —** menyalakan.

able sanggup; boleh, pandai; **to be —** sanggup boleh, dapat.

-able akhiran kata yang ertinya; dapat, patut, boleh.

ablution basuh, mandi wuduk.

ably dengan pandainya.

abnegation ingkar.

abnormal ganjil, luar daripada biasa.

abnormality keadaan ganjil.

aboard di kapal, di keretapi;

all —! semua penumpang naik ke kapal (dan sebagainya).

abode tempat tinggal.

abolish, to — menghapuskan, membatalkan, memansukhkan, membasmikan.

abolition pembatalan, penghapusan, pembasmian.

abominable makruh.

abomination kebencian.

aboriginal asli, purba; orang asli.

aborigine orang asli.

abort, to — (of child) menggugur(kan) (anak).

abortion (miscarriage) keguguran.

abortive gagal, ketinggalan.

about (around) berkeliling, di mana-mana; (approximately) lebih kurang, kira-kira; (concerning) darihal, berkeadaan dengan.

above (of position) di atas; (more than) lebih daripada; — all terutama, teristimewa.

abrasion lecet, jejas, luka pada kulit, hakisan.

abrasive penggosok, penjejas; an — ubat penggosok.

abreast berseiring; saeng; — of, with the times tahu akan segala kepentingan zaman.

abridge, to — memendekkan, meringkaskan.

abridg(e)ment pemendekan, ringkasan.

abroad (diluar negeri; to go — merantau, pergi keluar negeri.

abrupt tiba-tiba, sekonyong-konyong.

abscess bisul, tokak.

abscond, to — melarikan diri.

absence tidak hadir, ketiadaan.

absent tidak hadir, tidak ada; to — o.s. menjauhkan diri.

absentee seorang yang tidak

masuk bekerja, seorang yang tidak hadir.

absenteeism keadaan tidak masuk bekerja.

absent-minded lalai, alpa.

absolute (of power) mutlak, tak terbatas.

absolution ampun, pengampunan, maaf.

absolve, to — membebaskan.

absorb, to — meresap, menyerap.

absorbed (in) asyik, bertekun; — in work sedang asyik bekerja.

absorbent yang meresap, yang menyerap.

absorbing (interesting) mengasyikkan.

absorption resapan, serapan.

abstain, to — from menjauhkan diri daripada, memantang.

abstemious berpantang.

abstention hal berpantang.

abstinence pantang.

abstract I abstrek, mujarad.

abstract II, to — mengambil dari; meringkaskan.

abstraction hal yang kemujaradan.

abstruse sulit, musykil.

absurd bukan-bukan, mustahil, tidak termasuk akal.

absurdity hal yang bukan-bukan, hal yang tak termasuk akal.

abundance banyak kelimpahan.

abundant berlimpah-limpah, serba banyak, berlebihan, banyak.

abuse salah pemakaian; (evil) kejahatan, perkataan kasar; memaki; to — memaki.

abusive kasar, dengan maki.

abysmal amat dalam, tidak terduga.

abyss jurang yang tidak terduga dalamnya, keluburan.

acacia sejenis pohon.

academy (*school*) sekolah tinggi; (*society*) persatuan orang terpelajar, akademi.

accede, to — menyetujui; mengkabulkan.

accelerate, to — mempercepat, melajukan.

acceleration pencepatan, laju.

accent (*mark*) tekanan, tanda tekanan; (*of speech*) cara berkata, pelat.

accentuate, to — mementingkan, mengutamakan.

accentuation penekanan, pengutamaan.

accept, to — menerima; menyetujui.

acceptable yang dapat diterima.

acceptance penerimaan; persetujuan.

access jalan masuk, tempat masuk; to give — to memberi jalan masuk.

accessary (*helper*) penolong, pembantu.

accessible mudah dimasuki; lekas terpengaruh.

accession naik takhta.

accessory hal yang menyertai sesuatu; dress accessories segala kelengkapan pakaian.

accidence perubahan dalam perkataan.

accident sesuatu yang terjadi, kemalangan, nahas.

accidental yang terjadi dengan kebetulan.

accidentally (*unintentional*) kebetulan; sengaja; bukan.

acclaim, to — bersorak.

acclamation penerimaan dengan suka hati; voted by — diterima dengan sebulat suara.

acclimatize, to — menjadi biasa dengan iklim.

accolade istiadat pemberian pangkat.

accommodate, to — (*adjust*) menyesuaikan; (*find time*)

memberi kesempatan; (*comprise*) muat; (*find lodging for*) beri tumpang.

accommodating sudi menolong, bersifat lemah-lembut; menurut.

accommodation penyesuaian; perumahan.

accompaniment penyertaan.

accompany, to — menyertai, mengikut, mengiringi.

accomplice kakitangan, kawan berbuat syubahat.

accomplish, to — mencapai, menyempurnakan.

accomplished sempurna.

accomplishment kesempurnaan; kepandaian.

accord persetujuan, sesuaian.

accordance persetujuan, penyesuaian; in — with sesuai dengan; to be in — with berpatutan dengan.

accordingly oleh sebab itu.

accordion sejenis alat muzik, akordion.

accost tegur, sapa; to — menegur menyapa.

account cerita, ceritera; of little — tidak penting; on no — sekali-kali tidak.

accountable bertanggungjawab.

accountancy hal memegang buku untung-rugi; ilmu akaun.

accountant akauntan; jurukira.

accoutrement perlengkapan askar.

accredit, to — (*to envoys*) mengirim duta dengan surat tauliah.

accredited yang umum diterima dan dipercayai.

accretion hal tumbuh; pertambahan.

accrue, to — bertambah banyak.

accumulate, to — bertambah banyak.

accumulation penambahan, penghimpunan.

accumulative bertambah-tambah.

accumulator penghimpun letrik, beteri letrik.

accuracy betul, teliti, ketepatan.

accurate teliti, selidik, cermat, tepat.

accursed celaka, terkutuk, laknat.

accusation tuduhan, dakwa, pendakwaan.

accusatory penuduh.

accuse, to — menuduh, mendakwa, mengadu.

accused, the — yang didakwa, yang dituduh.

accustom, to — membiasakan.

accustomed biasa.

ace, air — seorang pahlawan penerbang; within an — of hampir-hampir.

acerbity rasa masam.

acetic acid cuka belanda.

acetylene gas kabait.

ache sakit; head — sakit kepala; stomach — sakit perut; to — sakit.

achieve, to — mencapai.

achievement kepandaian; hasil, kejayaan, pencapaian.

acid asam.

acidity kadar asam.

acknowledge, to — mengaku, mengakui; to — receipt (of a letter) mengaku penerimaan (surat).

acknowledgement pengakuan.

acme puncak.

acne bintit.

acorn buah pokok oak.

acoustic berkenaan dengan bunyi atau pendengaran.

acquaint, to — memperkenalkan; to — o.s. with membiasakan diri dengan.

acquaintance perkenalan.

acquiesce, to — menyetujui dengan tidak berkata; bersetuju.

acquiescence persetujuan dengan tidak berkata.

acquire, to — mencapai, memperoleh.

acquisition pencapaian.

acquisitive yang sifatnya hendak memperoleh; memilik.

acquit, to — menerangkan bahawa seorang tidak berdosa; melepaskan.

acquittal kelepasan, lepas.

acquittance pembayaran hutang.

acre ekar, ukuran tanah; (1.33 acre=1 relung).

acreage jumlah luas, ekar dalam sebidang tanah.

acrid asam; tajam.

acrimonious tajam.

acrimony sifat tajam, perkataan tajam.

acrobat penambul, gerakan badan.

across lintang; seberang; to come — (a thing) menemui; to take — menyeberangkan; with arms — berdakap.

act perbuatan; babak; (law) undang-undang, akta; to — berbuat; melakukan diri; bertindak.

acting (on the stage) berlaku; (substituting) pengganti; — (as) memangku sebagai.

action perbuatan, pergerakan, usaha, feel; to take — mengambil tindakan; in — sedang berjuang.

activate menghidupkan, menggerakkan, dengan giat, cergas.

active giat, ringan bergerak; — method kaedah cergas.

activity kesibukan, pergerakan, kegiatan.

actor anak bangsawan, pelakun.

actress pelakun.

actual yang sebenarnya, betul-betul.

actually asalnya, sebenarnya, sebetulnya.

actuate, to — menjalankan.

acuity, acuteness ketajaman.

acumen kepandaian.

acute tajam; an — angle sudut tirus; an — pain sakit yang pedih.

ad abbr of **advertisement** iklan.

A.D., Anno Domini tahun Masihi.

adage peribahasa, pepatah.

Adam Adam.

adamant amat keras.

Adam's apple halkum.

adapt, to — menyesuaikan.

adaptation penyesuaian.

add, to—memperbanyak(kan), melebihi, menambah, menjumlahkan, mencampurkan.

addendum tambahan.

adder ular bisa.

addict seorang yang ketageh sesuatu.

addicted ketagih; — to opium ketagihan candu.

addiction ketagihan.

addition penambahan; tambahan.

additional tambahan.

addle (of eggs) buruk, tembelang, busuk; to — menjadi busuk.

address (for letters etc) alamat; (greeting) tegur sapa; to — (direct one's course) mengarahkan; (greet) menyapa; (speak) berucap.

addressee kepada yang dialamatkan, penerima.

adenoids ketumbuhan dalam lidung.

adept pandai, ahli.

adequate cukup; sekadar, patut.

adequately dengan secukupnya, sepatutnya.

adhere, to — melekat kepada, bersangkut pada.

adherent yang berpautan dengan, yang bersangkutan.

adhesion keadaan sesuatu yang melekat.

adhesive sifat yang melekat; gam.

ad hoc istimewa untuk hal ini.

adieu selamat jalan, selamat tinggal.

ad infinitum terus-menerus, tidak berkeputusan.

adipose gemuk.

adjacent dekat, di sebelah, di sisi, berdampingan.

adjective sifat nama, kata-sifat.

adjoin, to — berpadu, bersatu, berdampingan.

adjourn menangguhkan, bersurai berpindah tempat.

adjournment penangguhan, persuraian.

adjudicate, to — menghukumkan, mengadili.

adjunct pembantu; tambahan.

adjust, to — menyesuaikan, melaraskan.

adjustment penyesuaian.

adjutant pegawai ajutan.

ad lib sekehendak hati.

administer, to — mentadbir, mengurus; to — the law mengadili to — medicine memberi ubat.

administration pemerintahan, pentadbiran.

administrative yang mengurus, yang mentadbir.

administrator pengurus, pengatur, pentadbir.

admirable terpuji, elok.

admiral laksamana, panglima laut.

Admiralty, the — Kementerian Angkatan Laut.

admiration pujian, kagum.

admire, to — memuji, menyanjong.

admirer pemuji.

admissible boleh diizinkan; boleh masuk.

admission kebenaran masuk, izin masuk.

admit, to — (*agree to*) mengaku memperkenankan; (*entrance*) masuk.

admittance pemberian izin masuk; no — dilarang masuk.

admixture tambahan.

admonish, to — menasihati, menegur.

admonition nasihat, teguran.

ad nauseam sampai mual.

ado kesusahan.

adolescence masa remaja.

adolescent anak muda teruna, puteri, remaja.

adopt, to — a child mengambil anak; to — **an idea** menerima, fikiran; adopted child anak angkat.

adoption pemungutan, pengangkatan.

adoptive kerana dipungut.

adorable terpuji, sangat menarik.

adoration pemujian, kemuliaan.

adore, to — memuliakan, sangat tertarik akan.

adorn, to — menghiasi.

adornment perhiasan.

adrift hanyut, timbul terapung.

adroit tingkas, pandai.

adulate, to — meleceh.

adult sempurna umur, dewasa, akil baligh.

adulterate, to — mencampuri.

adulteration campuran.

adulterer seorang yang berzinah.

adultery zinah; to commit — berzinah.

advance kemajuan; pendahuluan, wang muka, wang tempah; to pay in — membayar wang muka; to — maju, naik.

advanced (*extended*) lanjut.

advantage guna, laba, untung, faedah, kebaikan.

advantageous berguna, berfaedah, beruntung.

Advent masa beberapa minggu sebelum hari Natal.

adventure peristiwa, kejadian.

adventurer pengembara.

adventurous berani.

adverb kata keterangan.

adversary lawan, penentang; (*national*) musuh.

adverse melawan.

adversity keadaan malang, kemalangan.

advertise, to — mengiklankan.

advertisement iklan.

advice nasihat, syor, petua; to ask for — minta nasihat.

advisable yang boleh dinasihati.

advise, to — menasihati, memberi nasihat.

advisedly bijaksana.

adviser penasihat.

advocate penganjur, pengacara; to — menganjurkan; peguambela.

adze beliung, kapak.

aegis, under the — of di bawah perlindungan.

aeon suatu ketika yang berabad-abad lamanya.

aerate, to — memperanginkan.

aerial yang berkenaan dengan udara.

aerodrome padang kapalterbang.

aeronautical berkenaan dengan penerbangan.

aeroplane kapalterbang.

aesthete seorang yang mementingkan keindahan.

aesthetic yang berkenaan dengan keindahan atau kecantikan; — appreciation penikmatan rasa indah.

afar jauh.

affability ramah-tamah.

affable ramah-tamah, peramah.

affair hal, perkara.

affect perasaan; to — mempengaruhi.

affectation gaya.

affected pilu, hiba.

affection perasaan, kesukaan, sayang, kasih, kemesraan.

affectionate dengan amat suka hati.

affidavit kenyataan yang sah, surat sumpah.

affiliate, to — mengangkat sebagai anggota, bergabung bersekutu.

affinity pertalian, tali persaudaraan.

affirm, to — mengaku, membenarkan, menyetujui.

affirmation pembenaran.

affirmative yang menyetujui.

affix penambah, tambahan; to — meletak(kan).

afflict, to — menyakiti, mengganggu.

affliction kesakitan, sengsara.

affluent lempah; anak sungai; (wealthy) kekayaan.

afford, to — dapat, sanggup.

affray perkelahian.

affront nusta, penghinaan; to — menustakan, memberi malu.

afield di padang, di kebun, di luar rumah.

aflame terbakar, bernyala.

afloat terapung, hanyut; (in circulation) sedang berlaku.

afoot berjalan kaki; sedang berlaku.

afore di hadapan; lebih dahulu; tersebut di atas.

afraid takut, merasa gentar; to be — of takut akan.

afresh baharu, mulai lagi.

African orang Afrika.

Afrikaans bahasa orang Belanda di Afrika Selatan.

aft pada buritan kapal; fore and — dari haluan ke buritan.

after selepas; setelah, sesudah, kemudian; — two days lepas dua hari.

afterbirth tembuni, uri.

afterglow sesudah matahari terbenam.

aftermath akibat.

afternoon tengahari, petang.

afterthought fikiran kemudian.

afterwards sesudah itu, setelah itu, kemudian, kelak.

again pula, lagi, semula.

against lawan, melawan; (racing) bertentang dongan.

agape ternganga.

agate batu akek.

age baya, umur, usia; zaman; of — dewasa, sempurna umur; under — bawah umur; to — menjadi tua.

aged berumur, berusia, tua.

ageless sentiasa muda, tak tahu tua.

agency perwakilan.

agenda acara, tertib, ajenda.

agent wakil, perantaraan, anasir.

agglomerate kumpulan, kelompok; to — mengumpul sampai menjadi satu kelompok.

aggrandisement pembesaran.

aggravate, to — mempersukar, memburuk.

aggravation pemburukan.

aggregate kumpulan; to — menjumlahkan.

aggression serangan, penyerbuan, pencerobohan.

aggressive bersifat menyerang.

aggrieved sakit hati, kecil hati.

aghast terperanjat, ngeri.

agile tangkas, pantas.

agility ketangkasan, kepantasan.

agitate, to — merisaukan, menghasut, kacau.

agitated terharu, bingung.

agitation haru. kerusuhan, kebingungan.

agitator pengacau, pengharu, penghasut.

aglow bernyala.

agnostic murtad, ingkar.

ago yang lalu; **two days** — selang dua hari.

agog bersemangat, gembira.

agony sengsara, kesakitan.

agrarian yang berkenaan dengan pertanian.

agree menyetujui, mengiakan.

agreeable baik, sedap, nikmat, sesuai dengan.

agreement persetujuan, kerelaan, perjanjian, muafakat; **to make an** — berjanji.

agricultural yang berkenaan dengan pertanian; — **produce** hasil pertanian.

agriculture pertanian, tanaman.

aground terkandas.

ague demam nyamuk.

ah wah.

ahead di hadapan; lebih dahulu; **to go** — meneruskan sesuatu.

ahem deham, dehem.

ahoy seruan yang biasa dipakai dalam dunia perkapalan takkala memanggil kapal lain.

aid bantuan, pertolongan; **first** — pertolongan cemas.

aide-de-camp pengiring yang membantu penglima.

ail, to — mengidap.

ailment penyakit.

aim tujuan, maksud, niat; **to** — membidik; mengarahkan; memaksudkan.

aimless tidak tentu arah.

air hawa, angin, udara; lagu; **castles in the** — perawangan cita-cita; **open** — di luar rumah; (*radio*) **on the** —

sedang siaran; **to** — memperanginkan; **to** — **one's views** mengemukakan pendapat.

air base pengkalan udara.

airborne di(angkut) melalui udara; — **troops** tentera payung terjun.

air-conditioned berhawa dingin.

aircraft kapalterbang.

aircraft carrier kapal induk.

aircrew anak kapalterbang.

airfield lapanganterbang, padang kapalterbang.

air force angkatan udara.

airgun senapang angin.

air hostess pelayan perempuan dalam kapalterbang; peramugari.

airless pengap.

airlift pengangkutan udara.

airline perusahaan penerbangan.

airmail pos udara.

airman tentera udara.

air marshal laksmana udara.

airport lapanganterbang.

air pressure tekanan udara.

air raid serangan udara.

airstrip lapanganterbang kecil.

airtight kedap udara.

airy berangin.

ajar tergenggang, terbuka; **to leave** — membunakan.

akimbo, with arms — bercekak pinggang.

akin bersanak, saudara.

alabaster batu pualam yang putih warnanya.

alacrity kegiatan.

alarm perasaan cemas, kekejutan, kecemasan; **to** — menakutkan, mengejutkan, mencemaskan.

alarm clock jam loceng.

alarmed bimbang, gempar, terperanjat.

alarming menggemparkan, membimbangkan.

alarmist penakut, seorang yang selalu mengecutkan orang.

alas adohai.

albatross burung camar.

albeit biarpun, sungguhpun, walaupun, meskipun.

albino balar.

Albion negeri Inggeris.

album albem, buku penyimpan gambar, dll.

albumen zattelor; albumin.

alchemist alkemis.

alchemy ilmu kimia dahulukala.

alcohol alkohol, arak.

alcoholic yang berkenaan dengan atau mengandung alkohol; arak; **an —** seorang yang ketagihan minuman keras, kaki botol.

alcove lekuk di tembok jadi bilik dipakai untuk duduk atau tidur.

alder sejenis pohon.

alderman pembantu datuk bandar.

ale minuman bir.

alert giat, pantas, berjaga.

alfalfa sejenis rumput makanan lembu.

alfresco di luar rumah.

algebra ilmu aljibra.

alias nama samaran.

alibi berdalih, bahawa seorang yang dituduh berada di tempat lain pada waktu kejahatan terjadi.

alien asing, dagang; **an —** orang asing.

alienate memindahkan hak.

alienation pemindahan hak.

alight (of fire) bernyala; **to —** turun.

align menjajarkan.

alike sama, serupa.

alimentary yang berkenaan dengan pencernaan.

alimony nafkah zahir.

alive hidup, berjiwa; **look —!** bersemangat.

alkali alkali.

all segala, semua, sekalian, segenap; seluruh, samasekali; **— of them** semuanya.

allay meredakan.

allegation pernyataan, percakapan; tuduhan.

allege menyatakan, mengatakan, menuduh.

allegiance ketaatan.

allegoric dengan kiasan.

allegory cerita ibarat, kiasan.

alleviate meringankan, meredakan.

alley lorong, jalan kecil.

alliance persekutuan, perikatan.

allied bersekutu.

alligator buaya.

allocate memperuntukkan.

allot memperuntukkan, membahagikan.

allotment bahagian, pembahagian, peruntukan.

allow membiarkan, memberi; memperkenankan, mengizinkan.

allowance izin; nafkah, elaun, wang belanja; **to make — for** menyesuaikan.

alloy logam campur; suasa; **to —** mencampurkan dengan logam yang kurang baik kadarnya.

all right baik, dalam keadaan baik.

all-round baik dalam segala hal.

allude, to — (to) membayangkan.

allure amat menarik hati.

allusion sindiran, kias.

alluvium kukup, lanar, pembawaan pasir, lumpur.

ally sekutu; **to —** bersekutu.

almanac almanak, takwim.

almighty mahakuasa.

almond buah badam.

almoner pegawai masyarakat di rumahsakit.

almost hampir.

alms sedekah, derma, baksis.

aloft di atas, ke atas.

alone sendiri, seorang diri, sebatang kara; **to leave —** membiarkan.

along sepanjang; dan, bersama; **to go, come —** ikut serta.

alongside kepil, di sisi; lying **—** terkepil, berganding; **to come —** mengepil; **to bring —** mengepilkan.

aloof jauh, sombong, takabbur, hidung tinggi.

aloud dengan suara kuat, dengan nyaring.

alp alp, puncak gunung; **the A—s** gunung-ganang di antara negeri Perancis dengan Itali.

alpha huruf pertama dalam abjad Yunani.

alphabet abjad, huruf.

alphabetically menurut abjad; **to arrange —** mengabjadkan.

already telah; sudah, pernah.

also pun, juga, pula, lain daripada itu.

altar tempat pemujaan.

alter, to — berubah, berganti, bertukar; mengubahkan, menukar.

alteration perubahan, pengubahan, penukaran.

altercation pertengkaran.

alternate selang-selang; **to — menyelang, bergilir-gilir.**

alternating berganti-ganti, bergilir-gilir.

alternative pilihan antara dua.

although walaupun, meskipun.

altimeter pengukur tinggi.

altitude tinggi, ketinggian.

alto suara rendah.

altogether semua sekali, belaka.

altruism kelakuan yang mementingkan hal orang lain.

alum tawas.

aluminium aluminium.

always selamanya, selalu, sentiasa.

amalgamate bersatu, berkongsi; **to — menyatukan,** memadukan.

amalgamation perpaduan, persatuan.

amass, to — mengumpulkan, menghimpunkan.

amateur penggemar, pelaku yang tak menerima pembayaran untuk perlakuannya.

amaze, to — menghairankan, mengajaibkan, menakjubkan.

amazed hairan, ajaib, takjub.

amazement hairan.

amazing menghairankan.

ambassador duta, wakil.

ambassadress duta perempuan; *(wife of ambassador)* isteri duta.

amber ambar.

ambiguity yang bererti dua.

ambiguous tidak tentu, tidak tentu ertinya.

ambition cita-cita.

ambitious bercita-cita, mencari nama.

ambivalent mempunyai dua sifat yang bertentangan.

amble jalan perlahan.

ambrosia makanan dewadewi.

ambulance ambulan.

ambulant yang berganti tempatnya.

ambush pengadangan; **to — mengadang; serang hendap.**

ameliorate, to — menjadi baik; memperbaiki, membetulkan.

amen amin.

amenable penurut, taat.

amend, to — membetulkan, pinda; **to make —s** mengganti rugi, membalaskan.

amenity keadaan yang menyenangkan, kenikmatan, kemudahan.

America negeri Amerika.

American orang Amerika.

amethyst batu kecubung.

amiability kelakuan manis, kelakuan lemah-lembut, ramah-tamah

amiable lemah-lembut, manis, ramah-tamah.

amicable ramah-tamah, secara sahabat.

amid, amidst di tengah, di antara.

amiss (*wrong*) salah; (*off the mark*) tidak kena.

amity persahabatan.

ammonia amonia.

ammunition ubat bedil, peluru.

amnesia hilang ingatan.

amnesty pengampunan.

amoeba kuman, ameba.

amok = **amuck**.

among, amongst di antara, di tengah.

amoral sumbang.

amorous cinta, berahi.

amorphous tidak berbentuk; sebam.

amortize menghapuskan.

amount jumlah, banyaknya; to the — of . . . jumlahnya . . . .

amp, ampere amper.

amphibian binatang yang hidup baik di darat ataupun di air, dualam; amfibia.

amphibious yang baik di darat ataupun di air.

amphitheatre gelanggang bundar dengan tempat duduknya bertingkat-tingkat di sekelilingnya.

ample luas, longgar.

amplify to — mengeraskan, membesarkan, meluaskan.

amputate, to — mengudung, memotong.

amuck, to run — mengamuk.

amulet azimat, tangkal.

amuse, to — menggembirakan, menyukakan hati.

amused gembira, suka hati.

amusement kesukaan, kegembiraan.

anachronism yang tidak sesuai dengan zamannya, salah masa.

anaemia anemia, kurang darah, pucat.

anaemic kekurangan darah, pucat lesi.

anaesthesia pembiusan.

anaesthetic ubat bius.

anaesthetize, to — membiusi.

anagram kalimat yang susunan hurufnya terbalik.

anal yang berkenaan dengan dubur.

analogous sesuai, sama.

analogy persamaan, kias, ibarat, tamsil.

analyse, (*US*) **analyze,** to — menghuraikan, mengupas, cerakin, menganalisa.

analysis penghuraian, pengupasan, cerakinan, analisa.

analyst penghurai.

analytic(al) yang berkenaan dengan penghuraian, kaedah cerakinan.

anarchist perusuh.

anarchy haru biru, huru-hara, kerusuhan.

anathema dikutuk (Allah).

anatomical yang berkenaan dengan badan anatomi.

anatomy ilmu anggota tubuh, anatomi kajibinatubuh.

ancestor nenek moyang.

ancestral yang berkenaan dengan nenek moyang.

ancestry nenek moyang; asal usul.

anchor sauh, jangkar; to cast (drop) — melabuhkan sauh; to —, at — berlabuh.

anchorage pangkalan, pelabuhan.

anchovy ikan kecil, budu.

ancient purba, dahulukala.

ancillary rendahan, bawahan; (*auxiliary*) pembantu.

and dan, dengan, lagi.

anecdote cerita pendek.

anew sekali lagi.

angel malaikat, bidadari.

angelic seperti bidadari.

angelus, doa (ugama Katolik).

anger kemarahan, panas hati, murka; to — memarahan.

angle I (*geometric etc*) segi, siku, sudut, liku.

angle II, (*fish*) to—memancing.

angler pengail, pemancing ikan.

Anglican yang berkenaan dengan gereja Inggeris.

Anglicize, to — memelok ugama keristian gereja Inggeris.

Anglo— Inggeris.

angry marah, panas hati, murka; to be — with marah akan, gusar akan; to get, become — naik marah.

anguish dukacita yang amat sangat.

angular berpenjuru, bersiku.

aniline celupan; zat warna.

animal binatang, haiwan.

animate I hidup, bernyawa.

animate II, to — menghidup-kan, menggembirakan.

animated giat, gembira.

animosity kebencian, per-seteruan.

aniseed adas, jintan manis.

ankle pergelangan kaki.

annals buku (riwayat) sejarah.

annexation (*of land, country*) perampasan.

annexe sambilan, lampiran; to — merampas, memiliki.

annihilate menghapuskan, membinasakan, memusnahkan.

annihilation pembinasaan, penghapusan.

anniversary hari peringatan, hari ulang tahun.

Anno Domini, *abbr* **A.D.** tahun Masihi.

annotate, to — mentaf-sirkan, memberi keterangan.

announce, to — mengumum-kan, memberitahu.

announcement pemberi-tahuan, pengumuman, mak-lumat.

announcer (*radio*) pemberita, penyiar, juruhebah.

annoy, to — mengganggu, menyusahkan, mengusik.

annoyance gangguan.

annoying susah, menyakit-kan hati.

annual tahunan, tiap-tiap tahun.

annuity wang tahunan, cagak hidup yang diberi bertahun-tahun.

annul, to — membatalkan, menghapuskan.

annular seperti cincin.

Annunciation pengumuman (*teristimewa pengumuman akan lahirnya Nabi Isa*).

anoint, to — pembersihan dengan minyak.

anomalous ganjil, lain dari-pada biasa.

anomaly keadaan ganjil.

anon kelak.

anonymity hal tak memberi nama.

anonymous dengan tidak memberikan nama; — letter surat terbang.

another satu lagi, sebuah lagi.

answer jawab, balasan, sahutan; to — menjawab, menyahut, membalas; to — the door pergi melihat ada siapakah di luar pintu.

ant semut; white — anai-anai; large red — kerengga; —eater tenggiling; —hill busut.

antagonism perlawanan.

antagonist lawan.

antagonize melawan.

Antarctic Antartika; **A—** Pole kutub selatan.

ante— awalan kata yang er-tinya, sebelum.

antecedent yang terjadi lebih dahulu.

antedate, to — memberi tarikh yang lebih dahulu dari tarikh yang betul.

antediluvian yang berkenaan dengan zaman dahulu; berzaman.

antelope sejenis rusa.

ante meridiem, *abbr* **a.m.** pagi hari, sebelum tengahari.

antenatal sebelum lahir.

antenna sungut.

anterior di hadapan; lebih dahulu.

anteroom bilik di hadapan ruang lain.

anthem nyanyian kehormatan; **national** — lagu kebangsaan.

anthology bunga rampai, kumpulan sajak.

anthracite sejenis batu bara.

anthrax sejenis penyakit ternak.

anthropoid seperti manusia.

anthropology ilmu pengetahuan manusia; **physical** — ilmu bangsa; **social** — ilmu kebudayaan.

anthropomorphous berbentuk manusia.

anti— anti, lawan, tentang.

anti—aircraft meriam penangkis kapalterbang.

antibiotic ubat yang memusnah zat hidup istimewa kuman penyakit.

anticipate, to — mendahului; menjangka bernantinanti.

anticipation pendahuluan, jangkaan; **thanking you in** — terima kaseh terlebeh dahulu.

anticlimax kekecewaan.

antic(s) loncatan, kelakuan jenaka.

antidote nurbisa, penawar.

antipathy kebencian.

antipodes daerah-daerah yang terletak di sebelah setentang sebalik bumi.

antiquarian berkenaan dengan zaman purbakala.

antiquated kolot, kunu.

antique barang dari zaman purbakala.

antiquity zaman purba, purbakala.

anti—semite benci akan orang Yahudi.

antiseptic pembunuh kuman penyakit; **ubat** pembunuh kuman penyakit.

antisocial bertentangan dengan rukun masyarakat.

antithesis antitisis, pertentangan.

antler tanduk rusa.

antonym kata berlawan, kata pertentangan.

anus dubur, jubur.

anvil besi landasan.

anxiety kecemasan.

anxious bimbang, khuatir, rawan; **to be** — **about** membimbangkan.

any apa-apa juga, barang apa, sebarang; **at** — **rate** bagaimanapun juga.

anybody barang siapa, siapa pun juga.

anyhow biarpun demikian, juga.

anyone barang siapa, siapa pun jua.

anything barang apa, apa-apa jua, apa-apa sahaja.

anyway biarpun demikian.

anywhere barang di mana.

apart terpisah, selain; **to set** — memisahkan, asingkan.

apartment bilik.

apathetic rengsa, berasa lesu.

apathy mati rasa.

ape monyet yang tak berekor; berokera; **to** — meniru.

aperture lubang, liang.

apex puncak, kemuncak.

aphorism pepatah, pematah.

aphrodisiac ubat tenaga

kuat, ubat penambah syahwat.

apiary tempat pemeliharaan lebah.

apiece sebuah, sepotong, masing-masing.

apocalypse wahyu, firman.

apocryphal tidak tentu, tak dapat dipercayai.

apologetic dengan minta maaf.

apologize, to — minta ampun, minta maaf.

apology permintaan maaf.

apoplectic seperti sakit pitam.

apoplexy pitam, gila babi.

apostle rasul, pesuruh.

apostolic yang berkenaan dengan rasul.

apostrophe tanda: ' ; bunyinya seperti 'k', pertolehan.

apothecary tukang ubat.

apotheosis penjelmaan.

appal, to — mengerikan, mendahsyatkan; —ling yang mengerikan.

apparatus perkakas, alat, radas.

apparel pakaian.

apparent nyata, terang; —ly rupanya, pada zahirnya.

apparition hantu.

appeal permohonan; timbang semula, apel; to — memohon, menarik perhatian; to — to a higher court mengapel kepada mahkamah tinggi.

appear, to — (become visible) tampak; (to come out from) terbit, keluar, timbul.

appearance roman, rupa; to all —s rupanya.

appease, to — mendamaikan.

appellation pemberian nama.

append, to — menambahkan.

appendage sambungan, tambahan.

appendicitis sakit tali perut umbai usus.

appendix sambungan, tambahan, hujungan.

appertain, to — berhubungan dengan, berkenaan dengan.

appetite nafsu makan, selera; to have a good — berselera.

appetize, to — menghidupkan selera.

applaud, to — bertepuk tangan menunjukkan kegerangan dan pujian; memuji.

applause tepukan tangan sebagai tanda pujian.

apple buah epal.

apple pie sejenis kuih daripada epal; in — order teratur.

appliance alat, perkakas.

applicable yang dapat dipakaikan; mengenai.

applicant peminta, pemohon.

application pemakaian, pengenaan; permohonan.

apply, to — (employ) memakai, mempergunakan; (be relevant) mengenai, berkenaan dengan; to — for meminta, memohon.

appoint, to — menentukan; menjadikan, mengangkat menjadi; (to an office) melantik.

appointment penetapan; mengangkat, perlantikan.

apportion, to — membahagi, menguntukkan.

appraisal penghargaan, nilaian, taksiran.

appraise, to — menghargakan, menilaikan, mentaksirkan.

appreciable ternilai.

appreciate, to — menghargai, menilai.

appreciation penghargaan.

apprehend, to — menahan, mengerti, memahamkan.

apprehension pengertian; ketakutan, kecemasan.

apprehensive takut, cemas, perhatian.

apprentice pelatih, aprentis.

approach datang, hampir;

cara; to — mendekati, menghampiri.

approbation perkenankan, izin.

appropriate patut, layak, berpadanan dengan; as is — dengan kadarnya; to — memiliki.

approval kebenaran, pengesahan, kelulusan.

approve, to — memperkenankan, mengesahkan; meluluskan; to — of berkenan.

approximate lebih kurang, kira-kira; to — menghampiri.

apricot buah aprikot.

April bulan April.

apron sejenis pakaian alas luar yang gunanya supaya pakaian lain tidak menjadi kotor.

apropos, — of berkenaan dengan.

apt patut, layak; suka.

aptitude kecerdikan, bakat.

aquamarine sejenis batu yang biru atau hijau; (colour) warna biru-hijau.

aquarium kolam kaca ikan, akuarium.

aquatic yang berkenaan dengan air atau hidup dalam air.

aqueduct jalan air, saluran air akuadak.

aquiline, an — nose mancung hidung.

Arab orang Arab.

Arabian Arab.

Arabic Arab; bahasa Arab.

arable yang dapat dicucuk tanam; — land huma, tanah pertanian.

arbiter pemisah, pelerai.

arbitrary sebarang, dengan sesenang-senangnya.

arbitrate, to — mendamaikan, memutuskan dengan jalan perantaraan.

arbitration usaha perantaraan.

arbitrator juru damai.

arbor (tech) kaki mesin.

arbour tempat berteduh.

arc lengkung, lengkuk.

arch I (shape) relung; pintu gerbang; to — merelung.

arch II terutama.

archaeologic(al) purbakala.

archaeology ilmu pengetahuan zaman purbakala.

archaic dahulukala, purbakala.

archangel malaikat.

arch-enemy musuh ketat.

archer pemanah.

archetype bentuk asli.

archipelago kepulauan, gugusan pulau-pulau.

architect ahli senibena, akitek.

architecture ilmu senibena.

archives arkip.

archivist pemegang arkip, pegawai yang menguruskan arkip.

archway jalan beratap; pintu gerbang.

arclamp arclight, lampu melengkung, api pemotong.

Arctic Arktik.

ardent bersemangat, bernyala-nyala, gembira.

ardour semangat, kegembiraan.

arduous sukar, payah, susah.

are ialah, adalah.

area kawasan, daerah; luas.

areca nut pinang.

arena gelanggang, medan.

argosy bahtera, pelayaran yang merbahaya.

argue, to — berhujah; bersoaljawab.

argument hujah; perbahasan.

argumentation perbahasan.

aria nyanyian, lagu.

arid kering, kersang.

arise, to — bangun, bangkit, muncul, terbit, timbul.

aristocracy bangsawan, golongan (kaum).

aristocrat orang berbangsa.
aristocratic berbangsa,
bangsawan.
arithmetic ilmu hitung, ilmu
kira-kira.
arithmetical yang berkenaan dengan ilmu kira-kira.
ark, Noah's A— bahtera
Nabi Noh.
arm I (*limb*) lengan; — in —
bergandjing.
arms II (*weapon*) senjata; coat
of —s lambang; to — memberi
alat senjata.
armada armada, angkatan
kapal.
armament persenjataan.
armature baju zirah; (*elec-
trical*) suatu alat dalam
dinamo.
armed bersenjata.
armful serangkum, sepemeluk.
armistice perletakan senjata.
armlet ikat lengan.
armour baja, baju zirah;
— -plated berlapis baja; to —
melapiskan baja; — ed car
kereta perisai.
armourer pembuat alat senjata.
armoury tempat senjata.
armpit ketiak, kelek.
army angkatan tentera
aroma harum.
aromatic harum, wangi.
arose *pt of* arise.
around sekeliling.
arouse, to —membangunkan,
menghidupkan.
arrange, to — mengadakan,
menguruskan, menyusun,
mengatur.
arrangement penyelenggaraan, susunan; peraturan.
arrant betul-betul, samasekali.
array aturan, rangkaian; perhiasan; battle — ikatan
perang; to — mengaturkan.
arrear(s) tunggakan; in —s
menunggak, kebelakangan.

arrest pertahanan penangkapan; under — ditahan,
ditangkap; to — menahan,
menangkap.
arrival kedatangan, ketibaan.
arrive, to — datang, tiba,
sampai.
arrogance kesombongan,
congkak.
arrogant sombong, bongkak.
arrow anak panah.
arrowhead hujung panah.
arrowroot ararut, ubi belanda.
arsenal tempat penyimpanan
alat senjata pemerintah.
arsenic warangan.
arson perbuatan membakar
dengan sengaja.
art kepandaian, kesenian,
senilukis.
artefact buatan tangan manusia.
arterial berkenaan dengan
pembuluh nadi, urat darah.
artery salonadi, urat darah.
artesian — well telaga bor.
artful cerdik, panjang akal,
pintar.
arthritis sengal, penyakit
sendi.
article artikel; (*chapter*) bab;
(*paragraph*) fasal; (*sentence*)
ayat; (*composition*) rencana,
karangan; (*goods*) barang dagangan; benda; lajang — tajuk
rencana; manufactured —
barang sudah siap.
articulate (*jointed*) bersendi;
(*of speech*) dilafazkan baik
dengan.
articulation artikulasi, persendian; lafaz baik.
artifice rekaan, tipu daya.
artificer tukang, orang utas.
artificial buatan, palsu.
artisan tukang.
artist ahli seni pelukis.
artistic berbakat seni.
artless sederhana, bersahaja.
arty pura-pura berkesenian.

Aryan yang berkenaan dengan bahasa Indo-Eropah.

as seperti, sebagai, selaku, sebab, kerana; — follows sebagai berikut; — if seakan-akan, seolah-olah.

asbestos asbes; — plate papan asbes.

ascend, to — naik; (mountains) mendaki; (trees etc) memanjat.

ascendancy kekuasaan.

ascension (of Muhammad) mikraj.

ascent jalan naik, mendaki.

ascertain, to — dapat tahu; (make inquiries) siasat.

ascetic pertapa, yogi.

asceticism yogi, pertapaan.

ascribe, to — menganggap disebabkan oleh.

aseptic pembersihan hama.

ash I (tree) pohon ash.

ash II abu, debu.

ashamed malu, segan.

ashen seperti abu, kelabu, pucat.

ashes abu daripada pembakaran mayat.

ashore di darat, ke darat; to go — mendarat.

ashtray tempat abu rokok.

ashy penuh abu, berabu; pucat.

Asiatic berkenaan dengan benua Asia; orang Asia.

aside asing; di sebelah, ke sebelah; to put — mengasingkan.

ask, to — (for sth) meminta; (inquire) bertanya.

askance miring; to look — at memandang tidak percaya.

askew miring.

asleep tidur, terlena; to fall — tertidur.

asp sejenis ubun.

aspect aspek, rupa, segi.

asperity kekasaran.

aspersion fitnah; to cast — s memfitnahkan, mencelakan.

asphalt minyak aspal; to — membubuh minyak aspal.

asphyxia bebaug. lemas.

aspic daging dan sebagainya dalam agar-agar.

aspidistra tanaman dalam pasu.

aspirate bunyi huruf 'h'; to — menarik nafas.

aspiration pernafasan; cita-cita.

aspire, to — mengharapkan; mencita-cita.

aspirin ubat aspirin.

ass kaldai.

assail, to — menyerang.

assassin pembunuh.

assassinate, to — membunuh.

assassination pembunuhan.

assault serangan; to — menyerang, merampas.

assay pengujian; to — (gold) menguji (emas).

assemblage pengumpulan; perkumpulan.

assemble, to — berkumpul, menghimpunkan.

assembler pemasang.

assembly (council) sidang; (assemblage) majlis, perkumpulan, perhimpunan, jamaah.

assent kerelaan, izin; to — mengabulkan, memperkenankan.

assert, to — menuntut, mendesak.

assertion pernyataan.

assess, to — menilaikan, menaksirkan.

assessment penilaian, taksiran.

assessor penilai; (legal) pengapit hakim.

asset kepunyaan, harta, keuntungan, sifat baik; —s plutang.

assiduous rajin, bertekun.

assign, to — memperuntukkan, membahagi; menugaskan.

assignation penyerahan, pembahagian.

assignment pembahagian, penyerahan; tugas, pekerjaan yang diserahkan.

assimilate, to — (of food) mencernakan.

assimilation permesraan; pencernaian.

assist, to — menolong, membantu.

assistance bantuan, pertolongan; mutual — bertolong-tolongan, tolong-menolong.

assistant pembantu, penolong.

associate kawan, tolan, handai, rakan; to — menghubungkan, mempertalikan; to — (with) berkongsi dengan, bersekutu dengan.

associated bersekutu, serangkai.

association perhubungan, pergaulan; perkongsian, persatuan.

assortment pilihan, rangkaian.

assuage, to — meredakan, memuaskan.

assume, to — (suppose) mengirakan, menyangkakan; (office) memegang.

assuming (presumptuous) sombong; pura-pura.

assumption (supposition) sangkaan, andainya.

assurance perjanjian, jaminan.

assure, to — menjamin, meyakinkan.

assuredly tentu, bahawasenya.

aster sejenis bunga.

asterisk tanda bintang (*).

astern pada buritan kapal.

asthma penyakit bengek, lelah, semput.

asthmatic bengek, lelah, semput.

astonish, to — menghairankan, mentakjubkan.

astonished hairan, takjub.

astonishment kehairanan.

astound, to — mendahsyatkan.

astral berkenaan dengan bintang.

astray tersesat.

astride tercelapak, terkangkang.

astringent kelat.

astrologer ahli nujum.

astrology ilmu nujum.

astronomer ahli ilmu falak.

astronomic(al) berkenaan dengan bintang.

astronomy ilmu falak, ilmu bintang.

astute cerdik, bijak.

asunder terbelah, pecah ringkah.

asylum (shelter) tempat perlindungan; (hospital for the insane) rumah gila.

asymmetric(al) (yang) tak sebanding taksemukur.

asymmetry keadaan tidak sebanding, keadaan taksemukur.

at di, pada; kepada, akan; — home di rumah; — midday pada tengahari; he arrives — the airport ia sampai ke lapangan terbang; not — all sekali-kali tidak.

ate pt of **eat.**

atheism ilmu kufur, tiada percayayan tuhan.

atheist kufur, orang yang ingkar akan ugamanya.

athlete ahli sukan.

athletic kuat badan; yang berkenaan dengan segala gerak badan; — sports sukan; — s gerak badan.

at-home sambutan, ramah-tamah.

Atlantic Atlantik; the — Lautan Atlantik.

atlas buku peta, atlas.

atmosphere angkasa; hawa, udara; suasana.

atoll pulau karang. pulau cincin.

atom atom.

atomic yang berkenaan dengan atom; — bomb bom atom.

atomizer alat pemercik.

atonal tidak sesuai dengan laras muzik.

atone, to — membalas, mengganti rugi.

atrocious amat jahat, busuk.

atrocity kejahatan, perbuatan buruk.

atrophy lisut.

attach, to — menghubungkan; membubuhi; menarik hati; to — menyangkutkan kepada, mengepil.

attaché pembantu duta; — case tas buku.

attached berlekat, kepil, terlekap; tertarik kepada; to be — to bersangkut paut dengan.

attachment (liking for) kesukaan.

attack serangan, serbuan; to — menyerang.

attain, to — mencapai.

attainable tercapai.

attainment(s) kepandaian, pencapaian.

attempt percubaan; to — mencuba.

attend, to — menghadiri, merawat(i).

attendance kehadiran; — list jadual kedatangan.

attendant pelayan.

attention perhatian, hatihati, jaga; to draw the — menarik perhatian; to pay — to memperhatikan.

attentive beringat-ingat, berperhatian.

attenuate tipis, halus; to — meringankan.

attest, to — menyatakan dengan sumpah, naik saksi.

attestation penyaksian, kenyataan dengan mengangkat sumpah.

attic loting, para-para.

attire pakaian, dandanan.

attired berdandan, berpakaian.

attitude sikap, perangai, lagak.

attorney wakil mutlak; power of — kuasa mutlak.

attract, to — menarik.

attraction daya penarik.

attractive molek, menarik hati.

attribute sifat; to — menentukan asalnya.

attributive pertalian.

attrition pergesekan.

atypical tidak sesuai dengan model biasa.

auburn perang.

auction lelong; by — dilelong; to —, sell by — melelongkan.

auctioneer jurulelong.

audacious berani, gagah.

audacity keberanian.

audible terdengar, kedengaran.

audience para penuntut; — hall balai mengadap.

audit odit, pemeriksaan bukubuku; to — memeriksa bukubuku.

audition perdengaran; (theat etc) ujian menentukan kebolehan dan bakat penyanyi.

auditive yang berkenaan dengan pendengaran.

auditor pendengar.

auditory berkenaan dengan pendengaran.

auger penggerek, gurdi.

aught apa sahaja, barang apa.

augment, to — menambahkan, memperbesarkan.

augmentation penambahan, perkembangan.

augur tukang ramal; to — meramalkan.

augury ramalan.

August (*month*) bulan Ogos.
august luhur, mulia.
auk burung laut.
aunt emak saudara.
aura keadaan yang semerbak dari salah satu orang atau benda.
aural yang berkenaan dengan telinga (atau pendengaran), dengar-tutur.
aurora (*dawn*) fajar; (*polar*) cahaya kutub utara atau selatan.
auspice, under the —s of di bawah lindungan, di bawah ihsan.
auspicious bertuah.
austere keras hati, hebat.
austerity jimat-cermat, keadaan amat sederhana.
Australian orang Australia.
authentic sah; asli, tulin.
authenticity keaslian, ketulinan.
authoritative berkuasa.
author pengarang, penggubah.
authority kuasa, kekuasaan; (*an official*) pembesar; the authorities pemerintah, pihak berkuasa.
authorization pengesahan, surat kuasa.
authorize, to — memberi kuasa, mengesahkan, membenarkan.
authorized berhak, berkuasa.
autobiographer pengarang riwayat hidupnya sendiri.
autochthonous asli.
autocracy pemerintah mutlak, autokrasi.
autocrat seorang yang memerintah dengan mutlak.
autograph tandatangan; to — menandatangani.
automatic dengan sendirinya, otomatik.
automation jentera yang berjalan dengan sendirinya.
autonomous otonomi, mempunyai hak kuasa.

autonomy otonomi, hak kuasa.
autopsy periksa mayat.
autumn musim gugur.
auxiliary pembantu.
avail, to — berguna, mempergunakan; of no — tidak berguna, sia-sia.
availability hal tersedia.
available sedia, tersedia; to make — menyediakan.
avalanche (*of snow*) runtuhan salji.
avarice kikir, kedekut, bakhil.
avaricious kikir, kedekut, bakhil.
avenge balasan; to — membalas.
avenger pembalas dendam.
avenue jalanraya.
average biasa, sedang, rata; on the, an — purata, hitung panjang.
averse segan, enggan, tak rela.
aversion kesegananan, ketidakrelaan.
avert, to — (of face, eyes) memalingkan.
aviary tempat pemeliharaan burung.
aviation penerbangan.
aviator penerbang.
avid asyek, penuh keinginan.
avidity keinginan besar.
avocado buah apukado.
avoid, to — menjauhkan diri dari, menghindarkan; (a blow) mengelak.
avoidance penghindaran, pengelakan.
avoirdupois sistem menimbang menurut cara Inggeris (1 pound (453.6 gr) = 16 ounces).
avow, to — mengakui, mengikrarkan, bersumpah.
avowal pengakuan, sumpah.
avuncular yang berkenaan dengan bapa saudara.

await, to — menunggu, menanti.

awake jaga, bangun; **to** — berjaga; membangunkan.

awaken, to — berjaga, bangun; membangunkan, membangkitkan.

award (*of court*) keputusan hakim; (*fine*) denda; (*present*) hadiah; **to** — memutuskan, menghadiahkan.

aware (*know*), — **of** tahu, insaf akan, sedar akan.

awareness kesedaran.

awash terendam.

away (*distant*) jauh; (*be off*) pergi, enyah; (*go*) —! enyah dari sini!; **to chase** — mengejar; **to pass** — meninggal dunia.

awe perasaan dahsyat, gempar; gerun; —-**inspiring** dahsyat, hebat.

awesome dahsyat, hebat.

awful dahsyat, hebat.

awhile untuk sementara.

awkward janggal, kekok ganjil.

awl penggerek.

awning kajang, langit-langit.

awry tersilap; kusut, berliku-liku.

axe kapak.

axiom ketentuan.

axiomatic(al) berketentuan.

axis paksi, pasak.

axle gandar roda, pasak.

ay(e) ia.

azalea sejenis bunga.

azure biru.

B

baa bunyi kambing mengembik.

babble leteran; **to** — berleter, merepek.

babbler peleter; orang yang suka meleter.

babe anak kecil, kanak-kanak.

baboon monyet besar.

baby anak kecil, kanak-kanak, bayi.

bachelor bujang; **B**— **of Arts**, *abbr* **B.A.** sarjana muda.

bacillus kuman penyakit.

back (*of body*) belakang, punggung; (*return*) kembali, balik; **at the** — of di belakang, di balik; **to bring, give** memulangkan, mengembalikan; **behind one's** — di belakang; **to lie on one's** — terlentang.

backbite, to — memfitnahkan; mengumpat.

backbone tulang belakang.

backgammon sejenis permainan.

background dasar, latar belakang.

backhand(ed) dengan belakang tangan; tidak berketahuan.

backing sokongan, bantuan.

backlog pesanan yang ditangguhkan.

backside buntut, punggung.

backslide, to — mundur kembali ke suatu kehidupan tak berugama.

backward terkebelakang, ketinggalan; **to go** —s mundur.

backwash ombak surut.

backwater air mati.

bacon lemak babi.

bacterium bakteria, kuman.

bacteriology bakterialogi; ilmu kaji kuman.

bad (*inferior*) kurang baik; (*of animal matter*) busuk; (*of vegetable matter and inanimate articles*) buruk; (*evil*) jahat; (*unlucky*) malang; — **form** kurang patut, kurang sopan; **to go** — (*of food etc*) menjadi busuk.

badge tanda, lencana, pingat.

badger sejenis landak; **to** — mengganggu, mengusik.

badminton permainan badminton, bulutangkis.

badness keburukan, kejahatan.

baffle, to — menyusahkan, menggagalkan.

baffling mustahil.

bag pundi-pundi, beg, karung; **to let the cat out of the** — membuka rahsia.

baggage barang-barang; bag and — segala barang-barangnya.

baggy terlalu longgar.

bagpipes sejenis alat muzik bangsa Skot.

bah ceh.

bail jamin, penanggung; **to stand** — (for) menjadi jamin; **to** — melepaskan orang dengan terima jaminan.

bailiff juru mahkamah, bailip.

bait umpan, pikatan; **to** — memikat, mengumpan.

baize semacam kain tebal.

bake, to — menggoreng, membakar; **half —d** setengah masak.

bakelite bakelit.

baker pembakar roti, tukang roti.

bakery tempat membakar roti.

balance neraca, timbangan, imbangan.

balanced sebanding, seimbang.

balcony peranginan.

bald botak, gondol.

bale (*package*) bungkusan, karung; **to** — membungkus dalam karung.

baleful buruk, jahat.

balk, baulk (*of wood*) balak; **to** — meronta; merintangi.

ball (*for games*) bola; (*dance*) majlis tari-menari; — **of wool** puntalan, bulu.

ballad(e) sejenis syair, balad.

ballast tolak bara, tolak bahar.

ballbearings kacang-kacang, bering bebola.

ballerina penari perempuan (teristimewa dengan tari 'ballet').

ballet sejenis tari bersama.

ballistic yang berkenaan dengan gaya lempar, balistik.

balloon pelembungan, belon.

ballot pengundian (pemungutan) suara (yang rahsia); **to** — mengundi.

ballroom ruang tari-menari.

balm balsam.

balmy harum, menyedapkan.

balsam balsam.

balustrade birai, sokongan.

bamboo bambu, buluh.

bamboozle, to — memperdayakan.

ban pantang; **to** — menantangkan.

banal boyak.

banality keboyakan.

banana pisang.

band (*binding*) ikatan; tali; (*musical*) sekumpulan pancaragam; **to** — together mengikat; berkumpul.

bandage balutan, bebat.

bandit penyamun, penjahat, pengganas.

bandy, to — melempar, menyebar.

bandy-legged kakinya pengkar ke dalam.

bane (*poison*) racun; (*curse*) celaka.

bang dentum, degam; **to** — memukul; **to** — **the door** menutup pintu dengan kuat.

bangle gelang rantai.

banian, banyan, — **tree** pohon beringin.

banish, to — membuang dari negerinya.

banishment pembuangan.

banister(s) susuran tangga.

banjo banjo, sejenis alat muzik.

bank (*for money*) bank; (*of river*) tepi sungai; (*shoal*) beting; (*ridge*) permatang; cloud — awan-berarak; to — menyimpan wang di bank.

bank-book buku hutang piutang seseorang di bank.

banker bankir.

banknote wang kertas.

bankrupt putus wang, bangkerap; muflis; to — menjadikan bangkerap.

bankruptcy kepupusan, muflis.

banner tunggul, panji.

banns pengumuman perkahwinan di gereja.

banquet (*of royalty*) persantapan, perjamuan; to — memperjamukan.

bantam ayam katik.

banter kelakar, senda gurau; to — berkelakar.

banyan beringin.

baptism upacara baptis.

bar (*of wood etc*) batang; (*obstruct passage*) sekat; (*of river*) beting; to — (*impede*) merintangkan.

barb duri; onak; bulu; to — memberi duri; —ed wire kawat berduri.

barbarian orang biadab.

barbaric biadab, ganas.

barbarity keganasan; kebiadaban.

barbecue daging panggang; to — memanggang.

barber tukang cukur, tukang gunting.

bard penyanyi yang mengembara.

bare (*hairless, treeless*) gondol; (*naked*) telanjang; to lay — membukakan, menguraikan.

barefaced (*shameless*) muka papan.

barely hampir tidak, nyaris tidak.

bareness kegondolan.

bargain (*agreement*) persetujuan; (*haggle*) menawar; into the — sebagai imbuhan.

barge tongkang; to — into meradak kepada.

bargee pemimpin tongkang.

baritone bariton.

barium barium.

bark (*of trees*) kulit kayu; (*of dog*) to — menyalak.

barley sejenis jelai.

barman penjual minuman di bar.

barn (*rice granary*) rengkiang; (*shed*) gudang, bangsal.

barnacle teritip.

barometer barometer, alat pengukur tekanan udara.

baron gelar orang berbangsa.

baroness orang perempuan yang bergelar.

baronet gelar orang berbangsa.

barrack(s) asrama, rumah berek.

barracuda sejenis ikan besar.

barrage rintangan terhadap pasukan musuh.

barrel (*cask*) tong, pipa; (*gun*) laras, pucuk (*bedil*).

barren (*childless*) mandul; (*of soil*) kerusang.

barricade rintangan; to — membuat rintangan.

barrier rintangan, empang.

barring (*excepting*) kecuali.

barrister pengacara, peguam.

barrow gerabak dorong.

barter tukar-menukar, pertukaran; to — menukar.

basalt sejenis batu.

base (*foundation*, *support*) alas, dasar, kaki, pangkal perdu; (*infamous*) hina, keji, nusta; to — (on) mengalaskan mendasarkan.

baseball sejenis permainan bola.

basement alas sebuah bangunan, ruang di bawah tanah.

baseness kehinaan.

bash, to — memukul, menghentam.

bashful malu, kemalumaluan, tersipu-sipu.

basic dasar.

basil daun ruku-ruku; selasih.

basin pasu, bejana; besen; river — perut sungai, lembongan.

basis dasar, alas.

bask, to — berjemur.

basket bakul, keranjang; —ball bola keranjang; —work anyam-anyaman.

bass I (mus) suara rendah, bunyi rendah.

bass II (fish) sejenis ikan.

bassoon sejenis alat muzik.

bastard haram jadah; anak gampang, anak haram.

baste, to — (with fat) renjiskan minyak.

bastion baluarti, benteng.

bat (zool) kelawar.

batch sekelompok barang-barang yang serupa.

bath mandi; tempat mandi, permandian; to take a — mandi.

bathe, to — mandi di sungai (di laut) atau di tempat berenang.

bather seorang mandi.

bathing costume pakaian mandi.

bathroom bilik mandi.

batman pelayan pegawai.

baton tongkat waran.

battalion batalion, pasukan.

batten, to — menjadi gemuk; to — on makan dengan lahap; to — down (a hatch) tutup.

batter, to — memukul, menghentam; to — down (walls etc) merobohkan.

battery (electric) penghimpun letrik, beteri; (of guns) kesatuan pasukan meriam.

battle perang, peperangan; to — bertempur, berjuang.

battlefield medan peperangan.

battlement(s) bangunan baluarti.

battleship kapalperang.

bauble titik-bengkel.

baulk see **balk**.

bawdy (of talk) carut.

bawl, to — berteriak, berkata dengan suara kuat; to — out mengumpat.

bay teluk, rantau; (of dog) salak anjing besar; sick — ruang sakit.

bayonet sangkur, bayonet; to — menikam dengan mata sangkur.

bay window jendela lekuk.

bazaar bazar, pasar di negeri timur; pasar derma.

bazooka senapang penangkis tank.

be (also is, are, was, were, being, been) ada; there are no trees in the garden tidak ada pohon di kebun; he is a schoolteacher dia ialah (adalah) guru sekolah.

beach pantai, tepi laut, pesisir; to — mendaratkan.

beacon suar.

bead manik.

beadle pegawai gereja atau salah satu syarikat.

beak paruh, cotok.

beaker piala.

beam balak, bendul; (of light) sinar; to — bersinar, bercahaya.

beaming (smiling) tersenyum, dengan muka yang berseri-seri.

bean kacang; full of —s penuh kegiatan.

bear I (zool) beruang; (astr) the Great B— bintang biduk.

bear II, to — (carry) memikul; (endure, support) menahan, menderita; to — in mind mengingat.

bear III, to — (*produce children*) beranak, bersalin.

bearable tertahan; **un**— tak tertahan.

beard janggut.

bearer si pembawa; si pemukul.

bearing sikap, kelakuan; a proud — sikap angkuh.

beast binatang buas, haiwan.

beastliness kehewanan, keadaan amat buruk.

beastly seperti binatang; buruk.

beat, to — memukul, memalu.

beaten terpukul; (*defeated*) alah.

beating pemukulan; (*defeat*) pengalahan.

beatitude keadaan sangat berbahagia dan selamat.

beau seorang yang gila gadis.

beautiful indah, cantik, elok, permai, molik.

beautify, to — mengelokkan, mencantikkan.

beauty keindahan, keelokan, kecantikan.

beauty parlour tempat penyelenggaraan kecantikan.

beaver sejenis binatang yang pandai mengerat pohon.

becalmed kematian angin.

because sebab, oleh sebab, oleh kerana.

beck isyarat; to be at s.o.'s — and call di bawah perintah seseorang.

beckon, to — mengisyaratkan.

become, to — menjadi.

becoming (*to look well*) patut, layak; cantik, manis.

bed (*for sleeping*) tempat tidur, ranjang; dasar; (*flower*) — petak; river — alur sungai.

bedaubed bergelumang.

bedbug kepinding, pijat-pijat.

bedclothes alas tilam, cadar.

bedding alas; alas tilam, tilam dan bantal golek.

bedeck, to — menghiasi.

bedevil, to — mengerasi; memanterai.

bedlam rumah gila; huru-hara.

Bedouin orang Badui.

bedraggled kusut-masai.

bedridden terpaksa tinggal di tempat tidur kerana sakit.

bedroom bilik tidur.

bee lebah; **-line** garis lurus antara dua tempat.

beech sejenis pohon tinggi.

beef daging lembu.

beefy seperti daging lembu; (*strong*) kuat.

beehive sarang lebah.

beer minuman bir.

beet ubi gula.

beetle kumbang.

befall, to — terjadi.

befit, to — patut, pantas.

before (*in place*) di hadapan, di muka; (*in time*) lebih dahulu; sebelum.

beforehand lebih dahulu.

befriend, to — memperlakukan sebagai sahabat, menolong.

beg, to — (*ask for*) minta; memohon; (*alms*) minta sedekah.

beget, to — memperanakkan.

beggar peminta sedekah orang bangsat.

begin, to — mulai; bermula; to — with pertama-tama; memulai.

beginner orang yang baharu mulai, orang belum pandai.

beginning awal, pangkal, permulaan; (*source*) pokok.

begonia sejenis tumbuhan dengan bunga berwarna.

begrudge, to — iri hati akan, cemburu akan.

beguile, to — memikat.

behalf, on — of untuk kepentingan, bagi pihak.

behave, to — berkelakuan, melakukan diri; berkelakuan baik.

behaviour kelakuan, peri laku, perangai, tingkah laku.

behead, to — memancung leher, memenggal kepala.

behest perintah.

behind (of place) di belakang, di balik; (of time) lambat, lewat; to stay — tinggal, ditinggalkan.

behold, to — melihat, nampak.

beholden wajib.

beige warna duku.

being (a being) makhluk; wujud; zat; in — ada; hidup; the Supreme B— zat Allah.

belabour, to — menghentam, memukul.

belch sedawa, belahak; to — bersedawa.

beleaguer, to — mengepung.

belfry menara loceng.

Belgian Belgium.

belie, to — mendustakan.

belief (religious) iman, keimanan; (trust) percaya, kepercayaan.

believe, to — percaya, mempercaya(i), berpendapat.

belittle, to — memperkecil, mengecilkan.

bell loceng, genta; as clear as a — nyata terang.

bell buoy pelampung yang berbunyi.

belle perempuan yang cantik.

bellicose galak.

belligerence perang.

belligerent pihak yang berperang.

bellow, to — menguak, berdengung.

bellows (also pair of —) puputan.

belly perut; to — bergelembung.

belong, to — (to) kepunyaan . . .; masuk hitungan, masuk golongan.

belongings harta-benda, barang kepunyaan.

beloved kekasih, tercinta.

below di bawah; (downstream) di hilir; — one's breath hampir tak kedengaran.

belt ikat pinggang; lengkaran, lengkungan; kawasan; driving — tali keledar.

bemoan, to — meratapi.

bemuse, to — membingungkan.

bench bangku; (referring to court of law) mahkamah.

bend bentuk; lengkung, lengkar; to — membengkokkan.

beneath di bawah.

benediction doa selamat.

benefaction perbuatan baik; derma.

benefactor orang dermawan, orang yang memberi wang untuk sesuatu.

beneficence kedermawanan.

beneficent dermawan.

beneficial berguna, berfaedah.

beneficiary si penerima wang derma.

benefit guna, faedah, kebajikan; for the — of . . . untuk kepentingan.

benevolence kerelaan, kebajikan.

benevolent dermawan, murah hati.

Bengal negeri Benggala.

benign baik, lemah-lembut.

benignant baik hati, lemah-lembut.

bent bengkok, bengkung.

benumbed kebas kerana sejuk.

benzine minyak benzin cuci.

benzol bensol, benzin cuci.

bequeath, to — mewariskan, mewasiatkan.

bequest yang diwariskan.

bereave, to — mengambil dari; meninggalkan di dunia.

bereaved kematian, ditinggalkan oleh kematian seseorang.

beret kopiah.

berry buah kecil; biji.

berth (*for a ship*) tempat kapal di pelabuhan, pengkalan; (*bank*) tempat tidur di kapal; **to give a wide — to** mengelakkan.

beseech, to — memohon.

beset, to — (*inlaid*) bertatahkan; (*surround*) di kelilingi dengan, mengepung.

beside di sisi; dekat; di luar; **to put —** menyambilkan; **— the question** tidak mengenai dasar.

besides lain daripada itu, apalagi, dan lagi.

besiege, to — mengepung.

besmirch, to — mengotori; mengkaburkan.

besot, to — membingungkan.

best, the — yang terlebih baik; **to do one's — bersungguh-sungguh; to —** mengatasi.

bestial seperti binatang.

bestiality kehewanan.

bestir, to — menggiatkan.

best man pengapit mempelai laki-laki.

bestow, to — membubuh; **to — upon** memberi kurnia.

bestride, to — menunggangi.

bestseller buku yang banyak dijual.

bet taruh, pertaruhan; **to —** bertaruhkan.

betel (*vine*) sirih; **—nut** pinang.

betray, to — mencedera, berkhianat; menderhaka kepada, belot.

betrayal pengkhianatan, perbuatan derhaka.

betroth, to — mengikat dengan perjanjian akan kahwin; **—ed** pertunangan.

betrothal pertunangan.

better lebih baik; (*in health*) **to be (get) — sembuh; for —** for worse baik dalam untung mahupun dalam malang.

between antara; (*of informa-*

tion) **— you and me** ini hanya mengenai kita berdua sahaja.

betwixt antara; **— and between** setengah-setengah.

bevel lereng; (*instrument*) perkakas mengukur sudut.

beverage minuman.

bevy kumpulan, kawan.

bewail, to — meratapi.

beware berhati-hati, jaga, beringat.

bewilder, to — membingungkan.

bewildered bingung, tercengang.

bewilderment bingung tercengangnya.

bewitch, to — menghikmat; **—ing** sangat menarik hati.

beyond di luar, di seberang; **this is — me** ini tak dapat saya fahamkan.

bi- dua; **—monthly,** dua kali sebulan.

bias berat sebelah; kecondongan; **to —** mencondongkan.

bib barut gantung.

bible Kitab Injil.

biblical yang berkenaan dengan kitab Injil.

bibliography (*list*) daftar buku-buku yang dikumpulkan dengan salah satu maksud.

bicarbonate bikarbonat.

bicentenary ulang tahun yang ke 200.

biceps buah pangkallengan.

bicker, to — cerewet.

bicycle besikal; **to —** besikal, naik besikal.

bid (*offer*) penawaran; **to make a — for** mencuba akan memperoleh; **to — menawar;** (*order*) suruh.

bidding penawaran; (*order*) perintah.

bide, to — menunggu; to — one's time menunggu masa yang baik.

biennial sekali tiap-tiap dua tahun; dua tahun lamanya.

bier usungan mayat; *(of rajas)* jenazah.

biff pukulan.

bifocal berpusat dua, berfocus dua.

bifurcate bercagak, bercabang; to — mencabang.

big besar; *(fully grown)* dewasa; — business perniagaan besarbesaran; to talk — menyombong.

bigamist orang yang beristeri (bersuami) dua.

bigamy hal beristeri (berlaki) dua.

bigot seorang yang secara gilagila berpegang kepada sesuatu kepercayaan.

bigotry kegila-gilaan tentang sesuatu kepercayaan.

bigwig orang cabang atas.

bike *abbr of* bicycle besikal.

bilateral bersisi dua; bercabang dua.

bile hempedu.

bilge bahagian bawah ruang kapal; — water air ruang.

bilingual berbahasa dua.

bilious sakit hempedu.

bill I *(of bird)* paruh, patukan; to — and çoo bercumbucumbuan.

bill II *(legal)* rang undangundang; *(reckoning)* daftar; — of lading surat muatan.

billboard tempelan, pelekat.

billet *(quarters)* tempat penumpangan.

billiards sejenis permainan bola di atas meja.

billion biliun, sejuta kali sejuta.

billow ombak besar; to — mengombak, bergelombang.

billygoat kambing jantan.

bin tong; dust— tong sampah.

binary yang terdiri dari dua bahagian.

bind, to — mengikat; to — (books) menjilid.

binder pengikat; ikatan.

binding ikatan, jilid buku, pertambatan.

binge kesukaan minum.

binocular teropong.

biochemistry biokimia.

biography riwayat hidup.

biology ilmu kaji hayat.

bipartisan yang berkenaan dengan dua parti.

bipartite yang terdiri dari dua bahagian.

biped berkaki dua.

biplane kapalterbang yang bersayap dua.

birch sejenis pohon; *(rod)* seikat ranting-ranting pohon tersebut dipakai untuk memukul anak nakal dan sebagainya.

bird burung, unggas; —s of a feather orang yang serupa sifatnya.

birdcage sangkar burung.

bird fancier penggemar burung-burung; penjual burungburung.

birdlime pikatan burung, getah.

birdseed padi-padian yang dipakai sebagai makanan burung.

birth kelahiran, lahir; kejadian; to give — to bersalin, melahirkan.

birth control penjarang jumlah kelahiran.

birthday hari lahir, harijadi; hari peranakan.

birthmark tanda.

birth rate jumlah anak yang dilahirkan pada tiap-tiap ribuan penduduk.

birthright hak kelahiran, hak yang melekat kepada anak sulung.

biscuit biskut.

bisect, to — membelah dua, potong tengah.

bishop biskup.

bison sejenis banteng, seladang.

bit sepotong kecil, sedikit.

sebentar; — by — lambat laun, sedikit demi sedikit.

bitch anjing betina; (*pej: woman*) orang sundal.

bite sepotong, sesuap; (*some food*) makanan; to — menggigit.

biting (*of speech*) tajam; (*of food*) pedas.

bitter pahit; it was — cold sejuknya hampir tak terderita.

bitterness kepahitan, pahit.

bitumen aspal, minyak tar.

bivalve dengan sepasang kulit kerang.

bivouac berkhemah.

bizarre ganjil.

blab, to — membukakan rahsia.

black hitam; gelap; to — menghitamkan; to — out menggelapkan;(*faint*) pengsan.

blackberry sejenis buah yang warnanya biru tua.

blackbird sejenis burung.

blackboard papanhitam.

blacken, to — menghitamkan; (*with soot or charcoal*) memberi arang di muka.

blackguard orang jahat.

blackhead bintit.

blackleg zat hitam.

black list daftar nama orang jahat.

blackmail menggertak, mengugut.

black market pasar gelap.

black marketeer tukang pasar gelap.

blackout penggelapan; (*faint*) pengsan.

black sheep (*person*) muka dua, orang buruk.

blacksmith tukang besi.

bladder gelembung, (*urinary*) pundi-pundi kencing.

blade bilah, mata pisau.

blame aib, celaan, arang di muka; to — mencela.

blameless tidak bersalah.

blameworthy salah, tercela.

blanch, to — memutihkan; menjadi pucat.

bland ramah-tamah, sopan.

blandishment pembujukan.

blank kosong; (*in writing*) tidak bertulis; a — kosong.

blanket selimut; to — menyelimuti.

blare, to — berbunyi mersik.

blarney kata-kata manis, bujukan; cakap angin.

blaspheme, to — bersumpah, seraph.

blasphemous tidak patut, buruk.

blasphemy perkataan buruk.

blast (*of wind*) angin kencang; (*of explosion*) letusan; to — meletuskan.

blast-furnace peleburan.

blatant kurang sopan.

blaze (*flame*) nyala api; (*mark on tree*) takik pada pohonpohon; to — bernyala besar.

blazer sejenis baju luaran berwarna.

blazing bernyala; — hot panas terik.

bleach (*liquid*) obat pemutih; to — memutihkan.

bleak (*of weather*) sejuk; (*of the senses*) kurang nikmat.

bleat embik; to — mengembik.

bleed, to — berdarah.

blemish aib, cela, cacat; to — mengaibkan.

blench, to — mundur kerana takut.

blend campuran; to — mencampur.

bless, to — memberkati, menganugerahi.

blessed berbahagia, selamat.

blessing berkat, kurnia, anugerah.

blight penyakit tumbuhtumbuhan; to — menyakitkan.

blind I buta; — alley jalan buntu.

blind II (*for windows*) bidai, tirai gulung, tabir.

blindfold dengan mata ditutup; to — menutup mata.

blindly dengan butanya.

blindness buta.

blink kelip mata, kedip; to — terkedip-kedip.

blinker(s) *(horse)* tudung mata.

bliss bahagia.

blissful berbahagia.

blister lepoh, lecur; to — melepoh, melecur.

blithe riang, gembira.

blithering bodoh, tak bererti.

blitz serangan hebat (istimewa dengan kapalterbang); to — menyerang dengan hebat, merosakkan.

blizzard ribut salji.

bloated kembung, gembung.

bloater sejenis ikan asap.

blob gumpal; selekeh.

bloc persekutuan berbagai golongan dengan satu tujuan.

block keping; bongkah; kelompok; sekelompok rumah; to — merintangi.

blockade pembatasan, menghalang.

blockhead si bodoh, bebal.

blockhouse sejenis loji atau benteng kecil.

block letter huruf besar.

bloke orang, si anu.

blond(e) putih kuning; a — perempuan yang berambut kuning.

blood darah; *(lineage)* bangsa; blue — turunan bangsawan.

blood feud khasumat, kasemat.

blood heat suhu.

bloodhound anjing pemburu yang amat besar.

bloodless dengan tidak tumpah darah.

blood money diat.

bloodshed penumpahan darah.

bloodshot kemerah-merahan.

bloodthirsty ganas, buas.

blood transfusion pindah tuang darah.

blood vessel salur darah.

bloody berdarah.

bloom bunga; perkembangan; to — berbunga.

bloomer kesalahan, silap.

bloomers *(old)* seluar orang perempuan.

blooming berbunga; amat sangat.

blossom bunga; to — berbunga.

blot titik; *(blemish)* salah; to — out menghilangkan, membinasakan.

blotch bintik; coreng.

blotting paper kertas kembang, kertas sap.

blouse baju kebaya.

blow *(hit)* pukulan, paluan; *(of wind)* to — bertiup, berpuput, meniup.

blowlamp api lancip.

blowpipe buluh sumpitan.

blowy berangin.

blowzy merah muka.

blubber lemak ikan paus; *(weeping)* tangisan.

blue biru; true — setia; to feel or be — bersedih hati.

Bluebeard seorang yang membunuh beberapa orang isterinya.

blue book buku penyata pemerintah.

bluebottle lalat hijau, langau.

bluejacket kelasi angkatan laut.

blue ribbon tanda penghormatan.

bluestocking orang perempuan yang pura-pura besar keinginannya akan belajar.

bluff *(of land)* tabir tanah; *(of persons)* ramah, bersifat terus-terang; to — menggertak.

bluish kebiru-biruan.

blunder kesalahan; to — berbuat sesuatu dengan banyak kesalahan.

blunt tumpul, puntung; (of person) bersifat terusterang.

bluntness ketumpulan.

blur kabut, hal kabur; to — mengaburkan.

blurb kata-kata pujian oleh penerbit salah satu buku.

blurt, to — out berkata dengan lancar.

blush merah muka, seri muka; to — bermerah muka.

bluster percakapan angin; to — melakukan diri seperti angin.

boar babi jantan.

board (wooden) papan; (officials, council) badan; lembaga; sidang pengurus; above — terbuka, tidak tersembunyi; — and lodging tempat tidur dan makanan.

boarder tetamu; murid dalam asrama.

boarding-house rumah tumpangan.

boarding-school asrama, sekolah asrama.

boast sombong; —ful bersombong, cakap angin; to — menyombong, bercakap besar.

boaster penyombong, pelagak.

boat kapal, perahu, sampan; in the same — sama nasibnya.

boatswain serang.

bob sejenis potongan rambut perempuan; to — mengambul, memantul, angguk-angguk.

bobbin puntalan, gelendung kili-kili.

bobby nama polis di negeri Inggeris.

bobsled, bobsleigh sejenis alat pengangkut orang dan barang di atas air beku atau salji.

bode, to — membayangkan.

bodice sejenis baju dalam panjang.

-bodied berbadan.

bodily jasmani.

body (physical) badan, tubuh; in a — (all together) serempak, serentak; heavenly — bintang.

bodyguard pengiring.

Boer warna negara Afrika Selatan yang dahulu berasal dari orang Belanda.

bog rawa, paya; to — down membenamkan.

bogus tiruan, lancung; pura-pura.

Bohemian orang yang berkehidupan bebas seperti kebanyakan orang seniman.

boil I bisul, puru, barah.

boil II, to — merebus, mendidih, menggelegak; (boil over) meluap.

boiler periuk; tempat kukusan.

boiling point titik didih.

boisterous riuh.

bold gagah; lancang, berani.

boldness kegagahan; kelancangan, keberanian.

bolero (dance) sejenis tarian Sepanyol; (dress) sejenis baju pendek untuk perempuan.

bolster bantal peluk; to — (up) menyokong.

bolt pasak, palang, kancing; (arrow) anak panah; to — melarikan diri.

bomb bom, periuk api; to — membom.

bombard, to — membom; menyerang.

bombardment pemboman; penembakan.

bombast bual kosong.

bomber kapal udara pembom.

bombing mengebom.

bona fide jujur.

bond (all; (agreement) jaminan; surat perjanjian; in — disimpan sampai cukainya telah dibayar.

bondage perhambaan.

bonded diikat; — warehouse gudang penyimpan barang yang masih belum dibayar cukainya.

bondman, bondslave budak, hamba abdi.

bone tulang; — of contention pokok perselisihan; fish — tulang ikan.

bonfire api yang dinyalakan di sebuah lapangan atau bukit.

bonnet sejenis topi; tutupan kepala.

bonny sedap, indah, menyenangkan.

bonus wang jasa; untung pegawai; baksyisy.

bony banyak tulangnya, bertulang.

booby orang bodoh; — trap ranjau.

book buku, kitab; to be in s.o.'s book —s tidak disukai oleh seseorang; to — membukukan.

bookbinder penjilid.

bookcase almari buku.

book end penyokong buku.

booking pembukuan; penempahan; tempat yang telah dipesan.

book-keeper pemegang buku kira-kira, juru buku kira-kira.

book-keeping juru pengatur kira-kira, ilmu menyimpan kira-kira.

bookmaker juru bertaruh.

bookworm bubuk buku; seorang yang amat gemar akan membaca buku.

boom (noise) dentum; (naut) sangga layar; to — berdentum.

boon anugerah, kurnia.

boor orang dusun.

boost, to — memperkembangkan.

boot kasut, sepatu tinggi.

bootee sejenis sepatu tinggi untuk perempuan atau anak.

booth barung, bangsal.

bootlace tali sepatu.

bootlegger penyeludup minuman keras.

boots pelayan hotel yang membersihkan sepatu tamu-tamu.

booty barang rampasan.

booze minuman keras; to — minum banyak minuman keras.

borax boraks, pijar.

border tepi, pinggir, batas; to — membatasi.

borderland hampir batas.

bore I, to — (hole) menggerek menggurdi.

bore II (tidal) bina; (person) orang yang membosankan; to — menjemukan, membosankan.

boredom jemu, bosan.

borer penggerek, penggurdi; (insect) serangga yang mengeruk lubang.

born dilahirkan; he is a — fool memang orang bodoh.

Borneo Kalimantan.

borough kota atau sebahagian kota besar yang masih memegang segala hak yang dahulu diberikan kepadanya oleh raja.

borrow, to — meminjam.

borrower peminjam.

bosom dada; in the — of one's family di antara kaum keluarga; — friend sahabat karib, kawan sehidup semati.

boss majikan, tuan besar; to — menguasai, memerintah.

botanic(al) yang berkenaan dengan tumbuh-tumbuhan.

botanist ahli tumbuh-tumbuhan.

botany ilmu tumbuh-tumbuhan.

botch, to — menjanggalkan.

both berdua, kedua, keduaduanya; — of them keduanya.

bother susah; to — mengganggu, menyusahkan; to — about perduli akan.

bottle botol, peles; to — menyimpan (menuang) di botol.

bottleneck kesempitan, kesesakan; rintangan.

bottom dasar, alas, bawah; — up tunggang-langgang, songsang; —s up! selamat minum!; — layer alasan.

bottomless tak jejak, sangat dalam.

bough dahan.

boulder batu tongkol, batu yang besar dan bundar.

boulevard jalanraya.

bounce, to — mengambul, melanting, melantun; to — back (off) memantul.

bound I (*limit*) batas; (*leap*) loncatan; out of —s dilarang masuk.

bound II, — for mengarah, menuju; homeward — mengarah pulang.

bound III, — up with terikat oleh; — to come tentu datang.

boundary batas, perhinggaan, sempadan.

bounder pelagak.

boundless tidak terhingga, tidak bersempadan.

bountiful murah hati, dermawan.

bounty kemurahan hati; derma, kurnia.

bouquet karangan bunga.

bout suatu waktu yang singkat waktu terjadi sesuatu yang dahsyat.

bow I (*of ship*) haluan kapal.

bow II (*salutation*) tundukan kepala; to — menundukkan kepala, tunduk, sujud.

bow III (*for arrows*) busar, ibu panah; (*violin*) penggesek biola.

bowel(s) usus, tali perut.

bower punjung.

bowl batil, pasu; bola kayu.

bow-legged pengkar.

bowler hat sejenis topi tuan.

bowling alley tempat bermain bola kayu.

bowling green lapangan bola kayu.

bow window jendela merelung.

box kotak, peti; (*to fight with fists*) bertinju.

boxer ahli tinju.

Boxing Day hari yang berikut hari Natal.

box office tempat penjualan tiket di panggung wayang.

boy anak laki-laki; (*servant*) pelayan.

boycott bikot; to — memulaukan.

boyhood masa muda (anak laki-laki)

boyish seperti anak muda.

Boy Scout budak pengakap.

brace suatu pengikat, penguat; (*naul*) tali kelat.

bracelet gelang.

bracken sejenis pakis.

bracket (*support*) sandaran; (*in writing*) tanda kurung; to — memakai tanda kurung.

brackish payau, masin.

brag, to — bercakap angin, bual; to — about membualkan.

braggart penyombong, pelagak, pembual.

braid anyaman, jalin rambut; to — menjalin, menganyam.

braille tulisan dan bacaan untuk orang buta.

brain, —s otak; —wave fikiran yang cerdik.

brainy pintar, cerdik.

braise, to — memasak.

brake (*for wheels*) pekam; (*thicket*) belukar; to put on the —s pekam; menahan.

bramble sejenis semak; buahnya yang hitam dan manis.

bran dedak, sekam.

branch ranting, cabang dahan; (*of road*) simpang; — (office) pejabat cawang; to — bercabang.

brand (*of hot iron*) tanda selar; (*trademark*) tanda, cap; to — menyelar; menandai, mencapkan.

brandish, to — melimbai, melambai.

brand—new samasekali baharu, serba baharu.

brass kuningan, tembaga; a — band serombongan pemain muzik dengan alat muzik kuningan.

brassiere, bra baju kutang.

brassy seperti kuningan.

brat anak (kata menghinakan).

bravado kegagahan.

brave berani, perkasa, perwira; to — (storms, dangers etc) menempuh.

bravery keberanian.

bravo syabas.

brawl pertengkaran; to — bertengkar.

brawn (pickled meat) semacam daging asam; (strength) kekuatan.

brawny kuat.

bray, to — mengeluarkan bunyi seperti kaldai, menguak.

brazen dibuat dari kuningan; (of behaviour) tidak tidak malu.

brazier anglo, tukang kuningan.

breach pemecahan; pelanggaran; mungkir; — of promise mungkir janji.

bread roti; daily — rezeki, penghidupan sehari-hari.

breadfruit buah pohon sukun, keluik.

breadth kelebaran, lebar; to a hair's — sehelai rambut.

breadwinner yang mencari nafkah.

break I (smash) pecah; (interval: time or space) selang; (pause; rest) istirahat; — of day, day—fajar.

break II, to — putus, patah, pecah, berpecah-belah; memecahkan, mematahkan, merosakkan; to — out pecah.

breakdown keruntuhan, roboh, kegagalan; a nervous — penyakit saraf yang terjadi dengan tiba-tiba.

breaker pemecah; (waves)

ombak besar, ombak memecah.

breakfast makan pagi, buka puasa.

breakwater tembok, yang didirikan akan menahan kekuatan air, benting ombak.

bream sejenis ikan.

breast (chest) dada; (of woman) buah dada, susu, tetek; to make a clean — of it mengakui salahnya.

breastbone tulang dada.

breaststroke berenang kodok.

breath nafas, napas; with bated — dengan khuatirnya.

breathe, to — bernafas, menarik nafas.

breather (rest) waktu singkat untuk beristirahat sementara.

breathing pernafasan.

breathless putus nafas, tercungap.

breech bahagian belakang sebuah meriam atau senapang; —es seluar setengah panjang.

breed bangsa; to — (bear children, young of animals) beranak; (raise animals) memeliharakan; berternak.

breeder peternak, pemelihara.

breeding (manners) budi bahasa, keadaban.

breeze angin, bayu.

breezy berangin; (of manner) beria-rioh.

brevity keringkasan, pendek.

brew pembuatan minuman bir; minuman; to — membuat bir.

brewer pembuat bir.

brewery tempat pembuatan bir.

briar, brier pohon mawar (hutan); kayu mawar.

bribe wang suap, wang tumbuk rusuk; to — menyuap, rasuah.

brick dibuat dari batu; batu-bata.

bricklayer tukang batu.

bride pengantin mempelai perempuan.

bridegroom pengantin mempelai laki-laki.

bridesmaid pengiring pengantin perempuan, pengapit.

bridge (*of single logs or planks*) titi; (*large* —) jambatan; (*of ship*) panggung di tengah kapal; (*game*) sejenis permainan terup; — **of the nose** batang hidung.

bridle tali kekang; **to** — mengekang, mengendalikan.

brief pendek, ringkas, peraturan ringkas; **to hold** — **for** memberi bantuan.

briefly dengan pendek; ringkasnya.

brigade sebahagian tentera angkatan darat, satu pasukan.

brigadier pangkat seorang panglima atasan.

brigand penyamun, perompak.

bright terang benderang; cuaca, cerah; (*intelligent*) cerdik.

brightness kejernihan, kecerahan; kecerdikan.

brilliance cahaya, seri, kilau.

brilliant berkilau-kilauan; mulia; (*diamond*) berlian.

brim tepi, pinggir.

brimful penuh tepat.

brimstone belerang.

brindled belang.

brine air masin, air laut.

bring, to — **membawa; to** — **about** menyebabkan, mendatangkan; **to** — **back** mengembalikan.

brink tepi, pinggir, sisi.

briny masin; yang berkenaan dengan laut.

briquette abu batu bara yang dibuat bentuk batu.

brisk giat, pantas.

bristle bulu yang kasar; **to** — menggermang.

bristly menggermang.

Britain (*also* **Great** —) kerajaan Inggeris.

Britannia nama kiasan negeri Inggeris.

British Inggeris; — **Isles** Inggeris Raya.

Britisher seorang Inggeris.

Briton bangsa asli Inggeris.

brittle rangup, rapuh.

brittleness kerapuhan.

broach, to — (*barrel*) menembuk tong; (*subject*) membuka perkataan.

broad lebar; (*spacious*) luas; **in** — **daylight** waktu siang hari.

broadcast siaran, penyiaran, pancaran; **to** — menyiarkan, memancarkan.

broadminded lapang hati, murah hati.

broadness lebar, kelebaran.

brocade sejenis kain ditenun dengan benang emas dan perak.

broccoli sejenis bunga kubis.

brochure risalat.

brogue loghat; sejenis sepatu.

broil, to — (*meat*) memanggang.

broke (*without money*) tidak mempunyai wang.

broken, — English bahasa Inggeris yang tidak sempurna; **—hearted** sangat sedih.

broker dalal, berokar.

broking pekerjaan seorang berokar.

bronchitis bronchitis, demam paru-paru.

bronco kuda yang belum pernah dijekang.

bronze perunggu; gangsa; **to** — melapisi dengan perunggu, memberi berwarna perunggu.

brooch sejenis kerongsang kebaya, bros.

brood (*of chickens*) pengeraman, rindukan; **to** — **ber-peram**, memeram, mengeram; (*deep thought*) memikirkan (merenung) dengan bimbang hati, tafakkur.

brooding (*sad*) gundah-gulana, memeram hati.

brook anak sungai; **to** — (*endure*) menderita.

broom penyapu; new — penyapu baharu; (*person*) orang yang baharu diangkat dan masih giat dalam pekerjaan-nya.

broomstick tangkai penyapu.

broth bubur.

brothel rumah pelacuran, rumah sundal, rumah jahat.

brother abang, adik, saudara; elder — , —s in arms saudara seperjuangan.

brotherhood persaudaraan.

brother-in-law ipar-duai.

brow dahi; — of a hill puncak bukit.

browbeat, to — menggertakkan.

brown perang, merah tua, hitam manis; — bread roti merah; — paper kertas bungkusan.

brownie sejenis jin yang membantu orang; (*junior Girl Guide*) pandu puteri yang muda-muda.

browse, to — menggagut.

bruise bincul, lebam, luka memar; **to** — berbincul; membinculkan.

brunette perempuan yang berambut dan bermata hitam.

brunt bahagian yang utama; to bear the — ditimpa kesusahan yang terbesar, menempuh kesukaran.

brush berus, sikat; (*vegetation*) semak, belukar; **to** — menyikat.

brushwood semak, belukar.

brusque dengan pendek; dengan kasar.

Brussels Brussel; — sprouts sejenis sayuran.

brutal kasar; ganas.

brutalize, to — menjadikan kasar atau ganas.

brute orang ganas (kejam), binatang; — force semata-mata kekuatan sahaja.

bubble gelembung; to blow —s gelembung; to — bergelembung.

buck rusa jantan; (*US dollar*) ringgit (Amerika); to pass the — memindahkan susah kepada orang lain.

bucket timba, baldi.

buckle lentik; to — melentik.

bud pucuk, kuntum, kuncup, kudup, putik; to nip in the — membinasakan waktu baru-baru menguntum.

buddy saudara.

budge, to — bergerak sedikit, berganjak.

budgerigar semacam burung serindit.

budget anggaran belanja, belanjawan; to — for mengaturkan dalam belanjawan.

buff warna kulit kuning; in the — telanjang bulat.

buffalo sejenis kerbau; wild — seladang, banteng.

buffer gencetan; — state negeri yang letaknya antara dua buah negeri lain yang bermusuhan tampan.

buffet pukulan; to — memukul; menempuh.

buffoon banyol, kelakar.

bug kepinding, pijat-pijat.

buggy kereta kuda yang beroda dua.

bugle bugel, terompet (istimewa untuk tentera).

build (*appearance of persons etc*) rupa, bangun, roman; to — membuat, mendirikan, membangunkan, membina.

builder pembangun, pembina.

building rumah, bangunan, binaan.

bulb (*lamp*) balun lampu, bal lampu; (*plant*) umbi.

bulge bengkak, benggil; to — mengampul, membuncit.

bulging bergelembung.

bulk (*cargo*) muatan kapal; (*volume, size*) jumlah besar, besarnya; to load in — memuatkan barang sejumlah besar dengan tidak dibungkus dahulu.

bulky sangat besar, terlalu besar.

bull lembu jantan, binatang besar yang jantan.

bulldog sejenis anjing besar.

bulldozer sejenis pesawat besar akan meratakan tanah.

bullet peluru.

bulletin surat siaran, maklumat.

bullfinch sejenis burung.

bullfrog sejenis katak besar.

bullion emas dan perak yang belum dijadikan wang.

bullock lembu jantan.

bully orang kejam; to — menggertakkan.

bulrush sejenis gelagah.

bulwark baluarti.

bum belakang; orang miskin yang mengembara, petualang.

bumblebee kumbang.

bump bonjol, bengkak; to — berdentum, gedebak.

bumptious sombong, congkak.

bumpy penuh bonjolan, lekuk-lekak.

bun sejenis kuih; (*hair*) gulungan rambut.

bunch rangkai, ikatan rangkai; to — bergabung; menggabungkan.

bund batas.

bundle bungkusan, gabung, ikatan; to — menggabungkan.

bung sumbat; to — (up) menyumbat.

bunghole lubang pengisi tong.

bungle membuat sesuatu dengan kurang baik (sebab bodoh).

bunk tempat tidur di dalam kapal; (*of talk*) bual kosong.

bunker tempat penyimpan batu bara dalam kapal.

bunkum cakap angin, bual kosong.

bunny kelinci.

bunting kain bendera.

buoy pelampung, apung-apung; to — (up) menggerakkan seseorang.

buoyancy gaya mengapung; (*of manner*) sifat selalu riang gembira.

buoyant boleh mengapung; riang gembira.

burden beban; to — membebani, menekan.

bureau biro, pejabat.

bureaucracy birokrasi.

bureaucratic birokratik.

burglar pencuri (istimewa yang memasuki rumah orang).

burgle, to — memasuki rumah orang akan mencuri.

burgundy sejenis minuman air anggur.

burial penguburan, pemakaman.

burlesque pertunjukan buruk.

burly agam, bayak.

Burmese dari Burma, orang Burma.

burn I *pt and pp* **burnt** luka bakar; to — hangus; bernyala, menyalakan; membakar; terbakar.

burn II (*stream*) anak sungai.

burning bernyala; — question perkara hangat.

burnish, to — menggilap.

burnous pakaian panjang seorang Arab.

bur(r) duri-durian.

burrow lubang di dalam tanah, liang; to — menggali lubang; hidup dalam lubang.

bursar juruwang sebuah persekolahan tinggi.

burst celah; letusan; to — meletus; pecah; membuka; penuh.

bury, to — mengkuburkan, menanam, memakamkan; to — the hatchet mengakhiri permusuhan.

bus kereta bas; a —man's holiday cuti yang sama dengan pekerjaan sehari-hari.

bush (*shrub*) pokok kecil; (*scrub*) belukar; semak.

bushel sejenis ukuran gandum atau buah-buahan (k.l. 36 ltr.).

bushy (*of foliage*) semak; (*of hair and foliage*) lebat.

busily dengan asyek, sibuk.

business kewajiban; pekerjaan; perdagangan, perniagaan; to do — berdagang, jual beli, berniaga.

businesslike teratur, dengan tatatertib.

businessman pengusaha, saudagar.

bust patung orang (hanya kepalanya).

bustle keramaian; to — berkecoh-kecah.

busy asyek, sibuk, sedang berbuat sesuatu; to — o.s. with sedang berbuat.

busybody orang yang selalu bercampur tangan, yang selalu ambil tahu pekerjaan orang lain.

but tetapi; melainkan; we waited — he didn't come kami tunggu tetapi ia tidak datang.

butcher tukang sembelih; to — menyembelih, memotong; membantai.

butler pelayan rumah yang pekerjaannya mengenai segala rumahan dan makanan.

butt (*of gun*) pangkal senapang; gagang, hulu; (*target*) sasaran, tujuan.

butter mentega; to — menyapu mentega.

buttercup sejenis bunga kuning.

butterfly kupu-kupu, ramarama.

buttermilk air susu selepas diambil menteganya.

buttock(s) buntut, punggung.

button kancing, butang; to — mengancing.

buttonhole rumah butang; rumah kancing; (*in order to speak to s.o.*) to — mengajak berbual.

buttress sangga, sokong, pengampu; (*of tree trunk*) banir; to — menyangga, menyokong.

buxom segar, bugar, gemuk dan cantik rupanya.

buy, to — membeli; to — off membayar supaya tidak diganggu lagi, menebus.

buyer pembeli, pemesan.

buzz bunyi desing; keramaian; to — berdesing, mendesing.

buzzard sejenis burung helang.

buzzer sejenis alat letrik yang mengeluarkan bunyi desing.

by dengan atas; (*near*) dekat; (*during*) pada; to travel — rail berjalan dengan keretapi; request atas permintaan orang; — day pada hari.

bye-bye selamat tinggal.

bygone yang telah lalu; let — be — s biar semua dimaafkan supaya berbaikan balik.

by-law undang-undang kecil.

by-name nama samaran.

bypass simpangan.

by-product hasil sampingan.

byre kandang kerbau.

by-road lorong kecil.

bystander orang yang hadir.

byword pepatah, pematah.

Byzantine dari atau secara Bizantium (Rom, Istambul).

C

cab kereta sewa, teksi.

cabaret restoran dalamnya juga diadakan tari-menari dan nyanyi, kabret.

cabbage sayur kubis.

cabby, cabman pengendara kereta sewa atau teksi.

cabin pondok, petak; kabin, bilik, penumpang dalam kapal.

cabinet (*furniture*) almari; (*room*) bilik; (*pol*) jemaah menteri, kabinet.

cabinetmaker tukang kayu yang pandai membuat alat rumah.

cable tali besar, kawat, kabel; (*telegraph message*) surat kawat laut; to — mengirim berita dengan memakai kawat laut.

cablegram surat kawat laut.

caboose dapur kapal; sebahagian keretapi untuk menumpangkan buruh.

cacao (*also — tree*) (pohon) buah koko.

cache persembunyian, tempat penyimpan barang berharga.

cackle, to — berkeok.

cacophony bunyi buruk.

cactus pokok kaktas, pokok tak berduri.

cad orang yang kurang ajar, orang yang biadap.

cadaverous seperti mayat.

caddie pembantu dengan permainan golf.

caddy peti kecil, cepu (istimewa untuk menyimpan teh).

cadence irama.

cadet pelatih, calun pegawai.

cafe kedai makanan dan minuman, kafe.

cafeteria restoran yang dalamnya tetamu mengambil makanannya sendiri.

cage kurung, kandang, sang-

kar; (**bird**) — sangkar burung; to — mengurung(kan).

cairn tumpukan batu (ditumpuk untuk peringatan, kuburan dan sebagainya); — terrier sejenis anjing.

caisson (*for ammunition*) kereta ubat bedil; (*for working under water*) peti yang kedap air dalamnya orang dapat bekerja di bawah air.

cajole, to — membujuk.

cake kuih, penganan; (*lit*) a piece of — sepotong kuih.

calabash labu.

calamitous celaka.

calamity celaka besar.

calcify, to — menjadikan kapur; (*harden*) mengeras.

calculable yang dapat dihitung.

calculate, to — menghitung, menghisab, berkira-kira, mengira(-ngira).

calculating (*selfish and scheming*) tebal hati, tak berbelas kasihan.

calculation hisab, perkiraan, perhitungan.

calculator jentera mengira.

calculus (*concretion in body*) batu.

calendar takwim, kalendar, daftar tahunan.

calf I (*animal*) anak lembu (atau binatang besar yang lain); — kulit anak kerbau.

calf II (*of leg*) buah betis.

calibrate, to — memeriksa kaliber sebuah senapang, menguji alat pengukur.

calibre kaliber.

calico kain belacu, kain putih.

caliph khalifah, kalip(at).

call panggilan; bunyi seruan; kunjungan; to — menyebut, menamai; memanggil; membangunkan; to — at (*place*), make a — on (*person*) singgah, menemui.

caller penyeru; orang yang datang berkunjung, tetamu.

calligraphy tulisan elok (indah).

calling, call panggilan, ilham.

callipers alat pengukur benda bundar.

callous keras kulit; (of heart) tebal muka, keras hati.

calm tenang, reda; to — menyabarkan, meredakan.

calorie kalori.

calumny fitnah.

calve, to — melahirkan anak kerbau.

calves see **calf.**

camel unta.

camellia bunga kaca piring.

cameo batu berwarna yang dipahat dan dipakai untuk perhiasan perempuan.

camera alat ambil gambar, kamera.

camouflage selimut, samaran; to — menyelimuti, menyamarkan.

camp perkhemahan; —**bed** tempat tidur; to — berkhemah.

campaign peperangan; political — dikayuh politik.

camphor kapur barus.

campus halaman sekolah tinggi; kampus.

can (food) bekal; to — mengisi dalam tin.

can, could boleh, dapat sanggup.

Canadian orang Kanada, dari atau berkenaan dengan negeri Kanada.

canal terusan; parit.

canary sejenis burung nyanyi.

cancel, to — membatalkan, meniadakan.

cancellation pembatalan.

cancer (tumour) sakit raja, pekung; (any corroding evil) suatu kejahatan kemusyarakatan.

Cancer (Zodiac) soratan, makara; tropic of — garis saratan.

candid terus terang, jujur, tulus.

candidate bakal, calon.

candidature pencalunan.

candle dian, lilin, kandil.

candlestick kandil, kaki dian.

candour kejujuran.

candy kembang gula, gulagula; to — membuat manisan.

cane rotan; sugar — tebu; Malacca — semambu; (walking stick) tongkat; to — merotan, sesah.

cane sugar gula tebu.

canine (yang berkenaan dengan atau seperti) anjing.

canister bekas calung.

cannibal manusia yang makan sesama manusia.

cannon meriam.

canny bijak, sempurna akal, cermat.

canoe sejenis perahu; to — berperahu, bersampan; berkayuh.

canon (eccl) peraturan (undang-undang) gereja.

canonize, to — menyatakan (dengan rasmi) kesucian seseorang.

canopy langit-langit.

cant (speech) bahasa golongan istimewa; kepura-puraan; bual kosong.

can't=cannot tidak boleh (dapat, sanggup).

cantankerous cerewet, bantahan.

canteen kedai minuman dan makanan dalam (asrama, perusahaan dan sebagainya).

canter lari ligat, cara lari kuda yang cepat; to — berlari dengan cepat.

canticle nyanyian, mazmur.

canvas kain layar, kain terpal.

canvass, to — berkeliling akan memohon anugerah memungut suara.

canyon jurang dalam, ngarai besar.

caoutchouc karet, getah.

cap kopiah, songkok; tutupan, kepala; — in hand dengan hina.

capability kesanggupan, kecakapan, kemahiran.

capable cakap, arif, bijaksana, mahir; — (of) sanggup.

capacious luas.

capacity kesanggupan; kebijaksanaan; kedayaan muatan; kedudukan; filled to — sarat bermuat, penuh; keupayaan.

cape I (garment) sejenis pakaian luar.

cape II (geog) tanjung, hujung tanah.

caper loncatan, lompat; to — meloncat-loncat, melompat-lompat.

capillary seperti rambut; — blood vessel rerambut darah.

capital (big, important) yang besar, penting, utama; (chief city) ibu negeri; (of finance) modal, wang pokok, kapital; (concerning death penalty) yang berkenaan dengan hukum mati; — letter huruf besar.

capitalism faham kapitalis, pemodal.

capitalist orang kapitalis, pemodal.

capitalize, to — memakai sebagai wang pokok; membuat wang.

capitulate, to — menyerah diri, mengaku kalah.

capitulation penyerahan.

capon ayam jantan kembiri.

caprice tingkah.

capricious bertingkah.

Capricorn (Zodiac) (bintang) jadyi; tropic of — garis balik jadyi.

capsize, to — terbalik, telungkup, karam.

capstan alat penggulung tambang (istimewa pada kapal).

capsule kapsul, sarung; kelompang.

captain (naut) juragan, kapten, nakhoda; (Malay warrior) panglima, hulubalang; (sport) pemimpin pemain bola; sepak; to — memimpin.

caption penerangan di atas karangan dan sebagainya.

captivate, to — memikat hati, mengambil hati.

captivation pengambilan hati, gaya penarik.

captive tertawan; (seorang) (prisoner), tawanan.

captivity tawanan, pengurungan.

captor penangkap.

capture penangkapan; to — merebut, menangkap; tawan.

car kereta; kenderaan; motokar.

carafe balang, sejenis kendi gelas.

caramel gula bakar.

carat karat, ukuran intan, mutu intan.

caravan (in desert) kafilah; (house on wheels) kereta yang dipakai sebagai rumah.

carbine sejenis senapang.

carbon zat arang; karbon; — paper kertas karbon.

carbonic, — acid asam arang.

carbuncle (gem) batu merah; (med) bisul.

carburettor karburator.

carcass bangkai.

card (pasteboard) kertas tebal; to — play —s main terup; (visiting) surat nama.

cardboard kertas tebal.

cardiac (yang berkenaan dengan) jantung.

cardigan sejenis baju wol.

cardinal (important) yang terpenting, yang utama; (eccl) pembesar pada gereja katolik; — numbers angka pokok; — points mata pedoman yang utama (utara north, timur east, selatan south, barat west).

card index susunan kad mengandungi pengetahuan.

care (*anxiety*) susah, khuatir, kesusahan; (*attention*) penyelenggaraan, asuhan, pemeliharaan; (*with* —) dengan cermat; to take — hati-hati; to take — of mengasuh, memeliharakan.

career (*rush*) perjalanan cepat; (*occupation*) jalan hidup.

carefree sejuk hati.

careful hati-hati, berjaga, beringat-ingat.

careless alpa, lengah, lalai; — ness kelalaian, kealpaan.

caress cumbuan; to — mencumbui bersuka-suka.

caretaker penjaga rumah.

cargo barang muatan.

caricature gambar ejekan, gambar olok-olok.

carnage penyembelihan, pembunuhan.

carnal badani; berhawa nafsu.

carnation bunga teruki.

carnival sejenis sukaan sebelum puasa nasrani; waktu beriang gembira.

carnivore pemakan daging.

carnivorous yang makan daging.

carol nyanyian (istimewa nyanyian hari Natal).

carp (*fish*) ikan kalui; to — mengumpat.

carpenter tukang kayu; to — bekerja sebagai tukang kayu.

carpet permadani, hamparan; to — menutupi dengan permadani.

carriage kereta, kenderaan, kenaikan; pengangkutan; (*cost of sending*) harga pengangkutan; — paid, free tambang dibayar dahulu.

carrier pembawa, pengangkut; — pigeon burung merpati pembawa surat.

carrion daging busuk, bangkai busuk.

carrot lobak merah.

carry, to — membawa, memikul, menjinjing, menggandar; he carried a rifle ia bersenapang.

cart kereta, cikar pedati, gerabak; bullock — kereta lembu.

cartel syarikat kaum pengusaha besar akan berkongsi.

cartilage tulang rawan, tulang muda.

cartography pembuatan peta, juru peta-memeta.

carton kotak.

cartoon gambar lucu; —ist pembuat gambar lucu.

cartridge kertus, ubat peterum; blank — kertus yang tak berpeluru.

cartwright pembuat gerabak.

carve, to — memotong; meraut; mengukir, memahat; merajang, mengelar.

carving ukiran; — knife pisau daging.

cascade air terjun; to — menerjun, mengalir ke bawah seperti air terjun.

case I (*box*) peti; almari; (*covering*) sarung; to — memasukkan ke dalam peti.

case II (*circumstances*) hal, perkara, peristiwa; in — jikalau, sekiranya; in any — bagaimanapun juga.

casement sejenis jendela.

cash pembayaran tunai, kontan; wang tunai; — down dengan pembayaran tunai.

cashew, — nut biji jambu monyet, biji rajus.

cashier I pemegang wang, kasyer, tukang wang.

cashier II to — memecat; mengeluarkan dari jawatan (istimewa daripada tentera).

cashmere sejenis kain kasmiri.

casino tempat berjudi dan tari-menari.

cask tong kayu, pipa.

casket peti kecil, cepu.

cassava ubi kayu.

casserole basi kasar; en — dibasi kasar.

cassock sejenis pakaian padri, jubah.

cast (*mould*) acuan, tuangan; (*theat*) jumlah pemain dalam sandiwara (*dan sebagainya*); (*of eye*) juling; to — melempar, melambungkan; melabuhkan; membuang; menghitung.

castanet, —s ceracap, sejenis kelontongan kayu yang dipakai dengan tarian Sepanyol.

castaway seorang yang dihanyutkan ke darat.

caste kasta, puak.

castigate, to — menyeksa; memaki.

casting (*mould*) tuangan; — net jala.

casting vote suara yang memutuskan dalam pemilihan kalau jumlah suara yang mengiakan sama dengan yang tidak bersetuju.

cast iron besi tuangan.

castle kota, istana, ma(h)ligai; (*chess*) (dengan main catur) tir; —s in the air cita-cita, angan-angan.

castor roda kecil di bawah kerusi atau meja kecil.

castor oil minyak jarak.

castor sugar gula yang halus sekali.

castrate, to — mengembirikan.

casual (*careless*) lalai, pengabai; kebetulan; tidak biasa; —ly sambil lalu.

casualty orang cacat yang luka atau mati dalam kemalangan atau peperangan.

casuarina, — tree pohon cemara, pohon ru.

cat kucing; lain binatang yang bangsanya sama dengan kucing.

cataclysm gempa, gara-gara atau celaka besar yang terjadi tiba-tiba.

catacomb ruang di bawah tanah dalam mana disimpan mayat-mayat.

catalogue, (*US*) **catalog** daftar, buku-buku, senarai buku-buku, kataloges.

catalysis katalisis.

catalyst katalisator.

catapult ali-ali; pelanting, lastik.

cataract jeram, riam, air terjun besar; (*med*) penyakit mata bular.

catarrh sema-sema, selesema.

catastrophe balak, bencana, celaka besar.

cat call siulan (akan menunjukkan tidak senang).

catch penangkapan; yang ditangkap, tangkapan; (*trickery*) tipu daya; to — menangkap; mencapai; mendapat.

catching (*attractive*) menarik hati.

catchword kata yang menarik perhatian.

catechism pengajaran ugama Nasrani (dengan jalan soal jawab).

categorical dengan mutlak.

category jenis, bangsa, kategori, bahagian.

cater, to — menjual atau mengurus makanan.

caterer langganan.

caterpillar belencas, ulat mentadu.

caterwaul, to — mengiau (*seperti kucing*).

catharsis (*inner purification*) pembersihan batin.

cathartic ubat pencahar.

cathedral gereja Katolik, atau Anglikan yang besar dalam suatu daerah.

cathode katode.

Catholic Katolik; yang memeluk semua; luas.

catkin bunga berupa mayang kecil.

cattle ternak, haiwan, kerbau, lembu; — breeding peternakan lembu kerbau.

catwalk titian di sisi jambatan (atau di kilang).

cauldron periuk, kawah.

cauliflower kol kembang, bunga kubis.

cause sebab, asal, benih, mula; hal yang penting; to — menyebabkan, menjadikan, membangkit, mendatangkan.

causeway jalan tinggi, jalan tambak.

caustic yang membakar; pedas.

cauterize, to — menyelar, membakar.

caution hati-hati, kelakuan yang bijak; to — memberi ingat, mengingatkan.

cautious hati-hati beringat-ingat, panjang akal.

cavalcade rombongan besar orang berkuda; perarakan.

cavalier orang hulubalang, orang bangsawan.

cavalry pasukan berkuda.

cave gua, lubang; to — in roboh, runtuh.

cavern gua.

cavernous yang berlubang sangat besar; seperti gua.

cavity lubang, liang, rongga; nasal — rongga hidung; oral — rongga mulut.

cayenne lada merah.

cease, to — berhenti, menghentikan; to — fire meletakkan senjata.

ceaseless tak putus-putus, tak berkeputusan.

cedar sejenis pohon.

cede, to — menyerahkan.

ceiling langit-langit bilik.

celebrate, to — merayakan, mempermuliakan.

celebrated termasyhor, ternama, kenamaan.

celebration perayaan.

celebrity kemasyhoran; orang yang masyhor.

celery pokok seladeri, daun seladeri.

celestial yang berkenaan dengan langit; kedewaan; — sphere falak.

celibate orang bujang, tidak beristeri atau bersuami.

cell bilik kecil dalam pertapaan (atau) penjara.

cellar ruang gudang, di bawah tanah (istimewa untuk menyimpan minuman anggur).

cello selo, sejenis biola.

cellophane sejenis kertas yang terang kelihatan cahaya di sebelah.

celluloid damar seluloid, sejenis bahan pelastik.

cellulose bahan nabati.

cement simen, perikat; to — menghubungkan; *(affairs)* menyangkut-pautkan.

cemetery perkuburan, pemakaman.

cenotaph sejenis tugu peringatan untuk orang yang telah meninggal tetapi yang jenazahnya di kubur di tempat lain.

censer perasapan, ukupan.

censor sensor, badan pemeriksa pertunjukan, buku, filem, surat dan sebagainya.

censorship sensur.

censure cacat; to — mencacat.

census banci, membanci.

cent matawang, sen; $\frac{1}{100}$ dollar; per — satu per seratus.

centenarian orang yang berumur seratus tahun.

centenary peringatan hari ulang tahun keseratus.

centennial yang berusia seratus tahun; hari ulang tahun keseratus.

centigrade berdarjah seratus pengukur panas.

centipede halipan, sepesan.

central pusat; di tengah.

centralization perpusatan, pemusatan.

centralize, to — memusatkan.

centre titik pusat, titik tengah, pusat, mata; — **of gravity** pusat berat.

centrifugal empar; — **force** daya empar.

centripetal ke arah pusat, pusaran; — **force** daya pusaran.

century abad, kurun.

ceramic yang berkenaan dengan tembikar.

cereal(s) biji-bijian, bijirin, padi.

cerebral yang berkenaan dengan otak.

ceremonial dengan upacara.

ceremonious dengan upacara; berpegang kepada adat istiadat.

ceremony upacara, istiadat; **without** — dengan begitu sahaja.

cert ketentuan.

certain tertentu, sungguh, pesti; a — **man** sesuatu, seseorang.

certainly memang, nescaya, tentu, sesungguhnya.

certainty kepestian, ketentuan; keyakinan.

certificate surat akuan, surat lulusan; ijazah, sijil.

certified diakui; ditetapkan; berijazah.

certify, to — menetapkan, mengakui kebenaran sesuatu.

cessation istirahat, perhentian.

cession penyerahan.

cesspool pelembagan.

Ceylon negeri Selon.

chafe luka lecet; **to** — menggosok; melecet.

chaff sekam, dedak; **to** —

menyekamkan; (*make fun of*) berkelakar.

chaffinch sejenis burung.

chagrin kesedihan; perasaan kecil hati.

chain rantai; **to** — merantaikan.

chain smoker orang yang terus-menerus merokok sahaja.

chain store salah satu di antara kedai yang semuanya kepunyaan satu orang atau syarikat.

chair kerusi; kedudukan kehormatan; ketua; **to take the** — mengetuai.

chairman ketua, pengerusi.

chalice piala.

chalk kapur, kapur tulis; **to** — (up) mencatit dengan kapur.

chalky penuh kapur, mengandung kapur; seperti kapur.

challenge tentangan, cabar; **to** — menentang, mencabar.

chamber bilik; bilik tidur; ruang pengadilan; dewan, badan.

chameleon bunglon; sumpah-sumpah.

chamois I sejenis kambing gunung.

chamois II (*leather*) kulit penggosok.

champ, to — memamah (mengunyah) (dengan kecap-kecup).

champion pendekar; juara, jempulan, johan.

championship johan.

chance untung, nasib; peluang; kebetulan; **games of** — main judi (dan sebagainya).

chancellor pembesar lapangan kehakiman dan lain-lain; ketua perguruan tinggi; canselor.

chandelier sejenis lampu gantung yang bercabang, kandil.

chandler pembuat lilin; penjual lilin, (sabun dan sebagainya).

change perubahan, pertukaran, peralihan, penggantian; (*money*) wang kembali, wang kecil; to — berubah, beralih, berganti.

changeable mudah berubah, tak tentu.

changeling anak yang ditukar waktu kecil.

channel alur, selat, saluran, terusan; the (English) C—Selat Inggeris.

chant sejenis nyanyian; to — menyanyi, melagukan.

chaos keadaan kacau-bilau kekacauan.

chaotic kacau-bilau.

chap (*man*) kawan, kulup, sahabat; (*on skin*) lecet; rekah.

chapel tempat, sembahyang.

chaperon pengiring orang muda atau perempuan; to — mengiringi.

chaplain padri (istimewa untuk tentera, asrama dan sebagainya).

chapter (*of book*) fasal, bab; (rel) kumpulan pembesar gereja.

char I, to — membakar, membara.

char II, to — (*household work*) membersihkan rumah, membuat pekerjaan rumahtangga dengan menerima gaji.

character aksara, huruf; budi pekerti, perangai, watak.

characteristic khas, khusus; sifat.

characterize, to — menyatakan, menandai khasiatnya.

charade sejenis teka-teki.

charcoal arang.

charge (*burden*) beban; (*gun*) isi senapang; (*cost*) harga, biaya, amanat, tanggungan; (*accusation*) pendakwaan, tuduhan; (*onslaught*) serangan; to — mengisi senapang.

chargé d'affaires kuasa usaha.

charger kuda seorang askar.

chariot kenderaan, rata.

charitable murah hati, dermawan.

charity kemurahan hati, kedermawanan.

charlatan orang yang melakukan diri sebagai doktor sebetulnya penipu.

charm keelokan, kemolekan; daya penarik; hikmat; to — memberahikan.

charming elok, molek, cantik.

chart peta (pelajaran); rajah; to — memetakan.

charter piagam; to — memberi hak kepada.

charwoman orang perempuan yang kerjanya membersihkan rumah.

chary hati-hati, segan.

chase I (*hunt*) pemburuan; (*pursuit*) pengusiran; to—memburu, mengusir, mengejar(i).

chase II, to — (*engrave*) memahat, mengukir.

chasm belah, celah.

chassis bahagian bawah sebuah kereta.

chaste suci.

chasten, to — mengajar supaya mahir; menghaluskan.

chastise, to — menyeksa.

chastity kesucian.

chat ceramah; bual; to — berbual, berceloteh.

chattels, goods and — hartabenda, barang-barang.

chatter (*persons*) bual; to — merepet, berbual; (*teeth*) gemertak.

chauffeur sais, derebar.

chauvinism sayang terhadap tanahair.

cheap murah; tidak berharga.

cheapen, to — menjadikan murah.

cheapness kemurahan.

cheat pengecoh, penipu; to — menipu, mengecoh.

check I (*chess*) sah (pada main

catur); (*halt*) perhentian; (*inspect*) pemeriksaan; (*cloth*) kain genggang; to — (*halt*) menahan; (*inspect*) memeriksa.

check II (*US*) — cheque.

checkers (*US*) (*game*) permainan dam.

checkmate sah-mat (pengalahan pada main catur); (kalah dalam apa pun juga).

cheek pipi; (*impudence*) besar mulut; —bone tulang pipi.

cheeky selamba, tebal muka.

cheer (*gladness*) kegembiraan, kesukaan; (*shout*) sorak; to — bersorak.

cheerful gembira, gerang, ramai, ria, riang.

cheerfulness sukacita, keriaan, keriangan, kegembiraan.

cheerio selamat tinggal.

cheerless sedih.

cheery gembira, bersuka hati, riang.

cheese keju.

cheetah sejenis harimau.

chef juru masak laki-laki.

chemical kimia; bahan kimia.

chemist (*pharmacist*) ahli ubat; ahli kimia; —'s (*shop*) rumah ubat.

chemistry ilmu kimia.

cheque cek; a blank — cek yang tidak diisi jumlahnya.

cherish, to — (*to prize*) menghargai; berpegang kepada, memeliharakan.

cheroot cerutu.

cherry sejenis buah; — blossom bunga sakura.

cherub malaikat.

chess catur; to play — main catur.

chessboard papan catur.

chessman buah catur.

chest peti kotak; (*anat*) dada; — of drawers almari laci.

chestnut sejenis buah berangan; (*colour*) warna merah tua.

chevalier orang bangsawan.

chevron (*pattern*) bentuk pucuk rebung; (*badge of rank*) tanda pangkat dalam tentera.

chew, to — mengunyah, memamah; to — the cud memamah biak.

chewing gum sejenis gulagula yang berisi getah.

chic indah dan jelita.

chicanery penipuan.

chick anak ayam.

chicken ayam muda; daging ayam.

chicken feed (*food*) memakan ayam; (*trivial*) barang yang tak berharga.

chickenpox cacar air, peletung.

chicory sejenis tumbuhan yang akarnya dibuat kopi.

chide, to — memaki.

chief tuan besar, kepala, penghulu; (*pre-eminent*) yang terutama, yang terpenting.

chiefly istimewa terutama.

chieftain penghulu, ketua.

chilblain bengkak pada tangan dan lain-lain kerana sangat sejuk.

child, *pl* **children** anak; —'s play pekerjaan yang sangat mudah.

childhood masa muda; from — dari kecil.

childish nyanyok, seperti anak kecil.

childlike seperti anak kecil.

chili cabai, cili.

chill rasa sejuk, dingin.

chilly dingin, sejuk; (*of manner*) tak peramah.

chime bunyi genta, loceng; irama; to — membunyikan loceng.

chimney cerobong, corong; — sweep(er) tukang pembersih cerobong.

chimpanzee sejenis monyet besar di negeri Afrika; cimpanzee.

chin dagu.

China negeri China.

china (*porcelain*) tembikar.

Chinese China; orang China.

chink (*crack*) ganggang celah, renggang; (*sound*) bunyi kerting; to — mengerentingkan.

chintz sejenis kain cita.

chip bilah, sepotong kecil, serpih, keping; (*potato*) —s keripik kentang.

chiropodist pengubat sakit kaki dan tangan.

chiropody pengubat sakit kaki dan tangan.

chirp kicau, ciak; to — berkicau; menciak.

chirpy gembira, ria.

chirrup *see* **chirp**.

chisel pahat; to — memahat.

chit (*note*) surat pendek.

chit–chat percakapan, bualan.

chivalrous bahaduri, perwira.

chivalry keperwiraan.

chloride klorid.

chloroform klorofom, sejenis ubat bius.

chlorophyll zat hijau yang terdapat dalam tumbuh-tumbuhan; klorofil.

chock setongkol kayu.

chock–full penuh sesak, penuh pepak.

chocolate coklat.

choice pilihan, pemilihan; yang baik.

choir kumpulan penyanyi.

choke, to — tersedak, tersumbat, kebangkalan; —d to death mati kelemasan.

cholera kolera, penyakit taun.

choose, to — memilih; to pick and — memilih dengan adil.

chop sepotong daging yang tebal; (*stamp, seal*) cap; to — mengapak, memotong.

chopper pemotong; pisau besar, parang.

choppy (*of sea*) gelora, ribut, komcah.

chopsticks sepit, alat pemakan China.

chop suey sejenis makanan China.

choral yang dinyanyikan bersama-sama, yang berkenaan dengan penyanyian bersama.

chord tali, dawai (kecapi dan sebagainya); (*line joining ends of arc*) garisan rentas.

chore pekerjaan rumah.

choreography perancang tarian.

chortle, to — terkekeh-kekeh.

chorus sekumpulan penyanyi; nyanyian bersama, beramai, koros.

Christ Nabi Isa.

christen, to — memasukkan ke dalam ugama Nasrani; memberi nama.

Christian orang Nasrani; — name nama kecil; — era tarikh Masihi.

Christianity ugama Nasrani.

Christmas *abbr* **Xmas** hari Natal; — tree pohon Natal.

chrome sejenis warna kuning, keromiam.

chromium kromium, sejenis logam.

chromosome keromosom.

chronic kronik; (*of sickness*) idap.

chronicle babad, sejarah.

chronological menurut waktu.

chronometer loceng jam dan sebagainya yang tepat menunjukkan waktu.

chrysalis kepompong.

chrysanthemum sejenis bunga.

chubby montok, montel.

chuckle tertawa terkekeh-kekek; to — tersenyum tertawa, mengekek.

chum sobat, kawan; to — up

with merapatkan diri pada merapati.

chunk sepotong, bingkah, bongkah.

church gereja.

churchyard kuburan permakaman dekat gereja.

churlish biadab, tak berbudi bahasa, kurang sopan.

churn alat penumbuk susu (akan membuat mentega); **to —** menumbuk susu.

chute saluran air atau bahan lain ke bawah.

chutney sejenis acar mangga.

cicada cengkerik.

cider minuman yang dibuat dari buah epal.

cigar rokok, cerutu.

cigarette rokok; **— case** celepa.

cinch (*certainty*) apa-apa yang tentu; **it's a —!** tentu jadil, tanggung!

cinder bara yang telah padam.

cine— yang berkenaan dengan gambar hidup.

cinema wang gambar, layar putih.

cinnamon kayu manis.

cipher (*figure 0*) angka sifar; (*secret writing*) tulisan rahsia; **to —** menghitung; memaki tulisan rahsia.

circle lengkaran, bulatan, kalangan; (*group*) lengkungan, golongan; **to —** berlegar.

circuit lengkungan, keliling; peredaran; **short —** putus edaran.

circular bulat, bundar; (*letter or notice*) surat edaran.

circulate, to — beredar, mengedarkan.

circum— awalan yang ertinya; keliling.

circumcise, to — mengkhatankan, menyunatkan.

circumcision khatan, sunat.

circumference lengkongan, lengkaran, keliling, lilit.

circumlocution memerikan dengan panjang lebar.

circumnavigate, to — belayar berkeliling (mengelilingi).

circumscribe, to — (*limit or restrict*) membatasi.

circumscription pembatasan.

circumspect hati-hati; saksama.

circumstance hal, perihal, keadaan.

circumstantial, — evidence keterangan yang diperoleh dari segala selok-belok yang mengelilinginya.

circumvent, to — memintas, mengatasi.

circus wayang sarkis; (*road junction*) lapangan tempat berpusat beberapa jalan.

cissy (*sl*) orang pemuda yang seperti perempuan kelakuannya.

cistern tempat penyimpan air.

citadel baluarti, benteng.

citation penyebutan dalam surat rasmi.

cite, to — menyebut; (*extract quotation*) memetik, mengutip.

citizen warganegara; penduduk; **—ship** kewarganegaraan, rakyat.

citron jenis buah limau nipis.

city bandar besar; bandaraya.

civet—cat musang, jebat.

civic yang berkenaan dengan warganegara dan kewarganegaraan, tata-rakyat.

civil yang berkenaan dengan kewarganegaraan, berkenan dengan penduduk bandar; (*of conduct*) baik budi bahasanya; pereman; **— law** hukum muka-malat.

civilian orang awam pereman, yang tidak tergolong askar.

civilization peradaban, kebudayaan, tamadun.

civilize, to — membawa

kebudayaan, memperadabkan, bertamadun.

Civvy Street (*sl*) kehidupan orang pereman.

claim tuntut hak; tuntutan; (*lawsuit*) pendakwaan; to — menuntut; mendakwakan.

claimant pendakwa.

clairvoyance bakat terus mata.

clairvoyant terus mata.

clam kepah, remis.

clamber, to — memanjat.

clammy lembab, lengas, berkemal.

clamorous rioh-rendah.

clamour gempar, keriohan, hinggar-bangar; to — meriohrendah menyeru; (*call for noisily*) menuntut dengan rioh.

clamp (*grip*) ketam, pengikat, tupai-tupai; to — mengetam, membubuhi tupai-tupai.

clan kaum, suku bangsa.

clandestine tersembunyi, diam-diam.

clang kelening, kelenung, kelentang; to — mengelening, mengelentang.

clank kelentang, keroncong; to — mengelentang.

clap tepuk, kelepuk; to — mengelepuk, mengelepak.

clapper (*tongue of bell*) anak genta, anak loceng.

claret sejenis minuman air anggur merah.

clarify, to — (*make clear*) menerangkan, menjelaskan.

clarinet sejenis serunai.

clarion sejenis terompet; terang dan kuat bunyinya.

clarity keterangan, kehening-an.

clash bunyi kelentang; (*quarrel*) pertengkaran; to — bertengkar; (*fight*) berlawan.

clasp ketam, kancing, pengancing; (*embrace*) peluk; to — (*grasp hand*) menjabat; (*embrace*) memeluk.

class kelas, golongan, bangsa, lapisan masyarakat, kelas, jenis; **the upper** — **kaum** atasan.

classic kelasik, yang berkenaan dengan zaman dahulukala.

classical yang berkenaan dengan zaman dahulukala; — education pengajaran pendidikan yang berdasarkan zaman tersebut.

classification pembahagian, pengaturan, penjenisan.

classify, to — membahagikan, menjenis.

classmate teman sedarjah.

classroom bilik darjah.

classy (*col*) berkenaan dengan golongan atas.

clatter kerincing; to — mengerincing.

clause kalimat pendek; fasal; **principal** *or* **main** — indok kalimat; **subordinate** *or* **dependent** — anak kalimat.

claw kuku, cakar; (*instrument*) alat pencekam; to — mencakar, mencekam.

clay tanah liat; — **pipe** paip tembikar.

clean bersih, elok; (*entirely*) samasekali; to — membersihkan, mencuci.

cleaning pembersihan.

cleanliness kebersihan.

cleanly bersih, yang suka akan kebersihan.

cleanse, to — membersihkan, mencuci.

cleansing pembersihan.

clear (*bright*) terang; (*limpid*) hening, jernih; (*obvious*) terang, tegas, jelas, nyata; to — **keep** — **of** menjauhi; to — (*scrub, trees*) menebus.

clearance (*of obstructions*) penghapusan rintangan; certificate of — surat izin untuk melalui pejabat cukai.

clearly nyata.

clearness jernih, hening, cerah.

cleavage (*split*) lekah, celah.

cleave, to — membelah, membaji.

cleaver alat pembelah; kapak, parang.

clef laras muzik.

cleft celah, lekah, rekah.

clematis sejenis tumbuhan berbunga.

clemency kerahiman, kemurahan.

clement rahim, rahman, berbelas kasihan.

clench, clinch (*fist*) genggam kepal tangan; (*hard grip*) pemegang kuat; (*agreement*) persetujuan; to — mengepalkan tangan; memegang kuat.

clergy golongan padri.

clergyman padri, pendita.

cleric(al) yang berkenaan dengan padri atau pendita; yang berkenaan dengan tulismenulis jurutulis dan sebagainya.

clerk kerani, jurutulis, penulis.

clever pintar, pandai, bijak, berakal.

cleverness kepandaian, kepintaran.

click kertik, kertuk; bunyi dalam bahasa Afrika Selatan; to — mengertik, mengertuk.

olient langganan.

clientele para langganan, para tetamu.

cliff batu karang, tebing tinggi.

climate hawa, iklim; continental — hawa darat; marine or oceanic — hawa laut.

climax puncak.

climb pendakian; to — (*heights generally in grade*) naik, menaiki; (*trees, ropes*) memanjat; (*hills*) mendaki; to — down turun.

climber pemanjat; (*in social sense*) orang yang ingin naik pangkat; (*plant*) tumbuhan jalaran, ulan.

cling, to — melekat, berlekat; to — to berpaku kepada.

clinic klinik, rumahsakit atau bahagian, rumahsakit tempat doktor diajar penyelenggaraan orang sakit.

clinical yang berkenaan dengan penyelenggaraan orang sakit; — thermometer pengukur suhu.

clip kerting.

clip (*grip*) kepitan; to — mengepit; (*with scissors, shears*) menggunting.

clipper pemotong, gunting; (*ship*) kapal yang cepat atau kapaludara.

clique golongan terbatas, lengkongan.

clitoris kelentit.

cloak (*of pilgrim*) sejenis jubah; (*outer garment*) pakaian luar; (*covering*) tutupan; (*blanket*) selimut; under the — of dengan dalih.

clock jam, loceng; three o'— pukul tiga; —wise jalannya seperti jarum jam.

clod ketul, kepal, gumpal.

clog (*obstruction*) rintangan; (*wooden shoe*) terompah.

cloister (*rel*) pertapaan; (*anode*) sejenis serambi yang beratap.

close I (*shut*) tertutup; (*limited*) terbatas; (*of door, joinery*) rapat; (*of crowd*) sesak; (*narrow*) sempit; (*near*) dekat; a — friend sahabat karib.

close II, to — (*shut*) menutup, mengatupkan; (*settle*) menetapkan; to — one's eyes memejamkan mata.

closet bilik kecil; (*cupboard*) almari.

closure (*end*) akhir; (*shut*) tutup, penutupan.

clot gumpal, kepal; to — bergumpal.

cloth kain; kain sekelat.

clothe, to — memakai pakaian; (*cover*) menutupi.

clothes pakaian; bed— segenap alas tilam sarung bantal (dan sebagainya).

clothing pakaian.

cloud awan, mega, pokok hujan, keredupan; —ed mendung, berawan; —y kelam; (*confused*) kelam-kabut.

clout (*patch*) tampal; to — memukul.

clove bunga cengkih.

clover sejenis rumput.

clown banjol, kelakar, lawak.

cloy, to — mengenyangkan (sampai jemu).

club cokmar, gada; kayu pemukul; (*association*) persatuan; to — together (with) berkumpul, berhimpun.

clubfoot cepuh.

cluck ketuk (ayam); to — berketuk.

clue petunjuk, tanda.

clump serumpun, seperdu; to — (*feet*) menggedebak kaki.

clumsy janggal, kekok, kikok; (*from cold*) kaku.

cluster rumpun, kelompok, kumpulan; to — berkelompok, berkumpul.

clutch (*of eggs*) pengeraman; (*grasp*) genggaman; to — menggenggam, mencekau.

clutter keriohan, kebingungan; —ed up with penuh dengan.

coach (*vehicle*) kereta; (*instructor*) pelatih, pengajar; to — melatih, mengajar.

coachman sais kereta.

coagulate, to — membeku, mengental; —d kental, beku.

coal arang batu, batu bara, —mine lombong batu bara.

coalesce, to — (*be at one*) bersatupadu, berpadu-padan.

coalition persatuan, percantuman.

coarse (*of texture etc*) kasap, kesat, kasar; (*of manner*) kasar, biadab, kurang ajar.

coast pinggir laut, pantai; —guard peronda pantai; —line garisan pinggir laut.

coastal di pesisir, tepi laut; —area pesisir.

coaster kapal penyusur.

coat (*garment*) baju; (*covering*) tutupan; (*layer*) lapisan (bulu binatang, lapisan cat dan lainlain); over— baju luaran; —of arms lambang.

coax, to — membujuk, merayu, mencumbu.

cob sejenis burung undan jantan; (*horse*) sejenis kuda; (*lump*) bungkal; (*corncob*) tongkol.

cobalt sejenis logam, kobalt; warna biru.

cobble, —stone batu bundar; to — membetulkan sepatu.

cobbler tukang sepatu.

cobra ular senduk.

cobweb sarang laba-laba, (sesuatu yang menyerupai sarang tersebut).

cocaine sejenis ubat pembius.

cock ayam jantan, burung jantan; fighting — ayam sabungan.

cockatoo burung kakatua.

cockerel ayam jago muda; (*forward young man*) orang muda yang lakunya gagah.

cocker spaniel sejenis anjing.

cockeyed juling.

cockfight sabungan ayam.

cockiness kepungahan.

cockle sejenis remis; —shell kerang.

cockney orang asli kota London.

cockpit gelanggang sabungan ayam; (*pilot's seat in plane*) tempat penerbang di dalam kapalterbang.

cockroach lipas.

cocksure yakin; (*impudent*) sombong.

cocktail sejenis minuman keras beberapa macam anggur yang dicampur.

cocky sombong, pongah.

cocoa koko, coklat; minuman coklat.

coconut buah kelapa; nyior; — fibre sabut kelapa; — milk santan, air kelapa; — oil minyak kelapa; — tree, — palm pohon kelapa, pohon nyior.

cocoon sarang ulat, kepompong.

cod sejenis ikan laut; —**liver** oil minyak ikan.

coddle, to — memeliharakan baik-baik (orang sakit).

code (*legal*) susunan undang-undang; (*procedure*) tatacara; **to** — menyalin berita menurut sistem kod.

codify, to — membukukan hukum.

codicil kodisil, tambahan surat wasiat.

coeducation pendidikananak laki-laki dan perempuan bersama-sama.

coefficient awalan pendepan, penjodoh bilangan.

coerce, to — memaksa.

coercion paksaan.

coexist, to — ada bersama, hidup bersama.

coexistence kehidupan bersama.

coffee kopi, kahwa; — **house** kedai kopi; — **bean** biji kopi.

coffin keranda, peti mayat, long.

cog gigi roda; —**wheel** roda gigi.

cogent yang meyakinkan, yang memaksakan.

cogitate, to — mentafakkurkan memikirkan.

cognac sejenis minuman keras.

cognate bersaudara.

cognizance kesedaran; pemandangan; **to have** — **of** mengetahui (salah satu hal rasmi).

cohabit, to — bersekeduduk sebagai laki isteri.

cohere, to — berpaut rapat; (*of arguments*) kena.

coherence perpautan, perhubungan.

cohesion bersangkut.

cohesive berpaut.

coil belit, lengkaran, gelongan, puntalan; **to** — bergelung, berbelit.

coin matawang, duit; **to** — (*money*) menempa (membuat) wang; membuat sesuatu yang baharu (istimewa) kata-kata dan ungkapan.

coinage (*coining*) pembuatan matawang; (*currency*) sistem matawang; (*new words*) ciptaan kata-kata baharu.

coincide, to — (*of time*) terjadi pada ketika itu juga; (*be the same*) tepat sama, seia sekata, sekena; (*agree*) bersetuju.

coincidence pertepatan.

coke sejenis batuarang, arangkok.

cold dingin, sejuk; kedinginan, kesejukan; (*in head*) selesema; **to catch a** — selesema.

colic ucus mulas, mulas perut.

collaborate, to — bekerja bersama; (*dalam lapangan kesenian, dengan musuh*).

collaboration sekutu; pekerjaan bersama.

collaborator orang yang sekutu.

collapse keruntuhan, kerobohan; **to** — merebah, roboh, runtuh, merebahkan, meruntuhkan.

collapsible (*of articles*) dapat dilipat.

collar kerah, leher baju; taliieher; kalung; to — (*catch*) memegang seseorang pada lehernya; menangkap.

collarbone tulang selangka.

collate, to — membandingkan (dua surat, naskhah dan sebagainya; menyatukan.

collateral berdamping dengan, bersisi; (*akin of relatives*) bersanak.

colleague kawan sekerja, teman sejabat (sekerja) rakan.

collect, to — berkumpul, berhimpun, memungut, menghimpunkan, mengumpulkan.

collected (*calm*) tenang.

collection pemungutan, kumpulan, himpunan.

collective bersama, berhimpun.

collectivism faham bahawa pemerintah ialah pemilik segala tanah (perusahaan, hasil bumi dan sebagainya).

collector pemungut; pengumpul.

college badan, dewan; kuliah; sejenis sekolah lanjutan, maktab; kolej.

collide, to — (with) merentak, melanggar.

collier buruh tambang batuarang; kapal batuarang.

colliery tambang batuarang.

collision pelanggaran.

colloquial yang berkenaan dengan percakapan, pertuturan.

colloquy percakapan.

collywobbles bunyi dengkur yang terbit dari usus.

colon (*in punctuation*) titik dua; (*anat*) usus besar; kolon.

colonel pangkat kolonel.

colonial kolonial; penduduk koloni, penjajahan.

colonist penduduk koloni; (*one who opens new land*) orang meneroka.

colonization penerokaan.

colonize, to — menjajahi.

colonnade serangkaian turus.

colony koloni, jajahan; (kumpulan penduduk asing dalam suatu bandar; kumpulan burung dan sebagainya yang hidup pada suatu tempat).

colossal sangat besar.

colossus patung orang yang sangat besar.

colour, (*US*) **color** warna; complementary — warna penggenap; — bar pembezaan terhadap orang berwarna; —blind buta warna (tak dapat membeza-bezakan warna); —ed berwarna.

colouring warna; pemakaian warna.

colours (*ensign, flags etc*) tunggul-tunggul, bendera, lencana, panji-panji.

colt anak kuda jantan.

column (*pillar*) tiang, turus; (*list*) jadual; (*row*) garis, jajar, barisan; — (*in a newspaper*) ruangan.

coma pengsan, tiada sedarkan diri.

comb (*for hair etc*) sisir; sikat; (*of cock*) balung ayam; to — menyisir, menyikat.

combat perang, perjuangan; pertempuran, perkelahian; to — memerangi, memperjuangkan.

combatant sedang berjuang, berperang; pejuang.

comber (*large wave*) ombak besar.

combination rangkaian.

combine, to — merangkaikan, menggabungkan, bergabung.

combustible dapat membakar.

combustion pembakaran.

come, to — datang; to — about terjadi; to — across mendapati; to — along ikut serta.

come-and-go pulang balik.

comedian pemain sandiwara, lawak.

comedown (*fall etc*) keruntuhan, kejatuhan.

comedy sandiwara lawak, lakun gembira.

comet bintang berekor, bintang berasap, bintang ziarah.

comfort (*ease*) kenikmatan, kesenangan, kesedapan; (*solace*) penghiburan; to — melipur, menghiburkan.

comfortable nikmat, enak, sedap, selesa.

comforter penghibur; (*scarf*) selendang kain bulu.

comic menggelikan; jenaka; —al menggelikan.

comma koma; inverted —s tanda pengikat kata.

command (*order*) perintah, suruhan; (*military unit*) bahagian tentera.

commandant komandan, panglima.

commander panglima, komandan; —in-chief panglima besar.

commandment (*of God*) firman; (*order*) suruhan.

commando komando, pasukan istimewa.

commemorate, to — memperingati.

commemoration peringatan, kenang-kenangan.

commence, to — mulai.

commencement permulaan.

commend, to — berpesan; memuji.

commendable terpuji.

commendation pujian.

commensurate sepadan, sedarjat.

comment tafsir, kupasan, ulasan; to — (**on**) mentafsirkan, mengupas.

commentary tafsir, ulasan, kupasan.

commentator pengupas, jurutafsir, juruulas.

commerce perdagangan, perniagaan.

commercial yang berkenaan dengan perniagaan.

commiserate, to — turut berdukacita, berbelas kasihan, mengasihani.

commissariat bahagian militeri yang mengurus hal makanan.

commission perintah, peraturan, suruhanjaya; to — memberi kuasa kepada, mengamanahkan.

commissionaire suruhan, pelayan yang berdiri dekat pintu pejabat besar.

commissioned memegang kuasa; (*rank*) berpangkat.

commissioner, High C— Pesuruhjaya Tinggi.

commit, to — (*entrust*) mengamanatkan; (*to hand over*) menyerahkan; (*do*) berbuat (kejahatan dan sebagainya); to — to prison memenjarakan.

committee Jawatankuasa, badan menguasai.

commode (*chest of drawers*) almari laci.

commodious luas, besar.

commodity mata barang dagangan.

commodore komodor, angkatan laut atau udara yang tinggi.

common (*public*) umum, satu bersama; (*used in all*) sepakai; — factor pengisi rata; —room ruang duduk; — sense akal budi.

commoner orang kebanyakan, rakyat jelata.

commonly pada umumnya, pada ghalibnya.

commonplace lazim, biasa, kebanyakan.

commons rakyat jelata, orang banyak; House of C— Majlis Orangramai.

commonwealth persekutuan negeri, komanwel.

commotion kegemparan, kegaduhan, kerusuhan; to cause a — merusuhkan, menggemparkan.

communal satu bersama.

communicable yang dapat diberitahu (disiarkan).

communicant si penerima khabar suci.

communicate, to — (*give*) memberi; (*deliver over*) menyerahkan; (*inform*) memberitahu; (*to join with*) berhubungan dengan.

communication (*news etc*) pemberitahu, berita, khabar, warta; (*joining*) perhubungan.

communicative peramah, ceramah.

communion perhubungan suci.

communiqué maklumat.

communism faham komunis.

communist orang komunis.

community golongan, pergaulan, masyarakat.

commute, to — (*interchange*) tukar-menukar; (*reduce punishment etc*) mengurangi (hukuman yang berat).

commuter orang yang pulang balik berteket se-hari-hari.

compact I padat, padu, mampat; (*of figure*) begap; (*agreement*) perjanjian.

compact II, to — memandu, memadat.

companion teman, kawan, pengiring, saudara; — in arms saudara seperjuangan.

companionable peramah.

companionship persaudaraan, pertemanan.

company (*commerce*) rakanan, syarikat; (*group*) rombongan; in — tidak tersendiri.

comparable boleh dibandingkan.

compare, to — memper-

bandingkan; beyond — tidak ada bandingnya.

comparison perbandingan, persamaan; degrees of — tingkat perbandingan.

compartment (*small section, area, cube*) petak; (*room*) bilik.

compass (*for direction*) pedoman, kompas; pair of — es jangka.

compassion belas kasihan, rahmat.

compassionate berbelas kasihan.

compatible sepadan dengan.

compatriot saudara senegeri sebangsa, setanah air.

compel, to — memaksa, mengerasi.

compendium iktisar.

compensate, to — mengimbangi, membalas, mengganti, mengimbuh.

compensation gantirugi, penggantian, balasan, imbangan, imbuh.

compere pembicara pada pertunjukan tari-tarian (nyanyi dan sebagainya).

compete, to — beradu, berlawanan, bersaing, bertanding melawan; (*in race*) melomba; to — with menyaingi.

competence kecekapan, kesanggupan.

competent berhak; cekap; sanggup.

competition persaingan, perlombaan, perlawanan.

competitive bersaingan dengan.

competitor saingan.

compilation kumpulan, himpunan.

compile, to — mengumpulkan, menghimpunkan, menyusun.

complacence kepuasan akan dirinya.

complacent senang, puas akan dirinya.

complain, to — (*be worried*) mengeluh; (*state grievance*) mengadukan.

complaint dakwa, pendakwaan, pengaduan; to lodge a — mengadukan, mendakwa.

complement penggenap; to — menggenapkan, melengkapkan.

complementary penggenap, pelengkap.

complete genap, lengkap, sempurna; to — menyempurnakan, melengkapi.

completion penyelesaian, pelengkapan, kesudahan.

complex majmuk, bergabung, kusut, beragam; kompleks.

complexion warna roman, cahaya muka.

complexity kekusutan, kesulitan.

compliance penyesuaian; in — with sesuai dengan.

compliant lembut, beria-ia.

complicate, to — mencampurkan, membaurkan.

complicated kusut, sulit, campur-aduk.

complication kekusutan, kesulitan.

complicity hal menjadi kaki-tangan.

compliment pujian, perbahasaan; to — memuji.

comply, to — memenuhi (permintaan dan sebagainya); menurut.

component bahagian; komponen.

compose, to — merencanakan, menggubah, mengarangkan; (*arrange*) menyusun; to — o.s. menenangkan diri.

composer penggubah.

composite majmuk, bergabung.

composition (*arrangement, order*) penyusunan, pengaturan, susunan; (*literary*) karangan, rencana.

compositor penyusun huruf, pencetak.

compost baja campuran.

composure ketenangan.

compound (*house and garden*) kampung; majmuk; (*complex*) katamajmuk; — fraction pecahan majmuk.

comprehend, to — (*understand*) memahamkan, mengerti; (*comprise*) mengandung.

comprehensible dapat difahamkan.

comprehension faham, pengertian.

comprehensive yang berkenaan dengan pengertian; (*wide*) luas, lengkap.

compress (*med*) kompres; (*cold*) penjaram (dingin); (*hot*) tuam (panas); to — memadatkan, memampatkan.

compressed terpicit, padat.

compression pemampatan.

comprise, to — (*include*) mengandung.

compromise bertolak-ansur, perdamaian; to — berdamai; mendamaikan; kompromi.

compulsion kewajiban, keharusan, paksaan.

compulsive harus, perlu, wajib.

compulsory perlu, diwajibkan; to make — mengharuskan memaksakan; (*by religion*) mewajibkan.

compunction sesal, kesesalan.

computation perhitungan, hisab, perkiraan.

compute, to — mengira menghitung.

comrade teman, kawan, saudara.

comradeship persaudaraan.

con, to — mempelajari.

concave lekuk, bulat cekung.

conceal, to — menyembunyikan, menyamarkan.

concealment persembunyian.

concede mengakui, menga-bulkan.

conceit kesombongan.

conceited sombong, bongkak.

conceivable dapat difaham-kan.

conceive, to — (*become pregnant*) menjadi hamil, bun-ting, mengandung; (*imagine*) fikir, sangka.

concentrate, to — (*centralize*) memusatkan; (*of liquids*) me-mekatkan; to — (up)on memusatkan kepada.

concentrated pekat pati.

concentration pemusatan; pati kepekatan; — camp pertawanan.

concentric sama pusat, bula-tan.

concept faham, pengertian, tanggapan.

conception (*idea*) faham, pengertian, buah fikiran.

concern (*affair*) hal, perkara; (*concerning*) berkenaan de-ngan; (*apprehension*) kekhua-tiran, kemasygulan.

concert I (*agreement*) persetu-juan, persatuan; in — with sesuai dengan, setuju dengan.

concert II, to — menguruskan bersama-sama, bermuafakat.

concertina sejenis alat muzik.

concerto karangan muzik untuk suatu alat muzik de-ngan pengiringan pancaragam.

concession (*special approval*) keutamaan pengkabulan; (*of land*) sebidang tanah yang diberi kepada seseorang (atau salah satu perusahaan dan sebagainya).

conch kepah, siput.

conciliate, to — menda-maikan, berdamai.

conciliation perdamaian.

conciliatory berdamai.

concise ringkas, singkat, pen-dek.

conclave rapat, tertutup.

conclude, to — mengakhiri memutuskan, menarik kesim-pulan, menyimpulkan.

conclusion akhir, kesudahan, penghabisan; keputusan, ke-simpulan; **to draw a** — menarik kesimpulan.

conclusive yang meyakinkan.

concoct, to — (*drugs etc*) mencampur; (*to make up, invent*) mereka-rekakan, membuat-buat.

concoction campuran; reka.

concomitant yang menyer-tai; seiring dengan; a — sesuatu yang terjadi pada waktu itu juga.

concord kerukunan, per-sesuaian.

concourse perhimpunan.

concrete konkrit, berwujud; (*of evidence etc*) benar.

concubine gundik, madu.

concur, to — terjadi serentak; sela sekata, setuju.

concurrence persesuaian, persetujuan.

concurrent sejajar, seiring.

concussion goncangan, ge-garan.

condemn, to — menyalah-kan; menghukumkan.

condemnation penyalahan; (*judicial*) hukuman.

condensation (*physical*) pe-ngentalan, zat pekat.

condense, to — mengen-talkan; (*concentrate*) memusat-kan; (*shorten*) meringkaskan; —d kental; ringkas; pelowap.

condescend, to — meramahi orang secara orang golongan atas terhadap orang bawahan.

condescension keramahan terhadap orang bawahan.

condiment rempah, rencah, lauk.

condition (*stipulation*) syarat, janji; (*circumstances*) keadaan; **in good** — dalam keadaan baik.

conditional bersyarat.

condolence bela sungkawa, ucapan takziah.

condone, to — mengampuni, memaafkan.

conduce, to — membantu akan mencapai sesuatu, mendatangkan.

conducive yang membantu akan mencapai sesuatu.

conduct I (*lead*) pemimpinan; (*behaviour*) laku, kelakuan.

conduct II, to — (*send under escort*) menghantarkan; (*guide, lead*) memimpin; to — o.s. berlaku, berkelakuan.

conductor (*guide*) pemimpin; (*in charge of*) penghantar; lightning — penurun kilat.

conduit aliran, pipa, saluran, selokan.

cone (*conical leaf*) kerucut, kun; benda-benda yang menyerupai kerucut; —shaped (*of heap, pile*) runjung, kuncup.

confection manisan, kuih; (*clothing*) pakaian perempuan.

confectioner tukang kuih, pembuat kuih dan manis-manisan.

confectionery kuih-kuih, manisan.

confederacy persekutuan.

confederate sekutu; a — sekutu; (*accomplice*) kakitangan; to — bersatu, bersekutu.

confederation persekutuan.

confer, to — (*give*) memberi, menganugerahkan; (*debate*) berunding.

conference perundingan, muktamar, majlis.

confess, to — (*acknowledge*) mengikrar, mengakui; (*admit guilt*) terima salah.

confession ikrar, pengakuan.

confessor padri yang mendengarkan pengikraran dosa.

confetti kertas-kertas berwarna yang dilemparkan orang pada perkahwinan dan sebagainya.

confidant(e) orang yang diberi tahukan hal rahsia.

confide, to — mencurahkan kepercayaan, mempercayai.

confidence kepercayaan, keyakinan; (*fearlessness*) keberanian; in — dengan rahsia.

confident berkeyakinan; berani.

confidential dengan mencurahkan kepercayaan; dipegang rahsia.

configuration (*arrangement*) cara susunan; (*appearance*) rupa, bangun.

confine I, —s batas, daerah pembatas.

confine II, to — (*restrain*) menahan; (*imprison*) meringkukkan, memenjarakan.

confinement pengurungan; (*childbirth*) bersalin, beranak.

confirm, to — membenarkan, mengakui, mengesahkan.

confirmation pengesahan, pembenaran, penegasan.

confiscate, to — merampas.

confiscation rampasan.

conflagration kebakaran besar.

conflict I pertentangan, perselisihan, perkelahian.

conflict II, to — (*in meaning*) berselisih faham.

confluence (*esp of rivers*) kuala.

confluent bertemu.

conform, to — (to) menyesuaikan diri kepada, menyerupai menyerupakan.

conformable sebunyi, sekata, sebanding dengan.

conformity kesamaan, persesuaian.

confound, to — (*defeat*) mengalahkan; (*perplex*) membaurkan, mengusutkan.

confront, to — berhadapan

dengan, bersemuka dengan, menentang.

confuse, to — mengelirukan, mengacaukan.

confused bingung, terharu, kacau, kelam-kabut.

confusion haru-biru, kacau-bilau, kerusuhan; in — haru-biru.

congeal, to — membekukan, mengentalkan.

congenial sesuai, serasi.

congenital dari hari lahir.

conger, — eel sejenis belut besar.

congest, to — bermuat sarat-sarat; memuatkan surat-surat.

congestion keadaan penuh sesak.

conglomerate berkumpul, berkepal, kelompok, kumpulan; to — mengelompokkan.

congratulate, to — memberi selamat, mengucapkan selamat, tahniah.

congratulation ucapan selamat, ucapan tahniah.

congregate, to — berhimpun, berkumpul; menghimpunkan, mengumpulkan.

congregation (any assembly) kumpulan; (religious assembly) jamaah.

congress muktamar, kongres; dewan perwakilan rakyat di negeri Amerika.

congruent sesuai, patut, sama.

conic(al) mengerucut, runjung, berupa kun.

conifer sejenis pohon tirus.

conjectural yang bersifat terkaan, agakan.

conjecture terkaan, tebakan; to — menerka, memebak, mengagak.

conjoin, to — berkumpul, bersatu; mengumpulkan.

conjugal yang berkenaan dengan kahwin.

conjunction hubungan, rangkaian; (grammar) kata penyambung, sendi-kata.

conjuncture ketika (terjadinya beberapa peristiwa).

conjure, to — (juggle) bersulap, bersilap; (produce magical effects) menyihirkan.

conjurer tukang silap mata, penyilap.

connect, to — menghubungkan, merangkaikan, menyangkutkan.

connected, — (with) bersambung, tersangkut, berhubung; well — perhubungannya baik.

connective yang menghubungkan, penghubung.

connection, connexion rangkaian, sambungan, perhubungan, pertalian.

connivance pembiaran.

connive, to — membiarkan sahaja, mengabulkan sesuatu yang sebetulnya tidak patut dikabulkan.

connoisseur orang yang tahu-menahu akan hal yang baik.

connotation erti makna yang terkandung dalam sepatah kata.

connubial yang berkenaan dengan kahwin, yang berkenaan dengan suami isteri.

conquer, to — mengalahkan, mengatasi, menaklukkan.

conqueror penakluk, pengalah.

conquest pengalahan, penaklukan.

consanguinity darah daging, pertalian keluarga sedarah.

conscience suara hati, angan-angan hati; to have a bad — insaf bahawa kelakuannya tidak baik.

conscientious saksama, teliti; — objector orang yang

menolak kewajiban kerana kemahuan hatinya.

conscious sedar, insaf; **to be — of** sedar akan, menginsafi.

consciousness kesedaran, keinsafan; **to regain —** siuman, balik sedar.

conscript I orang yang diwajibkan masuk tentera.

conscript II, to — mengerahkan.

conscription keraban askar.

consecrate (rel), **to —** mewakafkan.

consecration perwakafan, persucian.

consecutive berturut-turut, berikut, beriring.

consensus persesuaian, persetujuan.

consent pengabulan, persetujuan kerelaan, izin; **to give one's —** merelai.

consequence akibat, lanjutan pembawaan; **in — of** disebab oleh.

consequent (noun) kejadian kemudian; sepadan dengan yang mendahuluinya.

consequently oleh sebab itu.

conservancy penjagaan (hutan, sungai dan sebagainya).

conservation pengekalan, perlindungan.

conservatism kekunoan, kekolotan.

conservative beradat; faham tua, kolot; **a —** orang yang berpegang kepada adat istiadat.

conservatory sejenis bilik gelas tempat memeliharakan tumbuh-tumbuhan yang tidak sesuai dengan tanah dingin.

conserve, to — simpan; **—s** barang dalam tin makan.

consider timbang; **to —** menimbang, mengagak-agak, menyangkakan; (to think of others) ingat akan orang lain.

considerable jadi-jadi, penting bukan kepalang; **a — part** sebahagian besar.

considerate bertimbang, perasaan murah hati.

consideration pertimbangan, perhitungan, balasan; (for another person) ingat akan orang lain; **under —** sedang ditimbang.

consign, to — (hand over) menyerahkan; (transmit) mengirim.

consignment barang kiriman barang amanat; **goods on —** barang-barang amanat.

consist, to — of terdiri dari, ada.

consistency darjah, kental, kekukuhan.

consistent teguh, kukuh, terus-terusan.

consolation lipur, penghiburan.

console, to — melipur, menghiburkan.

consolidate, to — mengekalkan, mengukuhkan.

consolidation penguatan; persatuan, peneguhan.

consonant (letter of alphabet) hurut benar; (in accord) serta bunyi, selaras dengan.

consort I suami atau isteri seorang raja.

consort II, to — (accompany) menyertai; (agree) seia sekata.

conspicuous tampak nyata, ketara.

conspiracy komplot, perkongsian rahsia dan jahat.

conspirator orang yang turut serta dengan jahat.

conspire, to — perkongsian, bermuafakat dengan maksud buruk.

constable mata-mata, polis.

constabulary badan polis.

constancy ketetapan, kekukuhan, keteguhan; (loyalty) setia.

constant tetap, mantap, ke-kal; a — tetapan.

constellation bintang rasi, nujum.

consternation kebingung-an, perasaan dahsyat, hairan.

constipate, to — menjadikan sembelit.

constipation sembelit.

constituency golongan pe-milih anggota badan pemerin-tah.

constituent juzuk, unsur; (part) penyusun; (voter) orang pemilih.

constitute, to — menyusun, mengadakan, merupakan, menjadikan.

constitution (physical) resam tubuh; (composition) keadaan, susunan; (legal) undang-undang dasar, undang-undang tubuh, perlembagaan.

constitutional yang ber-kenaan dengan keadaan (tu-buh, jiwa atau negara); — law hukum negera.

constrain, to — (compel) memaksa; (imprison) me-ngurungkan; (hold) menahan.

constraint paksaan, (of con-duct) ketegangan, kelakuan tertahan.

constrict, to — (densely packed) memampatkan; (shrink) me-nguncup, mengucut.

constriction keadaan kun-cup, mampat.

construct, to — membentuk, membangunkan, membina.

construction pembentukan, pembangunan, pembinaan, ra-ngkaian.

constructive yang memben-tuk, pembentuk, penyusun, pembangun, pembina.

constructor pembangun, pembentuk, pembina.

construe, to — (translate) menyalin, menterjemahkan; (interpret) mentafsirkan.

consul konsol.

consulate konsulat.

consult, to — (seek advice) minta penerangan, nasihat; to — (with) berbincang, bermuafakat.

consultation (deliberation) muafakat, perbincangan; (asking advice) permintaan nasihat.

consume, to — (eat) makan; (use) memakai; (finish) meng-habiskan.

consumer pemakai; — goods keperluan hari-hari sebagai makanan (pakaian dan se-bagainya).

consummate I lengkap, sem-purna.

consummate II, to — me-nyempurnakan, melengkap-kan.

consummation penyem-purnaan, tujuan yang di-kehendaki.

consumption (use) pema-kaian; (disease) penyakit paru-paru, batuk kering.

consumptive (disease) kena penyakit paru-paru, batuk kering.

contact (liaison) perhubungan; (touching) persentuhan, per-temuan; to be in (come in to)) — with bersentuhan; mengenai, berhubungan; to — ber-hubungan.

contagion penjangkitan, penjalaran.

contagious menjangkit, menjalar.

contain, to — berisi, mengan-dung, bermuat; (restrain) me-nahan.

container tempat penyim-panan (sesuatu).

contaminate, to — menjang-kiti; —d kejangkitan, kena hama.

contamination penjang-kitan.

contemplate, to — (*actually or mentally*) memandang; (*stare at*) merenungkan.

contemplation kemenungan; renungan; (*intention*) maksud, tujuan.

contemplative termenung, tafakkur.

contemporaneous sezaman (yang terjadi atau hidup pada zaman itu juga).

contemporary sezaman; — orang yang hidup pada zaman itu juga.

contempt penghinaan, pengejian, kehinaan; — **of court** melalaikan hukum.

contemptible hina, keji.

contemptuous congkak.

contend, to — melawan, berbantah; **to** — **that** menetapkan bahawa, menegaskan bahawa.

content I (*satisfaction*) kepuasan; (*after warm feelings*) puas sejuk hati; **to** — memuaskan; **to** — **o.s. with** mencukupi.

content II (*capacity*) muatan; —**s** isi, barang apa yang dimuat (di dalam sesuatu).

contention pertengkaran, ketetapan, hal yang ditetapkan.

contest I perlumbaan, pertandingan.

contest II, to — membantahi, berlawan, berlumba.

contestant pelumba.

context bahagian yang mendahului suatu kalimat (atau ayat) dan bahagian berikutnya.

contiguous rapat, dekat.

continent (*mainland*) benua, daratan; **the C**—(**of** Europe) benua Eropah.

continental yang berkenaan dengan benua; penduduk benua Eropah.

contingency sesuatu yang harus terjadi, suatu akibat yang belum tentu.

contingent tak tentu, kebetulan, harus; a — (*troops*) pasukan, tentera.

continual selalu, senantiasa.

continuation sambungan, lanjutan.

continue, to — meneruskan, menyambung, melanjutkan.

continuity penerusan.

continuous selamanya, selalu, senantiasa, terus, tidak bersela, tak berhentinya.

contort, to — meliuk lampai, memulas, membelit, memiluh.

contortion piuhan, belitan.

contortionist orang yang pandai meliuk lampai membelit-belitkan badannya.

contour garis luaran, sama tinggi; (*curved shape*) bentuk.

contra— lawan.

contraband (*goods*) barangbarang gelap; (*forbidden*) seludupan, larangan; — **trade** dagang gelap.

contraceptive pencegah penghamilan.

contract I (*agreement*) persetujuan, perjanjian, akad; — **of sale** akad jual beli.

contract II, to — (*enter an agreement*) berjanji, mengusahakan perniagaan, mengadakan perkahwinan; (*shrink*) mengecut.

contraction penguncupan, peringkasan.

contractor perusaha, pemborong.

contradict, to — menyalahi, melawan, menyangkal.

contradictory bersalahan, berlawanan dengan, bertentangan.

contralto suara perempuan yang terlebih rendah.

contraption perkakas yang ganjil.

contrary sebaliknya, berlawanan, bersalahan; **the** — lawan, kebalikan.

contrast I pertentangan, berlawan.

contrast II, to — bertentangan dengan; memperlawankan.

contravene, to — melanggar, melawani, berlawan, dengan.

contravention pelanggaran.

contribute, to — (*support*) menyokong; (*hand over*) menyerahkan; to — to membantu akan.

contribution sokongan, derma, yuran, bantuan; (*article in writing*) karangan.

contributive, contributory yang membantu, menyokong, menambah.

contrite sesal hati, bertobat.

contrition sesalan

contrivance (*thing contrived*) pendapatan; (*device*) muslihat, daya.

contrive, to — merancangkan, menciptakan.

control kawalan, pengamatan, pengendalian; pengaruh; to — memeriksa; (*restrict*) menahani.

controller pengawas

controversial bertentangan, berlawanan.

controversy pertentangan, pertengkaran.

contusion luka memar, lebam.

conundrum teka-teki.

conurbation kumpulan bandar-bandar.

convalesce, to — menjadi waras, sembuh.

convalescence keadaan hampir sembuh.

convalescent balik sembuh, waras; a — orang yang baharu sembuh.

convene, to — berkumpul, menghimpunkan, memanggil orang akan bermesyuarat.

convenience kenikmatan, kesenangan, untung; (*lavatory*) bilik jamban, tandas.

convenient nikmat, senang.

convent biara.

convention (*assembly*) perkumpulan; (*agreement*) persetujuan.

conventional menurut kebiasaan, yang telah lazim biasa.

converge, to — memusat, berkumpul, mengumpul.

convergence hal memusat, pertemuan.

conversant kerap bertemu dengan; berhubungan dengan; berpengetahuan akan.

conversation percakapan, perbualan.

conversational yang berkenaan dengan percakapan perbualan.

converse I, to — bercakap-cakap.

converse II (*opposite*) sebaliknya, berlawanan, lawan, perlawanan.

conversion perubahan, pemindahan; (*rel*) pemasukan ugama.

convert I orang yang baharu memeluk ugama.

convert II, to — mengubahkan, memindahkan; (*rel*) memasukkan ugama.

convertible dapat balik, dapat diubahkan.

convex bulat cembung, lungkum.

convey, to — menyampaikan, membawa, mengangkut.

conveyance penghantaran, pembawaan; (*vehicle*) kenderaan.

conveyor pembawa, pengangkut.

convict I orang hukuman, orang salah.

convict II, to — menghukum.

conviction (*verdict of guilty*) penghukuman; (*firm belief*) keyakinan.

convince, to — meyakinkan,

menginsafkan; —d yakin, insaf, percaya.

convivial riang gembira. suka-cita.

convocation panggilan akan berapat, perkumpulan.

convoke, to — memanggil akan mesyuarat.

convoy pengiringan, penghantaran; (*protective*) perlindungan.

convulse, to — menggeletarkan, menggeliatkan, menggeleparkan.

convulsion geliat, gelepar, sawan.

convulsive gelepar, kejang.

coo dekut, kukuran; to — mendekut, berkukur.

cook jurumasak; to — (*col: falsify*) mengakali.

cooker (*utensil*) pemasak, panci.

cookery masak-memasak, masak-masakan; — book buku masakan.

cookie kuih kecil.

cooking pot kuali, periuk.

cool dingin, sejuk; (*calm*) tenang, berani; to — (off) mendingin, menyejukkan.

cooler alat pendingin, penyejuk; (*col: gaol*) penjara.

coolie kuli.

coolness kesejukan.

coop sangkar reban; to — (up) mengurungkan, menyangkarkan.

cooperate, to — syarikat, bekerjasama.

cooperation syarikat kerjasama.

cooperative yang bersyarikat.

coordinate seimbang, selaras, setara; to — mengimbangkan, menyetarakan, mempersetujukan.

coordination penyesuaian penyelarasan.

coot sejenis burung meliwis.

cop, (*col*) to — menangkap.

cop(**per**) (*col*) mata-mata, polis.

copper lembaga merah; (*coin*) matawang tembaga.

copartner rakan.

copartnership rakan istimewa, jika para buruh juga mendapat syir.

cope, to — with menempuh dengan berhasil.

copious mewah, sangat banyak.

coppice, copse semak, belukar.

copra kopra, kelapa kering.

copula dalam tata-bahasa; kopula, kata menyatukan.

copulate, to — bersetubuh.

copulation setubuh, persetubuhan.

copy salinan; to — menyalin, meniru, mencontoh.

copyright hak pengarang, hakcipta.

coquette perempuan yang mempermainkan orang laki-laki.

coral batukarang; red — merjan; — reef benteng karang.

cord tali, tambang; (*ribbed fabric*) sejenis kain tebal; to — mengikat dengan tali tambang.

cordial (*drink*) ubat penyegar; (*of manner*) ramah-tamah.

cordon barisan lengkongan daripada polis atau military.

corduroy sejenis kain tebal.

core (*of fruit*) rumah biji (buah-buahan); (*inner part*) pusat, inti, teras.

co-respondent orang yang dituduh bersama dengan orang terdakwa dalam perkara perceraian laki jsteri.

coriander ketumbar.

cork (*spongy wood*) gabus; (*for bottle*) sumbat; —screw koterek; to — menyumbat.

corm umbi, ubi.

cormorant sejenis burung laut.

corn I biji, butir, biji-bijian, jagung, padi-padian; —**cob** tongkol jagung.

corn II (*on foot*) katimumul.

corner penjuru, liku, pelosok, sudut; —**stone** batu; dasar, bahagian penting.

cornet sejenis alat muzik.

corollary akibat yang pasti, balikan.

coronation upacara naik takhta, penabalan.

coroner pegawai negeri yang pekerjaannya memeriksa selok-belok suatu kematian yang disebabkan oleh kemalangan atau pembunuhan; —'s inquest pemeriksaan oleh pegawai tersebut.

coronet mahkota kecil.

corporal I yang berkenaan dengan badan, jasmani.

corporal II (*mil*) pangkat kopral.

corporate syarikat, sekutu, bersekutu, badan.

corporation persyarikatan, persekutuan, perbadanan.

corporeal jasmani, badan.

corps (*mil*) bahagian tentera; (*assembly*) kumpulan.

corpse mayat, jenazah, bangkai.

corpulence kegemukan, kebayakan.

corpulent gemuk, bayak, gendut.

corpuscle sel darah.

corral pagaran, kandang kuda, lembu dan sebagainya; to — memasukkan ke dalam kandang itu.

correct tetap, betul, benar; (*proper*) patut; to — memperbaiki, mematikan, membetulkan; (*adjust*) menyesuaikan; (*reprove*) mengajar.

correction pembetulan, perbaikan.

corrective pengajaran; sesuatu yang akan memperbaiki hal yang buruk.

correctness kebenaran.

correlate suatu yang berhubungan dengan sesuatu yang lain; to — berhubung dengan, bertalian dengan; memperhubungkan.

correlation perhubungan, pertalian, perantaraan.

correlative yang berhubungan, bertalian dengan.

correspond to — (*agree with*) sesuai dengan, sepakat dengan, sama dengan, berbetulan dengan; (*send letters*) berkirim surat.

correspondence (*agreement*) persesuaian, persetujuan; (*letters*) surat-menyurat.

correspondent (*regarding news*) pemberita, koresponden, pembawa berita; (*in trade*) orang atau perusahaan yang tetap berniaga dengan salah sebuah perusahaan yang lain; — with sesuai dengan.

corridor lorong jalan dalam rumah.

corrigible dapat diperbaiki.

corroborate, to — menetapkan menyungguhkan, menguatkan.

corroboration penyungguhan, penguatan.

corrode, to — dimakan karat, berkarat.

corrosion karat.

corrugate, to — beralur, bergelugur, mengerut.

corrupt (*rotten*) busuk, keruh; to — membusukkan merusakkan, membinasakan.

corruptible dapat disuapi.

corruption kebusukan, kekeruhan.

corset sejenis baju kutang, korset.

cortege pawai.

cosh (*col*) cokmar, penggada;

to — memukul dengan cokmar.

cosmetic bahan pemanis, alat kecantikan, bedak, celak.

cosmic duniawi yang berkenaan dengan alam.

cosmopolitan, a — city bandar yang penduduknya berasal dari berbagai-bagai negeri dunia.

cosmos alam dunia.

cost harga, biaya, pembelanjaan, perbelanjaan; at all —s tak boleh tidak.

coster(monger) penjaja.

costly mahal, berharga.

costume pakaian.

cosy sedap, nikmat; tea — tudung teh.

cot tempat tidur anak; kandang.

coterie kalangan masyarakat.

cottage pondok, rumah kecil.

cottager orang yang diam di sebuah pondok rumah.

cotton kapas; (cloth) kain kapas; — wool kapas; — yarn benang kapas.

couch ranjang, bangku, balaibalai.

cough batuk; to — batuk, berdaham.

council dewan, majlis; security — dewan keamanan.

councillor anggota dewan (majlis).

counsel nasihat, bicara; (person) pembicara, penasihat; — for the defence pembela.

counsellor penasihat.

count I hisab, kira, perhitungan jumlah; to — membilang, menghitung.

count II (title) gelar orang bangsawan.

countenance paras, air muka wajah.

counter (in shop) meja di kedai; (in gambling) biji (salah satu benda dari tulang atau gading yang dipakai se-

bagai matawang pada mainan terup), bertentangan; to — melawan.

counteract, to — menentangi, merintangi.

counter-attack serang balas.

counterbalance imbangan, timbalan; to — menimbali, menimbangi.

counter-clockwise perjalanan lawan jarum jam.

counter-espionage pekerjaan intip terhadap kepada intipan pihak musuh.

counterfeit lancung, falsu; to — melancung, memalsukan.

counterfoil pokok surat (surat tanda pada cek dan sebagainya yang dipegang oleh yang empunya).

countermand perintah akan membatalkan perintah lebih dahulu.

counterpane kain di atas tempat tidur.

counterpart (a double) pasangan; (an opposite) lawan.

counterpoint (in music) lagu yang menyertai lagu asli.

counterpoise imbangan; to — mengimbangi.

countersign tandatangan pada surat yang telah ditandatangani lebih dahulu.

countess gelar perempuan yang berbangsa.

counting house pejabat.

countless tidak terpermanai.

countrified di luar bandar.

country negara, negeri; hulu, desa; native — tanahair.

county jajahan negeri, daerah.

coup (d'état) rebutan kekuasaan, kudeta.

couple pasang; a — of dua; married — sekelamin, bini.

couplet satu bahagian dalam suatu syair.

coupling alat penghubung.

coupon sijil, carik, kopan.

courage keberanian, keperkasaan, kegagahan; **to take —** memberanikan hati.

courageous berani, gagah, perkasa, perwira.

courier (*messenger*) pengantar; (*for tourists*) pengurus rombongan pelancung.

course (*direction*) tujuan, arah, haluan; (*movement*) perjalanan, kursus; **of —** memang.

court I (*of royalty*) dalam, istana; (*of law*) pengadilan, mahkamah; **—yard** halaman, lapangan; **supreme —** mahkamah tinggi.

court II, to —, pay **— to** meminang, main muda.

courteous berbudi bahasa, tahu adat.

courtesan perempuan jalang, sundal.

courtesy budi bahasa.

courtier orang istana.

court-martial mahkamah tentera.

courtship peminangan.

cousin, (first) **—** saudara sepupu; **second —** saudara dua pupu.

cove teluk kecil.

covenant perjanjian, waad; **to —** bersetuju, berjanji.

Coventry, to send s.o. to — tidak mahu bercampur lagi dengan seseorang.

cover tutup tudung sarung, selimut; (*shade*) perlindungan; **to —** meliputi; melindungi.

covert tersembunyi rahsia.

covet, to — melubakan, mengingini.

covetous ingin, luba.

covey (*birds*) seperindukan ayam hutan, sekawan; (*a set*) kelompok, kawan.

cow lembu; (binatang betina, gajah, badak dan sebagainya); **to —** menakuti.

coward penakut, pengecut; **—ly** kecil hati.

cowardice kecut kecil hati.

cowboy, cowhand koboi, pembantu peternak lembu.

cower, to — berdekam, merangkung kerang ketakutan.

cowhide kulit lembu.

cowl (*of monk*) kerudung orang rahib; (*chimney*) cerubung; ketupung.

cox, coxswain pengemudi sampan.

coy tersipu-sipu, kemalumaluan.

crab kepiting, ketam.

crabbed, — handwriting tulisan cakar ayam.

crack (*of sound*) letus, tembakan; (*aperture*) retak, celah; **to —** (*break*) meretakkan, memecahkan.

cracker sejenis bunga api, petas, mercun; semacam biskut.

crackle, to — gemertak, gemerincik.

cradle ayunan, buaian; (*place of birth*) tempat lahir.

craft (*skill*) kepandaian; (*trade*) pertukangan; (*ship*) kapal.

craftsman tukang, orang utas, pandai.

craftsmanship kepandaian, kecakapan.

crafty pintar, busuk, akal kancil.

crag batu (karang) yang tinggi dan runcing.

cram, to — (*pack*) memadatkan; (*for exam*) menghafazkan sesuatu benar-benar (istimewa untuk ujian).

crammed penuh padat.

cramp ular-ular, kekejangan; **to —** menyempitkan.

crane (*machine*) jentera pengangkut; (*bird*) burung jenjang; **to —** one's **neck** menghulurkan leher.

crank (*handle of machine*) putaran, pemutar; **to — up** memutar jentera.

cranky pelik, setengah gila.

cranny celah, genggang.

craps sejenis judi.

crash (*noise*) dentum; (*crash down*) runtuh, roboh; to — jatuh, rebah, hancur.

crass sangat bebal.

crate pembungkus (bambu, kayu dan sebagainya).

crater kawah gunung berapi, lubang.

crave, to — (for) ketagih, mengingini mengidam.

craving tagih, idam, keinginan.

crawl (*swimming*) sejenis gaya berenang; to — merayap, merangkak, menjalar; (*sneak into*) menyelinap.

crayfish, crawfish udang karang.

crayon pensil atau kapur berwarna dipakai untuk melukis gambar.

craze kegilaan.

craziness kegilaan.

crazy gila, sakit ingatan; to be — about gila akan.

creak kertak, kersuk; to — mengertak, mengersuk.

cream kepala susu; (*for face*) pupuk muka, bahagian yang terlebih baik; —coloured putih kuning.

creamery tempat membuat, memakai atau menjual mentega.

crease kerut, kerdut, lipatan; to — berkerut, mengerutkan.

create, to — melahirkan, mengadakan, menjadikan.

creation kejadian, penjadian, ciptaan.

creative membina, pencipta, yang mencipta.

creator khalikul-alam, pencipta.

creature khalayak, makhluk.

creche tempat penjagaan anak kecil.

credence kepercayaan.

credentials surat kepercayaan.

credible boleh dipercayai.

credit (*belief*) kepercayaan; (*reputation*) nama baik; (*financial*) piutang, kredit; debit and — hutang piutang.

creditable yang membawa nama baik.

creditor penagih, orang perhutangan.

credulity sifat lekas percayakan orang.

credulous lekas percaya orang.

creed kepercayaan, syahadat.

creek teluk, rantau; caruk.

creep, the —s rasa seram ngeri; to — (*also* crept) merangkak, merayap, menjalar, gelangsar.

creeper (*plant*) tanaman yang menjalar, ulah.

creepy geli, seram, ngeri, mengerikan, menyeramkan.

creese keris.

cremate, to — membakar mayat.

cremation pembakaran mayat.

crematory, crematorium tempat pembakaran mayat.

creosote minyak kreosot.

crescent bulan perhani, bulan sabit, lengkungan bulan; barang apa yang menyerupai sabit.

crest (*hair, feather etc*) jambul; (*hill*) puncak, kemuncak; (*emblem*) lambang; (*aigrette*) tajuk; to — berpuncak, berjambul.

cretin kerdil dan pandir.

crevasse jurang airbatu.

crevice belah, celah.

crew (*of ship*) anak kapal; (*workmates*) orang yang bekerja sekelompok.

crib (*for horse etc*) tempat makanan untuk kuda (lembu dan sebagainya); (*child's cot*) tempat tidur anak.

cribbage sejenis main terup.

crick, a — in one's neck kejang leher; **to —** mengejangkan.

cricket (*grasshopper*) belalang, jangkerik; (*game*) sejenis main bola.

crier pencanang, penyeru.

crime kejahatan, kesalahan, jenayat.

criminal jahat, kriminil; penjahat; **—** code kitab undang-undang jenayat; **—** law hukum jenayat.

criminology ilmu jenayat.

crimp, to — mengerutkan.

crimson merah lembayung, merah padam.

cringe, to — (*stock*) tunduk, membongkok; (*abase o.s.*) menghinakan diri.

crinkle kisut; **to —** berkisut; mengisut.

cripple pincang, tempang; **a —** orang pincang, berjalan pincang.

crisis kegentingan, krisis.

crisp garing, rangup, mersik; **potato —s** kerepek kentang.

criss-cross pencong-mencong lintang-kedak.

criterion batujlan, ukuran, sukatan.

critic pengupas, pengeritik.

critical (*inquiring*) selidik; (*strained, dangerous*) genting, musykil, berbahaya; **—** situation kegentingan.

criticism kupasan, kritik.

criticize, to — mengupas, membahas, mengeritik, memecat.

croak, to — menguak, menggauk.

crochet, to — mengait, merenda.

crockery periuk belanga, barang, tembikar.

crocodile buaya; **to shed —** tears menangis pura-pura.

crocus sejenis bunga.

croft sebidang tanah sawah

atau kepunyaan orang tani.

crofter petani.

crone orang perempuan yang tua.

crony teman karib.

crook keluk; (*rogue*) penjahat, penipu.

crooked bengkok, bengkung; (*evil*) jahat; **—** legs pengkar.

croon, to — bersenandung, menyanyi, menyanyi secara perlahan-lahan.

crooner penyanyi secara perlahan-lahan.

crop (*of fowl*) tembolok; (*agriculture*) hasil bumi; (*plants*) tanaman; (*haircut*) potongan rambut; **to —** memotong, memangkas.

croquette keroket.

cross I (*crucifix*) salib; (*mark*) tanda silang; (*of animals etc*) perkahwinan antara binatang yang agak berlainan rupanya; **Red C—** palang merah.

cross II silang, melintang; (*thwart*) lawan, merengut, marah; **to —** melintangi, mengalangi.

crossbar sengkang, palang.

crossbeam palang, sengkang.

crossbred peranakan.

crosscut penampang, rentas.

cross-examine, to — memeriksa, menyelidiki jawaban dan perkataan orang sekali lagi dengan sangat teliti.

cross-eyed juling.

crossing persilangan; (**—** place) tempat penyeberang, tempat melintas.

cross-legged berhimpit kaki, bersila.

cross-purposes tujuan (maksud) yang belawanan.

crossroad(s) jalan simpang empat, persimpangan.

cross-stitch jahit silang.

crosswise lintang, silang.

crossword, — puzzle sejenis teka-teki, teka silangkata.

crotch (*anat*) pangkal paha; (*of branch*) pangkal dahan.

crotchet (*mus*) satu titinada.

crouch to — meringkok, membongkok.

croupier peraih wang dalam main judi.

crow burung gagak; to — (*of cocks*) berkokok.

crowbar perejang, pengumpil, tuil.

crowd orang banyak, khalayak ramai; to — berkerumun, berduyun-duyun.

crowded (*of persons*) ramai; (*of places*) penuh sesak.

crown tajuk, mahkota; puncak; (*Government*) raja, kerajaan; —prince putera mahkota.

crucial genting, kemelut.

crucifix patung salib.

crucifixion penyaliban.

crucify, to — menyalibkan.

crude (*raw*) mentah; (*rough*) kasar.

cruel zalim, kejam ganas; (*causing injury*) yang menyakiti.

cruelty keganasan, kekejaman, kebengisan.

cruise pelayaran; to — payar, memayari, belayar.

cruiser kapal pemayar, kapal penjelajah.

crumb remah.

crumble, to — meremahremah, merepih.

crumbly repih, kersai.

crumpet sejenis kuih.

crumple, to — (up) berkisut, merenyok, menggumalkan; (*collapse*) roboh.

crunch kerkah; to — mengkerkah.

crusade (*Christian*) perang salib; (*any campaign against evil*) gerakan akan mengatasi hal yang buruk.

crusader salah satu pejuang perang salib; pendekar.

crush penghancuran; (*crowd*) kumpulan ramai; to — menghancurkan; (*grind spices*) menggiling.

crust kulit, kerak; to — berkerak.

crusty berkulit keras; (*angry*) marah; (*of speech*) tajam perkataan.

crutch (forked stick) topang; (*of cripple*) tongkat ketiak.

crux kemusykilan, soal pati.

cry seruan, teriakan; (*weep*) tangis; to — berseru, menangis.

crypt gua permakaman.

cryptic rahsia, tersembunyi.

crystal hablur.

crystallize, to — menghablurkan.

cub anak serigala, anak harimau (atau binatang buas yang lain).

cube kubus, dadu, kiub.

cubic dadu; — measure ukuran isipadu.

cubicle petak, bilik tidur yang kecil sekali.

cubism salah satu gaya seni.

cubit hasta.

cuckoo sejenis burung; —clock sejenis loceng.

cucumber mentimun, ketimun.

cud makanan yang dimamah binatang; *see* chew.

cuddle rangkuman; to — merangkum, melekap.

cudgel gada, belantan.

cue (*signal to act etc*) tanda (isyarat) akan berbuat atau mengatakan sesuatu; alat pemain billiards.

cuff (*of coat*) lipat tangan; (*blow*) tempeleng; to — menempeleng, menggocoh.

culinary yang berkenaan dengan masak-memasak.

culminate, to — memuncak; culminating point puncak.

culmination puncak, hal memuncak.

culpable jahat, bersalah, tercela.

culprit orang yang bersalah (berdosa).

cult pemujaan, pujaan, penyembahan.

cultivate, to — (*plants etc*) menanami, menanamkan; (*practise*) mengusah.ukan.

cultivation tanaman, penanaman; (*use*) pengusahaan.

cultural budaya, yang berkenaan dengan kebudayaan.

culture (*of growth*) perkembangan; (*intellectual*) kebudayaan, peradaban; (*good manners*) budi bahasa; to — mengembangkan.

cultured berbudi, beradab.

culvert saluran air di bawah jalan dan sebagainya, pembetung.

cumbersome, cumbrous kaku, kekok, canggung.

cummerbund ikat pinggang.

cumulative bertambah-tambah.

cumulus (*heap*) longgok; (*clouds*) awan berkepul-kepul, awan kemawan.

cunning kelicikan; cerdik, licin, pintar busuk, pintar belit.

cup mangkuk, cangkir, cawan; (*prize* —) piala.

cupboard almari piring, gerobok.

Cupid salah satu dewa Runawi yang boleh dibandingkan dengan Kamajaya.

cupidity keloban.

cupola kubah, atap merelung.

cur anjing geladak.

curate seorang padri pembantu.

curator kurator, penyelenggara, pemelihara (buku, benda berharga dan sebagainya).

curb (*bridle*) kendali; (*of road*) pinggir jalan tepi; to — mengendalikan, menahan.

curd dadih.

curdle, to — dadih, bergumpal, membeku.

cure (*remedy*) ubat, pengubatan; (*healed*) kesembuhan; to — menyembuhkan.

curfew .am malam waktu larangan berjalan malam, berkurung.

curio barang (benda) ajaib.

curiosity keinginan tahu; (*article*) barang ajaib.

curious ingin tahu, kemahuan tahu; (*abnormal: of person*) pelik.

curl ikal; to — mengikal, mengeriting; (*roll*) bergulung.

curlew sejenis burung.

curly ikal keriting.

currant buah kismis.

currency lakunya wang, alat pembayaran wang.

current yang berlaku, karan, aliran, pengaliran, harus; alternating — arus ulangalik; direct — arus terus.

curriculum susunan (recana) mata pengajaran, bidang pelajaran.

curry I kari, gulai; to — memasak (atau menambah) kari.

curry II, —comb keruk; to — menggaruk, mengeruk.

curse laknat, kutuk sumpah, kecelakaan; to — mengutuki.

cursory sepintas lalu.

curt pendek singkat, ringkas.

curtail, to — memuntungkan mengudungkan, memotong.

curtain tirai, tabir.

curtsy, curtsey tunduk; to — tunduk, membongkok beri hormat.

curvature bentuk lengkung, garis bengkok.

curve garis lengkung, lentur, keluk; to — melengkung, melentur.

cushion bantal alas; to — memberi bantal, mengelilingi dengan bantal.

custard sejenis makanan manis.

custodian penjaga, wakil.

custody (*of unmarried girl*) perwalian; (*safe keeping*) pemeliharaan; (*imprisonment*) hukuman kurungan penjara.

custom adat, resam, kebiasaan, kelaziman.

customary biasa, lazim, adat.

customer langganan; a queer — orang pelek.

custom house pebean, pejabat kastam, rumah cukai.

cut I potongan, tampang; (*wound*) luka; a short — pintasan.

cut II, to — memotong, membelah, meraut, menyabit; to — down memotong, menebang; to — short memintas.

cut-away di depan.

cute (*clever*) pintar; (*charming*) manis, jelita.

cuticle kulit ari.

cutlass sejenis pisau belati.

cutler pembuat atau penjual pisau dan sebagainya.

cutlery alat pemotong, pisau, garpu, senduk dan sebagainya.

cutlet sepotong daging goreng.

cutter pemotong; sejenis kapal.

cutting (*in horticulture*) cangkuk; (*from newspaper*) potongan suratkhabar.

cuttlefish ikan kurita, sotong.

cyclamen sejenis bunga.

cycle peredaran, pusingan, lengkaran; (*abbr of bicycle*) besikal; to — berbesikal.

cyclist pengendara besikal, orang yang berbesikal.

cyclone punca beliung, pusaran angin, angin putar ke dalam.

cyclostyle sejenis alat pencetak, membuat salinan.

cygnet anak angsa swan.

cylinder selindar, toraktorak.

cylindrical panjang bulat, bulat torak.

cymbal gembereng, canang, gong.

cynic orang yang kelakuannya 'pedas-pedih'.

cynical bersifat 'pedas-pedih'.

cypress sejenis pohon.

cyst risa; (*urinary bladder*) pundi-pundi kencing.

D

dab persinggungan yang sedikit, sentuhan; to — at menolak sedikit.

dabble (*splash*) memerciki.

dachshund sebangsa anjing yang pendek kakinya.

dad, daddy ayah, pak.

daddy-long-legs sebangsa nyamuk yang panjang kakinya.

daffodil bunga kuning.

daft pandir, gila.

dagger tumbak lada, keris, pisau belati (dan lain-lain).

dago (*pej*) orang Sepanyol, Portugis atau Itali, orang Eropah Selatan.

daily tiap-tiap hari; (*newspaper*) khabar harian.

dainty elok, cantik, halus, baik; — bit makanan sedap, penganan.

dairy (*shop*) kedai susu; (*farm*) tempat memerah susu.

dairy farm ternak lembu susu.

dairymaid pemerah susu.

dairy produce penghasilan daripada susu.

dais (*throne*) anjung tempat singgahsana.

daisy bunga serunai Belanda.

dale lembah.

dam empangan, tambak, besa permatang; to — up menambak.

damage kerosakan, kerugian; —s ganti kerugian.

damask kimkha, dewangga; (*metal*) baja yang berpamur; (*colour*) warna merah muda.

damn mengutuki, menyumpahi, melaknati.

damnable patut dikutuki.

damnation kutukan, laknatan.

damned terkutuk, dilaknati.

damp (*vapour*) wap air; (*foggy*) kabut; (*wet*) lembab, banyak wap air; to — membasahi, membasahkan; to — down menimbun dengan abu api.

damper (*disappointment*) keciwa.

damp-proof tahan lembab.

damsel dayang.

dance menari, menyuruh menari.

dance hostess penari perempuan di rumah dangsa.

dancer penari.

dancing-master guru menari.

dancing-room bilik tari.

dandelion sejenis bunga kuning.

dandified pesolek.

dandruff kelemomor, kekotoran kepala.

dandy pesolek, elok sekali.

Dane orang negeri Denmark.

danger bahaya.

dangerous berbahaya.

danger signal tanda bahaya.

danger zone daerah berbahaya.

dangle berjuntai, bergoyang-goyang berayun-ayun.

dank lembab tak sedap.

dapper elok.

dapple berintik-rintik; rupa berintik-rintik.

dapple-grey kuda warna kelabu.

dare berani, mengadu untung.

daredevil pemberani, berani mati.

daresay kira; I — he will go saya kira ia mahu pergi.

daring berakah, candang, sangat berani, berani mati.

dark gelap, kelam; (*gloomy*) muram; (*obscured*) tersembunyi; D— Ages kurun gelap.

darken menjadi gelap, membuat gelap.

darling kekasih, manis, yang tercinta, yang dicintai.

darn menampal, membubul.

dart (*arrow*) anak panah; (*javelin*) seligi; (*leap*) lompat, loncat; (*throw arrows* etc) memanah, melemparkan.

dash, to — (*smash*) meremokkan, memukul menyerang; (*frustrate*) membatalkan; to — sth down melemparkan, menghempaskan; to — out mencoreng, mencorek; to — up datang berlari.

dashboard (*mud screen*) papan-papan roda penahan lumpur.

dashing gagah, berani.

data daripada datum.

date (*palm*) pohon kurma; (*time*) tarikh, haribulan; at an early — tak lama.

datum yang diketahui.

daub menyapu, memperkatakan.

daughter anak perempuan.

daughter-in-law menantu perempuan.

daunt menakutkan, menawarkan hati.

dauntless tak takut, gagah berani.

dawdle (*idle talking*) bual kosong, merepet; (*lingering*) leka, lengah.

dawn fajar (*of day*); terbit fajar.

day hari, siang; (*time*) hari waktu, masa; —s of grace hari mendapat tangguh.

dazed keliru bingung, tercengang.

dazzle kesilauan; to — menyilaukan mata.

deacon anggota pengurus orang miskin.

dead mati.

deaf pekak tuli.

deal (*large quantity, total*) jumlah; a great, good — banyak benar; to — with membeli pada.

dean kepala; kepala jabatan; pendita; dekan.

dear (*of price*) mahal, berharga; (*beloved*) yang dicintai.

death mati, kematian.

debar menghalangi, menyingkirkan dari.

debase merendahkan, menghinakan, memalsukan.

debasement pemalsuan.

debatable dapat dibahas.

debate bahas; to — menyangkal.

debauch, to — membujul, menipu, merosakkan; (*outrageous behaviour*) cabul.

debauchery kecabulan, kebiadapan.

debilitate melemahkan.

debility kelemahan.

debit hutang, ruang debet dalam pembukuan.

debonair manis, ramah-tamah.

debris robohan, ketinggalan.

debt hutang; (*obligation*) kewajiban; — of nature mati.

debunk menelanjangi orang; menurunkannya dari kemuliaan yang tak patut diterimaan.

debut permainan yang pertama daripada seorang pemain atau penyanyi.

decade sepuluh (hari, tahun sebagainya).

decadence kemunduran.

decadent mundur, dalam kemunduran.

decamp (*strike camp*) mem-

buka khemah; (*make off*) lari.

decant mencucurkan dari suatu bekas ke bekas yang lain dengan cermat.

decanter balang air anggor, kelalang.

decapitato memenggal kepala orang.

decarbonize menghilangkan zat karbon.

decay (*decline*) memundurkan, mundur; (*rot*) menjadi buruk dan busuk, reput.

decease meninggal, mati; the —d mendiang, marhum.

deceit dusta, tipu, penipuan.

deceitful dusta, menipu, menyesatkan.

deceivable mudah ditipu.

deceive menipu, mengecoh, menyesatkan; to be —d tertipu, salah.

December bulan Disember.

decency kesopanan.

decent (*respectable*) sopan; (*proper*) patut, pantas; (*pleasant*) manis.

decently dengan sopan.

decentralization pembahagian kekuasaan kepada daerah-daerah.

decentralize membahagibahagikan kekuasaan kepada daerah-daerah.

deception tipu, kecoh, penyesatan.

deceptive dusta, bohong.

decide memutuskan, menetapkan; to — against memutuskan melawan sesuatu.

decided tetap bermaksud.

deciduous luruh; trees pohon yang berdaun luruh; tidak kekal.

decimal perpuluhan; seperpuluhan.

decimate mengurangi, menghabiskan.

decimation pengurangan, pemusnahan.

decipher membaca mengertikan tulisan yang secara rahsia.

decipherable dapat dibaca dan diertikan.

decision (*setlement*) keputusan; (*decided in character*) ketetapan hati.

decisive menentukan, tentu, tetap.

deck dek kapal; geladak; **to —** (*adorn*) menghiasi.

deckchair kerusi dek.

declaim bercakap.

declaration keterangan, pengumuman, penyataan; (*for customs duty*) pemberitahu fasal barang-barang cukai.

declare menerangkan memberitahu, mengaku.

declension (*grammar*) keturunan, kemunduran.

decline (*fall back*) mundur; (*grammar*) menolak, mengikrabkan kata-kata.

decode membaca dan mengertikan code.

decompose (*separate*) menghuraikan; (*become rotten*) menjadi busuk.

decontaminate menghilangkan hama penyakit.

decorate menghiasi, memberi bintang.

decoration perhiasan, bintang, lukisan.

decorative menghiasi.

decorator pelukis rumah, perikat tembok.

decorous sopan, pantas.

decorum kesopanan.

decoy kandang itik, itik pemikat, burung pemikat; (*bait*) umpan.

decoy duck itik pemikat; burung pemikat.

decrease pengurangan; **to —** berkurang.

decree perintah, keputusan.

decrepit sudah dhaif, buruk.

decry mencela terang-terang, mencacat, membusuk-busukkan.

dedicate pentahbiskan, memujakan.

dedication tahbis, pujaan.

deduct memotong; **charges —ed** sesudah dipotong segala bayaran.

deduction potongan; (*conclusion*) kesimpulan.

deed perbuatan; **— of gift** penghebahan; menyerahkan sesuatu dengan surat.

deem mengira, memandang, menimbang; **to — highly of** memandang tinggi.

deep dalam, tinggi, keras, gelap; (*in thought*) dalam fikiran, tajam fikiran.

deep-rooted sudah berurat berakar.

deep-seated dalam letaknya.

deep-toned bersuara dalam.

deer rusa.

deerstalker (*person*) pemburu yang menghendap rusa.

deface merosakkan, mencacatkan, menggaris-garis.

defamation fitnah.

defame, to — memfitnahkan, memburukkan nama.

default kelalaian; **to —** tidak memenuhi kewajiban-nya.

defeat kekalahan, ketewasan; **to —** mengalahkan, menewaskan.

defeatism hal menerima kekalahan dengan sabar, kekurangan semangat.

defecate, to — buang air, berak.

defect kekurangan, cela, cacat.

defection penderhakaan.

defective bercacat; kekurangan.

defence pertahanan, pembelaan.

defenceless tak dipertahankan.

defend, to — membela, mempertahankan; **to — against** melindungkan.

defendant orang yang diduduh.

defender pembela.

defensive bertahan, penangkis, pertahanan; to be on the — bertahan, menangkis.

defer, to — menunda, mempertangguhkan.

deference turut-turutan, kehormatan.

deferential dengan hormat, berhormat.

defiance tantangan; (*against accepted Government*) penderhakaan.

defiant menentang.

deficiency kekurangan; (*defect*) cela.

deficient kurang, kekurangan.

deficit kekurangan wang.

defile (*pass*) genting; to — mencemarkan, mengotorkan.

define, to — mentakrifkan, menyatakan, memberi pengertian.

definite jelas, putus, tetap, tentu; —ly benar, betul, sungguh.

definition takrif, pengertian.

definitive tetap.

deflate, to — mengempiskan.

deflation kempis.

deflec., to — melentur, menyipi, membias.

deflection penyimpangan, pembiasan.

deflower, to — mempersunting.

deform, to — memburukkan, mencacat; —ed bercacat.

deformity cacat.

defraud, to — menipu.

defray, to — membayar, membelanjakan.

deft tangkas, pantas tangan.

deftness ketangkasan.

defunct mati, meninggal.

defy, to — menentang, melawan.

degenerate, to — makin

lama makin berkurang baik, mundur.

degeneration kemunduran.

degradation penurunan, kemunduran.

degrade, to — menurunkan pangkat, merendahkan.

degree kadar, darjah, tingkat; (*rank*) pangkat; by —s lambat laun.

degression pengurangan, hal berkurang.

dehydrate, to — mengeringkan, kontang.

deify, to — mempertuhankan.

deign, to — sudi akan, berkenaan akan.

deity dewata, Tuhan.

deject, to — memasyghulkan, menyusahkan hati, berdukacita.

dejection kemasyghulan, kemuraman.

delay kelambatan, tangguh, penangguhan; to — menangguhkan, melambatkan.

delectable menggembirakan, memuaskan.

delectation kesukaan.

delegate I wakil, utusan.

delegate II, to — mengutuskan; mengamanatkan.

delegation rombongan perutusan.

delete, to — menghapuskan.

deliberate I (dengan) sengaja; tenang, berhati-hati.

deliberate II, to — merunding kan, berbincang.

deliberation pertimbangan, perbincangan, perundingan.

delicacy (*fine; of work etc*) kehalusan; (*weakness*) lemah-lembut, kelemahan.

delicate (*fine*) halus; (*weak*) lemah.

delicatessen kedai makanan dan minuman.

delicious sedap, lazat cita.

delict pelanggaran hukum.

delight kesukaan, hal yang

sangat menyenangkan; to — menyukakan.

delightful lazat, sangat menyukakan.

delimit, to — menentukan batasnya.

delineate, to — melukiskan, menggambarkan.

delinquency *(carelessness)* kelalaian; *(misdeed)* kesalahan, salah langkah.

delinquent bersalah; *(person)* orang yang bersalah.

delirious kacau fikiran, racau; to be — meracau, meng(k)igau.

delirium keadaan kacau fikiran, iguan.

deliver, to — *(free)* membebaskan, membukakan; to — a blow memukul.

deliverance penyelamatan.

delivery *(things sent)* penghantaran; *(given)* pemberian; *(of child)* hal melahirkan anak.

dell lembah.

delta delta, beting pada kuala sungai.

delude, to — menipu.

deluge banjir.

delusion khayal(an), maya.

delve, to — *(dig)* menggali.

demagogue pemimpin (dan pengasut) rakyat.

demand *(request)* permintaan; *(claim)* tuntutan; in — laku, laris.

demarcation pembatasan, perenggan.

demean, to — o.s. berlaku, berkelakuan.

demeanour sikap, kelakuan.

demented gila.

dementia kegilaan.

demerit cela, salah.

demise mangkat raja; to — mewasiatkan, menyerahkan kepada.

demobilization pembubaran tentera.

demobilize, *abbr* **demob**, to —

— melepaskan dari kerahan, membubarkan tentera.

democracy kerakyatan, demokrasi; negeri yang diperintah secara kerakyatan.

democrat penganut faham kerakyatan.

democratic kerakyatan.

demolish, to — merobohkan, membinasakan.

demolition perombakan, roboh.

demon raksaksa, jin, syaitan.

demoniac seperti syaitan.

demonstrate, to — menunjukkan, menyatakan, menampakkan.

demonstration penunjukan, kenyataan, tunjuk perasaan.

demonstrative yang menunjukkan, membuktikan.

demonstrator orang yang mempertunjukkan sesuatu.

demoralize, to — merosakkan tata tertib, merosakkan semangat.

demote, to — menurunkan pangkat.

demur, to — meronta-ronta, melawan.

demure santun, lemah-lembut, malu.

den *(of wild boar)* jerumbun; *(room)* bilik kecil.

denationalize, to — menghapuskan hak kewarganegaraan.

denial peniadaan, keingkaran.

denigrate, to — memburukkan nama.

denim sejenis kain tebal.

denizen penduduk.

denomination *(name)* nama; *(class)* jenis.

denominator angka pembawah pecahan.

denotation *(sign)* tanda; *(meaning)* erti.

denote, to — *(indicate by a sign)* menandai, menandakan; *(mean)* bererti.

denounce, to — memburuk-
kan.

dense lebat, rapat, sesak,
padat, tumpat.

density padat, rapat, kele-
batan, ketumpatan.

dent lekuk; to — melekukkan,
kemok.

dental yang berkenaan de-
ngan gigi; — mechanic tukang
gigi.

dentifrice ubat pembersih
gigi.

dentist doktor gigi.

denture gigi buatan.

denude, to — menelanjang-
kan, membuka pakaian, gondol.

denunciation pemburukan.

deny, to — meniadakan,
membukankan, menolak,
mengingkari.

deodorize, to — menghilangkan baunya.

depart, to — berangkat,
pergi; (deviate) menyimpang,
bertolak; (home) berpulang;
meninggal.

department (branch) cabang,
bahagian; (office) jawatan,
jabatan.

departure kepergian, ke-
berangkatan, bertolak.

depend, to — on bergantung,
tergantung kepada.

dependable boleh dipercayai.

dependant anak buah.

dependence penggantungan.

dependency daerah jajahan.

dependent bawahan, takluk,
bergantung kepada; a —
(dependant) anak buah, orang
yang di bawah tanggungan
seseorang.

depict, to — melukiskan,
menggambarkan.

deplete, to — menghabiskan,
mengosongkan.

deplorable menyedihkan.

deplore, to — merapati,
menyesali.

depopulate, to — berkurang
penduduknya, mengurangi
penduduknya.

deport, to — membuang dari
tanahairnya; to — o.s. bersikap.

deportation pembuangan.

deportment laku, kelakuan,
sikap.

depose, to — memecatkan;
(state officially) menyatakan
dengan rasmi.

deposit (sediment etc) keladak,
endapan, timbunan; (security)
cagaran; to — mengendap.

deposition menaruhi (money
for safety) simpanan.

depositor penyimpan.

depository (store) gudang.

depot (store) penyimpanan,
gudang; (mil etc) tempat
pelatih soldadu, atau mata-
mata baharu.

deprave, to — merosakkan
iman.

depravity kebusukan.

deprecate, to — minta
supaya jangan.

depreciate, to — (belittle)
mengurangi; (fall in value)
berkurang.

depreciation (abuse) cacian;
(fall in price) pengurangan
harga.

depress, to — mengecilkan,
mengurangi; (make sad) menggundahkan.

depressed (overcast) redup;
(sad) masyghul.

depression (hollow) lekukan,
lembah; (low state) meleset,
masa kesempitan, musim merosot.

deprivation kehilangan,
pemecatan.

deprive, to — mengambil
sesuatu yang dihargai.

depth dalam; —s laut yang
dalam.

deputation utusan, wakil.

deputize, to — mewakilkan.

deputy wakil, naib timbalan, pengganti; — **chairman** naib pengerusi.

derail, to — mengakibatkan keretapi keluar rel.

derange, to — mengacaukan.

deranged (*mad*) gila.

derelict terlantar, (istimewa kapal yang ditinggalkan di tengah laut).

dereliction peninggalan.

deride, to — mengejek, mentertawakan.

derision ejekan.

derisive yang mengejekkan.

derivation terbitan, turunan, penurunan.

derivative (*of words*) kata jadian, kata bentukan, kata terbitan.

derive, to — from menurunkan dari.

dermatology ilmu penyakit kulit.

derogatory yang menghinakan mengecilkan mencacat.

derrick pemburan, jentera melubang.

dervish darwis.

descend, to — turun, menurun; to — upon menghinggapi.

descendant turunan, anak cucu.

descent penurunan; (*slope*) landaian; (*history, origin*) asal usul.

describe, to — memerikan, merencanakan, menghuraikan, melukiskan, menceritakan.

description (*verbal, written*) rencana, cerita; huraian; (*appearance*) macam, rupa; beyond — tiada terperikan.

descry, to — menampak.

desecrate, to — menajiskan, mengotorkan.

desert I padang pasir, tanah gurun.

desert II, to — meninggalkan, melari.

desertion lari.

deserve, to — patut menerima.

deserving berjasa.

desiccate, to — mengeringkan.

design (*pattern*) corak; (*programme, draft*) rencana, rancangan; (*end in view*) tujuan maksud; to — mcrangkakan.

designate bakal; to — (*name*) menamakan; (*appoint*) mengangkat menjadi.

designation (*nomination*) pengangkatan; (*name*) nama, gelar.

designer pelukis, perancang.

designing perancangan; (*wily*) p.ntar.

desirable yang dikehendaki, baik, patut.

desire keinginan, hasrat; (*carnal*) nafsu; to — berhajat, menginginakan.

desirous ingin; (*carnal*) bernafsu.

desist, to — berhenti, tidak meneruskan berbuat atau melakukan sesuatu.

desk bangku, meja tulis.

desolate sepi, pencil, sunyi senyap; to — memencilkan.

desolation keadaan sepi sunyi, keicngangan.

despair keadaan putus asa, kehilangan akal; to — putus asa.

despatch = **dispatch**.

desperado orang jahat.

desperate (*without hope*) putus asa; (*slender chance*) genting; (*dangerous*) berbahaya.

despicable hina, keji.

despise, to — mengeji akan.

despite biarpun, walaupun.

despoil, to — merampas merampuk.

despondency gundah-gulana, putus asa.

despondent pecah hati, putus asa.

despot raja yang zalim.

despotic yang memaksa.

despotism kelakuan atau peraturan maharaja lela.

dessert manisan yang dimakan pada akhir persantapan.

destination tujuan, tempat yang dituju.

destine, to — memperuntukkan, memaksudkan.

destiny nasib, untung nasib.

destitute fakir, miskin, papa, kekurangan.

destitution kemiskinan.

destroy, to — merosakkan, membinasakan.

destroyer pemburu; *(ship)* kapal perosak.

destruction kerosakan kebinasaan; *(accursed)* celaka.

destructive yang merosakkan.

desultory tidak berhubung.

detach, to — menghuraikan, mengasingkan, menceraikan; **—ed** *(by o.s.)* tersendiri; terpencil.

detachment *(mil)* bahagian; askar penyendirian.

detail I perihal, butir-butir; **in** — lebih lanjut, dengan selok-beloknya.

detail II, to — memerikan (dengan panjang lebar).

detain, to — menahan.

detect, to — mendapati.

detective mata gelap.

detector alat untuk mendapati sesuatu.

detention tahanan; *(prison)* hukuman berkurung.

deter, to — menghalangi, mencegah.

detergent pembersih.

deteriorate, to — mundur bertambah buruk, memburukkan.

deterioration kebusukan, kemunduran.

determinate yang tertentu, yang telah ditentukan.

determination *(cessation)* perhentian; *(fixing date etc)* penetapan; *(conclusion)* keputusan; *(of purpose)* berazam.

determine, to — menyelesaikan, menetapkan, memutuskan.

detest, to — menjijikkan, membencikan.

dethrone, to — menurunkan dari takhta kerajaan.

detonate, to — meletuskan.

detonation peletusan, letus.

detonator alat peletus.

detour simpangan, penyimpangan.

detract, to — mengurangi mengecilkan.

detriment *(loss)* kerugian.

detrimental yang merugikan; *(bringing misfortune)* celaka.

devastate, to — membinasakan, merosakkan.

devastation pembinasaan.

develop, to — berkembang, tumbuh, mengembangkan.

development perkembangan, kemajuan.

deviate, to — menyimpang melencong.

deviation simpangan, penyimpangan, lencongan.

device akal, daya.

devil iblis, hantu, syaitan.

devilish sebagai syaitan.

devilry jahatan keburukan.

devious bersimpang-siur bengkang-bengkok.

devise, to — *(invent etc)* menciptakan.

devitalize, to — melemahkan, mematikan semangat.

devoid, — of tidak mempunyai, kekurangan.

devolve, to — *(upon)* berpindah kepada, jatuh ke tangan; memindahkan, menyerahkan.

devote, to — *(give up wholly)* mencurahkan, menyerahkan; **—d** *(pious)* berbakti.

devotee penggemar.

devotion kebaktian, patuh, taat; —s doa.

devour, to — (*eat*) makan; (*destroy*) membinasakan.

devout berbakti, beriman.

dew embun; — drop titik embun; to form — berembun.

dewlap gembel lembu, gelambir.

dexterity ketengkasan.

dexterous tengkas, pantas.

diabetes penyakit gula, penyakit kencing manis.

diabetic yang berkenaan dengan penyakit gula.

diabolic(al) yang berkenaan dengan syaitan, seperti syaitan sangat jahat.

diadem mahkota, perhiasan kepala.

diagnose, to — menetapkan sifat penyakit.

diagnosis penetapan sifat penyakit.

diagonal garis pepenjuru.

diagram rancangan gambarajah.

dial piringan yang diberi angka-angka.

dialect dialik, loghat, bahasa daerah pelat.

dialogue kata-bual, soal jawab, percakapan, berdailog.

diameter garispusat, perepang.

diametrical tepat bertentangan.

diamond intan; a — wedding peringatan tahun perkahwinan yang ke 60.

diaper (*US*) popok, lampin, bedung.

diaphonous tembus cahaya, terang terus.

diaphragm sekat rongga badan, daiferam.

diarrhoea cirit, buangbuang air.

diary buku peringatan buku catitan perharian.

diatribe teguran yang kasar cacian.

dibble tugal; to menugal.

dice dadu; *see* **die;** to **play,** shoot — main dadu.

dichotomy pembelahan dua, pembahagian dua.

dictaphone alat yang menetapkan segala perkataan yang dirakamkan ke dalamnya.

dictate, to — (*settle*) menetapkan.

dictation (*writing*) rencana.

dictator diktator.

dictatorial memerintahkan secara bukubesi.

diction lagu, gaya berkata.

dictionary kamus, daftar perkataan.

did *pt of* **do.**

didactic pengajar, akan mengajar.

diddle, (*col*) to — menipu.

die I dadu; the — is cast hal sudah diputuskan.

die II, to — mati, berpulang ke rahmatullah, mangkat, sampai ajalnya, meninggal (dunia); to — in harness meninggal tengah bekerja.

diet I makanan; to — makan berpantang.

diet II (*assembly*) muktamar.

dietetics ilmu makanan.

differ, to — berbeza; berselisih.

difference (*be unlike*) perbezaan, (*disagree*) selisih.

different lain berbeza; to be — from berlainan daripada.

differential berlainan; — charges biaya yang berubah menurut keadaan yang berlainan.

differentiate, to — berbeza, membezakan.

difficult sukar, payah, susah.

difficulty kesukaran kesusahan.

diffidence malu.

diffident malu, tersipu-sipu, penyegan, tidak yakin diri.

diffuse I baur menyebar, resap.

diffuse II, to — menyebar; meresap, berbaur.

diffusion penyebaran, resapan.

dig (*prod*) jolokan; to — menggali, mencangkul.

digest (*summary*) ikhtisar, ringkasan

digest, to — (*assimilate*) mencerna; (*summarize*) meringkaskan; (*understand*) memahamkan.

digestion pencernaan.

digestive yang berkenaan dengan pencernaan, pencernaan.

digger penggali.

diggings (*mining*) penggalian.

digit angka.

dignify, to — menghormati, mempermuliakan.

dignitary pembesar, orang mulia.

dignity kebesaran, kemuliaan; (*rank*) pangkat.

digress, to — melentur menyimpang.

digression simpangan, pelanturan.

digs (*lodging*) tempat penginapan.

dike, dyke benteng, permarang, tambak.

dilapidated buruk.

dilapidation keadaan buruk.

dilate, to — membesarkan, melapangkan.

dilatory yang menangguhkan.

dilemma keadaan sukar.

diligence kerajinan.

diligent asyik rajin, ringan tulang.

dill sejenis jintan.

dillydally, to — berlengahlengah menyambalewa, dolakdalik.

dilute cair; to — mencairkan.

dim kabur, samar, kelamkabut.

dime seper sepuluh ringgit Amerika.

dimension ukuran, besar.

diminish, to — mengecilkan, turun, susut.

diminution perkecilan.

diminutive sangat kecil.

dimple cengkung, lesung pipit.

din riuh.

dine, to — makan, menyantap; (*give meal to*) memberi makanan kepada; to — out makan di tempat lain.

diner orang yang bersantap; (*dining car*) kereta restoran di keretapi.

dinghy sampan kecil (istimewa pada kapal besar atau pesawat udara).

dingo sejenis anjing hutan.

dingy berkemal.

dining room bilik makan.

dinner makan malam; — jacket sejenis pakaian lakilaki.

dinosaur sejenis binatang para sejarah yang sangat besar.

dint lekuk, kepuk; by — of oleh sebab, oleh kerana.

diocese daerah yang di bawah kuasa seorang 'bishop' (gereja Katolik).

dip (*slope*) condongan, lerengan; (*bathe*) mandi; to — mencelupkan.

diphtheria sakit rengkung.

diphthong bunyi kembar.

diploma diploma ijazah; to take one's — mendapat ijazah.

diplomacy kepandaian dalam urusan antarabangsa, siasat, diplomasi.

diplomat diplomat.

diplomatic yang berkenaan dengan kedutaan luar negeri.

dipsomania ketagih akan minuman keras.

dire celaka, malang.

direct (*directly*) langsung; (*straight*) lurus; (*precise*) tepat;

(*right through*) terus; to — menunjukkan, mengarahkan.

direction arah, jurusan, hala, tujuan, haluan; (*order*) perintah.

directive pedoman, petunjuk; (*order*) perintah.

director pemimpin, pengarah.

directory petunjuk, buku penunjuk, panduan.

dirge nyanyian sedih dinyanyikan dalam suatu istiadat permakaman.

dirk sejenis golok.

dirt kotor, kecemaran; (*mud*) lumpur; — cheap sangat murah.

dirty kotor, selekeh, cemar; (*of language*) carut; to make — mengotorkan, mencemarkan.

dis—awalan yang ertinya: cerai, tak, tidak.

disability kecacatan, kelemahan; (*unable*) tidak sanggup.

disable, to — mengalangalangi, melumpuhkan; —d person, orang cacat.

disadvantage kerugian, keadaan kurang baik.

disagree, to — berselisih, berlawanan, bertentangan.

disagreeable kurang elok, kurang peramah.

disagreement perselisihan, selisih faham.

disappear, to — hilang, lenyap; to make — menghilangkan.

disappearance lenyap, kelenyapan.

disappoint, to — mengeciwakan, mungkir; —d keciwa.

disappointment kekeciwaan.

disapproval tiada bersetuju.

disapprove, to — of menyalahi, mencela.

disarm, to — melucutkan senjata.

disarmament perlucutan senjata.

disarrange, to — merombakkan; —d tak urus.

disaster celaka, bencana, petaka.

disband, to — membubarkan.

disbelieve, to — tidak mempercayai.

disc piringan.

discard, to — membuang mencampakkan.

discern, to — mengecamkan, memperhatikan, mengenal.

discerning mengenal.

discernment perhatian, keadaan mengamati.

discharge pengeluaran; (*of gun*) tembakan; (*pus*) keluar nanah.

disciple murid, penganut, pengikut.

disciplinarian orang yang suka tata-tertib.

disciplinary yang berkenaan dengan tata-tertib.

discipline disiplin, tata-tertib; (*training*) mata pengajaran; to — melatihkan supaya tertib.

disclaim, to — mengingkari, memungkiri.

disclose, to — menyingkapkan, membukakan.

disclosure penyingkapan, pembukaan.

discolour, to — berubah warna.

discomfit, to — mengalahkan, menggagalkan.

discomfort keadaan tidak elok, kesusahan.

discompose, to — membingungkan; —d bingung.

discomposure kebingungan.

disconcert, to — menggagalkan, memalukan, membingungkan.

disconnect, to — menceraikan, menguraikan, memutuskan; —ed terputus-putus.

disconsolate sedih, putus asa.

discontent keadaan tidak puas; —ed kurang elok, tidak puas.

discontinue, to — menghentikan, tidak meneruskan.

discord *(disagreement)* perbantahan, kecederaan.

discordant janggal.

discount I potongan.

discount II, to — memotong harga.

discountenance, to — menolak, tidak berkenan.

discourage, to — menawarkan hati.

discourse I percakapan, perbincangan.

discourse II, to — mempercakapkan, memperbincangkan.

discourteous kurang ajar, biadab.

discover, to — menemui, mendapati; *(uncover)* membuka.

discovery pendapatan, jumpaan.

discredit *(disrepute)* nama buruk; *(not believed)* tidak percaya; to — memberi malu, tidak percaya.

discreditable yang membawa nama buruk.

discreet bijaksana.

discrepancy berlainan, tidak sesuai.

discretion siasat, kebijaksanaan.

discriminate, to — (from) memperbezakan, memperlainkan; to — (against) membelakangkan.

discriminating yang memperhatikan baik-baik, berakal halus.

discrimination *(difference)* pembezaan; *(fine observation)* perhatian baik; *(fine intelligence)* akal halus.

discus, disc cakera.

discuss, to — bercakap, ber-

bicara, berbincang, membicarakan.

discussion percakapan, pembicaraan, perundingan.

disdain penghinaan; to — menghinakan.

disease penyakit; —d kena penyakit.

disembark, to — turun kapal, turun darat, mendarat.

disembarkation pendaratan, turun kapal.

disembowel, to — mengeluarkan ususnya.

disengage, to — membuka, melepaskan; —d tidak beralangan.

disentangle, to — melepaskan, menguraikan.

disfavour keadaan tidak suka; to — tak suka akan.

disfigure, to — memburukkan rupanya, bentuknya; —d salah bentuk.

disgorge, to — *(vomit)* muntah, memuntahkan.

disgrace hina, keaiban; to — mempermalukan, memberi malu.

disgruntled tidak puas, tidak senang.

disguise samaran; to — menyamarkan, samar.

disgust perasaan mual, jijik; to — menjijikkan, membenci.

dish I *(pot)* pinggan, batil.

dish II *(food)* santapan, hidangan, masakan, sajian; to — up *(food)* menghidangkan, menyajikan.

disharmony kejanggalan, keadaan tidak sesuai.

dishearten, to — menawarkan hati, menggundahkan.

dishevelled *(of hair)* rambutnya kusut masai.

dishonest tak lurus, penipu.

dishonesty penipu, keadaan tidak lurus.

dishonour keaiban, kehina-

an, kekejian; to — meng-
hinakan, mengaibkan.
dishonourable hina, keji.
disillusion to — mengeciwakan.
disinclination keseganan.
disincline, to — menyegan-
kan, menjadikan segan.
disinfect, to — menghapuskan hama, membersihkan.
disinfection persucian, penghapusan hama.
disinherit, to — memecatkan dari warisan, membuang
saudara.
disintegrate, to — bercerai,
luluh, mencerai beraikan.
disinterested (*without seek-
ing profit*) dengan tidak mencari untung; (*uninterested*)
tidak menaruh perhatian.
disjoint, to — menceraikan,
merombakkan; —ed terputus-
putus.
disk, disc piringan, cakera.
dislike kebencian; to — tidak
suka akan, membencikan.
dislocate, to — (*loosen*) menguraikan; (*put out*) mengeluarkan; (*pull out*) mencabut; —d
terpelecuk, tergeliat.
dislodge, to — mengeluarkan, menghalaukan.
disloyal tidak setia, derhaka.
dismal sedih.
dismantle, to — membukakan (segala kelengkapannya).
dismay kecemasan, kedahsyatan; to — mendahsyatkan,
mencemaskan.
dismember, to — mencin-
cangkan.
dismiss, to — menghentikan,
mengeluarkan, memecatkan.
dismissal keberhentian;
notice of — surat lepas.
dismount, to — turun,
menurunkan.
disobedience tidak taat; (*as
treason*) derhaka.
disobedient tiada taat;

(*treachery*) derhaka.
disobey, to — tidak menurut;
menderhaka.
disorder kerusuhan, kekacauan; (*illness*) penyakit; **in** —
kacau.
disorderly tak urus, kacau.
disorganize, to — mengacau,
tidak teratur.
disown, to — (*deny*) menyangkal.
disparage, to — merendahkan, mengecilkan, mencacat.
disparagement penghinaan,
mencacat.
disparate berlainan, tak
seimbang; hal yang sangat
berlainan.
disparity tidak sama timbang.
dispassionate tenang, tawar
hati.
dispatch (*sending off*) pengiriman; (*official letter*) rasmi;
to — mengirimkan.
dispel, to — mengusir,
menghalaukan.
dispensable (*not obligatory*)
tak perlu.
dispensary rumah ubat.
dispensation (*arrangement*)
peraturan; (*exemption*) izin
supaya dibebaskan.
dispense, to — (*give*) memberi; (*relax*) memberi pembebasan dari sesuatu kewajiban;
to — **with** tidak memakai.
dispenser tukang beri ubat.
disperse, to — membubarkan, mencerai beraikan, bersurai, berserak.
dispersion, dispersal
(*scattering*) penghamburan; (*of
meetings etc*) pembubaran.
dispirit, to — menawarkan
hati, menggundahkan; —ed
tawar hati.
displace, to — memindahkan
dari tempatnya.
displacement pemindahan,
pengubahan.

display pertunjukan; to — mempertunjukkan.

displease, to — tidak menyenangkan; menyakitkan hati.

displeasure tidak senang, marah, gusar.

disport, to — (o.s.) bermain-main, bersenang-senang.

disposal (arrangement) pengaturan; (settlement) penetapan; (sale) penjualan.

disposition (arrangement) aturan, urusan; (temperament) perangai, sifat, budi pekerti.

dispossess, to — mengambil harta-benda seseorang.

disproportionate tidak setimbal tidak seimbang.

disprove, to — menunjukkan kesalahan sesuatu.

disputable yang dapat dilawankan.

disputation pertengkaran.

dispute perselisihan, guam; to — berselisih, bertengkar; membantahkan.

disqualification pembatalan.

disqualify, to — batal, tidak sanggup membatalkan.

disquiet khuatir, bimbang; to — membingungkan.

disregard mengabaikan, lalai; (scorn) penghinaan: to — mengabaikan, tidak peduli.

disrepair keadaan buruk.

disreputable buruk nama, keji hina.

disrepute nama buruk.

disrespect kurang hormat.

disrobe, to — membuka pakaian kehormatan.

disrupt, to — menghancurkan, memecahkan, ganggu.

disruption penghancuran, pemecahan, gangguan.

dissatisfaction tidak puas hati.

dissatisfactory yang tidak memuaskan.

dissatisfy, to — menyakitkan hati, tidak memuaskan.

dissemble, to — menyamarkan, menyembunyikan.

disseminate, to — menyebarkan, mencerai beraikan.

dissension perselisihan.

dissent perbantahan; (denial) keingkaran; to — membantahkan, mengingkari.

dissenter pengingkar.

dissertation karangan menerangkan sesuatu uraian.

dissident tidak sesuai, berselisih.

dissimilar tidak sama.

dissimulate, to — menyembunyikan, menyamarkan.

dissipate, to — (scatter) menghamburkan; (squander) memboros.

dissipation penghamburan; pemborosan.

dissociate, to — menceraikan, mengasingkan.

dissolute cabul; (perverse) nakal.

dissolution (as in smelting) peleburan; pembubaran.

dissolve, to — larut, meleburkan; (vanish) lenyap.

dissonance bunyi janggal.

dissonant janggal.

dissuade, to — menasihati supaya jangan.

distance kejauhan; (distance apart) jarak; to keep at a — menjauhkan.

distant jauh, renggang.

distaste tidak suka; (strong disgust) jijik.

distasteful memualkan, jijik.

distemper I (of dogs) penyakit anjing.

distemper II (on walls) sejenis kapur dinding; to — mengapur dinding.

distend, to — mengembangkan, mengembungkan.

distil, to — mengukus.

distillate suling.

distillation penyulingan.

distinct lain, berbeza, tak sama.

distinction (*difference*) perbezaan; (*mark of honour*) kemuliaan; (*insignia*) kebesaran.

distinctive (*special*) istimewa; (*clear*) nyata.

distinguish, to — memperbezakan; (*select*) memilih; to — o.s. memperoleh nama mulia.

distort, to — (*alter appearance*) mengubahkan rupa bentuknya; (*twist*) memulas, memutar.

distortion pengubahan rupa.

distract, to — melanturkan, menyesatkan.

distraction (*relaxation*) kelengahan; (*comforter*) penghiburan.

distress (*sorrow*) kedukaan, kesedihan; (*poverty*) kemiskinan; to — menyedihkan, mendukakan.

distribute, to — agih, membahagi, menyebarkan.

distribution pembahagian, pemberian taburan.

district daerah, tanah, bahagian, jajahan.

distrust kecurigaan, syak wasangka; to — mencurigai, tidak percaya.

disturb, to — (*interfere*) mengganggu; (*unsettle*) mencemaskan; (*annoy*) mengacaukan; (*quarrel*) mengga-duhkan.

disturbance kerusuhan, kekacauan, gangguan.

disuse, to — tidak memakai lagi.

ditch parit, lecah bandar; to — membuat parit.

ditto yang sama, seperti yang tersebut, dito.

ditty nyanyian, pantun.

diurnal yang berkenaan dengan hari siang malam.

divan (*couch*) bangku; (*court*) balai; (*council*) dewan (di negeri timur).

dive (*leap down*) terjun; (*in water*) selam; to — menyelam.

diver juruselam.

diverge, to — berpencar.

divergent pencar.

diverse berbagai bermacam-macam.

diversion (*road*) penyimpangan.

diversity berbagai ragam, pancawarna.

divert, to — menyimpangkan, mengalihkan.

divest, to — (*of*) (*take off*) menanggalkan; (*abandon*) meninggalkan.

divide, to — pisah, menceraikan; to — by four membahagi empat.

dividend angka yang dibahagi.

dividers (*also pair of* —) jangka.

divination ramalan nujuman.

divine kedewaan, ketuhanan; (*excellent*) sangat baik; — service upacara keugamaan.

diviner peramal, tukang ramal.

divinity kedewaan, ketuhanan.

divisible dapat dibahagi; — by five dapat dibahagi lima.

division bahagi; pemisahan; (*in ricefield*) batas.

divisor pembahagi.

divorce cerai; to — bercerai, menceraikan.

divorcee perempuan yang telah bercerai.

divulge, to — membuka rahsia.

dizziness pening, pitam, pusing kepala.

dizzy pusing, pening.

do (*thing, work*) buat, mem-bust; (*effect*) mengerjakan, mengusahakan, mengurus menyelenggarakan; —ing sedang berbuat; don't, — not jangan.

docile turut-turutan, patuh.

dock I (*naut*) dok, kalangan; —s pelabuhan; to — memasukkan kapal ke kalangan.

dock II (*law*) tempat untuk orang terdakwa di pengadilan, kandang.

dock III (*cut short*) buntut binatang (istimewa anjing dan kuda).

docker buruh pelabuhan.

docket (*list*) daftar; (*pawn ticket*) surat tebusan; to — mencatit dengan ringkas.

dockyard limbungan.

doctor tabib, doktor; pangkat tertinggi pada sekolah tinggi; to — mengubati.

doctrine (*teaching*) ajaran; (*religious*) asas ugama.

document naskhah, surat, dokumen.

documentary yang menegaskan dan membuktikan.

dodder to — gementar.

dodge (*stratagem*) akal, daya; to — mengelak, mengelakkan.

doe rusa betina, kijang betina.

dog anjing; (*person contemptuously*) orang hina; — days hari yang panas terik.

dogged degil.

doggerel sajak yang buruk dan tak lancar.

dogma (*doctrine*) rukun; (*principle*) pendirian, kepercayaan.

dogmatic yang berkenaan dengan rukun, menurut pendirian yang tetap.

doldrums keadaan tenang dan reda, keadaan redup, kawasan angin mati.

dole pemberian wang derma; to — out mencatukan, mendermakan.

doleful sedih, berdukacita.

doll boneka, anakan, patung; to — up berpakaian elok-elok.

dollar ringgit; — area daerah ringgit.

dolly anakan; (*maid*) gadis; (*machinery*) suatu alat jentera.

dolorous sedih, tawar hati.

dolphin ikan lumba-lumba.

dolt orang bodoh.

domain daerah, negara, tanah.

dome dom, kubah; (*curved*) lengkung.

domestic yang berkenaan dengan atau suka rumahtangga; school of — science sekolah urusan rumahtangga; — animals binatang ternak.

domesticate, to — menjinakkan; —d (*tame*) jinak; (*liking home life*) suka bekerja di rumah.

domesticity hal atau sifat berdiam di rumah, kehidupan senang di rumah.

domicile tempat kediaman, kediukman, rumah.

dominance keunggulan.

dominant yang memerintah, unggul; (*predominant*) istimewa.

dominate, to — mengusai, memerintahi.

domination penjajahan, pertuanan.

domineer, to — mengusai; (*oppress*) menganiayakan.

dominion perintahan, negeri, daerah, tanah dominion.

domino (*game*) sejenis permainan dalam.

don I, to — memakai pakaian.

don II (*academic*) guru pada perguruan tinggi.

donate, to — mendermakan.

donation derma, sokongan.

done selesai, habis; over— (*of cooking*) dimasak terlalu lama; well —! syabas!

donkey (*ass*) keldai; (*stupid person*) orang bodoh.

donor penderma; (*blood*) pemberi darah.

doodle coret, gorisan; to — mencoret, menggoris.

doom (*misfortune*) celaka, nasib malang; to — mencelakakan.

door pintu; front — pintu hadapan.

doorstep ambang.

dope (*anaesthetic*) ubat bius; to — memabukkan.

dormant sedang tidur, pendam.

dormitory ruang tidur.

dormouse sejenis tupai.

dorsal yang berkenaan dengan punggung.

dosage, dose (*of medicine*) sukatan ubat.

doss, (*col*) to — (down) tidur; — house rumah penginapan untuk orang miskin.

dossier segala surat-surat berkenaan dengan perkara seseorang.

dot bintik, noktah, titik; on the — tepat; to — memberi bertitik.

dotage masa tua nyanyok.

dote, to — (*old age*) nyanyok; (*foolish conduct*) berkelakuan bodoh; to — (up)on mempermanjakan.

doting tua, nyanyok.

double dua, ganda, kembar, rangkap; (*of things folded*) berlipat; (*twice*) dua kali; (*total*) jumlah yang dua kali sebesar; (*of person*) orang yang sama rupanya.

double-cross, to — menipu.

doublet (*garment*) sejenis baju laki-laki.

doubt kebimbangan, keraguan, ragu-ragu, syak waham; to — meragukan.

doubtful ragu-ragu, tak tentu; —ness waswas.

doubtless tak boleh tidak, tentulah.

douche pancut.

dough adunan; (*col: money*) wang.

doughnut sejenis kuih.

doughty perkasa.

dour keras hati.

douse membasahkan; (*extinguish light*) memadam lampu.

dove burung dara, merbuk.

dovetail tanggam; to — menanggam.

dowager janda berbangsa.

dowdy berpakaian buruk.

dower emas kahwin.

down I bawah, ke bawah, di bawah; (*descend*) turun; (*go downstream*) hilir; to bring — menurunkan; to — come — turun.

down II (*feeling down*) masyghul, tawar hati.

down III (*fine hair*) roma, bulu.

down IV, —s (*open high land*) dataran tinggi yang berumput.

down V, to — menurunkan; to — tools (*strike*) mogok.

downcast tawar hati, sedih.

downfall kejatuhan.

downgrade kemunduran.

downhill melandai, turun, ke bawah.

downpour hujan lebat.

downright lurus, terus terang.

downstairs ke bawah, di bawah (istimewa pada rumah bertingkat).

downstream hilir; to go — menghilir.

downtrodden tertindas.

downward ke bawah.

dowry emas kahwin, isi kahwin.

doze tidur sebentar; to — mengantuk, terkelap; to — off tertidur.

dozen dosen.

drab warna redup.

draft (*preliminary writing etc*) derap, rangka, rencana, rancangan; (of soldiers) pasukan.

draftsman penggambar, perancang, tukang lukis.

drag (grapnel) sauh; (in fishing) alat pemukat; to — menghela, menarik; to — (along) mengheret.

dragnet pemayang pukat.

dragon ular naga.

dragonfly capung, sibar-sibar.

dragoon soldadu berkuda.

drain parit, saluran; to — menyalurkan air, mengalirkan.

drainage pengaliran, tali air, saliran.

drake itik jantan.

dram sejenis timbangan berat.

drama lakun, sandiwara.

dramatic yang berkenaan dengan sandiwara, yang seperti sandiwara.

dramatist, dramaturge pengarang sandiwara.

dramatize, to — melakunkan, memainkan salah satu peristiwa.

drape, to — menggantungkan.

draper penjual kain-kain.

drapery (clothing linen) kain-kain; (curtains) tirai-mirai.

drastic dengan keras, kuat.

drat jahannam!

draught penghelaan, penarikan; (of ship) ukuran terbenannya kapal di dalam air; (of air) angin.

draughtsman penggambar, perancang.

draw (drawing of lots) penarikan undi; (tie) seri dalam pertandingan; to — menghela, menarik, tertarik; — one's attention menarik perhatian seseorang; to — lots membuang undi.

drawback (difficulties) kesukaran; (loss) rugi.

drawbridge jambatan jungkatan.

drawer (of table etc) laci.

drawers seluar dalam panjang.

drawing gambar, lukisan; — room bilik tamu.

drawl ucapan perlahan-lahan; to — berbual dengan perlahan, lahan.

dread ketakutan, kedahsyatan.

dreadful dahsyat, hebat, jahat.

dream buah mimpi; to — of memimpikan.

dreamer orang mimpi.

dreamy yang khayal.

dreary sabak, gabak.

dredge alat (galah) kerana mengeluarkan tiram dan sebagainya dari air; to — mengeruk.

dredger kapal korek, kapal keruk.

dregs sisa, keladak, hampas.

drench, to — membasahkan.

dress pakaian; full — pakaian mulia; to — berpakai, memakai; (decorate) berhias.

dresser (hospital) jururawat laki-laki, pembantu berpakai atau membalut.

dressmaker tukang jahit.

dressy suka berpakaian elok.

dribble (of mouth) meleleh; (at football) kelicik.

drift penghanyutan; pengaliran; to — mengapung; to — (about) terapung hanyut.

driftwood apung-apung, kayu apung.

drill (bore) penggerek, gurdi, bor; (of troops etc) pengajaran dan pelatihan dalam tentera; to — (bore) menggerek, menggurdi; (of troops etc) berbaris, berkawat.

drily dengan kering; (briefly) dengan pendek.

drink minuman; (alcoholic) minuman keras; to — minum.

drip titis, penitisan; to — menitis.

dripping penitisan; (*cooking fat*) lemak masak.

drive perjalanan kereta; **to — away** menghalau, mengusir.

drivel (*slaver*) air liur; (*talk nonsense*) bual kosong.

driver sais, pengemudi pembawa motokar.

drizzle hujan rintik-rintik, gerimis; **to —** gerimis, hujan rintik-rintik.

droll anih; jenaka.

dromedary sejenis unta.

drone (*male bee*) lebah jantan; (*noise*) bunyi berdengung.

drool, to — berliur.

droop lelai; **to —** terkulai, melelai.

drop (*of liquid*) titik, titis; (*fall*) kejatuhan.

droppings (*of birds etc*) tahi (burung dan sebagainya).

dross (*in smelting*) sanga.

drought musim kemarau, kekeringan; absolute **—** kemarau kontang.

drove I (*flock*) kumpulan, kawan.

drove II *pt of* **drive**.

drover gembala.

drown, to — mati tenggelam, mati lemas, menenggelamkan.

drowse, to — mengantuk.

drudge orang yang berat pekerjaannya; **to —** berpayah-payah.

drug (*medicine*) ubat; (*poison*) racun; (*anaesthetic*) ubat bius.

druggist ahli ubat, penjual ubat.

drum genderang, tabuh, beduk; **ear —** gendang pendengar.

drummer juru gendang.

drunk *pp of* **drink** mabuk; pemabuk.

drunken mabuk; **—ness** kemabukan.

dry kering, (*of fruit*) ringkai; (*of hair, soil*) kersang; (*of weather*) kemarau.

dryad peri yang berdiam di hutan.

dry-clean, to — mencuci dengan ubat-ubat (tidak memakai air atau —)

dryness kekeringan.

dual rangkap, bilangan dua.

dub, to — (*name*) member gelar, menamakan.

dubious tidak tentu; (*worried*) bimbang.

duchess perempuan berbangsa tinggi.

duck I (*bird*) itik.

duck II, to — seludup, menyelam; (*duck down*) bersembunyi.

duckling anak itik.

duct paip, saluran, pembuluh.

ductile liat, mudah dikerjakan.

dud sesuatu atau seseorang yang tak berguna.

dudgeon, in high — sakit hati, dendam.

due harus, mesti wajib, patut diberikan atau dilakukan; **— bia,** cukai.

duel perang, tanding; **to —** bertanding, berkelahi.

duet nyanyian atau permainan muzik untuk dua orang.

duffel, duffle sejenis kain tebal dan berbulu.

duffer orang dengu.

dug *pt and pp of* **dig**; (*nipple*) puting susu.

dugout jalur, perahu selit.

duke orang berbangsa tinggi.

dulcet manis, merdu.

dull (*of light*) pudar, redup; (*feeling*) berat kepala; (*stupid*) dengu.

dullness kedenguan.

duly dengan sepertinya, sepatutnya.

dumb bisu; (*keep silent*) diam.

dumbbell besi berat untuk melatih urat.

dumbfound, to — membisukan, mendahsyatkan.

dummy (*mere tool*) orang yang tidak penting yang hanya alat sahaja; (*counterfeit*) tiruan.

dump (*for stores*) penyimpanan; (*rubbish*) persampahan; to — membuang sampah.

dumpling sejenis gorengan tepung.

dumps, to be down in the — tawar hati, sedih.

dumpy tegap.

dunce orang bodoh.

dune bukit pasir.

dung (*manure*) baja; tahi.

dungarees sejenis pakaian bekerja yang kainnya kuat.

dungeon penjara di bawah tanah.

dunghill tumpukan tahi.

duo dua.

dupe orang yang ketipuan; to — menipu.

duplicate rangkap, kembar, berganda, pasangan yang tepat sama, salinan, pendua.

duplicity tidak jujur, sifat berdua muka.

durability daya tahan.

durable kekal, tahan lama.

duration panjang, lamanya.

duress paksaan.

during sedang, selama, tengah.

dusk senja kala.

dusky kesamaran; **a — skin** kulit hitam.

dust abu, debu, lebu.

dustbin persampahan.

duster lap abu.

dusty berdebu.

Dutch Belanda.

dutiful penurut.

duty kewajipan, keharusan; **to do one's —** menjalankan kewajipannya.

duty (*tax*) bia, cukai; export — bia keluar; import — bia masuk.

dwarf kecil, kerdil; to — mengecilkan.

dwell, to — tetap tinggal, berumah, berdiam.

dweller penduduk.

dwelling rumah, tempat kediaman.

dwindle, to — makin lama makin kecil, susut, berkurang.

dye celupan, pencelup; to — mencelup.

dying yang berkenaan dengan kematian, meninggal.

dyke benteng; *see* **dike**.

dynamic dinamis, giat, semangat.

dynamics pengetahuan yang berkenaan dengan pergerakan sesuatu hal.

dynamite dinamit, letupan, sepedo.

dynamo alat dinamo.

dynasty turunan raja-raja.

dysentery disenteri, cirit darah.

dyspepsia salah cerna.

E

each (*of persons*) masing-masing; (*of things*) tiap-tiap setiap.

eager asyik, ingin, tergesa.

eagle burung rajawali, helang.

ear I telinga; (*sense of hearing*) pendengaran; **to have an —** for music berbakat muzik.

ear II (*of grain*) bulir.

eardrum gendang pendengar, anak telinga.

earl gelar orang berbangsa.

earlier lebih dahulu, lebih awal.

early pagi-pagi; siang-siang pada awalnya; **to keep —** hours bangun dan tidur pada waktunya, tidak terlambat.

earmark, to — menandakan.

earn, to — mendapat wang upah; patut menerima; **to — a living** mencari nafkah.

earnest I kesungguhan, sungguh asyik.

earnest II (*pledge*) wang menentukan, cengkeram.

earnings pendapatan, pencarian.

earring anting-anting, subang.

earth bumi, tanah; **to run to —** memburu binatang sampai ia masuk ke lubangnya.

earthenware periuk belanga, barang pecah-belah.

earthly yang berkenaan dengan bumi, duniawi.

earthquake gempa bumi.

earthworm cacing.

earthy seperti tanah; (*worldly*) duniawi.

earwig tempiring.

ease (*facility*) kemudahan; (*comfort*) kesenangan; **at —** senang; **to —** memudahkan, meringankan.

easel kuda-kuda untuk papan hitam.

easily mudah.

easiness kemudahan.

east timur; **the far E—** timur jauh; **north —** timur laut.

Easter Paska.

easterly yang di(atau dari) timur.

eastern di sebelah timur.

easy senang, ringan, mudah; **— chair** kerusi malas; **—-going** tak bersusah.

eat, to — makan, santap; **to — one's words** menarik perkataannya balik.

eaves talang, tepi atap, cucur atap.

ebb air surut, pasang surut; **to — surut.

ebony kayu arang.

ebullient penuh riang gembira.

eccentric (*axis not central*) lengkaran yang tak sama pusatnya; (*of persons*) pelik, lain dari biasa; **an —** seorang yang pelik kelakuannya.

ecclesiastical yang berkenaan dengan gereja.

echo gema, gaung; **to —** bergaung, bergema.

eclair sejenis kuih.

eclipse gerhana; **to —** menggelapkan, mengelamkan.

ecology pengetahuan tentang tempat kediaman makhluk dan cara kehidupannya.

economic yang berkenaan dengan perekonomian; **—s** pengetahuan tentang perekonomian.

economical cermat.

economist orang yang jimat dan cermat.

economize, to — berjimat.

economy ekonomi, perekonomian.

ecstasy besar cita.

ecstatic yang besar cita.

eczema eksema, penyakit kulit.

eddy pusaran air, puting beliung; **to —** berpusar.

Eden (*Paradise*) firdaus.

edge pinggir, sisi, tepi, bibir; (*of knife*) tajam; **to take the —** off menumpulkan.

edible boleh dimakan.

edict undang-undang, maklumat.

edifice pembangunan.

edify, to — memberi menyunting, manfaat.

edit, to — menyunting karangan supaya boleh diterbitkan.

edition penerbitan, pengeluaran, cetakan, edisi.

editor penyunting.

editorial tajuk rancana, induk karangan.

educate, to — mengasuh, mendidik melatih.

education asuhan, pendidikan, pengajaran.

eel ikan belut.

eerie yang menakutkan, mendahsyatkan.

efface, to — menghapuskan.

menghilangkan; to — o.s. berkelakuan sopan.

effect (*result*) akibat; —s (*property*) harta; to take — berlaku.

effective berguna, tepat, benar.

effeminate seperti perempuan.

effervesce, 'o — meruap, mendidih.

efficacious mujarab.

efficiency kependaian, urusan baik.

efficient pandai berhasil, berguna.

effigy patung, gambar orang.

effloresce, to — berbunga.

effluence aliran, pancaran keluar.

effort percubaan, ikhtiar, usaha; to make an — mencuba, berikhtiar, berusaha.

effrontery kelakuan kurang ajar.

effusive dengan mencurahkan perasaannya.

egg telur; he is a bad — a orang jahat; —shell kulit telur.

ego diri, keakuan.

egocentric berpusat pada diri sendiri.

egoism pendirian bahawa segala sesuatu berpusat pada diri sendiri.

egoist orang yang mengutamakan diri sendiri.

egotism perasaan diri sendiri.

Egyptian yang berkenaan dengan (atau orang) Masir.

eiderdown bulu sejenis itik.

eight delapan.

eighteen delapan belas.

eighth yang kedelapan.

eighty delapan puluh.

either kedua-duanya, dalam dua; juga tidak; on — side sebelah-menyebelah; — of you salah satu antara berdua.

ejaculate, to — (*emit*) meman-

carkan; (*speech*) mengucapkan tiba-tiba.

ejaculation pancaran; ucapan tiba-tiba.

eject, to — menghalaukan, mengusir, mengeluarkan.

ejection pengusiran, pengeluaran.

eke, to — out mencari wang, mencari nafkah.

elaborate panjang lebar, lanjut; to — menghuraikan dengan panjang lebar.

elapse, to — lalu.

elastic bingkas, menganjal.

elasticity sifat bingkas, menganjal.

elate, to — menggembirakan, meriangkan; —d gembira, riang; (*proud*) bangga.

elation kegembiraan, keriangan.

elbow siku; at one's — dekat.

elder I (*older*) lebih tua; (*respected aged person*) orang yang patut dihormati, datuk.

elder II sejenis pohon.

elderly setengah baya.

eldest sulung.

elect terpilih; to — memilih.

election pemilihan.

elector pemilih.

electorate para pemilih (istimewa untuk perwakilan rakyat).

electric letrik, dengan jalan tenaga letrik; — shock sambar letrik.

electrician tukang letrik.

electricity letrik.

electrification memasang aliran letrik.

elec rify, to — memberi letrik.

electrocution kematian disebabkan letrik.

electron letron.

elegance kehalusan, kecantikan.

elegant halus, cantik, bergaya.

elegy nyanyian sedih, ratapan.

element unsur, elemen, anasir.

elementary unsur, awalan, rendah.

elephant gajah; a white —sesuatu yang sukar dipeliharakan.

elevate, to — menaikkan, mempertinggikan; —d tinggi; (honoured) mulia.

elevation penaikan, tinggi, ketinggian.

elevator pesawat untuk menaikkan barang atau orang.

eleven sebelas.

elevenses makan pukul sebelas.

elf peri, bidadari, orang halus.

elfin peri.

elicit, to — menarik, mengeluarkan.

eligible patut, layak akan dipilih.

eliminate, to — menghapuskan, melenyapkan.

elimination penghapusan.

elite bahagian yang terbaik, golongan atas.

elixir ubat istimewa, penyegar.

elk rusa besar di negeri Amerika.

ellipse (oval) bulat buntar, ilip.

elliptic(al) bulat buntar; (part left out) tidak sempurna; —question : oalan sampuk.

elm sejenis pohon.

elocution gaya berkata dan berucap, petah.

elongate panjang, memanjang.

elope, to — lari dari rumah dengan bakal suami.

eloquence kefasihan.

eloquent fasih, pasih.

else (otherwise) lain; (besides) lagi; nothing — lain tidak; what —? apalagi?; who —? siapa lagi?

elsewhere pada tempat lain.

elucidate, to — menjelaskan, menerangkan.

elude, to — mengelakkan.

elusive sukar ditangkap, sukar difahamkan.

emaciate, to — menguruskan; mengeringkan.

emaciation kekurusan.

emanate, to — keluar terbit, berpancar dari.

emancipate, to — memerdikakan, melepaskan.

emancipation kemerdikaan kelepa:an

emasculate lemah; to — mengembirikan.

embalm, to — merempahi mayat.

embank, to — menambak membenteng.

embankment tambak benteng.

embargo penahanan (kapal dan perniagaan); to — menahan.

embark, to — naik kapal; to — on mulai sesuatu.

embarrass, to — memberi malu, mempermalukan.

embassy kedutaan.

embellish, to — memperelokkan, menghiasi.

embellishment perhiasan.

ember bara api.

embezzle, to — mencuri barang yang diamanatkan.

embitter, to — memahitkan, menggusarkan.

emblazon memberi berlambang; (honour) memuliakan.

emblem lamb:ng.

embodiment penjelmaan.

embody, to — mengandung, berisi.

emboss, to — membuat pahatan timbul.

embrace rangkuman peluk; to — memeluk, merangkum.

embroider, to — merakam, menyulam.

embroidery sulaman.

embroil, to — membabitkan, mengacaukan.

embryo lembaga; **in** — belum jadi belum diperkembangkan.

emerald zamrud.

emerge, to — muncul, timbul; terbit.

emergence muncul, terbit.

emergency darurat; **state of** — keadaan darurat.

emery amril.

emetic ubat yang menyebabkan muntah.

emigrant orang pindahan.

emigrate, to — berpindah negeri.

emigration perpindahan.

eminence (*excellence*) keunggulan, keutamaan; **His E**gelar seorang pembesar ugama.

eminent utama, unggul.

emissary penyuruh, orang suruhan.

emission pemancaran, penyebaran.

emit, to — memencarkan.

emotion gerak hati, rasa hati, perasaan, kepiluan.

emotional yang berkenaan dengan perasaan hati.

emperor kaisar, maharaja.

emphasis tekanan, ketegasan.

emphasize, to — menekankan, mementingkan, mengutamakan.

emphatic(al) dengan tegas, dengan keras.

empire kerajaan.

empiric(al) berdasarkan penyelidikan.

employ, to — mempergunakan.

employee pegawai, pekerja, kakitangan.

employer majikan, pengusaha.

employment pekerjaan, gunatenaga.

empower to — memberi kuasa.

empress isteri kaiser; maharani.

emptiness kekosongan, kehampaan.

empty kosong, hampa; **to** — mengosongkan, menghampakan.

emu sejenis burung unta, burung kasawari.

emulate, to — berikhtiar akan menyamai (atau mengatasi) melawan.

emulsion campuran yang tak senyawa.

enable, to — memungkinkan, membolehkan.

enact, to — memerintahkan dalam peraturan (atau undang-undang); (*effect*) melakukan.

enamel sadur; **to** — menyadur.

enamour, to — (*inspire with love*) memberahikan; (*like*) menyukakan.

encamp, to — berkhemah.

encampment perkhemahan.

encase, to — memasukkan ke dalam bungkusan (peti dan sebagainya); (*cover*) melingkupi.

enchant, to — (*love, delight*) memberahikan, menyukakan; (*bewitch*) menghikmat.

enchantment (*magical*) pesona.

encircle, to — melengkari, mengepung.

enclave daerah yang letaknya di dalam negeri asing.

enclose, to — melengkari, melengkungi; (*in letter*) melampirkan, menyertakan.

enclosure (*land*) sebidang tanah yang dikelilingi pagar; (*of letter*) lampiran.

encompass, to — melengkari, mengelilingi.

encore sekali lagi, ulangan; **to** — meminta supaya nyanyian dan sebagainya diulangi sekali lagi.

encounter (*sudden meeting*) pertemuan tiba-tiba.

encourage to — menggiatkan; (*advance*) memajukan, menganjurkan.

encouragement (*comfort*) penghiburan; (*give a lead*) penganjuran.

encroach, to — (*spread*) menjalar; (*infringe*) melanggar.

encroachment pelanggaran.

encrust, to — menutupi dengan kulit (kerak dan sebagainya).

encumber, to — (*obstruct*) menghalangi; (*burden*) membebankan.

encumbrance beban, kesusahan.

encyclopaedia ensiklopedia, kamus langkap.

end (*limit*) hingga; (*conclusion*) akhir, penghabisan, kesudahan; (*aim*) tujuan; to come to an — berakhir; to — mengakhiri menyudahi.

endanger, to — membahayakan, menggentingkan.

endear, to — menyukakan, mencintakan.

endearment cumbuan.

endeavour percubaan; to — mencuba, berusaha.

endemic yang selalu didapati di antara sesuatu suku bangsa.

endless tidak habisnya, tidak sudah, tidak berkesudahan; (*eternal*) kekal.

endo— awalan kata yang ertinya; di dalam.

endorse, to — (*a cheque*) menulis tandatangan pada belakang cek; (*approve*) membenarkan mengesahkan.

endorsement (*signature*) tandatangan; pembenaran.

endow, to — (*bequeath*) mewariskan; (*give*) memberi.

endowment anugerahan, pemberian wang, kuasa.

endurance daya tahan, tahanan.

endure, to — merasai, menderita, menahan; terus berlaku.

enemy seorang lawan, musuh, seteru.

energetic bertenaga, bergaya, giat, ringan tulang.

energize, to — menggiatkan, mencurahkan semangat.

energy tenaga, daya, kegiatan, kekuatan.

enfold, to — meliputi; (*embrace*) memeluk.

enforce, to — (*put on pressure*) mendesak; (*compel*) memaksa.

engage, to — (*agree*) berjanji; (*retain*) menempah; (*attract*) menarik hati.

engaged (*in marriage*) bertunang; to be — in sedang berbuat sesuatu.

engagement pertunangan; perjanjian.

engaging mengambil hati.

engender, to — mengakibatkan.

engine jentera, pesawat, motor; — driver pemandu keretapi, lokomotif.

engineer, (civil) — jurutera.

English Inggeris; (*language*) bahasa Inggeris; the — orang Inggeris.

engrave, to — merakamkan, mengukir, memahat.

engraving gambar pahatan.

engross, to — menarik seluruh perhatian.

engulf, to — meliputi.

enhance, to — meninggikan, memperbesar.

enhancement peninggian.

enigma hal yang sulit dan sukar terfaham.

enjoy, to — menyukai, mengalami sesuatu yang menggembirakan.

enjoyable sedap, yang menyukakan.

enjoyment kesukaan.

enlarge, to — menjadi besar, memperbesarkan, memperluaskan.

enlargement pembesaran.

enlighten, to — menerangkan, menjelaskan.

enlist, to — masuk tentera.

enliven, to — menggiatkan, menggembirakan.

enmesh menjerat, menjala.

enmity perseteruan, permusuhan.

enormity kejahatan besar.

enormous sangat besar.

enough cukup, pada, sampai.

enrage, to — memarahkan, menerbitkan marah.

enrapture, to — sangat menyukakan hati.

enrich, to — memperkayakan.

enrol, to — (list name) mendaftarkan nama; (join a body) menjadikan seseorang angguta.

enrolment pendaftaran.

ensconce, to — (place) menempatkan; (hide) menyembunyikan.

ensemble seluruhnya, hal yang ditinjaukan sebagai satu.

enshrine, to — memasukkan dalam tempat suci.

ensign bendera, panji.

ensnare, to — memikat, memperdayakan.

ensue, to — terjadi sebagai akibat, disebabkan.

ensure, to — menentukan, menetapkan.

entail, to — menetapkan hak milik salah satu bidang tanah supaya tak dapat diwariskan kepada orang lain.

entangle, to — (implicate) membabitkan.

enter, to — (place) masuk; (write in) mendaftarkan, memacukkan; to — (up)on mulai.

enterprise usaha, pengusahaan.

enterprising (active) cerga; (bold) berani.

entertain, to — menamu, menjamu, menjamukan.

entertainment permainan, kesukaan, kesenangan.

enthral, to — menarik, mengambil hati.

enthrone, to — menabalkan; —d bertakhta.

enthusiasm kegembiraan, semangat.

enthusiast orang yang bersemangat.

enthusiastic menggelora, gembira, bersemangat.

entice, to — membujuk.

entire seluruh, segala, antero.

entirely samasekali, belaka.

entirety kesempurnaan, seluruhnya.

entitle, to — (name) menamakan memberi nama; (give claim to) memberi hak.

entity pati, kebenaran.

entomology kaji serangga.

entrails isi perut, usus.

entrance I pintu masuk, jalan masuk.

entrance II, to — sangat merawankan, merayukan, mengharukan.

entreat, to — memohon.

entreaty permintaan, permohonan.

entrée (dish) makanan yang dihidangkan di antara makanan ikan dan makanan daging.

entrench, to — mengelilingi dengan parit.

entrepot (storehouse) gudang untuk barang perniagaan; (centre) pusat perdagangan.

entrepreneur pengusaha, majikan perusahaan.

entrust, to — mengamanatkan.

entry masuknya; pintu masuk; pendaftaran.

entwine, to — membelitkan, menjalin.

enumerate, to — membilang, menghisab, menghitung.

enumeration hisab, penghitungan.

enunciate, to — mempermakalumkan, mengucapkan.

envelop, to — menyelubungi, memalut, meliputi.

envelope sampul, salut, sarung.

enviable yang menerbitkan cemburu, iri hati.

envious cemburu, iri hati, dengki; to be — of cemburu akan, mengiri.

environment lengkungan; suasana, keadaan alam sekeliling.

environs daerah kota, sekeliling.

envisage, to — berhadapan muka dengan, menghadapi, memandang.

envoy duta, utusan.

envy kecemburuan, iri hati, dengki; to — mengiri, mencemburui.

enzyme enjima, enzim.

ephemeral yang hidup hanya sehari sahaja, yang tak kekal.

epic syair pahlawan.

epidemic wabah.

epidermis kulit ari, kulit luar.

epigram pantun atau sajak pendek yang mengandung buah fikiran.

epilepsy sawan babi.

epilogue bahagian terakhir sebu h karangan.

epiphany penjelmaan.

episcopal yang berkenaan dengan gereja.

episode peristiwa.

epistle surat (istimewa yang disebut dalam Injil).

epitaph tulisan pada nesan.

epithet nama istimewa yang menyatakan sifat sesuatu.

epitome ikhtisar, ringkasan.

epoch jaman, zaman.

equable tetap; (calm) tenang.

equal samarata, sebidang, sepadan, setanding, banding, orang yang sepangkat.

equality kesamaan.

equalize, to — meratakan, menyamakan.

equally sama.

equanimity ketenangan hati, ketetapan hati.

equate, to — menyamakan, mempersamakan.

equator khatt ul-istiwa.

equatorial yang berkenaan dengan khatt ul-istiwa.

equerry salah seorang perwira pada istana raja.

equestrian yang berkenaan dengan menunggang kuda; (rider) penunggang kuda.

equilateral yang sama sempadannya.

equilibrium keseimbangan.

equine yang seperti atau berkenaan dengan kuda.

equinox waktu matahari melalui khatt ul-istiwa.

equip, to — berlengkap, melengkapi.

equipment peralatan, perlengkapan, kelengkapan.

equitable adil.

equity keadilan.

equivalent sama, seteraf imbangan, tanding(an) bentara beratara.

equivocal bererti dua.

equivocate, to — berdalih.

era masa, tarikh, zaman.

eradicate, to — membinasakan, memusnahkan.

erase, to — menghapuskan, memupuskan.

eraser penghapus.

erect tegak, tercancang; to — membangunkan, menegakkan, mendirikan.

erection penegakan, pembangunan.

ermine sejenis cerpelai; bulu binatang tersebut (yang sangat berharga).

erode, to — dimakan karat, dimakan hari.

erosion karat, hakisan; soil — penghanyutan tanah.

erotic yang berkenaan dengan cinta, asmara.

err, to — salah, berkhilaf.

errand perjalanan akan menghantarkan surat; — boy suruhan.

erratic tak tentu, melincah-lincah.

erroneous salah.

error salah, kesalahan, kekeliruan.

erudite terpelajar, pandai.

erudition keadaban pendidikan, kepandaian.

erupt, to — meletus.

eruption letusan, letupan; (of skin) timbulnya kudis.

escalator tangga yang bergerak akan menaikkan orang.

escape kelepasan; to — berlepas diri; (of stream etc) keluar.

escarpment batu karang yang curam.

escort pengiringan, pengantar, pengiring; to — menghantar, mengiringi.

esoteric maknawi, batin.

especial istimewa utama.

especially istimewa pula, terutama.

espionage pekerjaan penyuluhan.

esplanade jalan atau lapangan untuk melancung.

espouse (wed), to — nikah, menikahkan.

esquire, abbr **Esq.** gelar yang sekarang hanya dipakai pada alamat surat, ertinya: tuan yang terhormat.

essay karangan, risalat.

essence inti, pati.

essential pokok, perlu, keperluan; —ly pada hakikatnya.

establish, to — mendirikan; menentukan, menetapkan, menubuhkan.

establishment (settling) penetapan, penentuan; (a body) badan, perusahaan, penubuhan.

estate (land) tanah; (plantation) kebun; (property) harta.

esteem hormat; to — menghormati.

estimate taksiran, perkiraan, nilaian; to — menaksir.

estimation pendapat, timbangan; (respect) hormat.

estrange, to — merenggangkan.

estuary kuala, muara.

et cetera, abbr **etc.** dan sebagainya (dsb.) dan lain-lain (dll).

etch, to — menggambarkan secara memahat.

etching pahatan, gambar.

eternal abadi, kekal; (unbroken) tak putus-putusnya.

eternity kekekalan, negeri yang baka.

ethereal sangat halus.

ethical yang berkenaan dengan adat istiadat dan keadaban.

ethics ilmu adab, pengetahuan tentang adat dan segala rukun hidup.

ethnic(al) yang berkenaan dengan bangsa.

etiquette peraturan adat dan budi bahasa.

etymology ilmu pengetahuan tentang asal dan erti-kata.

eucalyptus kayu putih; — oil minyak kayu putih.

eulogy pujian, madah.

eunuch orang puntung, sida.

euphemism nama halus untuk sesuatu yang kurang baik, pemanis.

euphonic, euphonious yang bunyinya baik.

Eurasian peranakan bangsa Eropah dengan bangsa Asia, kacukan.

Europe Eropah.

European yang berkenaan dengan Eropah, orang Eropah.

evacuate, to — keluar, mengo.ongkan.

evacuation pencucian perut; (*withdrawal*) penyingkiran.

evacuee pelari, penyingkir.

evade, to — mengelak, menyingkiri.

evaluate, to — menilai.

evaluation nilaian.

evangelic(al) yang berkenaan dengan penyebaran ugama Nasrani.

evangelist guru injil.

evaporate, to — menguap, meruap, menghawa, sejat.

evaporation pengewap, menjadi wap, sejatan.

evasion pengelakan; (*equivocation*) dalih.

evasive yang mengelak; berdalih.

eve malam yang mendahului sesuatu peristiwa.

even I rata, datar, sama; (*of numbers*) genap.

even II (*adverb*) malahan, juga, pun, bahkan, biarpun; (*repay*) to — membalas.

evening malam, petang.

event hal, perihal, peristiwa, kejadian.

eventful ramai, penuh peristiwa.

eventide senjakala.

eventual yang harus akan terjadi, yang akhirnya terjadi.

eventuality hal yang harus akan terjadi.

ever pernah, selalu, sentiasa, selamanya; what— barang apa dan seterusnya.

evergreen pohon yang daunnya malar hijau.

everlasting kekal, tidak berkesudahan, abadi.

every setiap, tiap-tiap; — other day selang sehari; — now and again sekali-sekali.

evict, to — mengusir, menghalaukan.

eviction pengusiran.

evidence kenyataan, pernyataan; to give — naik saksi; to — menyatakan.

evident ternyata, terang.

evil keburukan, kejahatan.

evince, to — menunjukkan.

evoke, to — memanggil.

evolution perkembangan ubah ansur.

evolve, to — memperkembangkan ubah ansur.

ewe biri-biri betina.

ex— bekas, lepasan.

exacerbate, to — menggusarkan.

exact (*demanding*) saksama, berjangka; betul, tepat; —ly betul, tepat.

exacting menuntut banyak kemahuannya.

exaggerate, to — melebihlebihkan, membesar-besarkan.

exaggeration kelebih-lebihan.

exalt, to — menjunjung, menjulang, mempermuliakan.

exaltation permuliaan.

examination (*test*) ujian; (*investigation*) pemeriksaan; penyelidikan; to pass an — lulus dalam ujian.

examine, to — menyelidiki, memeriksa; menguji.

example umpama, ibarat, misal, tuladan, contoh; for — misalnya.

exasperate, to — memahitkan, memarahkan.

exasperation kepahitan, dendam.

excavate, to — menggali.

excavation penggalian.

exceed, to — melampaui, melebihi.

exceedingly terlalu, terlampau, terlebih.

excel, to — mengatasi, melampaui, melebihi.

excellence keutamaan.

Excellency, (Your, His, Her) — yang terutama.

excellent ulung, sangat baik.

except, —ing selain, kecuali terkecuali; **to —** mengecualikan.

exception kecualian; **without** — tidak terkecuali; **to take —** to membantah.

exceptional luar biasa, teristimewa, bukan main.

excerpt ringkasan.

excess (*increase*) kelebihan; (*abundance*) kemewahan; **in** — of lebih daripada.

excessive telanjur, tersangat, terlampau.

exchange pertukaran; (*money*) pertukaran wang; **to —** bertukar, menyilih, menukar.

exchangeable dapat ditukar, boleh ditukar.

exchequer perbendaharaan; **Chancellor of the E—** menteri kewangan kerajaan Inggeris.

excise bia, cukai; **to —** mencukai.

excitation perangsang; pengasutan.

excite, to — mengasut, merangsangkan, menggiatkan; **—d** gembira.

excitement kegembiraan; (*tumult*) gempar.

exclaim, to — berteriak, menyerukan.

exclamation seruan, penyeruan; **— mark** tanda penyeru(!),

exclude, to — mengeluarkan, tidak memberi masuk.

exclusion pengeluaran.

exclusive tidak termasuk, tergolong, kecuali.

excommunicate, to — membuang seseorang dari umat Nasrani.

excrement(s) tahi, cirit.

excrete mengeluarkan membuang.

excruciate, to — menyeksakan.

exculpate, to — memperlepaskan, membebaskan daripada tuduhan.

excursion melawat tempat-tempat, berkelah, makan angin.

excuse permintaan ampun, maaf; (*device*) dalih, helah; **to —** mengampuni; **— me** minta maaf.

execrable sangat buruk, celaka.

execute, to — melangsungkan, mengerjakan, melaksanakan, melakukan; (*death penalty*) melakukan hukuman mati.

execution penglaksanaan melakuan.

executioner pertanda, algoja.

executive yang berkenaan dengan melakukannya sesuatu hal.

executor pelaku; **— of a will** wasi.

exemplary patut dituladan.

exempt lepas, bebas; **to —** memperlepaskan, mengecualikan.

exemption pembebasan.

exercise (*use*) penggunaan; (*training*) latihan; **— book** buku campaian; **to —** melatih.

exert, to — (*use*) mempergunakan; (*strength*) berkuat, menguatkan; **to —** influence mempengaruhi.

exertion pengusahaan.

exhalation wap, pengeluaran nafas,

exhale, to — menguapkan, menafaskan.

exhaust tempat keluaran gas (wap dan sebaginya); **to —** (*tire out*) memenatkan, melelahkan; menghabiskan.

exhaustion keletihan, kelelahan kepenatan.

exhaustive habis-habisan, lengkap.

exhibit bukti, tanda, hal yang dipertunjukkan; to — mempertunjukkan.

exhibition pertunjukan, pameran.

exhilarate, to — menggembirakan, meriangkan, menyukakan hati.

exhilaration sukacita.

exhort, to — (admonish) menegur; (urge) mendesak.

exhortation desakan.

exhume, to — mengeluarkan semula dari tanah kuburan.

exigence, exigency kesesakan.

exile orang buangan, buangan, pengusiran; to — membuang dari negerinya.

exist, to — ada, terdapat, hidup.

existence kehidupan, keadaan, wujud.

existent ada, terdapat, hidup.

exit tempat (jalan) keluar.

exodus kepergian (istimewa beramai-ramai).

exonerate, to — membebaskan, memperlepaskan.

exorbitant terlalu mahal, besar.

exorcize, to — menjampikan, menyerapah.

exotic asing.

expand, to — meluas, mengembang, memperluaskan.

expanse daerah yang luas.

expansion perkembangan, perluasan.

expatriate, to — membuang, mengeluarkan dari negerinya.

expect, to — (think) menyangka; (hope) mengharap; (reckon) mengira, berpendapat.

expectancy pengharapan.

expectant harapan, berharapan.

expectation pengharapan.

expedience kecerdikan.

expedient berguna, bermanfaat; (suitable) patut.

expedite, to — memperlekaskan, menyegerakan.

expedition (for war etc) angkatan; (speed) kecepatan.

expel, to — mengusir, membuang.

expend, to — (money) membelanjakan; (give out) memberi.

expenditure perbelanjaan.

expense harga; —s perbelanjaan.

expensive mahal.

experience pengalaman; to — mengalami, merasai; —d berpengalaman.

experiment duga percubaan; to — mengadakan percubaan.

experimental dugaan berdasarkan percubaan dan penyelidikan.

expert (skilled person) ahli, pakar; (skilled) pandai mempunyai kepandaian istimewa.

expiration (breath) pengeluaran nafas; (end) selesai.

expire, to — (breathe out) mengeluarkan nafas; (die) meninggal, mati.

expiry akhir, selesai.

explain, to — menyatakan, menerangkan, menghuraikan; to — o.s. menjelaskan maksudnya.

explanation keterangan, penjelasan.

explanatory yang menerangkan, menjelaskan.

expletive kata yang melengkapkan, yang tak bererti.

explicit terang nyata, jelas.

explode, to — meletup, meletus; (error) mempertunjukkan kesalahannya.

exploit perbuatan yang mulia; to — mempergunakan.

exploitation penggunaan, penggunaan untuk kepentingan diri sendiri.

exploration pemeriksaan.

explore, to — memeriksa, menjelajah.

explosion letupan, letusan.

explosive peletup, yang meletup.

exponent seorang atau sesuatu yang menerangkan; (*example*) umpama, tamsil.

export pengeluar, ekspot; —s barang ekspot.

expose, to — (*open curtains etc*) menyingkap; (*show*) mempertunjukkan; (*open up*) membukakan.

exposition pertunjukan, penjelasan.

expostulate, to — membantah.

exposure keadaan terdedah di angin; (*display*) pertunjukan.

expound, to — menghuraikan, memaparkan.

express I (*exact*) tepat; (*specially done*) istimewa dibuat; (*fast*) cepat, lekas; (*train*) keretapi ekspres.

express II , to — (*emit*) mengeluarkan, melahirkan; (*speak*) mengucapkan, menyatakan.

expression (*phrase*) pengucapan, penyataan, kata; (*of face*) air muka.

expressive (*serving to show or reveal*) yang menunjukkan, melahirkan; (*of meaning*) mengandung erti.

expropriate, to — mengambil milik orang.

expulsion pembuangan.

exquisite sangat elok, sangat baik, sangat halus.

ex-service bekas ahli tentera.

extant yang ada, yang terdapat.

extempore dengan tidak dikarangkan atau difikirkan lebih dahulu.

extend, to — meluas, meman-

jang; to — kindness to menunjukkan ramah tamah.

extension keluasan, perluasan; sambungan.

extensive luas.

extent luas, keluasan; to a certain — sampai darjat yang tertentu.

extenuate, to — meringankan.

exterior luar, di luar, dari luar.

exterminate, to — membasmi, membinasakan.

extermination pembasmian, kebinasaan.

external luar, zahir.

extinct (*extinguished*) padam; (*vanished*) lenyap; mati.

extinction kehilangan, kematian.

extinguish, to — memadamkan, mematikan.

extinguisher pemadam.

extol, to — memuji.

extort, to — memperoleh sesuatu.

extortion pemerasan.

extra tambahan, lebih.

extra- di luar sesuatu; — mural di luar tembok.

extract (*from book*) kutipan dari buku; to — (*pull out*) menarik, mencabut.

extraction penarikan, pencabutan.

extradite, to — menyerahkan penjahat asing kepada yang berwajib.

extraneous tak masuk golongan.

extraordinary luar biasa, bukan kepalang.

extravagance sifat pemboros.

extravagant pemboros.

extreme (*furthest*) yang terjauh; (*especially*) istimewa, tersangat.

extremist orang yang berpendirian pelampau.

extremity hujung.

extricate, to — melepaskan, mengeluarkan.

extrovert orang yang mementingkan hal-hal zahir lebih daripada hal yang batin.

exuberance kemewahan.

exuberant (of plant growth) subur; (abundance) mewah; (overdране decoration) terlalu banyak perhiasan.

exude, to — bercucuran, mencucurkan.

exult, to — beria-ria, bergembira.

exultant ria, gembira, gerang.

exultation kegerangan, keriangan.

eye mata; apple of the — jantung hati; to keep an — on menjaga.

eyeball biji mata.

eyebrow alis, kening.

eyelash bulu mata.

eyelid pelupuk mata, kelopak mata.

eye-opener hal yang memberi keinsafan tentang sesuatu.

eyesight penglihatan.

eyewash sindir mata.

eye-witness saksi yang melihat sesuatu dengan matanya sendiri.

F

fable dongeng binatang, cerita hikayat, dongeng.

fabric (raw material) bahan; (cloth) kain.

fabricate, to — memperbuat; mereka.

fabrication (design) rekarekaan; (falsehood) pemalsuan.

fabulous mustahil.

façade hadapan, muka rumah.

face muka, paras, wajah; to his — di mukanya; on the — of it rupanya.

face powder bedak.

facet segi (istimewa pada intan).

facetious jenaka, melawak.

facial yang berkenaan dengan muka.

facile mudah, lancar; (easygoing) lemah lembut.

facilitate, to — memudahkan.

facility (easiness) kemudahan; (opportunity) kesempatan.

facing (opposite) bertentangan berhadapan, menghadapi.

facsimile salinan tepat.

fact (historical fact) peristiwa; (case, matter) hal; in —, as a matter of — sebenarnya.

faction golongan, badan.

factor (element in something) faktor, pengisi.

factory (trading station) loji; (industry) kilang.

factotum bujang yang membantu tuannya dalam segala hal.

factual yang berkenaan dengan kenyataan.

faculty (aptitude) bakat; (ability) kebolehan; (department of University etc) salah satu cabang sekolah tinggi, fakulti.

fade, to — turun warnanya, luntur, hilang warnanya.

fading pengurangan, menurun.

faeces tahi, cirit.

fag (sl: weary toil) pekerjaan yang menjemukan.

faggot kayu api yang diikat.

fail, without — tak mungkin, tak dapat tidak.

failing I (blemish etc) cacat, kesalahan.

failing II (in default of) kalau bukan demikian, jika tidak.

failure tidak terjadinya, terkandas; (financial) hal yang tidak berhasil.

fain, would — sudi, rela akan.

taint (not clear) tak nyata.

redup; (weak) lemah; —-hearted takut, penakut; (swoon) to — pengsan.

fair I (beautiful, fine) indah, bagus, elok; a — copy salinan yang bersih; — play adil dan teratur dengan tidak memakai tipu daya; the — sex kaum perempuan.

fair II (market) pasar malam derima.

fairly — well baik juga.

fairway sebahagian jalan (atau sungai) yang mudah dijalani.

fairy peri, bidadari; —land negeri antah berantah.

faith (religious) iman, keimanan; (reliance) kepercayaan.

faithful setiawan, berbakti; the — yang beriman.

faithfulness kesetiaan, khidmat.

faithless (untrustworthy) tak setia, tak dapat dipercayai.

fake cesuatu yang tak benar, barang palsu; to — memalsukan.

fakir orang fakir.

falcon burung helang.

fall kejatuhan, keruntuhan, keguguran; (autumn) musim buah; —c (waterfall) air terjun.

fallacious salah, tak benar.

fallacy kesalahan, buah fikiran yang tak benar.

fallible dapat bersalah.

fallow tandus; to lie — ditinggalkan, tidak dikerjakan.

false (not true) salah, tak benar; (counterfeit) palsu; pembohong, penipu.

falsehood (lie) bohong, dusta; sesuatu yang tak benar.

falsetto suara laki-laki yang tinggi seperti suara perempuan.

falsification pemalsuan.

falsify, to — memalsukan, memutar balikkan.

falter, to — (stumble) berjalan goyah, bergoyang; (of speech) bercakap tertahan-tahan (terputus-putus).

fame nama (buruk atau baik), nama baik, nama yang termasyhur.

famed (rumoured) konon, khabarnya; (illustrious) termasyhur.

familiar baik, jinak manja, terkenal, biasa; to be — with biasa dengan.

familiarity ramah-tamah.

familiarize, to — o.s. merapatkan diri, memperkenalkan.

family keluarga (ayah bonda dengan anaknya) sanak saudara, kaum keluarga.

famine bahaya kelaparan, kebuluran.

famish, to — laparkan.

famous termasyhur, terkenal, ternama.

fan I kipas, baling-balingangin.

fan II (enthusiast) penggemar

fanatic fanatik, gila-gilaan.

fanaticism fanatik

fancier peminat; bird — orang yang menggemari burung.

fanciful berbagai ragamnya.

fancy (idea) angan-angan, rekaan; (inclination) kecenderungan; (ornamental) berhias.

fanfare bunyi terompet.

fang taring.

fantastic ajaib.

fantasy khayal; (in writing) karangan berdasarkan anganangan.

far jauh, jauh lebih; as — as sampai, pada tempat itu, sejauh.

farce pekerjaan tak sungguhsungguh, main-main sahaja.

fare wang tambang; (food) makanan yang dihidang.

farewell perpisahan, selamat tinggal.

farinaceous yang mengandung pati, berpati.

farm kebun, tanah, rumah dan ladang; (of *livestock*) peternakan; to — bertani, bercucuk tanam.

farmer orang tani, petani.

fart kentut.

farther lebih jauh.

farthest yang terlebih jauh.

fascinate, to — sangat menarik hati, mengambil hati.

fascinating yang sangat menarik, pandai mengambil hati.

fascination dayapenarik.

Fascism faham fasis.

Fascist seorang yang menganut faham fasis.

fashion (style) ragam; (custom) kebiasaan, adat; to — membuat, membontok.

fashionable menurut cara, menurut adat kebiasaan.

fast I (fasting) puasa; to — berpuasa.

fast II (firm) keras, kukuh; (speedy) deras, cepat, lekas, laju; a — colour warna yang tak luntur; — asleep tidur nyenyak, nyedar.

fasten, to — (by stakes) memancangkan; (bind) mengikat; (stick on) melekatkan; (fil) memasang.

fastidious berpilih-pilih.

fat gemuk, berminyak, lemak; —head orang bodoh.

fatal yang mengakibatkan kematian.

fatalism faham sabar.

fatality nasib buruk, kecelakaan.

fate nasib; he was —d sudah nasibnya.

fateful nasib, yang sudah ditentukan.

father ayah, bapak.

fatherhood menjadi, ayah.

father-in-law bapa mentua.

fatherland tanahair.

fathom depa; to — mendepa.

fatigue kelelahan, lesu, kepenatan.

fatten, to — menambunkan, menggemukkan.

fatty gemuk, tembun.

fatuous tak berguna.

faucet (pipe) saluran.

fault (flaw) cacat, aib, cela; (error) salah, kesalahan, gelinciran.

faultfinding suka mengumpat, mencari salah.

faultless tidak bercela, tidak bergelinciran.

fauna segala haiwan, binatang, mergastua.

favour (gift) anugerah, kurnia; (approve) to — kenan.

favourable yang menguntungkan, baik, patut, yang mengkabulkan.

favourite yang terlebih disukai, kesayangan.

fawn I anak rusa.

fawn II, to — mengibaskan buntut; to — upon bermanismanis.

fear ketakutan, gentar; for — of kerana takut.

fearful yang menggentarkan, takut, segan.

fearless tak takut, tak gentar.

fearsome yang menakutkan.

feasible harus dapat dikerjakan.

feast (day) hariraya, hari besar; (banquet) perjamuan, kenduri.

feat perbuatan gagah atau ajaib.

feather bulu burung; (crest of bird) jambul.

feature sifat, kasiat, hal yang penting; to — menunjukkan hal yang penting.

febrile berkenaan dengan sakit demam.

February bulan Februari.

feckless tak berguna.

fecund subur, biak.

fecundity kesuburan, ke-adaan biak.

fed pp and pt of **feed**; — **up with** jemu, bosan.

federal sekutu, bersatu.

federate, to — berkumpul, bersekutu, bersatu.

federation menyatukan, per-sekutuan, kesatuan.

fee bayaran, biaya upah; (subscription) harga langganan; (school fees) bayaran sekolah.

feeble lemah, lemas, merang-kak-rangkak; —**minded** be-bal, bodoh.

feed pemberian makan; **to** — memberi makan; (put food into child's mouth) menyuapi; (supply) memberi; (satisfy) memuaskan; (fatten) **to** — **up** menambahkan.

feel rasanya, perasaan; **to** — (grope) meraba; (be conscious of) berasa; (realize) berpera-a-an, berpendapat; **to** — **fine** merasa senang hati.

feeler (antenna) sungut-sungut.

feeling rasa, perasaan, cita.

feet pl of **foot**.

feign, to — buat-buat, pura-pura.

feint serangan, pukulan yang dibuat-buat sahaja; **to** — menyerang pura-pura.

felicitous sangat baik dan pada tempatnya.

feline yang berkenaan dengan kucing, yang seperti kucing.

fellow kawan, teman, sahabat, saudara.

fellowship persahabatan; (scholastic) pangkat seorang; fellow, pada sekolah tinggi.

felony kejahatan, kesalahan besar.

felt I sejenis kain tebal dan panas.

felt II pp and pt of **feel**.

female (of persons) perempuan; (of animals) betina.

feminine yang berkenaan dengan perempuan.

femininity perempuan.

feminism faham perempuan.

femur, —**s** (atau) femora, tulang paha.

fence I, to — main bersilat.

fence II pagar; **to** — **in** mema-gari mengurungkan.

fence III (receiver) tukang tadah; **to** — menadah.

fencer (with sword) pendekar ahli silat.

fencing pagar-pagar, bahan untuk membuat pagar.

fend, to — menolak; **to** — **for o.s.** memelihara diri.

fender alat pencegah, penolak.

fennel adas.

ferment ragi; **to** — beragi, mendemam menapai.

fermentation peragian pena-paian.

fern pakis, paku.

ferocious buas, ganas.

ferocity kebuasan, keganasan.

ferret sejenis musang yang dipakai pada pemburuan.

ferric, ferrous mengandung besi, ferik.

ferry tambangan, perahu tam-bang, feri; **to** — menambang-kan, menyeberang.

fertile subur, biak.

fertility kesuburan.

fertilize, to — merabuki, membaja.

fertilizer pupuk, baja; **arti-ficial** — baja (pupuk) buatan.

fervent asyik, bersemangat, panas.

fervour kegiatan.

fester, to — membarah, ber-nanah.

festival perayaan yang ber-kenaan dengan hariraya.

festive yang berkenaan de-ngan keriaan; yang suka.

festivity perjamuan.

festoon karangan bunga, gu-

bahan; to — menghiasi dengan karangan bunga.

fetch, to — mengambil, membawa; *(be sold for)* dijual seharga.

fetching yang menyukakan.

fete hari-raya; **to —** menjamukan.

fetid kohong, pesing.

fetish jimat.

fetter(s) belenggu.

fettle keadaan; **in good (fine) —** dalam keadaan baik.

feud *see* **enmity.**

feudal, — system sistem yang mementingkan pertalian rapat antara tuantanah dengan penduduk tanah itu.

fever demam.

feverish sakit demam.

few sedikit; **a —** beberapa.

fez sejenis kopiah terbus.

fiancé(e) tunangan.

fiasco kegagalan.

fib bohong; **to —** membohong.

fibre sabut, serabut; **of coarse —** bersifat kasar.

fickle bertingkah, berubah-ubah.

fickleness sifat bertingkah.

fiction khayal; *(in literature)* karangan yang berdasarkan angan-angan.

fictitious khayalan; berdasarkan hal yang tak benar; *(pretending)* pura-pura.

fiddle biola, rebab.

fiddler pemain biola, rebab.

fiddling *(trifling)* tak berharga, tak berguna.

fidelity kesetiaan.

fidget tingkah, kegelisahan; *(person)* orang yang terlincah-lincah.

fidgety terlincah-lincah, gelisah.

field lapangan, tanah lapang, medan, halaman padang; *(of battle)* medan peperangan; *(in farm)* huma ladang, sawah.

fiend iblis, syaitan; *(addict)* seorang yang ketagih sesuatu; **dope —** orang yang ketagih dadah.

fierce galak, ganas; *(of heat)* hangat, panas.

fiery berapi-api, bernyala, panas; **— red** merah padam.

fifteen lima belas.

fifth yang kelima; **a —** seperlima.

fiftieth yang kelima puluh.

fifty lima puluh.

fig buah ara.

fight perkelahian, perjuangan, pertempuran.

fighter pendekar, pahlawan, pejuang; *(boxer)* peninju; *(aeroplane)* kapalterbang pemburu.

fighting cock ayam sabungan.

figment keterangan yang tidak betul.

figurative kiasan, ibarat.

figure *(appearance)* rupa; *(carriage)* sikap; *(cipher)* angka; *(diagram)* rajah; *(statue)* patung.

filament sabut, tali, tali pusar, filamen.

filch, to — mencuri.

file I kikir; **to —** mengikir.

file II *(papers)* alat *(buku)* tempat menyimpan surat; **to —** menyusun dan menyimpan surat.

file III *(row)* deret baris; **single —** satu baris sahaja.

filial yang berkenaan dengan kewajipan anak terhadap orang tuanya.

filigree sejenis pekerjaan emas perak.

filings kikir, tahi kikir.

fill kekenyangan; **to eat one's —** makan sampai kenyang.

fillet *(ribbon)* pita, jalur; *(piece of meat etc)* sepotong daging atau ikan yang tak ada tulangnya.

filling pengisi, isi gigi.

fillip (*with finger*) jentik; (*stimulus*) dorongan pendo-rong.

filly anak kuda betina.

film (*on eye*) selaput; filem, gambar hidup; — **star** bin-tang filem.

filter penyaring, penapis; to — menyaring, menapis.

filth kotor, kecemaran.

filthy kotor.

filtration penapisan.

fin sirip ikan.

final (*at the end*) terakhir; (*conclusive*) tak dapat diubah lagi, tentu; (*of a contest*) per-tandingan yang terakhir.

finale bahagian yang terakhir karangan muzik (sandiwara dan lain-lain).

finance kewangan, urusan wang; —s wang.

financial yang berkenaan dengan kewangan.

financier ahli kewangan.

finch sejenis burung bernyanyi.

find pendapatan; to — men-dapat, menemui, bertemu dengan; (*come to an opinion*) berpendapat; (*decide*) memu-tuskan.

finder orang yang mendapat (menemui) sesuatu.

finding (*of court*) keputusan hakim.

fine I (*delicate*) halus; (*of quality*) elok, indah, baik.

fine II (*penalty*) denda; to — mengenakan denda.

finery dandan, perhiasan.

finesse kehalusan, akal.

finger jari; index — jari telunjuk; little — jari koleng-keng; middle — jari hantu; ring — jari manis.

finger bowl kembukan.

fingerprint bekas jari.

fingertip hujung jari.

finish habis, akhir, perhen-tian, kesudahan.

finite terbatas.

fir sejenis pohon.

fire api, bara, kebakaran; (*of gun*) tembakan, penem-bakan; to cease — letak senjata; on — terbakar.

fire alarm alat yang me-nunjukkan bahaya api, sem-boyan kebakaran.

firearm senjata api.

fire brigade pasukan pe-madam api, pasukan bomba.

fire engine pesawat pema-dam api, jentera bomba.

fire escape sejenis tangga untuk lari kalau kebakaran.

firefly api-api kelip-kelip, kunang-kunang.

fireplace dapur, tungku, tem-pat api.

fireproof tahan api.

fireside tempat dekat api, bara.

firewood kayu bakar, kayu api.

firework petas, mercun, bunga api.

firing penembakan, temba-kan.

firm I tepat, kuat, kukuh, tegas.

firm II perusahaan, gudang.

firmness kekukuhan, kete-guhan, ketetapan.

first yang pertama; (*beginning*) mula; (*base*) dasar.

first aid pertolongan cemas.

first-born anak sulung.

first-class kelas pertama; yang sangat baik.

firstly pertama-tama.

first-rate sangat baik.

fiscal yang berkenaan dengan wang pemerintah (wang pa-jak).

fish ikan; dried — ikan kering; gold— ikan emas.

fisherman nelayan penang-kap ikan.

fishery perikanan.

fishing hook kail, pancing.

fishing rod pancing, joran.

fishmonger penjual ikan.

fishy penuh ikan; (*smell*) bau hamis; (*dishonest*) tak jujur.

fissure celah, belah, rekah.

fist genggam, kepal tangan; **to fight with one's —s** bertinju.

fit I (*convulsion*) sawan, pitam; (*sudden feeling*) perasaan yang terbit tiba-tiba.

fit II (*proper*) patut, pantas; (*healthy*) segar, dalam keadaan baik; (*of clothes*) potongan pakaian

fitment perkakas rumah.

fitness kesegaran keadaan patut dan baik.

fitter (*of machine*) pemasang, tukang jentera; (*tailor*) tukang menjahit.

fitting (*proper*) patut, layak, seharusnya; (*apparatus*) perkakas, alat-alat.

five lima; **a —day week** lima hari kerja dalam seminggu.

fiver wang kertas £5.

fix (*difficulty*) keadaan genting; (*fixed point etc*) tempat yang ditetapkan.

fixation penetapan, penentuan.

fixed tetap, tentu.

fixture (*house fitment*) perkakas rumah yang tetap ada di dalamnya; (*sporting event*) pertemuan permainan.

fizz minuman yang meruap; **to —** meruap.

fizzle, to — merenjis, meruap.

flabbergast, to — menjadikan tercengang, mentakjubkan.

flabby bonyok, lembik.

flaccid lemah, lembik.

flag I bendera, panji-panji.

flag II, —stone batu ubin; **to —** membatui dengan batu ubin.

flagellate, to — memukul dengan cambuk (rotan).

flagon sejenis botol besar.

flagrant nyata betul

flail pengirik; **to —** mengirik.

flair kepandaian, bakat.

flake serpih; **to —** berpusu.

flaky berserpih, berkeping, berpusu-pusu.

flamboyant sejenis pohon yang berbunga; (*florid*) berhiasa.

flame nyala, api marak; (*love*) kasih sayang.

flaming bernyala-nyala, berapi, panas terik; (*of colour*) berwarna terang; (*flagrant*) berlebih-lebihan.

flamingo sejenis burung bangau.

flank rusuk, sisi; (*wing of army etc*) sayap; **to —** menyisi.

flannel kain panas.

flap (*end of cloth etc*) punca; (*layer*) lapisan; (*to hang limp*) **to —** kelepak.

flare (*beacon*) suar; (*widening out*) perkembangan; **to —** berkembang; **to — up** (*rage*) tiba-tiba terbit marahnya, meluap.

flare path jalan keluar dan masuk pesawat udara yang disuar malam.

flash kilap, kilat, kelip-kelip, sinar; **to —** berkilap, berkilat mengkilat, mengkilap.

flashlight lampu penyuluh; suar.

flask sejenis botol air panas, buli-buli kelalang.

flat I rumah di dalam gedung yang terdiri dari bilik-bilik setingkat; (**a** *plain*) tanah datar, tanah berpaya.

flat II rata, datar, papar, papak.

flatfooted bertapak rata.

flatiron seterika.

flatness kedataran, cepernya.

flatten, to — memaparkan, memepat, menggiling.

flatter, to — membujuk, mengambil muka, melambungkan, memuji.

flatterer pemuji, pembujuk.

flattery bujukan, cumbu-cumbuan.

flatulent terkembung.

flaunt, to — menggembar-gemburkan, memperlihatkan dengan bangga.

flavour (*sensation of smell, taste*) rasa harum; (*special property*) khasiat; to — menambah rempah dan sebagainya supaya lebih sedap.

flaw cela, kecelaan, cacat; to — merosakkan, mencacat.

flawless tidak bercela atau bercacat, sempurna.

flax sejenis rami halus; — en yang dibuat dari rami halus; (*colour*) berwarna kuning.

flea kutu; —**bite** bekas digigit kutu.

fleck bintik, titik, rintik; (*freckles*) tahi lalat; to — menitiki.

fledge, to — memberi berbulu; **full—d** cukup berhak dan berijazah.

fledgeling anak burung; (*inexperienced person*) anak muda yang belum berpengalaman.

flee, to — lari, melarikan diri; (*vanish*) hilang lenyap.

fleece I, to — mengangkat bulunya; (*rob*) memperoleh wang orang dengan bermanis-manis.

fleece II bulu biri-biri, bahan yang rupanya seperti bulu biri-biri.

fleet sejumlah kapalperang (atau kapal udara); the — angkatan laut.

fleeting sepintas lalu, fana.

Fleet Street jalan di bandar London yang namanya bertalian dengan wartawan.

Flemish yang berkenaan dengan negeri Flanders.

flesh daging; the — badan; — and blood daging darah.

fleshy yang berdaging; (*fat*) gemuk.

flex tali dawai letrik; to — mengetulkan.

flexible melentuk, melentur.

flick jentik; to — menjentik.

flicker kejap, kelip; to — berkejap-kejap, berkelip.

flight (*flying*) penerbangan; (*flock of birds etc*) sekawan burung dan sebagainya.

flighty tak tetap, berubah-ubah.

flimsy (*paper*) kertas tipis; (*thin of cloth etc*) tipis; sangat halus; (*weak*) lemah.

flinch, to — mundur, mengundurkan diri.

fling, to — lontaran, lemparan.

flint batu api.

flip jentik; to —, —**ped** menjentik.

flippancy kekurangan sungguh-sungguh.

flippant tak bersungguh-sungguh.

flipper kaki yang digunakan untuk berenang (misalnya; kaki kura-kura), sirip lebar.

flirt orang yang suka bermain-main; to — main; (*ogle*) mata; (*with endearments*) bercumbu-cumbu.

flirtation cumbu-cumbuan.

flit perpindahan; to — berpindah cepat-cepat.

float pelampung; to — terapung, mengapung, timbul.

flock kawan puak, kelompok; a — of birds sekawan (burung).

flog, to — memukul dengan rotan, mendera.

flood banjir, air bah; —**gate** pintu air; —**light** lampu yang sangat terang benderang.

floor lantai, dasar, tingkat; first — tingkat atas yang pertama; (di Amerika) tingkat dasar to take the — mulai berucap.

flop (*sound*) bunyi depap; (*failure*) kegagalan.

flora flora, semua tumbuh-tumbuhan dalam salah satu daerah.

floral yang berkenaan dengan bunga dan tumbuh-tumbuhan.

florid (*ornate*) penuh perhiasan; (*reddish*) merah, kemerah-merahan.

florist (*student of flowers*) ahli bunga; (*seller*) penjual bunga.

flotilla beberapa kapal yang berkumpul, sekelompok kapal.

flotsam apung-apungan.

flounce (*movement*) gerakan tangan atau lengan; (*on garment*) jalur (kelim) pada pakaian.

flounder I sejenis ikan.

flounder II, to — (*in shallow water*) mengarung; (*in difficulties*) menempuh kesusahan.

flour tepung.

flourish (*ornament*) perhiasan; (*in speech or writing*) perkataan atau tulisan yang berhias.

flourishing (*healthy*) subur; (*prosperous*) makmur, berhasil.

flout ejekan; to — mengejek-kan.

flow aliran, pancaran; (*wave*) gelombang; ebb and — pasang dan surut.

flower bunga, kembang, puspa; in — berbunga; to — berbunga, berkembang.

flowery penuh bunga; (*fine words*) dengan berbagai kata indah.

flowing berhiliran; (*fluent*) lancar, bergaya baik.

flu selesema dengan demam.

fluctuate, to — bergoncang, turun naik.

fluctuation turun naik.

fluency kepasihan, kelancaran.

fluent pasih, lancar.

fluff bulu halus; (*faulty acting*) peranan di sandiwara yang tak betul dihapalkan; to —

menggerakkan badannya (sayapnya).

fluid cair, barang cair.

fluke (*lucky stroke*) untung, dapat durian runtuh.

fluorescent berpendar, kali-mantang.

flurry (*bustle*) hal keadaan gelisah; (*disturbance*) meru-sukkan.

flush I (*sudden flow*) aliran, banjir; (*of face*) kemerahan muka; (*excitement*) kegerangan.

flush II (*level etc*) penuh, sarat; — with sama rata dengan.

flush III (*of cards*) serangkaian kertas terup main yang sewarna.

fluster kegugupan; to — bingung, kelam-kabut.

flute suling, seruling.

flutter kegugupan, getaran; to — bergetar.

fluvial yang berkenaan dengan atau terdapat di sungai.

flux (*of bowels*) menceret, cirit; (*constant changes*) pasang naik; (*flow*) aliran.

fly I, to — terbang, melayang; (*of flags*) berkibar-kibaran.

fly II lalat; a — in the ointment salah satu peristiwa yang memburukkan suasana; — blow telur lalat.

fly III (*flying*) terbangnya; (*flap*) lapisan, kelepak; (*for tent*) tirai penutup khemah.

flyer, **flier** burung dan lain-lain yang terbang; (*airman*) penerbang.

flying, — boat kapalterbang air; — fox keluang, kelelawar.

foal anak kuda; to — melahir-kan anak kuda.

foam buih, busa; to — ber-buih, berbusa.

fob, to — menipu.

focal yang terletak pada pusat.

focus, to — berkumpul, mengumpulkan sinar, mene-patkan; fokus.

fodder makanan ternak.

foe musuh, seteru, lawan.

foetus janin.

fog halimun, kabut; **to —** menyelimuti, menyelubungi, mengkaburkan.

fogey, an old — orang kolot.

foggy kabur, kelam-kabut; *(of things etc)* tidak nyata.

foible sifat kurang baik, salah pada perangai seseorang.

foil *(layer)* lapis (emas, perak dan sebagainya); **to —** menggagalkan.

foist, to — memasukkan atau memberi sesuatu yang kurang baik dengan cara menipu.

fold lapis, lipat, pelipatan; *(for animals)* kandangan; **to —** melipatkan; **to — in one's arms** memeluk.

-fold akhiran kata yang ertinya: berlipat ganda.

folder surat edaran siaran yang dilipat.

foliage daun-daun rimbun.

folio ehelai kertas panjang yang dilipat, dua halaman yang bertentangan dalam buku khas.

folk orang; **young —s** orang muda; **—song** nyanyian orang dusun; **—lore** budaya rakyat; **— tale** cerita rakyat.

follow, to — berikut, mengikuti, turut, menurutkan (re-*sulting*) berakibat; **as —s** sebagai berikut.

follower pengiring, penganut, pengikut.

following pengiring, para pengikut; **the —** yang berikut.

folly perbuatan atau buah fikiran yang tak berguna, kebodohan.

foment, to — mendemah, menuami, *(instigate)* mengasut.

fond sangat mencintai; **to be —** of menggemari, sangat suka akan.

fondle, to — mencumbui.

font wadah, pasu, pasu tempat mempermandikan anak masa masuk ugama Kristian.

food makanan, hidangan, santapan.

foodstuff barang makanan bahan hidup.

fool si tolol, orang bebal; **a —'s cap** topi yang menunjukkan bahawa orang yang memakainya seorang bodoh.

foolhardy suka menempuh bahaya yang tak perlu dihadapi.

foolish bodoh, gila.

foolishness kebodohan, kegilaan.

foolproof sangat terang dan mudah sehingga tak dapat salah.

foolscap kertas panjang, kertas kajang.

foot kaki; *(bottom)* pangkal; sejenis ukuran Inggeris (12 inci).

foot-and-mouth (disease) sejenis penyakit lembu.

football bola (untuk sepakbola); sepakbola, main bola; **to play —** main bola.

footbridge titian.

foothold tumpuan.

footing tumpuan; *(position)* kedudukan, tingkat, pangkat.

footlights lampu panggung.

footman seorang pelayan orang besar yang berpakaian istimewa.

footnote catitan di bawah halaman.

footpath jalan kaki, lorong rintis.

footprint jejak kaki.

footstep jejak kaki; **to follow in someone's —s** berbuat seperti seseorang lain.

footstool penumpu kaki.

footwear sepatu, kaus kaki, kasut.

fop seorang pesolik.

for bagi, untuk, akan; **I bought**

this — you ini saya beli untuk kamu; (*because*) sebab, kerana.

forage makanan kuda (tentera); — cap sejenis kopiah soldadu.

foray penjarahan; to — menjarah.

forbear(s) nenek moyang.

forbid, to — melarang, tidak memperkenankan.

forbidden pantang, terlarang, haram.

forbidding rupanya tidak peramah, tak lemah lembut.

force (*strength*) kekuatan, kekerasan; (*power*) kuasa, kekuasaan; (*coercion*) paksaan; (*exertion*) tenaga; the —s (*troops*) angkatan perang.

forceful dengan kuat, dengan hebat.

forceps sejenis angkup, sepit.

forcible dengan kuat, hebat.

ford arungan; to — mengarungi.

fore di muka, di hadapan, hadapan; (*naut*) haluan; come to the — tampil ke muka.

forearm lengan bawah, lengan hasta.

foreboding alamat atau rasa sesuatu yang kurang baik akan terjadi.

forecast ramalan; to — meramalkan, menganggar lebih dahulu.

forecastle, fo'c's'le haluan kapal.

forecourt halaman di depan rumah.

forefather(s) nenek moyang.

forefinger jari telunjuk.

forefront bahagian yang terkemuka.

forego, to — terjadi lebih dahulu; the —ing facts hal yang disebut lebih dahulu.

foreign luar.

forelock rambut di dahi, jambul.

foreman mandur, tandil, kepala.

foremast tiang tupang.

foremost yang hadapan sekali, yang terutama; **first** and — terlebih dahulu.

forensic yang dipakai berkenaan dengan kehakiman.

forerunner seseorang atau sesuatu yang mendahului.

foresee, to — menilik, merasa lebih dahulu, menyangkakan.

foreshadow, to — membayangkan.

foreshore tepi pantai.

foreshorten, to — menggambarkan dengan pandangan.

foresight penilikan ke masa hadapan dan pemeliharaan untuk menghadapi masa itu, pandang jauh.

foreskin kulup.

forest hutan, rimba.

forestall, to — mendahului, memintas.

forester ahli perhutanan.

forestry kehutanan, perhutanan.

foretaste rasa dahulu; to — merasai dahulu.

foretell, to — meramalkan.

forethought fikiran dahulu.

forewarn, to — menasihati sebelum terjadi.

forewoman mandur perempuan.

foreword katapendahuluan.

forfeit (*fine*) denda; (*something redeemable*) tebusan; to — kehilangan hak, kena denda.

forge api pandai besi, api penempa; to — menempa.

forgery pemalsuan, tipu.

forget, to — lupa, melupakan; to — o.s. tak sedar akan dirinya.

forgetful lupa, pelupa, lalai.

forgetfulness pelupaan, kelalaian.

forgive, to — mengampuni, memaafi.

forgiveness pengampunan, ampun, permakafan.

forgo, to — (*leave*) meninggalkan; (*abstain*) berpantang, memantang.

fork (*cutlery*) garpu; (*branch etc*) cabang; tuning — garpu tala; **to** — bercabang.

forlorn putus asa, celaka.

form (*shape etc*) rupa, bentuk, bangun; (*class*) kelas; (*conduct*) kelakuan; (*bodily condition*) keadaan badan.

formal (*appearance*) yang berkenaan dengan bentuk, rupa; (*customary*) beradat, menurut adat.

formality peraturan, adat, upacara.

formation pembentukan susunan.

formative yang membentuk.

former dahulu, dulu, bekas, yang sudah-sudah; in — times masa dahulu, dahulukala.

formidable yang mendahsyatkan, hebat.

formless tak berupa, tak ada bentuknya.

formula rumus, formula.

formulate, to — merumuskan.

fornicate, to — bersundal, menyundal.

fornication persundalan.

forsake, to — memungkiri, mungkir daripada meninggalkan.

forswear, to — membuang dengan bersumpah.

fort benteng, kota, kubu.

forte kepandaian dalam sesuatu hal.

forth ke muka, keluar; back and — pulang; balik; to bring — menerbitkan, melahirkan.

forthcoming yang akan datang.

forthright lurus, terus, langsung, dengan jujur.

forthwith dengan langsung.

fortieth yang keempat puluh.

fortification kubu.

fortify, to — mengubui, berkubu; mengukuhkan.

fortitude keteguhan hati, ketetapan.

fortnight dua minggu; —ly tiap-tiap dua minggu.

fortress kota berkubu.

fortuitous kebetulan.

fortunate beruntung, bertuah; —ly untunglah.

fortune nasib, untung, tuah.

fortuneteller tukang ramal, juru (tukang) tenung, tukang telek.

forty empat puluh; over — lebih (tua); — winks tidur sebentar.

forum tempat untuk bertukar fikiran dan mempercakapkan segala hal.

forward di muka, ke muka; —s ke hadapan.

fossil fosil.

foster, to — mendidik memelihara; — child anak pungut; — mother pengasuh, inang.

foul busuk, kotor; buruk, keji; — language carut; **to** — mengotorkan.

foulness keburukan, kejahatan.

found, to — mengalaskan, mendasarkan.

foundation dasar rukun, alasan, pembentukan; — stone batu asas.

founder I pembangun, pembina, pengasas.

founder II, to — (*of a ship*) karam; (*collapse*) roboh.

foundling anak pungut.

foundry peleburan.

fount mata air; (*printing*) huruf-huruf sebentuk yang dipakai dalam percetakan.

fountain mata air, pemancar.

four empat; on all —s merangkak.

fourteen empat belas; **—th** yang keempat belas.

fourth keempat.

fowl unggas, ayam, daging unggas; **— run** kandang ayam itik, reban.

fox (*jackal*) rubah; (*crafty person*) orang yang berakal kancil; flying — keluang.

fox terrier sejenis anjing.

foxtrot sejenis dangsa, tari.

fraction pecahan, sebahagian sangat kecil; **a — of a second** sekejap mata.

fractious rusing.

fracture patah, patah tulang, retak.

fragile rangup, rapuh.

fragility kerapuhan.

fragment sepotong, sebahagian patahan, keping, serpih.

fragmentary terdiri atas potongan, serpih.

fragrance harum, wangi.

fragrant harum, wangi, semerbak.

frail lemah; (*morally*) mudah tersesat.

frailty kelemahan; (*moral*) kesalahan.

framboesia puru.

frame (*arrangement*) bentuk, bangun, susunan; (*body*) badan; (*construction etc*) birai, bingkai; **— of mind** perangai; **—work** rangka, rancangan; **to — membentuk.

franc kesatuan wang negeri Perancis.

France negeri Perancis.

franchise hak kewarganegaraan hak memilih.

Franco— Perancis.

frangipani bunga kemboja, bunga kubur.

frank terus terang; **—ly** dengan terus terang.

frankincense (*benzoin*) kemenyan; (*incense*) setanggi.

frankness sifat terus terang, kejujuran.

frantic sangat bingung.

fraternal yang berkenaan dengan atau seperti saudara laki-laki.

fraternity persaudaraan.

**fraternize, to — bercampur gaul, bergaul.

fraud penipuan, kecoh.

fraudulent yang menipu, penipu.

fraught, — with danger yang mengakibatkan bahaya, sangat berbahaya.

**fray, to — berjerumbai.

freak (*person*) tingkah; sesuatu yang sangat pelek, cacat rupa.

freakish bertingkah, ganjil.

freckle tahi lalat pada muka orang; to — menitik.

free bebas, merdeka, tidak terikat; (*freely*) percuma; (*liberal*) murah hati, tidak kikir.

freedom kemerdekaan, kebebasan; (*in conduct*) terlalu ramah-tamah.

freehand, — drawing menggambar dengan tidak memakai pandu.

freehold milik lengkap.

freelance pengarang yang tidak terikat kepada penerbit.

freemason anggota sesuatu persaudaraan rahsia.

freethinker orang yang tidak mengakui peraturan ugama.

**freeze, to — membeku, membekukan; to — on to memegang kuat-kuat; to — out menyingkirkan mengeluarkan.

freezing sangat dingin; (*of manner*) tidak peramah.

freight (*charge*) tambang (biaya) pengangkutan (laut); (*cargo*) muatan (kapal); to — mengangkut (dengan kapal).

freighter pengangkut barang, kapal pengangkut.

French yang berkenaan dengan negeri atau orang Perancis; (*language*) bahasa Perancis.

frenzy gila, kegilaan, mata gelap; to — menggilakan.

frequency jumlah kalinya, perulangan.

frequent I berulang-ulang, berkali-kali, banyak; —ly acap kali, kerap kali.

frequent II, to — merapati, pergi mengunjungi selalu.

fresco lukisan dinding, cara melukiskan dinding.

fresh (*new, recent*) baharu, baharu-baharu; (*of fruit etc*) mentah, sedap; (*fit*) segar.

freshen, to — menyegarkan.

freshness kesegaran.

fret, to — (*corrode*) makan karat; (*worry*) mendendam, makan darah.

fretful khuatir, rusing.

fretsaw gergaji sangat halus untuk mengerawang.

fretwork ukiran kerawang, terawang.

friar salah seorang anggota persaudaraan ugama.

friction pergeseran, pergesekan.

Friday hari Jumaat.

fried goreng.

friend saudara, sahabat, teman, kawan, handai, tolan; to be —s with bersahabat dengan.

friendliness sifat kelakuan ramah-tamah, kebaikan.

friendly dengan ramah-tamah, manis, bersahabat, mesra.

friendship persahabatan, persaudaraan.

frieze jalur yang berukir di atas gedung antara bumbung dan atap.

frigate sejenis kapalperang dahulukala, kapal pemayar.

fright kekejutan, ketakutan.

frighten, to — menggentarkan mengejutkan, menakutkan.

frightful menggentarkan, mendahsyatkan.

frigid (*cold*) dingin; (*of feeling*) dingin hati, tak peramah.

frigidity kedinginan hati mati rasa.

frill jumbai, gunjai; to — menghiasi dengan jumbai.

fringe rumbai, jumbai, gunjai, bilai, kelim, pinggir.

frisk loncatan; to — melompat-lompat, meloncat-loncat.

frisky ria, riang.

fritter goreng pisang dan sebagainya; to — away membuang waktu (wang dan sebagainya).

frivolity sifat dangkal, kebodohan.

frivolous dangkal, riah, bodoh.

frizz rambut keriting; to — mengeriting.

frizzle, to — mengeriting; (*fry*) menggoreng sampai garing.

frizzy keriting.

fro, to and — maju mundur, pergi balik.

frock pakaian perempuan, sejenis jubah.

frog katak, kodok.

frolic kelakar, main-main, gurau (*enda*).

from daripada, mulai daripada; (*cause*) kerana; apart — that lain daripada itu.

frond daun pakis, pelepah.

front (*forehead*) dahi; (*face*) muka; (*forward position*) depan, hadapan; (*front line*) garis depan; in — di muka.

frontage bahagian muka sesuatu bangunan dan lain-lain.

front door pintu muka depan.

frontier batas, perbatasan, sempadan.

frontispiece (*of book*) gambar pada halaman pertama di sebuah buku.

front-page halaman pertama suratkhabar.

front yard halaman.

frost keadaan membeku, darjah dingin di bawah titik air beku.

froth buih; —y berbuih.

frown kerut; to — mengerutkan muka.

frugal sederhana, ugahari.

frugality kesederhanaan, kecermatan.

fruit buah, buah-buahan; (*produce*) hasil; to —, bear — berbuah.

fruiterer tukang buah, penjual buah.

fruitful biak, subur; (*successful*) (sangat) berhasil.

fruition perolehan.

fruitless tak berhasil, hampa, sia-sia.

fruitshop kedai buah-buahan.

fruit tree pohon buah.

frustrate, to — membatalkan, mengandaskan, tawar hati, membantutkan.

frustration kegagalan, kekandasan, kecewaan.

fry I anak ikan; small — (*young children*) kanak-kanak; (*insignificant beings*) orang bawahan.

fry II daging goreng; to — menggoreng.

frying pan kuali penggoreng.

fuchsia sejenis bunga.

fuddle (*intoxicated*) mabuk; (*confused*) bingung; to — memabukkan.

fudge (*sweetmeat*) sejenis coklat lembik; to — mengakalkan, memalsukan.

fuel bahan bakar; to — memperoleh bahan bakar.

fuel oil minyak bakar.

fugitive orang pelari.

fugue karangan muzik yang berpusat pada satu lagu.

-ful akhiran kata yang ertinya; penuh.

fulcrum titik galang.

fulfil, to — (*accomplish*) melakukan, menyelesaikan.

fulfilment penetapan, penyelesaian.

full penuh; (*complete*) lengkap, sempurna, genap; (*exactly*) tepat; (*fully*) penuhnya; with — speed secepat-cepatnya.

full-blooded kuat, giat.

fullness keadaan penuh, kesempurnaan, kenyang.

fully samasekali, dengan sempurna; — fashioned samasekali menurut bentuk.

fulsome berlebih-lebihan.

fumble, to — (for) merabaraba.

fume ukup; to — mengukup; (*anger*) memarahi, gusar akan.

fumigate, to — mengukupi; (*disinfect*) menghapus hama dengan mengukup.

fun keriaan, jenaka, gurau senda.

function (*duty*) jabatan, jawatan; (*a gathering*) pertemuan; to — berlaku, berjalan.

functionary pegawai, penjabat, pemangku.

fund persediaan, pokok, modal, pokok amal, tabungan, kumpulan wang.

fundamental pokok, asli; —s pokok, dasar penting.

funeral pemakaman, penguburan, yang berkenaan dengan pemakaman.

funereal sedih.

fungus cendawan, kulat.

funk perasaan takut; (*coward*) orang penakut; to — takut akan.

funnel cerobong, corong, serombong.

funny jenaka, menggelikan; (*peculiar*) ganjil, pelik.

fur bulu binatang.

furious sangat panas hati, marah, geram.

furl, to — menguncup, menggulungkan.

furlong 1/8 batu.

furlough (*US*) tempoh beristirihat, cuti panjang.

furnace dapur leburan, relau.

furnish, to — memperlengkapi (rumah dengan segala alat); **to** — (with) menyediakan.

furniture perkakas rumah.

furrier penjual atau pembuat pakaian bulu binatang.

furrow alur, galur, parit; (*frown*) kerut; **to** — membuat alur.

further lebih lanjut, lebih jauh; (*moreover*) tambahan; (*in addition*) lagi; **to** — memajukan.

furtherance pembantuan, penolongan.

furthermore apalagi, tambahan pula.

furtive diam-diam, curi-curi.

fury berang, marah yang amat sangat.

fuse tali api, sumbu taup, sekatan.

fuselage rangka kapalterbang.

fusilier anggota salah satu pasukan Inggeris.

fusillade tembakan.

fusion perpaduan, menyatukan, taupan.

fuss cencung; kekacauan; **to** —, **make a** — banyak leteran, kekacauan.

fussiness sifat cerewet.

fussy cerewet.

futile tidak berguna, hampa, sia-sia.

futility kesia-siaan.

future masa yang akan datang, bakal, zaman depan; **for the** —, **in** — masa ke depan, seterusnya.

fuzzy (*indistinct*) kabur; (*of hair*) keriting, ikal.

G

gab percakapan, bualan.

gabardine sejenis kain yang kuat, kain gabardin.

gabble cakap cepat dan hampir tidak kedengaran; **to** — bercakap dengan cepat.

gable bahagian dinding muka yang terhimpit antara kedua belah atap.

gad, a —about seorang yang suka berkeliaran.

gadfly pikat.

gadget alat.

Gaelic yang berkenaan dengan orang Kelt; (*language*) bahasa Kelt.

gaff (*naut*) canggah, topang, serampang; (*fish spear*) tombak ikan, serampang; **to** — menyerampang.

gaffer bapa, orang tua.

gag sumbatan di mulut, cekek.

gaiety sukacita, keriaan, kegembiraan.

gain perolehan, kemajuan, keuntungan; **—s** untung, laba; **to** — memperoleh.

gait sikap, gaya berjalan, lenggok.

gala perayaan besar.

galaxy (*Milky Way*) jalan bintang susu; (*brilliant company*) kumpulan orang termasyhur.

gale topan, taufan, angin ribut.

gall (*bile*) hampedu; (*bitterness*) pahit; (*on a tree*) bonjol (pada pohon atau kulit); (*painful swelling*) bisul.

gallant perkasa, gagah.

gallantry kegagahan, gagah perkasa.

galleon kapalperang dahulukala.

gallery (*verandah*) serambi, selasar; (*in theatre*) kelas kambing di panggung wayang.

galley sejenis kapal dahulukala yang dikayuh oleh sejumlah orang, ghali.

gallivant, to — suka bermain.

gallon sejenis ukuran (*Brit* = 4.546 ltr; *US* = 3.7853 ltr), gantang, gelen.

gallop sejenis gaya pelarian kuda; to — berlaku atau terjadi sangat cepat.

gallows tiang penggantungan.

galore mewah, penuh, berlimpah-limpah.

galvanize, to — (*coat*) menampal.

gambit permulaan pada main catur.

gamble main judi; to — berjudi.

gambler penjudi.

gambol lompatan; to — berlompat-lompat.

game (*animals hunted*) perburuan, binatang (burung buruan; (*sport etc*) permainan, main; (*plucky*) berani, gagah.

gamecock ayam sabungan.

gamekeeper penjaga dan pemelihara binatang perburuan.

gaming house, gambling house rumah berjudi, tempat berjudi.

gammon kaki belakang babi yang diasap.

gander angsa jantan.

gang rombongan, kumpulan.

gangboard, gangplank papan titian untuk naik dan turun kapal.

ganger kepala kumpulan.

gangleader kepala kumpulan.

gangrene mati daging; kelemayuh, tak berdarah.

gangster penjahat, pengganas.

gangway jalan di antara deret kerusi, jalan pada kapal, titian papan untuk naik dan turun kapal.

gannet sejenis burung laut.

gaol penjara, jel, kurungan.

gaoler penjaga penjara.

gap celah, kancing, genting.

gape, to — (*of mouth*) ternganga; (*yawn*) menguapnguap; (*of rips, tears etc*) terbelah, terbahang.

garage bilik simpan kereta.

garbage kotoran, sampah; *US* —can persampahan.

garble, to — mengakali, memalsukan.

garden kebun, taman; botanical —s kebun bunga; experimental — kebun percubaan; to — berkebun.

gardener tukang kebun.

gardenia bunga kaca piring.

garden party perjamuan yang diadakan di kebun.

gargantuan sangat besar.

gargle ubat kumur; to — berkumur-kumur.

gargoyle sejenis patung orangorangan atau binatang yang dipakai sebagai pancuran air.

garland gubahan, kalungan bunga; to — menghiasi dengan kalung.

garlic bawang putih.

garment sehelai pakaian.

garnet batu merah, batu delima.

garnish, to — memperhias, menggubah.

garret bilik di bawah atap rumah, anjung.

garrison pasukan yang ditempatkan dalam kota.

garrulous ceramah, ramah mulut.

garter ikat kaus.

gas gas, wap; —**bag** orang yang bercakap angin.

gaseous bergas, seperti gas.

gash luka tetak; to — menetak.

gasoline (*US*) minyak bensin.

gasp bunyi nafas tertahan; to — ngap-ngap.

gassy seperti atau penuh gas.

gastric yang berkenaan dengan perut besar.

gastronome seorang yang suka akan makanan sedap.

gastronomy ilmu pengetahuan tentang makanan sedap.

gate, gateway pintu, pintu gerbang, pintu pagar.

gatecrasher jamu tamu yang tidak dijemput.

gatekeeper penjaga pintu.

gatepost tiang pintu.

gather, to — berkumpul, berhimpun.

gathering kumpulan perhimpunan.

gaudy berlebih-lebihan terlalu banyak perhiasan.

gauge ukuran isi, uji alat pengukur atau penguji; to — menguji.

gaunt sangat kurus, kurus kering.

gauze kain kasa.

gay ria, riang, suka hati.

gaze pandang; to — at memandang.

gazelle sejenis binatang yang menyerupai rusa.

gazette suratkhabar rasmi warta kerajaan.

gear (*harness*) pakaian kuda; (*tools etc*) perkakas, alat-alat.

gecko toke(k), tokai cicak kubin.

gelatine agar-agar.

gelding kuda kembiri.

gelignite sejenis ubat letupan.

gem makmjkam permata, jauhar; (*anything precious*) sesuatu yang sangat elok atau berharga.

gender jenis kelamin berkenaan dengan tata-bahasa.

gene salah satu anasir atau faktor sel lembaga.

genealogical yang berkenaan dengan asal-usul.

general I (*officer*) hulubalang, penglima.

general II umum, awam, am; in —, in a — way umumnya biasanya.

generality pokok fikiran asas, peraturan atau kenyataan dasar.

generalization kesimpulan mengenai kebanyakan hal atau orang.

generalize, to — menjadikan sesuatu pendapat kenyataan umum, mengatakan sesuatu yang mengandung erti umum.

generally pada umumnya, biasanya.

generate, to — menerbitkan, menjadikan, menimbulkan.

generation I (*breeding*) pembiakan; (*creation*) penjadian, pembuatan.

generation II (*descendants*) keturunan.

generosity kemurahan hati, elimpahan.

generous dermawan, murah hati, limpah.

genesis asal mula, awal; G— buku pertama pada Taurat.

genetic yang berkenaan dengan asal mula sesuatu; —s ilmu pengetahuan asal-usul.

genial baik hati, ramah-tamah.

genie jin.

genitals kemaluan, urat.

genitive bentuk genitif.

genius I (*spirit*) jin.

genius II (*power of mind*) bakat utama (istimewa), jinius.

genius III orang yang berbakat utama itu.

genteel yang berkenaan dengan orang berbangsa; berbudi bahasa.

gentile orang yang bukan daripada orang Yahudi.

gentle lemah lembut, manis.

gentleman orang yang baik budi bahasanya; (*general term*) tuan, laki, laki-laki.

gentleness sifat lemah lembut.

gently dengan budi bahasa, dengan lemah lembut; (*slowly*) perlahan-lahan.

gentry orang baik-baik, berbangsa.

genuine sejati, sungguh, betul.

genus jenis, macam, bangsa.

geographic(al) yang berkenaan dengan ilmu alam.

geography ilmu alam.

geologist ahli kaji bumi.

geology geologi, ilmu penyelidikan bumi, kaji bumi.

geometry ilmu ukur, ilmu jometri.

germ (*rudiment of new organism*) lembaga, benih, kecambah; (*of disease*) hama penyakit, kuman penyakit.

German yang berkenaan dengan negeri atau orang Jerman; (*language*) bahasa Jerman.

germinate, to — berkecambah; (*to cause to appear*) menimbulkan.

gerund salah satu bentuk tata-bahasa Inggeris.

gestation waktu hamil, bunting.

gesticulate, to — bermain tangan, bergerak tangan dan badannya sambil berkata.

gesticulation pergerakan tangan atau badan.

gesture gerakan tangan, isyarat.

get, to — (*obtain*) memperoleh, mendapat, mencapai, diberi; (*take*) mengambil; (*understand*) mengerti; (*cause*) menyebabkan, menjadikan; (*become*) menjadi; do you — it? kamu mengertikah?; I haven't

got the money saya tidak ada wangnya; to — well, better sembuh, betah.

getaway pelarian.

getup rupa pakaian dan sebagainya.

geyser mata air panas; (*water healer*) pesawat pemanaskan air.

ghastly mendahsyatkan, menakutkan.

gherkin timun acar.

ghetto daerah kediaman orang Yahudi di sebuah kota.

ghost hantu, mambang.

ghostly yang berkenaan dengan hantu.

ghoul hantu kubur.

giant raksasa, gergasi, bota.

gibber, to — merepet.

gibberish perkataan pelat.

gibbon siamang, ungka.

gibe, jibe, to — mengejekkan, memperolok-olokkan.

giblets bahagian ayam atau itik yang di sebelah dalam (seperti, hati, hempedal yang boleh dimakan).

giddiness pening.

giddy pening kepala.

gift bingkisan, hadiah, derma, pemberian.

gifted berbakat.

gigantic raksasa, sangat besar.

giggle ketawa terkekek-kekek.

gild, to — mengemasi, menyepuh.

gilding sadur emas, sepuh emas.

gill (*of fish*) insang; (*of fowl*) pial.

gimlet sejenis penggurdi, penggerik.

gin (*snare*) sejenis jerat; (*liquor*) minuman keras.

ginger (*plant*) halia; (*stimulation*) rasa bersemangat, kegiatan.

gingerbread roti halia.

gingerly dengan perlahan-lahan.

gingham kain genggang, sejenis kain cita.

gipsy, gypsy orang yang tergolong suku bangsa pengembara di Eropah.

giraffe zirafah.

gird, to — (*fasten*) mengikatkan; (*encircle*) mengelilingi, mengepung.

girder galang, gelegar.

girdle ikat (tali) pinggang, kendit.

girl anak, dara, gadis, budak perempuan; —**guide** pandu puteri, pengakap perempuan

girlhood masa gadis.

girlish seperti gadis.

girth (*of horse*) tali perut kuda; (*measurement round*) ukuran keliling.

gist inti, ringkas, dasar, pokok; **the** — **of one's thoughts** pokok fikiran.

give, to — memberi, menghadiahkan, mengurniai; (*give o.s. up*) menyerahkan diri; (*shrink*) surut.

glacier sejenis sungai air beku yang disebabkan oleh kumpulan ice dan salji di gunung.

glad suka hati, senang hati, sukacita, gerang.

gladden, to — menggerangkan, menyukakan hati.

glade tempat di hutan yang tidak berpohon.

gladiator seorang pendekar.

gladness suka ria, kegerangan, sukacita.

glamorous sangat elok, sangat menarik.

glamour keelokan yang sangat menarik hati.

glance sepintas kejap, pandang; **at a** — sepintas lalu.

gland kelenjar.

glare cahaya yang sangat

terang; to — bercahaya sangat terang.

glass (*substance*) kaca, gelas; (*drinking vessel etc*) alat gelas, gelas minum dan sebagainya.

glassy seperti gelas.

glaze ringas; to — meringas, menyepuh.

glazier pembuat kaca jendela.

gleam sinar, cahaya yang redup.

glean, to — mengumpulkan memungut padi seberapa ada sesudah sawah telah dituai.

glee keriangan, kegembiraan.

glen jurang.

glib lancar mulut, fasih.

glide, to — meluncur, melayang.

glider pesawat pelayang.

glimmer bayang-bayang, sekelip mata.

glimpse kilap, sekelibat; to — terlihat sekelip mata.

glint kilat, kerlip, gemerlap; to — mengerlip, gemerlapan.

glisten, to — berkilau-kilauan, gemerlap.

glitter, to — gemerlap, gilang-gemilang.

gloat, to — geli akan kesusahan orang lain.

global yang melengkapi seluruhnya.

globe bola, gelub; (*earth*) bumi.

globule titik kecil, until.

gloom muram.

gloomy sabak, muram.

glorify, to — memuliakan, mengagungkan.

glorious jaya, mulia; (*beautiful*) sangat elok.

glory kejayaan, megah, kemuliaan; to — sangat bangga membuat sesuatu.

gloss I kilau, gilap sepuh.

gloss II (*comment*) tafsiran; to — mentafsirkan, mengupas.

glossary daftar kata, loghat.

glossy menggilap.

glove sarung tangan.

glow seri, marak, cahaya; to — berseri, bercahaya.

glower, to — (at) memandang dengan marah.

glow-worm ulat kelip-kelip, kelimayar.

glucose sakar anggur.

glue perikat; to — merikat.

glum bermuram, muram, tak senang hati.

glut kepuasan, penawaran yang jauh melebihi permintaan.

glutton pelahap.

glycerine geliserin.

gnarled monggol, bongkong.

gnash, to — one's teeth berkertak gigi.

gnat sejenis agas.

gnaw, to — menggigit, mengerkah, mengunyah.

gnome sejenis jembalang.

gnu sejenis rusa.

go (doing, attempt) perbuatan, kejadian; come and — lalu-lintas; to have a — at mulai cuba berbuat; to — (depart) pergi; (go out) keluar.

goad (for elephant) kosa; to — merangsangkan.

go-ahead giat, bersemangat.

goal arah tujuan; (football etc) gol; —keeper penjaga gol.

goat kambing.

goatee janggut yang menyerupai janggut kambing.

gobbler ayam belanda.

go-between perantara, orang tengah, telangkai.

goblet piala.

goblin bota, jin, raksasa.

God, god Tuhan, Allah; by G—! demi Allah!

goddess betari, dewi.

godfather, godmother, god-parents ayah (ibu bapa) angkat.

godhead Tuhan, dewata.

godless tidak mengakui Tuhan; (evil) jahat, derhaka.

godlike seperti Allah, seperti dewa.

go-getter seorang yang sangat rajin.

goggle, —-eyed matanya belodok; —s sejenis kacamata.

going, —s-on kelakuan, peristiwa.

gold emas, kencana; (coin) wangemas; (precious) sangat baik sangat berharga; —smith pandai emas.

golden daripada emas, kencana, keemas-emasan.

golf golf, sejenis permainan dengan bola dan pukulan; — course padang bermain golf.

golly, by — ! astaga!

gondola sejenis sampan di negeri Itali.

gondolier orang yang mengayuh 'gondola'.

gone vp of **go** (disappeared) habis, hilang, lenyap; (past) lalu.

gong gung, gong, mongmong.

good (comp better, sup best) baik; (seemly) patut; (pleasant) manis yang menyukakan hati.

goodness kebaikan; (interjection) demi Allah!

goodwill kesudian, kebajikan.

goose angsa, daging angsa.

gooseberry sejenis buah.

gore lumuran darah; to — menanduk.

gorge gaung, jurang, tekak, tenggorok; to — menggelogok, makan dengan lahap.

gorgeous sangat elok, mulia.

gorilla sejenis monyet besar, gorila.

gorse sejenis semak.

gory berlumuran darah.

gosh wah!

gosling anak angsa.

gospel injil, sebahagian buku injil.

gossamer sesuatu yang sangat halus, sangat halus.

gossip orang yang bocor mulut istimewa yang suka mempercakapkan hal-ahwal orang lain, bual.

gouge pahat kuku; to — mencungkil, memahat.

gourd labu.

gourmand sangat suka akan makanan sedap dan mewah.

gourmet orang yang sangat halus cita rasanya berkenaan dengan hal makanan dan minuman.

gout sengal.

govern, to — menguasai, memerintah; —ing body badan yang berwajib, badan pemerintah.

governess pengasuh perempuan yang mengajar anak di rumah anak itu.

government pemerintah, pemerintahan, kerajaan.

governor gabenor negara; (employer) majikan; (father) ayah; G— General gabenor jeneral.

gown pakaian perempuan; (of Haji) jubah.

grab cekauan, pegangan; to — mencekau, (seize) merampas.

grace (charm) seri; (of appearance) sifat lemah gemalai; (breeding) budi bahasa; (favour) kurnia, anugerah; (pardon) ampun, maaf; by the — of God dengan kurnia Allah.

graceful jelita, indah, lampai.

gracious baik budi, ramah-tamah.

grade darjah, tingkat, tangga, kelas, taraf; on the up — sedang naik.

gradient cerunan, curamnya.

gradual(ly) perlahan-lahan, beransur-ansur, lama kelamaan, bertangga-tangga.

graduate graduate, siswazah tamatan sekolah tinggi.

seorang yang berijazah sekolah tinggi; to — memperoleh ijazah sekolah tinggi.

graft (in horticulture) cangkukan yang dimasukkan sebuah celah pada kayu pohon lain; (bribery) tumbuk rusuk, wang suap, raswah.

grail, Holy G— pasu yang dipakai Nabi Isa dan di situ darahnya ditadah.

grain biji, butir biji-bijian; (rice) padi.

grammar nahu tata-bahasa, ilmu saraf; —school sekolah pada mana bahasa Latin diajarkan, paramasastra.

grammarian ahli bahasa, ahli tata-bahasa, ahli nahu.

grammatical yang berkenaan dengan nahu tata-bahasa.

gramme, **gram** ukuran berat, gram.

gramophone peti nyanyi; — record piring peti nyanyi.

grampus sjenis ikan paus; (heavy breather) orang yang termengah-mengah.

granary rengkiang; lombong; (fertile region) daerah yang mewah padi.

grand utama, besar, mulia.

grandchild anak cucu; great— cicit.

gran(d)dad nenek, datuk.

grandeur kemuliaan.

grandfather nenek, datuk.

grandiose mulia.

grandmother nenek perempuan.

grandson anak cucu laki-laki.

grandstand panggung, rumah panggung.

grange rumah berserta dengan tempat ternak dan sebagainya.

granite batu besi, batu ubin.

granny nenek perempuan.

grant wang dan sebagainya yang diberi sebagai sokongan.

hadiah, biasiswa; to — (*bestow*) menghadiahkan; (*approve*) memperkenankan.

granule biji, butir.

grape daun anggur; — -sugar gula anggur; —vine pohon anggur.

grapefruit sejenis buah limau.

graph gerap, ruang.

-graph akhiran yang ertinya; tulisan atau penulis.

graphic(al) gerapik; (*vivid*) yang melukiskan dengan nyata.

grapple pegangan; to — mencekau, memegang kuat; grappling iron sauh terbang, sauh jangkar.

grasp genggaman tangkapan; (*understand*) iaham; to — menjabat, memegang.

grasping loba, tamak.

grass rumput; —hopper belalang.

grate (*fireplace*) sejenis alat besi (di bawah api) untuk menahan bara api; to — (*rasp*) kukur.

grateful bersyukur menerima kasih, tahu balas.

grater parut, kukur.

gratification kepuasan; (*a payment*) pemberian wang.

gratify, to — (*please*) menyukakan; (*satisfy*) memenuhi memuaskan.

grating kisi-kisi.

gratis percuma.

gratitude syukur hati, hutang budi.

gratuitous (*for nothing*) percuma; (*without grounds*) tidak berguna, tidak beralasan.

gratuity sagu hati, baksysis.

grave I kubur, makam; — -stone nesan; —yard tanah perkuburan.

grave II (*weighty*) penting, berat; (*strained*) genting; (*calm*) tenang.

gravel kerikil, kerakal, batu; to — menyebarkan kerikil.

gravitate, to — condong kepada.

gravity (*weight*) beratnya, keberatan; (*importance*) kepentingan.

gravy kuah.

graze, to — (*of animals*) makan rumput, memakankan rumput.

grease minyak; to — meminyaki.

greasy berminyak; (*of manner*) berkelakuan terlalu bermanis-manis.

great besar, raja, penting, mulia; (*excellent*) sangat baik; a — deal banyak.

greatly sangat, amat sangat.

Grecian yang berkenaan dengan orang Yunani; — nose hidung lurus dengan tiada lekok antara dahi dan hidung.

greed kelubaan.

greedy gelojoh, lahap, luba.

Greek Yunani, orang Yunani.

green hijau, berumput, berdaun; (*unripe*) belum masak; (*inexperienced*) muda.

greengrocer penjual sayur-sayuran.

greenhouse rumah atau bangsal gelas untuk pertanaman.

greens sayuran hijau.

Greenwich, — mean time waktu sesuai dengan waktu di bandar.

greet, to — memberi salam, tabik; (*receive*) menyambut.

greeting tegur, sapa, salam, sembah.

gregarious berkawan, berkelompok.

gremlin sejenis jin kecil yang menyebabkan segala gangguan.

grenade bom lempar.

grey, **gray** kelabu, abu-abuan; — hair beruban.

greyhound sejenis anjing yang sangat cepat larinya.

grid sejenis kisi-kisi; (*on map*) garis pemandu

gridiron sejenis salaian, kisi-kisi.

grief penderitaan, kedukaan, dukacita; **to come to —** kena celaka.

grievance (*burden*) keberatan; (*complaint*) pengaduan.

grieve, to — merawankan, merayu; **—d** sedih hati.

grievous menyusahkan, menyedihkan.

grill salai; (*food grilled*) makanan panggang; (*grill room*) tempat di mana makanan itu dipanggang dan dihidangkan; **to —** memanggang.

grille kisi-kisi.

grim keras hati, ganas, menakutkan.

grimace geringsing, gerenyot; **to —** menggeringsing, menggerenyot.

grime kekotoran, daki.

grimy comot.

grin gerenyut, gerenyeng; **to —** (*also* —**ned**) meringis.

grind, to — menggiling, mengisar; (*sharpen*) mengasah, mencanai.

grinding (*tedious work*) pekerjaan yang berat dan menjemukan.

grindstone batu pengasah, kiliran, batu canai.

grip genggaman, pegangan; **to —** menggenggam, memegang kuat; (*understand*) menarik perhatian.

gripe, to — mencekau, mencubit.

gripes usus mulas.

grisly menakutkan, mendahsyatkan.

gristle tulang muda, tulang rawan.

grit pasir, kerikil, hancuran.

grizzled beruban.

grizzly abu-abuan; (*of hair*) beruban.

groan orang kerana sakit; **to —** (*overloaded*) sarat dimuati.

grocer penjual segala bahan makanan.

grog sejenis minuman.

groggy mabuk, terhoyong-hayang.

groin lipat paha, kunci paha.

groom gembala kuda, sais; **bride—** mempelai laki-laki.

groove alur, parit, lurah.

grope, to — menggerayang, meraba, menggerapai.

gross dua belas dozen; (*coarse*) kasar; (*total*) berjumlah dengan tidak dipotong apa-apa.

grotesque ganjil, pelik.

grotto sejenis gua.

grouch peringut; **to —** meringut.

ground (*base*) dasar, alasan; (*earth*) bumi, tanah; (*place*) tempat, daerah.

grounding (*knowledge*) pengajaran.

groundless tidak beralasan.

grounds (*dregs*) hampas, endapan; (*land*) kebun halaman, lapangan, padang.

group kelompok, puak, kawan kumpulan.

grouse, to — bersungut-sungut, menggerutu.

grove sekelompok pohon, dusun.

grovel, to — meniarap; (*abase o.s.*) merendahkan diri.

grow, to — (*of plants*) menjadi; (*become*) tumbuh; (*increase*) bertambah besar, berkembang biak; (*to plant*) bertanam.

growl, to — menderam.

grown-up akil baligh, dewasa, orang dewasa.

growth tumbuhan, perkembangan.

grub (*of insect*) ulat; tempayak; (*sl.: food*) makanan; to — mencungkil, menyungkai.

grubby (*worm-eaten*) berulat; (*dirty*) kotor.

grudge sakit hati, dendam, benci; to — against) berdendam.

gruel sejenis bubur.

gruelling yang menyiksa, yang sangat memayahkan.

gruesome mendahsyatkan, menakutkan.

gruff merengus, kasar.

grumble to — merengut, merajuk, bersungut.

grumpy berleter marah, galak.

grunt bunyi meronseng; to — merungut.

guano sejenis baja tahi kelalawar.

guarantee jaminan, tanggungan; — fund wang jaminan, jamin, tanggung.

guarantor penanggung, penjamin.

guard pengawalan, penjagaan, kawal, pengawal; — of honour barisan kehormatan; to — berjaga, berkawal.

guardian (*for unmarried girl*) wali; (*watchman*) pengawal, penjaga; —ship penjagaan.

guerilla gerila.

guess pengiraan, terkaan, penerkaan; to — mengira, mengagak, menerka.

guest tamu, jamu; paying — orang yang menumpang; to have —s berjamu, tetamuan.

guffaw gelak berdekah; to — bergerak terbahak-bahak.

guidance pimpinan, asuhan.

guide pemimpin, penuntun, pandu; ranger —, girl — pandu perempuan, pengakap perempuan.

guild gabungan persyarikatan orang sekerja, syarikat kerja.

guile (*deceit*) tipu daya, peni-

puan; (*cunning*) cerdik; —ful bertipu-daya; —less tak bersalah, tak bertipu-daya.

guillotine sejenis alat untuk memancung kepala orang terhukum.

guilt salah, kesalahan.

guiltless tidak bersalah, tidak berdosa.

guilty salah, berdosa, bersalah.

guinea-fowl, **guinea-hen** sejenis ayam, ayam mutiara.

guinea-pig marmut.

guise cara pakaian, rupa.

guitar sejenis alat muzik.

gulf (*bay*) teluk; (*whirlpool*) pusaran air; to — (*engulf*) meliputi; (*swallow*) menelan.

gull sejenis burung camar.

gullet kerongkong, tekak.

gullible mudah tertipu.

gully alur, jurang, lurah.

gulp gelogok; to — menelan gelogok; to — down menelan lekas-lekas.

gum getah; — tree sejenis pohon kayu putih.

gummy bergetah.

gumption giat, cerdik.

gums gusi.

gun alat penembak, senapang; (*cannon*) meriam.

gunner soldadu atau pegawai yang pekerjaannya berkenaan dengan meriam.

gurgle, to — menggogok.

gush pancaran; to — terpancar, pancutan.

gusher (*oil well*) minyak yang terus terpancar tak usah dipompa.

gust angin keras yang terjadi dengan mendadak.

gusto kegiatan dan keinginan akan berbuat sesuatu, semangat.

gut, —s (*intestine*) usus; (*bravery*) keberanian; (*violin string*) tali biola (yang dibuat dari usus haiwan).

gutta-percha getah perca.

gutter saluran selokan, parit.

guttural yang berkenaan dengan tekak, (tenggorok).

guy I sejenis rantai atau tali penarik.

guy II gambaran orang yang menyerupai Guy Fawkes.

guzzlo, to — makan dengan lahap.

gymkhana lapangan sukan; pertunjukan sukan.

gymnasium tempat gerak badan, tempat latihan jasmani, tempat bersenam, jimnasiam.

gymnast orang yang pandai bergerak badan.

gymnastic yang berkenaan dengan latihan jasmani; —s latihan gerak badan jimnastik.

gynaecology ilmu penyakit alat kandungan.

gyrate, to — beredar, berkisar.

H

haberdasher penjual barang-barang kecil sebagai kancing, pita, dan sebagainya.

habit (*practice*) kebiasaan; (*bodily constitution*) keadaan badan atau jiwa, resmi.

habitable yang dapat didiami.

habitat tempat kediaman asli.

habitation tempat kediaman, tempat tinggal.

habitual kebiasaan, tetap.

habituate, to — membiasakan.

hack (*hoe*) cangkul; (*horse*) kuda sewaan.

hackney kuda sewaan.

haddock sejenis ikan.

Hades alam barzah.

haemorrhage cucur darah.

haemorrhoids puru sem-

belit, bawasir.

haft pegangan pemegang, ulu, gagang.

hag nenek yang rupanya buruk; (*witch*) hantu.

haggard rupanya liar dan payah.

haggle, to — tawar-menawar.

ha(h) kata seru: ah!

hail I (*greeting*) daulat, tabik; (*call*) seruan; 'o — memberi tabik, menyambut dengan hormat.

hail II (*rain*) hujan batu; to — terun hujan batu.

hair rambut, bulu; —cut potong rambut; curly — rambut keriting.

hake sejenis ikan.

halcyon, — days hari tenang, dan sentosa.

hale sihat.

half setengah, sebelah, separuh; one's better — isteri seseorang.

halfpenny matawang Inggeris.

halibut sejenis ikan.

hall balai; (*house of landowner*) rumah tuantanah.

hallmark cap pengesahan emas dan perak.

hallo kataseru; eh!; tabik.

hallow, to — mempersucikan.

hallucination khayalan, maya.

halo lengkaran cahaya di keliling matahari atau bulan.

halt I perhentian; to — berhenti.

halt II, to — (*limp*) berjalan pincang; —ing(ly) terputus-putus.

halter talileher kuda.

halve, to — membahagi dua, memperdua, membelah dua.

ham (*thigh*) paha; (*sl: poor actor*) pemain sandiwara yang kurang baik.

hamburger sejenis pergedel daging.

hamlet kampung, desa.

hammer palu, tukul, pemukul; **to come under the —** dilelongkan.

hammock ayunan, buaian.

hamper I (*basket*) rantang, keranjang.

hamper II, to — mengalangi, merintangkan, mengganggu.

hand tangan; **— of a clock** jarum; **at —** (*near*) dekat; (*ready*) sedia; **to have a — in** turut campur; **to — out** membahagikan.

handbag tas tangan.

handbill surat sebaran.

handbreadth, a — a sepelempap.

handcuff(s) belenggu, gari.

handful (*fistful*) sekepal; (*a few*) sejumlah kecil.

hand grenade bom tangan.

handicraft pekerjaan kerajinan tangan, pertukangan.

handiwork pekerjaan tangan, buah tangan.

handkerchief, hanky saputangan, selampai.

handle pegangan, pemegang, gagang, tangkai, hulu; **to — memegang.**

handmade buatan tangan.

handout (*gift*) derma; (*statement to press etc*) surat siaran; (*proffer*) diunjuk.

handrail susuran tangga.

handshake berjabat tangan.

handsome cantik, rupawan.

handwriting bekas tangan, tulisan.

handy sedia, mudah tercapai; (*adroit*) akas; **to come in —** sangat berguna.

hang cara bergantung; **to — bergantung, mengampai.**

hangar tempat penyimpan kapalterbang.

hanger, — on pengikut.

hangman pelebaya, pertanda.

hangover rasa sakit bekas mabuk.

hanker, to — (*after*) sangat ingin akan, merindukan.

hanky *see* **handkerchief.**

haphazard kebetulan, sebarang.

hapless malang.

happen, to — terjadi, berlaku.

happening(s) peristiwa, kejadian, hal-ahwal.

happiness kebahagiaan, sukacita.

happy senang hati, suka hati.

happy-go-lucky sesenangsenang, wenang.

harangue ucap mendesak.

harass, to — mengganggu, menggoda.

harbour pelabuhan, bandar; **— master** syahbandar; **to — berlabuh.**

hard (*firm*) keras; (*from cold etc*) kaku; (*difficult*) sukar; (*cruel*) bengis; **— cash** matawang; **— currency** wang yang harganya tetap.

hardboard sejenis kertas keras.

hard-boiled (*callous*) tidak malu, muka papan.

harden, to — mengeras, mengeraskan.

hard-headed dingin kepala, degil.

hard-hearted bengis.

hardly hampir tidak.

hardness kekerasan.

hardship kesukaran, kesengsaraan.

hardware barang-barang besi, perkakas dapur dan sebagainya.

hardy (*brave*) berani; (*of body*) kuat; **— plants** tumbuhtumbuhan yang tahan sejuk dan panas.

hare sejenis arnab; **—brained** kepala udang.

harem tempat kediaman gundik.

hark, to — mendengarkan.

harm (*loss*) kerugian; (*evil*) kejahatan; (*misfortune*) kemalangan; to — menjahati.

harmful yang merugikan.

harmless tiada ada salahnya, tidak merugikan.

harmonic, harmonious (*free from dissent*) selaras; (*sound*) serunai.

harmonica harmonika, sejenis alat muzik.

harmonize, to — (*agree*) menyelaraskan; (*singing*) bernyanyi bersama-sama dengan menyelaraskan suara.

harmony persesuaian, keseimbangan harmoni.

harness pakaian kuda, abah-abah; **to die in** — meninggal di tengah pekerjaannya.

harp sejenis alat muzik; to — on terlalu lama membicarakan sesuatu.

harpoon serampang.

harpsichord sejenis alat muzik dahulukala.

harrow garu, sisir tanah, penggaruk.

harry, to — (*destroy*) merosakkan; (*worry*) mengganggu.

harsh kasar.

hart rusa jantan.

harvest pemungutan, pengetaman; to — memungut.

harvester orang atau mesin pemungut hasil bumi.

has-been seseorang atau sesuatu yang sudah tidak penting lagi.

hash (*hashed meat*) makanan daging yang dicincang halus; (*mess*) bercampur-aduk.

hashish, hasheesh hasis.

haste kegopohan; to make — bersegera.

hasten, to — bersegera, tergopoh-gapah, tergesa-gesa.

hasty terburu-buru, tergopoh-gapah.

hat topi; — in hand berkelakuan rendah.

hatch I pintu bawah, lubang di dinding.

hatch II (*from eggs*) seperindukan, pengeraman; to — menetaskan.

hatchet kapak, beliung.

hate kebencian, dendam.

hateful yang membencikan.

hatred kebencian.

haughty tinggi hati, sombong.

haul (*catch*) tangkapan, penangkapan; to — menarik.

haunch pangkal paha.

haunt tempat yang selalu dikunjungi.

have, to — mempunyai, mendapat.

haven pelabuhan; (*shelter*) tempat terlindung.

haversack sejenis karung penyimpan barang yang dipakai soldadu untuk berpergian.

havoc pembasmian, kebinasaan; to make —, play — among membinasakan.

hawk helang, rajawali.

hawser rantai di kapal.

hay rumput kering.

haystack timbunan rumput kering.

haywire (*sl*) sesuatu yang kusut.

hazard permainan judi.

hazardous berbahaya, tak tentu.

haze halimun, kekaburan; to — mengaburkan.

hazel sejenis tumbuhan; warna merah tua.

hazy kabur, kelam-kabut, berkabut.

he dia, ia; (*male*) jantan; —-man orang yang sangat gagah dan kuat.

head kepala, jemala; (*upper portion of river etc*) hulu; (*top*) puncak; (*first portion*) bahagian pertama; (*leader*) pemimpin ketua.

headache sakit kepala.

headdress, head-gear perhiasan atau penutup kepala.

headhunter orang pengayau.

heading (of letter etc) kepala rencana (karangan dan sebagainya).

headland hujung tanah, tanjung.

headline kepala rencana (berita dan sebagainya) di suratkhabar.

headlong lintang pukang.

headman penghulu, kepala kampung.

headmaster Guru besar sekolah.

head office pusat pejabat besar.

headphones talipon kepala.

headquarters ibu pejabat.

headstrong keras kepala, keras batang leher.

headway perlajuan, kemajuan.

headwind angin sakal.

heady (awesome) hebat; (fiery) galak; a — wine minuman anggur keras.

heal, to — menjadi sembuh, menyembuhkan.

health kesihatan, kesegaran.

healthy segar, sihat, menyegarkan.

heap susun, timbunan; (a lot) sejumlah besar.

hear, to — mendengar; mendengarkan; to — from mendapat khabar dari.

hearing, sense of — pendengaran.

hearsay khabar angin, desasdesus.

hearse kereta mayat.

heart (anal) jantung; (seat of emotion) hati, hati sanubari, kalbu; to learn by — hapal, mengapalkan.

heartbeat debar jantung, denyut hati.

heartbreaking menyayat hati.

heartburn sendawa asam.

hearten, to — menggembirakan, melipur.

heartfelt sungguh-sungguh.

hearth batu dapur di dalam rumah.

heartily dengan sungguh dengan hebat; to eat — makan dengan sedap.

heartless kejam, tidak berbelas kasihan.

hearty dengan kuat, dengan gembira.

heat panas, kepanasan; (preliminary race) satu bahagian dalam perlumbaan atau pertandingan.

heath padang yang tidak ditanam; sejenis tumbuhan.

heathen (unbeliever) orang kafir; (uncivilized) orang tidak beradab.

heatstroke, to suffer from — dipanah matahari.

heatwave masa panas terik.

heave, to — mengangkat sesuatu yang berat; (of breath) menarik.

heaven (sky) langit; (abode of God) syurga; (paradise) kayangan.

heaviness berat, keberatan.

heavy berat, sarat, antap.

Hebrew Yahudi, Ibrani.

heckle, to — mengemukakan pertanyaan yang sukar dijawab.

hectic sangat ramai, ribut, riuh-rendah.

hedge pagar pohon; to — memagari, menutupi; (be shifty in argument) tidak sudi menjawab pertanyaan.

hedgehog sejenis landak.

heed perhatian; to — memperhatikan, mengindahkan, menghiraukan.

heedless dengan tidak diperhatikan (diendahkan), tidak perduli.

heel tumit.

hefty berat, tegap.

heifer sapi betina yang belum beranak.

height tinggi, ketinggian.

heighten, to — memperting-gikan, meninggikan.

heinous sangat jahat.

heir waris, turunan.

heirloom pesaka, barang warisan.

helicopter kapalterbang yang dapat naik tegak.

hell neraka, jahannam.

helm kemudi.

helmet topi besi, ketopong.

helmsman jurumudi, penge-mudi.

help pertolongan, pemban-tuan; (*household*) pembantu di rumahtangga; **to** — menolong, membantu.

helpful suka menolong; (*use-ful*) berguna, bermanfaat.

helping (*of food*) sebahagian makanan, hidangan.

helpless tidak berdaya, daif.

helter-skelter sempang-perenang, porak-parik.

hem bilai, kampuh, bibir, kelim; **to** — mengelim.

hemi— awalan kata yang ertinya; setengah.

hemisphere setengah bola bumi, setengah bulatan, hemis-piar.

hemp rami; Indian — ganja.

hen ayam betina; —pecked orang laki-laki yang menurut sahaja kemahuan isterinya.

hence (*from here*) dari sini; (*from now*) dari sekarang.

henceforth, henceforward ke hadapan, seterusnya, mulai dari sekarang.

henchman pengiring, kaki-tangan.

henna inai.

hepta— awalan kata yang ertinya; tujuh.

her dia, ia, akan dia, kepada dia; (*possessive*) -nya.

herald bentara penyiar; **to** — mengumumkan.

heraldry ilmu asal-usal dan lambang turunan.

herb rumput-rumputan; medi-cinal — jamu.

herbalist penjual ubat jamu.

herbivorous yang hanya ma-kan tumbuh-tumbuhan maun.

Herculean sangat kuat, sa-ngat sukar dilakukan.

herd kawan, kumpulan; herds-man, gembala.

here sini, di sini, tempat ini.

hereafter kemudian hari, pada masa yang akan datang.

hereby dengan jalan ini, dengan ini.

hereditary baka, turun-temurun.

heredity baka, sifat turun-temurun.

heresy faham (pendapat, per-kataan) yang berlawanan de-ngan faham resmi.

heretic orang yang mengucap-kan pendapat yang berlawan-an dengan faham resmi.

heritage barang warisan, pusaka.

hermaphrodite banci, kedi.

hermetic kedap udara.

hermit pertapa.

hernia burut, sakit bodek.

hero pahlawan; (*on stage*) pelaku utama dalam sandi-wara.

heroic yang berkenaan de-ngan atau seperti pahlawan, gagah perkasa.

heroin sejenis ubat penidur.

heroine pahlawan perem-puan; (*on stage etc*) pelaku perempuan yang utama dalam sandiwara (buku dan seba-gainya).

heroism kepahlawanan, ke-perwiraan.

heron sejenis bangau, burung pucung.

herring sejenis ikan laut; **to** —

draw a red — across the path menyimpangkan perhatian orang.

hers kepunyaan perempuan itu.

herself ia (perempuan) sendiri.

hesitant bimbang, ragu-ragu.

hesitate, to — berdua hati, ragu-ragu, bimbang.

hessian sejenis kain kasar.

hetero– awalan kata yang ertinya; lain, berlainan.

heterogeneous terdiri dari berbagai-bagai unsur, serba jenis.

hew, to — menebang, menetak.

hexa– awalan kata yang ertinya; enam.

hexagon segi enam.

hey kataseru: eh!

heyday puncak, masa raja, perkembangan.

hibernate, to — tidur nyenyak pada musim sejuk (binatang).

hibiscus kembang sepatu, bunga raya.

hiccup sedu; to — tersedu.

hide I, to — bersembunyi, menyembunyikan, menyelimuti, menyamarkan, memendamkan.

hide II (skin) kulit haiwan.

hideous seram, ngeri, mengerikan.

hiding tempat bersembunyi; (beating) pukulan.

hierarchy susunan beringkat-tingkat.

hieroglyph tulisan Masir pada masa purbakala; (secret script) tulisan rahsia.

higgledy-piggledy simpang-perenang, kacau-bilau.

high (of place) tinggi; (rank) mulia; — life kehidupan orang berbangsa; — seas laut lepas.

highborn berasal dari orang berbangsa.

highbrow sangat terpelajar.

hightalutin(g) dengan perkataan, yang tinggi-tinggi.

high-handed dengan memaksa, maharajalela.

highly amat sangat.

high-minded berbudi baik.

highness kebesaran ketinggian, mulia; His H— Maha Mulia.

high-pitched nyaring.

high school sekolah menengah.

high-spirited gembira, besar hati.

high-strung sangat halus rasa hatinya.

high tide air pasang.

highway jalan besar, jalanraya; —man penyamun.

hike perjalanan kaki; to — berjalan kaki.

hiker pelancong yang berjalan kaki.

hilarious gembira, riang, ria.

hill bukit.

hillock busut, anak bukit.

hilly berbukit-bukit.

hilt pangkal pedang, puting, hulu.

him dia, ia (laki-laki).

himself ia (laki-laki) sendiri.

hind I (deer) rusa betina.

hind II, hinder (rear) belakang.

hinder, to — menghalang.

Hindi salah satu bahasa India.

hindrance rintangan, gangguan.

Hindu Hindu.

Hindustani yang berkenaan dengan Hindustan; (person) orang Hindu; (language) bahasa Hindi.

hinge sendi, engsel; to — (on) bersendi kepada, memasang dengan sendi.

hint isyarat, sindiran, kiasan; to — mengisyaratkan; to — at menyindirkan.

hinterland daerah darat.

hip pangkal paha, panggul.

hip, hip, hurrah! sejenis sorak gembira.

hippopotamus sejenis badak berendam.

hire wang sewa, sewaan.

hirsute beramus, randuk, berbulu.

his dia, -nya, kepunyaannya laki-laki.

hiss, to — berdesau, berdesir, berdesus-desus.

historian ahli sejarah.

historic(al) bersejarah, berkenaan dengan sejarah, dahulukala.

history sejarah.

histrionic yang berkenaan dengan pemain atau permainan sandiwara.

hit pukulan; (*success*) hasil baik; **to** — memukul.

hitch (*jerk*) sentak; (*obstruction*) rintangan, alangan.

hitch-hike perjalanan dengan minta menumpang kereta dan sebagainya dengan percuma di tengah jalan, pukul kaki.

hive beehive, sarang lebah; (*crowded place*) tempat yang sangat ramai dan riuh.

hoar berubah, kelabu keputih-putihan kerana sudah tua.

hoard persediaan, timbunan; **to** — menyimpan.

hoarding pagar papan di sekeliling rumah yang sedang didirikan timbun simpan.

hoarse garau, serak.

hoary berubah; (*old*) tua.

hoax bukan-bukan; **to** — bersenda gurau, memperdayakan.

hob paku; (*of hearth*) papan besi di sisi tungku.

hobble pincang; **to** — berjalan pincang.

hobby kegemaran, kesukaan.

hobgoblin sejenis jin, polong.

hobnail paku rebana pada sepatu.

hob-nob, to — (*also* —bed) minum bersama-sama; bergaul dengan ramah-tamah.

hobo (*US*) pertualang, orang miskin.

hock sebahagian kaki kuda.

hockey sejenis permainan dengan bola dan kayu pemukul.

hod tempat pemikul kapur (simen dan sebagainya).

hoe cangkul, tajak; **to** — mencangkul, menajak.

hog babi, babi kembiri.

hoist pesawat penaikan barang dan sebagainya; **to** — menaikkan.

hold I (*cavity*) ruang.

hold II pegangan, genggaman; (*influence*) pengaruh; **to catch** — of memegang, mencapai; **to have a** — on mempengaruhi; **to** — out menghulurkan.

holdall sejenis bekas isi barang.

holder pemegang.

holding kepunyaan tanah, tanah milik.

holdup (*robbery*) mengadang di jalan, samun.

hole lubang, liang, rongga; **to be in a** — berada dalam keadaan susah.

holiday hariraya, cuti, hari besar.

holiness kesucian.

hollow lekuk, rongga; (*empty*) hampa, kosong; **—eyed** cekung.

holly sejenis tumbuhan.

hollyhock sejenis bunga.

holocaust pengorbanan atau pembasmian secara besar-besaran.

holster tempat menyimpan pistol.

holy kudus, suci; **— day** hari peringatan hal suci.

homage bakti, hormat, penghormatan; **to pay (do)** — to menghormati.

home tempat kediaman, rumah; (native place) tanahair; kampung halaman.

home country nusa dan bangsa, tanahair.

homely sederhana, tidak cantik.

homesick rindu, ingin pulang ke rumah.

homespun ditenun di rumah.

homestead rumah dengan segala rumah turutannya.

homeward(s) ke rumah, pulang; — **bound** arah ke rumah.

homicide pembunuhan manusia.

homily nasihat.

homing yang pulang istimewa; burung yang diajarkan pulang ke rumahnya.

homo— awalan kata yang ertinya; sama.

homoeopathy ilmu pengubatan penyakit dengan ubat yang mengandung zat penyakit itu juga.

homogeneous sama jenis; serba sama.

homonym kata yang sebunyi tetapi tidak seerti.

homo sapiens manusia.

homosexual tarikan antara sejenis.

hone batu asah; to — mengasah.

honest lurus, jujur, tulus, benar.

honesty kelurusan, kejujuran, ketulusan hati.

honey madu, manisan; (term of endearment) tangkai hati; — **-bee** lebah; **-comb** sarang lebah.

honk bunyi angsa; to — membunyikan hon kereta.

honorary yang diberi sebagaimana kehormatan; — **secretary** setiausaha yang tidak diupah.

honour kehormatan, kebesaran; kemuliaan, penghor-

matan; (reputation) nama baik.

honourable yang berhormat, terhormat, mulia, tulus dan ikhlas.

hood sejenis tudung kepala (segala yang menyerupai tudung).

hoodlum orang jahat, buaya darat.

hoodwink, to — menipu.

hoof kuku (kuda lembu dan sebagainya); to — (trample) menerajang.

hook kait, pemaut, sangkutan; by — or by crook dengan segala daya upaya.

hooked (bent) bengkok; (caught on hook) berkait.

hookey, to play — membolos.

hooligan buaya darat, samseng.

hoop simpai.

hoot teriak, seruan; I don't care a — tidak perduli.

hop I sejenis tumbuh-tumbuhan.

hop II (jump) loncat, lompat, jingkat.

hope pengharapan, asa; to — mengharap, berharap.

hopeful penuh pengharapan.

hopeless putus asa.

horde kelompok.

horizon kaki langit.

horizontal garis melintang.

hormone hormon.

horn (of animal) tanduk; (music) sejenis alat muzik (sesuatu yang berbentuk seperti tanduk).

hornet tebuan, penyengat, naning.

horoscope tenung, falakiah.

horrible, horrid ngeri, mendahsyatkan.

horrify, to — mengecutkan, mendahsyatkan.

horror kengerian, perasaan ngeri, sesuatu yang mengerikan; —**struck**, —**stricken** sangat terkejut dan dahsyat.

horse kuda.
horseback, on — berkuda; **to ride on** — menunggang kuda.
horseman orang berkuda, pensendara.
horseplay kelakar bergurau senda yang kasar.
horsepower daya kuda.
horse-race lumba kuda.
horse-radish sejenis lobak.
horseshoe sepatu kuda, ladam.
horticulture ilmu berkebun bunga.
hose kaus kaki; *(watering)* pembuluh penyiram.
hospitable murah hati, suka menerima tetamu.
hospital rumahsakit.
hospitality kemurahan tangan, kesukaan menerima tetamu.
host I tuanrumah.
host II *(crowd)* sejumlah besar.
hostage orang tahanan, jaminan.
hostel sejenis asrama.
hostess perempuan yang menyambut tamu.
hostile bermusuhan, berseteru.
hostility permusuhan, perseteruan.
hot panas, hangat, meradang; *(of spices)* pedas.
hotbed *(for plants)* persemaian (juga dalam erti kiasan).
hot-blooded galak.
hot dog roti dengan inti daging.
hotel hotel, rumah penginapan.
hotfoot dengan terburu-buru.
hotheaded panas hati, lekas marah.
hothouse rumah kaca untuk tanaman yang tidak tahan akan sejuk.
hot-tempered lekas meradang, pemarah.
hound anjing pemburu; **to** — memburu.

hour jam; — **hand** jarum jam; —**ly** tiap-tiap jam.
house rumah, tempat kediaman.
house agent wakil jual-beli dan sewa-menyewa rumah.
houseboat kapal yang dilengkapkan sebagai tempat tinggal.
housebreaker pencuri yang memasuki rumah, penceroboh.
household isi rumah, rumahtangga.
householder tuanrumah, kepala keluarga.
housekeeper pengurus rumahtangga.
housemaid pengemas rumah.
housewife suri rumah.
housework pekerjaan rumahtangga.
housing perumahan.
hovel teratak.
hover, to — mengambang-ambang, melayang di udara.
how bagaimana, macam mana; *(much)* berapa.
howdah rengga, rengka gajah.
however akan tetapi, pun, melainkan.
howl pekik; **to** — memekik, melolong.
howler pemekik; *(stupid mistake)* kesalahan, khilaf.
hoy hai!
hub gantang-gantang, pusat roda; *(centre generally)* pusat.
hubbub gempar.
huddle kerumun; **to** — menimbunkan; **to** — **together** berhimpit-himpit.
hue I warna, corak.
hue II, — **and cry** gempar.
huff *(sulk etc)* kecil hati, merasa dikecilkan hati; **to** — gusar perasaan tersinggung.
hug peluk; **to** — memeluk.
huge sangat besar.
hulk *(naut)* badan kapal.
hulking kekok.

hull I (*husk*) kulit, sekam; to — mengupas.

hull II (*naut*) badan kapal.

hullabaloo kerusuhan.

hullo wahai.

hum berdengung.

human manusia, kemanusiaan; — being manusia.

humane rahim, bebelas kasihan.

humanitarian berfaham manusia; (*compassionate*) berbelas kasihan.

humanity pari kemanusiaan.

humble rendah, hina, berkhidmat; to — merendahkan.

humbug bohong, penipu.

humdrum sederhana, menjemukan.

humid lembap lengas.

humidity keadaan lembap; absolute — kelembapan mutlak.

humiliate, to — merendahkan, menghinakan.

humiliation penghinaan.

humility kerendahan hati.

humming, —bird sejenis burung.

hummock anak bukit.

humorist orang yang suka berjenaka.

humorous jenaka.

humour keadaan geli hati, jenaka; out of — marah, tak senang hati.

hump bongkok; (*on camel*) kelasa; —back bongkok.

hunch bongkok; —back orang yang bongkok.

hundred seratus; —s of beratus-ratus.

hunger lapar, kelaparan.

hungry lapar; (*desire*) sangat ingin.

hunk bongkak.

hunt pemburuan; to — berburu, memburu.

hunter pemburu; (*horse*) kuda pemburu.

huntsman pemburu.

hurdle pagar; — -race lari lompat pagar.

hurl lontar, lemparan; to — melontar, melemparkan.

hurly-burly kekacauan.

hurrah hurray, syabus.

hurricane angin taufan.

hurried(ly) tergesa-gesa, tergopoh-gapah.

hurry kegopohan; in a — terburu-buru, tergesa-gesa; to — bersegera; — up! lekas!, segerahlah!

hurt luka; to — menyakiti, melukai.

hurtle, to — melemparkan lekas-lekas.

husband suami, laki.

husbandry (*farming*) pertanian.

hush kesunyian, ketenangan; (*be silent*) diam; — - — rahsia.

husk dedak, sekam; (*coconut*) — kulit sabut.

husky I bersekam; (*strong*) kuat.

husky II (*dog*) anjing Eskimo.

hussy perempuan nakal.

hustings pemilihan.

hustle keramaian; to — mendorong, mendesak.

hut pondok, teratak.

hyacinth sejenis bunga kiambang.

hybrid tumbuhan atau haiwan yang hasil perkahwinan antara dua jenis yang berlainan; kacukan.

hydrant paip air.

hydraulic dikerjakan dengan tenaga air; —ilmu tenaga air.

hydro- awalan kata yang ertinya: air.

hydrochloric, — acid asam garam, hidroklorik.

hydroelectric mengadakan karban letrik dengan air; hidro-letrik.

hydrogen zat air.

hyena hyaena, sejenis anjing hutan.

hygiene kebersihan, ilmu kesihatan.

hygienic bersih, menurut ilmu kesihatan.

hymn mazmur.

hyper— awalan kata yang ertinya: terlalu.

hyphen tanda penyambung sengkang.

hypno— awalan kata yang ertinya: tidur.

hypnosis tidur yang disebabkan oleh ilmu sihir.

hypnotic sesuatu yang menyebabkan tidur.

hypnotism penduran dengan jalan ilmu sihir.

hypnotize, to — menidurkan dengan jalan ilmu sihir.

hypo— awalan kata yang ertinya: di bawah, kurang.

hypochondria keadaan murung.

hypochondriac orang yang murung hati.

hypocrisy muka-muka, purapura.

hypocrite munafik, bermukamuka berpura-pura.

hypocritical bermuka-muka, munafik.

hypodermic di bawah kulit.

hypothesis andai-andai, pengiraan; hipotesis.

hysteria sejenis penyakit sarat.

hysterical terselap.

hysterics serangan selap, penyakit saraf.

I

I aku, sahaya, saya.

Iberian yang berkenaan dengan negeri Sepanyol dan Portugal; orang yang berasal dari negeri tersebut itu.

ice air beku; **to break the —** menjadikan ramah-tamah.

iceberg bukit air beku, bungkah air beku.

icicle titisan air beku.

icing kerak gula di atas kuih.

icon patung **atau** gambar orang suci.

iconoclasm penghancuran patung.

icy penuh air beku, ditutup air beku; (*very cold*) sangat sejuk.

idea buah fikiran, faham, pengertian angan-angan cita-cita.

ideal cita-cita, utama, unggul, yang terlebih diangan-angankan.

idealism faham idealis.

idealize, to — mencita-cita, mengangan-angankan.

identical yang sama tepat sama.

identify, to — (*as identical*) mempersamakan; (*establish identity*) memperkenalkan.

identity persamaan, kenyataan; **— card** kad pengenalan.

ideogram, **ideograph** huruf yang menyatakan faham sesuatu bukan bunyinya.

ideology ideologi, cita-cita yang merupakan dasar salah satu sistem politik.

idiocy kependiraan.

idiom (*natural way of language*) bahasa yang istimewa terdapat pada salah satu golongan orang; (*form of language*) simpulan bahasa, jalan bahasa, ungkapan.

idiomatic yang istimewa termasuk salah satu bahasa; yang termasuk bahasa sehari-hari simpulan bahasa.

idiosyncrasy perasaan atau kebiasaan yang boleh dianggap khasiat istimewa salah seorang.

idiot orang pandir, tolol.

idle (*useless*) tidak berguna, sia-sia, cuma-cuma; (*lazy*)

malas; (*not in use*) tak berjalan.

idler pemalas.

idol patung, berhala, arca.

idolatry penyembahan berhala.

idyll syair yang melukiskan
keindahan alam dan kampung
halaman; (*idyllic state*) keadaan seperti di kampung
halaman itu.

idyllic sempurna, sangat menarik.

if jikalau, jika, kalau, bila.

igloo rumah orang Eskimo.

ignite, to — memasang api,
menyalakan.

ignoble hina, cendala.

ignominious yang menghinakan.

ignominy kejian, penghinaan, kelakuan hina.

ignoramus orang yang tidak
tahu apa-apa, orang jahil.

ignorance kejahilan, kebodohan.

ignorant jahil, tidak tahu-
menahu.

ignore, to — tidak mengendahkan, memungkirkan.

iguana sejenis biawak.

ill sakit, kesakitan; (*bad etc*)
buruk, jahat, keburukan, kejahatan; to fall — jatuh sakit.

ill-advised tidak bijaksana.

ill-bred tidak beradab berbahasa kasar.

illegal tidak sah, melanggar
undang-undang.

illegible tidak dapat dibaca.

illegitimate tidak sah, tidak
menurut hukum; (*bastard*)
haram jadah, anak gampang.

ill-fated malang, celaka.

ill-favoured tidak menyukakan.

ill-gotten diperoleh secara
jahat.

illicit dilarang, haram.

illiteracy keadaan buta huruf.

illiterate buta huruf.

ill-judged tidak bijaksana.

ill-mannered kurang berbahasa, tidak beradab.

illness penyakit, sakit.

illogical tidak menurut ilmu
mantik, tidak lojik.

ill-omened sialan.

ill-starred malang, celaka.

ill-timed tidak pada waktunya.

ill-treat, to — menganiaya;
ill-treatment aniaya.

illuminate, to — menerangi,
menyinari, memberi cahaya.

illumination penerangan.

illusion khayalan, angan-
angan, silap.

illusionist orang yang berkhayal; (*conjurer*) penyilap.

illusive, illusory khayalan.

illustrate, to — (*make clear*)
menjelaskan; menerangkan;
(*with pictures*) menggambari.

illustration gambaran; (*example*) umpama.

illustrious mulia, agung,
termasyhur.

ill will sakit hati, dendam.

im— awalan kata yang ertinya;
tidak; di dalam.

image gambar angan-angan,
cermin, bayangan; (*statue*)
patung, imej.

imagery gambar-gambaran.

imaginable yang dapat diangan-angankan

imaginary khayal.

imagination angan-angan,
rekaan, khayal.

imaginative yang suka berkhayal.

imagine, to — berkhayal,
mengangan-angan; (*suppose*)
fikir.

imbecile bodoh, bebal; orang
bebal, tongong, tolol.

imbibe, to — minum; (*absorb*)
menyerap, menghirup.

imbue, to — membasahkan,
mencelup.

imitate, to — menurut.

menyama-nyama, meniru, mencontohi.

imitation tiruan.

imitative yang meniru, mencontoh.

imitator peniru.

immaculate bersih; tidak bercacat.

immanent batin, hadir dalam segala bahagian alam.

immaterial tidak penting.

immature masih muda, belum masak, belum sempurna.

immeasurable tidak berukur, tidak terduga.

immediate, —ly langsung, terus-menerus segera; (near) yang terlebih dekat.

immemorial abadi, azali, kuno.

immense sangat besar.

immensity keadaan sangat besar.

immerse, to — mencelup, rendam, membenamkan, menyelamkan.

immersion permandian.

immigrant orang yang masuk negeri asing hendak berpindah negeri.

immigrate, to — masuk negeri asing hendak berpindah negeri.

immigration perpindahan.

imminent yang kelak akan datang.

immobile tidak dapat bergerak.

immobilize, to — menjadikan tetap.

immoderate terlampau, melalui batas.

immodest tidak sopan, kasar.

immoral buruk, lacur, cabul.

immorality keburukan, kelacuran.

immortal kekal, abadi.

immortality kekekalan.

immovable tidak terganjak, tetap.

immune (from injury etc) kebal, lali tidak mempan; (from rules etc) bebas.

immunity kekebalan, kelalian.

immure, to — mengurungkan.

immutable tidak dapat diubah.

imp anak syaitan.

impact kena; to — menekan, mendesak.

impair, to — merugikan, melemahkan.

impale, to — menyulakan.

impalpable (not felt) tidak terasa; (not apprehended) tidak mudah difahamkan.

impart, to — (give) memberi; (make known) memberitahukan.

impartial adil.

impassable yang tidak dapat dilalui.

impasse jalan buntu.

impassible tidak dapat merasa.

impassion, to — menggiatkan.

impassive tidak berperasaan.

impatience tidak sabar.

impatient tidak sabar; (restless) gugup.

impeach, to — menuduh, mendakwa.

impeachment penuduhan, pendakwaan.

impeccable tidak berdosa, tidak bercela, tidak bercacat.

impecunious tidak mempunyai wang.

impede, to — mengalang, merintangi.

impediment rintangan, alangan; — in one's speech patah lidah.

impel, to — (drive) mendorong; (force) memaksa.

impend, to — kelak terjadi.

impenetrable kedap, tidak dapat ditembus.

imperative yang memaksa,

yang memerintah cara perintah; (by religion) wajib.

imperceptible yang tidak terlihat, tidak terasa.

imperfect (incomplete) tidak sempurna, tidak engkap; (defective) bercacat.

imperfection cacat.

imperial yang berkenaan dengan kerajaan.

imperialism faham imperialis.

imperil, to — membahayakan.

imperious yang suka memaksa.

impersonal tidak berkenaan dengan seseorang.

impersonate, to — menjelmakan (on the stage) memainkan peranan.

impertinence hal kurang ajar.

impertinent kurang ajar, tidak tahu adat.

imperturbable tidak terganggu, tenang.

impervious tidak dapat dilalui.

impetuous giat.

impetus daya bergerak.

impinge, to — (on) mengenai melanggar.

impish seperti anak syaitan.

implacable tidak dapat dipujuk.

implant, to — memasukkan menanami, menanamkan.

implement alat, perkakas; **to** — memenuhi, melengkapkan

implicate, to — membabitkan, mencampurkan.

implication perhatian, akibat.

implicit termasuk, terkandung.

implore, to — memohon, meminta.

imply, to — termasuk, mengandungi.

impolite biadab, kurang ajar.

import (matter of consequence) hal yang penting; pemasukan; —s barang impot, barang yang dimasukkan dari luar negeri.

importance kepentingan kebesaran.

important penting; (dignified) mulia.

importer pengimpot.

importunate yang mendesak, menyusahkan.

impose, to — mengenakan; (influence) mempengaruhi; to — upon memperdayakan.

imposing yang menghairankan.

imposition pengenaan; (forced work etc) pekerjaan atau pembayaran yang wajib.

impossibility tidak harus.

impossible tidak boleh jadi, mustahil

impostor penipu.

imposture perdayaan.

impotence kelemahan.

impotent tidak berdaya, tidak berkuasa; (sexual) mati pucuk.

impound, to — mengurungkan.

impoverish, to — menjadikan miskin.

impracticable tidak dapat dilakukan.

impractical tidak dapat dilakukan, tidak praktik.

impregnable yang tidak dapat dialahkan.

impregnate, to — (make pregnant) menghamilkan; (fill) memenuhi.

impresario pengurus pemimpin.

impress pencetakan, cap to — mencetak.

impression jejak, rakam, kesan; (on mind) pada perasaan.

impressionable mudah dipengaruhi.

impressive yang mengharukan.

imprint bekas, rakam, cap, kesan.

imprison, to — memenjarakan.

imprisonment penjara, pengurungan.

improbability hal mustahil.

improbable mustahil.

impromptu dengan tidak dipersiapkan lebih dahulu.

improper salah, tidak senonoh.

impropriety kesalahan, keadaan tidak patut.

improve, to — membetulkan, memperbaiki.

improvement perbaikan, pembetulan.

improvisation pengucapan dengan tidak disiapkan lebih dahulu.

improvise, to — mengucapkan dengan tidak dipersiapkan lebih dahulu.

imprudent tidak bijaksana.

impudence muka papan.

impudent kurang ajar, muka papan.

impulse (*force*) dorongan; (*of mind*) gerak hati.

impulsion dorongan.

impulsive gerak hati, mudah terpengaruh.

impunity kebebasan dari hukuman.

impure kotor, tidak suci.

impute, to — menuduh.

in dalam, di dalam, ke dalam, di, pada.

in- awalan kata yang ertinya: tidak; di dalam.

inability keadaan tidak mampu.

inaccessible tidak tercapai, tidak dapat dimasuki.

inaccurate tidak tepat.

inaction keadaan tidak ber-

gerak.

inactive tidak giat.

inadequate tidak menukupi kurang.

inadmissible yang tidak dapat diperkenankan.

inadvertent (*unintentional*) tidak sengaja; (*negligent*) lalai.

inane (*senseless*) tidak bererti.

inanimate tidak berjiwa.

inapt tidak cekap.

inarticulate tidak jelas, pelat.

inasmuch, — as oleh kerana.

inattentive kurang ingat, alpa, tidak berperhatian.

inaudible tidak terdengar.

inaugural merasmikan berkenaan dengan pelantikan, pembukaan.

inaugurate, to — melantik, membuka.

inauguration pelantikan, pembukaan.

inborn bawaan, pada dasarnya.

inbreeding perkahwinan ternak.

incalculable tidak terbilang.

incandescent terang.

incantation mantera, jampi.

incapable tidak cakap, tidak sanggup.

incapacitate, to — menjadikan tidak sanggup.

incarcerate, to — memenjarakan.

incarnate penjelmaan; **to** — menjelma.

incarnation penjelmaan.

incendiary pembakar.

incense I istanggi, ukup, kemenyan.

incense II, to — (*anger*) menyakitkan hati.

incentive perangsang, penggiat.

inception permulaan.

incertitude keadaan tidak tentu.

incessant tidak putus-putusnya, tidak berhenti.

incest perbuatan sumbang.

incestuous sumbang.

inch inci; give him an — and he'll take a mile diberi (betis) hendak paha.

incidence jatuhnya; *(affecting)* pengaruh.

incident peristiwa, kejadian.

incidental kebetulan.

incidentally sambil lalu.

incinerator tempat membakar sampah.

incision takek, kelar.

incisive yang memotong, mengiris; *(trenchant)* tajam.

incisor gigi kacip.

incite, to — mengajak, memberangsangkan, menghasut.

inclement berhawa buruk.

inclination kecondongan, kecenderungan.

incline, to — *(bend)* tunduk, membongkok; *(deviate)* memiring, mencondongkan.

include, to — mengandung, termasuk, meliputi.

inclusion termasuknya.

inclusive termasuk, tergolong.

incognito dengan menyamar.

incoherent tidak bersambung, tidak tentu hujung pangkal.

income pendapatan, peruntungan; *(salary)* gaji.

in-coming yang masuk.

incomparable tiada taranya, tidak terbanding.

incompatible bertentangan, berlawanan.

incompetence keadaan tidak cakap atau tidak upaya.

incompetent tidak cakap.

incomplete tidak sempurna, tidak lengkap.

incomprehensible tidak terfaham.

inconceivable tidak dapat difahamkan.

inconclusive tidak pesti.

incongruity tidak pada tempatnya.

incongruous tidak seimbang, bertentangan tidak sama.

inconsequence hal tidak bersambung.

inconsequent(ial) tidak menurut akal; *(unimportant)* tidak penting.

inconsiderable tidak besar, tidak berharga.

inconsiderate kurang hormat, tidak memikirkan orang lain.

inconsistent tidak sesuai, bertentangan.

inconspicuous tidak menarik perhatian.

inconstant tidak tetap, berubah-ubah.

incontestable yang tidak dapat dilawan.

incontinent *(unchaste)* tidak bertarak; *(of urine)* beser.

inconvenience gangguan, kesusahan.

inconvenient menyusahkan, susah.

incorporate dihubungkan dalam suatu badan, menuhuhkan.

incorporation perbadanan, persatuan.

incorrect tidak tepat, tidak benar.

incorrigible tidak dapat diperbaiki.

incorruptible yang tidak lapuk di hujan. tidak lekang di panas.

increase penaikan, tambahan.

incredible mustahil, tidak dapat dipercayai.

incredulous tidak percaya.

increment penambahan, kenaikan.

incriminate, to — menuduh.

incrustation kulit, kerak.

incubate, to — mengeram.

incubation pengeraman.

incubator alat pengeram.

inculcate, to — mendesakkan, memasukkan.

incumbent, it is — on me to . .kewajiban saya akan ....

incur, to — kena.

incurable tidak dapat disembuhkan.

incursion serangan, serbuan.

indebted berhutang.

indecency keadaan atau kelakuan yang tidak senonoh.

indecent tidak senonoh.

indecision tidak tetap.

indecisive bimbang, ragu-ragu.

indecorous tidak patut.

indeed sebetulnya sesungguhnya.

indefensible tidak dapat dipertahankan.

indefinable tidak dapat d-tentukan.

indefinite tidak tentu, tidak tetap.

indelible yang tidak dapat dihapuskan.

indelicate kasar.

indemnity wang pengganti rugi.

indent lekuk, bersuak.

indentation takuk, teluk, rantau.

indenture surat rangkap dua, surat perjanjian.

independence kemerdekaan.

independent bebas, merdeka berdiri sendiri.

indescribable tidak bergambarkan.

indestructible yang tidak dapat dirosakkan.

indeterminate tidak tentu, ragu-ragu.

index (*finger*) jari telunjuk; (*pointer*) petunjuk; to — membuat daftar.

India India, Hindia.

Indian Hindia, orang Hindia; Red — orang Indian di Amerika; — corn jagung.

indicate, to — menyatakan menandakan.

indication tanda, penunjukan.

indicator penunjuk.

indict, to — mendakwa.

indictment pendakwaan.

indifference perasaan tidak peduli, kelalaian.

indifferent (*careless*) masa bodoh, lalai; (*unimportant*) tidak penting.

indigenous asli, bumiputera.

indigestible yang tidak dapat dicerna, tidak hadam.

indigestion salah cerna.

indignant marah, berang.

indignation perasaan berang.

indignity perlakuan buruk, penghinaan.

indigo nila, tarum.

indirect cara tidak langsung.

indiscernible yang tidak dapat diperbezakan.

indiscreet kurang bijaksana.

indiscretion kelakuan tidak bijaksana.

indiscriminate campur-aduk, tidak memilih.

indispensable sangat perlu.

indispose, to — menjadikan tidak sanggup.

indisposition keadaan kurang baik, sakit.

indisputable yang tidak dapat dilawan.

indissoluble yang tidak dapat diurai; (*binding for ever*) kekal.

indistinct samar, kabur, tidak terang.

indistinguishable tidak dapat dibezakan.

individual keseorangan, perseorangan, individu.

individuality sifat perseorangan.

individually satu demi satu masing-masing.

indivisible tidak dapat dibahagi.

indolence kelengahan.

indolent lemas, malas, lengah.

Indonesian yang berkenaan dengan Indonesia; orang Indonesia.

indoor dalam rumah (keadaan); — games permainan dalam.

indoors di dalam rumah; I stayed — saya tinggal di rumah.

indubitable, indubitably yang tidak dapat diragu-ragukan, tentu.

induce, to — mengakibatkan, menerbitkan, mendatangkan.

inducement pendorong.

induct, to — memasukkan, menempatkan.

induction penarikan kesimpulan dari beberapa kenyataan.

indulge, to — memperkenankan; to — in menuruti kehendak hati.

indulgence kemanjaan.

indulgent yang mengulur, membiarkan.

industrial perusahaan, yang berkenaan dengan perusahaan.

industrialist pengusaha.

industrialize, to — mengusahakan.

industrious rajin, ringan tulang.

industry (*diligence*) kerajinan; (*manufacturers etc*) usaha, perusahaan.

inebriation kemabukan.

inedible tidak termakan.

ineffective tidak berhasil.

ineffectual hampa, tidak berhasil.

inefficient tidak cakap; tidak berhasil.

ineligible tidak dapat dipakai, tidak dapat masuk.

inept tidak pada tempatnya, mustahil.

ineptitude keadaan mustahil.

inequality keadaan tidak setimbal.

inert rengsa.

inertia kelembaman.

inescapable tidak dapat tidak, tidak ada jalan keluar.

inessential tidak penting.

inestimable tidak terharga, tidak ternilai.

inevitable tidak dapat dielakkan, tidak dapat tiada.

inexcusable tidak dapat dimaafkan.

inexhaustible yang tidak dapat dihabiskan.

inexorable keras, tidak terpujuk.

inexpensive murah.

inexperienced tidak berpengalaman.

inexplicable yang tidak dapat dielaskan, yang tidak dapat diterangkan.

inextricable yang tidak dapat dielakkan, tidak dapat diuraikan.

infallible tidak dapat salah.

infamous bernama buruk, keji.

infamy kekejian.

infancy masa bayi, masa kanak-kanak.

infant bayi, kanak-kanak; — school taman kanak-kanak.

infanticide pembunuhan anak yang baharu dilahirkan.

infantile yang berkenaan dengan kanan-kanak, keanak-anakan.

infantry pasukan askar berjalan.

infatuation kegilaan, berahi.

infect, to — menjangkiti.

infection jangkitan.

infectious, — disease penyakit berjangkit.

infer, to — menarik kesimpulan.

inference kesimpulan.

inferior (*lower*) lebih rendah; (*poor in quality*) kurang baik.

infernal yang berkenaan, dengan nuraka.

inferno nuraka.

infertile (*of soil*) tidak subur; (*of women*) mandul.

infertility hal tidak subur.

infest, to — penuh dengan.

infidel orang yang tidak beriman, kafir.

infidelity penderhakaan, keingkaran ugama; (*in marriage*) zina.

in-fighting tinju-meninju dengan sangat berdekatan.

infiltrate, to — menyusup, meresap.

infiltration penyusupan, resapan.

infinite tidak terbatas, sangat banyak, sangat besar.

infinitesimal sangat kecil.

infinitive cara tidak tentu.

infinity keadaan tidak terbatas.

infirm lemah.

infirmary rumahsakit.

inflame, to — menyala, meluap.

inflammable mudah dinyalakan.

inflammation bernyala; (*of the body*) sakit radang.

inflammatory yang menyalakan.

inflate, to — mengembungkan, melembungkan.

inflation kembung, inflasi.

inflexible kejang, tidak dapat dilekukkan.

inflexion bengkok ke dalam.

inflict, to — mengenakan.

infliction pengenaan.

influence pengaruh; to — mempengaruhi.

influential berpengaruh.

influenza penyakit influensa, selesema.

influx aliran ke dalam, kemasukan.

inform, to — memberitahu, mengatakan.

informal tidak rasmi, tidak dengan upacara.

informant pemberita, orang yang memberitahu.

information maklumat, perkhabaran khabar.

informative yang memberitahu menerangkan.

informed berpengetahuan.

informer penuduh, pengadu.

infra- awalan kata yang ertinya :di bawah.

infrequent tidak selalu, jarang.

infringe, to — melanggar.

infringement pelanggaran.

infuriate, to — memarahkan.

infuse, to — (*pour in*) menuang sedoh.

–ing akhiran kata yang menyatakan; bentuk sedang membuat salah satu kata kerja.

ingenious cerdik, berakal.

ingenuity kecerdikan.

ingenuous terus terang.

ingle tempat api di bilik; **–nook** penjuru dekat api.

in-going yang masuk.

ingot sebatang emas.

ingratiate, to — berminyak air, bermuka-muka.

ingratitude kekurangan terimakasih.

ingredient bahan, ramuan.

inhabit, to — mendiami, menduduki.

inhabitant penduduk, isi negeri.

inhale, to — menarik nafas, menghisap.

inherent berpautan dengan, terpaut.

inherit, to — mewarisi.

inheritance peninggalan, pesaka.

inheritor ahli waris.

inhibit, to — (*forbid*) melarang; (*restrict*) mengalangi.

inhibition rintangan, alangan.

inhospitable tidak suka menerima tetamu.

inhuman tidak seperti manusia; (*cruel*) tidak mengenal belas kasihan.

inimitable tidak dapat ditiru.

iniquity tidak adil; kejahatan.

initial bermula, mula-mula, permulaan.

initiate orang yang telah diterima dalam segala upacara; to — mulai, memulakan.

initiation (*start*) permulaan; penerimaan dengan upacara.

initiative dayausaha, langkah pertama; to take the — mulai, initiatif.

inject, to — menyuntik menyucuk.

injection suntikan, cucuk.

injunction perintah, amanat.

injure, to — (*wound*) melukai; (*damage*) merosakkan, mencacatkan.

injury (*wound*) luka; (*wrong*) perbuatan tidak adil.

injustice tidak adil; (*oppression*) aniaya.

ink dawat.

inkling rasa, faham.

inland darat, dalam negeri.

in-law bersemenda, keluarga semenda.

inlay tatahan; to — menatah.

inlet (*bay*) rantau, teluk, seruk.

inmate penduduk rumah.

inn rumah penginapan, kedai minuman keras.

innate dasarnya, pembawaan, semulajadi.

inner dalam.

innocence keadaan tidak bersalah.

innocent tidak bersalah, tidak berdosa.

innocuous tidak berbahaya, tidak merugikan.

innovation perbaharuan.

innuendo sindirian.

innumerable tidak terhitung, tidak tepermanai.

inoculate, to — menyuntik, mencucuk ubat.

inoculation suntikan, penyuntikan, cucuk ubat.

inoffensive tidak galak, tidak bersalah.

inopportune tidak pada tempatnya.

inordinate yang terlampau, berlewat, tidak teratur.

inquest penyelidikan rasmi (istimewa berkenaan dengan hal hukum).

inquire, to — bertanya; to — after menyanyi.

inquiry (*question*) pertanyaan; (*investigation*) penyelidikan.

inquisition penyelidikan.

inquisitive ingin tahu.

inroad serangan musuh.

insane gila sakit ingatan, bertukar akal.

insanitary tidak bersih.

insanity kegilaan.

insatiable tidak puas-puas.

inscribe, to — menulisi; (*enter in roll etc*) mendaftarkan.

inscription tulisan (istimewa pada batu).

inscrutable tidak terduga.

insect serangga.

insecticide ubat pembunuh serangga.

insecure tidak kukuh.

insensibility hal pengsan.

insensible tidak sedar.

insensitive mati rasa.

inseparable tidak terpisah.

insert, to — menyisip; to — an advertisement memasukkan iklan.

inset sisipan.

inshore dekat pantai.

inside di dalam, sebelah dalam.

insidious secara pengkhianat, penipu.

insight faham, pengertian, pandang-timbang.

insignia lencana, tanda kehormatan.

insignificance kekecilan.

insignificant tidak bererti, kecil.

insincere tidak tulus, serong hati, tidak jujur.

insinuate, to — (hint etc) menyindirkan, menganginanginkan; (introduce gradually) menyusupi.

insinuation sindiran.

insipid tawar, ambar.

insist, to — (urge) mendesak; (hold to) berpegang teguh pada.

insistence desakan.

insistent yang mendesak.

insolence besar mulut.

insolent mulut besar, biadab.

insoluble yang tidak dapat diselesaikan, yang tidak dapat diputuskan; tidak larut.

insolvent tidak sanggup membayar hutangnya, muflis.

insomnia penyakit tidak mahu tidur.

inspect, to — memeriksa, menyelidiki.

inspection pemeriksaan, penyelidikan.

inspector pemeriksa, penilik, nazir.

inspiration (breath) penarikan nafas; (divine) ilham.

inspire, to — menarik nafas; mengilhami.

instability keadaan tidak tetap.

install, to — melantik, menabalkan.

installation (of apparatus etc) pemasangan; (office) pelantikan, penabalan.

instalment angsuran; to pay by —s mengansur.

instance umpama, misal; for — misalnya.

instant (urgent) yang mendesak, penting; (current month) bulan ini.

instantaneous pada ketika itu juga.

instantly terus, langsung.

instead pengganti, melainkan; — of this pengganti ini.

instep kura-kura kaki.

instigate, to — menghasut, mengacum.

instigation penghasutan.

instigator penghasut.

instil mempengaruhi.

instinct nafsu tabiat, naluri.

instinctive pembawaan.

institute lembaga; to — (establish) mendirikan; (begin) mulai.

institution lembaga; (custom) adat istiadat.

instruct, to — mengajar; memberitahu.

instruction pengajaran; —s suruh, perintah.

instructive yang mengajar menasihat.

instructor pengajar.

instructress pengajar perempuan.

instrument alat; (legal document) naskhah rasmi; musical — alat muzik.

instrumental (promoting) yang memajukan sesuatu hal; yang berkenaan dengan alat muzik.

insubordination derhaka, melawan.

insubstantial tidak benar, tiada sungguh-sungguh.

insufferable tidak tertahan.

insufficient tidak cukup, kurang.

insular yang berkenaan dengan pulau.

insulate, to — (separate) mengasingkan.

insulin insulin, ubat penyakit gula.

insult nusta; to — menusta akan.

insuperable yang tidak dapat diatasi.

insurance insuran, pertanggungan; life — tanggungan jiwa, insuran nyawa.

insure, to — mempertanggungkan.

insurmountable tidak dapat diatasi.

insurrection pemberontakan.

intact tidak dirugikan.

intake (place) tempat masuk; (entrant) orang yang diterima.

intangible tidak terpegang; (eluding the mind) tidak terfaham.

integer angka bulat.

integral lengkap, sempurna.

integrate yang terdiri dari berbagai bahagian, sempurna.

integration hal bersatu.

integrity kejujuran, ketulusan hati, tidak terpengaruh.

intellect kecerdasan akal, intelek.

intellectual kecerdasan, yang berkenaan dengan akal; an — orang terpelajar.

intelligence akal, kebijaksanaan, kecerdasan.

intelligent berakal, cerdik, cerdas.

intelligible yang dapat difahamkan.

intemperate melewati batas.

intend, to — bermaksud, berniat.

intense sangat; (emotional) bersemangat.

intensify, to — mempersangat.

intensity kehebatan.

intensive hebat, sungguhsungguh.

intent maksud, niat.

intention maksud, tujuan.

intentional sengaja.

inter, to — menguburkan.

inter— awalan kata yang ertinya: antara, di antara.

interact, to — saling mempengaruhi.

interaction hal saling mempengaruhi.

interbreed, to — mengahwinkan dengan haiwan yang berlainan.

intercede, to — mengantara.

intercept, to — memintas, memotong.

interchange hal tukarmenukar, pertukaran.

interchangeable dapat ditukar.

intercourse pergaulan, pertemuan

interest (importance) kepentingan; (concern) minat, perhatian; (on money) bunga wang, faedah.

interesting menarik hati.

interfere, to — (intervene) menengah; (meddle) campurtangan.

interference camputangan.

interim (time between) antara, selang; (provisional) sementara.

interior di dalam.

interject, to — menyelang.

interjection kata seru.

interlace, to — menjalinkan.

interlock, to — jalin-menjalin.

interloper orang yang mencampuri perkara orang lain.

interlude antara.

intermarry, to — berhubungan dengan golongan keluarga lain dengan jalan perkahwinan.

intermediary perantaraan.

intermediate antara, sementara; to — mengantara.

interminable tidak putusputusnya.

intermingle, to — bercampur.

intermission selang.

intermittent terputus-putus.

intern, to — mengasingkan, mempertawankan.

internal di dalam; (as opposed to foreign) dalam negeri.

international antarabangsa.

internment pertawanan, perasingan.

interpellation permintaan keterangan.

interplay selang-menyelang.

interpolate, to — menyisipkan.

interpose, to — menengah.

interpret, to — menjelaskan, mentafsirkan.

interpretation penjelasan, tafsiran.

interpreter juru bahasa.

interrelation perhubungan antara dua belah pihak.

interrogate, to — menanyai.

interrogation pertanyaan.

interrogative menanyakan, penanya; — **pronoun** ganti-nama tanya.

interrupt, to — memintas, memutuskan.

interruption perputusan.

intersect, to — memotong.

intersection pemotongan, titik tempat pertemuan, garis pemotong.

intersperse, to — mencerai beraikan.

interval sela, selang; (*break in performance etc*) separuh waktu.

intervene, to — menengah, berada di antara.

intervention perantaraan, camputangan.

interview interbiu; **to** — temu-duga.

interweave, to — memperjalinkan.

intestate tidak berwasiat.

intestine, large — usus besar; **small** — usus kecil.

intimacy karib, mesra.

intimate mesra, karib, rapat, teman.

intimidate, to — menakutkan, menggertakkan.

intimidation penakutan, pengugutan.

into ke dalam; **to look** — **the matter** memeriksa hal itu.

intolerable yang tidak dapat dibiarkan sahaja.

intolerance sifat tidak membiarkan.

intolerant tidak suka membiarkan.

intonation pelaguan, lagu suara.

intone, to — melagukan.

intoxicant pemabuk.

intoxicate, to — memabukkan; **—d** mabuk.

intoxicating yang memabukkan.

intoxication mabuk.

intra— awalan kata yang ertinya: di dalam, sebelah dalam.

intractable tidak menurut; (*difficult*) sukar.

intransigent yang tidak suka menyesuaikan diri.

intransitive — verb kata-kerja yang tiada penyambut.

intravenous dalam pembuluh darah.

intrepid berani, gagah.

intricacy kesulitan.

intricate sulit, berselok-belok.

intrigue tipu-daya; (*love affair*) cinta rahsia.

intrinsic dasarnya, hakiki.

intro— awalan kata yang ertinya: ke dalam.

introduce, to — (*bring in*) memasukkan; (*make formally known*) memperkenalkan.

introduction (*of person*) perkenalan; (*to book etc*) permulaan, kata pengantar, pendahuluan.

introductory yang mengantar, yang mendahului.

introspective yang menyelidiki diri sendiri.

introvert orang yang selalu memusatkan fikiran akan diri sendiri.

intrude, to — (*infringe*) melanggar; **to** — **upon** mengganggu.

intruder pengganggu.

intrusion pengganggguan, jalar dalam.

intrusive yang mengganggu.

intuition gerak hati, perasa.

intuitive menurut gerak hati.

inundate, to — membanjiri, mengampuhkan, bah.

inundation pengampuhan, banjir, bah.

invade, to — melanggar, menyerbu.

invader penyerbu.

invalid I orang sakit.

invalid II (*not valid*) tidak sah.

invalidate, to — menjadikan tidak sah.

invaluable tidak terharga, tidak ternilai.

invariable tetap, tidak berubah.

invasion penyerbuan, pelanggaran.

invective celaan.

inveigle, to — membujuk.

invent, to — mendapati, menciptakan.

invention pendapatan, rekaan, ciptaan.

inventive yang suka menciptakan hal baharu.

inventor pencipta, pendapat.

inventory daftar barangbarang (alat rumah dan sebagainya).

inverse terbalik, balik lawan.

invert, to — membalikkan.

invertebrate tidak bertulang belakang; (*weak*) lemah; haiwan invertebrata.

invest, to — memakaikan, mengenakan; (*stake*) menaruh.

investigate, to — memeriksa, menyelidiki.

investigation pemeriksaan, penyelidikan.

investigator pemeriksa, penyelidik.

investiture pelantikan.

investment (*money*) penanaman wang; pelantikan.

inveterate tetap, berakar, berumbi.

invidious yang menyakiti, yang tidak menyenangkan.

invigorate, to — memperkuat; menggembirakan.

invincible tidak dapat dialahkan.

inviolate tidak dilanggar.

invisible tidak terlihat, tidak kelihatan.

invitation panggilan, jemputan.

invite, to — menjemput, mempersilakan.

invocation doa, seruan.

invoice daftar barang dagangan yang dikirim.

invoke, to — memanggil, menyeru kepada.

involuntary tidak sengaja, dengan sendirinya.

involve, to — mengenai, melibatkan, tersangkut terlibat.

invulnerable kebal, tidak lut.

inward(s) di dalam, ke dalam.

iodine iodin.

I.O.U.(= **I owe you**) surat pengakuan hutang.

irascible panas hati, lekas marah.

irate marah.

ire murka.

iridescent (*colour of rainbow*) berwarna pelangi; (*changing colour*) berubah-ubah warnanya.

Irish yang berkenaan dengan negeri Irlandia, bahasa Irlandia, orang Irlandia.

irksome boyak, menjemukan.

iron I besi; (*tools etc*) alat besi; (*flat* —) seterika, penggosok.

iron II, to — mencampur (atau menutupi) dengan besi; (*clothes etc*) menyeterika.

ironic(al) yang berkenaan dengan ejekan.

ironmonger tukang ayan.

irony kata sindir, kejadian yang sebetulnya baik tetapi mengandung kekeciwaan.

irrational bilangan yang tidak terukur.

irreconcilable tidak terbujuk, tidak setuju.

irrefutable yang tidak dapat disalahkan.

irregular (*not usual*) tidak seperti biasa; (*disordered*) tak teratur; (*uneven*) tidak rata.

irrelevant yang tidak mengenai pokok, tidak bersabit.

irreparable yang tidak dapat diperbaiki.

irreplaceable yang tidak dapat diganti.

irrepressible tidak tertahan.

irreproachable tidak bersalah, tak bercacat.

irresistible tidak tertahan.

irresolute bimbang.

irrespective, — of dengan tidak memandang.

irresponsible tidak bertanggungjawab.

irretrievable yang tidak dapat diperoleh kembali.

irreverent tidak menghormati.

irrevocable tidak dapat dipanggil kembali, hilang lenyap.

irrigate, to — mengairi.

irrigation pengairan, taliair.

irritable bengkeng.

irritant yang merangsang.

irritate, to — merangsang; menyakiti hati.

irritation perangsangan.

is see be ; there — ada.

-ish hujungan kata yang bererti: yang berkenaan dengan; seperti; kira-kira.

Islam ugama Islam.

Islamic yang berkenaan dengan ugama Islam.

island pulau.

isle pulau.

-ism akhiran kata yang menyatakan: faham.

isn't = is not tidak.

iso— awalan kata yang ertinya: sama, rata.

isolate, to — mencilkan, mengasingkan, memisahkan.

isolation asingan, perasingan, pemisahan.

issue (*outlet*) keluaran, pancaran keluar; (*offspring*) anak; (*point in debate*) perkara perbincangan.

-ist akhiran kata yang ertinya: orang pelaku pembuat.

isthmus sogenting tanah.

it dia, ia; perkara.

Italian Itali, yang berkenaan dengan negeri atau orang Itali, bahasa Itali.

italics huruf condong.

itch gatal.

item bahagian, butir.

itinerant yang berkeliling.

itinerary jalan perjalanan.

its kepunyaannya.

itself sendiri; by — dengan sendirinya.

ivory gading.

ivy sejenis tanaman menjalar.

J

jab radak; to — meradak.

jabber kecek, bual.

jack nama orang laki-laki.

jackal serigala.

jackass kaldai jantan; (*blockhead*) orang bodoh.

jackdaw sejenis burung gagak.

jacket baju; (*wrapper*) sampul, bungkusan.

jack-knife pisau lipat yang besar.

jackpot kumpulan wang yang dimenangi

jade I (*horse*) kuda tua; (*woman*) perempuan nakal atau jahat.

jade II (*stone*) sejenis batu permata berwarna hijau.

jaded payah, sangat letih.

jagged gerigi.

jaguar sejenis harimau di Amerika.

jail penjara, kurungan; to — memenjarakan.

jam I (*trouble, difficulty*) kesesakan kesukaran; to — (*squeeze*) mengapit, menyepit; (*stop up*) menyumbat.

jam II (*a preserve*) manisan.

jamboree perkumpulan besar pengakap-pengakap.

jangle, to — berbunyi janggal.

janitor penjaga pintu.

January bulan Januari.

Japanese orang Jepun, bahasa Jepun.

jar I kendi, mangkuk.

jar II bunyi janggal.

jargon istilah-istilah golongan yang susah difahamkan.

jasmin(e) bunga melur.

jasper sejenis batu permata.

jaundice sakit kuning, mambang kuning.

jaunt, to — pergi bersiar, bertemasya, makan angin.

jaunty solik.

Javanese Jawa; orang Jawa; bahasa Jawa.

javelin lembing.

jaw rahang; upper — rahang atas.

jazz jazz sejenis muzik dan tari yang berasal dari orang Negro di Amerika Syarikat.

jealous cemburu, dengki, iri hati.

jealousy dengki, cemburu, iri hati.

jeans seluar kain tebal itu.

jeep sejenis kereta.

jeer ejekan; to — memperolokkan.

jelly sejenis agar-agar; to — membekukan.

jellyfish ubur-ubur.

jemmy perejang.

jeopardize, to — membahayakan.

jeopardy bahaya.

jerk sentak, renggutan.

jerkin sejenis baju pendek.

jersey sejenis baju.

jest gurau; to — bergurau senda.

jester lawak.

Jesus nabi Isa.

jet I pancaran air, pemancar; —propelled aircraft kapaludara yang maju dengan jalan pancaran gas.

jet II sejenis batu hitam yang dibuat perhiasan; —black hitam legam.

jetsam barang hanyut yang dibuang dari kapal.

jettison pembuangan barang dari kapal.

jetty pangkalan, jambatan.

Jew, Jewish Yahudi.

jewel permata, ratna, maknikam.

jeweller tukang emas, jauhari.

jewellery permata, emas intan.

jib I (*naut*) jib; to — mengubahkan layar kapal dari sebelah satu ke sebelah lain.

jib II, to — tidak mau maju.

jibe = gibe.

jiff(y) sejurus, sebentar, sekejap mata.

jig sejenis tarian.

jigsaw sejenis gergaji halus.

jilt orang perempuan yang menolak kekasihnya.

jingle bunyi gemerincing.

jink, high —s suka ria, riang gembira.

jinx orang yang membawa nasib malang, orang malang.

jitterbug sejenis tarian.

jitters takut, kegugupan.

job I pekerjaan.

job II, to — meradak.

jockey pemacu kuda; to — memperdayakan, menipu.

jocular jenaka.

jocund sukacita, riang, gembira.

jodhpurs sejenis seluar untuk berkuda.

jog berjalan goyah, bergoyang-goyang.

joggle, to — bergoyang, bergoncang.

join penghubungan; to — menyambung, menyatukan.

joiner tukang kayu yang pakar.

joint hubungan; (of body) sendi, buku, persendian; (in rock) rekah batu; (by more than one person) bersama-sama; — menghubungkan menyambung.

joist pelancar, palang.

joke gurau, kelakar.

joker orang jenaka.

jollity gurau senda, suka ria.

jolly sukacita, riang gembira.

jolt goncangan; to — menggoncangkan.

jonquil sejenis bunga.

joss berhala, topekong; — stick setanggi ladan.

jostle singgung.

jot, to — down mencatit.

journal (daily record) buku harian; (newspaper) majalah.

journalism kewartawanan.

journalist wartawan.

journey perjalanan; to — berjalan.

journeyman tukang.

Jove, by —! Astaga!

jovial riang, suka hati.

jowl tulang rahang, pipi; (dew.ap) gelambir.

joy keriangan kesukaan, rasa ria.

joyful yang menggerangkan.

jubilation sorak, suka ria, riuh-rendah.

jubilee peringatan 50 tahun.

judge hakim; to — mengadili

memutuskan, menimbangkan, menghakimkan.

judg(e)ment putusan hakim; the last — day hari kiamat; to pass — on menghukum.

judicial berkenaan dengan kehakiman atau pengadilan.

judicious bijaksana.

jug bekas, kendi, mangkuk.

juggernaut kereta yang sangat besar (dipakai untuk menarik patung Krishna).

juggle, to — bermain silap mata.

juggler penyilap mata.

jugular yang berkenaan dengan leher.

juice air buah yang diperah.

juicy berair, bergetah.

July bulan Julai.

jumble campur-aduk, kekacauan.

jump lompat, loncat; (quick rise) penaikan tiba-tiba; high — lompat tinggi; long — lompat jauh.

jumper I pelompat.

jumper II sejenis baju pendek.

jumpiness kegugupan.

jumpy takut-takut, gugup.

junction penghubungan.

juncture (time) ketika.

June bulan Jun.

jungle rimba, hutan, belukar.

junior muda, bongsu; (lower) lebih rendah.

juniper sejenis tumbuhan.

junk (vessel) jong; (old stuff) barang lama.

junta golongan.

juridical yang berkenaan dengan hukum.

jurisdiction kuasa kehakiman, (territory) daerah yang di bawah kuasa itu.

jurisprudence ilmu hukum.

jurist ahli hukum.

juror anggota juri.

jury juri.

just I lurus, adil, patut.

just II (exactly) tepat; (almost)

nyaris, baharu sahaja; — now pada waktu ini.

justice keadilan; (*magistrate etc*) hakim; court of — pengadilan, kehakiman.

justifiable patut, boleh dikatakan benar.

justification pembenaran.

justify, to — membenarkan.

jut anjung; to — (out) menganjung.

jute guni.

juvenile muda; (*child*) anak muda.

juxtapose, to — menaruh bersisi-sisi, berdampingan.

juxtaposition tempat bersisi-sisi, tempat berdampingan.

K

kale sejenis kubis.

kangaroo binatang kanggaru, sejenis binatang di negeri Australia.

kaolin tanah liat yang dipakai untuk membuat tembikar.

kapok kapuk, kabu-kabu.

kayak sejenis perahu jalur.

keel lunas kapal.

keen (*sharp*) tajam; (*eager*) bersemangat; (*of wits*) akal; — on suka akan.

keen-sighted tajam mata.

keep, to — (*provide for*) memeliharakan; (*hold*) memegang; (*preserve*) menyimpan.

keeper penjaga, pengawas.

keeping penyimpanan; pemeliharaan.

keepsake tanda mata.

keg tong, pipa.

ken pengetahuan.

kennel kandang anjing.

kerb, curb pinggir jalan tepi.

kernel biji, isi.

kerosene minyak tanah bersih, minyak gas.

kestrel sejenis burung helang.

kettle cerek; —drum sejenis tabal, negara.

key anak kunci; (*pointer*) penunjuk; (*translation*) salinan; —hole lubang kunci.

khaki warna kuning abu.

kick tendang, terajang, sepak.

kid anak kambing; (*leather*) kulit anak kambing.

kidnap, to — mencolek, melarikan.

kidney buah pinggang.

kill pembunuhan; (*prey*) binatang yang dibunuh.

killer pembunuh.

killjoy orang yang menghapuskan suka ria.

kiln dapur, sabak.

kilogramme ukuran kilo.

kilt sejenis pakaian sarung dipakai oleh orang Skot.

kimono pakaian orang Jepun.

kin bangsa, keluarga.

kind I jenis, macam, rupa.

kind II ramah-tamah; —hearted baik hati.

kindergarten taman kanak-kanak.

kindle, to — menyalakan, menyala, pasang.

kindling kayu api yang kecil.

kindly dengan manis, dengan ramah-tamah.

kindness ramah-tamah, kebaikan hati.

kindred pertalian darah daging, kaum keluarga.

king raja, yamtuan.

kingdom kerajaan.

kingfisher burung raja udang, burung pekaka.

kink pintal, belit.

kinsfolk kaum keluarga, kaum kerabat.

kinship pertalian sanak saudara.

kipper ikan salai.

kiss cium, kecup, kucup; to — mencium.

kit barang-barang; —bag pundi-pundi barang-barang.

kitchen dapur.

kitchenette dapur kecil.

kite sejenis burung helang; layang-layang; **to fly a —** menaikkan layang-layang.

kith. — and kin karib dan baid.

kitten, kitty anak kucing.

klaxon semboyan.

kleptomania keinginan gila-gila hendak mencuri.

knack kecakapan, kebiasaan dalam percakapan.

knacker orang yang membeli dan membantai kuda.

knapsack sejenis sarung berisi berbagai keperluan; *(made of rattan)* ambung.

knave orang penjahat.

knead, to — meramas, menguli.

knee lutut; **to bring a person to his —s** mengalahkan.

kneecap tempurung lutut.

kneel, to — berlutut, bertelut.

knell bunyi loceng.

knickers sejenis seluar untuk perempuan.

knick-knack barang kecil dan halus.

knife pisau, parang.

knight sastria, kestria, pahlawan.

knighthood kekestriaan.

knit, to — merajut, mengait.

knitting rajutan, kaitan.

knob combol, bonggol, buku.

knock pukulan, ketuk.

knocker palu pintu.

knock-kneed pengkar keluar.

knoll anak bukit, busut.

knot simpul; *(ship's speed)* ukuran, kecepatan kapal.

knotty bersimpul; *(lumpy)* berbuku; *(difficulty)* sukar.

know, to — tahu, mengetahui; *(recognize)* kenal; *(comprehend)* faham akan.

know-all orang yang tahu dalam semua hal.

know-how pengetahuan, faham.

knowing berakal, pintar; **—ly** dengan sengaja.

knowledge pengetahuan, ilmu keahlian.

knuckle buku jari; **—bone** tulang buku.

kohl celak mata.

kosher makanan yang boleh dimakan oleh orang Yahudi (tidak najis).

kudos hormat, nama masyhur.

L

label lebal; *(party —)* nama atau tanda golongan; **to —** membubuh lebal.

laboratory makmal.

laborious dengan susah payah, dengan sukar.

labour usaha, kerja, pekerjaan; *(workmen collectively)* perburuhan, kaum buruh.

labourer buruh, pekerja.

laburnum sejenis pohon berbunga.

labyrinth tempat orang-orang mudah tersesat; *(state of perplexity)* keadaan kusut.

lace *(cord)* tali; *(braid)* renda.

lacerate, to — *(tear)* mengoyak; *(injure)* menyakiti.

lack kekurangan, kesempitan.

lackadaisical lemah-longlai.

lackey bujang orang besar.

lacklustre tidak bersinar.

laconic pendek, ringkas.

lacquer laka, sampang; **to —** membohi laka sampang.

lacrosse sejenis permainan bola.

lactation penyusunan, keluar susu.

lactic yang berkenaan dengan susu.

lad anak laki-laki, pemuda.

ladder tangga.

ladle pencedok, senduk; **to —** mencedok, menyenduk.

lady siti, nyonya, perempuan; *(of rank)* perempuan yang berbangsa.

ladylike sangat baik budi bahasanya.

lag kelambatan; **to —** jalan lambat-lambat.

lager, lagerbeer sejenis minuman bir.

lagoon danau air laut, lagun.

lair tempat tinggal binatang, jerumun.

laity orang awam.

lake tasik danau.

lamb anak kambing; *(gentle person)* orang yang dikasihi.

lame pincang, tempang.

lameness kepincangan, ketempangan.

lament ratap.

lamentable yang menyedihkan.

lamentation ratapan.

lamp lampu, pelita, kandil.

lance lembing, tombak; **— corporal** soldadu di bawah kopral.

land tanah, darat, bumi, negeri.

land agent ahli jual-beli tanah dan rumah.

landed bertanah, mempunyai tanah.

landholder pemilik tanah, penyewa tanah.

landing I pendaratan; *(arrival)* sampainya, tibanya; **— place** pangkalan.

landing II *(on stairs)* lataran antara tangga tingkat pertama dan tangga tingkat kedua.

landlady tuanrumah, induk semang.

landlord *(of house)* tuanrumah, *(of land)* tuantanah.

landmark *(boundary)* sempadan; *(conspicuous object)*

tempat yang mudah tertampak dalam salah satu daerah.

landmine ranjau darat.

landowner tuantanah, pemilik tanah.

landscape gambar alam yang indah, pemandangan.

landslide tanah runtuh; *(political)* kemenangan besar untuk satu pihak dalam pemilihan.

land tax cukai tanah, hasil.

lane lorong.

language bahasa; **spoken —** bahasa pertuturan; **— background** 'atar bahasa.

languid lemah.

languish, to — merana; **to — for** rindu akan.

languor kelemahan.

lank tinggi dan kurus, panjang lampai.

lantern, Chinese — tanglung; **— jaws** rahang cekung.

lanyard tali penyandang.

lap I *(turn of thread, fold etc)* seliit sebeli' kain atau benang, lipatan.

lap II *(person's knees etc)* pangku, riba, ribaan; **to hold in one's —** memangku.

lap III, to — *(drink)* sesap.

lapel kelepak baju.

lapidary yang berkenaan dengan batu; *(engraver)* pengukir batu.

lapse *(slip)* kekhilafan; *(fall)* kejatuhan; *(interval)* antara, selang.

larceny pencurian.

lard lemak babi.

larder bilik simpan makanan.

large besar, luas; **on a — scale** secara besar-besaran; **at — bebas.**

largely sebahagian besar.

lark sejenis burung; *(frolic)* senda gurau; **to — berkelakar.**

larva jentik-jentik.

laryngitis demam tenggorok.

larynx pangkal tenggorok, peti suara.

lascivious gatal, sundal.

lash (*stroke of whip*) pukulan cambuk; (*of whip*) tali cambuk.

lass gadis, anak perempuan.

lassitude kelelahan, kelemahan.

lasso jerat, tanjul; to — menanjul.

last I (*shoe last*) kelebut kasut.

last II (*rearmost etc*) yang terakhir, terkebelakang, penghabisan.

last III (*endure*) gaya tahan; to — terus berlaku, bertahan.

lasting tetap, kekal, tahan lama.

latch selak, kancing pintu; —key kunci pintu luar.

late terlambat, kesiangan; (*recent*) yang baharu lalu; (*deceased*) al-marhum, mendiang.

lately baharu-baharu ini, kemudian ini.

latent diam, pendam, tersembunyi.

later kemudian; two days — selang dua hari.

lateral pada sisinya, bahagian sisi.

latest yang terakhir.

latex getah.

lath belebas, bilah, pelupuh; to — memasang belebas.

lathe bindu, mesin, pelarik.

lather busa, buih; to — menyabun; —y berbuih.

Latin bahasa Latin.

latitude, parallel of — garisan lintang; degree of — darjah garisan lintang; (*freedom*) kebebasan.

latrine jamban, tandas, tempat buang air.

latter berkenaan dengan akhirnya waktu.

lattice kisi-kisi.

laudable yang patut dipuji, sangat baik.

laugh tertawa, gelak; to — ketawa, tertawa.

laughable menggelikan.

laughing tertawa; no — matter sesuatu yang tidak boleh ditertawakan, bukan main.

laughter tertawa, ketawa.

launch I sejenis kapal, lancaran.

launch II, to — melemparkan.

launder, to — mencuci.

laundress perempuan yang mencuci pakaian.

laundry tempat mencuci pakaian.

laureate patut dipuji.

laurel pohon (daun) salam; to reap — s mendapat pujian.

lava lahar.

lavatory tempat cuci tangan jamban, tandas.

lavender sejenis bunga yang sangat harum.

lavish sangat mewah.

lavishness kemewahan.

law (*case*) hukum; (*enactments*) undang-undang; (*regulations*) peraturan; (*custom*) adat.

law-abiding taat pada undang-undang.

lawful menurut hukum, menurut undang-undang.

lawless tidak menurut hukum.

lawn halaman yang berumput; —mower pemotong rumput.

lawsuit dakwa, bicara.

lawyer peguam, loyar.

lax lengah, lalai.

laxative pencahar, julap.

lay I (*concerning laity*) tidak berkenaan dengan hal ugama, bukan ahli.

lay II, to — (*lay down etc*) membaringkan, meletakkan, merebahkan; (*eggs*) bertelur.

layer lapisan; in —s berlapis-lapis.

layette segala pakaian, untuk anak kecil.

lay-off waktu tidak digunakan untuk bekerja.

layout susunan.

laze, to — bermalas-malas, melengah.

lazy malas; —bones orang malas.

lea tanah rumput.

lead I timah hitam; plumbum; (for sounding) batu duga; **to** — menutup dengan timah hitam.

lead II (guide) pedoman, pimpinan; (for dog) tali pemimpin anjing; **to take the** — mendahulukan, memimpin.

leaden seperti timah hitam; (heavy) sangat berat.

leader pemimpin; (in newspaper) tajuk rencana.

leadership pimpinan, daya pimpin.

leading besar, terpenting; — article rencana pengarang.

leaf daun; (thin sheet) helai; gold — perada.

leafless ranggas.

leaflet surat sebaran, risalat, siaran; (of plant) daun muda.

leafy rimbun, rendang, berdaun.

league (confederation etc) persekutuan, ikatan, gabungan.

leak bocor, tiris; **to** — bocor.

leaky bocor.

lean I (thin) kurus; — corps hasil sedikit; — **years** tahun-tahun kekurangan.

lean II condong, cenderung.

leaning kecondongan, kecenderungan.

lean—to sengkuap, bangsal, pisang cesikat.

leap lompat; **to** — melompat, meloncat.

leap year tahun lompat.

learn belajar, mempelajari; (hear) mendengar; **to** — **by heart** menghapalkan.

learned terpelajar, berpengetahuan.

learning pengetahuan, pelajaran.

lease sewa; **to** — menyewakan.

leasehold sewaan.

leaseholder penyewa.

leash tali anjing; **to** — memegang, mengikat dengan tali.

least yang terkecil, tersedikit; **at (the)** — sekurang-kurangnya.

leather kulit.

leave I (take one's leave) minta diri.

leave II (behind one) meninggalkan; (allow) membiarkan; (go out) pergi, keluar; (furlough) cuti.

lecher orang gatal.

lecherous gasang, gatal.

lectern sejenis mimbar.

lecture pembacaan, kuliah, syarah; **to** — bersyarah.

lecturer pensyarah.

ledge birai; (on cliff) tempat datar pada gunung atau karang; (reef) karang di bawah laut.

ledger buku besar.

lee tempat teduh, di bawah angin, perlindungan; —side, —ward di bawah angin.

leech pacat lintah, lintah darat.

leek bawang perai.

leer kerling, jeling.

left sebelah kiri; **on the** — **hand** pada sebelah kiri.

left—handed kidal (awkward) kekok.

leg kaki (binatang atau manusia dari pangkal paha sampai buku lali); (of chair etc) kaki kerusi (meja dan sebagainya).

legacy waris.

legal menurut hukum, menurut undang-undang, sah.

legality sahnya.

legalize, to — mengesahkan.

legation kedutaan.

legend hikayat dahulukala, dongeng sejarah, petunjuk.

legging kulit atau kain pembungkus kaki.

leggy berkaki panjang.

legible mudah dibaca.

legion soldadu dalam tentera Rom.

legislation undang-undang.

legislative yang membuat undang-undang, undangan.

legislature badan yang mengadakan undang-undang.

legitimate sah, berhak.

leisure waktu keluasan, senang; at — dengan keluas.

lemon limau; (colour) warna kuning muda; — squash air limau.

lend memberi pinjam, meminjami, meminjamkan.

length panjangnya, kepanjangan; (of time) lamanya; at — dengan panjang lebar.

lengthen, to — memperpanjangkan; melamakan.

lengthways, lengthwise membujur.

lengthy panjang, dengan panjang lebar.

lenience, leniency kemurahan, kelembutan hati.

lenient lembut hati, rahim.

lens lens, kanta.

lentil sejenis pokok kacang.

leopard harimau bintang, har'mau akar.

leper orang kusta.

leprosy kusta.

less kurang, tidak sebesar; more or — lebih-kurang, kira-kira.

-less akhiran kata yang ertinya; tidak mempunyai.

lessen, to — mengurangkan.

lesser tidak sebesar, yang lebih kecil.

lesson pelajaran, pengajaran.

lest jangan sampai, kalau-kalau.

let I, to — (allow to escape) melepaskan; (allow) membiarkan; to — alone membiarkan, tidak mengganggu.

let II, to — (lease) menyewakan.

lethal membawa maut.

lethargic ketagihan tidur.

lethargy tagih tidur.

letter (of alphabet) huruf; (written message) surat; capital — huruf besar; to the — tepat.

letterbox peti surat.

lettuce daun selada.

Levant bahagian timur daerah Lautan Tengah.

level rata, datar.

level-headed dingin kepala.

lever tuil, pengumpil; to — up menuil, mengumpil.

leverage umpil, daya pengumpil.

levity perbuatan atau sifat riak.

levy pemungutan wang, wang yang dipungut; (conscripted troops etc) jumlah orang yang dikerahkan.

lewd gasang, sundal.

lexicon kamus.

liability pertanggungan; limited — company syarikat berhad.

liable bertanggungjawab.

liaison (illicit intimacy) pertalian tidak sesonoh antara seorang laki-laki dengan perempuan; (connection) perhubungan; — officer pegawai penghubung.

liana kayu akar, sejenis tumbuhan menjalar, akar ulan.

liar pendusta, pembohong.

libel fitnah dengan tulisan.

libellous yang memfitnahkan.

liberal dermawan, luas, murah hati.

liberate, to — memerdekakan, membebaskan.

liberation pembebasan.

liberty kebebasan, kemerdekaan.

librarian pengurus perpustakaan, ketua kutub-khanah.

library taman pustaka, perpustakaan.

libretto cerita, hikayat yang

berhubungan dengan sebuah opera.

licence, US **license** lesen, izin.

license, to — mengizinkan.

licensee pemegang lesen.

licentious gatal.

lichen lumut.

lick jilat; to — menjilat; (sl: defeat) mengalahkan.

licorice see **liquorice.**

lid tutup; eye — kelopak mata.

lie I letak sesuatu; — of the land keadaan; to — berbaring, terbaring, tidur.

lie II (falsehood) bohong, dusta.

lieu, in — of pengganti.

lieutenant pegawai leftenan.

life hidup, hayat, nyawa, jiwa.

lifebelt, lifebuoy pelampung berenang.

lifeguard pengawal, pasukan pengawal.

lifeless tidak hidup, tidak bernyawa mati; (sluggish) tidak bersemangat.

lifelong selama hidup.

life preserver pemukul kayu diberatkan pada hujungnya.

lifetime umur hidup.

lift tumpangan; (elevator) alat penaikan orang dan barang; to get a — menumpang.

ligament ikat sendi, ligamen.

light I (opposite of dark) terang; (brilliancy) cahaya; (lamp) lampu, pelita gid.

light II (not heavy) ringan; (fine) halus; (not genuine) tidak sungguh-sungguh; (facile) mudah.

light III (of colour) warna muda; — -blue biru muda.

lighten, to — menerangi, mencahayakan; meringankan; memudahkan.

lighter (for setting alight) pemetik api; (barge) tongkang; (brighter) lebih terang; (of weight) lebih ringan.

light-fingered tangan panjang.

light-hearted riang gembira, senang hati.

lighthouse rumah api, semboyan.

lighting penerangan.

lightning kilat, halilintar.

lightship kapal yang memancarkan cahaya dengan lampu laut.

lignite sejenis arangbatu muda, lignit.

likable yang menyukakan hati.

like I sama, sebagai, seperti, semacam, laksana.

like II, to — suka akan, menyukai, berkenan.

-like akhiran kata yang ertinya: seperti.

likelihood harus; in all — boleh jadi.

likely harus; barangkali.

liken, to — menyamakan, mempersamakan.

likeness kesamaan, persamaan.

likewise begitu juga.

liking gemar, kegemaran, kesukaan; to have a — for gemar, suka akan.

lilac sejenis bunga.

lilt nyanyian berirama.

lily sejenis bunga teratai.

limb anggota badan, kaki, lengan; (of tree) dahan, cabang.

limber lemah lentur; to — (up) menjadikan lemah, lentur.

lime I asam, limau; — juice air limau.

lime II kapur; quick— kapur tohor, kapur mentah.

lime III (bird) getah perikat akan memikat burung; to — menggetahkan burung.

lime IV sejenis pohon.

limerick sajak, pantun.

lime(stone) batukapur.

limit hingga, batas, perhinggaan.

limitation pembatasan, per-hinggaan.

limousine kereta motokar yang tertutup.

limp I lembek.

limp II (*lame*) kepincangan, jalan pincang, tempang.

limpet sejenis remis.

limpid hening, jernih.

line (*drawn line, row*) garis, baris; (*cord*) tali; (*wire*) kawat; (*railway*) jalan keretapi; to draw up in — berbaris.

lineage keturunan.

linear yang berkenaan dengan atau, seperti garis.

linen kain linan; (*collectively*) segala pakaian dan kainkainan rumahtangga.

linesman pengawas sempadan (pada main bola).

linger, to — berlambat-lambat.

lingerie pakaian dalam perempuan.

lingo bahasa salah satu golongan masyarakat.

linguist ahli bahasa, orang yang faham akan berbagai-bagai bahasa.

linguistic yang berkenaan dengan bahasa; —s ilmu bahasa.

liniment ubat penggosok, minyak urat.

lining lapis, lapik, lapisan.

link gelang rantai, mata rantai; (*connection*) sambungan, pertalian; to — menangkaikan.

linoleum sejenis kain tebal dan kuat akan menutup lantai.

linseed biji bijan.

lint kain tiras.

lintel ambang (di atas pintu atau jendela).

lion singa; (*person*) orang gagah; (*astr*) bintang asad.

lip bibir; upper — bibir atas; lower, under — bibir bawah.

lipstick gincu, pemerah bibir.

liquefy, to — menjadi cair; mencairkan.

liqueur cairan, zat cair, barang cair.

liquid air.

liquidate, to — (*pay debt*) membayar hutang; (*wipe out*) menghapuskan.

liquidation pembubaran.

liquor (*alcoholic drink*) minuman keras.

liquorice, licorice sejenis zat hitam yang dipakai untuk ubat batuk atau manisan.

lisp hapalan pelat (istimewa dengan hurufs); to — berkata pelat.

lissom lampai, lunglai.

list I daftar, senarai; to — mendaftarkan, mencatit.

list II, to — (*lean*) condong, miring.

listen, to — mendengarkan.

listener pendengar.

listless lalai, lemah.

literacy boleh menulis dan membaca.

literal menurut huruf.

literary yang berkenaan dengan kesusastraan.

literate cakap menulis dan membaca.

literature kesusastraan.

lithe lemah lentur.

lithograph cetakan cap batu.

litigate, to — mendakwa, berguam.

litter (*stretcher etc*) tandu, usungan; (*bedding for animals*) rumput-rumput untuk tempat tidur haiwan; (*rubbish*) sampah sarap.

little (*small*) kecil; (*young*) muda; (*not much*) sedikit.

liturgy sejenis doa umum.

live I hidup; —stock ternak.

live II, to — hidup; (*exist*) berada, tinggal.

livelihood pencarian, nafkah, kehidupan.

lively gamat.

liven, to — **up** cerdas, menyukakan hati.

liver hati, limpa; **hot**—**ed** lekas berahi.

livery wang untuk membelanjakan makanan kuda.

livid berwarna muka kebiru-biruan kerana sangat marah atau takut.

living sedang hidup; (*means of subsistence*) kehidupan, rezeki.

lizard sejenis cicak, tok-kai.

'll kependekan will atau shall dalam; he'll, I'll dan seterusnya.

llama sejenis unta.

load beban, muatan, tumpangan.

loaf I sebuku roti.

loaf II, to — bermalas-masalan.

loafer perlente, pelengah.

loan pinjaman; to ask for the — of minta pinjam; **to** — meminjamkan.

loath, loth segan, tidak sudi.

loathe, to — menjijikkan, jijik akan, membencikan.

loathing benci, jijik.

loathsome menjijikkan.

lobby ruang muka, tempat tunggu; to — mempengaruhi.

lobe keping; (*of ear*) cuping.

lobster udang karang.

local tempatan, kedaerahan.

locality tempat, daerah.

locate, to — (*place*) terletak; (*discover*) mendapat (atau menentukan) tempatnya.

location tempat, letaknya.

loch danau, tasik (di negeri Skot).

lock I (*hair*) anak rambut, seikal rambut.

lock II (*for door*) ibu kunci; (*in river etc*) pintu air; —, **stock and barrel** semua lengkap.

locker kotak pada tembok untuk menyimpan (pakaian, buku dan sebagainya).

locket sejenis anting-anting yang berisi gambar.

lockjaw terkancing mulut.

locksmith †tukang kunci.

locomotive dapat bergerak; (*railway*) kepala keretapi.

locust belalang.

lodge pondok, teratak; to — memberi tumpang.

lodger penumpang di rumah penginapan.

lodging(s) pondok, perumahan.

loft (*pigeons etc*) kandang burung.

lofty tinggi.

log sebatang kayu; (*measure ship's speed*) alat untuk mengukur kecepatan kapal; —book buku harian pada sebuah kapal.

logarithm logaritzam; —ic table(s) jadual logaritzam.

loggerhead, at —s (with) berselisih, bertengkar.

logic ilmu mantik, lojik.

logical menurut akal, sampai masuk akal.

loin sepotong daging pinggang; —cloth cawat.

loiter, to — menyambalewa, berlambat-lambat.

loiterer pelengah, orang yang jalannya berlambat-lambat.

loll, to — duduk (atau berbaring) dengan lemah malas.

lollipop gula-gula.

lone tersendiri, sunyi.

loneliness kesunyian, keseorangan.

lonely sunyi, sepi.

lonesome sunyi-senyap.

long I (*in space, time*) panjang; (*of time*) lama; (*far*) jauh, luas; (*period*) ketika (waktu) yang lama; **all day** — sepanjang hari

long II, to — **for** merindukan, ingin akan.

longer, longest lebih panjang, yang terpanjang sekali.

longhand tulisan biasa (bukan tulisan ringkas).

longing keinginan, rindu.

longitude garisan bujur.

long-lived berumur panjang, lama.

long-suffering dapat menahan sakit; (*patient*) sabar.

long-winded sangat lama sampai membosankan.

loofah buah petola.

look (*gaze*) pandang; (*appearance*) rupa; (*watch*) jaga; —s roman, rupa, paras.

looker, good— orang rupawan, cantik.

looker-on penuntun.

look-in (*visit*) singgah.

looking-glass cermin muka.

look-out tempat tinjauan.

loom, to — terlihat sayup-sayup.

loop jerat, gelung; **to** — menjerat.

loophole lubang di tembok; (*means of escape*) jalan keluar.

loose longgar, tidak terikat; (*free*) bebas.

loosen, to — melepaskan, melonggarkan.

loot barang rampasan; **to** — merampas.

lop ranting; **to** — off memancing, menutuh.

lope, to — berlari dengan langkah panjang.

lopsided berat sebelah.

loquacious ceramah, suka berkecek-kecek.

lord, L— (*God*) Tuhan, Allah; (*noble*) orang bangsawan.

lore (*learning*) pengetahuan; (*tradition*) adat istiadat.

lorry kereta lori.

lose, to — (*cause to disappear*) menghilangkan; (*of property*) kerugian; (*defeat*) kalahkan.

loser orang yang kalah.

loss kerugian, kehilangan.

lost, lose hilang, kehilangan, binasa.

lotion air pembersih luka.

lottery loteri.

loud keras, nyaring.

loudspeaker alat pembesar suara.

louse kutu, tuma.

lousy penuh kutu; (*sl: nasty*) buruk.

lout orang dusun, orang kekok.

lovable manis, peramah.

love cinta, percintaan, kasih, asmara, kesayangan, kekasih.

love affair pertalian cinta.

lovebird burung serindit, burung bayan.

loveliness keelokan, kecantikan.

lovely cantik, manis, jelita.

love-making cumbu-cumbuan, berkasih.

love match perkahwinan semata-mata kerana kasih sayang.

love-potion ubat pengasih, guna-guna.

lover pencinta, kekasih.

lovesick sangat berahi, tergila-gila.

loving yang mengasihi, mencintai.

low rendah, pendek; (*of birth*) hina.

low-down hina, keji.

lower lebih rendah; **—** lip bibir bawah; **to** — menurunkan.

lowland dataran rendah.

lowly hina, rendah; (*in style*) secara rendah.

low-spirited sedih.

loyal setia, setiawan.

loyalty kesetiaan.

lozenge belah ketupat; (*for coughs*) sejenis ubat batuk.

lubricant minyak licin.

lubricate, to — meminyaki; minyak licin.

lucid terang; (*made plain*) jelas.

lucidity keadaan terang, sifat terang.

luck nasib, untung untung baik; good — kemujuran.

luckily baiknya, mujurlah, untungnya.

lucky beruntung, mujur.

lucrative beruntung, membawa untung.

ludicrous bebal, patut ditertawakan.

lug sentak, menyeret keraskeras.

luggage barang-barang penumpang.

lugubrious sedih.

lukewarm suam-suam kuku.

lull teduh reda.

lullaby dondang, nyanyian pengulit(-ulit); to sing a — mendadung, mendaduh.

lumbago sengal pinggang.

lumber (*junk*) barang yang tidak berguna lagi; (*timber*) kayu-kayuan.

lumberjack penebang pohon, pekerja balak.

luminous bercahaya, bersinar, berkilau-kilauan.

lump penggal, potong, bongkah, gumpal.

lumpy penuh gumpal-gumpal.

lunacy kegilaan, keadaan gila.

lunar yang berkenaan dengan bulan.

lunatic (*person*) orang gila; gila; — asylum rumah gila.

lunch, luncheon makan siang; to — makan siang.

lung paru-paru.

lunge hentak, terajang, gerak maju.

lurch I, to leave in the — meninggalkan dalam kesukaran.

lurch II condong; to — berhuyung-huyung.

lure umpan, pikat; to — memikat, mengumpan.

lurid yang mengerikan, menakutkan.

lurk, to — mengendap.

luscious manis, sangat mewah.

lush rimbun, subur.

lust hawa nafsu, syahwat.

lustful bernafsu, bersyahwat.

lustre gilang-gemilang, bercahaya, kilau.

lustrous berkilau-kilauan, bercahaya.

lusty sihat, dan kuat.

lute sejenis alat muzik, kecapi.

luxe, de — sangat mewah dan bagus.

luxuriant limpah-mewah, subur.

luxuriate, to — (*live luxuriously*) hidup mewah.

luxurious mewah.

luxury kemewahan.

lying tidak jujur, pendusta.

lynch, to — menghukum mati dan membunuh menurut kemahuan sendiri.

lyre sejenis alat muzik dahulukala.

lyric sajak, syair; (*meant to be sung*) patut dinyanyikan.

M

ma mama, emak.

ma'am *see* **madam.**

macabre yang menakutkan, ngeri.

macadam dikerjakan dengan lapisan batu tertumbuk.

macaroni makanan jenis meehoon.

macaroon sejenis kuih.

mace (*nutmeg*) bunga pala.

machete parang.

Machiavellian tidak jujur, penipu.

machine mesin, pesawat, jentera.

machinery mesin-mesin, alat jentera.

machinist ahli pesawat, penjahit mesin.

mackerel sejenis ikan laut; tenggiri.

mackintosh kain untuk baju hujan.

macro— awalan kata yang ertinya: besar.

mad gila, sakit otak; (angry) marah; to go — bertukar akal.

madam, ma'am encik, puan.

madden, to — menggilakan, menjadi gila.

made pt and pp of make, a — man orang yang berhasil dalam kehidupannya.

madhouse rumah gila.

madness kegilaan.

madonna lukisan, gambar pahatan Siti Mariam.

madrigal sejenis sajak atau nyanyian percintaan.

maelstrom pusaran air.

maestro pemimpin (atau pengarang) muzik.

magazine (periodical) majalah; (storehouse for arms) tempat penyimpan senjata; (in a gem) tempat peluru di dalam senapang.

magenta ubat pencelup.

maggot kuman, ulat, berenga.

magi, the (three) M— ketiga orang bijaksana dari negeri Timur yang datang mengunjungi Nabi Isa.

magic ilmu sihir, guna-guna.

magician ahli ilmu sihir.

magistrate hakim, pengadil.

magnanimity kemurahan hati.

magnanimous karim, murah hati.

magnate orang yang sangat kaya atau terkemuka, orang besar.

magnet batu berani, besi berani.

magnetic bersifat maknit; (power of attorney) sangat menarik.

magnetism daya penarik.

magnetize, to — menarik memberi daya penarik.

magnificence kemuliaan, kemewahan.

magnificent sangat elok, mulia.

magnify, to — membesarkan; magnifying-glass cermin pembesar.

magnitude besarnya, sifat penting.

magnolia sejenis pohon berbunga elok.

magnum botol berisi air anggur.

magpie sejenis burung murai.

maid gadis; old—anak dara tua.

maiden anak dara.

mail I (armour) baju zirah daripada rantai-rantai besi.

mail II pengiriman atau penghantaran surat.

maim, to — mengundungkan.

main I (power) kekuatan; (ocean) lautan; (pipe) saluran besar.

main II (principal) yang pokok, terutama, terpenting; — clause ibu kalimat; — road jalanraya.

mainland benua, tanah besar.

mainly istimewa, pada ghalibnya.

mainstay sangga yang terpenting, sokongan yang terpenting.

maintain, to — (keep up) memeliharakan; (stress) menetapkan, menegaskan.

maintenance pemeliharaan.

maize jagung.

majestic seperti gila, mulia, agung, dirgahyu.

majesty keagungan; His, Your M— Seri Paduka Baginda Yang Dipertuan Agung, dirgahyu.

major (greater) lebih besar.

majority kebanyakan, terbesar.

make buatan; to — membuat, membentuk.

make—believe dalih, rekaan.

maker pembuat, penjelma.

makeshift sesuatu yang dipakai sebagai pengganti sahaja.

make-up palit dan pupuk untuk perhiasan muka.

mal—awalan kata yang ertinya: tidak baik, buruk.

malacca, — cane tongkat semambu.

maladjusted tidak sesuai, tidak teratur.

maladjustment keadaan tidak teratur.

maladroit janggal, kaku.

malady penyakit.

malaise rasa tidak sedap badan.

malaria demam nyamuk, demam kura.

Malay Melayu, bahasa Melayu, orang Melayu.

male laki-laki; (*of animals*) jantan.

malediction laknat, kutuk, tulah.

malefactor penjahat.

malevolent jahat, buruk hati.

malformation bentuk salah.

malice dengki, dendam, benci, iri hati; **to bear — —** berdengki, berdendam.

malicious jahat, dengki, berdendam.

malign merugikan.

malignant jahat, merugikan.

mall pemukul.

malleable yang mudah dikerjakan; (*easily led*) bersifat penurut.

mallet pemukul, tukul.

mallow sejenis tumbuhan.

malnutrition keadaan kurang makan.

malpractice perbuatan salah.

malt padi-padian yang diolah sehingga boleh dipakai untuk membuat minuman keras.

mamma nama ibu.

mammal binatang yang tergulung bangsa mammalia.

mammoth sejenis gajah dahulukala; (*very large*) sangat besar.

mammy nama ibu.

man orang, manusia, orang laki-laki; **— and wife** suami isteri; **— of war** kapal perang.

manacle belenggu, gari; **to —** menggari.

manage, to — (*control, lead*) mengendalikan, mengurus, memimpin.

manageable penurut, jinak.

management pimpinan, badan pemimpin, pengurus.

manager pengurus.

mandarin I pegawai tinggi China; (*language*) bahasa rasmi China.

mandarin II (*orange*) sejenis limau.

mandate surat perintah, mandat.

mandatory yang mengandung perintah.

mandolin(e) mandolin, sejenis alat muzik.

mandrake sejenis tumbuhan racun.

mane bulu tengkuk.

manful gagah, berani.

manganese amang, manganum.

manger palung, tempat makan untuk ternak.

mangle I penggiling; **to —** menggiling.

mangle II, to — (*spoil*) merosakkan.

mango mangga, pauh.

mangosteen manggis.

mangrove pokok bakau.

manhandle, to — melakukan sesuatu dengan tenaga

orang sahaja; *(handle roughly)* memperlakukan dengan kasar.

manhole lubang pada lantai, saluran (dan sebagainya) lubang periksa.

manhood *(manly quality)* keberanian; — *(adult)* masa dewasa.

mania kegilaan.

maniac orang gila.

manicure mewarnakan kuku (tangan dan kakinya).

manifest *(clear)* ternyata, terang; — menyatakan.

manifestation penjelmaan.

manifesto maklumat, pengumuman.

manifold berlipat ganda, berganda-ganda.

manipulate, to — menggaya, memperlakukan.

manipulation perlakuan dengan tangkas dan cerdik.

mankind manusia, orang-orang.

manly bersifat laki-laki; *(brave)* gagah, berani.

manna makanan dari syurga (seperti tersebut dalam kitab suci).

mannequin orang perempuan yang memakai dan mempertunjukkan pakaian menurut cara yang terakhir.

manner macam, cara, laku, kelakuan, sikap; **—s** tatacara.

mannered, rough— tidak tahu adat, kurang ajar.

mannerism lagak, tingkah laku.

mannerly sopan santun, baik budi bahasanya.

manoeuvre pergerakan pasukan askar atau kapal perang.

manor tanah kepunyaan seorang bangsawan.

manpower tenaga orang.

manservant pelayan laki-laki.

mansion rumah besar; — house rumah tuantanah.

mantelpiece sejenis para yang didirikan di atas dapur api sebagai perhiasan.

mantle baju jubah; to — menutupi.

mantrap ranjau.

manual buku pedoman pemimpin; — activity kerja tangan.

manufacture pembuatan; to — mengerjakan, membuat.

manure baja.

manuscript naskhah.

many banyak; a good, great — sejumlah besar.

map peta: weather — peta cuaca.

maple sejenis pohon.

mar, to — merosakkan, membinasakan.

maraud, to — merompak, merampas.

marauder perompak, perampas.

marble marmar, pualam; *(playing)* — guli.

March bulan Mac.

march perjalanan berbaris; to — berbaris.

marchioness perempuan bergelar.

mare kuda betina.

margarine marjerin, mentega buatan.

margin sisi, susur, tepi, pinggir; *(limitation)* batas.

marginal yang berkenaan dengan sisi, pinggir.

marigold sejenis tumbuhan.

marine yang berkenaan dengan laut; yang berkenaan dengan angkatan laut dan perkapalan.

mariner kelasi; master — nakhoda sebuah kapal penambang.

marionette sejenis patung orang yang dapat dimainkan seperti wayang kulit.

marital yang berkenaan dengan hal suami isteri.

maritime yang berkenaan dengan laut.

mark (*target*) sasaran; (*sign*) tanda, kesan; (*examine*) memerikra; below the — kurang baik; wide of the — tidak kena.

marker (*pointer*) penunjuk.

market pasar, pekan; black — pasar gelap.

marking ink dawat yang tidak dapat dihilangkan.

marksman ahli menembak.

marmalade sejenis manisan, halwa limau.

marmot sejenis tikus.

maroon I warna merah tua; (*firework*) sejenis mercun.

maroon II, to — membuang seseorang pada tempat terpencil.

marquee sejenis khemah besar.

marquis gelar orang bangsawan.

marriage perjodohan, kahwin, nikah; to give in — menjodohkan.

married kahwin, berlaki, beristeri, berumahtangga.

marrow lemak tulang, sumsum.

marry, to — kahwin, nikah, menikahkan.

Mars dewata perang di negeri Rom dahulukala; (*astr*) bintang Marikh.

marsh rawa, paya.

marshal perwira berpangkat tinggi; to — mengatur.

martial yang berkenaan dengan perang; — law pemerintahan tentera.

martini nama minuman keras.

martyr syahid; to — mati syahid.

martyrdom mati syahid.

marvel sesuatu yang ajaib, menakjub.

marvellous menakjubkan, menghairankan, ajaib.

mascara celak mata.

mascot azimat.

masculine bersifat laki-laki; laki-laki; jantan, maskulinum.

masculinity jantan.

mash campuran; (*food for horse*) makanan campuran untuk kuda.

mask topeng; to — memakai topeng, menyamar.

mason tukang batu.

masonry pekerjaan tukang batu.

masque sandiwara dahulukala.

masquerade topeng; to — bertopeng, menyamarkan diri.

mass I upacara ugama katolik.

mass II (*crowd*) kelompok besar; (*large quantity*) banyak; the —es rakyat jelata, orang banyak; —meeting rapat raksasa.

massacre pembunuhan besar; to — membunuh secara besar-besaran.

massage, to — memicit, mengurut, lulut.

masseur juru lulut.

masseuse tukang picit perempuan, juru lulut.

massive besar dan berat; (*firm*) pejal.

mast tiang kapal.

master (*designation*) tuan; (*one in control*) kepala, pemimpin; (*employer*) majikan; (*teacher*) guru.

masterful tinggi hati, keras kepala.

master key kunci istimewa, kunci yang dapat membuka segala ibu kunci.

masterly sangat pandai.

masterpiece pekerjaan kesenian dan sebagainya yang sangat indah.

mastery (*authority*) penguasaan; (*expert*) keahlian.

masticate, to — memamah, mengunyah.

mastiff sejenis anjing.

masturbate, to — merancap.

masturbation rancap.

mat I tikar.

mat II (dull) kusam, redup.

matador pembunuh lembu dalam tanding antara lembu dengan orang.

match I (for lighting) api.

match II, (equal etc) lawan, tara, padan; (competition) pertandingan.

matchet, machete parang.

matchless tidak berbanding, tiada bandingnya.

mate, to — (zool) teman, kawan, teman hidup.

material bahan; (cloth) kain raw — bahan mentah.

materialism kebendaan keduniawian.

materialist orang berfaham kebendaan.

materialize, to — mewujudkan, menjelmakan.

maternal yang berkenaan dengan ibu; — uncle saudara lelaki yang laki-laki.

maternity ibu; — hospital rumahsakit beranak.

matey ramah-tamah.

mathematics ilmu hisab.

matinee pertunjukan siang hari.

mating season masa kelamin, waktu binatang kahwin, musim mengawan.

matins doa subuh dinihari.

matriarchy susunan masyarakat dalamnya ibu dianggap kepala keluarga.

matriculate, to — mengizinkan pelajar masuk sekolah tinggi.

matriculation lulus masuk sekolah tinggi sebagai mahasiswa.

matrimonial yang berkenaan dengan perjodohan.

matrimony perjodohan.

matrix (womb) kandung; (mould) tuangan, acuan.

matron perempuan yang telah bersuami; (in hospital etc) kepala urusan rumahtangga di rumahsakit (asrama dan sebagainya).

matter benda, zat, bakal, bahan; (pus) nanah; as a — of fact sebetulnya.

matting barang tikar.

mattress tilam.

mature masak; (understanding) masak akal; —ly dengan masak; to — menjadi masak, matang.

maturity hal keadaan masak, kematangan.

maty ramah-tamah.

maudlin bersifat (berkelakuan) penangis.

maul pemukul; to — memukul; (destroy) merosakkan.

mausoleum makam yang sangat indah.

mauve warna kemerah-merahan bercampur biru.

mawkish tawar, ambar.

maxim pepatah, pematah, peribahasa.

maximize, to — memperbesarkan, secara habis-habisan.

maximum maksima, jumlah ukuran dan sebagainya yang terbesar.

may, might boleh, harus; it — be true barangkali benar.

May bulan Mei.

maybe barangkali, boleh jadi, harus.

mayfly sejenis serangga.

mayor datuk bandar.

mayoress datuk bandar perempuan; (wife of mayor) isteri datuk bandar.

maze tempat sesat, tempat yang membingungkan; to — membingungkan.

me aku, saya, beta.

mead minuman madu; padang rumput.

meadow padang rumput.

meagre (*lean*) kurus; (*poor: of soil*) kersang; (*of means*) sempit, miskin.

meal I makanan.

meal II (*flour*) tepung.

mealy seperti tepung, **yang** mengandung tepung.

mean I (*medium*) sedang, tengah, pertengahan.

mean II (*base*) hina, keji; (*stingy*) kikir, lokek; no — feat hasil yang bukan kepalang.

mean III, to — bererti, bermakna.

meander belok, kelok, liku; to — berbelok-belok, berkelok-kelok, berbelit.

meaning (*sense*) erti, pengertian; (*intention*) maksud, tujuan.

meanness kehinaan, kekejian.

means jalan, ikhtiar, upaya.

meantime sementara itu.

meanwhile dalam pada itu, sementara itu.

measles sakit campak.

measurable terukur, dapat diukur.

measure ukuran, takaran, banyaknya, besarnya; (*due proportion*) kadar.

measured a — tread langkah tenang dan rata.

measurement ukuran.

meat daging.

meaty berdaging, penuh daging.

mechanic (*person*) ahli jentera; —s ilmu mekanik, ilmu jentera, mekanik.

mechanical yang berkenaan dengan atau seperti jentera yang dikerjakan dengan mesin, mekanik, kejenteraan.

mechanism sistem jentera, jalannya jentera, pesawat.

mechanization memberi

jentera.

medal medal, bintang tanda penghormatan, pingat.

medallion sejenis medal, benda yang rupanya seperti medal.

medallist (*maker*) pembuat medal; (*recipient*) penerima medal.

meddle, to — beramputangan, mencampuri, mengganggu.

meddlesome suka beramputangan.

mediaeval, medieval yang berkenaan dengan atau seperti kurun pertengahan.

median, — line garisan menengah.

mediate dengan perantaraan.

mediation perantaraan.

mediator perantara, orang tengah.

medical yang berkenaan dengan perubatan.

medicament ubat.

medicate, to — mengubati.

medicinal yang berkenaan dengan ubat, yang menyembuhkan.

medicine (*drugs*) ubatubatan; (*the science*) ilmu kedoktoran.

medicine-man dukun.

mediocre sedang, tidak berapa baik.

mediocrity keadaan atau sifat sedang, tidak berapa baik.

meditate, to — (*to o.s.*) berfikir; (*on a thing*) memikirkan, tafakkur.

meditation renungan.

Mediterranean Laut Tengah.

medium tengah-tengah, sedang, perantaraan.

medley campuran, rampaian.

meek patuh, rendah, penurut.

meet (*hunting*) pertemuan pemburu dengan anjing; to — bertemu, berjumpa.

meeting pertemuan, jumpaan; (*assembly*) mesyuarat.

mega- awalan kata yang ertinya: besar; —lith batu besar.

megalomania keinginan tergila-gila hendak membesar-besarkan diri.

megaphone alat pembesar suara.

melancholic sayu, rayu, murung, sendu.

melancholy sayu, sendu, gundah-gulana.

melee perkelahian, pertempuran huru-hara.

mellifluous manis sebagai madu.

mellow manis kerana masak; (*soft*) lembik.

melodious merdu, selaras.

melodrama sandiwara yang sangat ramai dan hebat dengan akhiran baik.

melody lagu, ragam.

melon sejenis semangka, temikai.

melt, to — melebur, mencairkan.

melting point panas pencair.

member anggota, ahli badan, ahli persatuan.

membership keanggotaan, ahli persekutuan.

membrane selaput, gendang-gendang; **mucous** — selaput lendir.

memento peringatan.

memoir(s) riwayat, rencana.

memorable patut, diingati.

memorandum memorandum, surat peringatan.

memorial yang memperingatkan, peringatan.

memorize, to — menghapalkan, mengingatkan.

memory ingatan, peringatan; (*fond recollection*) kenangan.

menace ancaman, ugutan; **to** — mengancam.

menagerie kumpulan binatang liar.

mend tambalan; **to** — (*patch*) menampal; (*put right*) memperbaiki, membetulkan.

mendicant meminta-minta; (*person*) orang meminta-minta, pengemis, bangsat.

menial yang berkenaan dengan atau seperti bujang rumah.

menopause mati haidh.

menstrual yang berkenaan dengan haidh.

menstruate, to — mendapat haidh.

menstruation haidh.

mental akal, rohani, yang berkenaan dengan hal jiwa; (*brains*) otak; — **arithmetic** kira-kira congak.

mentality hal kejiwaan; (*character*) tabiat.

mention sebutan, penyebutan.

mentor penasihat.

menu daftar makanan.

mercantile yang berkenaan dengan perdagangan, perniagaan; — **marine** perkapalan perniagaan.

mercenary hanya bekerja untuk upah, mencari untung sahaja.

merchandise barang dagangan.

merchant saudagar pedagang.

merciful rahim, berbelas kasihan.

merciless tidak berbelas kasihan, kejam.

mercury raksa; (*astr*) **M**—bintang Utarid.

mercy belas kasihan, rahim; **to have** — berbelas kasihan.

mere I semata-mata belaka, sahaja; —ly hanya, semata-mata.

mere II (*pool*) danau, kolam.

meretricious seperti oran sundal.

merge, to — memandu, bersatupadu, bercantum.

merger perpaduan, percantuman.

meridian garisan bujur; yang berkenaan dengan tenga-hari.

meringue sejenis kuih.

merino (*sheep*) sejenis kambing; (*its wool*) bulu kambing itu.

merit jasa, bakti; **to** — berjasa.

meritorious berjasa.

mermaid puteri laut, bintulbahar.

merman putera laut.

merriment sukacita, keriangan.

merry ria, riang gembira.

merry-go-round putaran, kisaran yang boleh dinaiki orang akan menghiburkan diri.

mesh mata jala, mata sirat; **to** — menangkap dalam jala, memukat.

mesmerism keadaan cuca.

mess (*food*) makanan; (*concoction*) campuran; (*confusion*) keadaan kacau-bilau.

message berita, warta, khabar.

messenger pesuruh, suruhan.

Messiah imam Mahdi.

messy kotor, kotor-bolor.

metabolism pertukaran zat.

metal logam; **road** — batu kerikil (untuk membuat jalan besar).

metallic yang berkenaan dengan atau seperti logam.

metallurgy ilmu mengerjakan logam.

metamorphosis penjelmaan perubahan rupa.

metaphor ibarat, kiasan, perumpamaan.

metaphysical yang berkenaan dengan mula jadi.

metaphysics ilmu mula jadi cesuatu.

mete, to — **out** membahagi, menakar.

meteor cirit bintang.

meteorite batu bintang.

meteorological yang berkenaan dengan udara hawa, angin dan sebagainya.

meteorology ilmu udara, kaji cuaca.

meter, metre pengukur, meter.

methinks pada pendapat saya.

method cara, jalan, aturan.

methodical bercara berperaturan.

Methodist anggota salah satu golongan ugama Nasrani.

meticulous terlalu hemat dan cermat.

metre meter (ukuran); (*rhythm*) irama, sajak.

metric menurut ukuran meter; — system sistem perpuluhan.

metrical bersajak; menurut sistem perpuluhan; menurut meter.

metronome alat yang menunjukkan irama salah satu karangan muzik.

metropolis ibu kota, kota yang besar dan ramai.

metropolitan yang berkenaan dengan bandar besar, penduduk bandar besar.

mettle semangat, kegiatan, keberanian.

mettlesome berani.

mews kandang kuda yang didirikan di sekeliling halaman.

mezzo—soprano suara perempuan yang antara tinggi dengan rendah.

miaow miaul, mengiau.

miasma kabut yang kurang sihat yang membawa penyakit.

mica sejenis galian, semendal.

micro- mikro, awalan kata yang ertinya: kecil.

microbe kuman, mikrob.

microcosm mikrokosmos, dunia kecil.

micron mikron.

microphone mikropon, corong radio.

microscope mikroskop, teropong halus.

microscopic yang berkenaan dengan mikroskop; (*very small*) sangat kecil.

mid tengah.

midday tengahari.

midden timbunan sampah atau baja.

middle tengah, di tengah, pertengahan; a — course jalan tengah.

middle-aged setengah baya, setengah tua.

Middle Ages abad pertengahan.

middling sedang, boleh juga.

midge nyamuk.

midget (*dwarf*) orang kerdil; (*very small*) sangat kecil.

midnight tengah malam, dinihari.

midriff sekat rongga badan.

midshipman bakal pegawai laut.

midst tengah; in the — of di antara.

midsummer waktu tengah-tengah musim panas.

midwife bidan.

midwifery ilmu bidan.

mien sikap.

might I kekuasaan; with all one's — sekuat-kuatnya.

might II *see* **may**.

mighty (*of power*) berkuasa; (*strong*) sangat kuat; (*large*) sangat besar.

migraine sakit kepala.

migrant yang berpindah, yang mengembara.

migrate, to — berpindah

negeri, berpindah tempat kediaman.

migration perpindahan.

mild lembut, halus, tidak kasar.

mildew cendawan, lapuk, lumut; to — berlapuk.

mile batu.

mileage batu jarak dihitungkan dengan ukuran batu.

milestone batu yang menunjukkan jauh.

militant yang sedang berjuang, berperang.

militarism faham tentera, sikap dan semangat tentera.

militarist orang yang berfaham tentera.

military, the — tentera.

militate, to — berjuang, melawan.

militia askar orang pereman.

milk susu; to — perah, memerah.

milk bar kedai susu dan segala minuman yang bukan minuman keras.

milkmaid pemerah susu.

milkman tukang susu.

milk powder tepung susu.

milky bercampur atau seperti susu.

mill giling, kilang; (*grinding*) kisaran; — ed (*of rice*) canai, ceruh.

millennium masa seribu tahun istimewa; masa seribu tahun tarikh Masihi.

millet jelai, sekoi, jagung gerbang.

milli- awalan kata yang ertinya seper seribu (1/1000).

milligram miligram.

milliner pembuat atau penjual topi perempuan.

millinery perusahaan topi perempuan.

million juta; —s and —s berjuta-juta.

millionaire melianar, orang kaya, jutawan.

millipede sejenis lipan, ulat mentibang.

millstone batu penggiling.

mime sejenis sandiwara yang dimainkan dengan gerak badan sahaja tidak dengan kata-kata.

mimeograph mesin akan memperganda-gandakan.

mimic orang yang pandai meniru dan mengajuk orang.

mimicry penyamaran mengajuk.

mimosa sejenis tumbuhan.

minaret menara.

mince daging halus lepas dicincang-cincang.

mincemeat campuran buah gula dan sebagainya untuk kuih.

mind (*recollection*) ingatan; (*opinion*) pendapat, perasaan.

minded (*disposition*) bertabiat, berperangai, cenderung kepada.

mindful, — (*of*) ingat akan, dengan menaruh perhatian.

mine I (*to dig out metals etc*) lombong galian; (*explosive*) periuk api ranjau.

mine II kepunyaan saya, saya punya.

miner pelombong, penggali, buruh tambang.

mineral barang galian, logam; **— water** air belanda.

mineralogy ilmu gali-galian.

mingle, to — mencampur; to **— with** bergaul dengan.

miniature (*painting*) lukisan yang sangat kecil; (*very small*) sangat kecil.

minimal sangat kecil, sekecil-kecilnya.

minimize, to — memperkecilkan sampai sedikit-dikitnya.

minimum minimum, jumlah ukuran yang terkecil atau tersedikit.

mining perlombongan.

minion anak emas, timangan.

minister menteri; to **— memberi.**

ministerial yang berkenaan dengan menteri.

ministry kementerian.

mink sejenis cerpelai; (*its fur*) bulu binatang itu.

minnow sejenis ikan kecil.

minor (*lesser*) lebih kecil; (*lower*) lebih rendah; (*of little importance*) kurang penting; (*person under 18*) belum dewasa.

minority golongan terkecil; (*under age*) keadaan belum dewasa.

minstrel biduan, penyanyi.

mint I (*coining*) tempat rasmi untuk membuat matawang; to **— membuat matawang.**

mint II (*plant*) pudina.

minuet sejenis tari dahulukala; (*music for it*) lagu untuk tari itu.

minus (*less*) kurang; negatif, tolak.

minuscule kecil.

minute I (*of time*) minit; (*notes*) rancangan.

minute II sangat kecil sangat sedikit, tidak penting.

minutiae selok-belok yang tidak penting.

minx gadis nakal.

miracle keajaiban, mukjizat.

miraculous ajaib.

mirage pembayangan udara.

mire paya, lumpur.

mirror kaca muka, cermin.

mirth keriangan, sukacita.

mis- awalan kata yangertinya: salah.

misadventure kecelakaan.

misalliance perkahwinan yang tidak sesuai dengan adat kebiasaan (yakni orang tinggi dengan orang rendah).

misanthropist orang yang benci akan orang lain.

misanthropy kebencian akan orang lain.

misapprehension salah faham.

misappropriate, to — memakai wang orang untuk kepentingan sendiri, mencuri.

misbehave, to — tidak berseiaku buruk laku.

misbehaviour kelakuan tidak baik.

miscalculate, to — salah menghitung.

miscalculation hitungan salah.

miscarriage keguguran anak, salah kenakan.

miscarry, to — (fail etc) gagal; (premature birth) gugur.

miscellaneous bermacam-macam, berjenis-jenis, rampai-rampaian.

miscellany campuran, bunga rampai.

mischance celaka, nasib malang.

mischief (injury) kerugian, kerosakan; (disturbance) kerusuhan.

mischievous (naughty) nakal; (injurious) merugikan.

misconception hal salah faham, hal salah anggap.

misconduct (behaviour) kelakuan buruk; (misguide) pim, pinan buruk.

misconstrue, to — salah mengerti tujuan orang.

miscreant jahat, hina, orang jahat.

misdemeanour pelanggaran, kelakuan buruk.

misdirect, to — salah menunjukkan.

miser orang kikir, kedekut, bakhil.

miserable celaka; sangat dukacita; melarat.

miserly kikir bakhil.

misery sengsara dukacita; (poverty) kemiskinah.

misfit pakaian dan lain-lain yang tidak sesuai.

misfortune celaka, nasib malang.

misgiving perasaan syak wasangka.

misguide, to — menyesatkan.

mishap celaka, kecelakaan.

misinform, to — salah menerangkan.

misinterpret, to — (wrongly explained) salah menjelaskan; (wrongly understood) salah menge tikan.

misjudge, to — salah memutuskan.

mislay, to — salah taruh sehingga sukar didapati.

mislead, to — menyesatkan.

mismanage, to — salah mengurus.

misnomer pemakaian nama atau istilah yang salah.

misogynist orang yang benci akan perempuan.

misplace, to — salah menaruh.

misprint salah cetak.

mispronounce, to — salah mengucapkan.

mispronunciation ucapan salah.

misquotation kutipan salah.

misquote, to — salah mengutip.

misread, to — salah membaca.

misrepresent, to — salah menggambarkan.

miss I (not hit) kegagalan, tidak kena.

miss II cik, puan.

missal buku sembahyang, buku doa.

misshapen salah bentuk, buruk bentuknya.

missile sesuatu yang dilemparkan.

missing kurang yang tidak ada pada tempatnya.

mission pengutusan.

missionary utusan ugama.

missis, missus nyonya, puan cik.

missive surat rasmi.

misspell, to — salah mengeja.

misspond, to — salah mengeluarkan, membelanjakan.

mist kabut, halimun; **to** — berkabut.

mistake salah, kesalahan, kekeliruan; **to make a** — keliru.

mister tuan.

mistletoe sejenis tumbuhan, api-api dedalu.

mistress kekasih madu.

mistrust, to — mencurigai, syak wasangka akan.

misty berkabut, sayup-sayup.

misunderstand, to — salah faham.

misunderstanding salah faham, salah terima.

misuse salah pemakaian; **to** — salah memakai.

mite sesuatu yang sangat kecil.

mitigate, to — (*lighten etc*) meringankan melonggarkan; (*console*) melipur.

mitigation ringan, kelonggaran.

mitre topi, tanda kehormatan seorang padri.

mitt(en) sejenis sarung tangan; **—s** sarung tangan seorang peninju.

mix, to — mencampurkan; **to** — **with** bergaul dengan.

mixed bercampur-aduk, campur-baur, rampai-rampaian.

mixer orang yang mencampurkan.

mixture campuran.

mnemonic yang menolong peringatan.

moan keluh, aduh; **to** — mengaduh, mengeluh.

moat parit.

mob rakyat hina dina; **to** — mengerumuni.

mobile mudah dipindahkan.

mobility hal mudah berpindah.

mobilization kerahan.

mobilize, to — mengerah.

mocha kopi yang baik mutunya.

mock (*sham*) tiruan, pura-pura.

mockery (*teasing*) ejekan, olokan.

mode cara, ragam, jalan.

model contoh, potongan, acuan.

moderate (*of price etc*) pantas, patut; (*mediocre*) sedang.

moderation keadaan atau sikap sedang.

moderator (*go-between*) perantara.

modern baharu, model baharu, moden.

modernism faham moden.

modernization pembaharuan.

modernize, to — memperbaharui.

modest rendah hati, sopan santun.

modesty kerendahan, kesopanan.

modicum sedikit, sejumlah kecil.

modification perubahan.

modify, to — (*alter*) mengubahkan; (*lighten*) meringankan.

modulate, to — mengatur, mengubahkan.

modulation perubahan suara.

modus, — operandi cara bekerja, berjalan.

mohair sejenis kain panas, kain bulu.

Mohammedan orang Islam.

moire sejenis kain sutera.

moist basah, lembab, lengas.

moisten, to — membasahkan, melembabkan.

moisture lembab, cairan, air.

molar, — tooth geraham.

molasses air tebu.

mole (*animal*) tikus mondok; (*on skin*) tahi lalat; (*wharf*) pangkalan.

molecule molekul.

molehill busut yang dibuat oleh tikus mondok.

molest, to — mengganggu; menganiaya.

mollify, to — melembutkan, membujuk, meredakan.

molluse kerang, siput, teritip.

mollycoddle pemuda yang terlalu lemah-lengah, anak manja.

molten terlebur, larut.

moment saat, detik, ketika.

momentarily untuk sejurus sahaja.

momentary sejurus lamanya, tidak lama.

momentous penting.

momentum kepesatan, laju.

monarch raja, yang dipertuan.

monarchy kerajaan.

monastery tempat orang rahib.

Monday hari Isnin.

monetary yang berkenaan dengan wang, kewangan.

money wang; **paper** — wang kertas.

moneybox tabung, peti pekak.

moneychanger penukar wang.

moneyed berwang, kaya, berada.

money market pasar wang. **-monger** penjual, pedagang.

mongoose sejenis cerpelai.

mongrel (*mixed*) bercampur, campuran.

monitor penasihat; (*at school*) pelajar, ketua kelas.

monk rahib.

monkey kera, monyet; **to** — **about** (*to fool*) memperolokkan; (*imitate*) meniru.

monkey wrench kunci Inggeris.

mono- awalan kata yang ertinya: satu, tunggal.

monochromatic berwarna satu.

monocle kaca mata untuk satu mata sahaja.

monogamy adat kahwin dengan satu isteri, suami sahaja.

monograph karangan yang mengenai satu pokok sahaja.

monolith batu tunggal.

monologue sebahagian dalam sandiwara yang dimainkan dan diucapkan oleh seorang sahaja.

monoplane kapal udara yang bersayap sepasang sahaja.

monopolize, to — memegang monopoli, memborong.

monopoly monopoli.

monosyllable kata yang hanya satu suku katanya.

monotheism ilmu tauhid, faham keesaan Allah.

monotone bunyi yang tidak berubah.

monotonous (*of sound*) tidak berubah bunyinya; (*boring*) bosankan kerana selalu sama.

monotony keadaan (atau bunyi) yang selalu sama.

monsoon musim monsun.

monster (*ogre*) raksasa; (*huge*) (binatang, manusia atau benda) yang sangat besar.

monstrosity sesuatu yang mengerikan atau mendahsyatkan.

monstrous sangat besar, raksasa, mengerikan.

month bulan.

monthly bulanan; majalah bulanan.

monument tanda peringatan.

monumental yang seperti tanda peringatan; (*vast*) sangat besar

moo, to — mengaum, menguak, meraung.

mooch, to — berlengah-lengah.

mood I keadaan hati; **to be in the** — (for, to) cenderung akan.

mood II cara

moody muram, murung.

moon bulan; **full** — bulan pernama.

moonbeam sinar bulan.

moonlight terang bulan.

moonstone sejenis batu perhiasan.

moor I padang yang kersang.

moor II, to — tempat menambatkan kapal, pertambatan.

mooring(s) tempat menambat kapal, pertambatan.

moose sejenis rusa besar.

moot yang dapat dipersoalkan; — point peguaman.

mop kain pencuci.

mope, to — bermuram hati.

moral berkenaan dengan hal baik dan buruk, akhlak; — training latihan akhlak.

morale semangat pasukan.

moralist orang yang selalu mementingkan kesusilaan.

morality kesusilaan; **moralities** adat sopan santun.

morass paya, rawa.

morbid tidak sihat, tidak sesuai dengan fikiran sihat.

morbidity keadaan tidak sihat fikiran.

mordant pedas, tajam.

more lagi, lebih, lebih banyak.

moreover dan lagi, lagi pula, lain daripada itu, tambahan pula.

morgue tempat menyimpan mayat.

moribund hampir mati.

Mormon anggota salah satu persaudaraan berugama.

morning pagi hari; **early in the** — pagi-pagi.

morocco sejenis kulit kambing.

moron orang tolol, pak pandir dungu.

morose murung, muram.

morphia, morphine morfine, ubat tidur, morfin.

morphology (of form) ilmu bentuk, kajibentuk; (of words) ilmu saraf, tata-bahasa.

morrow, the — keesokan harinya; **on the** — of the event keesokan hari lepas peristiwa itu.

morsel sepotong kecil, sesuap.

mortal yang akan mati; (mortal man) insan.

mortality (death) kematian; (number of deaths) bilangan maut.

mortar (for rice) lesung; (plaster) lepa.

mortar board papan lepa; (headdress) sejenis topi yang dipakai oleh mahasiswa.

mortgage gadai, cagaran.

mortify, to — mematikan hawa nafsu; (shame) menghinakan.

mortuary (place for corpses before burial) tempat menyimpan mayat.

mosaic lukisan yang dibuat daripada bermacam-macam potongan tembikar batu dan sebagainya yang berwarna-warni.

Moslem, Muslim orang Islam.

mosque masjid.

mosquito nyamuk; — net kelambu.

moss lumut.

mossy berlumut.

most terbanyak terlebih, kebanyakan.

—most akhiran kata yang ertinya: terlebih; top— yang tertinggi.

mostly pada umumnya, pada ghalibnya, kebanyakannya.

moth gegat.

mother ibu, bonda, induk;
— country negara tumpah
darah.

motherhood keibuan.

mother-in-law emak mentua.

motherly seperti ibu.

mother-of-pearl indung
(kulit) mutiara, gewang.

mother tongue bahasa ibu-
aida.

motif ragam, pokok, dasar
pada sebuah lukisan.

motion (*movement*) gerakan;
(*proposal*) usul, cadangan.

motion picture wayang
gambar hidup.

motivate, to — memberi
alasan.

motivation hal memberi atau
merupakan alasan, penggerak.

motive sebab, alasan, penggerak, motif.

motley (*parti-coloured*) anekawarna; (*mixture*) campuran.

motor motor, pesawat, jentera.

motorcar motokar.

mottled burek, berintik-rintik.

motto semboyan, cogan kata.

mould (*loose earth*) tanah gembur; (*for casting*) acuan.

moulder pembentuk, penu-
ang.

moulding tuangan.

mouldy lapuk, bercendawan.

moult to — meluruh.

mound busut, anak bukit.

mount I, to — (*horse*) tunggangan, kuda tunggangan.

mount II, mountain gunung, bukit.

mountaineer orang yang
pandaj mendaki gunung.

mountainous bergunung-
gunung.

mountain pass lorong celah gunung, genting.

mountain range mountain-
chain banjaran gunung.

mounted berkuda.

mourn, to — (*wear mourning*)
berkabung; (*lament*) meratap.

mourner orang yang berka-
bung.

mournful berdukacita, sayu.

mourning perkabungan.

mouse tikus.

mouse deer pelanduk, kancil.

mousetrap perangkap tikus.

moustache kumis, misai.

mouth mulut; (*of river*)
muara, kuala.

mouth organ tiup-tiup mulut.

mouthpiece (*spokesman*)
orang yang mengucapkan buah
fikiran orang lain, juru cakap.

movable yang dapat dipindahkan.

move (*take steps, action*)
tindakan; it's your — inilah
giliran tuan bergerak.

movement pergerakan.

mover penggerak; (*proposer*)
penganjur.

movies wayang gambar hidup.

moving (*of feelings*) merawankan hati.

mow, to — menyabit, memotong rumput.

mower penyabit, pemotong.

much (*great quantity*) banyak;
(*very*) sangat; how —? berapa?

muck tahi, baja; to — up
(*dirty*) mengotorkan.

mucous berkenaan dengan
lendir, berlendir.

mucus lendir; hingus.

mud lumpur, luluk.

muddle kekacauan; to —
mengacaukan.

muddy becak, berlumpur.

mudguard sayap roda.

muff sejenis sarung tangan
yang dibuat daripada bulu
binatang.

muffin sejenis kuih.

muffle, to — menutupi,
menyelubungi.

muffler sejenis selendang daripaaa kain bulu.

mufti (*priest*) ketua ugama Islam mufti; (*plain clothes*) pakaian preman.

mug I (*cup*) sejenis cawan.

mug II (*sl*) orang bodoh.

mug III, (*sl*) to — (up) bertekun.

muggy panas terik.

mulatto peranakan habsyi dengan orang bangsa kulit putih.

mulberry sejenis pohon.

mule sejenis binatang yang bapanya kaldai dan ibunya kuda, baghal.

mulish seperti kaldai; (*obstinate*) keras kepala.

mull, to — membuat minuman dengan mencampurkan bir atau air anggur dengan gula, telur, rempah-rempah dan sebagainya.

mullet sejenis ikan.

mullion tiang tegak di tingkap.

multi– awalan kata yang ertinya; bermacam-macam.

multicoloured pancawarna, berwarna-warni.

multifarious berjenis-jenis.

multiple berlipat ganda, bermacam-macam; (*arithmetical*) angka kandungan bulat.

multiplication darab; — table sifir darab.

multiplicity jumlah besar.

multiplier pendarab.

multiply, to — mendarab; (*prolific of animals*) menjadi biak.

multitude sejumlah besar; (*crowd*) orang banyak.

multitudinous sangat banyak.

mum diam, tenang.

mumble ucapan yang tidak terang.

mummify, to — merempahi mayat.

mummy ibu.

mumps penyakit bengok.

munch, to — mengunyah, memamah.

mundane duniawi, keduniaan.

municipal yang berkenaan dengan bandaraya.

municipality bandaraya, perbandaran.

munificence kemurahan hati.

munition alat perang.

mural yang berkenaan dengan tembok (dinding); (*decoration on wall*) lukisan dinding.

murder pembunuhan; to — membunuh.

murderer pembunuh.

murderous yang akan atau ingin membunuh, pembunuh.

murky gelap, kelam.

murmur bisik, sungut.

muscat sejenis buah anggur.

muscle otot, urat.

muscovy — duck itik manila.

muscular berotot, berurat daging.

muse I, the M—s dewi Yunani zaman purbakala.

muse II, to — (*contemplate, stare*) merenung; (*reflect*) berfikir.

museum muzium, sekolah gambar.

mush sejenis bubur.

mushroom cendawan.

mushy seperti bubur.

music muzik bunyi-bunyian.

musical pertunjukan bermuzik, berkenaan dengan muzik.

music hall dewan dipakai untuk mempertunjukan tari-tarian, nyanyi dan sebagainya.

musician pemain muzik.

musk kesturi, jebat.

musket senapang.

musketeer soldadu bersenapang.

Muslim *see* **Moslem.**

muslin kain khasa.

musquash bulu sejenis tikus.

mussel sejenis remis, kepah, siput.

must I *(new wine)* air anggur yang belum beragi.

must II mesti, perlu, wajib.

must III *(mould)* lapuk.

mustang kuda yang belum jinak di Amerika.

mustard, — **seed** biji sesawi.

muster pengumpulan orang untuk mengadakan pemeriksaan.

musty basi, berlapuk.

mutation perubahan, pergantian.

mute *(dumb)* bisu; *(silent)* senyap.

mutilate, to — mengudungkan.

mutilation pengudungan.

mutineer penderhaka.

mutinous derhaka, pemberontak.

mutiny pemberontakan.

mutter *(grumble)* sungut-sungut; **to** — bersungut-sungut.

mutton daging kambing.

mutual saling, satu sama lain.

muzzle *(snout)* moncong; **to** — memasang sarung.

my kepunyaan aku, saya.

myopia mata rabun.

myopic mata rabun, buta ayam.

myriad *(ten thousand)* sepuluh ribu; *(immense number)* sangat banyak.

myrrh sejenis kemenyan.

myrtle sejenis pohon.

myself saya sendiri.

mysterious ghaib, rahsia.

mystery rahsia.

mystic batin, ghaib; *(a —)* sufi.

mysticism ilmu batin, ilmu tasawuf.

mystify, to — merahsiakan.

myth cerita purbakala, hikayat.

mythical yang berkenaan dengan hikayat purbakala.

mythology ilmu hikayat lama, dongeng dewa-dewa.

N

nab, to — menangkap.

nabob orang yang sangat kaya, nawab.

nadir titik yang rendah sekali, ketika yang terlalu susah.

nag I kuda kecil.

nag II, to — membengkengi, menggoda, berleter.

nail *(finger)* kuku; *(iron)* paku; **to fight tooth and** — berkelahi dengan sekuat-kuatnya.

naive jujur dan sederhana.

naked *(bare)* telanjang; *(open)* terbuka; **with the eye** dengan mata kasar sahaja.

namby-pamby percakapan yang terlalu manis sehingga menjemukan.

name nama; **in the** — **of** atas nama; **to** — menamai.

nameless tidak bernama.

namely ialah, iaitu, yakni.

namesake orang senama.

nanny *(she-goat)* kambing betina.

nap I *(sleep)* tidur sebentar.

nap II *(card game)* permainan terup.

nape tengkok.

napkin tuala; *(for a baby)* bedung, lampin.

nappy bedung, lampin.

narcissism sifat memujikan diri sendiri.

narcissus sejenis bunga.

narcotic yang membiuskan.

narrate, to — berhikayat, menceriterakan.

narrative ceritera hikayat, riwayat.

narrator penghikayat, yang menceriterakan.

narrow sempit, sesak.

narrow-minded akal pendek, singkat akal.

nasal yang berkenaan dengan hidung; (of speech) bunyi sengau.

nasalize, to — menyengaukan.

nasturtium sejenis tanaman menjalar yang berbunga.

nasty (filthy) kotor; (shabby) buruk; (evil) jahat; (terrible) hebat.

natal yang berkenaan dengan kelahiran.

nation bangsa, kebangsaan.

national nasional, kebangsaan; — anthem lagu kebangsaan.

nationalism rasa (faham) kebangsaan.

nationalist nasionalis.

nationalist(ic) bersifat nasionalis.

nationality kewarganegaraan, bangsa.

nationalize, to — menjadikan milik negeri.

native bumiputera, dalam negeri.

nativity kelahiran Nabi Isa.

natty rapih.

natural (by nature) berdasarkan pembawaan; (normal) lazim, biasa; (spontaneous) sifat semulajadi.

naturalist ahli pengetahuan alam; (dealer in live animals) penjual binatang.

naturalize, to — memberi hak penduduk warganegara, menjadikan warganegara.

naturally memang, biasa, lazim.

nature sifat dasar; (character) tabiat pembawaan, perangai.

naught tidak apa-apa; (no value) tidak berharga.

naughty nakal.

nausea mabuk, pusing, rasa mual (muak).

nauseate, to — menjadikan mual.

nautical yang berkenaan dengan perkapalan dan pelayaran.

naval yang berkenaan dengan angkatan laut.

nave (of church) bahagian tengah sebuah gereja.

navel pusat.

navigable yang dapat dilayari.

navigate, to — (sail) berlayar; (steer) mengemudikan.

navigation pelayaran, ilmu pelayaran.

navigator ahli pelayaran.

navvy buruh yang menggali lubang membuat terusan.

navy angkatan laut; — -blue biru tua.

nay tidak.

neap, —tide air pasang perbani.

near, —(by) hampir, dekat; (nearly related) karib; to come — mendekati.

nearly dekat-dekat, hampir.

near-sighted buta ayam.

neat (clean, tidy) bersih, teratur.

nebula sekelompok bintang di langit yang kelihatan dari jauh seperti kabut bercahaya.

nebulous kabut.

necessary, **necessarily** perlu, terpaksa.

necessitate, to — memaksa, memerlukan.

necessitous miskin, melarat.

necessity keperluan, keharusan.

neck batang leher, tengkuk.

necklace kalung, rantai leher.

necro— awalan kata yang ertinya: mati.

necromancy ilmu ghaib istimewa yang berkenaan dengan roh orang yang telah mati.

necropolis perkuburan.

nectar minuman yang sangat sedap, manisan pada bunga.

nectarine sejenis buah.

née kata yang menunjukkan nama isteri sebelum kahwin.

need keperluan; (*difficulties*) kesukaran; (*poverty*) kemiskinan; to — perlu.

needful perlu; the — keperluan.

needle jarum, apa sahaja yang menyerupai jarum; — -work jahitan.

needless tak usah, tidak perlu.

needy miskin, melarat.

nefarious jahat.

negation peniadaan, ketiadaan.

negative negatif, yang meniadakan, kata yang menolak.

neglect kelalaian, kealpaan.

neglectful alpa, lalai.

negligence kelalaian, kealpaan.

negligent alpa, lalai, lengah.

negligible yang dapat dilalaikan, ringan.

negotiable yang boleh dibeli atau dijual.

negotiate, to — merundingkan.

negotiation perundingan.

negotiator perunding.

Negress orang habsyi perempuan.

Negro orang negro, habsyi.

negroid seperti orang negro.

neigh, to — meringkek, bunyi kuda.

neighbour tetangga, orang sebelah, jiran.

neighbourhood berhampiran, sekeliling, orang sekampung, berjiran, kawasan sekitar.

neighbouring yang dekat, damping, hampir, jiran.

neither salah satu, bukan.

neo— awalan kata yang ertinya: baru.

neolithic berkenaan dengan akhirnya zaman batu.

neologism, neology pemakaian atau pembentukan kata baharu.

neon gas neon.

neophyte orang yang baharu masuk ugama.

nephew kemanakan, anak saudara.

nephritis demam ginjal, sakit buah pinggang.

nepotism pemberian jawatan hanya kepada saudara-saudara sahaja.

nerve (*of body*) saraf; (*spirit*) keberanian, semangat.

nerveless tidak bersemangat lemah.

nervous darah gemuruh, gelisah; (*concerning nerves*) yang berkenaan dengan saraf; — system susunan saraf.

nervousness kegugupan.

nervy (*strong*) kuat.

—ness akhiran kata yang menunjukkan: keadaan, hal.

nest sarang.

nestle, to — duduk bersenang-senang.

nestling burung muda yang belum keluar daripada sarangnya.

net I jaring, jala; to — merajut, menyirat.

net II, — profit untung bersih.

nether yang di bawah, bawah.

netting kain kasa, jaring.

nettle daun gatal, jelatang; to — (*provoke*) merangsangkan.

network jaring.

neural yang berkenaan dengan urat saraf.

neuralgia sakit urat saraf (biasanya di kepala).

neuro— awalan kata yang ertinya: saraf.

neurology ilmu sakit urat saraf.

neurosis sakit urat saraf.

neurotic orang yang sakit urat saraf.

neuter laki-laki bukan perempuan bukan.

neutral sama tengah; (*indifferent*) tidak tentu, nutral.

neutrality sama tengah.

neutralize, to — menawarkan.

never belum pernah, tidak pernah; (*how can that be?*) masakan.

nevermore sekali-kali tidak lagi, tidak pernah lagi.

nevertheless meskipun begitu, walaupun demikian.

new baharu, baharu-baharu ini.

newcomer orang baharu.

new-fangled menurut contoh baharu.

newly baharu-baharu ini se karang ini.

news berita, khabar, warta.

newsagent penjual suratkhabar.

newspaper suratkhabar.

newsreel filem warta berita.

newt sejenis bengkarung air.

next yang hampir dekat; (*adjoining*) bersempadan; (*following*) yang kemudian; (*approaching of time*) yang datang.

nibble, to — mengunggis.

nibs, (*col*) his — orang pembesar.

nice (*neat*) teliti, cermat; (*fine*) bagus, manis, jelita, sedap.

nicety ketelitian.

niche ceruk, relung di tembok.

nick takek, kelar; in the — of time tepat pada waktunya.

nickel matawang Amerika Syarikat.

nickname nama ejekan, nama timangan, gelaran.

nicotine zat nikotin.

niece kemanakan perempuan, anak saudara perempuan.

nifty (*col*) pesolek.

niggard orang kikir; —ly kikir.

nigger (*pej*) orang negro, habsyi.

niggling sempit, picik.

nigh dekat, hampir.

night malam; good — selamat malam; last — semalam, malam tadi; to spend the — bermalam.

night club tempat makan malam dan berpesta-pesta.

nightfall senjakala.

nightingale burung jentayu.

nightly (*by night*) pada malam hari; (*every night*) tiaptiap malam.

nightmare kekau, igauigauan.

nihilism faham ingkar, pengingkaran semua susunan politik.

nihilist orang yang mengingkari semua susunan politik.

nil tidak apa-apa.

nimble cekatan, pantas, tingkas.

nimbus awan hujan, awan mendung.

nincompoop orang bodoh.

nine sembilan.

nineteen sembilan belas.

nineteenth yang kesembilan belas.

ninetieth yang kesembilan puluh.

ninety sembilan puluh.

ninth yang kesembilan.

nip I cubit, cepit; to — mencubit.

nip II (*drink*) seteguk minuman keras.

nippers sepit, angkup.

nipple (*anat*) puting, tetek; (*instrument etc representing a nipple*) tombol (dan lain benda) yang menyerupai puting tetek.

nippy tajam, pedih sejuknya.

nisi, decree — keputusan

dapat bercerai jika tidak ada halangan dalam waktu yang tertentu.

nit (*bug*) telur kutu.

nitric, — acid asid nitrik.

nitrogen zat sendawa, nitrojen.

nitwit (*col*) orang bodoh.

no tidak, bukan; —-one tiada seorang pun.

nobble, (*sl*) to — menipu, berbuat jahat istimewa pada perlumbaan kuda.

nobility kaum atasan.

noble (*by birth*) bangsawan, berbangsa; (*excellent*) mulia.

nobleman orang berbangsa.

noble—minded baik hati, mulia.

nobly mulia, bersifat mulia.

nobody tidak ada seorang pun; a — orang yang tidak masuk hitungan.

nocturnal yang berkenaan dengan malam hari, pada malam hari.

nod angguk kepala; to — mengangguk.

node bonggol, berbuku.

nodule bonggol kecil, buku tumbuhan.

noggin cawan mangkuk besar.

noise bunyi; (*uproar*) gaduh, riuh-rendah; (*of storm*) ribut.

noiseless yang tidak ada bunyinya.

noisome (*injurious*) yang merusakkan; (*of smell*) berbau bu-uk.

noisy bergaduh, riuh-rendah, gempita.

nomad suatu seorang daripada suku bangsa pengembara, nomad.

nomadic yang berkenaan dengan atau seperti pengembara.

nominal yang berkenaan atau seperti kata benda, yang berkenaan dengan nama.

nominate, to — mengangkat; (*political candidate*) mencalunkan.

nomination penamaan calun.

nominative nominatif tatabahasa.

non—awalan kata yang ertinya: tidak.

non—acceptance hal tidak menerima.

nonagenarian orang yang umurnya anatara 89 dengan 100 tahun.

nonchalance perasaan masa bodoh.

non—combatant orang yang tidak turut berperang.

non—committal yang tidak mengikat janji.

nonconformist orang yang tidak turut rukun syarat salah satu gereja rasmi.

nonconformity hal tidak menyesuaikan diri dengan susunan rasmi.

nondescript tidak mudah diperikan.

none suatu pun tidak.

nonentity sesuatu yang tidak ada, ketiadaan.

non—existent yang tidak ada.

nonplus, to be —sed keadaan tercengang.

nonsen.e bukan-bukan, yang tidak-tidak.

nonsensical yang bukanbukan

non sequitur sesuatu yang tidak masuk akal.

non—stop terus-menerus, tidak berhenti.

noodle sejenis misoa.

nook tempat duduk yang tersendiri; (*corner*) sudut.

noon tengahari.

noose jerat; to — menjerat.

nor juga tidak.

Nordic yang tergolong kepada bangsa yang mendiami negeri Skandinavia.

normal biasa, lazim.

Norman yang berkenaan dengan penduduk negeri Norman.

Norse yang berkenaan dengan Norway.

north utara.

north—east timurlaut.

northerly yang berkenaan dengan sebelah utara.

northern yang berkenaan dengan daerah utara.

north pole kutub utara.

north—west baratlaut.

Norwegian penduduk atau bahasa Norway.

nose hidung; to — menghidu, mencium.

nose—dive terjun dengan kepala dahulu ke bawah (kapal udara).

nose—ring cincin hidung.

nosey ingin tahu (atau ingin mencampuri) perkara orang lain.

nostalgia rindu, hiba hati.

nostril lubang hidung, liang hidung.

not tidak, tiada; (*implying an alternative*) bukan.

notability sesuatu atau seseorang yang menarik perhatian.

notable yang menarik perhatian; (*important*) penting.

notation sistem menulis angka; petunjuk.

notch takek, kelar; to — menakek, mengelar.

note (*music*) bunyi nada; (*mark*) tanda; (*reminder*) peringatan, catitan.

notebook buku catitan, peringatan

noteworthy patut diperhatikan.

nothing tidak apa-apa.

notice pemberitahu, pengumuman, kenyataan.

noticeable dapat diperhatikan, kelihatan.

notice board papan kenyataan.

notifiable yang harus diberitahu.

notification pemberitahuan, pengumuman, pengisytiharan.

notify, to — memberitahu.

notion faham, pengertian buah fikiran.

notoriety nama buruk.

notorious terkenal dengan nama buruk.

notwithstanding biarpun, walaupun.

nought tidak apa-apa; to come to — gagal, menjadi sia-sia.

noun kata benda, nama benda.

nourish, to — (*feed*) memberi makan; (*support*) memeliharakan.

nourishment makanan, pemberian makan.

novel hikayat, ceritera, nobel.

novelette cerita pendek.

novelist pengarang cerita.

novelty sesuatu yang baharu.

November bulan November.

novice orang baharu.

now sekarang ini; adapun; from — on mulai sekarang.

nowadays sekarang, masa sekarang.

nowhere di mana-mana pun tidak.

nozzle moncong.

nuance perbezaan halus warna.

nubile yang dapat kahwin.

nuclear yang berkenaan dengan pusat atom.

nucleus inti, pusat, pokok.

nude telanjang.

nudge sentuh; to — menyentuh.

nugget setongkol emas; in nuggets berbuku.

nuisance susah, gangguan; (*person*) orang yang mengganggu orang lain.

null batal, tidak sah.

nullify, to — membatalkan.
numb kebas tidak berasa.
number (*total*) jumlah; (*tale*) bilangan; (*numerical figure*) angka, nombor; a — of beberapa.
numeral angka; yang menunjukkan angka, bilangan.
numerator pembilang.
numerical yang berkenaan dengan atau menunjukkan angka.
numerous banyak.
numismatic yang berkenaan dengan matawang.
numskull orang bodoh.
nun rahib perempuan.
nunnery tempat untuk rahib perempuan.
nuptial yang berkenaan dengan perkahwinan.
nurse pengasuh jururawat; to — merawat, memeliharakan.
nursery bilik anak-anak; (*for plants*) semaian.
nursing rawatan; — home rumah perawatan orang sakit.
nurture pemeliharaan; to — memeliharakan, mendidik.
nut I buah berkulit keras.
nut II (*for screw*) kunci sekeru.
nutmeg buah pala.
nutrient yang mengandung zat makan.
nutrition pemberian atau penerimaan makanan.
nutritious yang banyak mengandung zat makanan.
nutshell kulit keras salah satu buah.
nutty penuh dengan buah berkulit keras.
nuzzle, to — mencium-cium.
nylon nylon, sejenis kain.
nymph bidadari, peri; (*insect*) kepompong.

O

o, oh wah!
oaf orang bodoh, orang bebal.
oak pohon kayu oak.
oar dayung.
oarsman pendayung.
oasis tempat berair di tengah padang pasir, oasis.
oast tempat pengering tumbuhan.
oat sejenis gandum.
oatmeal tepung gandum.
oath sumpah; to take (swear) an — mengangkat sumpah.
obduracy kekerasan kepala.
obdurate keras kepala.
obedience ketaatan.
obedient taat.
obeisance sembah.
obelisk sejenis tiang batu yang ditegakkan orang sebagai peringatan.
obese gemuk, bayak.
obesity rupa gemuk.
obey, to — menurut.
obituary pemberitahu kematian salah seorang.
object I (*thing*) benda, barang; (*intention*) maksud, tujuan.
object II, to — berkeberatan, tidak suka akan.
objection bantahan, bangkangan.
objectionable tidak disukai.
objective objektif, yang berkenaan dengan hal nyata dan lahir; (*aim*) tujuan.
objectivity hal atau sifat objektif.
objector orang yang berkeberatan.
oblate papar, dempak pada hujungnya.
oblation ibadat kepada Allah.
obligate, to — mewajibkan, memaksakan.
obligation kewajiban, tanggungan.

obligatory wajib, perlu.

oblige, to — mewajibkan; **to be —d (to)** berterima-kasih akan.

obliging suka menolong orang, peramah.

oblique mereng, serong.

obliterate, to — menghapuskan, memadam.

obliteration penghapusan.

oblivion lupa; **to fall into** — tidak diingatkan lagi.

oblivious pelupa, tidak ingat akan.

oblong bujur.

obnoxious buruk, busuk.

oboe sejenis serunai.

obscene cabul, carut.

obscenity kecabulan, kekotoran.

obscure gelap, kabur, kelam-kabut.

obscurity kegelapan, kesamaran.

obsequies kebumikan.

obsequious merendahkan diri.

observable yang dapat ditinjau, kelihatan.

observance penetapan, peraturan ugama.

observant cergas, giat, tajam pemerhatian.

observation peninjauan, penjelasan.

observatory bilik penunggu bintang (dan sebagainya).

observe, to — (*heed*) memperhatikan; (*see*) melihat, meninjau; (*follow*) menurutkan.

observer peninjau, pengamat.

obsess, to — menggoda.

obsession godaan, fikiran yang selalu menggoda hati orang.

obsolescence hal sudah tua (atau lama).

obsolescent sudah menjadi tua (lama).

obsolete tidak dipakai lagi, sudah tua.

obstacle rintangan.

obstetrical yang berkenaan dengan kelahiran.

obstetrician ahli ilmu bidan.

obstetrics ilmu bidan.

obstinacy kekerasan hati, kedegilan.

obstinate tegar, keras hati, degil.

obstreperous huru-hara.

obstruct, to — mengalangi, merintang.

obstruction alangan, rintangan, sekatan.

obstructive yang merintangkan, yang merupakan rintangan.

obtain, to — mendapat, memperoleh.

obtrude, to — menonjolkan diri.

obtrusion penonjolan diri.

obtrusive yang menonjolkan diri.

obtuse (*blunt*) tumpul; (*stupid*) bodoh, bebal; (*at obtuse angle*) cakah.

obverse lebih besar pada puncaknya daripada pangkalnya.

obviate, to — menyingkirkan.

obvious ternyata, terang.

occasion (*juncture*) tempoh, peristiwa, ketika; (*cause*) sebab; (*having time to*) kesempatan; **to give** — menyebabkan.

occasional terkadang, sekali-sekali.

occident, the O— Barat, negeri Barat.

occlude, to — menutupi, merintangi.

occult ghaib, rahsia.

occultism ilmu ghaib.

occupant penduduk rumah (tanah dan sebagainya).

occupation pendudukan, penempatan.

occupier orang yang menduduki rumah atau tanah.

occupy, to — menduduki, berumah.

occur, to — terjadi, berlaku.

occurrence kejadian, peristiwa.

ocean lautan, samudera.

oceanic yang berkenaan dengan atau seperti lautan.

ochre warna kuning tua.

o'clock jam; **seven** — pukul tujuh.

oct—, octa—, octo— awalan kata yang ertinya: delapan.

octagon segidelapan.

octave oktab.

octavo ukuran sehelai kertas atau buku.

October bulan Oktober.

octogenarian orang yang berumur 80 tahun.

octopus ikan kurita, doyak.

oculist doktor mata.

odd ganjil, ajaib; — **jobs** pekerjaan tidak tetap.

oddity sesuatu (atau seorang) yang ganjil.

oddments barang lebihan, sisa-sisa.

odds selisih, perbezaan.

ode sejenis nyanyian.

odious yang membencikan.

odium kebencian, cacat.

odour bau; bau harum.

Odyssey nama syair Yunani purbakala yang memerikan segala hal-ahwal suatu pelayaran.

oesophagus kerongkongan.

of (*from*) dari, daripada; (*about*) akan, mengenai; (*among*) di antara.

off (*far*) jauh; (*go*) pergi, keluar, di luar; (*broken*) putus.

offal sisa-sisa, lebihan.

off day hari kelepasan.

offence (*wrong*) kesalahan; (*sin*) dosa.

offend, to — bersalah, melanggar.

offensive penyerangan, penyerbuan.

offer penawaran, tawaran; **to** — memberi.

offering persembahan.

offhand dengan tidak diperiksa lagi.

office jabatan, pejabat, opis.

officer pegawai negeri; opsir.

official rasmi, resmi.

officialdom kaum pegawai.

officiate, to — melakukan (upacara ugama).

officious suka bercampurtangan.

offing laut yang tertampak jauh dari pantai.

offish berkelakuan kurang ramah-tamah.

off-licence izin menjual minuman keras tetapi minuman itu tidak boleh diminum pada tempat itu.

off-print cetakan tambahan.

offset (*compensation etc*) pengganti kerugian; (*print*) sejenis cetakan.

offshoot cabang.

offspring anak, anak cucu, turunan.

often kerap kali, berkalikali.

ogle kerling; **to** — main mata, mengerling.

ogre bota, gergasi, raksasa.

oil minyak.

oilcloth sejenis kain minyak.

oil colour cat minyak.

oil painting lukisan cat minyak.

oil palm kelapa sawit, kelapa bali.

oilskin sejenis kain minyak.

oily berminyak; (*unctuous*) bermanis-manis.

ointment palit, sapu.

O.K., okay baiklah.

okra sejenis tumbuhan.

old (*aged*) tua; (*ancient*) purba; (*former*) lama; (*past*) dulu.

—old akhiran kata yang ertinya: seperti, berupa.

olden dulu, dahulukala.

old-fashioned kolot kuno.

old-world seperti pada tempoh dulukala.

oleander sejenis pohon bunga.

oleo— awalan kata yang ertinya: minyak.

olfactory yang berkenaan dengan penghiduan bau.

oligarchy pemerintah yang terdiri daripada beberapa orang sahaja.

olive buah zaitun; — oil minyak zaitun.

olympiad waktu empat tahun.

Olympian salah satu dewadewi di gunung mahameru Olympos.

Olympic yang berkenaan dengan pertandingan sukan yang diadakan sekali tiaptiap empat tahun.

omega huruf terakhir abjad Yunani.

omelet(te) telur dadar.

omen tanda, alamat sesuatu akan terjadi, sempena.

ominous celaka sial.

omission hal tidak termasuk, penghilangan.

omit, to — tidak memasukkan.

omni- awalan kata yang ertinya: semua.

omnibus (*bus*) kereta bas; (*miscellaneous contents*) yang mengandungi bermacammacam perkara.

omnipotence kudrat Allah, maha kuasa.

omnipotent maha kuasa.

omnipresent yang hadir di mana-mana.

omniscient yang tahu akan segala hal.

omnivorous yang makan segala hal haiwan muserba.

on di atas, pada, di; akan; (*put on*) mengenai; — *fire* terbakar.

once sekali; (*formerly*) dulu.

oncoming yang mendekati, yang akan datang.

one satu, esa.

one-eyed matanya hanya satu, cemeh.

onerous berat, menyusahkan.

oneself diri sendiri.

one-sided berat sebelah.

one-time dulu, bekas.

one-way, — *street* jalan untuk lalulintas dari satu jurusan sahaja, jalan sehala.

onion bawang.

only hanya sahaja, cuma.

onomatopoeia kata-bunyi.

onset (*assault*) serangan, serbuan, penyerbuan.

onslaught serangan hebat.

onto = **on to** ke tempat, sedia.

onus beban, kewajiban.

onward(s) maju, kemuka.

onyx sejenis batu berwarna.

ooze lumpur.

opal batu baiduri.

opaque tidak terang, kabur, legap.

open terbuka; to — membuka.

open-handed murah hati.

open-hearted jujur.

opening pembukaan; permulaan.

openly dengan jujur, terus terang.

open-minded berpandangan luas.

opera opera, bangsawan, sandiwara.

operate, to — (*work*) berlaku, berjalan; (*be successful*) berhasil.

operatic berkenaan dengan atau seperti opera.

operation belah, bedah, cara berjalan, bekerja.

operative berlaku, yang berjalan.

operator orang yang menjalankan; *telephone* — pelayan talipon.

operetta opera pendek (biasanya gembira).

ophthalmic yang berkenaan dengan mata, kena penyakit mata.

opiate yang mengandung madat.

opinion pendapat, pendirian, perasaan.

opium madat, candu.

opossum sejenis tupai.

opponent yang melawan, lawan, penentang.

opportune baik, layak, pada tempatnya.

opportunity kesempatan, peluang baik.

oppose, to — melawan; menentang.

opposite bertentangan; (*oppose*) lawan.

opposition pertentangan, perlawanan, pembangkang.

oppress, to — menekan, mengempit, menindih, menganiayai.

oppression himpitan, penindasan.

oppressive terhimpit, sesak.

opprobrious menghina, mengejikan.

opprobrium kekejian; kehinaan.

optic, optical yang berkenaan dengan mata atau penglihatan.

optician pembuat atau penjual cermin mata dan sebagainya.

optimism faham optimis.

optimum yang terbaik.

option pilihan, kebebasan memilih.

opulence kekayaan, kemewahan.

opulent kaya, mewah.

opus karangan muzik.

or atau.

oracle tempat orang Yunani dahulukala meminta nasihat dewata.

oral yang berkenaan dengan mulut, lisan.

orange sejenis limau manis.

orangeade air limau.

orang–outang orang hutan, mawas.

oration ucapan, percakapan.

orator orang yang berucap.

oratorio sejenis karangan muzik dengan nyanyi-nyanyian.

oratory tempat sembahyang.

orb bulatan, bola dunia.

orbit (*of planet*) peredaran; (*course, beat*) jalan berkeliling.

orc sejenis ikan paus.

orchard kebun buah-buahan, dusun.

orchestra pancaragam.

orchestral yang berkenaan dengan pancaragam.

orchestrate, to — mengarang muzik untuk pancaragam.

orchid bunga anggerik.

ordain, to — mengangkat jadi padri.

ordeal percubaan yang berat.

order pangkat, tingkat; kelas, tertib.

order book buku pesanan.

order form borang untuk memesan barang.

orderly teratur, tertib; (*page*) budak kundang.

ordinal turutan.

ordinance peraturan, undang-undang.

ordinarily biasanya.

ordinary biasa, lazim; makanan yang diadakan dalam kedai atas harga dan waktu tetap.

ordination peraturan, pemerintahan.

ordnance (*cannon*) meriam; (*military stores*) jawatan yang menyelenggarakan perlengkapan askar.

ore bijih.

organ (*instrument*) alat; (*musical instrument*) sejenis alat muzik.

organdie sejenis kain kasa.

organic organik, yang berkenaan dengan dasar sesuatu.

organism susunan teratur yang terdiri atas bahagian tersendiri.

organist pemain organ.

organization urusan, penyelenggaraan; (a body) lembaga, pertubuhan.

organize, to — mengurus, mengatur, menyusun.

orgasm hawa nafsu, syahwat.

orgy sukaria yang melampaui batas.

oriel anjung pada tingkat atas sebuah rumah.

orient, the O— sebelah Timur, negeri Timur.

oriental dari Timur, yang berkenaan dengan Timur.

orientate, to — menempatkan atau menetapkan tempatnya menurut pedoman.

orientation penetapan tempat atau pendirian, penyesuaian, orientasi.

origin asal, asal-usul, pangkal, permulaan.

original asli, yang bermula, asal.

originality keaslian; (of conduct) sifat tabiat lain dari biasa.

originate, to — (initiate) mulai, terbit; (found) mendirikan; (create) mengadakan.

ornament perhiasan.

ornamental yang menghiasi, yang merupakan perhiasan.

ornate penuh perhiasan.

ornith(o)— awalan kata yang ertinya: burung.

ornithology kaji burung.

orphan anak piatu, anak yatim.

orphanage rumah anak yatim.

orth(o)— awalan kata yang ertinya: lurus.

orthodox berpendirian tetap dan patut menurut adat.

orthodoxy sifat, keadaan orthodox.

orthography ejaan baik.

orthopaedic yang berkenaan dengan ilmu salah bentuk.

oscillate, to — bergoyang berayun-ayun.

oscillation goyang, getar, ayun.

osier cabang salah satu pohon yang dipakai untuk anyaman.

osprey sejenis helang.

ossify, to — menjadi tulang.

ostensible rupa-rupanya, pura-pura.

ostentation hal menunjukkan kekayaannya.

ostentatious(ly) dengan bermegah-megah.

osteo— awalan kata yang ertinya: tulang.

ostracize, to — membuang dari pergaulan masyarakat.

ostrich burung unta, burung kasawari.

other lain; — than lain daripada.

otherwise lain, dalam hal lain, secara lain.

otter anjing air, berangberang.

ottoman bangku berbantal yang tidak ada sandarannya.

ouch aduh.

ought, — to patut, harus, seharusnya.

ounce timbangan ounce.

our kepunyaan kita.

ours kepunyaan kita.

ourselves kita sendiri.

oust, to — mengenyahkan, menghalaukan.

out keluar, di luar; (go) pergi.

out— awalan kata yang bererti: keluar, di luar.

outbalance, to — lebih berat, melebihi.

outbid, to — menawar lebih mahal.

outbreak (of war) pecah peperangan.

outbuilding rumah turutan.

outburst (*explosion*) letusan.

outcast orang yang dibuang daripada pergaulan masyarakat.

outclass, to — termasuk golongan lebih baik.

outcome (*result*) akibat; (*profit*) hasil.

outcry teriakan kerana marah.

out—distance, to — berjalan lebih cepat, melumbai.

outdo, to — melebihi.

outdoor di luar rumah.

outer luar, lahir.

outermost yang di sebelah luar sekali.

outfit kelengkapan, perlengkapan.

outfitter penjual segala rupa kelengkapan.

outgoing yang keluar, pergi; (*expenses*) —s belanja.

outgrow, to — tumbuh (atau menjadi besar) lebih cepat.

outing temasya, berjalan untuk menghiburkan diri.

outlandish asing, luar negeri.

outlast, to — tinggal lebih lama daripada.

outlaw orang terbuang yang tidak terkawal oleh hukum pemerintah.

outlay belanja, perbelanjaan.

outlet jalan keluar.

outline garis yang jadi sempadan salah satu bentuk.

outlive, to — hidup lebih lama.

outlook pandangan, tinjauan.

outlying jauh, terpencil.

outmanœuvre, to — melebihi dengan siasat baik.

outmoded tidak berbanding dengan masa.

outnumber, to — jumlahnya lebih besar.

outpatient orang sakit yang datang ke rumahsakit untuk ambil ubat sahaja bukan tinggal di sana.

outpost pasukan pengawal jauh daripada pasukan ibu.

outpour(ing) tumpah, curah.

output jumlah yang dihasilkan.

outrage (*offence*) pelanggaran; (*evil*) perbuatan jahat.

outrageous (*extremely*) terlalu; (*immoderate*) yang melampau batas; (*very evil*) terlampau jahat, terlampau cabul.

outrigger kapal yang berbatang bingkai.

outright semua sekali, sekaligus.

outrival, to — melebihi dalam persaingan.

outrun, to — berlari lebih cepat.

outset permulaan, awal.

outshine, to — sinar (cahaya) nya lebih terang.

outside luar, sebelah luar.

outsider orang luar, orang yang bukan dalam lengkongan.

outskirts bahagian luar.

outspoken jujur, terus terang.

outstanding terkemuka.

outstay, to — tinggal lebih lama.

outstretched terhulur.

outstrip, to — berlari lebih cepat.

outward di luar, luaran, lahir; —bound kapal yang keluar dari pelabuhan asalnya.

outwear, to — memakai sampai jejas dan usang.

outwit, to — menang kerana lebih cerdik.

outworn sudah tidak dipakai lagi, usang.

oval bulat bujur, bujur telur.

ovary indung telur, obari.

ovation sambutan meriah, tepuk sorak.

oven dapur, sabak.

over (*above*) di atas, ke atas; (*over there*) ke sana; di sana; (*too*) terlalu, terlampau.

over—awalan kata yang ertinya:

luaran, atas, melebihi, terlebih.

overabundant berlimpah-
limpah, terlalu banyak.

overactive terlalu giat.

overall(s) pakaian kerja.

overanxious terlalu khuatir.

overawe, to — sangat mempengaruhi sehingga ditaati.

overbalance, to — (lose
balance) hilang keseimbangan;
(over weight) lebih berat daripada.

overbear, to — (exceed)
melebihi.

overcast berawan, redup,
mendung.

overcharge, to — melebih-
lebihi, minta harga yang
terlalu mahal.

overcoat baju luar.

overcome, to — mengatasi.

overcrowd, to — penuh
sesak, memenuhi sarat-sarat.

overdo, to — melampau; (in
cooking) terlalu lama dimasak.

overdraft mengeluarkan cek
harganya lebih daripada modal yang tersimpan dalam
Bank itu.

overdraw, to — menulis cek
sejumlah lebih besar daripada
modal dalam Bank.

overdress, to — berpakaian
terlalu indah-indah.

overdue terlambat.

overeat, to — makan terlalu
banyak.

overestimate, to — menilai
(menaksir) terlalu tinggi.

overflow, to — melempah,
meluap, sebak.

overgrown (of scrub) semak;
(of youths) bagur.

overhang bergantung di atas.

overhaul membuka dan memperbaiki apa yang kurang
baik.

overhead di atas, di udara.

overhear, to — terdengar,
kebetulan mendengar.

overjoyed sangat riang.

overland melalui daratan.

overlap, to — menutupi
sebahagian, melampau se-
·bahagian.

overleaf pada sebalik halaman buku.

overloaded (of ship) sarat.

overlook, to — (see from
above) memandang dari atas;
(forget) lupa.

overlord maharaja, tuan besar.

overnight malam yang sudah lalu; (by night) pada
malam.

overpower, to — menewaskan, menggagahi.

overreach, to — (trick) memperdayakan.

overrule, to — membatalkan,
mengatasi.

overrun, to — (of crowds)
mengerumuni; (defeat) me-
ngalahkan.

overseas di seberang laut.

oversee, to — mengawasi.

overseer pengawas, mandur
tandil.

overshadow, to — mene-
duhi, meredupkan menaungi.

oversight kekhilafan, kesalahan.

oversleep, to — kesiangan,
tidur terlalu lama.

overstate, to — menyatakan
dengan berlebih-lebihan.

overstay, to — tinggal lebih
lama.

overt nyata, terang, terbuka.

overtake, to — (catch up)
mendapatkan; (pass) memo-
tong akan.

overthrow (destruction) roboh; (defeat) pengalahan; (removal) pembuangan.

overtime lebih masa.

overtone nada tambahan.

overture lagu muzik yang
dimainkan pada permulaan
opera dan sebagainya.

overweight berat yang melebihi; (of authority) pengaruh yang lebih besar.

overwhelm, to — meliputi.

overwork pekerjaan yang terlampau berat.

overwrought gugup dan lelah.

ovoid hal yang menyerupai telur.

ovum telur (ilmu hayat), obam.

owe, to — berhutang; (for a kindness) berhutang budi.

owing, — to — berhubung dengan, oleh kerana.

owl burung hantu.

owlet anak burung hantu.

own sendiri, kepunyaannya sendiri.

owner pemilik, tuanpunya.

ownerless tidak ada pemilik, tidak yang mempunyainya.

ownership hak milik.

ox lembu, sapi.

oxide oksid.

oxygen zat asam, zat pembakar, oksijan.

oyster tiram.

ozone ozon.

P

pace langkah; (gait) cara atau gaya berjalan.

pacemaker pelari dan lainlain yang berjalan di hadapan sambil pelari lain mencuba hendak menyamai kecepatannya.

pacific suka damai; **the P—** (Ocean) Pasifik, Lautan Teduh.

pacification perdamaian, hal mendamaikan.

pacifism faham aman damai, faham bahawa semua peperangan harus dihapuskan.

pacifist orang yang berpegang kepada faham aman damai.

pacify, to — mendamaikan.

pack (bundle) bungkusan, pak; (crowd) kumpulan; (of dogs etc) sekawan anjing (serigala dan sebagainya).

package bungkusan, pak; to — membuat bungkusan.

packer orang (atau alat) pembungkus.

packet bungkusan kecil; — boat kapal mil.

packhorse kuda beban.

packing pembungkusan, bungkusan.

pact persetujuan, perjanjian.

pad alas, bantal; (layer) lapisan.

padding bahan pengisi pakaian, lapisan.

paddle dayung, kayuh, pengayuh.

paddle wheel kincir air.

paddock halaman atau lapangan untuk melatih kuda.

paddy padi.

padlock kunci mangga.

padre padri tentera.

pagan orang yang tidak termasuk ugama rasmi, orang jahil.

paganism jahiliah.

page I bidunda.

page II halaman, mukasurat; to — memberi bernombor.

pageant pertunjukan atau perarakan indah-indah.

pageantry pertunjukan mewah.

pagoda kuil yang berupa seperti menara.

pah cehi

pail baldi.

pain sakit, pedih kesakitan.

painful sakit; (of work) susah.

painless tidak berasa sakit.

painstaking sangat rajin.

paint cat; to — mengecat.

painter (artist) pelukis; (decorator) tukang cat.

painting lukisan, melukis gambar.

pair pasang; (married couple) kelamin.

pajamas see **pyjamas.**

pal (col) teman, kawan.

palace istana, mahligai.

palaeo–, paleo– awalan kata yang ertinya: lama, dahulu, tua.

palaeontology ilmu pengetahuan hal masa yang lampau.

palanquin, palankeen tandu, kereta pelangkin.

palatable lazat, sedap.

palate langit-langit, tekak; (sense of taste) rasa mulut.

palatial seperti atau berkenaan dengan istana.

palaver percakapan panjang lebar, mesyuarat.

pale I (wan) pucat; (faded) pudar.

pale II (stake) sula.

paleness rupa pucat.

palette papan pencampur cat yang dipakai oleh pelukis.

paling pagar (yang terdiri atas pancang).

palish sedikit pucat.

pall kain tutup untuk peti atau usungan mayat.

pallet tempat tidur daripada jerami.

palliative sesuatu yang meringankan.

pallid pucat.

pallor rupa pucat, pucat.

palm I palma; (as symbol of victory) daun palma sebagai tanda kemenangan.

palm II (of hand) pelempap, tapak tangan.

palmist tukang ramal daripada retak tangan.

palm oil minyak daripada salah satu pohon palma, minyak kelapa sawit.

palm sugar gula kabung, gula enau.

palpable yang dapat diraba, berwujud.

palpitate, to — berdebar-debar, gementar.

palpitation hal berdebar, hal gementar.

palsy kebas, lumpuh.

paltry tidak berharga, hina.

paludal yang berkenaan dengan paya.

pampas padang rumput yang luas di Amerika Selatan.

pamper, to — memanjakan.

pamphlet surat siaran, buku sebaran, risalat.

pan panci, kuali, periuk, belanga.

pan– awalan kata yang ertinya: seluruh.

panacea ubat untuk segala penyakit.

Panama, — hat topi pandan.

pancake sejenis kuih dadar.

pancreas pankreas, hati.

panda sejenis binatang yang rupanya seperti beruang kecil.

pandemic yang menjalar pada seluruh negeri atau dunia.

pandemonium (hall of evil spirits) tempat kediaman semua iblis; (uproar) haru-hara.

pander, to — menjadi kakitangan dalam hal jahat atau hawa nafsu.

pane kaca jendela.

panegyric puji-pujian, yang memuji-muji.

panel papan tipis di tengah pintu (dan sebagainya).

pang sakit pedih, kepedihan.

panic kegemparan gugup, bingung.

panicky bingung, tergugup, gempar.

pannier sejenis keranjang.

panoply alat senjata yang lengkap.

panorama pemandangan alam.

pansy sejenis bunga.

pant ngap-ngap, nafas yang ngengap.

pantaloon, —s sejenis seluar panjang.

pantheism pemujaan Tuhan dalam segala hal yang ada di dunia.

pantheon kuil untuk pemujaan semua dewata.

panther harimau kumbang.

panties seluar anak atau perempuan.

pantomime pertunjukan sandiwara yang tidak ada tutur kata atau nyanyiannya.

pantry bilik penyimpan alat makan dan makanan.

pants seluar, ceiana, seluar dalam.

papa ayah.

papacy kedudukan Pope.

papal yang berkenaan dengan Pope atau jabatannya.

papaw betik, kepaya, papaya.

paper kertas; (*newspaper*) harian, suratkhabar.

papist nama ejekan orang berugama Katolik.

paprika sejenis lada.

papyrus sejenis lontar.

par, to put on a — **(with)** menyamaratakan, menyerupakan; **on a** — **(with)** sama rata.

parable ibarat, perumpamaan, cerita tamsilan.

parabola parabola.

parachute payung untuk mendarat setelah menerjunkan diri daripada kapalterbang.

parachutist soldadu berpayung terjun.

parade, to — berbaris; (*display*) mempertunjukkan dengan bangga.

paradise syurga; **bird of** — burung cenderawasih.

paradox sesuatu yang rupanya mustahil tetapi sebetulnya memang benar, lawan asas.

paradoxical perkara yang

betul tetapi rupanya sahaja mustahil.

paraffin parafin; — **oil** minyak tanah.

paragon umpama, tuladan yang utama.

paragraph ceraian, perenggan, fasal pasal dalam buku atau suratkhabar.

parakeet, paroquet burung bayan.

parallel sejejar, selari; — **of** latitude garisan lintang.

parallelism keadaan sejajar, pergandingan.

parallelogram rajah segi empat selari.

paralyse, to — melumpuhkan.

paralysis kebas, layuh, kelumpuhan.

paralytic orang yang kebas, orang yang lumpuh.

paramount utama, tertinggi, terbesar, mulia.

paranoia keadaan gila.

parapet tembok rendah di tepi jambatan (di atas atap rumah dan sebagainya).

paraphernalia segala alat perkakas kepunyaan seseorang; barang-barang.

paraphrase ubahan (salah satu fasal dan sebagainya) dengan kata lain; uraikata; — menjelaskan sesuatu dengan kata-kata sendiri.

parasite parasit; (*mistletoe*) pokok dedalu.

parasol payung (untuk matahari).

paratroops tentera berpayung terjun.

parboil, to — memasak setengah masak; — **rice** beras keling.

parcel bungkusan.

parch, to — menjadi kering dan panas; (*roast*) memanggang.

parchment kulit kambing

yang dipakai jadi kertas tulis dan sebagainya.

pardon ampun, maaf; **I beg your** — maaf.

pardonable yang dapat dimaafkan.

pare, to — (*cut*) memotong; (*lop*) menutuh; (*peel*) mengupas.

parent ayah, ibu; (*origin*) asal; —s ibubapa.

parentage keturunan, asalusul.

parental berkenaan dengan ibubapa.

parenthesis (*brackets*) tanda kandung; kata atau kalimat yang diberi bertanda kandung.

parenthetic(al) yang disisipkan.

pariah paria, bangsa rendah.

parish bahagian negara yang mempunyai gereja sendiri.

Parisian penduduk bandar Paris.

parity persamaan.

park kebun besar, taman.

parley muafakat, mesyuarat; to — bermesyuarat.

parliament parlimen.

parliamentarian yang berkenaan dengan parlimen.

parliamentary yang berkenaan dengan atau menurut adat parlimen.

parlour bilik duduk.

parochial yang berkenaan dengan parish; (*narrow*) picik.

parody ejekan, olok-olok.

parole perjanjian bahawa seorang tawanan tidak akan melarikan diri.

paroquet see **parakeet.**

paroxysm (*fit*) sawan; (*madness*) kegila-gilaan.

parquet lantai yang terdiri daripada potongan kayu kecil-kecil.

parricide pembunuhan ayah.

parrot burung nuri, burung kakatua.

parry, to — menangkis.

parse, to — menghuraikan kalimat.

parsimonious hemat dan cermat, lokek.

parsnip sejenis ubi.

parson pendita, padri.

parsonage rumah pendita.

part bahagian separuh.

partake, to — mengambil bahagian, turut serta.

partial berat sebelah.

partiality memihak.

participate, to — menyekutui, turut serta, mengambil bahagian.

participation pesertaan, hal mengambil bahagian.

participator pengikut, peserta.

particle butir, biji, hujungan.

parti-coloured belang, anekawarna.

particular istimewa, khusus.

particularize, to — menyebut satu demi satu.

parting (*part, put aside*) perpisahan; (*in hair*) belahan (penceraian) pada rambut.

partisan orang yang mengikut (menganut) salah satu gerakan.

partition sekatan, petak; **to** — off menyekat.

partly sebahagian.

partner (*in trade*) rakan, sekutu; (*in marriage*) jodoh.

partnership persekutuan, persyarikatan.

partridge sejenis ayam hutan.

party (*group etc*) rombongan, parti, pihak.

parvenu orang yang seumpama pipit hendak menjadi enggang.

pass (*in exam*) hal lulus dalam ujian; (*approval*) izin jalan; **to come to** — berlaku; **to** — (*proceed*) berjalan; (*go by*) lalu.

passable boleh juga, baik juga.

passage jalan terus, terusan, selat, tembusan; (*voyage*) pelayaran.

passenger penumpang, penambang.

passer—by orang yang lalu lalang.

passing sepintas lalu; (*death*) kematian.

passion asmara, kegairahan, dendam, hawa nafsu.

passionate bernafsu, keburu nafsu.

passionflower sejenis bunga.

passive (*suffering*) menderita; (*unresisting*) tidak melawan, pasif.

Passover salah satu perayaan orang Yahudi.

passport surat paspot.

password semboyan.

past lalu, lewat, sudah; (*past time*) masa yang lalu.

paste perekat; to — tampal.

pasteboard kertas tebal.

pastel sejenis kapur berwarna yang dipakai untuk menggambar; gambar yang dilukis dengan kapur berwarna itu.

pasteurize, to — membunuh segala kuman penyakit.

pastille sejenis ubat batuk.

pastime penghiburan, permainan.

pastor pendita, padri.

pastoral yang berkenaan dengan gembala dan kehidupan dusun.

pastry adunan, kuih; —cook pembuat dan penjual kuih.

pasture perumputan, padang rumput; to — menggembalakan, makan rumput.

pasty —faced pucat mukanya.

pat (*clap*) tepuk tangan; (*small lump*) setepek.

patch tampal, tampung; (*plot*) sebidang tanah.

patchouli minyak nilam.

patchwork tampalan.

patchy bertampal.

pate kepala.

patella tempurung lutut.

patent nyata, terang; protected by — terjamin, terlindung, khas.

patentee pemegang paten.

paternal yang berkenaan dengan ayah, seperti seorang ayah.

paternity ayah, kedudukan ayah.

path jalan, lorong.

pathetic yang menerbitkan belas kasihan.

pathfinder perintis jalan.

patho— awalan kata yang ertinya: sakit, penyakit.

pathological yang berkenaan dengan penyakit.

pathology ilmu penyakit.

pathos sifat yang menerbitkan belas kasihan.

pathway jalan kecil, lorong.

patience sabar, kesabaran.

patient I (*sick person*) orang sakit, penderita.

patient II sabar.

patois loghat daerah.

patriarch ayah dan kepala keluarga, orang tua.

patriarchy aturan masyarakat yang berdasarkan ayah sebagai kepala keluarga.

patrician orang bangsawan zaman Rumawi dahulukala, berbangsa.

patricide pembunuhan ayahnya.

patrimony waris dari keturunan ayah.

patriot orang yang sangat cinta kepada tanahairnya, bumiputera.

patriotic sangat cinta kepada tanahairnya.

patrol pengawalan, peronda.

patron pelindung, penaung, penunjang.

patronage penaungan, pertolongan.

patronize, to — menaung, menolong.

patronymic nama ayah atau keturunan ayah.

patter (*speak quickly*) percakapan cepat; bahasa golongan istimewa.

pattern (*example*) contoh, umpama; (*on cloth*) corak.

paunch perut gendut; (*bird's crop*) tembolok.

pauper orang miskin, papa.

pauperism keadaan rakyat miskin, kepapaan.

pause jeda, sela; **to** — berhenti, menanti.

pave, to — mengalasi, membubuh batu.

pavement batu ubin pada tepi jalan, kakilima.

pavilion (*tent*) khemah besar; (*hall etc*) balai.

paw cakar, kaki; **to** — mencakar, menggeragas.

pawn (*at chess*) bidak; **to** — menggadaikan.

pawnbroker pajak gadai.

pawnshop rumah gadai, pajak gadai.

pay pembayaran, gaji, upah; **to** — membayar, memberi.

payable yang dapat atau harus dibayar.

payday hari pembayaran, hari gaji.

payee si penerima wang.

paymaster pembayar (gaji dan sebagainya).

payment pembayaran.

pay office pejabat pembayaran wang.

pea kacang.

peace (*after strife*) perdamaian; (*national*) aman.

peaceful damai, sejahtera.

peach I buah persik.

peach II, (*sl*) **to** — (*inform against*) mengadukan.

peacock burung merak.

peahen burung merak betina.

peak I hujung, puncak.

peak II, to — berkurang kuat; —ed kurus kering mukanya.

peal (*of bell*) bunyi loceng; (*laughter*) bunyi tertawa gelak-gelak.

peanut kacang tanah, kacang goreng.

pear buah per.

pearl mutiara, mutu; mother-of- — gewang, indung mutiara.

peasant orang tani, petani.

pease kacang.

peat sejenis tanah gambut subur yang digunakan sebagai bahan pembakar.

pebble batu kerikil, pasir kasar.

peck patuk, cotok; **to** — mencotok, mematuk.

pecker, wood— burung belatuk.

peckish lapar.

pectoral yang berkenaan dengan dada.

peculiar (*special*) khas, khusus; (*odd*) ganjil, pelek.

peculiarity (*special property of drugs etc*) khasiat; hal yang ajaib, ganjil, pelek.

peculiarly terkhusus, pada khususnya.

pecuniary yang berkenaan dengan wang, kewangan.

pedagogue ahli didik, ahli latih.

pedal (*foot lever etc*) pemijak kaki, pedal, injak-injak, kayuh.

pedant orang yang terlampau mementingkan pengetahuan dan peraturan.

pedantic yang terlampau mementingkan peraturan dan pengetahuan.

peddle, to — (*hawk*) berjaja, menjaja, menggalas.

pedestal kaki, alas, lapik.

pedestrian orang yang berjalan kaki.

pedigree asal usul, susur galur, keturunan.

pedlar penjaja penggalas.

peek, to — (*peep*) mengintip, mengintai.

peel kulit; to — mengupas.

peep (*noise*) bunyi kicap-kicau; (*pry*) intipan, intai.

pephole lubang kecil untuk mengintai.

peep show pertunjukan gambar-gambar yang boleh diintai melalui lubang kecil.

peer I orang bangsawan di negeri Inggeris.

peer II, to — melihat dengan tajam.

peerage kaum bangsawan.

peerless tidak berbanding, tidak ada taranya.

peeved (*col*) gusar.

peevish terharu, runsing.

peg pasak, paku; to — memasak.

pejorative kata yang merendahkan.

pelargonium sejenis bunga.

pelican burung undan.

pellet butir, gintil.

pell-mell haru-biru, porak-peranda.

pellucid terang cuaca, jernih.

pelt I kulit binatang.

pelt II, to — melempar, melontar.

pelvis panggul.

pemmican sejenis daging dendeng.

pen I pena, kalam; to — menulis, mengarang.

pen II (*for cattle*) kandang lembu.

penal yang berkenaan dengan hukuman; — laws undang-undang jenayat.

penalize, to — memutuskan bahawa sesuatu akan dihukum.

penalty hukuman, denda.

penance tapa, pertapaan, penebusan dosa.

penchant kecenderungan.

pencil pensel.

pendant (*for ear*) anting-anting.

pending (*not settled*) belum diputuskan; (*during*) seraya, sambil.

pendulous tergantung, berayun-ayun.

pendulum buaian, batu jam.

penetrate, to — (into) membual, menerusi

penetrating terus-menerus.

penetration penembusan.

penguin sejenis burung laut di kutub selatan.

penholder batang pena.

penicillin ubat penicillin.

peninsula semenanjung.

peninsular yang berkenaan dengan atau seperti semenanjung.

penis zakar, butuh.

penitence sesal, kesesalan.

penitent sesal hati, bertobat.

penknife pisau kecil, pisau lipat.

penman pengarang.

penmanship (*writing*) gaya menulis; (*authorship*) gaya mengarang.

pen name nama samaran, nama pena.

pennant panji-panji, gada-gada.

penniless miskin, tidak mempunyai wang.

penny matawang Inggeris.

penology pengetahuan tentang hukuman penjara dan lain hukuman.

pension pencen, sara; to — memberi pencen.

pensionable yang berhak mendapat pencen, yang berpencen.

pensioner orang yang menerima pencen.

pensive termenung.

penta — awalan kata yang ertinya: lima.

pentagon segilima.

pentathlon aduan lima.

penthouse sengkuap.

pent(-up) dikurungkan.

penultimate yang kedua daripada akhir.

penurious (*poor*) miskin, papa; (*mean*) kikir.

penury kemiskinan, kepapaan.

peon pelayan, pekerja.

people rakyat, orang, bangsa, penduduk.

pep kegiatan, semangat.

pepper lada; red — cabai.

peppermint permen, poho.

peppery penuh lada; (*pungent*) pedas.

peptic yang berkenaan dengan pencernaan.

per- awalan kata atau kata hadapan yang ertinya: terusmenerus, seluruhnya.

perambulate, to — berjalan berkeliling.

perambulator, *abbr* **pram** kereta pendorong anak kecil.

perceive, to — (*see*) melihat; (*feel*) merasa; (*understand*) mengerti.

per cent peratus.

percentage persen, peratus.

perceptible yang terlihat, berwujud.

perception penglihatan, harus melihat, pengamatan.

perceptive mudah melihat, mudah mengerti.

perch I sejenis ikan.

perch II, to — hinggap, bertenggek.

perchance barangkali.

percipient orang yang melihat atau merasa.

percolate, to — tiris, menapis.

percolator alat penapis kopi.

percussion (*striking*) pemukulan; (*drumming*) penabuhan, genderang.

perdition kebinasaan, keruntuhan.

peregrination perjalanan berkeliling.

peremptory yang tetap dan pesti, yang tidak dapat diubahkan lagi.

perennial bertahun-tahun lamanya; (*permanent*) kekal, abadi.

perfect sempurna.

perfection sempurna, penyempurnaan.

perfectionist orang yang mementingkan harus mencapai kesempurnaan.

perfidious berkhianat.

perfidy khianat.

perforate, to — membuat lubang, menembus.

perforation hal melubangkan.

perform, to — menjalankan, melaksanakan.

performance pekerjaan, perbuatan, pertunjukan.

perfume minyak wangi, baubauan.

perfunctory sepintas lalu tidak bersungguh-sungguh.

perhaps barangkali, kalaukalau.

peri- awalan kata yangertinya: keliling.

peril bahaya; in — of one's life dalam bahaya maut.

perilous berbahaya.

perimeter sekeliling, lengkaran, lengkong.

period zaman, kala, masa ketika; (*full stop*) noktah.

periodic berkala.

periodical berkala; (*journal*) surat berkala, majalah.

periphery garis keliling, lengkaran.

periphrasis cara bercakap dengan panjang lebar.

periphrastic dengan panjang lebar.

periscope sejenis teropong dengannya orang yang didalam laut atau lubang dapat melihat hal yang di atas muka air atau bumi.

perish, to — mati, tewas, binasakan.

perishable yang boleh rosak, yang lekas menjadi busuk.

perisher (sl) orang celaka.

periwinkle (flower) sejenis tumbuhan; (shellfish) sarang unam.

perjure, to — o.s. bersumpah bohong.

perjurer orang yang bersumpah bohong.

perjury sumpah bohong.

perk, to — menegakkan kepala.

perky sombong, besar mulut.

permanence, permanency kekekalan, keadaan tetap.

permanent tetap, kekal; — wave, perm keriting rambut (yang tahan lebih kurang enam bulan).

permeate, to — menyerap.

permeation penyerapan.

permissible yang boleh diperkenankan.

permission izin, kebenaran.

permit izin, surat lesen.

permutation pengubahan susunan sesuatu.

permute, to — mengubahkan turutannya.

pernicious jahat, celaka, yang mencelakakan.

pernickety sangat teliti, sukar disenangkan.

peroration ucapan akhiran.

perpendicular tegak, betul.

perpetrate, to — (do something bad) melakukan sesuatu yang tidak baik.

perpetration hal melakukan sesuatu yang tidak baik.

perpetual abadi, kekal.

perpetuate, to — mengekalkan.

perpetuity kekekalan.

perplex, to — membingungkan, mengelirukan.

perplexity kebingungan, kekusutan.

perquisite pendapatan sambilan.

persecute, to — menganiayakan.

persecution aniaya.

perseverance ketetapan hati, ketekunan.

persevere, to — bertekun, tetap hati.

Persian Parsi, penduduk negeri Iran.

persist, to — berkeras, berkukuh.

persistence ketetapan, ketekunan.

persistent tetap, kukuh, tekun.

person orang, diri, awak; in — sendiri.

personable rupawan, cantik.

personage orang besar, pembesar.

personal diri sendiri, perseorangan.

personality keperibadian, wujud, tabiat, peribadi, sahsiah.

personally sendiri; peribadi.

personate, to — memainkan peranan.

personification penjelmaan.

personify, to — menjelma.

personnel pekerja, ahli-ahli.

perspective tinjauan, perspektif.

perspicacious berakal, bijaksana.

perspicacity kecerdikan, kebijaksanaan.

perspicuity sifat terang.

perspicuous terang, mudah difahamkan.

perspiration keringat, peluh.

perspire, to — berkeringat, berpeluh.

persuade, to — memujuk.

persuasion pemujukan, keyakinan.

persuasive yang memujuk, sesuatu yang meyakinkan.

pert kurang sopan.

pertain, to — bertalian, berhubung dengan, termasuk, tergulung.

pertinacious keras kepala, keras hati.

pertinacity ketegaran, sifat keras kepala.

pertinence, pertinency keadaan tepat, kena.

pertinent berhubung dengan, berkenaan dengan, tepat.

perturb, to — membingungkan.

perturbation kebingungan.

perusal pemeriksaan.

peruse, to — memeriksa dengan saksama.

Peruvian yang berkenaan dengan negeri Peru, penduduk Peru.

pervade, to — menyerap, meresap.

pervasion penyerapan.

pervasive yang menyerap.

perverse jahat, salah.

perversity keadaan jahat, keadaan salah.

pervert orang yang batinnya terputar balik; (*renegade*) orang murtad.

pervious mudah dimasuki; termasuk akal.

pessimism sifat (faham) cemas.

pessimist orang pencemas, pesimis.

pessimistic suka cemas.

pest seseorang atau sesuatu yang dikira sebagai gangguan, binatang yang merugikan, perosak.

pester, to — mengganggu.

pestiferous yang merosakkan.

pestilence penyakit sampar, hawar.

pestilent(ial) yang merosakkan, yang membinasakan.

pestle alu, pengentak, penumbuk; **to** — menumbuk dengan alu.

pet binatang yang disukai (didik); — name nama timangan.

petal kelopak bunga.

peter, to — out berakhir perlahan-lahan.

petersham sejenis pita tebal dan bergelugur.

petite berbadan kecil serta halus.

petition surat permintaan, surat permohonan, surat rayuan.

petrel sejenis burung laut.

petrify, to — membatu.

petro— awalan kata yang ertinya: batu.

petrol minyak bensin, petrol.

petroleum minyak tanah.

petticoat baju dalam untuk perempuan.

pettish bengkeng.

petty kecil, tidak penting.

petulance kebengkengan.

petulant lekas marah, bengkeng.

petunia sejenis bunga.

pew bangku gereja.

pewit, peewit sejenis burung paya.

pewter timah putih bercampur timah hitam; (*articles of* —) mangkuk kendi dan lain-lain yang dibuat daripada logam itu.

phantom (*ghost*) hantu; (*vision*) khayalan.

Pharaoh Firaun.

Pharisee orang farisi, orang munafik.

pharmaceutical yang berkenaan dengan ilmu ubat-ubatan.

pharmacist ahli ubat.

pharmacology ilmu khasiat ubat.

pharmacy ilmu membuat ubat; (*drug store*) rumah ubat.

pharynx tekak.

phase ketika, jangka; (*grade*) tingkat.

pheasant burung pegar, burung kuau.

phenomenal (being) berwujud; (wonderful) ajaib.

phenomenon perwujudan; hal ajaib.

phew ceh!

phial botol kecil.

phil(o)-, -phil(e) awalan dan akhiran kata yang ertinya: suka akan, penggemar.

philander, to — main perempuan.

philanthropic berbelas kasihan akan sama-sama manusia.

philanthropist orang dermawan, orang murah hati.

philanthropy dermawan, murah hati.

philatelist pengumpul setem.

philately pengumpulan setem.

philharmonic penggemar muzik.

philologist ahli bahasa.

philology ilmu bahasa, Filoloji.

philosopher ahli fikir, orang yang pandangan hidupnya berdasarkan falsafah.

philosophic(al) yang berdasarkan seperti atau suka falsafah.

philosophize, to — berfalsafah.

philosophy falsafah, filsafat, pandangan hidup.

phlegm dahak, lendir.

phlegmatic dingin kepala, berdarah dingin.

phobia ketakutan atau segan yang amat sangat.

phone abbr of **telephone** talipon.

phonetic menurut bunyi dalam bahasa; **—s** ilmu bunyi bahasa, ilmu fonetik.

phonetician ahli fonetik, ahli ilmu bunyi bahasa.

phoney (col) palsu, lancong.

phono- awalan kata yang ertinya: suara.

phonograph (US) alat yang mengeluarkan bunyi yang lebih dahulu dirakamkan pada piring hitam.

phosphate posfat, kalimantang.

phosphorescence pendar, kalimantang.

phosphorescent bercahaya sayup-sayup, berpendar.

phosphoric mengandung fosfor, posforik.

phosphorus fosfor, posforus.

photo abbr of **photograph** gambar, foto.

photograph gambar, foto; **to — menggambar.**

photographer tukang gambar.

photographic yang berkenaan dengan gambar, foto.

photography gambar, foto.

phrase ayat, kalimat, ujar, rangkaikata; **to — mengucapkan.**

phraseology susunan kata, cara berkata.

phut bunyi batuk kering; **to go — roboh; gagal.**

physic pengubatan; **—s** ilmu fizik.

physical badani, jasmani, tubuh, fizik.

physician tabib, doktor.

physicist ahli ilmu alam.

physio- awalan kata yang ertinya: alam.

physiognomy firasat, perasat.

physiological yang berkenaan dengan ilmu faal alat tubuh.

physiology ilmu faal alat tubuh, fisioloji; kaji tugasorgan.

physique keadaan badan, tubuh.

pianist pemain piano.

piano, pianoforte piano; **grand — piano besar.**

piccalilli acar campur-campur.

piccaninny anak kecil.

piccolo sejenis seruling.

pick (*tool*) cangkul cungkil; (*choice*) pilihan; to — (*collect*) memungut; the — of the bunch yang paling baik.

pickaback mendukung.

pickaxe beliung.

picket (*stake*) pacak, pancang; (*guard*) kawal, pengawalan; (*of strikers*) orang pemogok yang mengajak pekerja lain mogok juga.

pickings punguton.

pickle acar.

pickpocket tukang seluk poket.

picnic (*pleasure excursion*) temasya; berkelah.

picnicker orang yang berkelah.

pictorial bergambar; (*journal*) majalah bergambar.

picture gambar.

picture book buku gambar.

picture gallery balai untuk lukisan dan gambar.

picture postcard pos kad bergambar.

picturesque elok, indah, patut digambarkan.

pidgin, — English bahasa kacuk yang berdasarkan bahasa Inggeris.

pie, to have a finger in the — bercampurtangan.

piebald belang.

piece potong, pecahan, penggal.

piecemeal potongan, sepoto.ig demi sepotong.

pier pangkalan, jambatan.

pierce, to — menembus, menebuk, menerusi, menusuk.

piety kesalehan, ketaatan, ibadat.

pig babi; (*uncouth person*) orang kurang ajar, yang tidak tahu adat.

pigeon burung merpati, punai.

pigeonhole kotak, lubang pada meja tulis.

piggery tempat pemeliharaan babi, peternakan babi.

piggy anak babi.

pigheaded tegar, keras kepala, degil.

pig iron besi jongkong.

piglet, pigling anak babi.

pigmy see pygmy.

pigskin kulit babi.

pigsty kandang babi.

pigtail anyam rambut, tocang.

pike (*weapon*) tombak; sejenis ikan.

pikestaff gagang tombak; as plain as a — terang dan nyata.

pilchard sejenis ikan laut.

pile (*heap*) timbunan, longgok; (*stake*) pancang.

piles (*of bridge*) tiang; (*haemorrhoids*) buasir.

pilfer, to — mencuri.

pilgrim orang yang berziarah ke tanah suci.

pilgrimage ziarah ke tanah suci; (*to Mecca*) Haji.

pill gentel, gintil, pel.

pillage perampasan; to — merampas.

pillar tiang, turus; driven from — to post dihalaukan dari suatu tempat ke tempat lain.

pillar box sejenis kotak pos.

pillion tempat duduk di belakang pengendera kuda atau motosikal.

pillory papan di dalamnya seorang hukuman diikat dan ditunjukkan kepada orang banyak.

pillow bantal.

pillowcase, pillow–slip sarung bantal.

pilot (*guide*) pandu; (*of plane*) juruterbang.

pimento cabai.

pimp alku, pinang muda.

pimpernel sejenis tumbuhan.

pimple bintil, jerawat.

pin peniti, semat, penyemat.

pinafore sejenis baju luar untuk kanak-kanak yang gunanya menutupi pakaiannya supaya tidak kotor.

pincers (*also* pair of —) sepit angkup, kakaktua.

pinch piat, cubit.

pincushion bantal kecil kerana menusuk dan menyimpan peniti.

pine I sejenis pohon kayu.

pine II, to — merana; to — for, alter merindukan.

pineapple buah nenas.

ping bunyi ting, kenting.

pinion hujung sayap; (*wheel*) sejenis roda berigi-rigi.

pink I (*colour*) warna merah jambu, merah muda.

pink II (*pierce*) menembus, berketuk.

pinnacle mercu, puncak.

pint ukuran Inggeris (0.568 ltr).

pioneer perintis jalan, pembuka; to — membuka jalan.

pious saleh, beribadat.

pip biji; (*of rank on uniform*) bintang pada bahu.

pipe paip, saluran; (*of bamboo*) buluh-buluh.

pipeline (*oil*) saluran minyak tanah.

piper pemain seruling.

piping (*whistling*) bersiul; (*tubing*) sekumpulan saluran (pembuluh).

pipit sejenis burung.

piquancy kepedasan.

piquant pedas.

pique kegusaran, sakit hati.

piqué (*fabric*) kain pike.

piracy perompakan.

pirate perompak laut.

pirouette putaran, pusingan dengan tari-menari.

pisciculture peternakan ikan, pemeliharaan ikan.

pistil putik bunga.

pistol pistol.

piston piston, kodok-kodok, omboh.

pit (*hole*) lubang; (*of ear, nose*) rongga; —ted (*pock-marked*) bopeng.

pitapat berdebar-debar.

pitch I gala-gala; —black hitam pekat.

pitch II (*of voice*) tinggi suara; laras suara, tingkat suara.

pitcher sejenis kendi, buyung.

pitchfork sejenis serampang besar yang dipakai untuk menimbun dan memindahkan rumput kering.

piteous yang memilukan, yang menimbulkan belas kasihan.

pitfall lubang penangkap binatang buas, perangkap.

pith isi batang kayu, empulur.

pithy penuh empulur; (*terse*) singkat.

pitiful yang menimbulkan kasihan, hiba.

pitiless tidak menaruh belas kasihan.

pittance pendapatan yang kecil, upah yang kecil.

pity belas kasihan, kehibaan.

pivot pasak, paksi, pusat.

pixie, pixy sejenis peri.

placard surat tempelan.

placate, to — (*soften*) melembutkan.

place tempat; (*residence*) tempat kediaman.

placid (*of temper*) sejuk hati.

plagiarism cedok.

plagiarist pencedok.

plagiarize, to — mencedok.

plague wabak.

plaice sejenis ikan.

plaid sejenis kain selendang yang berwarna-warna.

plain I (*clear etc*) jelas, terang, jujur; (*flat*) rata.

plain II (*level tract*) padang datar.

plaint (*lament*) kelohan; (*accusation*) tuduhan.

plaintiff pendakwa, penuduh.

plaintive sayu, sedih.

plait (*fold*) lipatan; (*braid hair*) jalin rambut.

plan rencana, rancangan.

plane I sejenis pohon.

plane II (*level*) latar, tanah datar; (*grade*) tingkat.

plane III (*of carpenter*) ketam; *see* aeroplane.

planet bintang.

planetarium pertunjukan jalan bintang.

plank papan, pelang.

plant tanaman, tumbuhan; (*machinery etc*) segala alat mesin yang perlu dalam suatu kilang.

plantain pisang.

plantation perusahaan kebun.

planter penanam, pengusaha kebun.

plaque sepotong logam (batu dan lain-lain) yang digunakan sebagai tanda peringatan.

plasma plasma darah.

plaster lepa, turap; sticking — pelekat; to — melepa, menampal, menurap.

plastic liat, plastik.

plasticine plastisin, sejenis tanahliat.

plate piring, pinggan.

plateau dataran tinggi.

platform (*for sleeping*) pentas; (*stage*) panggung.

plating sadur, lapisan emas (perak dan lain-lain).

platinum pelatinum, emas putih.

platitude perkataan yang selalu dikatakan sehingga tidak bererti.

Platonic yang berkenaan (atau sesuai) dengan pengajaran Plato; — love cinta rohani bukan jasmani.

platoon pasukan askar.

platter piring.

platypus sejenis binatang yang didapati di Australia sahaja.

plausible yang dapat dipercayai.

play (*game, amusement*) main, permainan; (*on stage*) sandiwara, lakunan.

playbill surat tempelan untuk mengumumkan pertunjukan sandiwara dan sebagainya.

player pemain.

playful jenaka.

playground halaman, tempat bermain, padang.

playhouse panggung bangsawan.

playing bermain; — cards daun terup.

playmate sebaya, kawan bermain.

playwright, play writer pengarang sandiwara.

plea keterangan (kenyataan) dalam pengadilan.

plead, to — mengemukakan, memohonkan.

pleasant lazat; sedap.

pleasantry gurau senda, kelakar.

please, to — menyukakan.

pleased senang hati, gembira, suka.

pleasing sedap, menyenangkan.

pleasurable yang menyenangkan, menyukakan.

pleasure kesukaan.

pleat pelipatan.

plebeian hina dina; rakyat jelata.

plebiscite pemungutan suara daripada segenap pemilih dalam sebuah negara.

pledge ikrar, jaminan, tanggungan; to — memberi jaminan.

plenipotentiary wakil yang berkuasa mutlak.

plenteous mewah.

plentiful mewah, limpah.

plenty kelimpahan, banyak.

pleurisy demam selaput dada.

pliability kelembutan; (*compliant*) keadaan sifat liat.

pliable, pliant lembut, lemah; (*supple*) liat.

pliers pelayar, sepit angkup.

plight I (*distressing state*) keadaan buruk, sedih.

plight II (*promise*) perjanjian.

plinth (*of column*) alas tiang; (*of wall*) bahagian bawah sebuah tembok yang menganjung.

plod, to — berjalan dengan susah payah.

plop celepuk, celempung.

plot (*of ground*) sebidang tanah yang kecil; (*stratagem*) daya; (*plan*) rancangan.

plotter perancang.

plough bajak, tenggala; (*astr*) the P — bintang biduk.

plover sejenis burung.

pluck I, (*courage*) **to — up** keberanian, kegagahan.

pluck II, to — memetik, menggentas.

plucky berani, gagah berani.

plug sumbat.

plum sejenis buah.

plumage bulu jambul burung.

plumb unting-unting, batu duga.

plumber yang memperbaiki paip air dan sebagainya.

plumbline tali penduga tegak.

plume bulu burung, jambul.

plummet batu duga.

plump (*stout*) gemuk, sintal; (*fall abruptly*) terjun.

plunder barang rampasan; to — merampas, menjarah.

plunderer perompak, perampas.

plunge cebur; to — mencebur, menyelam.

plural bilangan banyak.

plus ditambah; tanda tambah.

plush sejenis kain yang rupanya sebagai baldu.

plutocracy pemerintahan orang kaya-kaya.

pluvial yang berkenaan dengan hujan.

ply I lapisan (kain, kayu dan lain-lain).

ply II, to — (*use*) memakai; (*work at*) menjalankan.

plywood kayu pakisan.

p.m. *abbr of post meridiem.*

pneumatic yang berkenaan dengan angin atau hawa.

pneumonia demam paru-paru.

poach I, to — (*cook*) merebus telur tidak berkulit.

poach II, to — melanggar hak tuantanah kerana pergi berburu di situ.

poacher orang yang pergi berburu di tanah orang lain dengan tidak mendapat izin.

pocket kantung, saku.

pocketbook buku catitan.

pocket money wang belanja.

pockmarked bopeng.

pod kulit kacang.

podgy gemuk dan pendek.

poem sajak, syair.

poet penyair, penyajak, pujangga.

poetic(al) seperti dalam syair.

poetry puisi, persajakan; to write — menyair bersyair.

poignant pedas, pedih, tajam.

point (*dot*) titik, noktah; (*item etc*) hal, fasal, perkara.

point-blank ditembak lurus; he refused — ia menolak dengan terus terang.

pointed rancang, runcing.

pointer jarum penunjuk.

pointless (*blunt*) tumpul; (*meaningless*) tidak bererti.

poise (*bearing*) sikap tenang.

poison racun, bisa.

poisoner peracun.

poisonous beracun, bisa.

poke jolok, sentuh.

poker (*fire*) alat penggalak; (*cards*) api; sejenis permainan terup; —**work** sejenis ukiran yang dikerjakan dengan jarum panas.

poky sesak sempit.

polar yang berkenaan dengan daerah kutub.

pole (*of wood*) pancang, tiang.

poleaxe kapak penyembelih.

polecat musang.

polemic pertengkaran.

pole star bintang kutub.

police polis.

police court mahkamah untuk pelanggaran peraturan polis.

policeman mata-mata.

police office pejabat besar polis di sebuah bandar.

police officer pengawal polis.

police station balai polis.

police warrant waran tangkap.

policy siasat, dasar, polisi.

polish ubat penggosok.

Polish yang berkenaan dengan negeri atau penduduk negeri Poland.

polite sopan santun, beradab.

politic bijaksana, berakal; —**s** politik.

political politik, siasah, tatanegara.

politician ahli politik, politikus.

polity (*government*) susunan tata negara; (*state*) negara.

polka sejenis tarian.

poll I pemungutan suara, pengundian suara.

poll II kepala.

pollen tepung bunga, debunga, serbuk bunga.

pollinate, to — menyerbukkan, mendebungakan.

pollination penyerbukan pendebungaan.

pollute, to — mengotorkan, mencemarkan.

pollution pengotoran.

polo sejenis permainan bola dengan naik kuda.

poltergeist hantu yang membingungkan dan mengganggu, alimun.

poly — awalan kata yangertinya: banyak.

polyandry aturan kahwin satu isteri dengan beberapa orang suami.

polychromatic berbagai warna.

polygamist orang yang mempunyai beberapa orang isteri.

polygamous beristeri banyak.

polygamy hal kahwin seorang suami dengan beberapa orang isteri.

polyglot orang yang faham akan banyak bahasa.

polygon banyak segi.

polymorphous berbentuk banyak, pancabentuk.

Polynesian yang berkenaan dengan kepulauan di Lautan Pasifik sebelah timur benua Australia.

polyp(e) sejenis binatang yang hidup di laut.

polytechnic yang berkenaan dengan bermacam-macam teknik, politeknik.

pomade minyak rambut; **to** — meminyaki rambut.

pomegranate buah delima.

pommel bonjol pada pelana.

pomp kemuliaan.

pompon, pompom jambul perhiasan.

pompous (*magnificent*) mulia; (*self-important*) sombong.

pond telaga, kolam.

ponder, to — berfikir, mengenang.

ponderous berat, boyak.

pony kuda kecil.

poodle sejenis anjing.

pool I lopak, palung; (*in a river*) lubuk.

pool II (*in betting etc*) jumlah taruhan.

poor miskin, papa, melarat.

poorly (*inadequately*) tidak cukup; (*degraded*) hina; (*sick*) sakit.

poorness kekurangan, kemeskinan.

pop I dentur, letus.

pop II (*col*) ayah, pak.

popcorn jagung yang dibembam.

pope Paus; —'s nose cenonggeng ayam.

popeyed dengan mata terbelalak.

popgun bedil angin permainan kanak-kanak.

popinjay burung nuri.

poplar sejenis pohon.

poplin sejenis kain.

poppy bunga madat, bunga apium.

poppycock bual kosong.

populace rakyat jelata.

popular populer, digemari, disukai ramai.

popularity hal disukai oleh orang ramai.

popularize, to — menjadikan terkenal dan disukai oleh orang banyak.

populate, to — meramaikan negeri, menduduki, mendiami.

population penduduk suatu negeri.

populous sangat banyak penduduknya.

porcelain tembikar.

porch serambi.

porcupine binatang landak.

pore I lubang kulit, liang.

pore II, to — over (*stare*) merenungkan; (*work etc*) bertekun.

pork daging babi.

porker babi peliharaan, babi muda yang ditambunkan.

porky yang berkenaan dengan atau seperti babi.

pornography karangan mengandungi perkara karut.

porous berlubang-lubang, berliang-rongga, serap air.

porpoise ikan lumba-lumba.

porridge bubur.

port I (*harbour*) pelabuhan; (*left side of ship*) kiri kapal.

port II (*wine*) sejenis anggur.

portable yang dapat dipindahkan.

portage wang pengangkutan.

portal (*gateway*) pintu gerbang.

portcullis kisi-kisi pada pintu gerbang yang boleh dinaik turunkan.

portend, to — menandakan, meramalkan.

portent tanda, alamat; (*marvel*) keajaipan.

portentious sangat penting dan bererti.

porter (*gatekeeper*) jaga pintu; (*carrier*) kuli pemikul barang.

porterage pekerjaan atau bayaran pengantaran.

portfolio (*case for papers*) tas surat-surat; (*office of minister*) jabatan menteri.

porthole pintu angin, tingkap pada kapal.

portico serambi yang bertiangtiang.

portion bahagian.

portly (*stout*) gemuk; (*stately*) tampan.

portrait potret, gambar seseorang.

portray, to — melukiskan, menggambarkan.

portrayal lukisan, gambaran.

Portuguese yang berkenaan dengan negeri atau penduduk negeri Portugal.

pose (*bearing*) sikap; to — (*put forward*) mengemukakan; (*assume attitude*) bersikap.

posh (*col*) bagus.

position (*site*) kedudukan; (*bearing*) sikap; (*state*) keadaan; (*place*) tempat.

positive positif, tentu, yakin.
possess, to — punya, mempunyai, memiliki.
possession milik, kepunyaan.
possessive berkenaan dengan kepunyaan, suka menunjukkan hakmiliknya.
possibility harus berlaku.
possible harus boleh.
possibly barangkali, boleh jadi, harus.
post I (*pillar etc*) tiang, tonggak.
post II (*letter etc*) pos, surat-surat.
post- awalan kata yang ertinya: belakangan, sesudah.
postage meterai, bayaran pengiriman; — **stamp** stem yang dicap.
postal yang berkenaan dengan pos.
postbag karung surat.
postcard pos kad.
poster (*also* bill—) pelekat, gambar pelekat.
posterior terkemudian, belakang.
posterity anak cucu.
postgraduate setelah memperoleh ijazah perguruan tinggi.
posthaste dengan cepat, terburu-buru.
posthumous anak yang dilahirkan sesudah meninggalnya ayah, sesudah mati.
postman pengantar surat, posmen.
postmark cap pos.
postmaster kepala pejabat pos; **P—** **General** kepala segala urusan pos.
post meridiem, p.m. waktu dari pukul 12 tengahari sampai 12 tengah malam.
post-mortem periksa mayat.
postnatal sesudah dilahirkan.
post-office pejabat pos.
post paid sudah dibayar stemnya.

postpone, to — menangguhkan.
postponement penangguhan.
postscript ringkasan; (*abbr*) **P.S.** tambahan pada akhir surat.
postulate, to — menerima sebagai dalil.
posture sikap, perawakan.
posy segabungan bunga.
pot jambangan, pasu, periuk, belanga.
potable dapat diminum.
potash zat dalam air abu, kaliam karbonat.
potato ubi kentang; **sweet —** ubi keledek.
potbelly orang yang perutnya buncit, si bujal.
potency kuasa, kekuatan.
potent berkuasa, kuat bertenaga.
potentate raja, yang dipertuan.
potential sanggup, harus.
potentiality keharusan, keupayaan.
potion minuman.
potpourri bunga rampai.
potter, to — (about) bekerja bertatih-tatih.
pottery barang pecah belah, tembikar.
potty (*col*) tidak bererti, gila.
pouch sarung, saku.
poulterer penjual ayam itik.
poultice alin, tuam.
poultry ayam itik.
pounce sambaran; **to —** (upon) menyambar.
pound I, (*abbr*) **lb** = ukuran berat (453.6 gr).
pound II (*also* — **sterling**: **£**) wang luggeris.
pound III kandang untuk mengurung lembu.
pound IV, to — menumbuk, melumatkan, menghancurkan.
poundage wang dalal dalam setiap pound.

pounder, a three— meriam yang berat pelurunya 3 pound.

pour, to — menuangkan, mencurahkan.

pout, to — mencebik, mencebil, merajuk.

poverty kemiskinan, kemelaratan, papa.

powder serbuk, tepung; (*cosmetic*) bedak; (*gun*) ubat bedil.

powder puff sepotong kain dan sebagainya untuk berbedak.

power (*authority*) kuasa, kekuasaan; (*strength etc*) kekuatan, daya, tenaga.

powerful kuat, bertenaga.

powerless tidak berdaya, lemah.

power station rumah letrik.

practicability harus boleh.

practicable yang dapat dilakukan.

practical berguna.

practice (*custom*) adat kebiasaan; melakukan.

practise, to — (*carry out*) melakukan; (*train*) melatih.

practitioner orang yang menjalankan kerja sebagai pengacara atau tabib.

pragmatic(al) berdasarkan hal berguna.

pragmatism sifat memperlakukan segala hal secara membuat.

prairie padang rumput yang tidak ada pohon-pohonnya.

praise puji-pujian; to — memuji.

praiseworthy patut dipuji.

praline sejenis gula-gula.

pram *abbr of* **perambulator**.

prance lompatan; to — melompat.

prank kelakar.

prattle percakapan yang tidak bererti.

prawn udang.

pray, to — berdoa, sembahyang; (*entreat*) bermohon.

prayer doa, sembahyang; permohonan.

pre— awalan kata yang ertinya: sebelum daripada.

preach, to — berkhutbah, bersyarah.

preacher khatib; (*of the Bible*) guru injil.

preamble kata pendahuluan.

precarious (*uncertain*) tidak tentu; (*difficult*) musykil; (*perilous*) berbahaya.

precaution hal beringatingat, tindakan yang diambil untuk lebih dahulu mencegah akibat buruk.

precautionary secara beringat-ingat.

precede, to — mendahului, berjalan dahulu.

precedence hal mendahului.

precedent hal yang terjadi lebih dahulu dan boleh dipakai sebagai ibarat.

precept peraturan, ajaran.

precinct halaman; —s lengkungan.

precious (*costly*) berharga, indah, bermutu.

precipice tebing curam.

precipitate I tergopoh-gopoh, lintang pukang.

precipitate II endapan.

precipitation kegopohan; turunnya hujan (atau salji).

precipitous curam.

précis keringkasan.

precise (*exact*) tepat; (*careful*) teliti.

precision ketepatan.

preclude, to — mencegah, menghindarkan.

preclusive yang mencegah, menghindarkan.

precocious terlalu cepat tumbuhnya.

preconceive, to — memahamkan lebih dahulu.

preconception pengertian lebih dahulu.

precondition syarat yang harus dipenuhi lebih dahulu.

precursor pembuka jalan.

predecessor orang yang lebih dahulu memegang jabatan.

predestination takdir.

predestine, to — mentakdirkan.

predicament keadaan sulit atau berbahaya, gendala.

predicate penyambut, sebutan tata-bahasa.

predicative penyambut sebutan tata-bahasa.

predict, to — meramalkan, menujumkan.

prediction ramalan.

predilection kecondongan.

predispose, to — mempengaruhi sehingga mudah kena penyakit.

predisposition rentan.

predominance hal terlebih banyak.

predominant (*in power*) lebih berkuasa; (*in numbers*) lebih banyak.

predominate, to — menguasai; lebih banyak.

pre-eminence keadaan sifat terutama.

pre-eminent istimewa, terutama.

pre-empt, to — memperoleh lebih dahulu.

pre-emption hak pembelian lebih dahulu.

preen, to — menyelisik bulunya (burung); (*smarten o.s.*) menghiasi diri.

prefabricate, to — membuat bahagian rumah dan lain-lain sehingga hanya mesti dipasang sahaja.

preface kata pengantar, kata pendahuluan.

prefect pembesar dalam masyarakat Rumawi zaman dahulu; (*in school*) ketua murid.

prefer, to — lebih suka akan.

preferable lebih disukai.

preference hal lebih suka akan, kecenderungan, pilihan.

preferential yang memilih, yang lebih suka akan.

prefix awalan.

pregnancy keadaan hamil, bunting.

pregnant hamil, bunting, mengandung.

prehensile yang dapat memegang.

prehistoric sebelum sejarah, azali.

prejudice prasangka; kerugian yang diakibatkan oleh salah satu perbuatan.

prejudicial yang mempengaruhi; (*injurious*) yang merugikan.

preliminary (*preparatory*) yang mendahului; (*initial*) permulaan.

prelude (*mus etc*) karangan muzik, temasya yang mendahului pertunjukan; (*beginning*) permulaan.

premature sebelum waktunya.

premeditate, to — memikirkan (atau merancangkan) lebih dahulu.

premeditation fikiran, (rancangan) lebih dahulu.

premier yang pertama, yang terpenting; (*prime minister*) perdana menteri.

premise pendirian dinyatakan dahulu yang merupakan dasar.

premises halaman.

premium (*reward*) hadiah; (*payment*) bayaran premium.

premonition alamat akan terjadi sesuatu prarasa.

premonitory yang merupakan tanda, alamat akan terjadi sesuatu.

preoccupied termenung, tafakur.

preoccupy, to — meliputi fikiran, meliputi hati.

pre-ordain, to — menetapkan lebih dahulu.

preparation persiapan, persediaan.

preparatory yang menyiapkan, yang mendahului.

prepare, to — menyediakan, menyiapkan.

prepay, to — membayar lebih dahulu.

preponderance jumlah yang lebih besar.

preponderate, to — (in numbers) lebih banyak daripada; (in influence) lebih besar pengaruhnya.

preposition kata tempat sendi nama, menunjuk kedudukan.

prepossess, to — (inspire with) mendatangkan; (impress) mempengaruhi.

prepossessing yang mengambil hati.

preposterous mustahil.

prerequisite sesuatu yang merupakan syarat yang harus dipenuhi lebih dahulu.

prerogative hak istimewa.

presage tanda, alamat bahawa sesuatu akan terjadi.

Presbyterian seorang anggota gereja Presbiter.

prescience pengetahuan lebih dahulu sesuatu hal akan terjadi.

prescient mengetahui lebih dahulu apa yang akan terjadi.

prescribe, to — menyuruh, menentukan.

prescript suruhan, perintah.

prescription surat ubat doktor.

prescriptive yang menyuruh.

presence kehadiran; — of mind akal budi.

present I (being present) yang hadir; (happening) yang berlaku sekarang.

present II (time) masa sekarang; at — sekarang.

present III (gift) pemberian, hadiah.

present IV, to — memperkenalkan.

presentable yang patut ditunjukkan atau dihadiahkan.

presentation (thing presented) pemberian; (act of presenting) pengenalan, penyampaian.

presentiment perasaan yang sesuatu akan terjadi.

presently nanti, kelak.

preservation pemeliharaan.

preservative ubat; penjagaan supaya baik.

preserve (jam etc) manisan; to — (care for) memelihara.

preside, to — mengetuai.

presidency jabatan ketua atau presiden.

president presiden, dipertua, ketua.

presidential yang berkenaan dengan presiden atau dipertua.

press (pressure) tekanan; (for squeezing) pemeras, kilang; (printing) mesin pencetak; (newspapers etc) suratkhabar.

press agent pembantu pengarang atau pemain sandiwara dan sebagainya.

pressing (pressure) yang mendesak; (momentous) penting.

pressure tekanan, desakan.

prestidigitator penyulap, pemain sulap.

prestige pengaruh, marwah, martabat.

presumably agaknya, rupanya.

presume, to — menyangka, menduga, mengira.

presumption sangkaan, kira.

presumptive yang boleh disangka.

presumptuous sombong, pongah.

presuppose, to — menyangka lebih dahulu.

presupposition sangka lebih dahulu.

pretence dalih, semu.

pretend, to — pura-pura, berdalih.

pretender yang menuntut pangkat dan sebagainya.

pretension tuntutan; hak.

pretentious mengada-ngada, pelagak.

preter- awalan kata yang ertinya: di luar.

preterite masa yang telah lampau.

pretext dalih.

prettily dengan manis.

prettiness kecantikan.

pretty cantik, molek.

prevail, to — menang, lebih banyak berlaku.

prevalence jumlah atau pengaruh yang melebihi.

prevalent lazim, lebih banyak terdapat.

prevaricate, to — berputar balik, berdalih.

prevent, to — mencegah, menghalangi.

prevention pencegahan.

preventive pencegah, penangkis.

preview pertunjukan (atau pemeriksaan) lebih dahulu.

previous yang lebih dahulu.

prewar sebelum perang.

prey mangsa, perburuan tangkapan.

price harga; cost — harga pokok.

price control kawalan harga.

priceless tidak ternilai.

prick cucuk; to — mencucuk.

prickle duri; to — mencucuk.

prickly berduri, gerutu; — heat miang peluh.

pride sombong, rasa bangga.

priest padri, pendita.

priestly patut untuk seorang pendita.

prig orang yang mementingkan kebaikan atau pengetahuan dirisendiri.

prim terlalu sopan santun, beradab.

prima donna seri panggung, penyanyi perempuan yang terbaik dalam bangsawan.

primal (*original*) asli; (*important*) terpenting; (*famous*) utama.

primarily pertama-tama.

primary mula-mula, asli peringkat awal pertama; — school sekolah rendah.

prime (*in quality*) keadaan sempurna, bahagian yang terbaik; (*beginning*) permulaan; (*important*) terutama, terpenting.

primer buku pelajaran yang pertama.

primeval asli, dahulukala.

primitive primitif, asli.

primogeniture hak anak sulung.

primordial mula-mula, permulaan, asli.

primrose sejenis bunga.

primula sejenis bunga.

prince putera, anak raja.

princedom kerajaan, tanah yang di bawah kekuasaan seorang raja kecil.

princely seperti seorang anak raja.

princess puteri.

principal pokok, terutama, terpenting.

principality daerah yang di bawah kekuasaan seorang anak raja.

principally pada ghalibnya.

principle dasar, pokok, asas, petua, lunas, prisip.

print (*impression*) bekas, jijak, kesan.

printer pencetak.

printing hal mencetak.

prior (*earlier*) terlebih dahulu; — to sebelum.

priority keutamaan hak melakukan atau memperoleh sesuatu lebih dahulu daripada yang lain.

prise, to — (*open*) membuka dengan keras.

prism perizam.

prison penjara, kurungan.

prisoner orang tahanan.

privacy keadaan atau kediaman tersendiri dan sunyi.

private (*not public*) pereman; (*to an individual*) prebet, tersendiri; (*secret*) tersembunyi.

privation (*absence of*) ketiadaan; (*lack*) kekurangan.

privet sejenis tanaman.

privilege hak istimewa, keutamaan.

privy tersembunyi, rahsia.

prize I hadiah.

prize II (*ship*) kapal rampasan.

prize III *see* prise.

prize fight pertandingan tinju.

prize money wang yang diperoleh lepas sebarang rampasan perang dijual.

prize ring gelanggang tinju.

pro- awalan kata yang ertinya: di hadapan; untuk kepentingan.

pro, —s and cons yang setuju dan yang melawan.

proa perahu.

probability kemungkinan, harus.

probable mungkin.

probably harus, barangkali.

probate pengesahan, surat wasiat.

probation percubaan, pemeriksaan; on — sedang dicuba.

probationary yang berkenaan dengan percubaan.

probationer orang yang masih dalam cubaan.

probe sejenis alat kedoktoran untuk memeriksa dalamnya luka.

probity kejujuran.

problem (*question*) soal; (*enigma*) masaalah.

problematic(al) tidak tentu, yang merupakan soal.

proboscis belalai, muncung.

procedure aturan, tata-cara, cara bekerja.

proceed, to — berjalan terus, maju.

proceeding (*conduct*) kelakuan; —s (*action*) tindakan.

proceeds hasil, pendapatan, perolehan.

process (*going*) perjalanan, jalannya; (*way of doing*) cara pembuatan; (*action of law*) perkara pengadilan, proses.

procession perarakan; **to** walk, go in — berarak.

proclaim, to — mempermaklumkan; isytiharkan; (*make clear*) menyatakan.

proclamation maklumat, permakluman, perisytiharan.

proclivity kecenderungan.

procrastinate, to — berlengah-lengah, berlambat.

procrastination kelengahan, kelambatan.

procreate, to — memperanakkan, menerbitkan.

procreation hal memperanakkan.

procurator wakil berkuasa.

procure, to — memperoleh, menghasilkan; berlaku sebagai alku, pinang muda.

procurer alku, pinang muda.

prod jolokan; to — menjolok.

prodigal pemboros, suka membuang wang.

prodigious luarbiasa; (*very fine*) sangat elok.

prodigy keajaiban; (*person*) orang yang bakat kepandaiannya luarbiasa.

produce hasil, pendapatan, perolehan; **to —** menghasilkan.

producer penghasil; (*maker*) pembuat.

product hasil, keluaran.

production (*producing*) pembuatan; (*thing produced*) hasil.

productive yang menghasilkan, yang banyak hasilnya, pengeluaran.

productivity daya menghasilkan.

profanation pemburukan.

profane tidak suci, buruk; — language mencarut.

profanity carut.

profess, to — (*mention*) menyatakan; (*declare*) mengaku; (*insincerely*) pura-pura.

professed diakui, dikatakan, rupanya.

profession (*declaration*) kenyataan; (*occupation*) jabatan, pekerjaan.

professor mahaguru, profeser.

proffer, to — mempersembahkan; (*extend a hand*) menghulurkan.

proficiency kepandaian, keahlian, kecakapan.

proficient pandai, cakap.

profile tampang muka.

profit laba, untung, keuntungan, faedah.

profitable berlaba, menguntungkan, berfaedah.

profiteer orang yang terlalu banyak makan untung.

profitless tidak berguna, tidak ada labanya.

profligate (*person*) pemboros; risau, cabul.

profound dalam, yang mendalam; a — sleep tidur nyenyak.

profundity keadaan sifat yang dalam.

profuse limpah mewah.

profusion kemewahan, kelimpahan.

progenitor datuk.

progeniture turunan.

progeny anak cucu, turunan.

prognosis kenyataan tabib

tentang jalannya penyakit pada waktu yang akan datang.

prognostic alamat sesuatu akan terjadi; ramalan.

prognosticate, to — meramalkan.

programme, (*US*) **program** acara, program, rancangan.

progress kemajuan, perkembangan; in — sedang berlaku.

progressive maju, yang suka mengemukakan perkembangan masyarakat.

prohibit, to — melarang.

prohibition larangan, pantang.

prohibitive yang melarang.

project (*plan etc*) rancangan, projek, maksud.

projectile benda yang dapat dilontarkan; peluru.

projection (*protrusion*) unjuran; (*opinion*) pandangan.

projector pembuat rancangan; (*for film*) alat penunjukan gambar filem.

prolapse, to — tergelincir keluar.

proletarian salah seorang rakyat jelata.

proletariat, the — rakyat jelata.

proliferate, to — berkembang biak dengan mempergandakan unsur asli.

proliferous yang berkembang biak dengan mempergandakan unsur asli.

prolific (*plants*) subur; (*dense*) lebat; (*abundant*) limpah.

prologue kata pendahuluan.

prolong, to — memanjangkan.

promenade perjalanan, tempat berjalan.

prominence keutamaan.

prominent yang terkemuka; — person orang besar.

promiscuity (*mixed*) percampuran.

promiscuous bercampur, berkacau bilau.

promise janji, perjanjian.

promising ada pengharapan baik.

promissory note surat perjanjian hutang.

promontory hujung tanah, tanjung.

promote, to — memajukan, mengangkatkan.

promoter penganjur.

promotion kenaikan pangkat; **to get** — naik pangkat.

prompt cepat, tangkas, langsung.

prompter seseorang yang membisikkan kata-kata lakun sandiwara kepada si pemain.

promptitude, promptness ketangkasan, hal langsung dan cepat.

promulgate, to — mengumumkan, mengisytiharkan.

promulgation pengumuman.

prone meniarap; — **to** cenderung akan.

prong serampang besar; **—ed** bergigi.

pronoun ganti nama.

pronounce, to — mengucapkan, melafazkan.

pronto (col) cepat, lekas, langsung.

pronunciation ucapan, lafaz, sebutan.

proof pruf, tanda dalil, keterangan.

proof reader pembaca pruf.

prop sangga, galang, tiang, tongkat; **to** — menyangga, menggalang.

propaganda propaganda, diayah.

propagandist orang yang berpropaganda, pendiayah.

propagate, to — berkembang biak, membinkkan.

propagation pembiakan.

propel, to — mendorong.

propeller kincir angin, baling-baling, kipas.

propensity kecondongan, kecenderungan.

proper (correct) yang betul, benar; (qualified) layak; (filling) patut, sepatutnya.

property kepunyaan, milik, harta-benda.

prophecy ramalan, nujum.

prophesy, to — meramalkan, menujumkan.

prophet rasul, nabi.

prophetic yang berkenaan dengan atau seperti rasul.

prophylactic tangkal penyakit.

propinquity keadaan dekat, keadaan hampir; (equality) persamaan.

propitiate, to — mendamaikan.

propitiation perdamaian.

propitious baik, mujur; (fitting) patut.

proportion nisbah, bahagian; (comparison) perbandingan.

proportional setimbang, berbanding dengan, nisbah.

proportionate seimbang, sebanding, berbanding dengan.

proposal cadangan, anjuran, rancangan; (of marriage) peminangan.

propose, to — menghadapkan, menganjurkan, mengemukakan, mencadangkan.

proposition (at a meeting) usul; (intention) maksud.

propound, to — mengemukakan, mengusulkan.

proprietary yang berkenaan dengan pemilik.

proprietor yang empunya.

propriety hal patut, kebenaran.

props alat sandiwara.

propulsion mendorongkan.

prorogation hal tidak meneruskan sidang mesyuarat dan sebagainya.

prorogue, to — tidak meneruskan sidang mesyuarat dan sebagainya.

prosaic seperti prosa.

proscribe, to — (expel) membuang; (reject) menolak.

prose prosa; to — mengarang prosa.

prosecute, to — (carry on) meneruskan; (legal) mendakwa.

prosecutor pendakwa; public — jaksa, pendakwa raya.

proselyte orang yang baharu memeluk ugama.

prosody ilmu persajakan.

prospect pengharapan; to — menyelidiki daerah untuk mencari gali dan lain-lain.

prospective bakal, yang akan datang.

prospector pencari gali (dan lain-lain).

prospectus prospektas, surat edaran yang memberi keterangan tentang sesuatu rancangan.

prosper, to — mendapat untung berhasil kekayaan.

prosperity kemakmuran, kekayaan, untung.

prosperous makmur, beruntung.

prostitute orang pelacuran, perempuan jalang.

prostitution pelacuran, persundalan.

prostrate meniarap; (in prayer) sujud.

prosy menjemukan.

protagonist pemimpin, pemuka.

protect, to — memelihara, mengawal, melindungi.

protection perlindungan, penjagaan.

protective yang melindungi.

protector pelindung, pemelihara.

protectorate negeri yang di bawah perlindungan negeri lain.

protégé seseorang yang di bawah perlindungan orang lain.

protein zat protin.

protest bantahan; to — membantah.

protestant protestan; orang yang membantah.

proto— awalan kata yang ertinya: asli.

protocol protokol, naskhah perjanjian politik.

protoplasm zat cair hidup, protoplasma.

prototype hal (atau orang) yang asli.

protract, to — melanjurkan, melanjutkan.

protracted kepanjangan, lanjur.

protrude, to — menjulur, menganjur.

protrusion hal menganjung, anjungan.

protuberance bonjol, bengkak.

protuberant menjulur, membengkak.

proud besar hati, bangga; (arrogant) sombong.

prove, to — mengesahkan, menunjukkan.

proverb peribahasa, pepatah, perumpamaan.

proverbial yang berkenaan dengan atau seperti pepatah dan sebagainya; terkenal.

provide, to — menyediakan, menyelenggarakan, memperlengkapi.

provided asalkan, dengan syarat.

providence pemeliharaan baik dan hemat.

provident hemat, panjang akal.

providential yang sebagai ditakdirkan tuhan.

province daerah, bahagian.

provincial yang berkenaan dengan kedaerahan.

provincialism faham kedaerahan.

provision perlengkapan; —s bekal, perbekalan.

provisional sementara, untuk sementara waktu; (*emergency*) darurat.

proviso dengan syarat.

provisory bersyarat.

provocation pengasutan, peransang.

provoke, to — merangsangkan; (*cause*) menyebabkan.

provost — marshal kepala polis militari.

prow haluan kapal.

prowess kegagahan, keberanian.

prowl, on the — sedang mencari mangsa; to — berkeliling mencari mangsa.

proximate yang terlebih hampir, yang berikut.

proximity hampirnya.

proxy wakil; (*letter authorizing*) surat kuasa.

prude perempuan yang terlalu mementingkan sopan santun.

prudence kebijaksanaan, kehati-hatian.

prudent bijaksana, berbudi.

prudential bijaksana.

prudish terlalu mementingkan sopan santun.

prune I buah perun yang dikeringkan.

prune II, to — memangkas, menutuh, memerun.

prurient condong akan hal cabul, gasang.

pry, to — mengintip, mengintai.

psalm mazmur, zabur.

psalmist pengarang muzmur.

psalter kitab mazmur.

pseudo— awalan kata yang ertinya: rupanya, pura-pura.

pseudonym nama samaran.

psychiatrist doktor penyakit jiwa.

psychiatry ilmu penyakit jiwa.

psychic berkenaan dengan hal jiwa.

psycho— awalan kata yang ertinya: jiwa.

psychological kejiwaan.

psychology ilmu jiwa.

psychosis penyakit jiwa.

pub=public house.

puberty cukup umur; age of — masa remaja, akil baligh.

pubic yang berkenaan dengan kemaluan, ari-ari.

public orang banyak, rakyat, sidang ramai, umum.

publican yang empunya kedai minuman.

publication pengumuman, penerbitan, terbitan.

public house kedai minuman.

publicist pengarang tentang hukum antarabangsa, wartawan.

publicity pengumuman, kenyataan.

public school sekolah umum.

publish, to — mengumumkan, menyiarkan.

publisher penerbit.

pucker, to — mengerut.

pudding puding, sejenis kuih.

puddle paluh, kubang.

pudgy pendek dan gemuk.

puerile seperti kanak-kanak.

puerility sifat kanak-kanak.

puff tiupan, puputan; (*breathe hard*) nafas panjang.

puffin sejenis burung laut.

puffy (*panting*) termengahmengah; (*distended*) kembung.

pug sejenis anjing; —nosed hidung pesek.

pugilist peninju.

pugnacious suka berkelahi, suka melawan.

pugnacity sifat galak.

pull hela, penarikan; (*influence*) daya penarik; to — menarik, menghela, menjerit.

pullet ayam muda.

pulley kerek, takal; to — mengerek.

pullover sejenis kemeja kain panas yang dipakai melalui kepala.

pulmonary yang berkenaan dengan paru-paru.

pulp daging, isi buah; (*gruel*) bubur; to — menjadikan bubur.

pulpit mimbar.

pulpy lembik.

pulsate, to — berdebar-debar.

pulsation debar jantung, denyut nadi.

pulse I nadi, denyut nadi.

pulse II (*beat*) aneka kacang.

pulverize, to — membubuk, menghancurkan.

puma sejenis harimau.

pumice (*also* — **stone**) batu timbul, batu apung.

pummel, to — memukul-mukul.

pump I bomba; to — membomba.

pump II (*light shoe*) sepatu yang tidak berkancing atau bertali.

pumpkin sejenis labu.

pun sindiran, perkataan jenaka.

punch I (*blow*) pukulan; (*drive*) kekuatan; (*tool for boring*) sejenis penggerik, alat pembuat lubang.

punch II (*drink*) sejenis minuman anggur.

punch bowl sejenis pasu untuk membuat minuman anggur.

punctilious sangat teliti dan terlalu mementingkan segala hal.

punctual (*careful*) teliti; (*on time*) tepat pada waktunya.

punctuality teliti, ketepatan pada waktu.

punctuate, to — membubuh tanda-tanda bacaan.

punctuation tanda bacaan.

puncture bocor; to — menembus.

pundit orang yang terlalu terpelajar.

pungency pedas.

pungent sengit, pedas.

punish, to — menghukum, mendera.

punishment denda, hukuman.

punitive yang menghukum, menyeksa.

punt I sejenis perahu yang lebar dan papar dan yang harus digalah.

punt II, to — (*pole a boat*) bergalah; (*bet*) bertaruh, berjudi.

punter pengggalah perahu; penjudi.

puny (*feeble*) lemah; (*small*) kecil.

pup anak anjing.

pupa kepompong, lembaga.

pupil (*scholar*) murid; (*of eye*) biji mata.

puppet boneka; (*puppet show*) wayang.

puppy anak anjing.

purchase pembelian; belian; to — membeli.

pure murni, jernih, suci; (*unmixed of metals etc*) benar.

purée bubur.

purgative pencahar, julap.

purgatory tempat arwah harus disucikan; yang mencucikan.

purge pembersihan; to — (*aperient*) mencahar; (*make clean*) membersihkan.

purification persucian.

purify, to — mencucikan, menjernihkan.

purist orang yang ingin membersihkan bahasa dengan membuang segala kata asing.

puritan orang yang mementingkan kehidupan sederhana dan adat asli.

purity kesucian, murni.

purl I rantai perhiasan.

purl II, to — (*flow*) air yang mengalir cepat dan berbunyi.

purl III, to — (*capsize etc*) jatuh telangkup, lintang pukang.

purloin, to — mencuri.

purple merah kehitam-hitaman, ungu.

purplish keungu-unguan.

purport erti, makna; **to —** bererti, menyatakan.

purpose maksud; **on —, —ly** dengan sengaja.

purr, to — berdengkur (kucing).

purse pundi-pundi, bekas.

purser pengurus hal kewangan pada kapal penumpang.

pursuance perlakuan; **in —** of sedang melakukan.

pursuant sedang melakukan, menuntut; **— to** berkenaan dengan.

pursue, to — memburu, mengejar, menyusul.

pursuit I pemburuan, pengejaran, penuntutan.

pursuit II, — plane kapalterbang pemburu.

purulent bernanah.

purvey, to — memperlengkapi dengan.

purveyance perlengkapan.

purveyor orang yang memperlengkapi (dengan makanan dan minuman).

pus nanah.

push (*shove*) dorongan; (*pressure*) desakan; (*activity*) kegiatan.

push–bike basikal.

pushing cerkas, menderas.

pusillanimous cabar hati, takut.

puss kucing.

pussy (*also —cat*) kucing.

put (*cast*) pelemparan peluru (dan sebagainya); **to —** menaruh, meletakkan, membubuh.

putative yang disangka.

putrefaction busuk.

putrefy, to — menjadi busuk, reput.

putrescent menjadi busuk, bangar.

putrid bangar, busuk.

putty dempul, pakal, galagala; **to —** memakal.

puzzle (*riddles*) teka-teki, tebakan; (*query*) soal; (*secret*) kesulitan; **to —** membingungkan.

pygmy, pigmy kerdil.

pyjamas baju tidur.

pylon pintu gerbang di negeri Masir; bangunan tinggi (tiang dan sebagainya).

pyramid limas, piramid.

pyre timbunan kayu untuk membakar mayat.

pyro— awalan kata yang ertinya: api.

pyrometer alat pengukur panas api.

pyrotechnic yang berkenaan dengan bunga api.

python ular sawa.

Q

quack I, to — bunyi itik.

quack II orang yang berlaku sebagai tabib tetapi sebetulnya tak mempunyai kelulusan.

quadrangle segi empat.

quadrangular bersegi empat.

quadrant seperempat lengkaran; (*instrument*) alat pengukur sudut.

quadrate bersegi empat.

quadrennial yang berlaku sekali dalam tiap-tiap empat tahun; yang empat tahun lamanya.

quadri— awalan kata yang ertinya: empat.

quadrille sejenis tarian.

quadruped binatang yang berkaki empat.

quadruple yang terdiri dari pada empat; (*verse*) rangkap empat.

quadruplet anak kembar empat.

quadruplicate rangkap empat, empat kali.

quaff, to — minum banyak dan dengan teguk besar.

quagmire paya, becak.

quail, to — mengundurkan diri kerana ketakutan.

quaint (*abnormal of person*) pelek; yang menarik perhatian kerana kuno atau ajaib.

quake, to — gementar, gempa.

qualification kepandaian, kelayakan.

qualified berhak, berkelayakan.

qualify, to — (*describe*) menentukan sifatnya; (*make a stipulation*) memenuhi syarat.

quality (*attribute*) mutu; (*eminence*) keutamaan, keahlian; (*kind*) jenis.

qualm rasa pusing.

quandary bingung, kesulitan.

quantitative yang berkenaan dengan banyaknya.

quantity jumlah, banyak kuantiti.

quarantine kerantin; to — masukkan ke dalam kerantin.

quarrel pertengkaran, perselisihan; **to** — berselisih, bertengkar.

quarrelsome bantah.

quarry I (*object of hunt*) perburuan; (*prey*) mangsa.

quarry II (*for stone*) galian batu.

quart sukatan (Inggeris= 1.136 ltr).

quarter seperempat (jam, tahun dan lain-lain), suku.

quarter–deck bahagian geladak tempat kediaman opsirlaut.

quarterly terjadi tiap-tiap tiga bulan sekali.

quartermaster pegawai rendah angkatan laut atau darat yang menguruskan alat-alat kelengkapan.

quartet(te) empat serangkai, karangan muzik untuk empat penyanyi.

quarto ukuran kertas atau buku.

quartz batu baiduri.

quash, to — membatalkan, meniadakan.

quasi pura-pura, seakan-akan.

quaternary berempat.

quaver salah satu tanda muzik; (*tremble*) getaran.

quay pangkalan.

queasy (*of food*) yang memualkan; lekas mual; (*weak*) lemah.

queen raja perempuan, permaisuri.

queer anih, ajaib.

quell, to — (*crush*) menindas; (*overcome*) mengalahkan.

quench, to — (*a light etc*) memadamkan; (*abolish*) menghapuskan.

quern kisaran, gilingan.

querulous bengkeng, runsing.

query pertanyaan; to — bertanya.

quest pertanyaan, penyelidikan rasmi.

question pertanyaan, soal.

questionable yang menimbulkan keraguan.

questionnaire daftar pertanyaan.

queue orang atau kenderaan yang sedang menunggu; to — (up) menunggu beriring-iring.

quibble (*evasion*) dalih; (*play on words*) kata-kata yang putar belit; to — berdalih.

quick cepat, lekas; (*vigorous*) giat, bersemangat.

quicken, to — mencepatkan, menggiatkan.

quicklime kapur tohor.

quickness kecepatan; kegiatan.

quicksand pasir hanyut.

quickset pagar yang terdiri daripada tumbuh-tumbuhan.

quicksilver air raksa.

quickstep sejenis tarian dengan langkah cepat, langkah cepat.

quick–tempered darah panas, berangsang.

quick–witted cerdik.

quid sugi, seketul tembakau yang disongel.

quiescence tenang sunyi.

quiescent diam tenang, sunyi.

quiet (of water) tenang; (silent) diam; (moderate) sederhana.

quietly (gently) perlahanlahan; (silently) diam-diam.

quill (of bird) batang bulu burung yang besar; (of porcupine) duri landak.

quilt sejenis selimut rangkap dua yang dijahit seluruhnya sehingga jadi satu.

quince sejenis buah.

quinine kina, kinin, ubat demam.

quinqu(e)– awalan kata yang ertinya: lima.

quinquina pohon kina.

quinsy sejenis demam sakit tekak.

quintessence saripati, inti.

quintet(te) muzik untuk 5 alat muzik atau 5 suara.

quintuple yang terdiri daripada lima, rangkap lima kembar lima.

quintuplet anak kembar lima.

quip (banter) sindiran; (precise saying) yang tepat.

quirk (quip) sindiran; (flourish in writing) lempai dalam tulisan (atau gambar).

quit, — (of) bebas daripada, terlepas daripada.

quite samasekali, belaka.

quits seri, rata.

quittance (cancellation) penghapusan; (requital) pembalasan.

quiver I tempat penyimpan anak panah, tabung.

quiver II, to — menggetar.

quiz (questioning) tanya jawab; to — menanyakan.

quizzical yang mengejekkan; (jocular) jenaka.

quoit sejenis cincin besi (atau dari bahan lain) untuk dilempar dalam permainan.

quorum kuorum, jumlah anggota yang perlu untuk mengesahkan keputusan mesyuarat.

quota bahagian rata yang mesti diberi atau diterima.

quotation (extract) petekan, kutipan; (of price) tawaran; — marks tanda kutip.

quote, to — mengutip, memetik; (price) menawar harga.

quotidian tiap-tiap hari, setiap hari.

quotient hasil bahagi.

R

rabbi ulama Yahudi.

rabbit kelinci, arnab, kucing Belanda.

rabble kumpulan penderhaka, hina-dina.

rabid gila-gila; hebat.

rabies penyakit anjing gila.

race I golongan (orang, haiwan dan lain-lain) yang keturunannya sama, bangsa.

race II (running etc) perlumbaan; to — berpacu, berlumba, perlumbaan.

racecourse tempat perlumbaan kuda.

racehorse kuda lumba.

race meeting perlumbaan kuda.

racetrack tempat perlumbaan.

racial yang berkenaan dengan bangsa, kebangsaan.

rack I (*driving clouds*) awan berarak.

rack II (*shelf*) para-para.

rack III (*torture*) sejenis alat penyeksa; to — menyeksa.

racket I, racquet raket.

racket II (*riot*) kerusuhan; (*col*) (*swindle*) tipu daya.

racketeer orang yang melakukan pemerasan wang dengan segala muslihat.

racoon sejenis beruang yang hidup di pohon di negeri Amerika.

racy (*spirited*) giat.

radar radar.

radial yang berkenaan dengan sinar.

radiance seri, cahaya.

radiant berseri, bercahaya, bersinar.

radiate bersinar, mempunyai sinar.

radiation sinaran, pancaran.

radical (*root*) akar; (*origin*) asli, pokok; (*root word*) umbikata.

radio radio.

radio— awalan kata yang ertinya: akar.

radiogram khabar yang diperoleh dengan jalan radio.

radiograph alat pengukur sinar matahari.

radio operator pengurus radio.

radiotelegram kawat radio.

radish sejenis lobak.

radium radium.

radius jari-jari.

radix akar.

raffia sejenis daun pandan yang dibuat segala anyam-anyaman.

raffish busuk, cabul.

raffle pengundian; **to —** mengadakan mengundi.

raft rakit.

rafter kasau.

rag I kain buruk, perca; in —s koyak-koyak.

rag II (*teasing*) pengusikan; to — mengusik.

rage kemarahan, murka.

ragged (*toothed*) bergerigi, gerigi; (*tattered*) cobak-cabik.

ragtime sejenis muzik.

raid (*charge*) penyerbuan; (*police raid*) penyerkapan; to — menggelidah.

raider penyerbu, penjarah.

rail I (*handrail*) susuran tangga; (*railroad*) landasan keretapi.

rail II, to — (*abuse*) mencaci, memaki.

railing (*paling*) pagar; susuran tangga.

raillery (*mocking*) ejekan; (*fun*) kelakar.

railway, (*US*) **railroad** jalan keretapi, landasan keretapi.

railway station stesen, perhentian keretapi.

rain hujan; to — hujan turun.

rainbow pelangi, benang raja.

raincoat baju hujan.

raindrop titik hujan.

rainfall banyaknya hujan yang turun.

rainy banyak hujannya; to provide against a — day menyimpan untuk masa sempit.

raise naik; to — (*hoist*) menaikkan; (*set erect*) menegakkan, mendirikan; to — cattle berternak lembu.

raisin sejenis kismis.

rajah raja negeri Timur.

rake I (*tool*) pencakar, penggaruk; to — mencakar.

rake II orang yang suka main-main.

rake III (*slope*) miringnya, kecondongan.

rally I perkumpulan.

rally II (*joke flirt*) bergurau senda.

ram I biri-biri jantan.

ram II (*ramrod*) alat pelantak; to — melantak.

ramble pengembaraan; to — mengembara.

rambler pengembara; (*rose*) sejenis bunga mawar yang menjalar.

rambling tidak teratur susunannya; (*of plants*) menjalar.

ramification percabangan.

ramify, to — bercabang.

ramp lerengan.

rampage amuk; to — mengamuk.

rampageous yang mengamuk.

rampant (*aggressive*) galak; (*unrestrained*) maharaja lela.

rampart baluarti, benteng, kubu; to — melindungi dengan benteng.

ramrod pelantak.

ramshackle buruk.

ranch padang ternak, peternakan di Amerika; to — berternak.

rancid tengek.

rancour dendam, iri hati, dengki.

random, at — sebarang mana-mana satu.

ranee raja perempuan, permaisuri.

range deret, banjar, barisan.

ranger (*wanderer*) pengembara; (*forest*) penjaga hutan; (*soldier*) soldadu berkuda.

rank I (*row*) baris, saf; (*grade*) pangkat.

rank II (*of plants*) terlalu subur, mewah.

rankle, to — bersakit dalam hati.

ransack, to — membongkar-bongkar kerana mencari sesuatu; (*plunder*) merampas.

ransom pembebasan tawanan dengan wang tebusan; to — menebus orang tawanan.

rant, to — bergembar-gembur.

rap ketuk, sakal.

rapacity kelobaan, tamak; sifat suka merampas.

rape perkosaan; to — memperkosa, mencabuli, rogol.

rapid laju, deras, cepat; (*in river*) jeram.

rapidity kecepatan kederasan.

rapier sejenis pedang halus.

rapport perhubungan pertalian.

rapt asyik.

rapture kegairahan, besar cita.

rapturous gairah, besar hati.

rare (*seldom*) jarang; (*unusual*) ajaib, garib; (*precious*) sangat baik.

rarefaction, **rarefication** penghalusan.

rarefy, to — (*make fine*) menghaluskan; (*soften*) melembutkan.

rarity sesuatu yang ajaib (yang tidak seperti biasa).

rascal buaya, bangsat, bedebah.

rash I kurang fikir, lancar, telanjur, cepat mulut.

rash II (*of skin*) ruam.

rasher sepotong yang tipis daging ham.

rasp sejenis parut, kukur.

raspberry sejenis buah.

rat tikus besar; to smell a — menaruh syak akan sesuatu.

ratable harus membayar cukai.

ratchet, **ratch** roda yang dibubuh alat bergigi yang menyebabkan jalannya kepada satu jurusan sahaja.

rate (*proportion*) kadar; (*cost*) biaya; (*tax*) cukai; (*price*) harga.

rather juga, agak, sedikit.

ratification pengesahan.

ratify, to — mengesahkan.

rating (*sailor*) kelasi yang tiada berpangkat.

ratio perimbangan, kadar.

ration catuan, pelabur, rangsum.

rational masuk akal, menurut akal, bijak.

rationale alasan.

rationalize, to — menghuraikan segala hal menurut akal.

rat(t)an rotan.

rattle kerek-kerek.

rattlesnake ular di negeri Amerika yang sangat bisa.

ratty (col) bengkeng.

raucous parau, garau.

ravage kerosakan, pembinasaan; to — merosakkan, membinasakan.

rave, to — meraban, meracau.

ravel simpulan; to — menjadi kusut.

raven burung gagak; (jet black) warna hitam.

ravenous kemaruk, sangat kelaparan.

ravine jurang, ngarai.

ravish, to — (snatch) merebut; (rape) memperkosa, mencabul.

ravishing sangat menarik hati.

raw (uncooked) mentah; (inexperienced) kasar, tidak berbudi.

ray I sinar.

ray II sejenis ikan laut, ikan pari.

rayon sejenis kain sutera buatan.

raze, rase, to — (cancel) menghapuskan; (destroy) membinasakan.

razor pisau cukur; — edge mata pisau cukur.

re mengenai, tentang.

re— awalan kata yang ertinya: kembali, membalas; melawan; mengulang.

reach (encircling) lengkungan; (of river) rantau; beyond one's — tidak dapat dicapai.

react, to — (requite) membalas; tindak balas; (influence) mempengaruhi.

reaction balasan; tindak balas; (opposition) penentangan.

read membaca; to — (understand) memahamkan; (study) mempelajari.

readable karangan yang menarik hati.

reader pembaca; (book) buku bacaan.

readily bersedia, sudi.

readiness kerelaan, kesudian, sedia.

readjust, to — mengatur semula.

ready siap, sedia, selesai, lengkap.

reaffirm, to — menyetujui, membenarkan sekali lagi, meneguhkan.

real nyata, benar, sungguh.

realism faham sungguh, betul.

realistic betul.

reality kenyataan, hakikat.

realization pelaksanaan.

realize, to — mengerti, insaf, sedar akan, menyedari.

really betul-betul, sungguh-sungguh.

realm kerajaan; (sphere) lapangan.

realty barang tetap.

ream I rim kertas 480 helai.

ream II, to — (enlarge the bore) membesarkan lubang dengan penggerik.

reanimate, to — menghidupkan kembali.

reap, to — (crops) mengetam, menuai, menyabit padi; (profit) memungut hasil.

reappear, to — terbit, timbul balik.

rear bahagian sayap belakang.

rear admiral salah seorang pegawai laut yang berpangkat tinggi, laksamana muda.

rearguard sayap belakang yang melindungi bahagian belakang tentera.

rearm, to — berlengkap semula.

rearmost ke belakang sekali.

rearrange, to — mengatur semula.

reason (cause) sebab, alasan, pokok; (understanding) taakulan.

reasonable menurut akal, masuk akal; (fitting) patut; (just) adil.

reassemble, to — mengumpulkan semula.

reassure, to — mengaku, menegaskan.

rebate potongan harga.

rebel pemberontak, penderhaka.

rebellion pemberontakan, gerak derhaka.

rebellious derhaka, memberontak.

rebound pengambulan; to — mengambul, menganjal.

rebuff (rejection) tolakan; (snarl, snub) tengking; to — menolak; menengking.

rebuild, to — mendirikan, membangunkan semula.

rebuke cela; to — mencela.

rebus sejenis teka-teki.

rebut, to — (reject) menolak; (refute) menyalahkan.

rebuttal penolakan; persalahan.

recalcitrant yang melawan, menolak.

recall (summon back) panggilan kembali; to — memanggil kembali; (remember) mengingatkan.

recant, to — mengakui bahawa perkataan atau pendapatnya tidak benar, mungkir.

recapitulate, to — meringkaskan.

recapitulation ringkasan.

recapture, to — menawan semula.

recast, to — menuang semula.

recede, to — (retreat of men) mundur; (of tide etc) surut.

receipt (thing received) penerimaan, jumlah yang diterima; (acknowledgement) tanda terima, surat rasip.

receive, to — menerima; (guests) menyambut.

receiver penerima; penyambut.

recent baru; —ly baharu-baharu ini.

receptacle tempat menyimpan, sesuatu bekas.

reception penerimaan; (of guests etc) sambutan, jamuan.

receptive ringan kepala, pantas akal.

recess waktu beristirahat; (vacation) cuti.

recession pengunduran, penarikan kembali.

recidivist orang yang sekali lagi melakukan kejahatan.

recipe ramuan untuk makanan.

recipient si penerima.

reciprocal berbalas-balasan, balikan, saling.

reciprocate, to — (give and receive mutually) membalas; (move back and forward) tukar-menukar.

recital (statement) riwayat; (speech) pengucapan; (recite Koran) pengajian.

recitation pengucapan; pengajian.

recite, to — menceritakan; mengaji.

reckless berani candang, tiada hirau akan sesuatu.

reckon, to — (count) menghitung, memperhitungkan; (consider) menganggap, berpendapat.

reckoning perhitungan; day of — hari pembalasan.

reclaim, to — mengembalikan daripada keadaan buruk kepada keadaan baik; (reform) memperbaiki.

reclamation pembukaan tanah; pengembalian daripada kejahatan atau keadaan buruk.

recline, to — (*recumbent*) berbaring; (*lean against*) bersandar.

recluse orang pertapa.

recognition (*valid*) pengakuan; (*know again*) pengenalan; (*respected*) penghargaan.

recognizable yang dapat dikenal.

recognize, to — mengenal; mengakui.

recoil, to — membingkas ke belakang.

recollect, to — mengingat, terkenang akan, mengenangkan.

recollection peringatan, kenangan.

recommence, to — mulai semula.

recommend, to — (*praise*) memujikan; (*advise*) mengesyur cadang.

recommendation pujian; letter of — surat kenalan, surat pujian, sokongan.

recompense balasan; — to membalas.

reconcile, to — mendamaikan, menyesuaikan.

reconciliation perdamaian, perbaikan.

recondite dalam, sulit.

recondition, to — membaharui, memeriksa dan memperbaiki.

reconnaissance peninjauan, pengintipan.

reconnoitre, to — mengintai, mengakap.

reconsider, to — menimbang semula.

reconstruct, to — membangunkan semula.

reconstruction pembangunan semula.

record (*note*) rekod, catitan rasmi; (*gramophone*) piring hitam.

recount, to — menceritakan dengan panjang lebar.

re-count, to — (*of numbers*) membilang semula.

recoup, to — mengganti rugi, memperoleh wang dan sebagainya sebagai penggganti rugi.

recourse, to have — to minta pertolongan atau nasihat pada.

recover, to — (*get back*) mendapat kembali; (*from illness*) sembuh.

recovery pemulihan, hal mendapat kembali; kesembuhan.

re-create, to — menciptakan semula.

recreation penghiburan.

recriminate, to — tuduhmenuduh, menyalahkan.

recrudescence hal pecah semula.

recruit soldadu yang baharu masuk tentera dan belum dilatih, orang baharu.

recruitment pengerahan; (*of candidates*) hal menjadi calun.

rectal yang berkenaan dengan atau melalui pelepasan, dubur.

rectangle empat persegi bujur selari.

rectangular bentuk empat segi bujur.

rectify, to — membetulkan, memperbaiki.

rectilinear, rectilineal yang berkenaan dengan garis lurus.

rectitude kejujuran.

rector pendita; ketua sekolah tinggi (dan sebagainya).

rectory rumah rector.

rectum bahagian usus besar pada dubur.

recumbent berbaring.

recuperate, to — sembuh, waras.

recur, to — berulang, kembali lagi, terjadi lagi.

recurrence hal kembali semula, perulangan.

recurrent yang terjadi ber-ulang-ulang.

red merah; **R—** **Cross** palang merah; fiery — merah padam.

redden, to — menjadikan merah.

reddish kemerah-merahan.

redeem, to — (*from pawn*) menebus; (*get back*) mendapat kembali; menyelamatkan.

redemption penebusan.

rediscover, to — mendapati semula.

redolent (*of smell*) berbau.

redouble, to — mempergan-dakan.

redoubt kubu, perkubuan.

redoubtable (*valiant*) per-kasa; (*dreaded*) yang men-dahsyatkan.

redound, to — (*contribute successfully*) berhasil.

redress penggantian; **to** — membetulkan, memperbaiki.

reduce, to — (*in size*) me-ngecilkan; (*alter*) mengubah-kan, menjadikan.

reduction perkecilan, pe-ngurangan; (*in price*) potongan harga.

redundancy kelimpahan ke-mewahan, kemewahan, ber-ulang.

redundant limpah mewah, berlimpah-limpah, berlebih-lebih.

reduplicate, to — meng-gandakan.

reed buluh; (*mus*) alat yang menerik dalam beberapa ma-cam seruling.

reedy penuh buluh, seperti buluh.

reef I batu karang, terumbu.

reef II, (*naut*) to — mengun-cupkan layar.

reefer sejenis baju pendek.

reek (*vapour*) wap; (*bad smell*) bau busuk; **to** — mengeluar-kan wap.

reel I (*for winding*) gelendung kili-kili.

reel II (*stagger*) gerakan siah layah; **to** — berjalan simpang-siur.

reel III (*dance*) sejenis tarian.

re-elect, to — terpilih semula.

re-enact, to — menjalankan lagi, melakunkan lagi.

re-enter, to — masuk semula.

re-examine, to — menyeli-diki semula, memeriksa se-mula.

refectory ruang makan (di tempat banyak orang dapat makan).

refer, to — (*to*) (*point to*) menunjukkan; (*hand over*) menyerahkan; (*concerning*) berkenaan dengan; (*reference*) rujukan kepada.

referee pengadil, pemisah.

reference (*handing over*) pe-nyerahan kepada; (*connection*) perhubungan; (*direction*) pe-nunjuk; (*referring*) rujuk ke-pada.

referendum pemungutan suara mengenai salah satu hal penting di antara se-mua penduduk, pengundian raya.

refine, to — (*of liquids*) menjernihkan; (*of language etc*) menghaluskan.

refinement kehalusan, adab, sopan santun.

refinery pembersihan.

reflect, to — (*flash*) berkilau-kilauan; (*rebound*) memantul.

reflection gambar cermin.

reflective yang mencermin-kan; (*pensive*) termenung, ta-fakur.

reflector benda yang me-mantulkan sinar, cermin.

reflex (*reflected*) pantulan; (*image*) bayangan, gambar cermin.

reform I pembaharuan, per-baikan; **to** — membaharui, memperbaiki.

reform II, to — (*form again*) membentuk semula.

reformation perbaharuan, perbaikan.

reformative yang bermaksud memperbaiki.

reformatory sekolah untuk memperbaiki anak yang telah menjadi jahat.

reformer pembaharu, orang yang ingin memperbaiki keadaan buruk.

refract, to — membias (cahaya).

refraction bias cahaya.

refractory degil, keras kepala.

refrain I ulangan pada akhir nyanyian.

refrain II, to — (from) menahan diri.

refresh, to — menyedapkan, menyegarkan.

refresher, — course kursus untuk memperbaharui dan mengulangi pengetahuan, ulang kaji.

refreshing sedap, segar.

refreshment sesuatu yang menyegarkan; —s makanan dan minuman yang menyegarkan.

refrigeration penyejukan.

refrigerator peti penyejuk.

refuel, to — mengisi minyak lagi.

refuge tempat perlindungan, pernaungan.

refugee orang pelarian.

refund pengembalian, pembayaran kembali.

refurbish, to — menggilap lagi.

refusal penolakan.

refuse I, to — menolak, tidak mau.

refuse II (*rubbish etc*) kotor, sampah sarap.

refutable yang dapat disalahi.

refutation penyalahan.

refute, to — menyalahi, membuktikan bahawa sesuatu tidak benar.

regain, to — memperoleh kembali.

regal yang berkenaan dengan raja, yang patut untuk raja.

regale makanan atau perjamuan yang sangat baik.

regalia alat kerajaan.

regard (*gaze*) pandang; (*keep in mind*) perhatian; (*esteem*) hormat, penghargaan.

regardless dengan tidak mengendahkan.

regatta perlumbaan kapal layar.

regency jabatan wakil raja.

regenerate, to — menghidupkan.

regent wakil raja.

régime pemerintahan, cara memerintah.

regiment pasukan, salah satu bahagian tentera.

regimental yang berkenaan dengan tentera.

regimentation pelaksanaan sistem yang teratur.

region daerah, tanah; (*portion*) bahagian, kawasan.

regional kawasan.

register daftar; (*of voice*) tingkat bunyi suara.

registrar pendaftar.

registration pendaftaran.

registry pejabat pendaftaran.

regress kemunduran; to — mundur.

regression kemunduran, pengembalian, rusutan kembali; (*of tide*) susutan laut.

regret (*sorry for*) sesal, penyesalan; (*pity*) sayang.

regretful sangat sesal akan sesuatu hal.

regrettable yang menyedihkan, yang patut disesali.

regroup, to — mengumpulkan semula.

regular (*according to rule*)

teratur; (*usual*) biasa; (*steady*) tetap; (*really*) benar-benar, sungguh-sungguh.

regularity ketetapan, hal teratur dan tetap.

regulate, to — mengatur.

regulation peraturan, susunan biasa.

regulator alat pengatur.

regurgitate, to — (*flow back*) mengalir kembali; (*vomit*) muntah.

rehabilitate, to — (*make right again*) membetulkan; (*restore to livelihood*) mengembalikan kepada kehidupan.

rehabilitation pengembalian, pemulihan.

rehearsal latihan sebelum mempertunjukkan sandiwara dan lain-lain.

rehearse, to — (*repeat*) mengulangi; (*practise*) mengadakan latihan.

reign kerajaan, pemerintahan; to — over merajai, memerintah.

reimburse, to — mengganti wang yang dibelanjakan.

reimbursement wang yang telah dibelanjakan.

rein tali kekang, kendali; to — mengendalikan.

reincarnate, to — menjelma balik.

reindeer sejenis rusa yang hidup di bahagian sejuk dunia.

reinforce, to — memperkuat, menebalkan.

reinforcement perkuatan; —s pasukan dan sebagainya yang merupakan kekuatan tentera.

reinstate, to — mengembalikan kepada keadaan yang dahulu.

reintegrate, to — menjadi satu semula.

reissue penerbitan (keluaran) ulangan; to — menerbitkan semula.

reiterate, to — mengulangi.

reiteration pengulangan.

reject sesuatu yang telah ditolak; to — menolak, membuang.

rejection penolakan.

rejoice, to — bergerang hati, menggembirakan.

rejoicings kegerangan, riang gembira.

rejoin I, to — (*retort*) menjawab dakwaan; (*accompany*) menyertai semula.

rejoin II, to — mengumpulkan balik.

rejoinder jawaban.

rejuvenate, to — memudakan, menjadi muda balik.

rejuvenation hal menjadi muda balik.

rekindle, to — menyalakan.

relapse hal runtuh lagi.

relate, to — menceriterakan, meriwayatkan.

related bertalian dengan; (*of family*) sekeluarga; — to berkeluarga dengan.

relation perhubungan, pertalian, sangkutan; (*family*) keluarga, saudara.

relationship persaudaraan.

relative berhubung dengan; (*family*) keluarga, sanak saudara.

relax, to — (*make slack*) berkurang tegang; (*enfeeble*) menjadi lemah.

relaxation hal berkurang tegang; keadaan rehat.

relay kuda (atau orang baharu) untuk mengganti yang lama; by —s bergilir-gilir.

re-lay, to — menaruh balik, meletakkan balik.

release pembebasan, kelepasan; to — membebaskan.

relegate, to — (*banish*) membuang, mengasingkan; (*in rank*) menurunkan pangkat.

relent, to — berkurang keras menjadi lembut hati.

relentless keras hati, ganas, tiada berbelas kasihan.

relevance, relevancy hal berhubungan, pertalian.

relevant bertalian, berhubungan, kena bersabit.

reliable yang dapat dipercayai, setia.

reliance kepercayaan, sesuatu yang dipercayai.

reliant yang percaya.

relic bekas (yang disimpan sebagai azimat atau tanda mata); **—s** (*deceased prince*) jenazah; (*remains*) peninggalan.

relief I (*help*) pertolongan, bantuan; (*of the poor*) sokongan kepada orang miskin.

relief II ukiran timbul; bentuk mukabumi; **—** map peta bentuk mukabumi.

relieve, to — meringankan.

religion ugama.

religious berugama, beriman.

relinquish, to — (*abandon*) meninggalkan; (*surrender*) menyerahkan.

relish (*taste*) rasa; (*savoury taste*) rasa sedap; **to —** kesukaan.

reluctance enggan, keseganan.

reluctant tidak suka, segan, enggan.

rely, to — on percaya, mempercayai.

remain, to — tinggal, ditinggalkan.

remainder lebih, bekas, sisa.

remains bekas, sisa; (*dead body*) jenazah.

remake, to — membuat (membentuk) semula.

remand pengiriman kembali ke penjara dan sebagainya.

remark (*comment*) perkataan; (*opinion*) pendapat; **to —** menyatakan.

remarkable yang menarik perhatian.

remedial yang menyembuhkan, pemulihan.

remedy ubat, penawar; **to —** menyembuhkan.

remember, to — ingat, teringat.

remembrance ingatan, kenangan; (*keepsake*) cendera mata.

remind, to — memperingatkan.

reminder peringatan.

reminiscence (*fond memory*) kenangan.

reminiscent ingat, terkenang, yang memperingatkan.

remiss lalai.

remission (*pardon*) permaafan; (*lessening*) pengurangan.

remit, to — (*pardon*) memaafkan; (*lessen*) mengurangi; (*transmit*) mengirim (wang dan sebagainya).

remittance (*money*) pengiriman wang.

remnant bekas, sisa, baki.

remodel, to — membentuk semula.

remonstrate, to — melawan.

remorse sesal penyesalan.

remorseful sangat sesal.

remorseless tidak sesal; (*pitiless*) tidak mengenal belas kasihan.

remote (*distant*) jauh; (*separated*) terpencil; (*in time*) lama.

remould, to — menuang (atau membentuk) semula.

removable yang dapat dipindahkan.

removal pindahan, pemindahan.

remove (*promotion in class*) penaikan kelas; **to —** memindahkan; (*change abode*) mengangkat.

remunerate, to — (*pay*) mengupah; (*compensate*) mengganti rugi.

remuneration upah; ganti rugi

remunerative (profitable) yang menguntungkan.

renaissance masa perkembangan.

renal yang berkenaan dengan buah pinggang.

rend, to — mengoyak, mencarik.

render, to — (give in return) membalas; (give) memberi; (arrange) mengaturkan.

rendez-vous tempat berkumpul, tempat pertemuan.

rendition (translation) terjemahan, salinan.

renegade (apostate) orang murtad; (deserter) pembelot.

renew, to — (make new) membaharui; (start again) mulai semula.

renounce, to — (surrender) menyerahkan; (repudiate) meninggalkan; (cast off) membuang.

renovate, to — memperbaiki, membaharui.

renovation pembaharuan.

renown nama harum; **—ed** termasyhor.

rent I sewa, wang sewa; **to** — menyewa.

rent II (torn) koyak.

rental wang sewa.

renunciation pembuangan, penolakan.

reopen, to — membuka semula.

reorganize, to — mengatur semula; menyusun semula.

repair I pembetulan, perbaikan; **to** — membaiki.

repair II, to — to mengunjung berulang-ulang.

reparable yang dapat diperbaiki.

reparation perbaikan; (compensation) penggantian rugi.

repartee jawaban yang tepat.

repast santapan.

repatriate, to — pulangkan ke tanahairnya.

repatriation pemulangan.

repay, to — (refund) mengganti.

repeal, to — membatalkan, memansukhkan.

repeat ulangan, pesanan ulangan; **to** — mengulangi.

repeatedly berulang-ulang.

repel, to — menolak.

repellent (distasteful) yang menjijikan.

repent, to — sesal akan, menyesalkan, tobat.

repentance sesalan, tobat.

repercussion hal kembali semula, gema.

repertoire persediaan cerita sandiwara (dan sebagainya) yang boleh dipertunjukkan kepada orangramai.

repetition ulangan.

replace, to — (put back) mengembalikan; (substitute) mengganti.

replacement penggantian.

replant, to — menanam semula.

replenish, to — menambah, memenuhkan.

replete (filled) penuh; (sated with food) kenyang.

repletion kekenyangan.

replica (duplicate) pendua; (copy of painting etc) salinan satu lukisan (dan sebagainya).

reply jawaban, balasan, sahut; **to** — membalas, menjawab.

repopulate, to — mengisi penduduk lagi.

report (news) khabar, berita, warta, repot, laporan.

reporter wartawan, juru warta.

reposo (rest) istirahat; **to** — beristirahat, rehat.

reprehend, to — mencela, menyalahkan.

reprehensible salah, tercela.

represent, to — (assume

form) merupakan; (*portray*) menggambarkan; (*be agent for*) mewakili.

representation gambaran.

representative (*agent*) wakil.

repress, to — (*oppress*) menindas; (*restrain*) menahan.

repression penahanan; penindasan, penekanan.

reprieve (*postponement*) pertangguhan; to — menangguhkan hukuman.

reprimand, to — mencela dengan rasmi, memberi amaran.

reprint cetakan ulangan; to — mencetak semula.

reprisal, to make —s membalas.

reproach cela; to — mencela.

reproachful yang mencela.

reprobate (*person*) orang busuk, orang jahat.

reproduce, to — (*propagate*) melahirkan membiak, memperanakkan; (*produce a copy*) membuat salinan.

reproduction (*copy*) salinan; (*display*) pertunjukkan.

reproof celaan, teguran.

reprove, to — mencela, menegur, mengherdik.

reptile (*animal*) binatang merayap; (*creeping*) yang merayap, reptilia.

republic republik, jamhuriah.

repudiate, to — (*reject*) menolak; (*deny*) menyangkal.

repudiation penolakan; penyangkalan.

repugnance pertentangan, perlawanan.

repugnant yang bertentangan, berlawanan.

repulse tolakan; to — menolak.

repulsion (*repulsing*) penolakan; (*disgust*) rasa jijik.

repulsive yang menjijikkan.

reputable yang baik namanya, kenamaan.

reputation nama, harum.

repute nama; to be —d disangka, dikatakan orang.

request permohonan, permintaan.

requiem doa untuk orang mati yang diadakan di gereja dengan upacara.

require, to — menghendaki; (*obligatory for Muslims*) memerlukan.

requirement kehendak; keperluan.

requisition tuntutan rasmi; to — menuntut dengan rasmi.

requital pembalasan.

requite, to — mengganti, membalas.

rescind, to — membatalkan.

rescript surat jawaban rasmi; (*of ruler*) titah.

rescue (*deliverance*) penyelamatan; (*help*) pertolongan; to — menyelamatkan.

research penyelidikan menurut ilmu pengetahuan.

researcher penyelidik.

resemblance kesamaan, persamaan.

resemble, to — menyerupai, merupai.

resent, to — kecil hati, gusar akan.

resentment sakit hati, dendam.

reservation (*clause*) syarat; (*of seat etc*) penyimpanan tempat (pada kapal dan sebagainya).

reserve (*thing laid by*) sesuatu yang disimpan; (*thing in readiness*) persediaan.

reserved (*laid by*) disimpan.

reservoir (*for water*) kolam air; (*store*) tempat penyimpan.

resettle, to — (*rearrange*) mengatur, (menyusun) semula; (*settle persons on a site*) menduduki.

reshuffle, to — mencampur semula.

reside, to — berdiam, ber-kedudukan.

residence tempat kediaman, kedudukan.

residency residency.

resident yang berdiam tinggal, bertempat tinggal, penduduk.

residual (*what is left*) yang ketinggalan; (*remains*) sisa, bekas.

residue sisa, bekas.

resign, to — minta berhenti, menyerahkan, meninggalkan.

resignation (*submissive*) sabar, kesabaran.

resilience kekuatan pelenting.

resilient bingkas, mengantul, melenting.

resin damar, gala-gala.

resinous yang mengandung damar.

resist, to — (*face*) menentang; (*withstand*) menahan; (*oppose*) melawan.

resistance pertentangan, penentangan, tahanan.

resolute tetap hati, tabah.

resolution (*analysis*) penghuraian; (*disposal*) penyelesaian; (*decision*) keputusan; (*opinion*) pendapat.

resolve keputusan, (*determination*) ketetapan hati.

resonance turut getar.

resonant (*quiver*) turut getar; (*resound*) bergema.

resorption penyerapan semula, resapan semula.

resort (*sheltered place*) tempat berlindung; (*frequented place*) tempat yang kerap dikunjungi orang.

resound, to — bergema, menggema; (*repeat*) mengulangi keras-keras.

resource akal, daya.

resourceful berakal, panjang akal.

respect hormat, kehormatan, penghargaan.

respectability keadaan atau sifat yang patut dihormati.

respectable yang patut dihormati.

respectful dengan hormat, berkhidmat.

respecting berkenaan dengan, mengenai.

respective(ly) masing-masing, tiap-tiap.

respiration pernafasan.

respirator alat penyaring hawa yang dipakai pada hidung atau mulut.

respiratory yang berkenaan dengan pernafasan.

respite pertangguhan, tempoh; to grant a — melegankan.

resplendence cemerlang, gilang-gemilang, bercahaya.

resplendent gilang-gemilang, bercahaya.

respond, to — menjawab, membalas.

respondent yang menjawab; (*in suit*) dakwaan.

response gerak-balas, jawaban, balasan, sambutan; in — to membalas.

responsibility tanggungjawab.

responsive I bertanggungjawab.

responsive II yang menjawab, membalas.

rest I (*pause*) istirahat, rehat; (*calm, peace*) ketenangan, ketenteraman.

rest II (*remainder*) lebih, sisa, bekas; to — (*remain*) tinggal.

restaurant restoran, kedai makan.

restful tenang, tenteram.

rest house pasanggerahan, rumah menginap.

restitution pemulihan, pengembalian; (*of a loss*) penggantian rugi.

restive tidak menurut, keras kepala.

restless gelisah, resah.

restock, to — melengkapkan semula.

restoration pemulihan, pembentukan kembali.

restorative yang menyembuhkan, menyegarkan.

restore, to — memulihkan, mengembalikan.

restrain, to — menahan.

restraint penahanan diri; without — dengan luasnya.

restrict, to — membatasi, menyempitkan; —ed terbatas.

restriction pembatasan.

restrictive yang membatasi, yang menyempitkan.

result (*product*) hasil; (*consequence*) akibat; (*earnings*) pendapatan.

resume, to — mulai semula.

résumé ringkasan.

resumption permulaan balik.

resurgence hidup semula, terbit semula.

resurgent yang hidup (terbit) semula.

resurrect, to — membangkitkan dari kubur, menghidupkan.

resurrection pembangkitan.

resuscitate, to — menghidupkan semula.

retail perdagangan runcit-runcit.

retain, to — memegang; (*adhere to promise etc*) berteguh.

retainer (*follower*) pengiring orang besar.

retake, to — mengambil kembali.

retaliate, to — membalas dendam.

retaliation pembalasan dendam.

retard, to — melambatkan, berlambat; (*of work, plant growth*) tergencat.

retch jeluak; to — menjeluak.

retentive yang memegang, menahan.

reticence sifat pendiam, sifat penahan.

reticent pendiam.

retinue pengiring.

retire, to — (*withdraw from*) mengundurkan diri; (*be pensioned*) bersara.

retirement pengunduran diri; bersara.

retiring malu, penyegan, manduk.

retort I sejenis labu gelas yang dipakai di makmal.

retort II (*reply*) jawaban yang tepat; to — menjawab dengan tepat.

retouch, to — mengubah sedikit untuk memperbaiki.

retrace, to — (*investigate*) menyelidiki sesuatu; (*go back*) kembali balik.

retract, to — menarik ke dalam, memasukkan lagi.

retreat (*withdrawal*) penguduran; (*place of privacy*) tempat untuk diri.

retrench, to — mengurangi, memotong perbelanjaan.

retribution pembalasan.

retrieve, to — (*regain*) mendapat kembali; (*dog*) —r anjing pemburu.

retro— awalan kata yang ertinya: ke belakang; di belakang, kembali.

retroaction perbuatan berbalik.

retrocession penyerahan kembali.

retroflected terkedek.

retrograde berbalik, mundur, mengundur.

retrogress, to — mundur.

retrospect (*survey of past*) tinjauan kepada waktu atau kejadian yang telah lalu.

retrospection kenangan.

retrospective (*looking back*) memandang ke belakang; yang meninjau atau berkenaan dengan hal yang telah lalu.

return (*go home*) pulang, kembalinya.

reunion hal bersatu atau berkumpul semula.

revaccinate, to — mencacar semula.

revalue, to — menilaikan semula.

reveal, to — membukakan, melahirkan maksud.

reveille bunyi terompet pagi-pagi hari kerana membangunkan soldadu.

revelation (*divine*) ilham, wahyu; (*of secret*) pembukaan rahsia.

reveller orang yang bersuka ria.

revel(s) kesukaan, suka ria.

revenge pembalasan; **to** — membalas.

revengeful ingin membalas dendam.

revenue pendapatan, hasil.

reverberate, to — bergaung, bergema.

reverberation gema, gaung.

revere, to — menghormati, mentakzimkan.

reverence hormat, takzim, pemujaan, penghormatan.

reverend yang dihormati, yang terhormat tuan.

reverent yang menghormati, mentakzimkan.

reverential yang berkenaan dengan penghormatan, yang menghormati.

reverie angan-angan.

reverse yang terbalik, yang pada baliknya; **—d** terbalik, songsang.

reversible dapat balik.

reversion pengembalian.

revert, to — kembali kepada keadaan dahulu; (*recur to*) balik.

review periksa ulangan, pemeriksaan semula.

revile, to — mencaci memaki, mencerca.

revise, to — (*examine*) memeriksa semula; (*amend*) memperbaiki.

revision perbaikan.

revisit, to — mengunjungi lagi, melawat semula.

revival hal hidup semula, penghidupan semula.

revive, to — hidup kembali, balik sedar, menghidupkan kembali.

revocation pembatalan.

revoke, to — membatalkan.

revolt pemberontakan; **to** — memberontak, menderhaka.

revolting jijik, menjemukan.

revolution (*rotation*) peredaran, putaran, perkisaran.

revolutionize, to — mengubahkan salah satu keadaan samasekali.

revolve, to — beredar, bermutar, mengedari.

revolver pistol.

revue sandiwara bercampur, pertunjukan yang terdiri daripada segala rupa tari-tarian.

revulsion perubahan yang tiba-tiba.

reward ganjaran, hadiah; **to** — membalas, menghadiahkan.

rewrite karangan yang diubahkan sehingga patut diumumkan, karang semula.

rhapsody karangan muzik yang sangat menarik hati.

rhetoric karangan mengenai ilmu berucap.

rhetorical, — question pertanyaan yang tidak payah dijawab kerana hanya cara berucap.

rheumatic sakit sengal.

rheumatism penyakit sengal.

rhinoceros, rhino badak.

rhododendron sejenis pokok seperti senuduk berbunga.

rhubarb sejenis pokok yang dimakan sebagai sayur.

rhyme sajak; **to —** bersajak.

rhythm irama.

rhythmic(al) berirama.

rib (of body) tulang rusuk; (of boat) ganding-ganding.

ribald carut; pencarut.

ribbon pita.

rice (in husk) padi; (husked) beras; (cooked) nasi.

ricefield sawah.

rich kaya; (of soil) subur; (of dress) mulia; (valuable) berharga; (abundant) mewah.

riches kekayaan, harta-benda.

richly dengan jaya.

rick longgok, timbunan.

rickets penyakit kanak-kanak yang menyebabkan kelemahan tulang.

rickety (feeble) lemah.

rickshaw langca, beca.

ricochet pengambulan sepi.

rid, to — melepaskan, membebaskan.

riddance pembebasan.

riddle I teka-teki.

riddle II, to — (sieve) menapis, mengayak.

ride perjalanan kereta; **to —** berjalan, berkereta.

rider (of horse) orang berkuda; (problem) masaalah (yang maksudnya menyelidiki pengetahuan si murid).

ridge (of roof) perabungan, rabung, bubungan; (between ricefields) batas; (on land) rabung bukit, permatang.

ridge pole bubungan.

ridicule ejekan, olok; **to —** mengejek, mengolok-olok.

ridiculous patut ditertawakan, menggelikan.

rife (prevalent) banyak terdapat, umum.

riffraff rakyat jelata.

rifle I bedil, senapang; **to shoot with a —** membedil, menembak dengan senapang.

rifle II, to — (rob) mencuri, menggeledah.

rifle range padang tembak, sasaran.

rift celah, belah; **to —** menceraikan, membelah.

rig I (ropes etc) tali temali; (equipment) perlengkapan.

rig II (manipulate unscrupulously) muslihat, tipu daya.

rigging temberang.

right (straight) lurus; (angle) siku; (correct) tepat, benar, patut; (just) adil; (good) baik.

right-about turn balik ke belakang, pusing belakang.

right-angled siku-siku, sudut tepat.

righteous patut, adil.

rightful (of possession) yang berhak; (proper) patut; (just) adil.

rightly dengan patut, dengan baik, sapatutnya.

right-minded berkelakuan baik, baik budi.

rigid (from cold etc) kaku; (stiff of leaves, hair) kejur, (obstinate) tegar.

rigidity kaku, ketegaran.

rigmarole cakap angin, percakapan merepet.

rigorous keras, kejam.

rigour, (US) **rigor** kaku; (harshness) kekerasan.

rile, to — menggusarkan, merangsangkan.

rim (edge) tepi; (edging) bingkai; (of wheel) lengkaran roda.

rind kulit buah.

ring I (finger) cincin; (circle) bulatan; (bracelet, hoop etc) gelang, simpai; (coil) lengkaran; (arena) gelanggang.

ring II (of bell) bunyi loceng.

ring finger jari manis.

ringleader kepala, salah satu kumpulan penjahat.

ringlet ikal rambut.

ringmaster pemimpin pertunjukan kuda.

ringworm kurap.

rink lapangan yang ditutupi

air beku yang dipakai untuk meluncur.

rinse membasuh; to — membasuh; (of mouth) berkumur-kumur.

riot kerusuhan, gaduh.

riotous rusuh, merisau.

rip (tug) renggutan; to — mencabik, mengoyak; to — open meretas.

ripe masak, matang.

ripen, to — menjadi masak.

riposte (in fencing) tangkisan; (retort) jawaban; to — menangkis; menjawab.

ripple riak; to — meriak.

rise (of land) tanah tinggi, bonggol, bukit; (a rise) kenaikan, naiknya; to — bangun; to give — to mengakibatkan.

rising sedang naik, bangkit; pemberontakan.

risk bahaya, tanggungan, harus rugi.

risky berbahaya; (unseemly) tidak sopan.

rite upacara.

ritual yang berkenaan dengan atau disertai upacara lazim, adat istiadat.

rival tanding, saing, lawan.

rivalry persaingan, pertandingan, singgitan.

river sungai, kali, batang air.

riverside tanah sebelah-menyebelah sungai.

rivet paku sumbat; to — menyumbat, memaku dengan paku sumbat.

rivulet anak sungai.

roach sejenis ikan.

road jalan; high— jalan raya.

road metal batu kerakal.

roam, to — mengembara.

roan kuda atau lembu yang berwarna burik belang.

roar bunyi mengaum; to — mengaum, meraung; (of thunder) menderam.

roast sesuatu yang dipanggang, sesuatu yang disalai.

rob, to — merampas, merompak, menyamun.

robber pencuri, perampas, penyamun.

robbery kecurian, perampasan, perompakan.

robe jubah.

robin sejenis burung murai.

robot jentera yang dapat melakukan pekerjaan orang.

robust agam, kuat, tegap.

rock I batu, karang; (of ship) to run upon the —s karam.

rock II, to — berayun-ayun, mengayun, buai.

rocket cerawat; to — naik seperti cerawat.

rocky berbatu, penuh batu karang.

rod batang, tongkat.

rodent binatang tikus.

rodeo pengumpulan lembu pada suatu peternakan di Amerika.

roe I (of fish) telur ikan.

roe II sejenis rusa; —buck rusa jantan.

rogue anak nakal, buaya.

roguish nakal.

role peranan, bahagian.

roll (thing rolled up) gulung; (manuscript) naskhah; (list) daftar, daftar hadir.

roller (instruments) gulungan, penggiling; (wave) ombak besar.

rollick, to — bersuka ria; —ing riang gembira ria-rioh.

roly-poly sejenis kuih.

Roman Rumawi, Rumi; — characters (letters, type) huruf Rumi.

Roman Catholic orang yang beragama Katolik.

romance cerita, hikayat.

romantic romantik.

Romany orang pengembara yang berbangsa Romani; bahasa Romani.

Rome kerajaan Rom.

romp bergurau.

roof atap; (of mouth, ceiling) langit-langit.

rook sejenis burung gagak.

rookery tempat burung gagak suka bersarang.

room (place) tempat; (space) lapangan; (apartment) bilik, ruang.

roomy longgar, luas, lapang.

roost (for fowls) reban.

rooster ayam jantan, ayam jago.

root I (of plant) akar; (origin) pangkal, mula pokok.

root II, to — menyungkur, menyodok tanah; — word akar-kata.

rope tali; to know the —s tahu akan selok-beloknya.

rosary tasbih.

rose bunga mawar; a bed of —s kehidupan atau keadaan mewah dan senang.

rosebud kuntum bunga mawar.

rosemary sejenis tumbuhan yang daunnya harum.

rosette perhiasan berbentuk bunga mawar.

rose water air mawar; (of conduct) kelakuan lemah-lembut.

roster daftar pekerjaan.

rostrum panggung; (pulpit) mimbar.

rosy berwarna kemerah-merahan.

rot kebusukan; to — menjadi busuk.

rota daftar pekerjaan, daftar giliran bekerja.

rotary yang berputar.

rotate, to — berputar, berkisar, berpusar; (in turn) bergilir.

rotation berputaran, perkisaran; giliran.

rote, by — dihafazkan sahaja (tidak difikirkan dalam-dalam).

rotor bahagian mesin yang berputar.

rotten bangar, busuk.

rotter orang busuk, orang jahat, orang keji.

rotund (round) bundar, bulat; (fat) gemuk.

rouge gincu, pemerah pipi dan bibir.

rough kasap, kesat, kasar.

roughly dengan kasar; (approximately) lebih kurang; — speaking selayang pandang.

roulette alat putar dadu main judi.

round (circular) bulat; (numbers) genap; (object) sesuatu yang bulat; (circuit) peredaran.

roundabout keliling; (not direct) tidak langsung, berputar.

rounders sejenis permainan bola dengan pemukul, bola keliling.

roundly dengan terus terang.

rouse, to — menggiatkan, menggalakkan, memberangsangkan.

rout (uproar) kerusuhan; (dispersion) pembubaran; to — semua sekali.

route jalan, perjalanan.

routine aturan biasa, tertib.

rove gembara; to — mengembara, berkeliling.

rover pengembara.

row I (line) deret, jajar, baris, banjar.

row II (use oars) dayung; to — berdayung, berkayuh.

row III (dispute) perselisihan, pertengkaran; to make a — berbantah, bergaduh.

rowboat, rowing boat sampan, perahu.

rowdy orang yang kasar dan suka merusuh.

rowlock keliti.

royal yang berkenaan dengan raja, diraja.

royalist pengikut sistem kerajaan.

royalty kedudukan atau kuasa

raja; salah satu di antara keluarga raja; (fee) cukai.

rub gosok; to — menggosok, menggesek.

rubber getah.

rubbish kotoran, sampah sarap.

rubble kerobohan.

rubicund kemerah-merahan.

ruby batu delima, sejenis batu merah yang berharga.

ruck kumpulan (pelomba).

rucksack sejenis sampul yang dipikul pada punggung.

rudder kemudi.

ruddy merah muka.

rude kasar, biadab.

rudiment bahagian yang tidak sempurna; —s dasar mula.

rudimentary dasar, tidak sempurna.

rue, to — menyesali.

rueful sesal, yang menimbulkan belas kasihan.

ruff, ruffle sejeni perhiasan berenda pada leher ropol.

ruffian orang jahat dan kasar.

rug (carpet) sejenis permadani; (blanket) selimut.

rugged kasar, kesat; (not flat) tidak rata.

ruin kejatuhan, keruntuhan.

ruinous celaka, binasa.

rule peraturan kaedah; (government) pemerintahan.

ruler orang yang memerintah, raja, yamtuan; (for drawing lines) pembaris.

ruling (judgement) keputusan hakim.

rum sejenis minuman keras.

rumble bunyi gerebak-gere-buk.

rumbustious riuh-rendah.

ruminant memamah biak, binatang menceruh.

ruminate, to — (chew cud) memamah biak; (meditate) berfikir.

rummage (contents) pembongkaran; (search) penggeledahan; to — (turn over) membongkar; (search) menggeledah.

rumour khabar angin.

rump tongkeng, belakang.

rumple, to — mengerut, menggumalkan.

rumpus huru-hara.

run lari, pelarian; (journey) perjalanan; in the long — lama kelamaan.

rung (kayu yang dipasang sebagai) anak tangga.

runner pelari; (messenger) pesuruh; (of plant) sulur.

running yang sedang lari.

running board injak-injak, tempat pijak.

runt sejenis lembu kecil.

runway landasan terbang.

rupee wang di negeri India.

rupture (hernia) burut; (severing) perputusan; to — pecah.

rural yang berkenaan dengan desa, dusun, luar bandar.

ruse reka, rekaan, muslihat.

rush I (very busy) kesibukan; (crowd) keramaian; (charge) menyerang.

rush II (plant) sejenis rumput purun.

russet kuning kemerah-merahan, perang.

Russian yang berkenaan dengan negeri atau orang Rusia.

rust tahi besi, karat; (disease of plants) sejenis penyakit tumbuhan; to — berkarat.

rustic yang berkenaan dengan desa (dan orang desa).

rustle bising; to — meresek.

rustless yang tidak berkarat.

rusty dimakan karat, berkarat.

rut (in road) bekas roda; (settled habit) jalan biasa.

ruthless keras hati, bengis kejam.

rye gandum hitam.

S

sabbath hari berisytirehat (hari Sabtu untuk orang Yahudi hari minggu untuk orang Nasrani).

sabotage perosakan; to — merosakkan, sabotaj.

sabre, (US) **saber** sejenis pedang; (cavalry) askar berkuda.

saccharine sakarin, gula tiruan.

sack karung, guni; (col) to get the — diberhentikan dari jabatannya.

sackcloth kain karung, guni.

sacrament upacara yang mewujudkan salah satu hak suci.

sacred suci, kudus.

sacrifice korban; to — mengurbankan.

sacrificial yang berkenaan dengan korban.

sacrilege pelanggaran hal atau tempat suci.

sacrilegious yang melanggar hal (tempat) suci.

sacrosanct sangat suci dan kerana itu tiada dapat dilanggar.

sad susah hati, sedih, sayu.

sadden, to — menyedihkan, menyusahkan hati.

saddle pelana.

saddler pembuat atau penjual pelana (dan segala rupa pakaian kuda).

sadism keinginan akan menyakiti orang, bengis.

sadistic ingin menyakiti orang, bengis.

sadness sedih, sayu.

safari perburuan dengan sekumpulan pemburu.

safe aman, tidak berbahaya, selamat, sejahtera.

safe conduct surat jalan, surat perlindungan.

safeguard perlindungan, surat jalan; to — melindungi.

safeguarding pemeliharaan, penghindaran.

safe keeping penyimpanan.

safety keamanan, selamat, kesejahteraan.

saffron kunyit; (colour) warna kuning.

sag lentur, lendut; to — melentur, melendut.

saga hikayat, kisah.

sagacious bijaksana, berakal, cerdik.

sagacity bijaksana.

sage I sejenis tumbuhan yang harum daunnya.

sage II (wise) bijaksana, cerdik; (wise person) orang bijaksana.

sago sagu.

sail layar; (sailing) pelayaran; to — belayar.

sailboat, **sailing-boat** perahu layar.

sailer, **sailing-vessel** kapal layar.

sailor anak kapal, kelasi.

saint suci, orang suci wali.

saintly seperti orang suci, saleh.

sake, for the — of kerana, bagi, untuk kepentingan.

salacious gasang.

salad makanan sayuran atau buah-buahan mentah, selada.

salary gaji.

sale penjualan; (auction) lelong.

salesman penjual.

salesmanship kepandaian menjual, kecekapan menjual.

salient yang menganjur, yang terpenting.

saline yang mengandung garam; (salty) asin, masin.

saliva air ludah air liur.

sallow pucat, pudar.

saloon ruangan tempat duduk.

salt garam; (salty) asin; **an old** — anak laut.

saltcellar tempat garam.

saltern pegaraman.

saltish masin.

salt lick tempat sesapan garam di hutan sira, jenut.

salt mine tambang garam.

saltpetre sendawa.

salubrious sihat, yang menyihatkan.

salutary baik, yang menyegarkan.

salutation salam.

salute salam, tabik; to — memberi tabik.

salvage pembayaran untuk penyelamatan kapal (atau muatannya); to — menyelamatkan barang atau kapal dari kerugian.

salvation keselamatan.

salve (ointment) koyok, palit; to — membubuhi koyok.

salver talam, baki.

Samaritan orang Samaria; a good — orang yang murah hati.

same sama; the — yang sama, yang serupa.

Samoan orang atau bahasa Samoa.

sample contoh, tuladan; to — mengambil (atau memberi) contoh.

sampler pencuba.

sanatorium, (US) **sanitarium** peranginan, sanatorium.

sanctification persucian.

sanctify, to — mengkuduskan, mencucikan.

sanctimonious pura-pura saleh, munafik.

sanction (penalty) pengukuhan, hukum; (permission) izin; to — mengizinkan.

sanctity kesucian.

sanctuary (holy place) tempat suci; (shelter) tempat perlindungan.

sand pasir.

sandal lapik kaki, cerpu.

sandalwood kayu cendana.

sandbag karung berisi pasir.

sandpaper kertas pasir; to — mempelas.

sandpiper sejenis burung kedidi.

sandstone batu paras.

sandwich dua potong roti dengan daging (ikan dan sebagainya) di antaranya.

sandy berpasir, penuh pasir.

sane sihat ingatannya, berakal; (sensible) bijaksana.

sanguinary berdarah, penuh darah.

sanguine (of complexion) merah muka; penuh harapan dan selalu giat.

sanitary menurut ilmu kesihatan; (clean) bersih.

sanitation hal memperbaiki keadaan kesihatan.

sanity (of health) keadaan sihat; (of mind) kesihatan akal.

Sanskrit, Sanscrit sanskrit.

Santa Claus orang padri dalam cerita dongeng yang membawa hadiah untuk kanak-kanak.

sap getah (dalam tumbuh-tumbuhan dan buah).

sapling pohon muda.

sapphire (stone) batu nilam; (colour) warna biru.

sarcasm bahasa ejek, ucapan kata-kata yang tajam, kias, sindiran.

sarcastic tajam, kias, sindiran.

sarcophagus peti mayat batu.

sardine ikan sadin.

sardonic tajam, sengit.

sari sari.

sarong sarung.

sartorial yang berkenaan dengan pembuatan pakaian laki-laki.

sash (round waist) ikat ping-

gang; (across breast) selempang.
Satan syaitan, iblis.
satanic yang berkenaan atau
seperti syaitan.
satchel sampul, karung, saku.
satellite (follower) pengiring,
pengikut; (planet) bintang
yang beredar di sekeliling
salah satu bintang lain, satelit.
satiate kenyang.
satin sutera yang berkilat,
antelas.
satire sajak sindiran.
satirical yang suka menyindir.
satirist orang yang suka
menyindir.
satirize, to — mengarang
sindiran, menyindir.
satisfaction hal kepuasan
hati.
satisfactory memuaskan.
satisfied, to be, rest — puas.
satisfy, to — memuaskan,
memenuhi.
saturate, to — (soak) merendamkan; (fill) memenuhi dengan; (absorb) menyerap.
saturation penyerapan.
Saturday hari Sabtu.
Saturn bintang.
saturnine (sluggish) lengah;
(gloomy) muram.
sauce kicap, kuah; (col)
(impudence) sifat besar mulut.
sauceboat tempat kicap.
saucepan kuali.
saucer piring, pinggan kecil.
saucy muka tebal, lancang
mulut.
saunter, to — berkeliaran,
melancong.
savage (wild) liar; (fierce)
ganas; orang biadab.
save I, to — (rescue) menyelamatkan; (lay by) menyimpan.
save II (except) kecuali.
savings wang simpanan, wang
tabungan; Post Office S—
Bank tabungan pos.

saviour penyelamat.
savour (taste) rasa; (special
property of drugs etc) khasiat;
to — merasa, rasanya.
savoury enak, lazat, sedap;
(dish) hidangan sedap.
savvy (col) tahu, mengerti.
saw gergaji; **hand**— gergaji
yang dikerjakan dengan satu
tangan sahaja.
sawdust habuk kayu, tahi
gergaji.
sawfish ikan todak, yu
gergaji.
sawmill kilang papan.
saxophone seksafon, alat
muzik.
say yang dikatakan, kata-
kata, ujar.
saying (words) perkataan;
(maxim etc) peribahasa, pepatah, bidal.
scab (over sore) keropeng;
(skin disease) kudis.
scabbard sarung keris, pedang dan sebagainya.
scabby berkeropeng.
scabies kudis.
scaffold (for gallows) panggung di atasnya mana di-
lakukan hukuman mati.
scaffolding bangunan sementara hampir rumah yang
sedang didirikan.
scald, to — (blister) melecur;
(dip in boiling water) mencelur.
scale I (of fish) sisik; (chip)
serpih; **to** — menyisiki.
scale II (balance) daun neraca;
—s neraca, timbangan.
scale III (grade) darjah, pang-
tingkat, sekil.
scallop (oyster) sejenis tiram;
(cockle) kerang.
scallywag orang keji.
scalp kulit kepala dengan
rambutnya.
scalpel pisau belah.
scaly bersisik.
scamp orang celaka, anak
nakal.

scamper lari, perjalanan cepat; to — berlari.

scan, to — (*scrutinize*) menatapi meninjau.

scandal sesuatu yang menerbitkan kemarahan dan fitnah orang banyak, fitnah.

scandalize, to — melanggar perasaan sopan santun.

scandalous keji.

scant sangat sedikit.

scanty sangat sedikit atau jarang.

scapegoat orang yang menanggung dosa orang lain.

scapula tulang belikat.

scar parut, bekas luka; to — meninggalkan parut, merupakan parut.

scarab sejenis kumbang yang dikira suci di Masir masa dahulukala.

scarce jarang, tidak cukup.

scarcely (*hardly*) hampir tidak; (*just; of time*) baharu sahaja; (*surely not*) masakan; he had — arrived baharu sahaja ia tiba.

scarcity kekurangan, kesempitan.

scare takut; to — menakutkan.

scarecrow orang-orangan (yang ditaruh di kebun untuk menghalau burung), selagut.

scarf sejenis selendang.

scarlet merah padam.

scathe, to — (*harm*) merosakkan, menyakiti.

scatter, to — menghamburkan, menabur.

scatterbrain orang yang fikirannya melincah-lincah, kepala angin.

scattered berhamburan, cerai-berai, bertaburan.

scavenger buruh yang membersihkan jalan; (*animal*) binatang yang memakan bangkai.

scene (*stage*) adegan, panggung, layar sandiwara; (*view*)

pemandangan; (*place*) tempat kejadian.

scenery layar dan lain alat sandiwara; pemandangan.

scent harum, bau, wangi.

sceptic orang yang menaruh syak akan salah satu kepercayaan.

sceptical yang menaruh syak akan salah satu kepercayaan.

sceptre tongkat sebagai tanda kerajaan atau kekuasaan.

schedule daftar, jadual; to — menyusun daftar.

scheme rancangan; to — merancangkan, sekim.

schism perpisahan.

schizophrenia salah satu penyakit jiwa.

scholar ahli, orang terpelajar; (*scholarship holder*) pelajar yang menerima biasiswa.

scholarship biasiswa; sekolarship.

scholastic yang berkenaan dengan pengajaran guru-guru.

school sekolah, perguruan; (*building*) rumah sekolah; (*subject taught*) pelajaran di sekolah; (*pupils*) murid-murid sekolah.

schoolbook buku sekolah, buku pelajaran.

schoolboy murid laki-laki.

schoolmaster guru laki-laki.

schoolmistress guru perempuan.

schoolroom bilik sekolah.

schoolteacher guru sekolah rendah.

schooner sejenis kapal layar.

sciatica sengal pinggang.

science ilmu sain, ilmu pengetahuan.

scientific berilmu, berdasarkan ilmu pengetahuan.

scientist ahli ilmu pengetahuan, ahli ilmu sain.

scintillate, to — berkilau-kilauan.

scissors gunting.

scoff I, to — mengejek.

scoff II, (col) to — (food) makan dengan lahap.

scold, to — mencaci-maki, mengherdik.

scone sejenis kuih.

scoop gayung, sauk-sauk.

scoot, to — lari, pergi lekas-lekas.

scope tinjauan, kawasan kelonggaran.

scorch, to — menghanguskan; —ed earth policy faham bumi hangus.

score (notch) takek, takuk; (count reckoning) mata, perhitungan.

scorn penghinaan, cacian; to — menganggap hina.

scornful penuh rasa penghinaan.

Scorpio bintang Kala.

scorpion kala jengking.

Scot orang bangsa Sekot.

Scots = Scottish.

Scotsman orang Sekot.

Scottish yang berkenaan dengan orang atau bahasa Sekot.

scoundrel bangsat.

scour I, to — (rub) menggosok, menggesel.

scour II, to — (run in search of) berkeliling cepat-cepat kerana mencari sesuatu.

scourer penggosok.

scourge, to — (pester) merundung; (flog) mendera.

scout I peninjau, pengakap, pengintai; boy — budak pengakap.

scout II, to — (reject) menolak dengan mengejekkan.

scowl pandang marah, bermuka masam.

scrabble, to — mencakar-cakar.

scraggy kurus kering.

scram (col) enyah!

scramble (climb) mendaki

ragang; (rough play) perjalanan yang sukar; to — berjalan atau mendaki dengan susah payah.

scrap (piece) carik, keping; (thing picked up) kutipan; (col) (quarrel) perkelahian.

scrape (scratch) garuk; (earth, gravel) kersik; (difficulty) keadaan genting; to — menggaruk.

scraper cakar, kukur.

scratch (line) goris; (as fowl) cakar, garuk; (starting line) garis permulaan.

scrawl tulisan cakar ayam; to — menulis secara cakar ayam.

scream jeritan, pekek, teriak.

screech jeritan; to — menjerit.

screen sekat, dinding, kajang; (curtain) tabir; (like a sail) layar.

screw (for fastening etc) sekerup; there is a — loose gila betul.

scribble tulisan cakar ayam; to — menulis secara cakar ayam.

scribbler orang yang menulis secara cakar ayam; (petty author) pengarang yang kurang baik.

scribe (writer) penulis; (instrument) alat penulis.

scrip akuan sementara.

script (manuscript) naskhah; (handwriting) tulisan tangan.

scriptural yang berdasarkan kitab suci.

scripture kitab suci.

scroll (roll of paper etc) naskhah yang digulung; (ornament) perhiasan dengan garis yang merupakan awan-awan.

scrotum kandung buah pelir.

scrounge, to — mencapai dengan kelicikan.

scrub I (brushwood) semak, belukar, samun.

scrub II (*rub to clean*) gosok; to — menggosok.

scruff (*of neck*) tengkok.

scruffy kotor.

scrumptious sangat enak.

scruple (*small weight*) ukuran berat.

scrupulous teliti, saksama.

scrutinize, to — meneliti, mengamat-amati, menatapi.

scrutiny siasat, telaah.

scud, to — berlari (atau melayang) cepat; (*with the wind*) turut angin.

scuffle perkelahian haru biru; to — berkelahi.

scull salah satu dari sepasang dayung.

scullery dapur tambahan.

scullion anak muda yang membantu juru masak.

sculpt, to — memahat.

sculptor ahli patung.

sculpture (*art of sculpture*) seni pahat; (*bas relief*) arca; (*statue*) patung.

scum (*on river*) kekat; (*froth*) buih; (*infamous thing*) hal yang sangat hina dan keji; (*rubbish*) sampah.

scurf (*dandruff*) kelemumur.

scurrilous kasar; carut.

scurry jalan atau lari cepat; to — berlari tergopoh-gopoh.

scurvy keji, hina.

scuttle I (*coal*) tempat penyimpan sedikit batu bara.

scuttle II (*in ship*) lubang di sisi kapal.

scuttle III, to — (*run*) berlari cepat-cepat tergopoh-gopoh.

scythe sejenis sabit besar; to — menyabit.

sea laut, segara, lautan.

seaboard pantai, tepi laut.

sea cucumber teripang.

seafaring yang belayar di laut; a — man anak laut.

seagull burung camar.

seal I anjing laut; (*skin*) kulit anjing laut itu.

seal II (*for letters etc*) meterai, cap; (*mark*) tanda.

sealing wax lakeri.

sea lion sejenis anjing laut.

seam kampuh, kelim.

seaman pelaut; able-bodied — kelas.

seamanship kepandaian (keahlian) belayar, ilmu pelayaran.

sea mile ukuran mile laut.

seamstress tukang jahit perempuan.

seance perkumpulan untuk pemanggilan roh orang yang telah meninggal.

seaplane kepalterbang laut.

sear, to — melayukan; (*cauterize*) menyelarkan.

search penyelidikan, penggelidahan.

searching sedang menyelidiki, sedang mencari.

searchlight lampu suluh.

search warrant izin penggelidahan.

seashore pantai, tepi laut.

seasick mabuk laut.

season musim, masa; (*proper time*) waktu yang tepat.

seasonal yang berkenaan dengan salah satu musim, tiap-tiap musim.

seat (*for sitting*) tempat duduk; (*chair*) kerusi; (*bench*) bangku. **—seater** yang bertempat duduk.

sea urchin bulu babi.

seaweed agar-agar laut.

seaworthy yang sanggup melayari laut.

secede, to — menarikkan diri dari salah satu badan rasmi.

secession penarikan diri, pemisahan.

seclude, to — memisahkan, menyencilkan; to — o.s. bersendiri.

seclusion pengasingan, menunggal.

second I (*in time*) detik, saat.

second II (*number*) yang kedua.

second III, to — membantu, menyangga.

secondary yang kedua; (*additional*) tambahan; — **school** sekolah menengah.

second-best yang kedua dari atas.

second hand tua, lama, yang pernah dipakai.

secondly kedua.

second-rate mutu kedua, tidak berapa baik.

second sight bakat terus mata.

secrecy pemegangan rahsia.

secret tersembunyi, rahsia; **to keep** — memegang rahsia.

secretarial yang berkenaan dengan pekerjaan setiausaha.

secretariat pejabat setiausaha.

secretary setiausaha.

secrete, to — (*hide*) menyembunyikan; (*issue of gland etc*) mengeluarkan (getah, darah dan lain-lain).

secretion pengeluaran (getah, darah dan lain-lain).

secretive yang suka merahsiakan atau menyembunyikan; (*silent*) diam-diam.

sect mazhab, badan berugama.

section belah, tampang, bahagian.

sector sektor; (*area*) kawasan, lengkongan.

secular seabad lamanya, sangat lama, abadi.

secure (*safe*) aman; (*of forts etc*) kukuh, teguh.

security (*deposit*) amanat, jaminan, tanggungan; (*safety*) keamanan, keselamatan.

sedan — chair pelangkin.

sedate tenang dan santun.

sedative ubat yang meredakan, ubat menenangkan sakit.

sedentary sedang duduk, suka duduk atau terpaksa duduk.

sediment endapan, mendak, keladak.

sedition penderhakaan.

seduce, to — (*persuade*) memujuk; (*lead astray*) menyesatkan.

seduction pemujukan; sesuatu yang menyesatkan.

seductive yang memujuk; yang menyesatkan.

see melihat, memandang; (*understand*) mengerti.

seed biji, benih.

seedless tidak berbiji.

seedling semaian.

seedy (*full of seed*) penuh biji; (*shabby*) berpakaian buruk; (*poor in health*) sakit, tidak sedap badan.

seek, to — (*search*) mencari; (*try for*) mencuba; (*claim*) menuntut.

seeker pencari.

seem, to — rupanya, tampaknya, agaknya.

seeming(ly) rupanya, tampaknya, kelihatannya, pada lahirnya.

seemly patut, sopan santun.

seep, to — merengat, tiris.

seer orang yang sanggup menilik hal yang akan terjadi pada masa yang akan datang.

seersucker sejenis kain lurik.

seesaw jungkang-jungkit, unggang-unggit.

seethe, to — mendidih, meruap, menggelegak.

segment (*of fruit*) pangsa, penggal; (*section*) temberang; (*of circle*) lengkaran; **to** — berpangsa, segmen.

segregate terpencil, terpisah; **to** — memisahkan, mengasingkan.

segregation pemisahan, pengasingan.

seismic yang berkenaan dengan gempa bumi.

seismograph alat yang mencatat gempa bumi.

seize, to — (*hold*) memegang; (*arrest*) menangkap.

seizure penangkapan.

seldom jarang.

select terpilih, pilihan; **to** — memilih.

selection pemilihan; pilihan.

selectivity kesanggupan menerima bunyi.

self diri sendiri.

self-acting bergerak atau berjalan dengan sendirinya.

self-assertion hal menuntut haknya sendiri, hal mementingkan harga dirinya.

self-assurance perasaan harga diri.

self-assured penuh harga diri.

self-centred berpusat kepada diri sendiri, mementingkan diri sendiri.

self-command hal menahan diri.

self-composed tenang.

self-confidence kepercayaan akan diri sendiri.

self-confident percaya akan diri sendiri.

self-conscious malu, tidak sanggup melakukan diri dengan tenang.

self-contained berpusat kepada kepentingan dirinya; (*reserved*) tidak suka bergaul.

self-control kesanggupan mengawal diri sendiri.

self-deception pembohong diri sendiri, penipu diri sendiri.

self-defence pembelaan diri sendiri.

self-determination hal menentukan sendiri.

self-evident sudah tentu.

self-explanatory yang tidak usah dijelaskan lagi.

self-expression hal membukakan batinnya.

self-government pemerintahan sendiri.

self-indulgence hal memuaskan hawa nafsunya.

self-indulgent memuaskan hawa nafsunya.

self-interest hal mementingkan diri sendiri.

selfish berpusat kepada diri sendiri sahaja.

selfless tidak mementingkan diri sendiri.

self-made dibuat sendiri; (*of person*) yang mencapai pangkat kerana kerajinan dan kepandaiannya sendiri.

self-pity kasihan akan diri sendiri.

self-possessed berkelakuan tenang.

self-possession ketenangan.

self-preservation pembelaan diri, pelihara diri.

self-respect mutu diri.

self-restraint pertahanan diri.

self-righteous yang mementingkan kebaikan sendiri.

self-sacrifice pengkorbanan diri.

selfsame yang tepat sama.

self-satisfaction kepuasan akan diri sendiri.

self-satisfied bangga akan diri sendiri.

self-service berdasarkan layanan diri.

self-sufficient sanggup melengkapkan diri.

self-supporting sanggup mencari kehidupannya sendiri.

self-willed keras kepala, degil.

sell, to — berjual, menjual, memperniagakan; laku.

seller penjual.

selvage tepi tenunan.

semantic yang berkenaan dengan erti kata, ilmu simantik.

semaphore tiang (atau lain alat) untuk memberi semboyan.

semblance persamaan, kesamaan.

semen mani.

semi— awalan kata yang ertinya: setengah.

semicircle separuh bulatan.

semicolon koma bernoktah.

semidetached bersambung pada satu sisi sahaja.

semifinal pertandingan yang mendahului pertandingan yang terakhir.

seminar perkumpulan mahasiswa dengan mahagurunya.

seminary madrasah, sekolah perguruan padri; setinbar.

semitone separuh titinada.

semolina isi gandum.

senate senat, badan pemerintah, badan pembuat undang-undang.

senator anggota senat.

send, to — berkirim, mengirim, menghantar.

sender pengirim.

senescence hal menjadi tua.

senile tua renta, tua bangka.

senior tua; *(in rank)* lebih tinggi pangkatnya, kanan.

sensation rasa, perasaan peka.

sensational hebat, menggemparkan.

sense *(feeling)* perasaan; deria; *(meaning)* erti; *(concept)* pengertian; *(mind)* akal; —s ingatan.

senseless *(unfeeling)* mati rasa; *(swoon)* pengsan; *(stupid)* bodoh.

sensibility kesanggupan merasa.

sensible berakal, berbudi.

sensitive lekas berasa, peka, mudah tersinggung; *(delicate)* halus.

sensitivity sifat lekas terasa, lekas terharu, lekas tersinggung.

sensory yang berkenaan dengan perasaan atau panca indera, deria.

sensual bernafsu; — pleasures kelazatan.

sensuous yang berkenaan dengan perasaan; *(sensual)* bernafsu.

sentence *(judgement)* keputusan, hukuman; *(in grammar)* kalimat; compound — kalimat majemuk.

sententious singkat dan tepat.

sentiment perasaan; sentimen.

sentimental bersentimen, lekas terharu.

sentimentality hal lekas terharu.

sentry pengawal, penjaga.

separate terpisah, tersendiri; to — berpisah, memisahkan.

separation pemisahan, penceraian.

sepia air hitam yang dipancarkan oleh ikan kurita; *(colour)* warna merah tua.

sept— awalan kata yang ertinya: tujuh.

September bulan September.

septic yang berkenaan dengan perbusukan; — tank tempat pemusnahan najis.

septuagenarian orang yang berumur 70 (antara 69 dengan 80).

sepulchral yang berkenaan dengan kubur, yang seperti kubur.

sepulchre kubur.

sequel *(construction)* sambungan; *(result)* akibat.

sequence turutan, rangkaian.

sequestrate, to — mencita.

sequin kelip-kelip yang dijahit pada pakaian dan sebagainya.

seraph malaikat.

serenade nyanyian yang dilagukan untuk memuji-muji gadis yang dicintai.

serene tenang dan terang, teduh, reda.

serf hamba, budak.

serge sejenis kain kuat.

sergeant sarjan.

serial yang merupakan rang-kaian; nombor siri.

series siri, deret.

serious (*sincere*) sungguh-sungguh; penting; (*important*) sungguh; penting; (*terrible*) hebat.

sermon khutbah; **to — ize** berkhutbah.

serpent (*dragon*) naga; (*snake*) ular.

serpentine yang seperti ular; (*coiled*) berbelit-belit.

serrated gerigi, biku.

serum sirim, sejenis ubat.

servant orang gaji, bujang; (*slave*) abdi.

serve, to — (*wait upon*) me-layani; (*fill a glass*) memenuhi; (*for wages*) makan gaji.

service jabatan, khidmat, pekerjaan, jawatan.

serviceable yang dapat di-pakai; (*profitable*) berfaedah.

serviette saputangan, tuala.

servile yang merendahkan diri.

servility sifat merendahkan diri.

servitude perhambaan.

sesame bijan.

session (*council*) sidang; (*school*) pengajaran sekolah tinggi setahun.

set I pasang, perangkat, leng-kap, susun.

set II, to — menaruh, meletak-kan, membubuhi; (*make ready*) memasang; (*arrange*) menga-tur.

setback pengunduran, ke-munduran.

settee bangku, kerusi pan-jang.

settle, to — (*live*) tinggal, berdiam; (*make certain*) me-nentukan; (*price, decision*) memutuskan.

settlement ketentuan, ke-tetapan; (*agreement*) penyele-saian, persetujuan; (*reconcile-ment*) perdamaian; (*place*) kam-pung, penempatan.

settler orang yang berpindah negeri dan hidup dalam tempat yang baharu itu.

set to perkelahian, pukul-memukul.

set up (*person's carriage*) sikap; (*arrangement*) susunan, aturan.

seven tujuh.

seventeen tujuh belas.

seventeenth yang ketujuh belas.

seventh yang ketujuh.

seventy tujuh puluh.

sever, to — (*part*) memisah-kan, menceraikan; (*rope etc*) memutuskan.

several (*of persons*) masing-masing; (*some*) beberapa.

severe (*of sentences*) berat; (*of persons, rule*) keras; (*ter-rible*) hebat.

severity kekerasan.

sew menjahit.

sewage sampah, kekotoran, najis.

sewer air selokan; (*open*) longkang.

sewing jahit-menjahit.

sex jenis kelamin, bangsa, jantina; the fair, gentle, weaker — kaum ibu.

sex— awalan kata yang ertinya: enam.

sextant alat pengukur tinggi bintang dibandingkan dengan kaki langit.

sexton pegawai gereja.

shabby (*worn*) buruk; (*dis-honourable*) keji.

shack pondok, teratak.

shackle belenggu, kongkong; **to —** membelenggu.

shade naung, teduh, tempat teduh; (*darker part*) bahagian gelap.

shadow (*figure*) bayang-bayang; (*in shade*) tempat teduh; (*shelter*) perlindungan.

shady rendang, teduh; (*dubious*) buruk; (*dishonest*) tidak jujur.

shaft batang, tangkai; a — of light batang cahaya.

shaggy berambut kusut.

shake goyang, geleng kepala; goncang.

shaky (*quaking*) gemetar; (*unsteady*) tidak tetap.

shale sejenis batu.

shall menunjukkan waktu yang akan datang; akan, hendak, mahu.

shallot bawang.

shallow dangkal, cetek, tohor; (*water*) tempat tohor, beting.

sham sesuatu yang tidak benar, pura-pura sahaja; to — pura-pura.

shamble hal berjalan bertatih-tatih.

shambles pembantaian, penyembelihan.

shame malu, aib, keaiban; to —, put to — mempermalukan, memberi aib.

shamefaced kemalu-maluan.

shameful yang memberi aib, yang menghinakan.

shameless tidak malu, muka tebal.

shampoo ubat langir; to — berlangir, melangir.

shamrock sejenis tumbuhan.

shank (*shin*) kaki dari lutut ke mata kaki, tulang kering.

shanty teratak, pondok.

shape (*form*) bangun, bentuk, rupa; (*substance*) wujud; (*mould*) acuan.

shapeless tidak berbentuk.

shapely rupawan.

share bahagian; (*of company*) syir; to — membahagi, berkongsi.

shareholder pemegang syir.

shark ikan yu.

sharp tajam, runcing; (*of taste etc*) pedas, pedih; (*active*) giat, galak.

sharpen, to — mengasah, merancang, menajamkan.

sharp-sighted tajam mata, bermata tajam.

sharp-witted penjang akal.

shatter, to — menghancurkan, meremukkan.

shave, to — bercukur, mencukur.

shaving(s) tatal, pengetaman.

shawl selendang, kain sal.

she dia, ia (perempuan).

sheaf berkas, ikat; to — mengikat-ikat, membuat berkas.

shear, to — memotong, menggunting.

shears gunting.

sheath (*of weapons etc*) sarung; (*of palm blossom*) kelopak, seludang.

sheathe, to — memasukkan ke dalam sarungnya, menyarungkan.

shed I gudang, bangsal.

shed II, to — (*leaves*) meluruh; (*spill*) menumpahkan.

sheen seri, cahaya.

sheep biri-biri.

sheepdog anjing penggembala.

sheepish malu, bingung.

sheepskin kulit kambing.

sheer (*mere*) hanya; (*unmixed*) tidak bercampur; (*obviously*) semata-mata; (*steep*) curam.

sheet (*bed*) alas tilam; (*of paper*) lembaran.

sheik(h) syaikh.

shelf papan, rak, para.

shell kulit; (*explosive*) bom; to — mengupas, menguliti.

shellfish kerang-kerangan, kepah; lokan.

shellproof tahan bom.

shell shock gugat sebagai akibat pemboman.

shelter tempat teduh, tempat perlindungan; **to take —** berlindung.

shepherd gembala; **to —** menggembalakan.

sherbet air serbat.

sheriff pegawai negeri tertinggi di daerah; kepala polisi disalah satu daerah di Amerika.

sherry sejenis minuman anggur.

shield perisai; **to — melin**dungi.

shift (*change*) pertukaran, perubahan; **to make —** berdaya upaya.

shiftiness sifat pintar busuk.

shifty penuh tipu daya, pintar busuk.

shilly–shally keragu-raguan; **to —** tidak sanggup memutuskan.

shimmer cahaya sayup-sayup; **to —** bercahaya sayup-sayup.

shin kaki sebelah muka dari lutut di bawah; **—bone** tulang kering.

shine kilap, kilau, cahaya seri.

shingle (*for roof*) sirap.

shingles ruam saraf.

shiny berseri-seri, menggilap.

ship kapal, perahu, bahtera; **to board —** naik kapal.

–ship akhiran kata yang ertinya: hal; keadaan; keahlian.

shipbuilder pembuat kapal.

shipload muatan kapal.

shipmate kawan sekapal.

shipment (*articles sent*) keriman; (*cargo*) pemuatan.

shipper pengangkut, pengirim.

shipping perkapalan, pengangkutan.

shipshape dalam keadaan baik dan teratur.

shipwreck kerosakan; **to —** merosakkan, kapal karam.

shipwright pembuat kapal.

shipyard kalangan membuat kapal.

shire salah satu bahagian negeri di Inggeris.

shirk, to — menjauhkan diri, menyingkiri.

shirker orang yang menjauhkan diri daripada kerjanya.

shirt kemeja.

shiver getaran, gigil; **to —** gementar, menggigil.

shoal I beting.

shoal II (*of fish*) sekelompok ikan.

shock I (*reaction*) pembidasan; (*fright*) kejutan.

shock II (*hair*) rambut tebal dan banyak.

shocker (*col*) cerita yang mengejutkan.

shocking yang mengejutkan; tidak sopan.

shoddy (*shabby*) buruk; (*imitation*) tiruan; (*poor quality*) mutunya buruk tetapi rupanya baik.

shoe sepatu, kasut; (*for horse*) ladam kuda.

shoehorn alat memakai sepatu.

shoemaker tukang sepatu.

shoo bunyi hendak mengusir ayam.

shoot (*of plant*) pucuk, cambah, taruk; **to —** (*of gun*) menembak.

shooting penembakan; (*hunting*) hak pemburuan.

shop kedai.

shopkeeper pekedai.

shoplifter orang yang mencuri barang di kedai.

shop window almari kedai.

shore I tepi laut, pantai; (*as opposed to sea*) darat.

shore II (*prop*) sangga, topang; **to —** menyangga, menopang.

short (*of persons, objects*) pendek; (*of time*) tidak lama; (*concise*) ringkas, singkat.

shortage kekurangan, kesempitan.

shortbread sejenis kuih.

short-circuit putus aliran, putus lirar.

shortcoming hal tidak memuaskan pengharapan.

shorten, to — memendekkan, menyingkatkan, meringkaskan.

shorthand tulisan terengkas.

short-handed tidak cukup pekerja.

short-lived tidak lama hidupnya, pendek umur.

shortly sedikit hari, tidak lama lagi.

shortness kependekan.

short-sighted (*lacking foresight*) akal pendek; (*eyesight*) buta ayam, mata dekat.

short-tempered darah panas, lekas marah.

shortwinded nafas lelah.

shot I (*for guns*) tembakan, peluru, penabur.

shot II (*of colour*) bercampur warnanya.

shoulder bahu; to — (*hang over shoulder*) menyangdangkan; (*carry*) memikul pada bahu.

shoulder blade tulang belikat.

shoulder strap sandang, selepang.

shout teriak, tempek sorak.

shove sorong; to — menyorong.

shovel (*spade*) penggali; (*ladle*) penyenduk.

show (*display*) pertunjukan; (*exhibition*) pamiran; to — memperlihatkan, menunjukkan.

showboat kapal yang padanya dipertunjukkan sandiwara dan sebagainya.

showcase almari kaca akan mempertunjukkan barang.

showdown pembukaan segala hal yang sulit atau rahsia.

shower pancaran air untuk mandi; (*rain*) hujan.

showman pengurus pertunjukan sandiwara dan sebagainya.

showroom tempat pertunjukan barang-barang.

shrapnel sejenis bom yang meletus.

shred (*of paper, cloth etc*) carik; to — mencarik.

shrew sejenis tikus, cencorot; (*woman*) perempuan bising.

shrewd tajam, panjang akal bijaksana.

shriek teriak, pekek, jeritan; to — berteriak, menjerit, memekek.

shrill nyaring, langsing.

shrimp udang; to — menangkap udang.

shrine tempat suci, tempat keramat, candi.

shrink, to — mengecut; to — from segan akan, takut akan.

shrinkage susut, hal berkurang.

shrivel, to — berkeriput, mengerut; —led keriput, kecut.

shroud kapan; to — mengapani, menyelubungi.

shrub (*woody plant*) pokok kecil; (*scrub*) semak.

shrug gerak mengangkat bahu.

shudder gementar.

shuffle (*cards*) kocok; (*feet*) salah satu gerak kaki; to — (*of walk*) berjalan merangkak-rangkak.

shun, to — menjauhkan diri pada, mengelakkan.

shunt, to — (*diverge*) menyimpangkan.

shut, to — (*lock*) mengunci; (*close*) menutup.

shutter penutup jendela.

shuttle puntalan, anak torak.

shuttlecock bola bula ayam

yang dipakai dalam permainan badminton.

shy malu, segan, tersipu-sipu.

Siamese orang atau bahasa Thai.

sick (*ill*) sakit; (*nausea*) mual, mabuk.

sick bay bilik orang sakit di kapal.

sickbed tempat tidur orang sakit.

sickle sabit.

sick leave cuti kerana sakit.

sickly penyakitan, kesakitan.

sickness penyakit.

side segi, sisi, belah; (*party*) pihak.

side arms pedang atau mata sangkur.

sideboard gerobok.

side dish lauk-pauk.

side issue perkara sambilan.

sideline pekerjaan sambilan.

sidelines garis batas pada padang bola tenis dan sebagainya.

sidelong miring, sisi; a — glance kerling.

sideslip, to — menggelincir, tergelincir.

side-step langkah menyimpang; to — menyimpang.

sidewalk (*US*) jalan tepi.

sideways sebelah, dari sebelah.

sidle, to — berjalan merusuk.

siege kepungan.

sienna warna merah tua.

siesta tidur pada tengahari.

sieve ayakan, penapis, ayak; to — menapis, mengayak.

sift, to — mengayak, menapis.

sigh keluh; to — mengeluh berkeluh-kesah.

sight penglihatan, mata; (*observation*) tinjauan; (*scene*) pemandangan.

sightless buta.

sightseeing melihat-lihat, bersiar.

sign tanda, alamat, lambang;

(*signal*) semboyan; to — menandatangani.

signal (*striking*) yang sangat menarik perhatian; (*sign*) tanda, semboyan isyarat.

signal box rumah semboyan.

signatory pihak yang turut bertandatangan.

signature tandatangan, sain.

signboard papan nama.

signet cap.

significance erti, makna.

significant bererti, bermakna, penting.

signify, to — (*be sign for*) menandakan; (*mean*) bererti, bermakna.

signpost papan jalan pada simpang.

silence sunyi; —! diam!; to — mendiamkan.

silencer penyenyap bunyi.

silent (*of persons*) senyap; (*lonely*) sunyi.

silhouette gambar orang yang tampak bayang-bayangnya sahaja.

silk sutera.

silken yang terjadi daripada atau seperti sutera.

silkworm ulat sutera.

silky seperti sutera halusnya.

sill ambang jendela.

silly tolol, bodoh.

silo tempat kedap udara menyimpan gandum.

silt lumpur, mendap, kersik lumut; —ed up terkambus.

silver perak; to — (*to plate*) menyadur perak.

silverfish (*insect*) gegat.

silversmith tukang perak.

silver wedding hari ulang tahun ke 25 hari perkahwinan.

similar serupa, sama, sesuai.

similarity kesamaan.

simile persamaan, tamsil.

simmer, to — mendidih perlahan-lahan; (*of rage etc*) menahan marahnya (atau tertawanya).

simper senyum simpul; to — tersenyum simpul.

simple (*ordinary*) sederhana; (*inexperienced*) tidak berpengalaman; (*easy*) mudah.

simple-hearted, simple-minded jujur, lurus hati.

simpleton orang bebal, orang bodoh, orang tolol.

simplicity kesederhanaan.

simplify, to — memudahkan.

simply sahaja, betul-betul, belaka.

simulate, to — buat-buat, pura-pura.

simultaneous serentak dengan, serempak dengan.

sin dosa; to — berdosa.

since dari, semenjak, sejak.

sincere lurus, tulus, betul, ikhlas.

sincerity kelurusan hati, keikhlasan hati, ketulusan hati.

sinecure jabatan yang bergaji tetapi hampir tidak ada kerjanya.

sinew otot, urat.

sinful berdosa.

sing, to — menyanyi, melagu.

singe, to — menggosongkan, siut.

singer penyanyi, biduan.

single (*one*) satu; (*solitary*) tunggal; (*not married*) bujang.

single-handed sendiri, dengan tidak dibantu ole horang lain.

single-minded jujur, tulus, ikhlas.

singlet baju dalam.

singly berdiri sendiri, satu-satu.

singsong (*of tune*) lagu yang selalu sama iramanya; (*droning*) berdendang.

singular (*solitary*) tunggal; (*strange*) ajaib; (*special*) istimewa.

singularity keajaiban; keadaan istimewa.

sinister (*ill-omened*) celaka; (*evil*) jahat.

sink persampahan, pelimpahan; to — tenggelam.

sinking (*feeling*) merasa hampa dada; — fund wang cadang untuk pembayar hutang.

sinner orang yang berdosa, berbuat dosa.

sino— awalan kata yangertinya: orang China.

sinuous berbelit-belit.

sinus rongga hidung (dada dan lain-lain).

sip sesap, teguk; to — minum berteguk-teguk tetapi sedikit.

sir tuan.

sire bapa salah satu haiwan (biasanya: kuda); tuanku.

siren sejenis bidadari laut; (*alluring woman*) perempuan cantik yang pandai membujuk dan mengambil hati; (*signal*) peduit, semboyan.

sirloin sepotong daging di atas atau di bawah tulang belakang lembu.

sirocco angin panas di negeri Itali yang asalnya dari padang pasir (gurun) Sahara.

sister saudara perempuan; (*younger*) adik; (*elder*) kakak.

sister-in-law ipar perempuan.

sit, to — duduk.

site letaknya salah satu bangunan.

sitting waktu duduk; — -room tempat duduk.

situated bertempat, terletak.

situation (*place*) letak; (*circumstance*) keadaan, hal.

six enam.

sixteen enam belas.

sixteenth keenam belas.

sixth keenam.

sixtieth keenam puluh.

sixty enam puluh.

sizable besar rupanya, besar ukurannya.

size besarnya, ukuran; to — memilih (atau mengatur) menurut besarnya.

sizzle bunyi berdesus.

skate I sejenis ikan, pari.

skate II sepatu yang dibubuhi besi untuk gelincir di air batu.

skedaddle, to — lari terburu-buru.

skein unting, tukal.

skeleton rangka; (of howdah) rengka, baluhan.

sketch (drawing) gambar; (plan) rancangan; to — menggambar dengan garisan besar; merancangkan.

skewer cucuk daging.

ski papan peluncur di atas salji; to — meluncur di atas salji dengan 'ski'.

skid penyangga; to — tergelincir, meluncur.

skiff sejenis perahu pendayung.

skilful pandai, cakap.

skill keahlian, kepandaian, kecakapan, kemahiran.

skilled pandai, cakap.

skim, —(med) milk susu bawah, susu yang telah diambil kepalanya.

skimp sedikit; to — (great care) menghematkan.

skimpy sedikit, kurang; (stingy) kikir.

skin kulit; he is — and bone ia sangat kurus.

skinflint kikir pari.

skinny kurus kering.

skip lompatan; to — melompat-lompat.

skipper nakhoda, juragan.

skirmish perkelahian, pertengkaran; to — berkelahi bertengkar.

skirt (dress) sarung, kain; to — menyusur, menyisi.

skit sindiran; (in theatre) sandiwara lucu.

skittish suka bercanda.

skittles sejenis permainan dengan bola dan sembilan pancang.

skulk, to — menyembunyikan diri, mengendap-ngendap.

skull tengkorak, tempurung kepala.

skunk sejenis binatang yang mengeluarkan bau busuk.

sky langit, angkasa, awang-awang.

skylark sejenis burung; to — berkelakar.

skylight jendela di atap rumah.

skyline yang terlihat pada kaki langit.

skyscraper pencakar langit.

slab (stone) papan batu; (off a log) papan yang ditebak dari sebelah luar batang pohon.

slack (of rope) kendur; (remiss) lalai; (quiet) sepi.

slacken, to — mengendurkan, mengulur; (delay) melengah, melalai.

slackness kekenduran.

slacks seluar panjang.

slag terak sanga.

slake, to — memuaskan.

slam (sound) gerdam; (winning) kemenangan.

slander fitnah, umpat; to — memburukkan nama, memfitnahkan.

slanderer pengumpat.

slanderous secara umpat, fitnah.

slang bahasa yang tidak tergolong bahasa rasmi.

slant miring, senget, gendeng.

slanting miring. gendeng. senget.

slap pukulan, tampar; to — menampar, memukul, menepuk, tangankan.

slapdash (offhand) dengan sebarang; (terrible) dengan hebat.

slapping (col) sangat baik, bukan main.

slapstick sandiwara dan sebagainya yang kurang halus aturannya.

slash potongan parang, luka tetak; to — menetak.

slat beruti.

slate (*stone for roofing*) sejenis batu berwarna kelabu kebiru-biruan yang selalu digunakan sebagai atap rumah; (*school*) papan batu luh.

slate pencil kalam batu.

slattern perempuan kotor, perempuan lucah.

slaughter pembantaian, sembelih.

slaughterhouse rumah bantai.

Slav orang berbangsa Slav.

slave hamba, sahaya, abdi.

slave driver orang yang keras dan bengis terhadap orang bawahannya.

slaver (*spittle*) air ludah, air liur; to — berludah.

slavery perhambaan.

slavish (*servile*) sangat merendahkan diri.

Slavonic bahasa orang Slav, yang berkenaan dengan orang Slav.

slay *pt* slew, to — membunuh.

sled kereta untuk membawa penumpang atau barang melalui padang bersalji, pedati.

sledge (*also* —hammer) pemukul besar.

sleek licin, halus dan mengkilap; to — melicinkan.

sleep tidur; to — tidur, terlena.

sleeper orang yang tidur.

sleepily mengantuk.

sleeping draught ubat tidur.

sleeping partner rakan yang tidak mencampuri perjalanan perusahaan.

sleeping sickness penyakit lena.

sleepless tidak dapat tidur.

sleepwalking berjalan dalam tidur.

sleepy mengantuk, terlena.

sleepyhead penidur.

sleet hujan bercampur salji.

sleeve lengan baju; to laugh up one's — tertawa diam-diam.

sleeveless tidak berlengan.

sleight akal kancil.

slender ramping, lampai.

slew, to — (*twist*) memutar.

slice hiris, keping; a — of bread keping roti.

slick (*sleek*) licin dan teratur; (*exactly*) tepat; (*directly*) langsung.

slide peluncuran.

slight I (*slender*) ramping, lampai; (*a little*) sedikit.

slight II (*neglect*) pelalaian; to — melalaikan, tidak mengendahkan.

slim lampai, ramping.

slime lumpur, lanyau.

slimy berlumpur, becak.

sling (*like cradle*) ambin, ayunan; (*for throwing*) umban, ali-ali; (*for broken arm*) anduhan.

slink, to — menyelinap.

slip (*mistake*) kesilapan, kesalahan; (*error in print etc*) ralat; (*for pillow*) sarung bantal; to — tergelincir; to — down (*of clothes etc*) jatuh.

slipknot simpul pulih.

slipper kasut selipar.

slippery licin, lincir.

slipshod tidak teratur.

slip-up salah bebal.

slipway galangan kapal.

slit belah, celah; to — (*split*) membelah; (*slice*) mengiris.

slither jalan terhuyung-hayang.

slobber air liur; to — meleleh.

sloe sejenis buah.

slog pukulan yang keras; to — memukul dengan keras.

slogan semboyan, cogan kata.

sloop sekuci.

slop, —s air kotor; (*some liquid food*) bubur.

slope cerun, landaian, lereng-an; to — melereng, melandai, curam.

sloppy (wet) basah; (muddy) becak; (dirty) kotor.

slosh, (col) to — memukul, menghentam.

slot I (slit) celah, lurah; to — membuat celah, membuat lurah.

slot II (track) bekas; kesan.

sloth I kemalasan; —ful malas.

sloth II (animal) binatang kongkang.

slouch sikap lemas rengsa.

slough I (bog) paya, rawa.

slough II (of snakes) selumur.

Slovak orang berbangsa Slovak.

Slovene orang berbangsa Slovenia.

slovenly tidak sempurna.

slow (behind time) lambat; (slowly) perlahan-lahan; (inactive) tidak giat.

slowcoach orang lembap, pelengah.

slowness kelambatan perlahan.

slow worm sejenis binatang yang rupanya seperti ular.

sludge lumpur; kotoran.

slug (snail) sejenis siput yang tidak ada rumahnya; (shot) peluru kecil.

sluggish lembap.

sluice pintu air.

slumber tidur; to — tidur.

slump (in prices) kejatuhan harga; to — jatuh harga.

slur cacat, aib.

slush lumpur bercampur dengan saiji basah.

slut perempuan jahat dan kotor.

sly pintar busuk, licik; on the — diam-diam.

smack I (slap) pukulan, tampar.

smack II (taste) rasa; to — rasanya, berbau.

smack III (sailing vessel) sejenis perahu menangkap ikan.

small (of size) kecil; (of quantity) sedikit; — change wang pecah.

small arms senjata api yang dapat disandang.

small fry (of no importance) orang kecil, golongan bawah.

smallholding sebidang tanah kecil yang disewakan.

smallish agak kecil.

small-minded picik.

smallpox cacar, ketumbuhan.

small talk kecek-kecek, bual.

smart (active) giat; (mentally) tajam, pintar pandai, berakal, cerdas.

smarten, to — mengelokkan, menjadikan elok dan bersih.

smash hancur; (heavy blow) pukulan yang hebat.

smashing (col) (superlative) terlalu elok.

smattering pengetahuan tentang sesuatu yang serba sedikit sahaja.

smear coreng, selekeh; to — membit.

smell (odour) bau; (nasal sense) penciuman, hidung; to — mencium, menghidu.

smelt I sejenis ikan.

smelt II, to — meleburkan logam; —ing furnace relau.

smile senyum, tersenyum.

smirk tertawa yang dibuat-buat sahaja; to — pura-pura tertawa.

smite, to — (hit) memukul; (defeat) mengalahkan.

smith tukang besi.

smithereens keping, pecahan.

smithy kedai tukang besi.

smock kemeja atau baju yang dikerut sebahagian.

smoke asap; (cigarette) rokok; to — (cigarettes) merokok.

smoker orang yang merokok.

smokestack cerobong, corong asap.

smoky berasap, penuh asap.

smooth rata, datar, papar, paras, licin; (*of reading*) lancar.

smother, to — mencekek, melemaskan.

smoulder api yang tidak meluap.

smudge selekeh; **to** — menyelekeh, mencoreng.

smug kemas dan sangat puas dengan diri sendiri.

smuggle, to — menyeludupkan.

smuggler penyeludup.

smuggling dagang gelap, menyeludup.

smut (*soot*) jelaga; (*obscene talk*) carut; (*disease of grain*) hama penyakit gandum.

smutty kotor.

snack makanan kecil alas perut.

snaffle sejenis tali kendali (kekang).

snag (*difficulty*) bonjol yang merupakan halangan; (*in river*) bangkar.

snail siput.

snake ular; **a** — **in the grass** bahaya atau musuh yang tidak diketahui.

snake charmer juru menyihirkan ular, silap mata.

snap (*bite*) gigitan tiba-tiba; (*sound*) bunyi meletik.

snapdragon sejenis bunga.

snappish bengkeng.

snappy sangat giat.

snapshot menggambar lekas-lekas.

snare jerat; **to** — menjerat.

snarl I (*growl*) menderam; **to** — menggertak.

snarl II (*tangle*) kekusutan; **to** — kusut, menjadi kusut.

snatch rebut, renggut; (*small piece*) bahagian kecil; **to** — merebut.

sneak, to — (*slink*) menyelinap; (*steal*) mencuri.

sneakers (*col*) sepatu.

sneer cupar; (*mock*) ejekan; (*insinuation*) sindiran; **to** — mengelek.

sneeze, to — bersin; **not to be** — **d at** bukan kepalang, bukan main.

snicker, to — tertawa tersembunyi.

sniff penciuman; **to** — mendium.

snigger, to — tertawa tersembunyi.

snip guntingan; **to** — menggunting.

snipe burung berkik; tetiruk; **to** — menembak dari tempat jauh dan tersembunyi.

sniper penembak dari tempat jauh dan tersembunyi.

snippet guntingan, potongan.

snivel (*snotty*) hingus; (*crying*) tangis tersedu-sedu.

snob orang yang sangat mengendahkan segala hal golongan atas dan tidak mahu bergaul dengan golongan bawah, sombong, bongkak.

snobbery hal atau sifat sombong bongkak.

snobbish bersifat sombong (bongkak).

snoop, to — mengintai-intai.

snooper orang yang suka mengintai-intai.

snooze, to — tidur ayam.

snore dengkur; **to** — dengkur, berdengkur.

snort dengus; **to** — mendengus.

snot ingus.

snotty beringus.

snout (*of fish, ship*) jongor; (*of animal, fish*) muncung.

snow salji; **to** — salji turun.

snow-blind buta kerana cahaya salji.

snowbound terkepung oleh salji.

snow-capped gunung yang puncaknya-tertutup salji.

snowdrift salji yang bertumpuk ditiup angin.

snowdrop sejenis tumbuhan yang berbunga pada akhir musim sejuk.

snowflake salji sekeping.

snowman patung orang yang dibuat daripada salji.

snow-white putih salji sebagai salji.

snub I gertak; to — menggertak, menghendik.

snub II, —-nosed berhidung pesek.

snuff I (*tobacco*) sedut tembakau dengan hidung.

snuff II (*charred wick*) sumbu yang telah terbakar.

snuffbox sejenis cepu untuk tembakau hidung.

snuffle (*sniff*) dengus.

snug senang, nikmat.

snuggle, to — merapati, merapatkan diri.

so (*in that way*) begitu; (*much*) sekian; (*moreover*) juga; (*thus*) demikian.

soak, to — (*absorb*) menyerap; (*immerse*) merendam; (*absorb*) meresap.

soap sabun.

soap bubble buih sabun.

soapy penuh sabun; (*of speech*) manis mulut.

soar, to — terbang tinggitinggi, mengawan.

sob sedan, sedu.

sober (*not drunk*) tidak mabuk; (*moderate*) sederhana, ugahari.

sobriety sifat, keadaan ugahari

sociability keramahan, halsuka bergaul.

sociable suka bergaul, peramah, ramah-tamah.

social yang suka bergaul.

socialism faham sosialis.

socialist orang berfaham sosialis.

socialize, to — menjadikan sosial.

society pergaulan, masyarakat; (*association*) golongan.

sociological yang berkenaan dengan ilmu masyarakat.

sociology ilmu masyarakat.

sock I sarung kaki pendek.

sock II (*col*) pukulan; to — memukul.

socket (*hole*) lubang; (*hollow*) lekuk; eye — lekuk mata.

sod ketul tanah berumput.

soda soda; — water air belanda.

sodden lecah, lecak, lembap.

sodium sodium, natrium.

sodomy semburit.

sofa bangku.

soft (*too soft of what should be crisp or hard*) lembek; (*tender, gentle*) lembut; (*weak of bodily character*) lemah.

soften, to — melemahkan, melembutkan.

soft-hearted lembut hati, menaruh belas kasihan akan orang lain.

softness kelembikan; kelembutan.

soft-spoken lemah lembut suara atau perkataannya.

soggy lecah, lembap.

soil I tanah.

soil II, to — mengotorkan, melumurkan.

sojourn persinggahan, tumpangan; to — singgah, menumpang.

solace lipur, penglipur lara.

solar yang berkenaan dengan matahari; — plexus jalin urat saraf di hulu hati.

solder pateri; to — memateriakan.

soldier soldadu, perajurit, askar.

sole I (*one*) satu-satunya; (*solitary*) tunggal; (*self*) sendiri.

sole II (*of foot*) tapak kaki.

sole III (*fish*) sejenis ikan, ikan lidah.

solely melulu, semata-mata.

solemn (*dignified*) tenang dan sopan; (*formal*) dengan upacara.

solemnity keadaan atau sifat tenang dan sopan; upacara.

solemnize, to — melaksanakan dengan upacara; (*of marriage*) mengijabkan nikah.

solicit, to — memohon, meminta dengan sungguh-sungguh.

solicitor pengacara.

solicitous (*desirous*) sangat ingin; (*apprehensive*) cemas.

solicitude kekhuatiran kecemasan.

solid (*having contents*) berisi; (*crammed*) padat; (*massive*) padu; (*firm*) pejal.

solidarity kerukunan, gotong-royong.

solidify, to — menjadikan teguh, menjadikan keras, menjadikan padat.

solidity keadaan padat, kekukuhan, keteguhan.

soliloquize, to — bercakap dengan diri sendiri.

soliloquy percakapan dengan diri sendiri.

solitary (*of places*) sunyi; (*alone*) bersendiri, tunggal.

solitude kesunyian, lengang.

solo tunggal, sendirian.

soluble dapat dilarut.

solution penyelesaian soal, jawab, larutan.

solve, to — menyelesaikan, menghuraikan.

solvency kesanggupan membayar hutangnya.

solvent (*for dissolving*) ubat pelarut; (*able to pay*) sanggup membayar hutangnya.

sombre (*of weather*) redup.

some ada yang . . .; (*a little*) sedikit; (*several*) beberapa; (*approximately*) lebih kurang.

somebody seseorang, salah seorang; (*prominent person*) orang terkemuka.

somehow entah bagaimana, bagaimanapun juga.

someone salah seorang, seseorang.

somersault tunggang balik.

something apa-apa, barang sesuatu.

sometime (*some time*) beberapa waktu; (*at some time*) pada suatu waktu.

sometimes kadang-kadang terkadang, adakalanya.

somewhat harus sedikit.

somewhere pada salah satu tempat.

somnambulism hal berjalan (atau melakukan hal lain) sambil tidur.

somnolent mengantuk.

son anak laki-laki.

sonata sejenis karangan muzik.

song nyanyian, lagu.

songster penyanyi; (*singing bird*) burung penyanyi.

son-in-law menantu laki-laki.

sonnet sejenis syair.

sonny (*col*) adik, kulup.

sonorous nyaring, dengan bunyi yang mempengaruhi.

soon (*quickly*) lekas, cepat, segera; (*in a short time*) tidak lama lagi; (*presently*) kelak; as — as selekas.

soot arang para-para.

soothe, to — meredakan.

soothsayer ahlun-nujum, tukang ramal.

sooty seperti atau penuh jelaga.

sop sepotong roti yang dicelup dalam air.

sophisticate, to — (*lead astray*) menyesatkan; (*lose one's standards*) menghilangkan sifat sederhana; —d (*worldly*) banyak berpengalaman dalam hal masyarakat dan duniawi.

sophistication pengalaman dalam hal duniawi.

sophomore (*US*) mahasiswa yang masuk tingkat pengajaran yang kedua.

sopping basah kuyup.

soprano soprano, suara perempuan tingkat tertinggi.

sorbet serbat.

sorcerer ahli sihir.

sorceress tukang sihir perempuan.

sorcery ilmu sihir.

sordid (*degraded*) hina, keji; (*stingy*) kikir; (*filthy*) kotor.

sore luka, sakit; (*grief*) sesuatu yang menyakiti hati.

sorghum jelai, sekoi.

sorrel sejenis tumbuhan; (*horse*) kuda yang berwarna merah tua.

sorrow penderitaan, kesedihan, dukacita.

sorrowful berdukacita.

sorry (*regret*) sesal; (*tearful*) sedih; —! (*pardon*) minta maaf!

sort macam, rupa, jenis.

S.O.S. isyarat minta pertolongan dalam keadaan sengsara.

so-so boleh juga.

sot orang yang ketagih akan minuman keras.

S(o)udanese yang berkenaan dengan negeri Sudan; penduduk negeri Sudan.

souffle dadar telur.

soul jiwa, nyawa, roh.

soulful yang menunjukkan perasaan dalam-dalam.

soulless tidak berperasaan.

sound I (*healthy*) sihat; (*not rotten*) bulk; (*correct*) benar.

sound II bunyi; (*voice*) suara; to — bersuara; membunyikan.

sound III (*strait*) teluk sempit, selat; to — (*find depth, probe*) menduga.

sounding sedang membunyikan; sedang menduga.

soundproof kedap bunyi, tidak memasukkan bunyi.

soup sup; to be in — dalam keadaan susah.

sour masam; to — menjadi masam.

source (*spring*) mata air; (*origin*) mula, asal.

souse (*pickle*) acar; (*soak*) celupan; to — membuat acar.

south selatan.

south-east tenggara.

southerly arah ke selatan; (*wind*) angin selatan.

southern berkenaan dengan selatan.

South Pole kutub selatan.

southward(s) ke arah selatan.

south-west daya.

souvenir cendera mata, tanda mata, kenang-kenangan.

sovereign raja, yamtuan; (*divine power of Ruler*) berdaulat; (*old*) matawang emas Inggeris.

sovereignty kedaulatan.

Soviet Soviet.

sow I, to — menyemai, menaburkan.

sow II babi betina.

sower penabur.

soy(a) kecap.

soy(a) bean kacang kedelai.

sozzled (*col*) sangat mabuk.

spa tempat yang ada pancut air panas.

space (*between earth and sky*) awangan; (*gap*) ruangan, keluasan; (*area between objects, places etc*) jarak.

spacing perenggang, penjarak.

spacious luas, longgar.

spade penggali; (*in cards*) salah satu jenis daun terup.

spadework pekerjaan berat.

spaghetti spageti, meehoon.

span jarak dari satu tempat

sampai ke tempat lain; (of thumb and finger) jengkal.

spangle kelip-kelip; —d berkelip-kelip.

Spaniard orang Sepanyol.

Spanish negeri atau orang Sepanyol.

spank tepuk, tampar; to — menepuk, menampar.

spanner sejenis kunci sekeru.

spar I (of ship) tiang kapal.

spar II (mineral) sejenis logam yang menghablur.

spar III (boxing) tinju; to — bertinju sebagai latihan.

spare I (of pearl) bahagian penganti pada mesin; (scanty) sangat sederhana.

spare II, to — (pity) menyayangkan; (pardon) memaafkan.

sparingly (carefully) dengan cermat.

spark I bunga api; not a — sedikit pun tidak.

spark II, bright - peeolik, orang yang suka bermain.

sparkle kilau, kilat; to — berkilau-kilauan, gemerlapan.

sparrow burung pipit; —hawk burung helang.

sparse jarang.

spasm (convulsion) kejang; (movement) gerak tiba-tiba.

spasmodic kejang.

spat, —s sarung kaki yang menyelubungi buku lali.

spate air bah.

spatial yang berkenaan dengan ruang.

spatter percik; to — memercik.

spatula sudip.

spawn telur ikan; to — bertelur.

speak, to — bercakap, berkata; (language) berbahasa; to — for bercakap sesuatu atas nama seseorang.

speaker penutur, pencakap; (of Council) pengerusi mejlis mesyuarat negeri, speaker.

speaking sedang bercakap; not on — terms tidak mahu bercakap.

spear lembing, tombak; to — menikam.

spearhead pemimpin.

spearmint sejenis tumbuhan yang pedas rasanya.

special istimewa, khas; (not trivial) bukan main, bukan kepalang.

specialist ahli.

speciality keistimewaan, hal istimewa, sesuatu yang diberi perhatian istimewa.

specialize, to — in menjadi ahli dalam salah satu bahagian.

species jenis, bangsa.

specific (pertaining to a kind etc) menurut jenis tertentu; (special) khas.

specific(ally) istimewa, khusus.

specification perukuran, perincian.

specify, to — menentukan.

specimen contoh.

specious yang baik rupanya.

speck bintik, borek; to — membuat bintik-bintik.

speckle bintik; to — membuat bintik-bintik; —d borek.

spectacle pertunjukan; pair of —s cermin mata.

spectacular yang mengajaibkan, yang sangat menarik perhatian.

spectator pemandang, penuntun.

spectre hantu.

speculate, to — (meditate) memikirkan; (invest) mengusahakan.

speculation (meditation) renungan; mengadu untung.

speculative (of investment) yang berkenaan dengan mengadu untung; (liable to loss) yang mengandung bahaya rugi.

speculator orang yang meng-adu untung.

speech pertutur, ucapan, ujar kata; (*language*) bahasa; **figure of** — kiasan.

speechless tergemap, ter-kelu.

speed kecepatan, kepantasan, laju, deras; **to** — (*hasten*) bersegera; (*go quickly*) berjalan terlalu cepat.

speedboat perahu bermotor yang sangat cepat jalannya.

speed cop (*US*) polis pengawas kecepatan lalu lintas.

speedway tempat perlumbaan motor, jalan besar yang istimewa untuk kendaraan bermotor.

speedy segera, lekas, cepat.

spell I (*enchantment*) pesona, jampi; —binder ahli yang pandai menarik perhatian.

spell II, to — (*words*) mengeja; (*result in*) mengakibatkan.

spell III (*short time*) waktu yang singkat.

spelling sejenis baju pendek.

spend, to — membelanjakan, mengeluarkan wang.

spendthrift pemboros.

sperm mani, seperma.

spew, spue, to — muntah.

sphere (*ball*) bola; (*range, province*) lengkongan, lapangan, sepiar.

spherical bulat, berbentuk bola.

sphinx (*Greek*) sejenis raksasa Yunani purbakala; (*Egyptian*) patung raksasa di Masir.

spice rempah-rempah; **to** — membubuhi rempah-rempah.

spick, — and span sangat elok dan teratur.

spicy pedas; (*of conduct*) nakal, tidak sopan santun.

spider labah-labah.

spike (*nail*) paku; (*stake*) pancang; **to** — memaku, memancang.

spill tumpah.

spin putaran, kisaran; **to** — (*thread, ropes*) memintal, mengantih.

spinach sejenis bayam.

spindle buluh pasak, gelendung.

spindly kurus lampai.

spindrift buih laut.

spine tulang belakang, tulang punggung.

spineless (*no spine*) tidak bertulang belakang; (*weak*) lemah, tidak kuat.

spinner pemintal, pengantih.

spinning pemintalan.

spinning top gasing.

spinning wheel pemintal, jentera.

spinster perempuan yang belum bersuami, anak dara.

spiny berduri, bercerancang.

spiral pilin.

spire hujung menara.

spirit I (*life, soul*) budi, jiwa, roh; (*genie*) jin; (*ghost*) hantu.

spirit II, —s minuman keras, sepirit.

spirited giat, bersemangat.

spiritless kurang giat; (*afraid*) takut, tawar hati.

spiritual batin, rohani, kejiwaan.

spiritualism ilmu wasitah.

spiro— awalan kata yang ertinya: nafas.

spirt, spurt (*jet of water*) pancaran, pancuran; **to** — memancarkan.

spit I (*for cooking*) pacak; (*tongue of land projecting into sea*) hujung tanah, anak tanjung.

spit II, to—berludah, meludah.

spite dendam, dengki, iri hati; **in** — **of** meskipun.

spiteful berdengki, iri hati.

spittle air ludah, liur.

splash cebar-cebur; **to make a** — sangat menarik perhatian orang banyak.

splatter, to — mencebarcebur.

splay yang condong, keluar, yang mengarak keluar.

spleen limpa, kura.

splendid sangat elok, mulia.

splendour elok; (*magnificence*) kemuliaan.

splice sambungan; **to** — menyambung.

splint kayu belat, kayu bidai.

splinter serpih; **to** — pecah memecahkan.

split (*fissure*) celah, rekah; (*separation*) penceraian; (*piece split in two*) belahan; — **second** sejurus sebentar.

splotch coreng.

splutter, to — gemercik, merecik.

spoil I, —s rampasan.

spoil II, to — (*damage*) merosakkan; (*go bad*) menjadi busuk.

spoke (*of wheel*) jari-jari, anak jenter.

spokesman juru cakap.

sponge bunga karang; yang seperti bunga karang, sepan.

spongy seperti bunga karang; (*of wood*) lempung.

sponsor orang yang bertanggungjawab, penaung.

spontaneous dengan sendirinya.

spool hantu.

spool puntalan, gelendung, kili-kili.

spoon senduk, sudu.

spoor kesan, jejak; **to** — mencari kesan.

sporadic jarang berlaku.

spore (*seed*) benih.

sport (*pastime*) permainan; (*merriment*) riang gembira; —**s** sukan, permainan; —**s ground** padang.

spot (*place*) tempat; (*round mark*) bintik; (*a little*) sedikit.

spotless bersih.

spotted belang, burik, berintik-rintik.

spouse (*wife*) isteri; (*husband*)

suami.

spout pancaran.

sprain, to — terpelecok, tergeliat, salah urat.

sprat sejenis ikan.

sprawl (*of shrub*) dahan kecil yang beranting dan berbunga; **to** — lintang pukang, bergelimpangan.

spray (*of shrub*) dahan kecil yang beranting dan berbunga; (*boom*) brick; **to** — menyemburkan.

spread (*spread out*) bentang, hampar; (*blossom*) perkembangan; (*space*) luasnya, lebarnya.

spread-eagle gambar burung rajawali terbentang.

spree suka ria.

sprig ranting.

sprightliness keriangan, kegembiraan.

sprightly riang gembira.

spring I (*of water*) mata air, perigi.

spring II (*season*) musim bunga.

spring III (*elasticity*) daya menganjal.

spring IV (*leap*) melompat.

springboard papan untuk terjun ke dalam air.

spring-cleaning pembersihan rumah.

spring tide pasang keling, air pasang besar.

sprinkle percik; **to** — memerciki, merenjiskan.

sprinkler alat penyembur, penyiram.

sprinkling, a —**of** sedikit di sana sini.

sprint lari jarak pendek; **to** — melari sejarak pendek.

sprite sejenis jin, polong.

sprout pucuk, tunas, rebung, cambah.

spruce (*tidy*) bersih dan baik rupa; (*careful*) cermat; **to** — **o.s. up** membersihkan diri, berpakaian bersih.

spry giat.

spunk (*bravery*) keberanian; (*rage*) kemarahan; —y berani, gagah.

spur (*for horseman*) pacu; (*of fighting cock*) taji; (*of hill*) susuh bukit; (*stimulus*) perangsang; on the — or the moment pada waktu itu juga.

spurious palsu, lancung.

spurn, to — (*reject*) menolak dengan menghinakan.

spurt (*run*) lari cepat; see spirt.

spy pengintai, suluh; to — mengintai, mengintip; to — out menyelidiki dengan diam-diam.

squabble pertengkaran; to — bertengkar.

squad rombongan, sekuad.

squadron pasukan askar, pasukan pesawat udara.

squalid jembel.

squall angin ribut yang datang tiba-tiba serta dengan hujan atau salji.

squalor kekotoran.

squander, to — boros, membuang.

squanderer pemboros.

square (*four-sided*) empat persegi; (*open space*) lapangan, tanah lapang, halaman; (*right angle*) bersiku.

squashy empuk, lembik.

squat cangkung; to — bercangkung.

squatter orang yang bercangkung; (*unlawful occupier of land*) orang yang menduduki tanah dengan tidak mempunyai kebenaran, setinggan.

squaw perempuan bangsa asli Amerika (bangsa Indian).

squawk jeritan, bunyi burung; to — berteriak.

squeak keciut, menciak; to — memekik.

squeal pekik, teriakan; to — memekik, berteriak.

squeamish lekas mual.

squeeze (*press hand*) tekanan; (*packed*) keadaan penuh sesak; to — menekan, memicit.

squelch bunyi celepuk, lecup-lecap; to — melecup; (*crush a flea or insect*) menindas.

squib petas, mercun.

squid ikan kurita, ikan sotong.

squint mata juling.

squire (*country gentleman*) tuantanah.

squirm gerak liat-liut, belit.

squirrel tupai.

squirt air yang memancut; to — bepancar, memancut.

stab tikam; to — menikam, meradak.

stability seimbangan, ketetapan, setabil.

stabilization keseimbangan, tetap.

stabilize, to — menjadikan tetap, kesetabilan.

stable I kandang kuda.

stable II (*firm*) kukuh, tetap, setimbang, tenteram.

staccato terputus-putus.

stack longgok, susunkan; smoke — cerobong kapal atau keretapi.

stadium tempat main sukan, stadium.

staff tongkat, tiang.

stag rusa jantan.

stage (*platform*) panggung; landing — pangkalan, bagan; (*grade*) peningkat.

stagecoach kereta yang membawa pos dan penumpang dari suatu tempat ke tempat lain.

stage fright perasaan takut menghadapi orang banyak, darah gemuruh.

stage whisper bisikan kuat supaya kedengaran oleh orang ramai.

stagger, to — (*toddle of infants*) bertatih-tatih; (*as drunk man*) jalan terhuyung-huyung.

stagnant mati, terhenti.

stagnate, to — tidak menga-lir, mati.

staid bertabiat tenang.

stain lumuran, renjis; *(flaw)* cacat; *(dirty)* mengotorkan.

stainless *(flawless)* tidak ber-cacat; *(not corroded)* tidak dimakan karat.

staircase tangga rumah; winding — tangga pusing.

stair(s), flight of —s tangga rumah.

stake *(pole)* pancang, rancang; *(for impaling)* sula; *(in betting)* taruhan, tagan.

stale *(musty)* apak, basi.

stalemate, to — *(frustrate)* menggagalkan.

stalk I batang, gagang, tangkai.

stalk II *(long pace)* langkah panjang, cara berjalan dengan langkah panjang.

stall *(for cattle)* kandang; *(for sale of goods)* kedai.

stallion kuda jantan.

stalwart *(strong)* kuat, tegap; *(forceful)* gagah.

stamina ketahanan.

stammer, to — gagap.

stammerer orang yang ga-gap.

stamp *(postage)* alat stem pengecap; *(seal)* cap, meterai; to — *(with foot)* hentam.

stamp collector pengumpul stem.

stampede pelarian kacaubilau (kuda, lembu dan lainlain).

stanch, to — *(support)* mena-han; *(stop bleeding)* menasak.

stand *(up)* berdiri; *(ending)* perhentian; *(hold out)* per-tahanan; *(position)* kedudukan.

standard *(grade)* darjah; *(flag)* panji, cogan; *(measurement)* ukuran.

standardize, to — menye-suaikan dengan harkat, mem-buat menurut ukuran.

stand-in pengganti, wakil.

standing kedudukan; *(of long —)* lamanya; *(firm)* tetap; *(— up)* yang berdiri.

stand-offish tidak beramah-tamah.

standpoint pendirian.

standstill perhentian tetap.

stanza pantun, bait.

staple *(important, basic)* uta-ma, pokok; *(produce)* hasil pokok, bahan mentah.

star bintang; *(celebrated person)* orang terkemuka dalam salah satu lapangan masyarakat.

starboard sebelah kanan kapal.

starch *(of coconut milk)* pati; kanji; to — menganji.

starchy kaku kerana baharu dikanji.

stare pandangan, renungan; to — *(of eyes)* terbuntang matanya; *(gaze)* memandang.

starfish bintang laut, tapak-tapak nabi sulaiman.

stark *(stiff)* kaku; *(downright)* belaka; *(completely)* sama-sekali; *(naked)* telanjang.

starling sejenis burung perl-ing.

start *(move)* gerak mendadak; *(starting place)* tempat per-mulaan.

starter orang yang memula-kan perlumbaan dan lain-lain.

starting keberangkatan; — point pangkal, tempat permulaan.

startle, to — mengejutkan, terperanjat.

startling yang mengejutkan, memeranjatkan.

starvation kelaparan, kebu-luran.

starve, to — *(to death)* mati kelaparan; *(very hungry)* san-gat lapar, bulur.

state I *(condition)* keadaan; *(country)* negara, yang ber-kenaan dengan negara; *(rank)* pangkat; *(pomp)* kemuliaan, kebesaran; **to lie in** — mayat diperlihatkan umum dengan upacara.

state II, to — menerangkan, menyatakan.

stately mulia, santun.

statement sebutan, perkataan, ucapan.

statesman ahli tata-negara.

static beku, berkenaan dengan hal yang seimbang dan yang tidak bergerak.

station (*place*) tempat; (*railway*) stesen.

stationary tidak bergerak, diam; (*fixed*) tetap.

stationer penjual kertas buku tulis dan sebagainya.

stationery keperluan tulis-menulis, alat tulis.

station house pejabat polis.

station master kepala stesen.

statistical menurut berdasarkan statistik, perangkaan.

statistician ahli statistik.

statistics statistik, perangkaan, ilmu statistik.

statue patung, arca.

statuesque seperti patung.

statuette patung kecil.

stature tinggi seseorang.

status pangkat, kedudukan, keadaan, taraf.

statute undang-undang; — **law** undang-undang yang termaktub.

statutory berdasarkan undang-undang.

staunch (*loyal*) kukuh, setia, patuh; *see* stanch.

stave papan samping (sebuah tong); (*of ladder*) anak tangga.

stay (*remain*) tinggal, kediaman; (*check action*) tahan (salah satu hukuman); (*endure*) daya tahan; tinggal.

stead, in a person's — pengganti seseorang.

steadfast (*firm*) tetap; (*determined*) tabah.

steady tetap, mantap; **to** — menjadi tetap.

steak sepotong daging atau ikan.

steal, to — (*rob*) mencuri; (*creep into*) menyelinap.

stealth hal tersembunyi, hal diam-diam.

stealthily tersembunyi, diam-diam.

steam wap air, kukus.

steam engine jentera kukus, jentera wap.

steamer (*ship*) kapal api.

steamroller penggelek jalan.

steed kuda, kenaikan.

steel baja; **to** — mengerasi.

steelyard dacing.

steep I terjal, curam; (*of place*) lereng yang curam.

steep II, to — mencelup, merendam.

steeple menara; —**chase** perlumbaan kuda melalui lapangan, parit, pagar dan sebagainya.

steer I, to — memegang kemudi, mengemudikan.

steer II (*castrated ox*) lembu jantan yang telah dikebirikan.

steersman jurumudi.

stellar yang berkenaan dengan bintang.

stem I (*of tree*) batang (*stalk*) gagang, tangkal; (*root wood*) pokok; (*of ship*) haluan.

stem II, to — (*check*) menahan; (*breast, change etc*) menempuh, melawan.

stench bau busuk.

stenograph huruf atau tulisan ringkas, teringkas.

stenographer juru teringkas.

stenography hal menulis ringkas.

stentorian dengan suara kuat.

step (*pace*) langkah; (*tread on*) jejak; (*action*) tindakan; (*of ladder*) anak tangga.

stepbrother saudara tiri.

stepchild anak tiri.

stepfather bapa tiri.

stepmother ibu tiri.

steppingstone batu loncatan.

stereotype, to — menetapkan bentuknya, jenis seacuan.

sterile (*free of germ*) suci hama; (*barren*) mandul; (*unprolific*) tidak kembang biak.

sterility keadaan mandul.

sterilize, to — menjadikan suci hama.

sterling (*genuine*) jati.

stern I (*of ship*) buritan; (*rear*) bahagian belakang.

stern II (*severe*) keras hati, herdik.

sternness kekerasan.

stevedore tukang punggah, ahli pemuat dan pemunggah kapal.

stew rebusan; **to** — merebus perlahan-lahan.

steward (*agent*) wakil; (*on ship*) pelayan kapal.

stick (*for walking*) tongkat; (*pole*) batang; **to** — melekatkan.

sticking plaster pita perekat.

stick-in-the-mud orang lambat.

stickleback sejenis ikan.

stickler, a — for orang yang berpegang kepada sesuatu dengan sekuat-kuatnya.

sticky bergetah, melekit; (*col: unpleasant*) keras hati.

stiff kaku, keras; (*overformal*) tidak ramah-tamah; (*difficult to do*) sukar.

stiffen, to — menjadi kaku.

stifle, to — mencekek; **—d** lemas.

stifling yang mencekek.

stigma (*blemish*) cacat.

stigmatize, to — mencacat.

stile penjejak kaki.

still I (*yet*) pula, juga, lagi; (*to this time*) masih.

still II (*silent*) diam; (*calm*)

tenang; (*quiet of places*) sunyi; in the — of night pada malam yang sunyi.

still III (*for distilling*) alat penyuling.

stillborn yang lahir mati, mati kebebang.

still life lukisan yang pokoknya salah satu susunan benda-benda seperti buah bunga alat rumah dan sebagainya.

stilt kaki-kaki, tinjau.

stimulant (*med*) yang merangsang, ubat perangsang; (*stimulus*) pendorong.

stimulate, to — mendorong, merangsang.

stimulation dorongan, perangsang.

stimulus pendorong, perangsang.

sting (*by wasp etc*) sengat; (*of pain*) pedihnya, sakitnya; **to** — menyengat; (*cause pain*) menyakiti.

stinginess kekikiran.

stingy kikir, bakhil, lokek.

stink, to — berbau busuk, kohong, bangar.

stint (*limit*) pembatasan; (*fixed amount of work*) pekerjaan yang ditetapkan.

stipend gaji (pendita).

stipendiary orang yang menerima gaji.

stipple, to — membubuhi titik-titik.

stipulate, to — (*demand fulfilment*) menuntut; (*settle*) menetapkan.

stipulation syarat.

stir (*move*) gerak; **to** — bergerak; menggerakkan; (*with spoon etc*) mengacaukan.

stirrup pemijak kaki, injak-injak.

stitch, to — menjahit.

stock (*main stem*) batang; (*source*) pokok; (*lineage*) turunan; (*stores*) persediaan; live-— ternak.

stockade benteng, kubu.

stockbroker saudagar jual beli syir.

stock exchange pasar wang, tempat jual beli syir.

stocking sarung kaki.

stocks (for boats) galang; (fetters) pasung.

stocky gemuk, pendek dan degap.

stockyard kurungan ternak.

stodgy (indigestible) yang sukar dicernakan, payah hadam; (heavy) berat.

stoic orang yang sanggup mengendalikan diri, orang sabar dan tenang.

stoke, to — menyala dan memeliharakan api.

stoker tukang api.

stole (garment) sejenis selendang.

stolid (inactive) kurang giat; (obtuse) dungu.

stomach perut; (inclination for) kecenderungan; pit of the — hulu hati.

stomach ache sakit perut.

stone (rock, pebble) batu; (of fruit) biji; (weight) ukuran berat Inggeris (14 lb); to — merejam.

stony penuh batu, seperti batu; (hard: of feelings) keras, kejam.

stooge (col) kakitangan.

stool (backless chair) bangku tidak bersandar; foot— alas kaki.

stoop I, to — bungkuk, bongkok, tunduk.

stoop II (verandah) panggung di hadapan rumah, serambi.

stop perhentian, berhenti; full — (grammar) noktah; to — berhenti, terhenti; (up a hole) menyumbatkan.

stopcock alat pengunci.

stopgap sesuatu yang mengisi untuk sementara waktu.

stoppage penghentian.

stopper sumbat; to — menyumbat.

stop-press berita yang dimuat ke dalam suratkhabar pada waktu yang terakhir.

stopwatch jam diberi beralat berhenti.

storage penyimpanan, tempat penyimpanan.

store (shed etc) gudang; —s persediaan, penyimpanan.

storey tingkat, loteng, berloteng.

storied termasyhur dalam cerita dan hikayat.

stork sejenis burung bangau.

storm (wind) angin ribut, taufan; (of rain) hujan lebat.

storm cloud awan hujan, pokok hujan.

storm troops pasukan penggempur.

stormy hebat, ribut, yang banyak taufannya, berkenaan dengan angin ribut.

story cerita, kisah, riwayat, dongeng.

stout (fat) gemuk; (resolute) berani.

stove dapur.

stovepipe corong yang mengalirkan asap keluar rumah.

stow, to — memuatkan, mengemaskan; to — away mengemaskan, menempatkan.

stowaway orang yang mencuri naik kapal sehingga ikut dengan tidak membayar tambang pelayaran.

straddle, to — (with legs apart) mengangkang; (bestride) duduk terjelapak.

strafe penembakan; to — menembaki.

straggle, to — (stray) sesat; (separate) bercerai-cerai; (of plant growth) tumbuh di sana sini.

straight lurus; (right through) terus langsung.

straighten, to — menjadi

lurus, menjadikan lurus, meluruskan.

straightforward jujur, terus
terang.

strain (*stretch*) ketegangan;
(*of speech etc*) gaya bercakap
atau mengarang; to — tegangkan.

strainer penapisan.

strait (*narrow*) sempit; —s
(*channel*) selat.

strand I (*shore*) tepi laut, pantai; to — (*run ashore*) kandas,
mengkandaskan.

strand II (*of rope etc*) helai,
unting.

strange anih, ajaib, ganjil.

stranger (*not known*) orang
yang tidak kenal atau di-
kenali; (*foreigner*) orang asing,
orang dagang.

strangle, to — mencekik.

strangulation cekikan,
kebebangan.

strap tali kulit, ambin kulit;
to — mengikat dengan tali
kulit.

strapping (*strong, big, stout*)
kuat, besar, gemuk.

stratagem tipu daya, muslihat.

strategic bersiasat, menurut
siasat.

strategy siasat, ilmu perang.

stratification susunan bertingkat, susunan berlapis-
lapis.

stratum lapisan, tingkat,
petala.

straw jerami.

strawberry buah strawberry.

stray tersesat; (*animal*) binatang yang berkeliaran; to —
(*lost*) sesat; (*wander*) berkeliaran.

streak corek, coreng; to —
mencoreng.

streaky berjalur.

stream (*river*) kali, sungai;
(*flow*) aliran, arus; to —
mengalir.

streamer ular-ular, panji-
panji.

street jalan, lorong yang ada
rumahnya; **the man in the** —
orang biasa.

strength kekuatan, keteguhan, kekuhan.

strengthen, to — bertambah
kuat, memperkuatkan.

strenuous sangat giat dan
rajin.

stress (*force*) tekanan; (*emphasis*) tegas; to — memberi
tekanan; (*emphasize*) mementingkan.

stretch regangan, menganjur;
(*of land etc*) luasnya (salah
satu tanah dan sebagainya).

stretcher peregang; (*litter*)
usungan.

strew menghamburkan, menaburkan.

strict (*careful*) teliti; (*exact*)
tepat, (*stern*) keras.

stride langkah; to — melangkah.

strident lantang, langsing.

strife perselisihan, pertengkaran.

strike (*blow*) pukulan; (*cease
work*) pemogokan; (*a find*)
pendapatan tiba-tiba.

striker pemogok.

striking (*noteworthy*) yang
menarik perhatian, pelek.

string (*cord*) tali; (*wire*) dawai;
(*form a line of*) rangkai.

stringency kekerasan.

stringent (*strict*) keras; (*binding*) yang mengikat.

stringy (*fibrous*) berserabut.

strip bilah, jalur; to —
(*undress*) membuka pakaian.

stripe jalur, corak.

stripling anak, muda, pemuda, teruna.

strive, to — (*contest*) berjuang;
(*contrive means*) berdaya-daya,
mengikhtiarkan.

stroke I (*blow*) pukulan, tam-
paran.

stroke II (*wipe*) usap; to — mengusap.

stroll bersiar-siar, berjalan-jalan sebentar; to — berjalan-jalan.

strong (*in general*) kuat; (*of buildings*) kukuh; (*of mind, smell etc*) keras; (*active*) giat, bersemangat.

strongbox peti besi penyimpan barang berharga.

stronghold benteng yang kukuh.

strong-minded tabah dan cerdas.

strongroom bilik kuat tempat penyimpan barang berharga.

structure susunan, bangun, rangkaian, struktur.

struggle (*contest*) perjuangan; to — (*in order to get free*) meronta.

strum, to — memetik.

strut, to — (*as peacock*) mengigal.

strychnine ubat racun strychnin.

stub (*stump*) tunggul; (*of cigar, torch etc*) puntung.

stubble jerami.

stubborn keras kepala, degil, tegar.

stuck-up bongkak sombong.

stud I (*for collar*) kancing; to — (*adorn with*) menatahkan; —ded with bertatahkan.

stud II (*of horses*) peternakan kuda.

student pelajar, penuntut, mahasiswa.

studio tempat bekerja seorang seniman.

studious rajin, bersemangat.

study telaah, pelajaran, ruang belajar, pengajian.

stuff (*material*) bahan; (*things*) barang; to — mengisi padat-padat.

stuffing pengisi.

stuffy apak, pengap.

stumble, to — tersandung tergelincuh.

stumbling block rintangan.

stump (*of tree*) tunggul; (*of cigar etc*) puntung; to — berjalan seperti berkaki buatan.

stumpy pendek dan tegap.

stun, to — (*deafen*) menulikan. (*bewilder*) membingungkan.

stunt I usaha istimewa, pertunjukan yang sangat menarik perhatian.

stunt II, to — (*check*) membantut; —ed terbantut; (*dwarfed*) kerdil.

stupefy, to — membiuskan, memabukkan.

stupendous yang sangat mentakjubkan.

stupid bodoh, dengu.

stupidity kebodohan, kependiran.

stupor pembiusan.

sturdy kuat, begap.

stutter percakapan gagap.

sty kandang babi.

sty(e) (*in eye*) tembel.

style gaya, cara; (*of speech*) jalan (gaya) bahasa; (*type*) jenis.

stylish berdasarkan budi bahasa; menurut gaya.

stylist pengarang yang baik gaya bahasanya.

suave halus, manis; (*in speech*) manis mulut.

sub- awalan kata yang ertinya; bawah; kurang; tidak sepenuh penuhnya.

subcommittee jawatankuasa kecil.

subconscious bawah daripada sedar.

subconsciousness keadaan bawah daripada sedar.

subdivide, to — membahagi lagi.

subdivision bahagian yang lebih kecil lagi.

subdue, to — menaklukkan, menundukkan

subject I (*dependent*) takluk, di bawah kekuasaan.

subject II (*of state etc*) anak negeri, anak buah; (*matter*) pokok; (*of discussion*) hal pembicaraan.

subject III, to — menaklukkan.

subjection penaklukan, penundukan.

subjective yang berdasarkan pandangan sendiri.

subject matter buah fikiran yang diuraikan di dalam karangan dan sebagainya.

subjoin, to — menyambung pada akhirnya.

subjugate, to — menakluki.

sublease penyewaan bukan dari yang empunya tetapi dari seseorang penyewa.

sublime maha mulia, akhbar.

submarine di dalam laut; (*warship*) kepal selam.

submerge, to — menenggelamkan, merendam.

submersion rendam; selam.

submission tunduk.

submissive (*docile*) lembut; (*serving as in forces*) berkhidmat.

submit, to — (*surrender*) menyerahkan; (*represent facts etc*) mempersembahkan.

subnormal di bawah keadaan biasa, kurang daripada sedang.

subordinate orang bawahan.

subpoena panggilan dari pengadilan, akan menghadiri sidang.

subscribe, to — (*sign*) menandatangani akan; (*make payment*) beryuran.

subscriber yang bertandatangan; (*to club, paper etc*) pelanggan.

subscription tandatangan; harga langganan.

subsequent kemudian, yang berikut; —ly kemudian.

subservient (*useful*) berguna

(untuk salah satu tujuan); (*servile*) yang menghinakan diri.

subside, to — (*of storms*) reda; (*lessen*) berkurang; (*of water, floods*) surut; (*shrink*) susut.

subsidence hal berkurang, hal susut, hal reda.

subsidiary tambah bantuan, hal tambahan.

subsidize, to — memberi sokongan.

subsidy sokongan.

subsist, to — (*be alive*) hidup; (*find means of existence*) mencari nafkah.

subsistence penghidupan, nafkah, mata pencarian.

substance (*essence*) wujud, zat; (*origin*) pokok; (*material*) benda; a man of — orang berada.

substantial (*real*) benar; (*being*) bewujud; (*big*) sejumlah besar.

substantiate, to — (*prove*) membenarkan; (*bring into being*) mewujudkan.

substitute ganti, pengganti; to — mengganti.

substitution pengganti.

subterfuge dalih.

subterranean di bawah muka tanah.

subtle (*tenuous*) halus; (*crafty*) cerdik.

subtlety sifat halus, kehalusan.

subtract, to — mengurangi, tolak.

subtraction pengurangan, tolak.

suburb pinggir bandar, daerah luaran sebuah bandar.

suburban yang berkenaan dengan hujung bandar.

suburbia semua hujung bandar atau seluruh penduduknya.

subvention sokongan tunjangan.

subversion (destruction) penrosakan; (overturning) penggulingan.

subversive yang bermaksud merosakkan kerajaan, subversib.

subway jalan di bawah muka tanah.

succeed, to — (take place of) mengganti akan; (be profitable) berhasil baik.

success hasil baik keuntungan, sesuatu atau seseorang yang berhasil baik, maju jaya.

successful berhasil baik, beruntung, berjaya.

succession (in sequence) turutan; (take place of) penggantian.

successive berturut-turut.

successor ganti, pengganti.

succinct ringkas, singkat, pendek.

succour pertolongan, menolong, memberi pertolongan.

succulence sifat, berair, hal banyak airnya.

succulent berair, bergetah, banyak airnya, banyak getahnya.

succumb, to — (be defeated) tewas, kalah; (die) mati.

such demikian, sebagai itu, begitu, sebesar itu, sebanyak itu.

suck tetek, hisap; **to** — mengisap, menyedut.

suckle, to — meneteki, menyusui.

suckling anak (manusia atau binatang) yang masih menetek.

suction penghisapan; — pipe paip pengisap.

sudden(ly), all of a **sudden** tiba-tiba, sekonyong-konyong.

suds air, buih sabun.

sue, to — mendakwa; (claim) menuntut.

suede sejenis kulit.

suet lemak.

suffer, to — menderita, merasai.

sufferance (patience) hal menyabarkan; (gift) pemberian; (in pain) kesakitan.

suffering penderitaan.

suffice, to — mencukupi, memadai.

sufficient sampai, cukup, mencukupi.

suffix akhiran kata.

suffocate, to — (strangle) mencekek; (feel choked) merasa tercekek; (stifle to death) mati lemas.

suffrage (concerning voting) hak memilih.

suffragette perempuan yang menuntut hak memilih untuk kaum perempuan.

suffuse, to — (as bruise) berbekam.

sugar gula, sakar; refined — gula pasir.

sugar basin tempat gula.

sugar cane tebu.

sugar mill kilang gula.

sugar palm kabung, enau.

suggest, to — (whisper) membisikkan; (advise) menasihatkan; (hint at) membayangkan; (propose) mencadang.

suggestion bisikan, nasihat, anjuran, cadangan, saran.

suggestive yang menganjurkan salah satu hal, yang mengingatkan.

suicidal yang berkenaan dengan bunuh diri, yang merupakan pembunuhan diri.

suicide (act) bunuh diri; (person) orang yang membunuh diri.

suit (request) permohonan; (marriage proposal) peminangan; (complaint) pengaduan.

suitability kepatutan, hal patut, kelayakan.

suitable patut, pantas, layak.

suitcase beg pakaian.

suite (*retinue*) pengiring, (*a set*) rangkaian, turut.

suited patut, sepadan.

suitor (*one who sues*) pendakwa; (*of marriage*) peminang, pelamar.

sulk, to — merajuk, merongseng.

sulky (*sullen*) muram, murung.

sullen murung, merengus, masam.

sulphate garam asam belerang, sulfat.

sulphur belerang, sulfur.

sultan sultan.

sultana ibu (*isteri, anak*), sultan; (*raisin*) sejenis kismis besar.

sultry panas pengap.

sum (*total*) jumlah; (*of money*) sejumlah wang; (*reckoning*) hitungan; to — up menghitung, menjumlahkan.

summarily ringkas.

summarize, to — meringkaskan.

summary ringkasan, ikhtisar, ringkas, rumusan.

summer, —time musim panas.

summit puncak, kemuncak.

summon, to — menyuruh datang, memanggil; (*to forced service*) mengerah.

summons (*call*) panggilan; (*for forced service*) kerahan; (*law*) pendakwaan surat dakwa.

sump takung tempat air (minyak dan lain-lain).

sumptuous mewah.

sun matahari.

sunbath jemur.

sunbather orang yang suka berjemur tengah panas.

sunbeam sinar matahari.

sunburned, sunburnt hitam oleh sinar matahari.

Sunday hari minggu, hari Ahad.

sun–dried salai.

sundry berbagai, bermacam; all and — segenap orang; sundries serba-serbi.

sunflower bunga matahari.

sunken (*of eyes, cheeks*) cengkung.

sunny yang disinari matahari; (*high spirits*) riang, ria.

sunrise matahari terbit.

sunset matahari mati, matahari turun.

sunshade payung, alat lindung sinar matahari.

sunshine cahaya matahari.

sunstroke dipanah matahari.

sup, to — menyenduk atau minum berteguk-teguk.

super— awalan kata yang ertinya: lebih, yang melebihi.

superabundant berlimpah-limpah.

superannuate, to — memberhentikan kerana tinggi umur.

superb (*of dress, bearing*) mulia; (*very good*) sangat baik.

supercilious sombong, congkak.

superficial tipis, cetek, tohor, tidak dalam.

superfluous terlebih, berkelebihan.

superimpose, to — mengecapkan di atas sesuatu yang lain.

superinduce, to — menambah sesuatu lagi.

superintend, to — mengawasi, menjaga, menguasai.

superintendence pengawasan.

superintendent pengawas; (*police*) pegawai polis pangkat tinggi.

superior (*better etc*) lebih baik (tinggi, besar); (*eminent*) utama; (*person*) orang atasan.

superiority kelebihan, keutamaan.

superlative tingkat perbandingan yang tertinggi.

supernatural sakti ghaib, keramat.

supernumerary lebih daripada jumlah tetap atau biasa.

superscribe, to — menulis di atas sesuatu.

supersede, to — (*substitute*) mengganti; (*put aside*) membuang.

superstition takhyyul, kepercayaan karut.

superstitious bertakhayyul.

superstructure bangunan sebelah atas.

supervene, to — terjadi tibatiba, terjadi sebagai tambahan.

supervise, to — mengawasi, mengatur.

supervision pengawasan, penjagaan.

supervisor pengawas, penyelia.

supervisory yang mengawasi.

supine (*lying on back*) terlentang; (*indolent*) sangat malas; (*sleepy*) mengantuk.

supper makan malam.

supplant, to — mengganti dengan mendesakkan orang atau hal lain.

supple gemalai, lemah, liat lentur.

supplement tambahan, sambungan.

suppliant yang memohon.

supplication permohonan.

supplier orang yang menyediakan langganan.

supply persediaan, perlengkapan, pembekalan.

support (*prop of wood etc*) sandaran, ongak; (*assistance*) pertolongan, sokongan bantuan.

supporter pengikut, penyokong.

suppose, to — menyangka, mengira; —, supposing seandainya, andai kata, sekiranya.

supposition sangka, andaiandai.

suppress, to — (*crush*) menindih, menindas; (*extinguish*) memadamkan.

suppression penindihan, penindasan, penyingkiran.

suppurate, to — bernanah.

supra— awalan kata yang ertinya: di atas.

supremacy keutamaan.

supreme agung, utama.

surcharge biaya (cukai, jumlah, muatan) tambahan.

sure tentu tanggung.

surely memang sudah tentu, tentulah.

surety penjamin, orang tanggungan.

surf buih (ombak), pecahan ombak; **to** — main berselancar di ombak laut.

surface sebelah muka, di muka, di luar.

surge (*of sea*) gelombang, ombak yang melambung; **to** — bergelombang.

surgeon ahli belah, doktor belah, tabib belah.

surgery ilmu belah; (*consulting room*) bilik pengubatan.

surgical yang berkenaan dengan pembelahan atau ahli belah.

surly merengus.

surmise sangkaan; **to** — menyangka.

surmount, to — mengatasi.

surname nama keluarga.

surpass, to — melampaui, melebihi.

surplus lebihan; (*remains of food*) sisa.

surprise, (*astonishment*) a — kejadian tiba-tiba; **to** — menghairankan, terpanjat.

surprising yang menghairankan.

surrealism aliran kesenian yang mengutamakan hal bawah sedar.

surrender penyerahan; **to** — menyerah diri.

surreptitious diam-diam curi-curi, gelap.

surround, to — mengelilingi, melengkungi, mengepung.

surroundings sekeliling, lengkungan, daerah.

surtax cukai tambahan.

surveillance penjagaan.

survey (*view*) pemandangan, pandang; (*inspection*) pemeriksaan; (*measur... map land*) pengukuran, sukat.

surveyor pengukur, menteri ukur, penyukat.

survival hal masih hidup.

survive, to — masih hidup terus hidup.

survivor orang yang masih hidup.

susceptible (*easily affected*) mudah kena sesuatu; (*easily influenced*) mudah terpengaruh.

suspect tersangka; orang yang disangka, orang yang disyaki.

suspend, to — (*hang up*) menggantung; (*postpone*) menangguhkan; (*stop for a time*) menghentikan untuk sementara.

suspense kebimbangan, hal ternanti-nanti.

suspension gantung, penangguhan

suspicion syak wasangka, waham.

suspicious berasa syak hati, yang menimbulkan syak hati.

sustain, to — (*hold up*) menahan; (*endure*) menderita.

sustenance (*food*) makanan; (*livelihood*) penghidupan.

swab kain kapas.

swag (*plunder*) barang rampasan.

swagger jalan bergaya; to — berjalan dengan bergaya.

swain pemuda dusun, pelamar.

swallow I burung layang-layang.

swallow II, to — menelan, meneguk.

swamp paya, rawa; to — ampuh .ir.

swampy becak, berpaya.

swan sejenis burung yang berleher panjang, undan.

swanky (*col*) sombong, berlagak.

swarm kawan, kelompok; to — berkerumun berkumpul.

swarthy berkulit hitam.

swashbuckler orang sombong.

swat, to — menampar (lalat dan sebagainya).

swathe, to — membalut, membarut.

sway (*swing unsteadily*) goncangan; (*swing arms*) lenggang; (*rule*) perintah; to — bergoncang bergoyang.

swear, to — bersumpah.

sweat peluh.

sweater kemeja kain panas.

sweaty berpeluh.

Swede orang bangsa Sweden.

Swedish yang berkenaan dengan negeri atau bahasa, Sweden.

sweep (*move in a curve*) gerak yang melengkungi; (*brush*) penyapu; (*oar*) dayung.

sweeping yang luas, besar-besaran; s kotoran, sampah.

sweepstake sejenis main judi loteri.

sweet manis; (*of voice*) merdu; (*fragrant*) harum; (*confection*) gula-gula, kuih.

sweetbread kelenjar ludah perut.

sweeten, to — memaniskan.

sweetheart kekasih, tangkai hati.

sweetmeat manisan, gula-gula.

sweetness kemanisan.

sweet pea sejenis bunga.

sweet-tempered manis, lemah-lembut.

swell (col) (person) orang golongan atas; (fine) baik dan cakap; to — berkembang, membengkak, kembung.

swelter panas terek; to — panas.

swerve simpangan; to — menyimpang.

swift cepat, laju; (of horses) tangkas.

swig (col) teguk; to — minum berteguk-teguk.

swill (with water) pembasuhan.

swim, to — berenang.

swimmer ahli berenang.

swimming pool kolam berenang.

swindle penipuan; to — menipu, mengecoh.

swindler penipu, pengecoh.

swine babi; (wild pig) babi hutan

swing ayunan, buaian.

swipe pukulan keras; to — memukul keras.

swirl (eddy) olakan, olak air; (whirlwind) puting beliung; to — berolak.

swish bunyi desir desau.

Swiss orang negeri Swis; bahasa Swis.

switch ranting, rotan; (of electric light etc) pemetik letrik.

swivel kili-kili; to — memutar dengan kili-kili.

swollen bengkak, bakup, busung.

swoon pengsan; to — pengsan.

swoop sambar; to — menyambar.

swop tukaran; to — menukar.

sword pedang, parang, kelewang.

swordfish sejenis ikan todak.

swordsman ahli pedang.

swot (col) (hard study) pelajaran yang sukar; (person) orang yang belajar dengan rajin.

sycamore sejenis pohon.

sycophant peleceh, orang yang pandai bermuka-muka.

syllable suku kata.

syllabus sukatan mata pengajaran dan sebagainya.

sylph sejenis peri, bidadari.

symbol simbol, lambang, tanda alamat.

symbolic(al) berkenaan dengan lambang.

symbolize, to — melambangkan.

symmetric(al), symmetry setangkup, semukur.

sympathetic yang menunjukkan belas hati, bertimbang rasa.

sympathize, to — turut merasa (sakit, sedih dan lain-lain).

sympathy simpati, belas kasihan, belasungkawa; (in agreement) hal bersetujuan dengan.

symphonic yang berkenaan dengan simfoni.

symphony simfoni, semacam karangan muzik untuk panca ragam.

symposium percakapan beberapa pengarang atau pendita untuk menghuraikan salah satu pendapat, simposium.

symptom tanda, alamat.

symptomatic berdasarkan tanda.

syn- awalan kata yang ertinya: bersama-sama; sama.

synagogue rumah, sembahyang kaum Yahudi, kanisah.

synchronization penyelarasan.

synchronize, to — terjadi serentak, menyelaraskan.

syncopate, to — menghilangkan suku kata atau huruf dalam salah satu kata.

syndicate kongsi, perkongsian, gabungan orang atau perusahaan.

synonym kata seerti.

synonymous yang seerti.

synopsis ikhtisar, ringkasan.

syntax ilmu nahu, ilmu tata-kata, aturan cakap, sintaksis.

synthesis perpaduan, sintisis.

synthetic(al) sintetis, yang berdasarkan sintisis.

syphilis penyakit raja, penyakit jahat.

Syrian orang negeri Siria.

syringe buluh-buluh; to — menyumpit.

syrup seterup, air gula, sirap.

system sistem, susunan, cara.

systematic menurut sistem, susunan atau cara.

systematize, to — menyusun.

T

tab punca; (of shoelace) hujung tali sepatu.

tabby (of cats etc) cecak.

tabernacle (for prayer) tempat persembahyang.

table meja; (flat board) papan; (list) daftar jadual.

tableau (picture) gambar.

tablecloth alas meja.

tablet papan tulis loh; (pill) tablet.

tableware alat makan.

taboo larangan, pantang; to — melarang.

tabular (flat) atur; yang disusun dengan aturan.

tabulate, to — menyusun.

tacit dengan tidak payah diucapkan; (silent) yang berdiam.

taciturn pendiam, tidak suka bercakap-cakap.

tack (nail) paku rebana; to — (change course) berpal-pal.

tackle takai; to — (grasp) memegang; (undertake) berusaha untuk mencapai sesuatu.

tact budi, bijaksana.

tactful bijaksana, bersiasat.

tactical berkenaan dengan siasat.

tactics siasat, ikhtiar.

tactless tidak berbudi, buta akal.

tadpole berudu.

taffeta sejenis kain sutera.

tag (of shoelace) hujung tali sepatu; (loose end) punca.

tail bantut, ekor; (rear portion) bahagian belakang.

tailor tukang jahit; to — memotong dan menjahit pakaian.

taint cacat; to — mencemari.

take pemegang; to — (grasp) memegang; (capture) menangkap; (get) mengambil; (accept) menerima.

taken up of take (influenced) terpengaruh; — aback terperanjat; — ill 'atuh sakit.

taker pengambil, penerima.

taking (alluring) yang mengambil hati.

talc serbuk wangi.

talcum, — powder sejenis bedak halus.

tale cerita dongeng, hikayat.

talent bakat orang yang berbakat.

talisman azimat.

talk percakapan perbincangan, ceramah; small — kecek-kecek.

talkative suka bercakap, ceramah, peramah.

tall tinggi yang berlebih-lebihan.

tallboy sejenis almari laci.

tallow lemak (untuk membuat lilin).

tally catatan perhitungan.

talon kuku, cakar.

tamarind pohon asam jawa.

tambourine rebana, tamborin.

tame (not wild) jinak; (feeble) lemah; to — menjinakkan.

tamper to — with mencampuri.

tampon sumbat.

tan (for tanning) samak; (colour) warna perang, warna kehitam-hitaman; to — menyamak.

tandem (dua) berbuntut-buntut.

tang (pungent taste) rasa yang tajam

tangent garisan sentuh.

tangible nyata, berwujud.

tangle (of hair rope etc) kekusutan; (disturbance) kekacauan; to — menjadi kusut.

tango ejenis tarian.

tank (for liquid) tangki; (armoured vehicle) kereta kebal, tank.

tankard mangkuk besar.

tanker kapal tangki pembawa minyak.

tantalize, to — menggoda.

tantamount — to sama erupa, berjumlah.

tantrum tinkah, kemarahan.

Taoism kepercayaan akan pengajaran Lao-tsze.

tap I (for water etc) cerat; salur.

tap II (noise, tap) detik, ketuk; to — mendetik mengetuk

tap-dancing sejenis tarian dengan mengentak-entakkan kaki.

tape pita; to — mengikat dengan pita.

taper dian; to — (off) melancip, melonjong, meninrus.

tapestry sejenis tenunan (yang biasanya dipakai untuk permadani).

tapeworm cacing pipih.

tapioca ubi kayu.

tapir tenok, cipan.

tar I minyak tar pelangkin, belangkin.

tar II (sailor) kelasi, anak kapal.

tarantula laba-laba yang besar.

tardy lambat, lengah.

target sasaran.

tariff cukai.

tarmac sejenis minyak aspal; (on aerodrome) jalan aspal itu pada lapangan kapal udara.

tarn tasik, danau.

tarnish kekusaman; to — hilang cahayanya, menjadi kusam, menjadi suram, menjadi buruk.

taro talas, keladi.

tarpaulin kain terpal.

tarry I penuh tar, seperti tar.

tarry II, to — (remain) tinggal; (wait) menunggu; (dawdle) melengah.

tart I (harsh) hardik; (sour, of aste, looks) masam.

tart II (col) (low woman) perempuan nakal.

tartan kain bulu yang warnanya genggang.

tartar (in wine barrel) kerak anggur di dalam tong.

task tugas, pekerjaan.

task force kesatuan yang disuruh melakukan tugas istimewa.

taskmaster pengawas.

tassel rumbai, jumbai.

taste rasa, cita-rasa; (smacking lips) pengecap; to — mengecap; merasai.

tasteful bagus, indah, dipilih dengan budi bahasa.

tasteless (of taste) tawar, ambar; (of other matters) tidak bagus, tidak indah.

tasty sedap, lazat, cita rasanya.

tatter kain secabik; in —s cobak-cabik, compang-camping.

tattoo I tanda rajah; to — merajah; —ed bercacah.

tattoo II (military signal) panggilan kembali askar; (display) pertunjukan askar.

taunt celaan; to — mencela.

Taurus salah satu nujum zodiak.

taut (*tight*) kencang, tegang.

tavern kedai minum.

tawdry sesuatu yang baik rupa tetapi tidak berharga.

tawny kuning tua, perang.

tax pajak, cukai.

taxation pajak, bea, cukai.

taxi(**=cab**) teksi; **to take a —** naik teksi.

taxidermy hal menyedia kulit binatang dan memasangkannya sehingga rupanya seperti binatang hidup.

tea teh, ca; (*afternoon meal*) makanan dengan minum teh.

teach, to — mengajar.

teacher guru.

tea chest peti teh.

teaching pengajaran.

teacup cawan teh; **storm in a —** gempar mengenai hal yang tidak penting.

teak(**wood**) kayu jati.

team (*of two beasts*) sepasang (lembu dan lain-lain); (*of people*) pasukan.

teapot tekoh.

tear I (*of eye*) air mata.

tear II koyakan; **to —** merobik, mencabik, koyakkan.

tearful sangat sedih.

tease, to — mengganggu, menggiat, mengusik.

teaser pengganggu, penggiat, pengusik; (*problem*) masaalah.

teat puting susu.

technical teknik.

technicality hal teknik, selokbelok teknik.

technician ahli teknik.

technique cara atau kepandaian membuat sesuatu, teknik, cara.

technology ilmu tentang segala kepandaian membuat sesuatu, teknoloji.

tedious menjemukan.

tedium rasa jemu.

teem, to — (**with**) berkerumun.

-teen akhiran bilangan antara 12 dan 20, -belas.

teenage umur antara 13 sampai ke 19

teeth *pl of* **tooth.**

teethe, to — mendapat gigi.

teetotal berpantang minuman keras.

teetotaller, (*US*) **teetotaler** orang yang berpantang minuman keras.

tele— awalan kata yang ertinya: jauh.

telecommunications perhubungan dari jauh, talikom.

telegram kawat taligram.

telegraph taligrap; **to —** mengetuk kawat.

telegraphic yang berkenaan dengan taligrap.

telepathy perhubungan rohani dari jauh dengan tidak melalui pancaindera.

telephone talipon; **— operator** pelayan talipon.

telescope teropong besar; **to —** mendorong sehingga sebahagian menutupi sebahagian lain sampai seluruhnya menjadi kecil.

television talivisyen, penyiaran gambar dengan gelombang radio.

tell, to — mengkhabarkan, mengatakan.

telltale pengumpat pengadu; (*betray a secret*) yang membuka rahsia.

temerity kegagahan dengan tidak memikirkan segala selokbeloknya.

temper (*frame of mind*) tunjuk perangai, keadaan hati, tabiat, perangai; **in a bad —, out of —** panas hati, berang; **to —** (*steel*) membaja; (*mitigate*) meringankan; (*restrain*) menahan.

temperament tabiat, perangai.

temperamental berkenaan dengan tabiat; (*easily annoyed*) mudah terharu.

temperance kesederhanaan; (in use of alcohol) hal berpantang minuman keras.

temperate sedang, sederhana, ugahari; (of climate) yang berhawa sederhana.

temperature (degree of heat) darjah panas; (of climate generally) hawa; (of body) suhu.

tempest angin ribut, taufan.

tempestuous (terrible) hebat; (of storm) ribut.

temple I (of forehead) pelipis.

temple II kuil, tempat berhala.

tempo kecepatan.

temporal (worldly) duniawi; (of time) yang berkenaan dengan waktu.

temporary sementara, untuk sementara waktu.

tempt, to — (urge) menggoda; (entice) membujuk, memikat.

temptation godaan; (advancement) pendorongan.

ten sepuluh; by —s berpuluh-puluh.

tenable yang dapat dipertahankan, yang dapat dipegang.

tenacious bertekun, melekat.

tenacity ketekunan.

tenancy sewa.

tenant penyewa.

tend, to — (take care of) memeliharakan; (animals) menggembalakan.

tendency kecenderungan, kecondongan.

tender I (of locomotive) kereta di belakang kepala keretapi pembawa bahan pembakar.

tender II (offer) penawaran; legal — alat pembayar yang sah.

tender III (fine) halus; (of food) empuk, lembut; (gentle) lemah-lembut; of — age muda teruna.

tendon otot, urat.

tendril sulur.

tenement (land) tanah milik, tanah sewa; (part of house)

bahagian rumah yang disewakan.

tenet kepercayaan, rukun.

tenfold lipat sepuluh, sepuluh kali ganda.

tenor (general course) tujuan, arah; (voice) suara tinggi laki-laki.

tense I regang, tegang.

tense II (in grammar) masa, waktu (tata-bahasa).

tension (of manner) gaya tegang; regangan ketegangan.

tent khemah.

tentacle sungut.

tentative secara percubaan.

tenth yang kesepuluh; (tenth part) sepersepuluh.

tenuous tipis, halus.

tenure (of land) hak milik; (of office) masa berjawatan.

tepid hangat, panas kuku, suam-suam kuku.

term (period) waktu terbatas; (word) istilah, kata; —s syarat, perjanjian.

terminable yang dapat diputuskan masanya.

terminate, to — mengakhiri.

termination pengakhiran, keputusan.

terminology istilah-istilah.

terminus perhentian, penghabisan.

termite anai-anai, rayap.

terrace tingkat; to — membuat tingkat; —d bertingkat.

terracotta barang tanah liat.

terrain tanah daerah.

terrestrial (of land) yang berkenaan dengan tanah; (of the earth) yang berkenaan dengan bul bumi.

terrible (awful) dahsyat, hebat; (very) terlalu.

terribly (very) amat sangat.

terrier sejenis anjing.

terrific dahsyat, hebat, mendahsyatkan.

terrify, to — mengejutkan, menakutkan, mengerikan.

territorial yang berkenaan dengan daerah, kedaerahan.

territory daerah, kalangan kawasan.

terror dahsyat kengerian.

terrorist perusuh, pengacau, penjahat, pengganas.

terrorism pengacauan, keganasan.

terrorize, to — menggentarkan mengugut.

terse ringkas, singkat, pendek.

tertiary yang ketiga.

test percubaan pengujian.

testament wasiat; **the New T**— Injil; **the Old T**— Taurat.

testicle buah pelir.

testify, to — naik saksi, menyaksikan.

testimonial (*certificate*) surat keterangan; (*gift*) hadiah sebagai tanda penghargaan.

testimony saksi, tanda.

test pilot juru terbang yang mencubai kapalterbang.

testy bengkeng.

tetanus tetanus, terkancing mulut.

tête-à-tête pertemuan antara dua orang sahaja.

tether (*rope*) tali tambat; to — mengikat, menambat.

tetra— awalan kata yang ertinya: empat.

text (*original*) naskhah; (*main body of work*) pokok (perkataan atau) buku; —**book** buku pelajaran.

textile barang tenunan, kain.

texture jaringan, susunan.

than daripada; better — lebih baik daripada.

thank, —**s** terimakasih, syukur; to — berterimakasih.

thankful berterimakasih, bersyukur.

thankless (*of person*) tidak berterimakasih; (*of tasks*) siasia, cuma.

that (*conjunction*) bahawa, yang, supaya, sehingga; (*de-*

monstrative pronoun) begitu, demikian; so — sehingga.

thatch atap (yang dibuat daripada bermacam-macam rumput) nipah; to — mengatapi.

thaw waktu menjadi cair, hancur.

the itu, ini.

theatre panggung, sandiwara, wayang.

theatrical yang berkenaan dengan atau seperti sandiwara.

theft kecurian.

their mereka, mereka punya.

them kepada, akan, mereka.

theme pokok (pembicaraan, fikiran, lagu dan lain-lain), thema.

themselves mereka sendiri.

then pada waktu, ketika masa itu, tatkala itu.

theo— awalan kata yang ertinya: Tuhan.

theologian ulama, alim.

theology ilmu ugama.

theorem soal, dalil, tiorem.

theoretical berdasarkan teori.

theorize, to — berteori, memakai teori.

theory teori.

therapeutic yang menyembuhkan; —s pengubatan, ilmu pengubatan.

–therapy akhiran kata yang ertinya: pengubatan, penyembuhan.

there di sana, di situ; ke sana; (*col*) he isn't all —! la gila.

thereabout(s) kira-kira, lebih kurang.

thereby oleh kerana itu.

therefore oleh kerana itu.

thereof dari itu.

thereupon sesudah itu, kalakian, hatta maka.

therewith dengan itu.

thermal yang berkenaan dengan panas; — unit kesatuan panas.

thermo— awalan kata yang ertinya: panas.

thermometer termometer; clinical — pengukur suhu.

Thermos flask botol termos.

thermostat alat pengimbang panas.

thesaurus daftar kata-kata.

these ini.

thesis dalil, tesis.

they mereka, dia; — say khabarnya, katanya, konon.

thick (of materials) tebal; (of fluids) kental; (of hair, leaves) lebat; (of foliage) rimbun; in the — of the fight di tengah-tengah pertempuran.

thicken, to — (of liquids) menjadi pekat, kental.

thicket belukar.

thickhead orang bodoh.

thickness ketebalan; kekentalan.

thickset (of plants) lebat; (of persons etc) gemuk.

thick-skinned tebal hati, tebal muka.

thief pencuri.

thieve, to — mencuri.

thigh paha; —bone tulang paha.

thimble bidal, sarung jari.

thin tipis, pipih; (fine) halus; (lean) kurus; —skinned mudah terharu.

thing (inanimate object) benda, barang; (affair) hal.

think, to — berfikir, berpendapat.

thinker ahli fikir.

third ketiga, pertiga; one — sepertiga.

thirst haus, dahaga.

thirsty haus, kehausan.

thirteen tiga belas.

thirteenth ketiga belas, pertiga belas.

thirtieth yang ketiga puluh.

thirty tiga puluh.

thistle sejenis tumbuhan berduri.

thong sejalur kulit, tali kulit.

thorn duri, onak.

thorny berduri.

thorough benar-benar, sungguh-sungguh.

those hal-hal atau orang-orang itu.

though walaupun, meskipun; as — seperti.

thought fikiran; (idea) angan-angan; (feeling) cita.

thoughtful termenung; (considerate) sangat memikirkan orang lain.

thoughtless kurang fikir, lalai.

thousand seribu; —s of beribu-ribu.

thousandth yang keseribu.

thrash, to — memukul, membanting.

thrashing pemukulan.

thread benang; to resume the —s meneruskan lagi pokok bual; to — memasukkan benang ke lubang jarum.

threadbare (shabby) buruk.

threat gertak, ugutan.

threaten, to — mengancam mengugut, mengacu.

three tiga.

threefold berangkap tiga.

three-ply (layers) berlapis tiga; (strands) berlembar tiga.

three-quarter(s) tiga perempat, tiga suku.

thresh, to — menebah gandum

threshold ambang pintu, pintu.

thrift jimat, penghematan.

thriftless tidak jimat, pemboros.

thrifty jimat, cermat.

thrill (tremor) kegentaran; to — menggentarkan; (pester) mengharukan.

thriller (buku, filem) yang mengerikan.

thrive, to — berkembang biak.

throat (gullet) kerongkongan; (neck) batang leher.

throaty diucapkan dalam kerongkongan.

throb debar, denyut; to — berdebar-debar, berdenyut-denyut.

throe (anguish) sakit, sengsara.

thrombosis trombosa, tersekat.

throne takhta, singgahsana.

throng orang banyak, keramaian; to — beramai-ramai.

throttle, to — mencekek.

through (end to end) terus; (because) kerana; to be — with selesai.

throughout terus-menerus; (all together) samasekali.

throw lempar; to — melemparkan; (discard) membuang.

thrush I sejenis burung.

thrush II (disease) sakit guam.

thrust tikam; to — (stab) menikam, meradak; (push) tolak.

thud debuk, gedebur.

thug (murderer) pembunuh; (ruffian) penjahat.

thumb ibu jari; —print cap jari.

thump celam-celum, gedebak-gedebuk; to — mencelam-celum.

thunder petir, guntur, guruh; to — bergemuruh.

thunderbolt kilat disertai dengan petir.

thunderclap petir.

thundering bergemuruh.

Thursday hari Kamis.

thus begini, begitu, demikian.

thwart, to — melintang.

thyme sejenis tumbuhan.

thyroid, — gland kelenjar, tairoid.

tiara (crown) sejenis mahkota; (head ornament) perhiasan kepala; (worn by bride) gandik.

tick I (zool) sengkenit.

tick II (sound) detik, ketik; (small mark) tanda, catitan; to — mendetik.

tick III, (col) on — membeli atau menjual berhutang.

ticket tiket.

tickle gelitik; to — menggelitik, menggelikan; —d geli.

ticklish lekas geli.

tidal yang berkenaan dengan pasang surut.

tide (time) waktu; (of sea) air pasang; high — air pasang; low — air surut.

tidiness kebersihan.

tidings berita, khabar.

tidy kemas; to — berkemas.

tie (cord etc) tali; (connection) pertalian; (necktie) tali leher; to — (fasten) mengikatkan; (tether) menambatkan; (in knot) menyimpul.

tier tingkat, deret bertingkat.

tiff (quarrel) perselisihan.

tiffin makan tengahari.

tiger harimau.

tight (close fitting) rapat; (taut) regang; (cramped) sempit, sesak; (col) (drunk) mabuk; in a — spot dalam keadaan sukar.

tighten, to — menjadi regang.

tigress harimau betina.

tile (floor) ubin; (roof) genting; to — memasang genting.

till I (until) hingga, sampai.

till II (for money) laci wang di kedai.

till III, to — (cultivate) mengerjakan membajak, mencangkul tanah.

tiller (rudder) celaga kemudi.

tilt letak miring, sendeng.

timber (baulk) kayu balak; (boards etc) papan.

time waktu, ketika, tempoh, masa, zaman, saat; (having —) to) kesempatan; (—s) kali.

timid (afraid) takut; (bashful) malu, tersipu-sipu.

timidity sifat takut, sifat malu.

timorous takut-takutan.

tin timah; —foil daun timah.

tinder rabuk.

ting bunyi; teng.

tinge warna; to — mewarnai.

tingle gelenyar; to — menggelenyar.

tinker tukang barang ayan.

tinkle bunyi; kerencing.

tinsel (*gold, silver*) perada; (*sham and showy*) rupanya bagus dan mengkilap tetapi tidak berharga.

tint warna; to — mewarnai, membubuhi warna.

tiny sangat kecil.

tip I hujung; finger— hujung jari.

tip II (*rubbish dump*) tempat membalikkan sampah.

tip III (*small present*) hadiah, wang rokok; (*private information*) isyarat, keterangan rahsia.

tipple minuman keras; to — selalu minum minuman keras.

tipster seseorang yang memberi keterangan tentang perlumbaan kuda dan lain-lain.

tipsy mabuk.

tiptoe, to walk on — menjingkit, melanjak.

tirade teguran yang diucapkan dengan panjang lebar.

tire I, to — menjadi lelah, melelahkan; —d penat; (*sated*) jemu.

tire II (*US*) =tyre.

tiredness kelelahan, kepenatan.

tireless tidak tahu lelah letih.

tiresome (*boring*) menjemukan; (*difficult, heavy*) susah, berat.

tissue (*woven finely*) tenunan halus; — paper kertas halus.

tit I sejenis burung kecil.

tit II, — for tat pukulmemukul, balas-membalas.

titbit penganan nikmat.

titillate, to — menggelitik.

title (*name*) gelar, nama; (*head of page etc*) kepala;

(*to property*) hak; — page halaman pada awalan buku.

titter, to — tertawa terkekekkekek.

tit(t)ivate, to — menghiaskan, memperelokkan.

tittle—tattle desas-desus.

titular yang berkenaan dengan nama, berdasarkan nama. **to** (*denoting place*) ka, kepada; (*until*) sampai; (*so as to*) bagi, untuk; (*following*) menurut; (*compared to*) berbanding dengan.

toad katak, kodok.

toady peleceh.

toast (*bread*) roti panggang; (*honouring*) penghormatan seseorang dengan minum, minum ucap selamat.

tobacco tembakau.

tobacconist penjual tembakau.

tobacco pouch tempat tembakau, celepa.

toboggan sejenis kereta pelucur yang dipakai pada lereng gunung yang bersalji.

toby sejenis cawan bergambar orang.

today pada hari ini.

toddle cara berjalan bertatih-tatih; to — bertatih-tatih.

toddler anak kecil yang jalannya masih bertatih-tatih.

toddy (*palm wine*) tuak.

toe jari kaki.

toff (*col*) pentolan.

toffee sejenis gula-gula.

tog, (*col*) —s pakaian.

together bersama-sama, berkumpul.

toggle sejenis pasak yang kerap dipakai pada kapal akan menetapkan tali.

toil susah payah, pekerjaan berat; to — membanting tulang.

toilet (*latrine*) tandas.

token tanda.

tolerable (*bearable*) yang dapat ditahan; (can do) boleh juga.

tolerance kesabaran.

tolerant sabar.

tolerate, to — membiarkan, menyabarkan.

toleration pembiaran.

toll I (tax) bea, cukai.

toll II (of bell) bunyi loceng; to — berbunyi, membunyikan loceng.

tomato buah tomato.

tomb kubur, makam; — stone batu nesan.

tome jilid buku yang besar dan berat.

tomorrow besok, esok hari.

ton tan, sukatan berat Inggeris.

tone bunyi; (healthy condition) keadaan badan yang kuat dan sihat.

tongs sepit, penyepit.

tongue lidah, lisan; (language) bahasa.

tonic yang menguatkan, yang menggiatkan.

tonight malam ini.

tonnage (of ship) ukuran muatan salah satu kapal; (of cargo) jumlah tan yang dapat dimuatkan ke dalam ruang kapal.

tonsil tonsil, tekak.

too (— much) terlalu terlampau; (also) juga.

tool alat; — s perkakas.

toot bunyi terompet; to — berbunyi, membunyikan terompet.

tooth gigi; armed to the teeth bersenjata dengan lengkap.

toothache sakit gigi.

toothbrush berus gigi.

toothpaste ubat gigi.

toothpick cungkil gigi.

top I (of mountain) puncak, kemuncak; (— part) bahagian atas; (of book, page etc) kepala.

top II (spinning) gasing; to whip, spin a — main gasing.

topaz sejenis batu permata berharga.

topcoat baju luaran.

top-heavy terlalu berat bahagian atasnya.

topic buah mulut, perkara bualan.

topical yang berkenaan dengan perkara percakapan orang.

topography topografi, perpetaan.

topple, to — roboh runtuh.

topsy-turvy lintang-pukang, kacau-bilau.

torch suluh, andang; (electric) lampu picit.

torment sengsara, kesakitan, seksaan; to — menyakiti, menyeksa.

tormentor penyeksa.

tornado topan puting beliung.

torpedo torpedo, periuk api atau bom laut.

torrent sungai yang harusnya sangat deras; (waterfall) air terjun.

torrential dengan deras dan lebat, dengan berderai-derai.

torrid panas terek, sangat panas dan kering.

torso patung badan manusia dengan tidak berkaki lengannya.

tortoise kura-kura, baning.

tortuous bengkang-bengkok.

torture seksaan; to — menyakiti, menyeksa.

Tory parti Inggeris yang berfahaman konservatif.

toss (of coin) pelemparan wang dengan pengundian.

tot I anak kecil; (of drink) minuman keras seteguk.

tot II (add up) beberapa bilangan yang harus dijumlahkan; to — menjumlahkan.

total (sum) jumlah; (all over) seluruh, samasekali; to — berjumlah.

totality seluruhnya, keseluruhan.

tote, to — mengangkut, memikul.

totter, to — berjalan bertatih-tatih, terhuyung-huyung.

toucan burung enggang.

touch sentuhan; to — kena; a — of sedikit; to keep in — berhubung dengan.

touched (of feelings) pilu, terharu.

touching memilukan hati, merindukan.

touchy bengkeng, tipis telinga.

tough (of meat, pliable) liat; (strong) kuat; (hard) keras; (difficult) sukar.

toupée rambut palsu, sejenis cemara.

tour perjalanan, temasya; to — bertemasya, mengelilingi.

tourism pelancungan.

tourist pelancung, pelawat.

tournament pertandingan.

tourniquet alat penasak darah dengan menekan pembuluh nadi.

tousle, to — mengusutkan.

tout, to — mencuba menarik langganan.

tow tunda, penundaan; to have in — menarik, menunda.

toward(s) ke arah, terhadap kepada.

towel tuala; to throw in the — menerima kealahan.

tower menara; to — membubung tinggi.

town bandar.

town hall dewan bandaran.

toxic bisa, beracun, mabuk.

toy benda permainan; to — with bermain-main dengan.

trace I (footprints) jejak, bekas, kesan; to — meracangkan.

trace II (of harness) tali kuda untuk menarik kereta.

tracing paper kertas kalkir.

track denai, jejak, kesan; off the — tidak kena.

tract I (region) daerah.

tract II (religious) risalah.

traction penarikan penghelaan; — engine jentera penarik.

tractor jentera penarik, motoran.

trade perdagangan perniagaan.

trademark cap perusahaan.

trader saudagar, pedagang.

tradesman pedagang.

trade union persyarikatan buruh persyarikatan orang sekerja.

trade wind angin paksa, angin timuran.

trading company syarikat perniagaan.

tradition adat kelaziman, kebiasaan, tradisi.

traditional menurut adat, beradat.

traffic (trade) perdagangan; (passing to and fro) lalu-lintas.

tragedy sandiwara sedih.

tragic sedih, menyedihkan.

tragicomedy sandiwara (atau hal) yang setengah sedih setengah gembira.

trail (track) bekas kesan, jejak; (path) jalan; to — mengikuti jejak.

trailer (tracker) pengikut jejak; (creeping plant) tumbuhan menjalar.

train (of dress) pancung pakaian; (queue) buntut; (rail) keretapi.

trainer pelatih.

training (education) pendidikan; (training generally) latihan.

traipse see **trapse**.

trait sifat, khasiat.

traitor pengkhianat, pembelot.

traitorous secara pengkhianat.

tram, car kereta terem.

tramp pertualang, pengembara.

trample, to — memijakkan.

trance keadaan khayali.

tranquil (*of water*) tenang; (*peaceful*) sejahtera, sentosa.

tranquillity (*calmness*) ketenangan; (*peace*) keadaan aman.

trans- awalan kata yang ertinya: seberang, terus.

transact, to — menjalankan, to — with berniaga dengan.

transaction perjanjian perdagangan.

transatlantic di seberang Lautan Atlantik.

transcend, to — melampaui, mengatasi.

transcendent yang melampaui, yang mengatasi.

transcendental yang berdasarkan kesedaran rohani.

transcribe, to — menyalin dengan huruf lain.

transcript salinan.

transfer (*move*) pemindahan; (*hand over*) penyerahan.

transferable yang dapat dipindahkan.

transference pemindahan; penyerahan.

transfiguration penjelmaan, pengubahan rupa.

transfigure, to — menjelmakan, mengubahkan rupanya.

transfix, to — (*go through*) menembus; memacak.

transform, to — mengubah rupanya, menjelma.

transformation perubahan rupa, penjelmaan.

transfusion pindah tuang.

transgress, to — (*break law etc*) melanggar; (*exceed*) melampaui.

transgression pelanggaran, maksan laut.

transgressor pelanggar.

transience sementara.

transient fana.

transit jalan terus, perjalanan.

transition perubahan, peralihan; — period masa peralihan.

transitive kata kerja yang ada penyambut.

transitory fana; (*temporary*) sementara.

translate, to — menterjemahkan.

translation terjemahan.

translator penterjemah.

translucence, translucent hening, jernih.

transmission pemindahan.

transmit, to — (*send*) mengirim; (*transfer*) memindahkan.

transmitter, transmitting set pemancar.

transparence jernih, sifat tembus cahaya, lutsinar.

transparent jernih, tembus cahaya, lutsinar.

transpire, to — (*sweat*) berpeluh.

transplant, to — memindahkan ke tempat lain, menganjak.

transport, —ation pengangkutan.

transpose memindahkan tempat.

transposition pemindahan, pertukaran.

transversal garis yang melintang.

transverse yang melintang.

trap perangkap, jebak.

trap door lubang pintu (ke loteng dan sebagainya).

trapeze sejenis ayunan untuk berbuai.

trapper orang yang menangkap binatang dengan jerat.

trappings (*for horse*) pakaian kuda; (*decoration*) perhiasan.

trapse, traipse, to — berjalan dengan susah payah.

trash (*rubbish*) sampah.

trauma luka, keadaan kesakitan.

traumatic yang berkenaan dengan kesakitan.

travel perjalanan; **to —** berjalan.

traveller orang yang mengembara musafir.

traverse (*crossbar*) palang yang melintang; (*of road, path*) jalan, simpang siur.

trawl, — net sejenis pukat tarik; **to —** menarik pukat.

trawler kapal penangkap ikan dengan pukat tarik.

tray tala, dulang.

treacherous secara pengkhianat, cedera.

treachery kecederaan khianat.

treacle air gula yang keluar daripada tebu dan lain-lain.

tread (*sound of step*) bunyi melangkah; (*pace*) langkah; (*step on*) jejak.

treason khianat, derhaka.

treasure emas intan dan lain barang berharga.

treasurer bendahari.

treasure trove harta terpendam yang didapati.

treasury perbendaharaan khazanah.

treat (*entertainment*) jamuan; (*exciting event*) hal yang menggembirakan.

treatise risalah.

treatment perlakuan; medical — pengubatan.

treaty perjanjian, persetiaan.

treble ganda tiga, lipat tiga, rangkap tiga.

tree pohon, pohon kayu; **family, genealogical —** susur galur, asal-usul, terumba.

trefoil tumbuhan yang daunnya tiga serangkai.

trek perjalanan dengan pedati dan sebagainya.

trellis kisi-kisi **to —** membubuh kisi-kisi.

tremble getaran, gementar; **to —** menggetar, gementar.

tremendous hebat, yang mendahsyatkan.

tremor gementaran, gerak gempa.

tremulous dengan gementar; takut-takut.

trench parit.

trenchant tajam.

trench coat baju tajam.

trend arah, tujuan.

trepidation gementar, getaran.

trespass, to — melalui, melanggar; **to — on** melanggar, ceroboh.

trespasser pelanggar.

tress ikal rambut, anyaman rambut; **—s** rambut perempuan.

trestle kuda-kuda.

trial (*attempt*) percubaan; (*of endurance*) penderitaan; (*in court*) pengadilan.

triangle segitiga, alat bersiku tiga, besitiga.

triangular berbentuk segitiga, bersegitiga.

tribal yang berkenaan dengan suku bangsa.

tribe suku bangsa, puak.

tribesman saudara sesuku, anggota salah satu suku.

tribulation sengsara, penderitaan.

tribunal pengadilan.

tribune I (*popular leader*) pemimpin rakyat.

tribune II (*platform*) panggung; (*pulpit*) mimbar.

tributary (*under the authority of*) orang yang di bawah kekuasaan, bawahan; (*of river*) anak sungai, cawangan.

tribute persembahan (sebagai tanda penghormatan), ufti.

trice menaikkan dan mengikat; **in a —** dengan serta-merta.

trick akal, tipu, daya, muslihat; (*habit*) kebiasaan; **to play —s** main akal.

trickery tipu daya.

trickle cucur; to — bercucuran, berlinang.

trickster penipu.

tricky pintar busuk, berakal kancil.

tricolour bendera yang berwarna tiga.

tricycle kenderaan beroda tiga.

triennial tiga tahun lamanya; yang terjadi tiap-tiap tiga tahun.

trier (*one who tries*) pencuba.

trifle perkara kecil, hal yang tidak penting.

trifling tidak penting.

trigger pemetik senapang, picu.

trigonometry trigonometri.

trilateral bersegitiga.

trill (*tremble*) getaran; (*certain consonants*) huruf getar; to — menggetar.

trilogy karangan atau sandiwara tiga serangkai.

trim (*neat*) teratur, cermat, keadaan baik dan teratur; to — (*prune*) memangkas; (*balance*) timbang.

trimming (*arranging*) pengaturan; (*clippings*) pemotongan; (*ornaments*) perhiasan.

trinity tiga bersatu.

trinket barang perhiasan yang tidak tinggi harganya.

trio tiga serangkai; karangan muzik untuk tiga orang penyanyi.

trio- awalan kata yang ertinya: tiga.

trip perjalanan, pelancungan, temasya.

tripartite (*in three*) dibahagi tiga; (*three parts*) berpihak tiga.

tripe (*col*) bual kosong.

triple lipat tiga, rangkap tiga; (*three parties*) berpihak tiga; (*three times*) berganda tiga.

triplet tiga serangkai; (*one of*

three born together) kembar tiga.

triplicate rangkap tiga.

tripod kakitiga bangku yang berkaki tiga.

trite biasa, ambar.

triumph kemenangan, kejayaan; to — menang.

triumphal yang berkenaan dengan kemenangan, jaya.

triumphant yang menang, berjaya.

trivial tidak penting.

triviality keadaan tidak penting.

trolley gerabak sorong.

trollop perempuan sundal.

trombone sejenis alat muzik.

troop kumpulan, kelompok; —s pasukan; troop-ship kapal pengangkut askar.

trooper soldadu berkuda; kuda tentera.

trophy peringatan berkenaan dengan kemenangan.

tropic kawasan hawa panas; T— of Cancer garisan sartan; T— of Capricorn garisan jadi; the —s daerah berhawa panas, tropika.

tropical yang berkenaan dengan daerah berhawa panas, tropika.

trot berlari, gerak badan; to — berlari.

trotter pelari; (*horse*) kuda yang kuat berlari.

troubadour penyair yang menyanyikan syairnya.

trouble (*difficulty*) kesukaran, kesusahan, susah; (*disturbance*) kerusuhan; to — (*disturb*) mengacaukan.

troublesome yang menyusahkan.

trough (*sluice etc*) palung; (*between waves*) tempat lembang antara dua pucuk gelombang.

trounce, to — memukul keras-keras.

troupe rombongan pemain sandiwara.

trouser, pair of —s seluar.

trousseau semua pekaian dan lain keperluan seseorang pengantin perempuan.

trout sejenis ikan air tawar.

trowel sudip.

truant orang yang malas, lengah; to play — malas, lari sekolah.

truce perletakan senjata, perdamaian.

truck I gerabak, pengangkut barang.

truck II (barter) tukar-menukar, penukaran.

truculence galak, garang.

truculent galak, garang.

trudge, to — berjalan dengan susah payah.

true benar, betul, sungguh.

truffle sejenis cendawan yang terdapat di dalam tanah.

truism kebenaran yang tidak payah dinyatakan lagi.

truly benar-benar, betul-betul.

trump (in cards) terup, main terup; to — mengalahkan dengan daun terup.

trumpery (of talk) bual kosong.

trumpet terompet; — call bunyi terompet; to — membunyikan terompet.

truncate kudung; to — mengudungkan.

truncheon sejenis tongkat, belantan.

trundle (wheel) sejenis roda kecil dan lebar; (cart) sejenis gerabak dan dorong.

trunk (tree) pokok, punggur, batang; (of body) tubuh; (box) peti.

truss (roof elc) bangunan penahan yang seperti kuda-kuda.

trust kepercayaan, pengharapan; (responsibility) tanggungan.

trustee wakil, wali.

trustful sangat percaya akan, penuh kepercayaan.

trustworthy yang dapat dipercayai, setia.

truth kebenaran, kesungguhan.

truthful tulus, benar.

try (attempt) percubaan; (plan) ikhtiar; to — mencuba.

trying sedang berikhtiar; (difficult) susah.

try-on (col) percubaan akan menipu.

tryout (attempt) percubaan; (practice) latihan.

tsetse sejenis lalat bisa di Afrika.

tub (wooden) tong; (earthenware bathing jar) tempayan.

tuba sejenis alat muzik.

tubby buncit, gemuk.

tube tiub, pipa pembuluh; (of lamp) corong.

tuber ubi.

tubercular berbenjol, berbonjol.

tuberculosis penyakit paru-paru, batuk kering.

tubing sistem pembuluhan.

tubular yang berkenaan dengan atau seperti pembuluh dan sebagainya.

tuck (fold) lipatan; (food) makanan.

Tuesday hari Selasa.

tuft jambak, jambul.

tug (boat) kapal penunda; to — menunda, menarik.

tuition pengajaran.

tulip sejenis bunga.

tulle sejenis kain jaringan yang halus.

tumble (headlong) jatuh lintang-pukang; to — jatuh lintang-pukang.

tumbledown jatuh.

tumbler (acrobat) penambul, orang yang pandai tunggang balik; (glass) sejenis gelas minum.

tummy perut.

tumour tumbuh; benign — tumbuh tenang; malignant — tumbuh ganas.

tumult huru-hara, kegemparan.

tuna sejenis ikan.

tundra padang rumput di Rusia utara, tundra.

tune (melody) lagu; (concord) laras, persesuaian; out of — salah laras.

tuneful (concordant) selaras; (melodious) merdu.

tuneless salah laras, janggal.

tungsten batu kawi, sejenis zat logam.

tunic sejenis baju kebaya yang panjangnya sampai ke lutut.

tuning fork penala.

tunnel lubang, tembusan; to — menembusi.

turban serban.

turbid (of liquid) keruh; (very confused) kacau-bilau.

turbulence pergaduhan kerusuhan.

turbulent rusuh bergaduh.

tureen mangkuk besar untuk sup (sayur dan sebagainya).

turf tanah datar yang berumput; the — lawan kuda.

turgid (swollen) bengkak; (bombastic etc) berlebihan.

turgidity bengkak.

Turk orang Turki.

turkey ayam belanda.

Turkish Turki; — bath penangas.

turmeric kunyit.

turmoil kerusuhan, kekacauan.

turn (revolve) putaran, pusaran; (circulation) peredaran; (curve) kelok; in — s bergilir; to — (sitting round) pusingkan; (on lathe) melarik membubut.

turncoat orang yang memutar-mutar haluan jika dikiranya lebih baik.

turner pembubut, pelarik.

turnip sejenis lobak.

turnout (produce yielded) jumlah barang yang dibuat dalam salah satu waktu.

turnover (reversal) pembalikan; (rotation) putaran; (cake) sejenis kuih.

turnpike palang melintang jalan pada tempat (bayar cukai).

turnstile sejenis pintu putar sehingga orang-orang dapat masuk satu demi satu.

turpentine (minyak) tarpentin.

turpitude kejahatan, kekejian.

turquoise batu pirus.

turret menara kecil; (for gun) bangunan pada kapal atau benteng untuk meriam.

turtle penyu, biuku, kurakura; to turn — terbalik, telungkup.

turtledove ketitir.

tusk gading taring; —ed bergading.

tussle perkelahian.

tussock (hump) bonggol; (tuft) jambul.

tut, —! ah!, masakan!

tutelage kuasa wali, perwalian.

tutor guru; to — mengajar; (control) menahan.

tutorial berkenaan dengan pekerjaan guru.

twaddle, to — berkecek.

twain dua.

twang (sound) bunyi; (of string) deting; (talk through nose) bunyi sengau.

tweak renggutan; to — merenggut.

tweed sejenis kain bulu.

tweet bunyi mencicit.

tweezer, —s penyepit, angkup.

twelfth yang kedua belas perdua belas.

twelve dua belas.

twentieth yang kedua puluh.

twenty dua puluh; —**one** dua puluh satu.

twice dua kali.

twiddle putaran; **to** — memutar-mutar.

twig I ranting.

twig II, (col) **to** — mengerti, memahamkan.

twilight senjakala.

twill kain kipar, sejenis kain tenunan.

twin kembar; **to** — mengembarkan.

twine (twist) pilin, pintal; (coil) belit; **to** — memintal; (wind round) berlilit.

twinge sakit mengejut.

twinkle kelip, gemilap; **to** — menggerlip.

twirl putaran, pusaran; **to** — berputar.

twist pilin, pintal; (coil) belit; gulung.

twitch kejang; **to** — berkejang.

twitter, to — berkicau.

two dua; **to cut in** — membelah dua.

two-edged tajam bermata dua.

two-faced bermuka dua.

twofold dua lipat, rangkap.

two-handed untuk kedua belah tangan.

two-ply pilin dua.

two-seater motokar yang bertempat duduk dua.

two-sided bersegidua.

twosome permainan dan sebagainya untuk dua orang.

two-step sejenis tarian.

two-way bermata dua, yang harusnya dua.

tycoon saudara yang sangat kaya.

type (specimen) contoh; (kind) jenis, macam.

typescript karangan yang ditaip.

typewriter mesin taip.

typhoid seperti penyakit tipus; — **fever** demam kepialu.

typhoon taufan.

typhus penyakit demam panas.

typical yang menjadi contoh (tuladan).

typify, to — menjadi contoh.

typist jurutaip.

typographical yang berkenaan dengan ilmu cetak.

typography ilmu cetak.

tyrannic(al) bermaharajalela.

tyrannize, to — bermaharajalela.

tyranny aniaya, kelakuan zalim.

tyrant raja zalim.

tyre tayar.

U

U-boat kapalselam Jerman.

ubiquitous yang hadir terdapat di mana-mana.

ubiquity hal terdapat di mana-mana.

udder ambing, susu.

ugh cehi, cisi

ugliness keadaan atau rupa buruk.

ugly buruk.

ukulele ukulele, sejenis gitar.

ulcer bisul, puru, barah.

ulcerate, to — berpuru, membarah.

ulcerous berbisul, berbarah.

ulterior (further) lebih jauh; (in the future) pada masa yang akan datang.

ultimate penghabisan, terakhir; —**ly** akhirnya.

ultimatum kata dua.

ultra- (excessively) terlalu; (beyond) lebih dari.

ultramarine (blue colour) warna biru terang.

umbilical yang berkenaan dengan pusat; — **cord** tali pusat.

umbrage (sense of injury) rasa tersinggung, kecil hati.

umbrella payung.

umpire orang tengah; **to** — menjadi pengadil.

umpteen (col) beberapa, sejumlah yang tidak tentu.

un— awalan kata yang ertinya: tidak; sebaliknya.

unable tidak sanggup; tidak cakap.

unabridged tidak diringkaskan.

unaccommodating tidak sudi menurut.

unaccountable tidak dapat diterangkan, atau difahamkan.

unaccustomed tidak biasa.

unadorned sederhana, tidak dihiasi.

unanimity kebulatan suara.

unanimous dengan suara bulat, sepakat.

unassuming sopan santun.

unattainable tidak tercapai.

unavoidable tidak dapat dielak.

unaware tidak sedar, tidak insaf; —s (suddenly) tiba-tiba.

unbalance, to — menghilangkan keseimbangan; —d tidak seimbang.

unbearable tidak tertahan.

unbecoming (not pretty) tidak elok; (unsuited) tidak patut.

unbeliever (not trusting) orang yang tidak percaya; (of religion) orang yang tidak beriman; (infidel, non-Muslim) kafir.

unbend, to — melepaskan, membuka.

unbias(s)ed tidak memihak.

unbolt, to — membuka palang pintu.

unbosom, to — (disclose) membuka rahsia.

unbounded tidak terbatas.

unburden, to — melepaskan, membukakan.

ubutton, to — membuka kancing.

uncalled—**for** tidak pada tempatnya.

uncanny sangat pelik dan menakutkan.

unceasing tidak berkesudahan.

unceremonious tidak memakai adat sopan santun.

uncertain tidak tentu; (unstable) tidak tetap.

uncertainty tidak tentu; (perplexity) ragu-ragu.

uncivil biadab, kurang ajar, kurang hormat, kasar.

uncivilized biadab, kuno.

uncle bapa saudara.

unclean (dirty) kotor; (defiled) najis.

uncomfortable tidak sedap, tidak nikmat.

uncommon tidak biasa, ajaib.

uncommunicative tidak suka bercakap-cakap, pendiam.

uncompromising tidak suka berdamai keras hati.

unconditional tidak bersyarat, mutlak.

unconscious tidak sedar, tidak insaf; (unintentional) tidak sengaja; (swoon) pengsan.

unconstitutional tidak menurut undang-undang tubuh.

uncontrollable tidak tertahan, tidak dapat dikawal.

uncork, to — membuka sumbat.

uncouth (coarse) kasar; (ungainly) kekok.

uncover, to — membuka tutupnya; —ed (opened) terbuka; (not covered) tidak ada tutupnya.

unctuous seperti minyak, bersifat bermuka-muka.

undaunted berani dan keras hati.

undecided belum diputuskan; (*dubious*) ragu-ragu.

undeniable tidak dapat disangkal.

under bawah; (*of place*) di bawah; (*of direction*) ke bawah; (*less than*) kurang.

under age belum cukup umur.

undercarriage bahagian bawah sebuah kereta (pesawat udara dan sebagainya).

underclothes pakaian dalam.

undercut (*of meat*) daging lembu yang dipotong dari tulang belikat; (*of price*) menawarkan sesuatu seharga lebih rendah.

underdog (*person defeated*) orang yang kalah; (*in adversity*) orang yang termasuk golongan rakyat hina dina.

underdone setengah masak.

underestimate, to — mengecilkan, mencapak.

underfoot di bawah kaki.

undergo, to — (*experience*) mengalami; (*endure*) menderita menahan.

undergraduate mahasiswa yang belum berijazah.

underground di bawah tanah; (*secret*) rahsia, tersembunyi.

undergrowth semak belukar.

underhand dengan tangan terbalik; (*unfair*) belat-belit, curi-curi.

underlie terletak di bawahnya; (*basic*) merupakan dasarnya.

underline, to — menggoris.

underling orang bawahan.

underlying yang merupakan dasarnya.

undermine, to — menggali di bawahnya; (*intrigue*) melemahkan dengan diam-diam.

underneath di bawah.

undernourish, to — tidak cukup memberi makanan.

underpin, to — menopang rumah dengan batu dan sebagainya.

underprivileged tidak mempunyai hak kemasyarakatan sepenuhnya.

undersell, to — menjual lebih murah, menjual terlalu murah.

undershirt baju dalam, anak baju.

underside sebelah bawah.

undersign, the — ed yang bertandatangan.

undersized kurang dari ukuran biasa atau sedang.

understand, to — mengerti, faham akan.

understandable yang dapat difahamkan.

understanding pengertian, faham.

understate, to — mengecilkan erti sesuatu.

understatement perkataan yang mengecil erti sesuatu.

understudy pemain simpanan yang dapat menggantl pemain pertama.

undertake, to — (*promise*) berjanji; (*support*) menanggung.

undertaker (*funeral*) orang yang mengurus menanam mayat.

undertaking pengusahaan, perusahaan.

undertone bunyi suara rendah, bunyi kasar.

underwater di bawah muka air.

underweight kurang berat.

underworld neraka, alam barzah.

underwriter penanggung.

undesirable tidak disukai.

undo, to — (*open*) membuka; (*annul*) membatalkan.

undoing (*destruction*) keruntuhan; (*failure*) kegagalan.

undone tidak disempurnakan.

undoubted(ly) nescaya, tidak boleh tidak.

undress, to — membuka pakaian.

undue tidak pada tempatnya, tidak patut.

undulate berombak; to — menggelombang, bergelombang.

unduly tidak patut, tidak pada tempatnya.

undying tidak mati; (*neverending*) tidak berhenti.

unearth, to — mengeluarkan dari tanah; (*secret etc*) membuka rahsia.

unearthly yang mengerikan, ngeri.

uneasiness kegelisahan, kebimbangan.

uneasy (*awkward*) kekok; (*restless*) gelisah.

unemployed menganggur; — person penganggur.

unemployment pengangguran.

unending tidak putus-putusnya, tidak berkesudahan.

unequalled tidak berbanding, tiada taranya.

unequivocal nyata, terang.

unerring tidak dapat salah.

uneven (*rough*) kasap; (*different*) tidak sama; (*of numbers*) ganjil.

unexpected tidak disangka-sangka, tiba-tiba.

unfailing tidak putus-putus.

unfair tidak jujur tidak adil.

unfaithful tidak setia.

unfamiliar tidak biasa.

unfasten, to — membuka; terbuka.

unfavourable, (*US*) **unfavorable** tidak baik, tidak menguntungkan.

unfeeling tidak berperasaan, mati rasa.

unfetter, to — membuka belenggu; (*give independence*) memerdekakan.

unfilial tidak dengan hormat kepada ayah bonda.

unfit (*not able*) tidak cakap; (*improper*) tidak patut.

unflagging tidak putus-putus.

unfledged tidak berbulu; (*of early youth*) belum dewasa.

unflinching tidak takut, berani.

unfold, to — berkembang, mengembangkan.

unforgettable yang tidak dapat dilupakan.

unfortunate celaka, malang.

unfounded tidak beralasan.

unfriendly tidak ramah-tamah.

unfurl, to — (*unroll*) membentangkan.

ungainly kekok, canggung.

ungodly tidak beriman; (*evil*) jahat.

ungracious (*unfriendly*) tidak ramah-tamah; (*rude*) kurang hormat, kasar.

ungrateful tidak berterimakasih.

unguent palit.

unhallowed tidak suci, tiada beriman.

unhampered bebas, tiada terharu.

unhappy sedih, tidak mujur, malang; tidak patut.

unhealthy kurang kesihatan; (*infectious*) tidak sihat, sakit.

unheard, — of mustahil.

unheeding lalai.

unhinge, to — mengangkat dari sendinya; (*unbalance*) menghilangkan keseimbangan.

unhitch, to — membuka ikatannya.

unholy tidak suci tidak beriman; (*evil*) jahat.

unhook, to — terlepas daripada cangkuknya.

unhurried tidak terburu-buru, tenang.

unhurt tidak (kena) luka.

uni— awalan kata yang ertinya: satu tunggal.

unicorn sejenis binatang khayalan yang bertanduk satu dipakai sebagai lambang.

unification perpaduan, persatuan.

uniform serupa, samarata, bersamaan, yang selalu sama, tetap; (dress) pakaian seragam.

uniformity hal sama (rupanya atau sifatnya).

unify, to — mempersatukan.

unilateral berkenaan dengan satu pihak sahaja.

unimpaired kukuh, kuat.

unimpeachable yang tidak dapat dicela, tidak bercacat.

unintelligent tidak berakal; tidak bijaksana.

uninterrupted tidak putus, tidak bersela.

uninviting tidak menyukakan, tidak menarik.

union persatuan, persekutuan, ikatan, gabungan; **U—** Jack bendera Inggeris.

unique (sole) tunggal, tersendiri; (unequalled) tidak ada tarafnya.

unison persamaan bunyi, serentak.

unit satu, yunit, se.

unite, to — menyatukan, mempersatukan, berpadu.

united bersatu, berpadu.

unity kesatuan, persatuan.

universal yang melengkungi seluruh alam dunia, umum.

universality hal atau sifat umum sedunia.

universe alam dunia, cakerawala.

university sekolah tinggi, universiti.

unjust tidak adil.

unjustifiable tidak patut, tidak beralasan.

unjustified tidak benar, tidak beralasan.

unkempt (of hair etc) kusut masai; (uncared for) tidak terpelihara.

unkind tidak ramah-tamah, tidak manis.

unlace, to — membuka talinya.

unlawful tidak menurut hukum dan undang-undang, salah; (by religion) haram.

unless jika tidak, kecuali jika.

unlike tidak sama, tidak serupa.

unlikely tidak besar harusnya, takkan.

unlimited tidak terbatas, tidak terhingga.

unload, to — membongkar memunggah, menurunkan.

unlock, to — membuka kunci.

unloose(n), to — membuka, melepaskan.

unlucky malang, sial.

unmanly tidak seperti seorang laki-laki.

unmentionable tidak patut disebut.

unmistakable yang tidak dapat diwahamkan lagi.

unnatural tidak menurut tabiat, tidak menurut dasar alam; (wrong) tidak bersalahan.

unnecessary tidak perlu; tidak mustahak.

unnerve, to — melamahkan.

unobtrusive tidak menyuaikan diri.

unoccupied kosong, tidak diduduki; (of work) tidak bekerja.

unorganized tidak teratur, tidak bersusunan tetap.

unparalleled tiada bandingnya, tiada bertara.

unpleasant kurang elok, tidak ramah-tamah, tidak berbudi bahasa.

unpopular tidak disukai orang.

unprecedented belum pernah terjadi lebih dahulu.

unpredictable tidak dapat diramalkan, tiada disangka.

unprincipled tidak menurut asas, keji, jahat.

unqualified tidak memenuhi syarat, tidak bersyarat.

unquestionable tidak tersangkal.

unravel, to — menguraikan benang yang terpilin; (*settle*) menyelesaikan.

unreal tidak benar.

unreasonable tidak menurut akal budi.

unrelenting (*not stopping*) tidak putus-putus; (*harsh*) tidak mengenal belas kasihan.

unremitting tidak putus-putus.

unresponsive tidak menyambut, tidak membalas.

unrest kegelisahan.

unrestrained tidak terbatas, dengan luasnya.

unripe mentah, muda.

unrivalled tiada berlawan, tiada bandingnya.

unroll, to — membuka gulungan.

unruffled tenang, tidak terganggu.

unruly galak; (*hair*) kusut.

unsafe tidak selamat; (*not strong*) tidak kuat.

unsatisfactory tidak memuaskan.

unsavoury, (*US*) **unsavory** tawar, tidak ada rasanya.

unscrupulous tidak berdasarkan adat atau iman, jahat.

unseat, to — melemparkan dari tempat duduknya.

unseemly tidak patut, tidak pantas.

unsettle, to — merisaukan, membingungkan.

unsightly tidak elok, rupanya buruk.

unskilled tidak diberi pengajaran, tidak memerlukan kepandaian istimewa.

unsociable tidak suka bergaul, tidak ramah-tamah.

unsophisticated sederhana, tidak berpengalaman dalam hal duniawi.

unsound (*of health*) tidak sihat; (*not true*) tidak benar.

unsparing (*abundant*) mewah; (*harsh*) tidak mengenal belas kasihan.

unspeakable tiada terkatakan; (*bad*) sangat buruk.

unstable tidak tetap, tidak tenteram.

unsteady bergoncang, tak tetap.

unstrung tidak terikat; (*bewildered*) bingung; (*worried*) bimbang.

unsubstantiated tidak terbukti.

unsuccessful tidak berhasil, gagal.

unsuitable tidak patut, tidak padan.

unswerving tidak menyimpang.

untenable tiada dapat dipertahankan.

untidy kotor, tak kemas, lalai.

untie, to — membuka ikatan.

until sampai, sehingga.

untimely tiada pada waktunya.

untold tidak dikatakan, tidak terkatakan.

untouchable yang tidak dapat atau boleh disentuh.

untoward (*not good*) tidak baik; (*clumsy*) canggung; (*unlucky*) malang.

untried tidak dicuba, tidak dialami.

untroubled tenang, tidak bingung.

untrue tidak benar; (not honest) tidak jujur; (not loyal) tidak setia.

untruthful bohong berdusta, pendusta.

unusual luarbiasa.

unveil, to — membuka tudung; (secret) membuka rahsia.

unwary tidak hati-hati.

unwavering tetap.

unwieldy canggung, kekok; (heavy etc) berat, sukar dipikul atau dipegang.

unwilling tidak suka, tidak sudi, segan.

unwind, to — terbuka atau membuka gulungnya.

unwise tidak bijak.

unwitting (not intentional) tidak sengaja; (unconsciously) tidak insaf, tidak sedar.

unwonted tidak biasa, luarbiasa, ajaib.

unworthy tidak patut, tidak dengan sepertinya.

unwritten tidak ditulis; — law hukum adat.

up di atas; ke atas; bangun.

upas racun, ipuh; — tree pohon ipuh.

upbraid, to — mencela.

upbringing pendidikan.

upcountry hulu.

upend, to — (set upright) menegakkan; (invert) membalikkan.

upgrade naik pangkat.

uphill ke atas, mendaki gunung; (difficult) sukar.

uphold, to — menyokong, berpegang kuat.

upholster, to — memberi bertirai (berbantal dan sebagainya).

upholstery perusahaan mengisi alas kerusi (dan sebagainya).

upkeep pemeliharaan.

upland tanah tinggi.

upper (higher) lebih tinggi;

(up river) lebih ke hulu; (above) atas.

uppercut pukulan tinju dari bawah ke atas.

upper hand, to get the — — menang, mencapai kemenangan.

uppermost yang amat tinggi, tertinggi; terkeatas.

uppish sombong.

upright tulus, jujur, dengan tulus.

uprising naiknya; (struggle) pemberontakan.

uproar gaduh, haru-biru.

uproarious gegak gempita.

uproot, to — membantun, membongkar dengan urat akarnya.

upset (confusion) kacau-bilau; (upturned) terbalik.

upshot akhir, hasil.

upside down terbalik, songsang.

upstanding tegak; (sincere) tulus.

upstart orang kaya baharu.

upstream mudik, ke hulu; to go — menghulu, mudik.

uptake pengangkatan; quick on the — pintar.

up-to-date sesuai dengan aliran sekarang.

upward(s) arah ke atas; (placed upwards) terletak di tempat yang lebih tinggi.

uranium uranium.

urban yang berkenaan dengan bandar.

urbane berbudi bahasa, sopan santun.

urchin anak laki-laki.

urge desakan, gerak hati; to — mendesak.

urgency hal sangat perlu.

urgent sangat perlu, mendesak, segera.

urinal jamban kencing.

urinate, to — kencing.

urine kencing.

urn sejenis kendi; (for ashes of

dead) sejenis tempayan untuk menyimpan debu jenazah.

us kami, kita.

U.S.A. Amerika Syarikat.

usage (_using_) pemakaian; (_custom_) adat, kebiasaan.

use (_using_) pemakaian; (_putting to a purpose_) guna, faedah; (_custom_) kebiasaan; to make — of mempergunakan.

used I telah memakai, telah dipakai.

used II, he — to come every day biasa ia datang setiap hari; to be — to biasa.

useful berguna, berfaedah.

useless tidak berguna, tidak berfaedah, sia-sia.

user pemakai.

usher (_at door_) pengantar masuk; (_attendant_) pengiring; to — mengantar masuk; — ette pengantar masuk perempuan.

usual biasa, lazim.

usually biasanya, pada ghalibnya.

usurp, to — merebut kuasa, merampas kuasa (mahkota dan sebagainya).

usury riba; to practise — makan riba.

utensil perkakas, alat.

uterus kandung peranakan, rahim.

utilitarian yang berkenaan dengan hal berfaedah.

utility guna, faedah; (_thing_) hal yang berguna.

utilization pemakaian, penggunaan.

utilize, to — mempergunakan, memakai.

utmost seboleh-bolehnya, sekuat-kuatnya; (_greatest_) terbesar.

utter I (_complete_) samasekali; (_extreme_) amat sangat; — misery sengsara yang amat sangat.

utter II, to — mengucapkan.

utterance ucapan, kata, ujar.

V

vacancy kekosongan.

vacant kosong.

vacate, to — meninggalkan, mengosongkan.

vacation (_quitting_) peninggalan; (_leisure_) waktu tiada bekerja; (_holiday_) cuti.

vaccinate, to — menanam cacar.

vaccination pencacaran.

vaccine benih cacar.

vacuous kosong, hampa.

vacuum hampa udara, hampagas.

vagabond pengembara, pertualang, orang bangsat.

vagary tingkah.

vagina lubang peranakan, faraj.

vagrancy hal mengembara, pengembaraan.

vagrant yang mengembara; (_person_) pengembara, orang bangsat.

vague samar; (_uncertain_) tidak tentu.

vain (_empty_) hampa; (_useless_) sia-sia, tidak berguna; (_conceited_) sombong, bongkak; in — sia-sia.

vale (_valley_) lembah.

valet, to — melayani seseorang laki-laki.

valiant gagah berani.

valid sahih, sah, laku, berlaku.

validate, to — mengesahkan, membenarkan.

validity keadaan sah, sahih; (_in use_) lakunya.

valise beg kecil.

valley jurang, lembah, lurah.

valour keberanian.

valuable hal yang berharga.

valuation penghargaan, nilaian.

value (_cost_) harga; (_utility_) guna; hal yang berharga atau berguna; *(appraisal)* nilai; to — menghargai, menilaikan.

valueless tidak berharga.

valuer penilai, juru taksir.

valve injab, katup; *(radio)* lampu radio.

vamp *(col) (woman)* perempuan yang suka membujuk dan memikat laki-laki.

vampire hantu pelesit, pontianak.

van *(leading row)* garis depan; *(cart)* sejenis kereta.

vandalism perosakan.

vane baling-baling.

vanguard baris depan.

vanilla pewangi.

vanish, to — menghilang, lenyap.

vanity sifat pelagak.

vanquish, to — mengalahkan.

vantage untung, keuntungan.

vapid ambar, tawar.

vapourization, *(US)* **vaporization** penguapan, tangas.

vapourize, *(US)* **vaporize, to** — menguap, menguapkan.

vapour, *(US)* **vapor** asap; wap air, kukus.

variability keadaan berubah-ubah, hal dapat diubah.

variable yang dapat diubah, berubah-ubah.

variance perselisihan; at — with berlawanan dengan.

variant hal yang berlainan.

variation perubahan.

varicose, — veins pembuluh mekar.

varied berjenis-jenis, aneka warna, pelbagai.

variegate, —d aneka warna.

variety hal berjenis-jenis, hal aneka warna, berjenis-jenis keragaman.

various berjenis, berbagai, pelbagai.

varnish minyak bernis; **to —** membubuhi bernis.

vary, to — berubah, berlainlainan; *(diverge)* menyimpang.

vase jambangan.

vast sangat luas, maha besar.

vat tong.

Vatican tempat kediaman Pope.

vault I *(burial chamber)* gua pemakaman.

vault II *(leap)* sejenis lompatan; pole — lompat bergalah.

vaunt bual-bual; to — berbual.

V.C. Victoria Cross, Bintang V.C.

veal daging anak lembu.

veer, to — berubah hala, memutar; *(dubious)* ragu-ragu.

vegetable sayur-sayuran.

vegetarian orang yang berpantang makan daging.

vegetation segala tumbuh-tumbuhan.

vehemence kekerasan.

vehement hebat, keras, kuat.

vehicle kereta, kenaikan.

vehicular yang berkenaan dengan kenaikan.

veil tudung, kelubung.

vein pembuluh darah, urat darah; —ed berurat.

velocity kecepatan, kederasan, laju.

velvet baldu, lembut.

venal *(for sale)* yang dapat dibeli; *(taking bribes)* yang makan suap.

vend, to — *(sell)* menjual; *(hawk)* berjaja.

vendetta pembalasan dendam secara membunuh.

vendor penjual, penjaja.

veneer lapisan cantik untuk bahagian luaran; to — melapisi dengan sepuh.

venerable patut diberi hormat.

venerate, to — menghormati.

veneration takrim, takzim.

venereal yang berkenaan dengan setubuh; — disease penyakit angin perempuan.

Venetian orang Venetia; — **blind** bidai; — **window** tingkap rangkap tiga.

vengeance pembalasan dendam.

vengeful menaruh dendam.

venison daging rusa.

venom bisa, racun.

venomous berbisa, racun.

vent pintu angin, jalan keluar; **to give** — to mengeluarkan.

ventilate, to — mengedarkan (memasukkan) udara, ganti udara.

ventilation kemasukan udara, peredaran udara, gantian udara.

ventricle rongga.

ventriloquist orang yang pandai cakap dengan tidak bergerak bibirnya.

venture (*daring act*) perbuatan yang berbahaya; (*speculation*) perniagaan yang sekali-kali tidak tentu; **to** — (*try*) mencuba.

venturesome berani.

veracity kesungguhan, kebenaran.

veranda(h) serambi, beranda.

verb kata ubat, kata kerja.

verbal yang berkenaan dengan kata buat.

verbatim sepatah demi sepatah.

verbose dengan memakai banyak kata.

verbosity hal cakap dengan panjang lebar.

verdant (*green*) hijau; (*green grass*) berumput hijau.

verdict keputusan hakim hukuman.

verdigris tahi tembaga yang warnanya hijau.

verge tepi, batas; **to** — condong, cenderung; **to** — on mendekati, hampir-hampir.

verger pegawai gereja yang mengiringkan orang ke tempat duduknya.

verify, to — memeriksa benar

tidaknya, menentukan.

verily bahawa sanya.

veritable bina betul.

verity kebenaran, hal atau kenyataan yang benar.

vermicelli sejenis meehoon.

vermilion warna merah terang.

vermin (*animal*) bintang yang merosakkan; (*in clothes*) kutu, tuma.

verminous penuh kutu (dan sebagainya).

vermouth sejenis minuman daripada air anggur.

vernacular bahasa daerah, asli.

vernal yang berkenaan dengan musim dunia.

verruca kutil.

versatile yang mudah menyesuaikan diri dengan ber bagai pekerjaan dan golongan masyarakat, pantas akal.

verse baris-baris sajak.

versed, — in ahli dalam, berpengalaman.

versification pengarang syair.

versify, to — mengarang syair.

version salinan, terjemahan.

versus (*huruf*, ringkasnya; v. atau vs.) melawan.

vertebra tulang belakang.

vertebrate bintang bertulang belakang, vertebrata.

vertex puncak.

vertical tegak.

vertigo pusing kepala, pening kepala.

verve semangat, kegiatan.

very (*true*) benar-benar, betul; (*most*) sekali, sangat, amat.

vesper malam; —s sembahyang malam.

vessel (*ship*) kapal, bahtera; (*basin*) behana; (*tube*) pembuluh.

vest (*garment*) baju; —ing (*securing legally*) memberi kuasa dan sebagainya.

vestal perempuan suci.

vestige kesan, bekas; not a — of evidence tiada keterangan biar sedikit pun juga.

vestry ruang penyimpan pakaian rasmi di gereja.

vet doktor haiwan.

veteran orang yang telah bertahun-tahun bekerja dalam salah satu jabatan.

veterinary yang berkenaan dengan kedoktoran haiwan.

veto hak beto.

vex, to — menyakiti hati, membengkengi.

vexation penggangguan; kekesalan.

via melalui, dengan perantaraan.

viable yang dapat hidup.

viaduct jambatan di atas jalan, jejambat.

vibrant yang menggetar.

vibrate, to — menggetar, gemetar.

vibration getaran.

vicar padri.

vicarage tempat kediaman seorang 'vicar'.

vicarious yang mengganti, yang mewakili.

vice I (evil) kejahatan, kebusukan; (blemish) cacat.

vice II (clamp) ragum.

vice— awalan kata yang ertinya: penganti, wakil.

vice—admiral laksamana muda.

vice–president wakil, naib presiden, naib yang dipertua.

viceroy raja muda, bizurai.

vice–versa dan sebaliknya, pulang balik.

vicinity dekat, hampiran.

vicious (evil) busuk, jahat; (fierce) ganas.

vicissitude perubahan nasib, hal-ahwal.

victim (of sacrifice) korban.

victimize, to — mengorbankan.

victor yang menang.

victorious yang menang.

victory kemenangan.

victual, —s barang makanan, perbekalan, rezeki.

vie, to — bersaingan, berkawanan.

view (observation) pemandangan; (opinion) penglihatan.

viewer penjinjau.

vigilant berjaga.

vigorous kuat, perkasa.

vigour, (US) vigor kekuatan, tenaga; (health) kesihatan badan.

vile keji, hina.

vilify, to — memburukkan; (name) mencemarkan.

villa rumah indah dengan kebun.

village desa, dusun, kampung.

villager orang dusun, orang kampung.

villain penjahat, bangsat.

villainous jahat, keji, buruk.

villainy kejahatan, keburukan.

vim (col) kekuatan, kegiatan, semangat.

vindicate, to — (defend successfully) mempertahankan; (validate) mengesahkan, membenarkan.

vindictive berdengki, hendak membalas dendam.

vine (climber) tanaman menjalar; (grape) pohon anggur.

vinegar cuka.

vineyard kebun pohon anggur.

vintage musim buah anggur.

vintner penjual anggur.

viola (musical instrument) biola besar.

violable yang dapat dilanggar.

violate, to — (infringe) melanggar.

violation pelanggaran; perkosaan.

violence kekerasan; (oppression) aniaya.

violent (harsh) keras; (terrible) hebat.

violet sejenis bunga; (colour) warna ungu muda.

violin biola; **to play the —** menggesek biola.

violinist penggesek biola.

viper ular bisa; (person) orang busuk.

virago perempuan galak.

virescent menghijau, kehijau-hijauan.

virgin anak dara; **— soil** tanah yang belum dikerjakan.

virginal seperti anak dara.

virginity keadaan anak dara, yang seperti dara, anak suci.

virile (manly) berkenaan dengan hal laki-laki, seperti laki-laki; (strong) kuat.

virility sifat laki-laki; kekuatan.

virtual sebetulnya.

virtue kebaikan, kebajikan; (duty) jasa.

virtuosity kepandaian dalam teknik salah satu kesenian.

virtuoso orang yang pandai dalam teknik salah satu lapangan kesenian.

virtuous baik, kebajikan.

virulence kejahatan.

virulent (poisonous) berbisa; (evil) jahat.

virus (poison) bisa; (malignity) kejahatan, vairas.

visa catitan pengesahan pada surat pas dan sebagainya.

visage muka, wajah, rupa.

vis-à-vis orang yang berhadapan muka.

viscid, —ity kental, pekat.

viscosity kental, pekat.

viscount orang bangsawan.

visibility penglihatan; hal boleh tampak.

visible tampak, kelihatan, terpandang.

vision penglihatan; (divine revelation) wahyu; **to —** melihat seperti dalam khayal.

visionary yang mendapat wahyu.

visit kunjungan; **to —, pay a — to** mengunjungi, singgah, lawat.

visitation kunjungan rasmi, lawatan.

visiting yang mengunjungi, yang melawat.

visitor tetamu, pelawat.

vista pemandangan.

visual yang berkenaan dengan penglihatan, yang kelihatan.

visualize, to — menggambarkan.

vital (affecting life) yang berkenaan dengan hal hidup; (very important) sangat penting.

vitality daya hidup, tenaga hidup.

vitamin bitamin.

vitreous yang seperti kaca.

vitrify, to — menjadikan kaca.

vitriol (sulphuric acid) asam belerang, terusi; (scathing criticism) kupasan yang sangat tajam.

vituperate, to — mencela, mencaci.

viva hiduplah!

vivacious gembira bersemangat.

vivacity kegembiraan, semangat.

vivid (bright) terang; (animated) bersemangat.

vivify, to — menghidupkan, mengiatkan.

vivisect, to — memotong-motong haiwan hidup (untuk penyelidikan kedoktoran).

vixen (female fox) rubah betina; (spiteful woman) perempuan galak.

vocabulary daftar kata, senarai kata-kata, loghat, perbendaharaan kata.

vocal berkenaan dengan suara, bersuara; (of vowels) huruf hidup.

vocalist penyanyi.
vocation bakat istimewa untuk salah satu pekerjaan, pekerjaan, bakat kerja.
vociferous dengan rioh-rendah.
vogue hal berlaku, hal menurut; **in —** sangat laku.
voice suara.
voiceless diam, tidak bersuara.
void (*vacant*) hampa, kosong; (*invalid*) tidak sah, batal; **to —** membatalkan.
volatile (*flying*) terbang; (*readily evaporating*) yang mudah menjadi wap.
volcanic yang berkenaan dengan atau seperti gunung berapi.
volcano gunung berapi.
vole sejenis tikus.
volition kemahuan, kehendak, bertujuan.
volley tembakan serentak.
volt volta (letrik).
voltage kekuatan letrik diukur dengan volta.
volubility kefasihan, kepetahan.
voluble fasih, petah lidah.
volume (*book*) jilid; (*contents*) isi padu; (*number*) banyaknya.
voluminous besar; (*of books*) terdiri daripada banyak jilid.
voluntary dengan suka rela.
volunteer orang yang berbuat sesuatu dengan suka rela.
voluptuous berlazat, nikmat dan mewah.
vomit muntah.
voodoo (*philtres*) guna-guna; (*sorcery*) ilmu sihir.
voracious lahap, gelojoh.
voracity kelahapan.
vortex pusaran, puting beliung.
vote suara pemilih; pendapat; **—s** suara para pemilih.
voter pemilih.

vouch, to — (*approve*) membenarkan; (*support*) menanggung; **to —** for menjamin.
voucher surat penetapan pembayaran, bocar.
vouchsafe, to — menganugerahkan.
vow ikrar, nazar; **to —** bernazar.
vowel huruf saksi.
voyage pelayaran; **to —** belayar.
voyager penumpang kapal, orang yang belayar.
vulgar (*coarse*) kasar; (*foul: of language*) carut.
vulgarity kekasaran.
vulnerability keadaan lekas kena luka.
vulnerable yang lekas kena luka.
vulpine (*foxy*) cerdik.
vulture burung hering.

W

wad segumpal kapas untuk jadi pengisi atau penyumbat; (*for gun*) nal.
wadding mengisi, menyumbat.
waddle, to — berjalan terkedek-kedek.
wade arung; **to —** mengarung.
wader burung pucung.
wafer sejenis biskut.
waffle sejenis kuih sepit.
waft (*scent*) bau harum yang semerbak.
wag (*shake*) kibas; (*joker*) orang jenaka; **to —** mengibas.
wage I upah, gaji; **— earner** orang upahan, buruh.
wage II (*war*) menjalankan perang, melakukan perang.
wager petaruhan.
waggle goyang; **to —** bergoyang.
wag(g)on gerabak.

waif binatang atau orang terlantar.

wail ratap; to — meratap, mengaduh.

wainscot lapisan kayu pada dinding.

waist pinggang; —band ikat (tali) pinggang.

wait tunggu; to — menanti, menunggu.

waiter pelayan.

waiting room bilik tunggu.

waitress pelayan perempuan.

waive, to — meninggalkan, tidak mempergunakan.

wake I jaga, berjaga; (*cause to wake*) membangunkan.

wake II, in the — of mengikuti.

wakeful (*vigilant*) berjaga; (*not asleep*) tidak dapat tidur.

waken, to — bangun, membangunkan.

walk (*gait*) cara berjalan; to — jalan kaki.

walker pelancung, orang yang berjalan.

walking sedang berjalan.

wall dinding; (*of stone*) tembok.

wallaby sejenis binatang kangaru.

wallet celepa wang kertas, saku.

wallflower sejenis bunga.

wallop pukulan yang keras.

wallow kubang; to — in berkubang.

wallpaper kertas dinding.

walnut sejenis buah yang berkulit keras.

walrus sejenis duyung.

waltz sejenis tarian.

wan pucat.

wand tongkat.

wander, to — beredar, mengedar, mengembara.

wanderer pengembara.

wane, on the —, to — berkurang, susut.

wangle, to — memperoleh dengan segala daya upaya atau tipu daya.

want (*deficiency*) kekurangan; (*poverty*) kemiskinan.

wanting kurang.

wanton (*mischievous*) nakal; (*playful*) suka bermain-main.

war perang, peperangan; civil — perang saudara.

warble (*of birds*) siul burung; (*sing with trills*) nyanyian yang bergetar-getar bunyinya; to — bersiul.

warbler sejenis burung.

ward (*guarding*) penjagaan; (*child*) anak tanggungan.

warden penjaga, pengawas.

warder penjaga penjara.

wardrobe (*cupboard*) almari pakaian.

wardroom bilik dalam pegawai kapal perang.

–wards akhiran kata yang ertinya: ke arah.

warehouse gudang.

ware(s) barang dagangan.

warfare perang, peperangan.

warily dengan tenang, dengan hati-hati.

warlike (*concerning war*) berkenaan dengan perang; (*eager for war*) suka berperang.

war lord kepala pasukan yang berperang untuk kepentingannya sendiri.

warm (*hot*) panas, hangat; (*cordial*) peramah; (*lively*) bersemangat.

warm-blooded berdarah panas.

warm-hearted baik hati.

warn, to — memberi ingat, memberi amaran.

warning amaran, nasihat.

warp keadaan bengkok.

warpath, to be on the — sedang berperang.

warrant (*guarantee*) jaminan; (*authority*) kuasa; (*to authorize payment*) surat yang memberi hak menerima wang.

warrant officer pegawai rendahan yang tertinggi.

warranty jaminan.

warren tempat yang terdapat banyak arnab.

warrior penglima, perajurit.

warship kapal perang.

wart kutil; —**hog** sejenis babi hutan.

war victim korban perang.

wary hati-hati.

wash pencucian; (*sweep of water*) harus air; **to** — membasuh; (*cleanse articles*) mencuci.

washbasin tempat basuh tangan.

washer (*metal ring*) lapik wasir logam.

wash–out sebahagian jalan yang berlubang disebabkan air bah.

wasp penyengat, tabuan.

waspish bengkeng.

wastage (*shrinking*) susut; (*loss*) kerugian kerana susut.

waste susut; (*remain*) sisa, bekas; **to lay** — membinasakan.

wasteful pemboros.

wastepaper basket bakul sampah.

waster pemboros.

wastrel sesuatu yang tiada berguna.

watch I (*guarding*) penjagaan; (*observation*) perhatian; **to be on** — berkawal.

watch II (*for telling time*) arloji, jam.

watchdog anjing penjaga.

watchful berjaga-jaga.

watchmaker tukang jam.

watchman penjaga, kawal, pengawal.

watch spring sepering jam.

watch tower menara untuk berkawal.

watchword semboyan.

water air; **by** — (*of travel*) dengan kapal; **fresh** — air bersih.

water buffalo kerbau.

water closet jamban tarik.

watercolour, (*US*) **water-color** cat air.

watercourse anak air, anak sungai.

watercress sejenis tumbuhan air yang dimakan sebagai ulam.

waterfall air terjun.

watergauge pembuluh kaca yang menunjukkan tinggi air.

water level paras air; (*water table*) muka air di dalam tanah.

water lily bunga teratai.

waterline batas air pada sisi kapal.

water main saluran paip air.

waterman tukang sampan.

watermark sejenis cap pada kertas (wang kertas dan sebagainya).

watermelon semangka, tembikai, mendikai.

water mill kincir air.

waterproof kedap air, tahan air.

watershed batas air, batas antara dua aliran air.

waterside tepi laut atau sungai.

watertight kedap air.

water wag(g)on kereta penyiram; (*col*) **to be on the** — tidak minum minuman keras.

waterway jalan air; (*canal or cut*) terusan.

waterwheel kincir.

waterworks (*reservoir*) kolam air.

watery cayir; (*insipid*) tawar.

watt kesatuan tenaga letrik.

wattle I (*of cocks*) pial.

wattle II (*for fencing*) ranting untuk pagar.

wave ombak, gelombang; (*coiling*) belit; (*of hair*) ikal; (*of flags in breeze*) berkibaran.

waver (*of*) — (*quiver*) bergetar; (*sway*) beroyang; (*undecided*) bimbang, ragu-ragu.

wavy berombak; (*of hair*) berikal, keriting.

wax I lilin, malam; — **paper** kertas lilin.

wax II, to — bertambah besar; (*become*) menjadi; to — **and wane** pasang surut turun naik.

waxen diperbuat daripada lilin, seperti lilin.

waxy seperti lilin.

way (*road*) jalan; (*style*) cara, ragam; (*custom*) adat, kebiasaan.

wayfarer pengembara, pelancung.

wayfaring perjalanan kaki.

waylay, to — mengadang, serang hendap.

-ways akhiran kata yang ertinya: ke arah.

wayward (*stubborn*) keras kepala; (*mischievous*) nakal.

we kami, kita.

weak daif, lemah, tidak kuat.

weaken, to — menjadi lemah, melemahkan.

weak-headed bebal, dengu.

weak-kneed lemah (badan atau jiwa).

weakling orang lemah.

weak-minded dengu, bebal.

weakness kedaifan, kelemahan.

wealth (*property*) harta benda; (*riches*) kekayaan.

wealthy hartawan, kaya.

wean, to — (*separate*) menjarangkan.

weapon senjata.

wear (*clothing*) pemakaian, pakaian; (*worn out*) kerosakan.

weariness kelelahan, kepayahan.

wearisome (*weakening*) yang melemahkan; (*boring*) yang menjemukan.

weary lelah, penat, payah.

weasel sejenis cerpelai.

weather hawa, hari, cuaca.

weather beaten dimakan hari.

weather bureau pejabat kaji-cuaca.

weather chart peta cuaca.

weathercock baling-baling.

weather forecast ramalan tentang keadaan hawa.

weather glass barometer.

weather station pusat kaji-cuaca.

weave cara bertenun; to — bertenun, menenun.

weaver tukang tenun; —**bird** burung tempua.

web tenunan; (*spider's*) sarang labah-labah; (*membrane between toes*) selaput di antara jari kaki.

webbed berselaput.

wed, to — kahwin, nikah.

wedding perkahwinan, nikah; — **day** hari perkahwinan.

wedge baji; to — memasang baji.

wedge-shaped berupa baji.

wedlock perjodohan, kahwin, keadaan suami isteri.

Wednesday hari Rabu.

wee kecil.

weed I rumput; to — merumput.

weed II, —**s** (*widow's*) pakaian janda.

week minggu; **today** — 7 hari lagi.

weekday hari yang bukan hari Minggu, hari kerja.

weekly (*every week*) tiap-tiap minggu; (*once a week*) sekali seminggu.

weep, to — menangis, meratap.

weevil kumbang, serangga, bubuk (yang merosakkan hasil bumi).

weft pakan.

weigh penimbangan; to — menimbang; (*it weighs*) beratnya; to — **anchor** membongkar sauh.

weighbridge alat penimbang kereta dan sebagainya.

weighing machine alat penimbang.

weight berat; (1 oz gold-smith's) bungkal; (on scales) batu timbang

weighty (heavy) berat; (important) penting; (influential) berpengaruh, besar pengaruhnya.

weir tambak menyeberang sungai.

weird (mysterious) ghaib; (fearful) yang mengerikan; (abnormal) pelik.

welcome (hail) selamat datang; (receive) sambutan.

weld, to — menyambung besi, memandu, mengimpal.

welder tukang pateri.

welfare keadaan baik, keadaan senang, keadaan sihat, keselamatan.

well I (water) mata air; perigi, telaga.

well II dengan baik, baik-baik; (of health) sihat.

well- awalan kata yang ertinya: baik-baik; sangat.

well-advised bijaksana.

well-behaved baik budi bahasanya.

well-being keadaan baik.

well-beloved yang sangat dikasihi.

well-bred baik budi bahasanya, sopan santun.

well-connected perhubungannya baik.

well-disposed baik hati.

well done telah dilaksanakan dengan baik.

well-informed yang pengetahuannya baik.

well-knit baik susunannya; (of body) baik badan.

well-known terkenal, termasyhur.

well-mannered baik budi bahasanya, sopan santun, beradab.

well-off berada berwang.

well-read banyak yang telah dibacanya.

well-spent yang dibuat, dipergunakan baik-baik.

well-spoken perkataannya halus.

well-to-do berada, kaya.

well-wisher teman baik, orang yang perasaannya baik terhadap seseorang.

well-worn usang, buruk.

Welsh orang bangsa Wales.

welt (of shoe) jalur kulit sepatu; (weal) bilur; **to** — memukul keras-keras.

welter huru-hara, kekacauan; **to** — berguling, berkubang.

wench anak perempuan, anak dara.

wend, to — menuju ke, mengarah ke.

werewolf manusia yang berubah menjadi serigala dan lain-lain.

west barat, sebelah barat.

westerly arah ke barat, dari sebelah barat; — **wind** angin barat.

western yang berada di barat.

westernize, to — menyesuaikan dengan adat barat.

westward(s) ke barat, arah ke barat.

wet basah, air; (rain) berhujan.

wettish agak basah.

whack pukulan hebat; (col) (share) membahagi.

whacking (very large) sangat besar; (beating) pukulan hebat.

whale ikan paus.

whalebone tulang insang.

whaler kapal penangkap ikan paus.

whaling penangkapan ikan paus; — **gun** meriam untuk menambakan serampang kepada ikan paus, dermaga.

wharf pengkalan.

what apa; apa?; (in which way) mana; (how, why) betapa.

whatever barang apa, apapun.

whatsoever barang apa, apa-pun.

wheat gandum; (*flour*) terigu.

wheedle, to — membujuk.

wheel roda, jentera; (*change direction*) putaran.

wheelbarrow kereta sorong beroda satu.

wheelwright pembuat roda, pembuat kereta.

wheeze nafas terengah, bernafas terengah-engah.

whelk sejenis remis.

whelp (*dog*) anak anjing; (*lion*) anak singa.

when bila; bila?; (*on the occasion*) apabila; (*at the time*) pada kala, tatkala, ketika, waktu, waktu mana.

whence dari mana.

whenever bila mana juga.

where di mana, ke mana; di mana?; — to ke mana; — from dari mana.

whereabouts kira-kira di mana.

whereas sedangkan, padahal.

whereby yang kerananya.

wherefore untuk apa; (*became*) kerana itu.

wherein di mana.

whereof dari apa; (*concerning*) tentang apa.

whereon di mana, pada mana.

whereupon padahal, yang kerana itu.

wherever barang di mana, di mana pun, ke mana-mana, ke mana pun.

wherewith dengan mana.

wherewithal dengan mana; (*the means*) apa yang perlu untuk membeli atau membuat sesuatu.

whet, to — mengasah, mencanai.

whether apa, -kah; I don't know — he is here saya tidak tahu adakah ia di sini atau tidak.

whetstone batu pengasah, batu canai.

whew! wah!, celaka!

whey air yang tinggal sesudah susu dadih.

which (*interrogative pronoun*) yang mana?, hal mana?; (*relative pronoun*) yang.

whichever mana sahaja, mana pun.

whiff (*smoke*) sekepul asap; (*of breeze*) angin sepoi.

while I (*space of time*) sebentar, waktu; once in a — sekali-sekala.

while II (*of simultaneous action*) sambil, seraya; (*actually*) padahal; (*as long as*) selama.

whim tingkah, olah.

whimper, to — merepek, merenyeh.

whimsical bertingkah; (*odd*) anih.

whimsy tingkah.

whine, to — merenyeh, merengek.

whinny, to — merengkek.

whip pecut, cemeti; (*in political party*) pengawas dan pengurus salah satu parti politik dalam parlimen.

whip hand, to have the — — of menguasai.

whipper-snapper (*child*) anak kecil; tidak orang muda (*ignorant young person*) orang muda dan tidak berpengalaman.

whirl pusingan; to — berpusing.

whirligig (*toy*) sejenis permainan yang berpusar; (*thing that revolves*) peredaran.

whirlpool pusaran air.

whirlwind pusaran angin.

whirr dengung, desing; to — mendengung, mendensing.

whisk sejenis bulu ayam (cemara dan lain-lain) untuk mengebas.

whisker cambang, jambang.

whisky, (*US*) **whiskey** minuman wiski.

whisper bisikan; (*rumour*) desas-desus; to — berbisik-bisik, membisikkan.

whist sejenis permainan terup.

whistle (*instrument*) seruling, peluit; (*sound*) siulan.

whit hal yang terkecil atau sedikit.

white warna putih; (*pale*) pucat; (*conduct*) berkelakuan baik.

white-hot panas putih.

white-livered pengecut.

whiten, to — memutihkan, menjadikan putih.

whitening kapur untuk menyapu rumah dan lain-lain.

white paper kertas putih; (*of Government*) usul pemerintah.

whitewash kapur untuk menyapu rumah.

whither ke mana.

whiting sejenis ikan.

whitish keputih-putihan.

whittle, to — meraut.

whizz bunyi desau, desir.

who siapa; siapa?; (*relative*) yang.

whoa berhenti!

whoever barang siapa.

whole (*complete*) bulat-bulat, sempurna, lengkap.

wholehearted bulat-bulat hati, dengan sekuat tenaga.

wholesale perdagangan secara memborong.

wholesome yang menyegarkan, menyihatkan.

wholly semua sekali.

whom kepada siapa, yang kepadanya.

whoopee, (*col*) to make — bersuka ria.

whooping cough batuk rejan, batuk ayam.

whopper (*very large*) sesuatu yang sangat besar; (*monstrous lie*) dusta besar.

whopping bukan main besar.

whore sundal.

whorl (*of leaves*) lengkaran daun; (*in fingerprint, hair*) pusar-pusar.

whose kepunyaan siapa, **yang** empunya.

whosoever barang siapa.

why mengapa, kenapa, apa sebabnya.

wick sumbu.

wicked jahat; (*naughty*) nakal.

wickedness kejahatan.

wicker ranting yang dianyam.

wickerwork anyam-anyaman.

wicket (*gate*) pintu kecil; (*cricket*) pancang yang dipakai dalam permainan cricket.

wide lebar; (*spacious*) luas, lapang.

wide-awake (*on watch*) jaga; (*of comprehension*) faham.

widen, to — meluas, melebarkan.

widow janda; to — menjadi janda.

widower janda laki-laki.

width lebar, keluasan.

wield, to — (*hold*) memegang; (*use, act*) melakukan.

wife bini, isteri.

wig (*artificial hair*) rambut palsu, rambut cemara.

wiggle lenggang; to — melenggang.

wigwam khemah orang Indian.

wild liar, buas, jalang, tidak jinak; (*unmannerly*) tidak beradab.

wilderness (*forest*) hutan, rimba, belantara.

wildness kebuasan.

wile tipu daya, muslihat.

wilful (*deliberate*) sengaja; (*obstinate*) keras kepala.

will I (*desiring*) kehendak, kemahuan; (*the faculty*) hati; at

— semahunya; to — (*compel*) memaksakan.

will II (*law*) surat wasiat.

willing reda, rela, sudi.

willingness kesudian, kemahuan.

will-o'-the-wisp cahaya api yang kelihatan pada tanah berpaya; (*elusive person*) orang yang tidak tetap hatinya.

willow sejenis pohon.

willy-nilly mau tak mau.

wilt, to — layu, melayukan.

wily licik, berakal, kancil.

wimple (*coil*) belit; (*crease*) kerut.

win kemenangan; to — (be *victorious*) menang; to — over mempengaruhi.

wince gerak ngeri; to — gerenyit kerana kesakitan.

wincey sejenis kain kuat.

winch puturan roda.

wind I angin, bayu.

wind II, — up penyelesaian, akhir; to — berbelit-belit, berputar, bergulung.

windbag orang yang suka berucap dengan panjang lebar.

windfall (*fruit*) buah yang gugur.

winding berkeluk-keluk, berbelit-belit.

winding up (*settlement*) penyelesaian; (*dispensing*) pembubaran.

wind instrument alat muzik yang ditiup.

windjammer kapal layar besar.

windlass putaran.

windmill kincir angin.

window jendela, tingkap.

window dressing perhiasan sahaja.

windpipe batang tenggorok.

windscreen cermin di muka kereta (pesawat udara dan lain-lain).

wind sock sejenis sampul

panjang yang berkibar pada hujung tiang untuk menunjukkan arah angin.

windswept banyak kena angin.

windy banyak kena angin; (*empty*) hampa; (*wordy*) yang suka bercakap angin.

wine air anggur, wain; (*colour*) warna merah tua; to — minuman air anggur.

wineglass gelas minuman air anggur.

winepress alat pemeras anggur.

wing sayap kepak; (*of house*) bahagian rumah.

wing beat kepak sayap.

wing commander pegawai angkatan udara.

wingspan jarak antara kedua hujung sayap.

wink kejap; (*glance*) kerling; (*hint*) isyarat; to — mengejapkan mata; mengerling.

winkle sejenis siput laut; to — out mengeluarkan.

winner pemenang.

winnings hasil kemenangan, untung.

winnow penampi, nyiru; to — menampi.

winsome yang menarik hati.

winter musim dingin, musim sejuk.

wintry yang berkenaan dengan musim dingin.

wipe, to — out, off menghapuskan, menghilangkan.

wire kawat, dawai; (*telegram*) surat kawat.

wire-haired berambut keriting.

wireless tiada berkawat; taligram radio; radio.

wiring pemasangan kawat.

wiry dibuat daripada kawat, seperti kawat; (*tough*) liat.

wisdom bijaksana, arif.

wisdom tooth geraham bongsu.

wise arif, bijaksana, budiman.

wisecrack perkataan pedas.

wish kehendak, keinginan, kemahuan.

wishful ingin, keinginan.

wisp unting.

wistful sayu, hiba.

wit (*intelligence*) akal, budi.

witch perempuan yang pandai dalam ilmu sihir.

witchcraft ilmu sihir.

witch doctor tukang sihir.

with dengan; (*along* —) serta; (*together* —) berserta dengan.

withdraw, to — menarik diri, mengundurkan diri.

withdrawal penarikan diri.

wither, to — layu, melayu, kering.

withers (*of ox*) lembusir.

withhold, to — tidak memberi.

within di dalam.

without di luar, sebelah luar.

withstand, to — (*oppose*) melawan; (*resist*) mempertahankan diri.

witless tidak berakal, dengu.

witness (*evidence*) saksi; (*explanation*) kenyataan; eye — penyaksi mata; to — naik saksi.

witness box, witness-stand tempat angkat sumpah.

witticism perkataan jenaka.

witting(ly) berketahuan, setahu; (*on purpose*) sengaja.

witty jenaka, lucu.

wizard tukang sihir.

wizened kurus kering.

wobble goyang, gerak tergoyang.

wobbly bergoyang, tatih.

woe (*agony*) sengsara; (*misfortune*) bencana; (*grief*) duka.

woebegone muram durja.

woeful sedih.

wolf anjing serigala; (*a eedy person*) orang tamak; (*col*) (*pursuer of women*) yang gila perempuan.

wolf cub anak serigala.

wolfish seperti serigala; tamak.

woman perempuan.

womanish seperti perempuan.

womankind kaum perempuan, wanita.

womanly seperti perempuan.

womb rahim, peranakan.

wombat sejenis binatang di Australia.

wonder hairan keajaiban, pelik.

wonderful ajaib, sangat elok.

wonderland negeri ajaib.

wonder-struck takjub, tercengang.

wondrous ajaib; (*very fine*) sangat elok.

wont biasa, kebiasaan.

woo, to — (*formally*) meminang; (*coax*) membujuk.

wood (*forest*) hutan; (*timber*) kayu; —work kerja perkayuan.

woodbine sejenis tumbuhan.

wood-carving ukiran kayu.

woodcut gambar ukiran kayu.

woodcutter (*feller*) penebang; pengukir kayu.

wooden kayu, dibuat daripada kayu; (*stiff*) kaku.

woodland tanah berhutan, tanah yang banyak pohon-pohon kayu.

woodpecker burung belatuk.

woodwork benda-benda yang dibuat daripada kayu.

woody banyak pokok-pokok kayu.

woof pakan.

wool bulu kambing.

woolgathering kelengahan, keadaan teringa-inga.

woollen, (*US*) **woolen** pakaian yang dibuat daripada bulu kambing.

woolly, (*US*) **wooly** berbulu, seperti bulu.

word kata, perkataan; (*news*) khabar.

wordy dengan panjang lebar.

work pekerjaan, kerja; to — (be engaged in) bekerja; (execute) mengerjakan; (cause to act, manage) menjalankan.

workaday sehari-hari.

workday hari kerja.

worker pekerja, buruh, pegawai.

workman buruh, pekerja.

workmanship kepandaian membuat sesuatu.

workshop bengkel, wokshop.

work-shy malas, tidak suka bekerja.

world dunia, alam, jagat.

worldliness keduniawian.

worldly duniawi.

worldwide yang terdapat dalam seluruh dunia.

worm cacing.

worm-eaten dimakan ulat; (old) tua, lama.

worried khuatir, cemas.

worry gangguan, keluh-kesah.

worse lebih buruk, kurang baik.

worsen, to — menjadi buruk, menjadi kurang baik.

worship puja, pemujaan.

worshipper pemuka, penyembah.

worst yang terburuk, yang sangat buruk, kurang baik sekali.

worsted sejenis kain bulu.

worth (price) harga; (use) guna, faedah; (proper) patut.

worthily dengan baik, dengan patut.

worthiness kebaikan; kepatutan.

worthless sekali-kali tidak berharga.

worthwhile yang patut diberi perhatian; (profitable) yang berfaedah.

worthy (suited to) patut; (of fit price) sesuai dengan harga; (deserving respect) patut dihormati.

would-be pura-pura

wound luka; to — melukai, melukakan.

wrack rumput-rampai dan lain sisa-sisa yang hanyut di laut.

wraith khayal (semangat) yang terlihat kalau seseorang baharu meninggal, hantu.

wrangle pergaduhan.

wrap, —s kain pembungkus, selendang; to — (with paper, bandage) membalutkan.

wrapper kain yang menyelubungi.

wrath murka, marah.

wreak, to — (anger, hate) melepaskan marah (dendam); (vengeance) membalas dendam.

wreath (garland) rangkaian bunga; (ring form) rangkaian.

wreathe, to — berkerut; menganyam, merangkaikan.

wreck (destruction) kerosakan, (kapal dan lain-lain); (ship foundering) kapal yang karam; (thing wrecked) sesuatu yang rosak.

wreckage kaparan.

wren sejenis burung.

wrench rengguttan; (sorrow at parting) kesedihan kerana berpisah; to — merenggut.

wrest, to — merengkuh, memulas.

wrestle, to — bergomol, gusti.

wrestling adu gomol.

wretch orang celaka, bedebah.

wretched (grieving) sedih; celaka, malang.

wriggle belit, lilit; to — berbelit, melilit.

wring, to — (the hand) menjabat tangan; (twist) memulas.

wrinkle kerut; to — berkerut, mengerutkan.

wrist pergelangan tangan; watch jam tangan.

writ perintah rasmi.

write, to — menulis, menyurat.

writer pengarang, penulis.

writhe belit, geliang-geliut; to — berbelit.

writing (*in act of*) sedang menulis; tulisan, karangan; —desk meja tulis.

wrong salah; (*confused*) keliru; (*wicked*) jahat.

wrongdoer pelanggar, orang yang bersalah.

wrongful salah; (*unjust*) tidak adil.

wrought dibuat, dihias, ditempa; — iron besi tempa.

wry miring, gerinyut.

X

xenophobia kebencian terhadap orang asing.

Xmas = Christmas.

X-ray, X-rays pancar.

xylophone sejenis alat muzik.

Y

yacht kapal layar (untuk masuk) perlumbaan.

yachtsman orang yang pandai belayar dalam kapal layar.

yak sejenis lembu di negeri Tibet.

yam ubi, keladi.

yank renggutan; to — merenggut.

yap dengking; to — mendengking, menyalak.

yard I (*garden, courtyard*) pekarangan, halaman.

yard II (*unit of measure*) ela.

yarn (*thread*) benang; (*tale*) cerita.

yawn kuap, hal menguap; to — menguap.

yaws puru.

year tahun, sanat; (*age*) umur, usia.

yearling binatang (lembu, kuda dan lain-lain) yang umurnya antara setahun dengan 2 tahun.

yearlong yang setahun lamanya.

yearly bertahun-tahun, tahunan.

yearn, to — rindu akan, merindukan.

yearning sedang merindukan, rindu.

yeast ragi.

yell jerit, pekek; to — berteriak, menjerit.

yellow kuning, warna kuning; (*shrivelled*) pengecut; to turn — menguning.

yellow fever sejenis penyakit demam.

yellowish kekuningan.

yelp dengking; to — berdengking.

yeoman pemilik sebidang tanah.

yeomanry para tuan tanah; (*volunteer cavalry*) pasukan berkuda yang terdiri daripada orang petani.

yes ya.

yester— yang lalu.

yesterday kelmarin, semalam; day before — kelmarin dahulu; — morning kelmarin pagi.

yet (*still*) masih; (*in addition*) lagi, pula; (*although*) meskipun, demikian; (*but*) akan tetapi.

yew sejenis pohon, kayu pohon itu.

Yiddish bahasa orang Yahudi Eropah tengah.

yield (*profit*) hasil; to — menghasilkan; (*deliver up*) menyerahkan.

yielding sedang menyerahkan; menghasilkan; (*soft*) lembut.

yodel sejenis nyanyian secara orang gunung di negeri Swis.

yoga yoga.

yogi penganut yoga.

yoke galas; (*bullock cart*) igu; (*authority*) kuasa; (*oppressor*) penindasan.

yokel orang dusun.

yolk kuning telur.

yonder di sebelah sana.

yore masa dahulu; of — pada masa dahulu.

you awak, engkau, kamu, tuan.

young muda; (*offspring*) anak.

youngster anak muda, pemuda.

your (kepunyaan) awak, kamu, tuan.

yours (kepunyaan) kamu, awak, tuan; (*letter ending*) dengan, hormat.

yourself engkau, kamu, tuan sendiri.

youth belia, masa muda; (*young persons*) anak muda, pemuda.

youthful muda.

Z

zany pelawak.

zeal kegiatan, semangat.

zealot orang fanatik, orang yang semangatnya sangat meluap.

zealous giat, bersemangat.

zebra sejenis kuda belang.

zebu sejenis sapi.

zenith (*peak*) kemuncak, puncak; (*of sun*) rembang.

zephyr (*breeze*) angin sepoi-sepoi, angin sepoi bahasa.

zero titik sipar; — hour saat permulaan salah satu serangan dan lain-lain.

zest (*relish*) rasa sedap; (*enthusiasm*) semangat.

zigzag bengkang-bengkok.

zinc zeng, timah sari.

Zionism faham yang bertujuan mendirikannya kembali negeri Yahudi di Palestine.

zip (*col*) (*energy*) semangat, kegiatan.

zodiac mintakulburuj, zodiak.

zombi(e) mayat yang dihidupkan balik dengan ilmu ghaib.

zone daerah (hawa), kawasan; polar — lengkungan, (kawasan) kutub utara dan kutub selatan; temperate — kawasan sederhana.

zoo taman binatang, zoo.

zoo—awalan kata yang ertinya: yang berkenaan dengan haiwan.

zoological yang berkenaan dengan ilmu haiwan; — gardens kebun binatang.

zoology kaji haiwan.

zoom terbang ke atas; to — terbang dalam kapalterbang ke atas dengan cepat.